BIOFEEDBACK
and SELF-CONTROL 1973

EDITORS

NEAL E. MILLER

Professor
Laboratory of Physiological Psychology
The Rockefeller University
New York, New York

T. X. BARBER

Director of Psychological Research
Medfield State Hospital
Medfield, Massachusetts

LEO V. DiCARA

Professor of Psychiatry and Psychology
Department of Psychiatry
University of Michigan
Ann Arbor, Michigan

JOE KAMIYA

Director, Psychophysiology Lab
The Langley Porter Institute
University of California Medical Center
San Francisco, California

DAVID SHAPIRO

Senior Associate
Department of Psychiatry
Massachusetts Mental Health Center
Harvard Medical School
Boston, Massachusetts

JOHANN STOYVA

Associate Professor
Department of Psychiatry
University of Colorado Medical Center
Denver, Colorado

BIOFEEDBACK
and SELF-CONTROL 1973

*an Aldine Annual on the
regulation of bodily processes
and consciousness*

ALDINE PUBLISHING COMPANY
Chicago

Production Editor
Nanci Connors

First published 1974 by
Aldine Publishing Company
529 South Wabash Avenue
Chicago, Illinois 60605

ISBN 0-202-25108-X
Library of Congress Catalog Number 74-1551109

Printed in the United States of America

CONTENTS

PREFACE

This fourth volume of *Biofeedback and Self-Control,* like its predecessors and like other Aldine Annuals, presents an authoritative selection of the most important work on the subject that appeared in the past year. The criteria of selection are those of the scholars making up the Editorial Board, whose interests reflect the several main trends in this field of study as well as its general scope and breadth.

The final selection and organization of material to be included is each year made by a member of the editorial board, who also presents an overview of work and trends in the field. Neal Miller, Director of the Laboratory of Physiological Psychology at the Rockefeller University assumed these responsibilities for the current volume, and his Introduction follows. In this, as in previous volumes, several papers appear that were originally published prior to the specific year that the Annual covers but which the Editors regard as exceptionally important.

We gratefully acknowledge the cooperation of the various authors, journals, organizations and publishers who granted their permission to reprint the selections included in this volume. Each selection has been reproduced exactly as it originally appeared in order to publish each year's Annual as soon as possible. The editors will greatly appreciate any comments and suggestions from readers to help make these volumes a more valuable reference work.

INTRODUCTION
Current Issues and
Key Problems

Two of the most urgent current needs in the burgeoning new area of biofeedback are for studies of therapeutic effects that are far more rigorous than those published to date, and for studies of the laws governing this new type of learning situation. We need to discover these laws in order to improve the efficiency of training.

I shall concentrate on these urgent needs in this introduction and therefore will not be able to comment on each significant study in this volume. Some of the general articles and reviews that are reprinted also deal with these needs as well as with additional issues.

NEED FOR RIGOROUS REPLICATION OF THERAPEUTIC STUDIES

In trying out a radically new therapeutic approach, it is natural for investigators first to see whether they can get any effect at all before investing time and effort on elaborate controls that may turn out to be irrelevant if there is nothing to be controlled. Unfortunately, however, the public media have seized upon and characteristically exaggerated such exploratory results. There is therefore a real danger of arousing impossible hopes that will result in inevitable disillusionment and that will interfere with the hard work needed to discover and evaluate the therapeutic potentialities of this new approach.

In order to avoid such a boom and bust, too often characteristic of new types of therapy, it is essential that the exploratory studies that have yielded the most promising therapeutic results be repeated, ideally in other laboratories, with more rigorous controls to avoid the possibility of the spurious conclusions that can be produced by the action of some of the factors discussed below. We need more instances, like the excellent example by Stunkard in article 36, in which a group of rigorous studies all replicate the same result.

NEED TO CONTROL FOR SPONTANEOUS FLUCTUATIONS

One factor for which better controls are needed is regression to the mean. In many chronic conditions, such as headaches and hypertension, the patient's symptoms tend to fluctuate between periods of exacerbation and those of ame-lioration. Under such circumstances, a patient is much more likely to seek out a treatment when he is feeling worse. But if treatment is started at this extreme point in the cycle, any further spontaneous change is likely to be improvement; in other words, a regression toward the mean. Such regression is illustrated in a recent study of hypertension by Johnson *et al.* (1973), in which they found that 70 percent of those who were treated experienced a decline in systolic pressure, but 62 percent of those who were untreated experienced a similar decline. Such figures illustrate the necessity of using suitable control groups.

If patients are treated until they improve and are then discharged, there is a second selective factor; not only is the treatment likely to be started when they are feeling worse than usual but it also is stopped when they are feeling better than usual. Thus, a comparison between the beginning and the end of treatment inevitably may be expected to regress toward the mean again, which, in this case, would be to get worse.

Another serious selective error is the fact that only the studies with positive therapeutic effects are published. One out of twenty of these will be expected to be significant at the 5 percent level by chance.

POWERFUL PLACEBO EFFECTS

In addition to the foregoing selective errors, there may be a genuine therapeutic effect from the patient's own mechanisms for recovery. Further, there may be another genuine therapeutic effect which, however, is not a specific result of the type of treatment but rather a nonspecific placebo effect elicited by the hope aroused, the attention received, and/or the suggestions given. The power and ubiquity of placebo effects is described by A. K. Shapiro in article 17 of this volume. Shapiro's paper merits thoughtful reading reading by anyone who is interested in evaluating therapeutic effects.

In order to avoid the placebo effect in evaluating the therapeutic action of drugs, pharmacologists have evolved the double-blind technique. In it, neither the patient nor the physician knows whether the coded medication is a presum-ably active agent or an inert placebo. This model should be followed as closely as possible in studies evaluating the effects of biofeedback. But it is more difficult to apply this technique in biofeedback studies than in those involving drugs. In a study of tension headache, Budzynski *et al.* (article 19) have made a commend-able attempt to include a control group who were exposed to a tape-recording of the clicks that told a feedback patient how successfully he was relaxing. But they could not tell the control patients that the clicks reflected tension levels because the patients could easily have determined that this was not true. Therefore, the control group differed from the experimental one in that the controls did not believe they were receiving feedback. The other provocative study on headache, by Sargent *et al.* (article 21), has no control for placebo effects, for concentrating on a distracting task, or for other possibly confounding factors. These authors' preliminary results are good enough to demand a study with suitable controls since, as A. K. Shapiro (article 17) points out, "headaches respond flagrantly to placebo medication."

That placebo effects are not limited to verbal reports but can affect objectively measured physiological processes is shown by 48 patients to whom Grenfell *et al.* (1963) gave placebos as a part of a double-blind evaluation of anti-hypertensive drugs. For these patients receiving only placebos, the average decreases were 25 mm Hg for systolic and 12 mm Hg for diastolic blood pressure. Furthermore, the decrease was progressive, with the maximum effect not being reached until after approximately 7 weeks.

As A. K. Shapiro's article in this volume and a study by A. P. Shapiro *et al.* (1954) point out, the effectiveness of both active and placebo medications can be markedly affected by the enthusiasm of the therapist administering them. Thus, if either the therapist or the patient knows when the procedure is being shifted from baseline to experimental, the effects of the baseline procedure cannot be used as a control. Furthermore, if the therapist is less enthusiastic with the control patients, they are not an adequate control group, a feature that is taken care of by the double-blind procedure.

Finally, as the study by Luparello *et al.* (article 18) shows, the effects of a suggestion can determine whether a nasal spray of isotonic saline produces an increase or a decrease in the physically measured airway resistance of an asthmatic patient. This study shows that Alexander (1950) underestimated the autonomic nervous system when he claimed that, because psychosomatic symptoms are under its control, they cannot be subject to the higher type of symbolic influence involved in hysterical and other symptoms.

While placebo effects may be a nuisance in evaluating the effectiveness of a new type of therapy, they do demonstrate the significant power of psychological factors and the ways in which these can influence autonomically mediated processes that have been thought to be purely automatic. Thus, the powerful placebo effect is a significant phenomenon in its own right, and certainly merits much more investigation than it has received.

One of the characteristics of placebo effects is that they often are transient. As A.K. Shapiro (article 17) has pointed out, Trousseau is credited with the admonition, approximately 100 years ago, "You should treat as many patients as possible with the new drugs while they still have the power to heal." It is quite possible, however, that some placebo effects may be relatively permanent; we need more research on this problem.

From the scientific point of view, it is important to know whether the effects of a technique are due to its specific rationale or to a nonspecific placebo effect. Additional research on the mechanism of a treatment often leads to significant improvements and to new applications, but it is a waste of time to investigate the mechanism of a treatment as though the effects were specific to its rationale, when in fact they are due to nonspecific placebo effects.

COMPARISON WITH ALTERNATIVE THERAPIES:
LONG-TERM FOLLOW-UP

From the practical point of view, a rigorous test of a new therapeutic technique is how its results compare with the best available alternative treatments. Since a new technique is often administered with a new enthusiasm, it is important to try to equate for this factor. Furthermore, in view of the transcience of many placebo effects and, of course, also of the regression of spontaneous fluctuations to the mean, a history of failure of treatment by other techniques is not a valid basis for comparison unless a careful investigation shows that these previous therapies did not produce any transient beneficial effects and that the new technique has considerably more long-lasting beneficial effects.

One of the impressive things about the Weiss and Engel (1971) study of the use of operant conditioning to treat premature ventricular contractions is the fact that some of these patients have been followed-up for considerable periods of time, as indicated by Engel and Bleecker (1974). The same is true of Engel's study of fecal incontinence (1974).

Perhaps a resolution of the conflict between the natural desire of authors to publish a study within a reasonable time and the scientific necessity for long-term follow-up data will be for editors to accept articles only if authors promise to make a serious attempt to follow up as many of the patients as possible at a reasonable later date. Alternatively, authors should voluntarily try to publish very brief follow-up articles, referring to the original article for all of the details and reporting the status of their patients at least one year and ideally two or more years later. For example, it would be extremely significant to know about the long-term follow-up status of the headache subjects in articles 19, 20, and 21. Fortunately, Sargent *et al.* (article 21) have promised such follow-up data.

EPILEPSY: REWARDING DIFFERENT PARTS OF EEG SPECTRUM

Sterman reports (article 32) that training epileptic patients to produce a sensorimotor rhythm of 12-14 Hz reduces the number of epileptic seizures, a finding that is confirmed by Finlay (article 34). But Kaplan (article 33) failed with two patients to get therapeutic effects for rewarding 12-14 Hz activity, and subsequently succeeded with two patients by rewarding 6-12 Hz activity. She believes that her results may not have been due to a specific effect on the EEG spectra but rather from training the patients to relax. These results are promising enough to merit a larger study in which the effects of rewarding different frequencies of the EEG and also of rewarding relaxation aided by feedback from the EMG are compared. With a little ingenuity it should be possible to reward different frequencies of the EEG in a double-blind design. Any differences in the effectiveness of training different frequencies would be nicely controlled for placebo effects.

BI-DIRECTIONAL VOLUNTARY CONTROL

In their efforts to train patients to control their premature ventricular contractions (PVCs), Weiss and Engel (1971) and Engel and Bleecker (1974) have taught patients to turn off their PVCs, turn them back on again, and then turn them off again on request. They believe, as do I, that such bi-directional training facilitates voluntary control. Furthermore, such specific control can scarcely be a mere nonspecific placebo effect. In work that is in progress, Dr. Thomas Pickering in my laboratory has replicated this aspect of their earlier work by succeeding in teaching two patients to turn PVCs on and off (Miller, 1974a).

TRANSFER FROM LABORATORY TO LIFE

One of the important problems of therapeutic training is whether it transfers from the laboratory situation to the life one. For example, patients trained to lower their blood pressure may do so only when it is being measured but not during stressful incidents of life. Thus, it is conceivable that they might mislead their physicians into taking them off an antihypertensive drug which they still need. While a portable device for securing continuous records of blood pressure is available (Bevan *et al.*, 1961), it involves a catheter into an artery. Although, such a catheter is not dangerous, it is not entirely without hazard. Therefore, one should hesitate to use this device until one is reasonably sure that the reduction in hypertension is more than might be expected from a placebo effect.

In studies of cardiac arrhythmias, it is possible to secure objective evidence by having the patients carry around a portable tape-recording ECG device that is completely without hazard. Engel and Bleecker (1974) have secured some follow-up measures of this type on their PVC patients; additional studies should secure such evidence both before and after training. The availability of a device for achieving such objective before-and-after measurements on patients with cardiac arrhythmias is one of the reasons that makes studies of the effects of biofeedback training on such patients attractive.

Finally, the two reports on torticollis (articles 23 and 48) are encouraging because this is reputed to be a stubborn condition, and there are some good before-and-after data, especially in the article by Brudny *et al.* (1974) that is a follow-up to the abstract (article 48). Some of these patients clearly transferred their improved control of head position from the laboratory to daily life.

LARGE VISCERAL CHANGES

Discovering how to teach subjects to learn large changes in visceral responses is potentially valuable therapeutically; it also greatly facilitates purely scientific studies. The second and third articles in this volume describe experiments producing large changes in a visceral response. In the study by Wells (article 3), relatively large increases in heart rate were produced by selecting highly motivated human subjects. In the study by Harris *et al.* (article 2), impressive increases in the blood pressure of baboons, approximately 30 mm Hg, maintained during a 12-hour period, were secured by using an ingenious schedule involving escape and avoidance of electric shock as well as food reward for an extensive period of training. In this study baboons rewarded for decreases did not show decreases but they did not increase, and thus served as a control for the effect of electric shocks since they received somewhat more shocks (personal communication) than did the increase animals.

INCREASES VS. DECREASES

In heart rate, Wells (article 3) also was more successful in producing increases than in producing decreases. These findings are in line with the rest of the literature and fit in with the fact that Wells *et al.* (article 7) find that a decrease in salivation, a change also involving a shift from parasympathetic activity, appears to be easier to learn than is an increase. This last result, however, may be due to the fact that the experimenters artificially stimulated the baseline rate of salivation by injecting into the mouth a weakly acidic solution. In fact, all comparisons of this type may depend on whether the baseline conditions are nearer the upper or lower extremes of possible variability.

SPECIFICITY AS THE BEST CONTROL FOR MEDIATION

In the efficient function of the organism, visceral and skeletal responses are intimately interrelated in adaptive patterns. From the practical points of view of therapy or of the etiology of psychosomatic symptoms, it may be important to understand these interrelationships and even to exploit them. The fact that a visceral change is accompanied by, or even produced by, a skeletal response does not necessarily detract from the effectiveness of that change. For example, for some patients, taking a sudden deep breath will stop an attack of paroxysmal tachycardia.

From the theoretical point of view, a hotly debated question has been whether or not the autonomic nervous system is qualitatively inferior to the somatic one so that the only way that instrumental learning can affect a visceral response is via the mediation of a skeletal one, as when a person speeds up his heart rate by running up a flight of stairs. At first, the paralysis of skeletal muscles by curare was used as a control for the effects of gross overt skeletal responses. And indeed, it does control for the demands on the cardiovascular system that are caused by the greater production of heat and carbon dioxide by overt skeletal activity. But in our first paper, DiCara and I realized that subjects may learn to send out from the motor cortex central impulses for skeletal responses, such as struggling, and that these impulses might elicit innate or classically conditioned changes in heart rate (Miller and DiCara, 1967, p. 17). In that paper, we presented various arguments against such an interpretation of the results.

As work progressed, however, it became obvious that, just as training can make skeletal responses more specific, it also can make visceral responses become more specific. In one experiment, rats were rewarded for and learned a difference between the vasomotor responses in the two ears (DiCara and Miller, 1968). It is hard to imagine any neural impulses to a paralyzed skeletal muscle, or even any emotional thoughts, that would cause a rat to blush in one ear and not the other. If one wants to consider the possibility of using the imagery of one ear being warm and the other cold as a mediating response, the notion becomes indistinguishable from the ideomotor hypothesis of the voluntary movement of skeletal muscles (Miller, 1969, p. 445). I now consider the many examples for learned specificity (Crider *et al.*, 1969; Miller, 1969; Shapiro *et al.*, 1970) as the best evidence that it is possible to learn direct control of such responses.

Although work by six different experimenters in my laboratory produced apparently very robust learning of a variety of visceral responses by rats paralyzed by curare (Miller, 1969), and this work was confirmed in two other laboratories (Hothersall and Brener, 1969; Slaughter *et al.*, 1970), a retrospective look at the data revealed that the size of these effects was declining progressively with time (Miller, 1972). Results on rats paralyzed by curare have since declined to virtually zero, so that, despite extensive efforts, we have been unable to find what went wrong and to replicate the earlier results from our laboratory (Dworkin, 1973; Miller and Dworkin, 1974), nor have Brener *et al.* (1974) or DiCara (personal communication) been able to replicate the results from their laboratory. Two studies by Thornton and VanToller (articles 4 and 5) could be the beginning of a reversal of the downward trend. Since slight errors in the adjustment of the respirator can cause the heart rate to drift progressively up or down, it would have been better if these investigators had made all adjustments before the beginning of training and then flipped a coin to decide whether the rat would be reinforced for increases or decreases. This procedure has been used routinely in my laboratory to eliminate any possibility of an unconscious error by the experimenter.

Fortunately, while the results on curarized rats have declined, studies on nonparalyzed animals and people have yielded better results.

Some of the most convincing studies are those demonstrating extreme specificity. In addition to those mentioned directly above, the study by Bleecker and Engel (article 25) is an interesting example of teaching a patient to control independently either cardiac rate or cardiac conduction.

PERIPHERAL VASOMOTOR RESPONSES AS A MODEL

Perhaps the most convincing studies of specificity to date are a series, patterned after the above-mentioned two-ear experiment, in which human subjects have been able to produce a difference between the temperature of the two hands, often by causing the temperature of the two hands to change in opposite directions. The first of these studies (Maslach *et al.*, 1972) involved only hypnosis. The next, by Roberts *et al.* (article 1), involved hypnosis along with improved performance during training with feedback. And a still more recent report by Roberts *et al.* (1974) used feedback to train nonhypnotized subjects over a period of 16 daily sessions to produce a difference between the temperature of the two index fingers first in one direction, then in the other direction, and then back in the first direction on immediately successive trials in each daily session. Finally,

Lynch, Hama, and Kohn in my laboratory have succeeded in repeating this experiment with two 10-year-old children and in carrying the specificity still further, so that these children are able to produce differences between the first and third fingers of the *same* hand reliably. We have been unable to discover any skeletal responses that can produce such differences, but are proceeding to use EMG recordings in an attempt either to discover or to rule out such responses.

While Taub *et al.* (1974) have not attempted specifically to reward specificity of temperature change, they report that a considerable amount of it develops spontaneously during advanced stages of training.

Although a learned change in temperature could conceivably be caused by a change in perspiration, evidence secured by Roberts *et al.* (article 1) and also by Lynch and Kohn (Miller, 1974b) shows that the learned change in temperature involves abrupt changes in peripheral circulation.

Because of the encouraging results secured to date, the benign nature of the response, its relative accessibility, and the great possibility for specificity, I believe that the control of temperature (or of peripheral circulation measured in other ways) is likely to be an especially good model situation for discovering and studying the various factors that have significant effects on the learning of a visceral response. Heart rate, as studied systematically by Brener (1974) and by Lang (1974), and heart rate and blood pressure, as studied by Schwartz and Shapiro (articles 29 and 41), are among the other models that have been investigated.

SIGNIFICANT FACTORS FOR FURTHER STUDY

We urgently need further study of problems and variables such as the following: the bases for the large individual differences in visceral learning that almost everyone reports encountering; the effects of motivation and of the as yet intangible variables in the relationship between the experimenter and the subject; the effect of the type of attitude that the subject takes, whether active or passive; the possible advantage of teaching skeletal relaxation first; the opposite possibility of first eliciting visceral changes via skeletal maneuvers and then, if necessary, gradually phasing the skeletal responses out; the possibility of first eliciting visceral changes by classical conditioning and then shifting over to an instrumental (operant conditioning) paradigm; the use of imagery; the use of specific training in visceral discriminations, as studied so extensively in Eastern Europe (Adám, 1967); the use of different types of feedback or of a less cognitive, more primitive type of reward than money or the knowledge of success; the possible use of a drug or other procedure to loosen up the tightness of homeostatic controls. It should be obvious that there is much important work to do in this new area of research.

In conclusion: "This is a new area in which investigators should be bold in what they try but cautious in what they claim."

NEAL E. MILLER

REFERENCES

Adám, G. *Interoception and Behaviour.* Akadémiai Kiadó, Budapest, 1967.

Alexander, F. *Psychosomatic Medicine: Its Principles and Applications.* W. W. Norton, New York, 1950, pp. 40-41.

Bevan, A. T., Honour, A. J., and Stott, F. H. Direct arterial pressure recording in unrestricted man. *Clin. Sci.* 1961, *36,* 329-344.

Brener, J. A general model of voluntary control applied to the pheno ena of learned cardiovascular change. In *Cardiovascular Psychophysiology* (P. A. Obrist *et al.,* eds.). Aldine, Chicago, 1974, 365-391.

Brener, J., Eissenberg, E., and Middaugh, S. Respiratory and somatomotor factors associated with operant conditioning of cardiovascular responses in curarized rats. In *Cardiovascular Psychophysiology* (P. A. Obrist *et al.,* eds.). Aldine, Chicago, 1974, 251-275.

Brudny, J., Grynbaum, B. B., and Korein, J. Spasmodic torticollis: Treatment by feedback display of EMG—a report of nine cases. *Arch. Phys. Med. Rehabil.* 1974. (In press)

Crider, A. B., Schwartz, G. E., and Shnidman, S. On the criteria for instrumental automatic conditioning: A reply to Katkin and Murray. *Psychol. Bull.* 1969, *71,* 455-461.

DiCara, L. V. and Miller, N. E. Instrumental learning of vasomotor responses by rats: Learning to respond differentially in the two ears. *Science* 1968, *159,* 1485-1486.

Dworkin, B. R. An effort to replicate visceral learning in curarized rats. Ph.D. Thesis, The Rockefeller University, 1973.

Engel, B. T. and Bleecker, E. R. Application of operant conditioning techniques to the control of the cardiac arrhythmias. In *Cardiovascular Psychophysiology* (P. A. Obrist *et al.,* eds.). Aldine, Chicago, 1974, 456-476.

Engel, B. T., Nikoomanesh, P., and Schuster, M. M. Operant conditioning of recto-sphincteric responses in the treatment of fecal incontinence. *New Engl. J. Med.* 1974, 646-649.

Grenfell, R. F., Briggs, A. H., and Holland, W. C. Antihypertensive drugs evaluated in a controlled double-blind study. *Southern Med. J.* 1963, *56,* 1410-1415.

Hothersall, D. and Brener, J. Operant conditioning of changes in heart rate in curarized rats. *J. Comp. Physiol. Psychol.* 1969, *68,* 338-342.

Johnson, B. C., Karunas, T. M., and Epstein, F. H. Longitudinal change in blood pressure in individuals, families and social groups. *Clin. Sci. Molec. Med.* 1973, *45,* 35s-45s.

Lang, P. J. Learned control of human heart rate in a computer directed environment. In *Cardiovascular Psychophysiology* (P. A. Obrist *et al.,* eds). Aldine, Chicago, 1974, 392-405.

Maslach, C., Marshall, G., and Zimbardo, P. G. Hypnotic control of peripheral skin temperature: A case report. *Psychophysiology* 1972, *9,* 600-605.

Miller, N. E. Learning of visceral and glandular responses. *Science* 1969, *163,* 434-445.

Miller, N. E. Interactions between learned and physical factors in mental illness. *Semin. Psychiat.* 1972, *4,* 239-254.

Miller, N. E. Applications of learning and biofeedback to psychiatry and medicine. In *Comprehensive Textbook of Psychiatry,* 2nd edition (A. M. Freedman, H. I. Kaplan, and B. J. Sadock, eds.). Williams & Wilkins, Boltimore, 1974. (In press) (a)

Miller, N. E. Clinical applications of biofeedback: Voluntary control of heart rate, rhythm, blood pressure. In *New Horizons in Cardiovascular Practice,* 1974. (In press) (b)

Miller, N. E. and DiCara, L. Instrumental learning of heart-rate changes in curarized rats: Shaping, and specificity to discriminative stimulus. *J. Comp. Physiol. Psychol.* 1967, *63,* 12-19.

Miller, N. E. and Dworkin, B. R. Visceral learning: Recent difficulties with curarized rats and significant problems for human research. In *Cardiovascular Psychophysiology* (P. A. Obrist *et al.,* eds.). Aldine, Chicago, 1974, 312-331.

Roberts, A. H., Schuler, J., Bacon, J., and Zimmermann, R. L. Individual differences and autonomic control: Absorption, hypnotic susceptibility, and the unilateral control of skin temperature. Paper read at Biofeedback Research Society Annual Meeting, February 1974.

Shapiro, A. P., Myers, T., Reiser, M. F., and Ferris, E. B. Comparison of blood pressure response to Veriloid and to the doctor. *Psychosom. Med.* 1954, *16,* 478-488.

Shapiro, D., Tursky, B., and Schwartz, G. E. Differentiation of heart rate and systolic blood pressure in man by operant conditioning. *Psychosom. Med.* 1970, *32,* 417-423.

Slaughter, J., Hahn, W., and Rinaldi, P. Instrumental conditioning of heart rate in the curarized rat with varied amounts of pretraining. *J. Comp. Physiol. Psychol.* 1970, *72,* 356-359.

Taub, E., Emurian, C., and Howell, P. Further progress in training self-regulation of skin temperature. Paper read at Biofeedback Research Society Annual Meeting, February 1974.

Weiss, T. and Engel, B. T. Operant conditioning of heart rate in patients with premature ventricular contractions. *Psychosom. Med.* 1971, *33,* 301-321.

BIOFEEDBACK
and SELF-CONTROL 1973

I

VISCERAL LEARNING

Voluntary Control of Skin Temperature: Unilateral Changes Using Hypnosis and Feedback

1

Alan H. Roberts, Donald G. Kewman,
and Hugh MacDonald

To demonstrate the ability of human subjects to achieve control over specific autonomic functions, hypnosis and auditory feedback were used to train a select group of hypnotically talented subjects to produce a difference in skin temperature in one hand relative to the other in a direction specified by the experimenter. Large and reliable effects were shown demonstrating that some individuals are capable of achieving a high degree of voluntary control over the autonomic processes involved in peripheral skin temperature regulation. Individual differences between subjects were noted, and variables that might account for these are discussed.

The recent work of Miller (1969) and his associates has demonstrated that glandular and visceral responses in animals can be modified by instrumental learning procedures without the mediation of skeletal responses. Using curare to control skeletal responses, he noted that it was apparently easier for paralyzed than unparalyzed animals to learn. He suggested that therapeutic training in humans might be enhanced by using hypnotic suggestion to increase learning and the transfer of training. Maslach, Ma.shall, and Zimbardo (1972) reported an exploratory study testing this hypothesis.

The purpose of this article is to demonstrate that subjects can learn to control voluntarily the skin temperature of one hand relative to the other, a task more specific and more difficult than simply raising or lowering skin temperature. This task was chosen because of its potential for producing differences of a magnitude that might have practical value and application. Some reports of attempts to control temperature by means of hypnotic suggestion or other means (Chapman, Goodell, & Wolff, 1959; Green, Green, & Walters, 1970; Hadfield, 1920; Luria, 1969; Maslach et al., 1972) suggested that large changes in skin temperature are possible. It is important to demonstrate that autonomic functions in man can be brought under cognitive volitional control and also that the magnitude of the changes are large enough to account for the psychosomatic symptoms observed in clinical settings.

[1] This study was conducted at the Laboratory of Hypnosis Research, Department of Psychology, Stanford University, and was supported by National Institute of Mental Health Grant 03859 to Ernest R. Hilgard, and Social and Rehabilitation Services Grant RT-2.

[2] Requests for reprints should be sent to Alan H. Roberts, Department of Physical Medicine and Rehabilitation, University of Minnesota Medical School, 860 Mayo Memorial Building, Box 297, Minneapolis, Minnesota 55455.

We are particularly grateful to Ernest R. Hilgard for his advice and encouragement. Eugene M. Farber, Dermatology Department, Stanford Medical Center, kindly provided the facilities of the constant temperature room. We thank Gary Marshall and Philip Zimbardo for their suggestions and, of course, A. Goodman, N. Hendrick, A. Lee, N. Morris, J. Petersen, and D. O'Brien who served as subjects in this study.

METHOD

Subjects

A select group of four female and two male university students, ages 20–24 years, served as subjects. Five subjects were able to pass all items of Form C of the Stanford Hypnotic Susceptibility Scale (Weitzenhoffer & Hilgard, 1962). They had received extensive hypnotic training and experience prior to this experiment. One (Subject 5), while having minimum prior hypnotic experience, was able to pass all but one item of Form C. Only two (Subjects 4 and 6) smoked cigarettes. All but Subject 4 and Subject 6 had some practice and experience in meditation; Subject 1 and Subject 2 were currently practicing meditation excerises during the period this experiment was conducted.

Procedure

Each subject received from five to nine individual one-hour training sessions (see Table 1). During early training sessions a cold pad was placed on one hand and a warm pad was placed on the other hand for a few minutes; then the subject was asked to maintain the difference between the two hands after pads were removed. During these early training sessions, skin temperature was monitored as described later, but no feedback information was provided to subjects. Additional training sessions provided feedback to subjects and were similar to later experimental sessions. Data from these training sessions were not analyzed. Hypnosis was used during training as described below for experimental sessions.

Following training sessions, each subject individually participated in three consecutive experimental sessions with from one to four days intervening between each session. The subject was seated in a comfortable chair in a room of about 22.5° centigrade, and apparatus was hooked up and calibrated. Skin temperature was recorded on a Grass Model-7 Polygraph with two 10,000-ohm Fenwall Uni-curve Interchangeable Curve-matched Thermistors taped to the pad of the subject's middle finger on the left and right hands. The resistance of each thermistor was recorded independently on Grass low-level dc Model-7P1 preamplifiers in skin resistance mode. The two signals were then compared, their difference amplified five times and recorded on a fourth channel with a thermistor located near but not touching the subject's hands.

The compared signal was fed to a combined voltage-controlled oscillator and voltage-controlled "volume control" producing a tone that changed frequency and moved from one earphone to the other in a stereo headset. Thus, as the right hand became warmer relative to the left, the frequency of the tone increased, and the tone moved toward the right earphone. As the left hand became warmer relative to the right, the frequency of the tone decreased and it moved toward the left earphone.

Each subject underwent a 10-minute hypnotic induction followed by a 5-minute period of rest and relaxation. Hypnotic induction procedures were individualized for each subject, but the length of the induction was 10 minutes for all subjects. The feedback signal was then started, and the subject was instructed as follows via an intercom from the separate monitoring room where the experimenter remained following induction:

For the next several minutes, left [right] hand and finger are cold and right [left] hand and finger are warm. Left [right] is cold and right [left] is warm. Left [right] finger cold, right [left] finger warm. Left [right] cold, right [left] warm. Tone to the right [left] side and up [down] in pitch.

This was followed by eight minutes without interruption by the experimenter, and then the instruction was repeated for the opposite hand. This was again followed by eight uninterrupted minutes, a third reversal of instruction, and another eight uninterrupted minutes. The feedback signal was then turned off and the subject was instructed to rest, relax, equalize the temperature of both hands, and make both hands comfortable. Finally the hypnotic trance was removed.

The hand chosen to start was different for each subject for each session, and subjects alternated between two experimenters in a predetermined balanced design. Thus, over three sessions, each subject was asked to perform nine consecutive simultaneous alternations in skin temperature.

In order to determine whether the response, once learned, could occur without external feedback or other external reinforcing stimuli, and to further demonstrate the independence of the response from other environmental stimuli such as physical setting or room temperature, Subject 1 and Subject 2 participated in two additional experimental sessions. The format of these sessions was identical to that previously described except that subjects were tested in a specially designed constant temperature room in the Laboratory of Dermatology at the Stanford Medical Center.

Room temperature was set about 28° centigrade. Copper constantan thermocouples were taped to identical sites on the fingers as described previously. Skin temperatures and room temperature were monitored by a Honeywell recording system that printed temperatures directly in degrees centigrade. No feedback of any kind was provided during these sessions, but experimenters and instructions were alternated as previously described providing data from six consecutive simultaneous alternations over the two sessions. Following the completion of all experimental sessions, subjects wrote responses to a number of open-ended questions concerning previous hypnotic experience, general background and experience, subjective impressions and ratings of experimental training, and general reactions.

RESULTS

Skin Temperature Changes

Data were analyzed at 25-second intervals during each eight-minute trial providing 19 data points for each subject. Results are shown for each subject separately in Table 1 and Figure 1 for right- and left-hand trials combined. Differences in hand temperature at the beginning of each trial were equated to a base line of zero. Mean changes in skin temperature from this base line, with negative scores indicating changes in the wrong direc-

TABLE 1

SEX, NUMBER OF TRAINING TRIALS PRIOR TO EXPERIMENTAL TRIALS, MAXIMUM TEMPERATURE DIFFERENCE ATTAINED ON ANY ONE EXPERIMENTAL TRIAL, AND MAXIMUM OF MEAN TEMPERATURE DIFFERENCES ATTAINED DURING ALL TRIALS FOR NINE EXPERIMENTAL TRIALS WITH FEEDBACK (*N* = 6) AND SIX EXPERIMENTAL TRIALS WITHOUT FEEDBACK (*N* = 2)

Subject number	Sex	Training trials	Maximum temperature difference, any one of nine trials with feedback[a]	Maximum temperature difference, any one of six trials without feedback[a]	Maximum of mean temperature differences for nine trials with feedback[a]		Maximum of mean temperature differences for six trials without feedback[a]	
					M	SD	M	SD
1	F	8	5.6	9.2	2.96	1.84	4.92	3.17
2	F	8	2.8	3.7	2.12	.58	2.37	1.14
3	F	5	2.5	—	1.97	.57	—	—
4	M	9	2.4	—	.99	.71	—	—
5	M	5	1.9	—	.37	.26	—	—
6	F	8	1.5	—	.18	.76	—	—

[a] In degrees centigrade.

tion, were compared to a hypothetical mean of zero change using *t* tests. Subjects 1, 2, 3, and 4 each showed statistically reliable changes in the correct direction for each of the nineteen 25-second intervals separately, averaged across the nine experimental trials.

Subject 5 (who had only five training sessions) showed significant changes (*p* < .05 or better) on each of the first eight 25-second

intervals but not for the remaining 11 data points. This suggests that he was able to change his skin temperature in the correct direction initially when asked to do so but was unable to maintain the change during the entire eight-minute trial.

Subject 6 showed no significant differences for any of the 19 individual data points in this analysis. However, the overall results for all

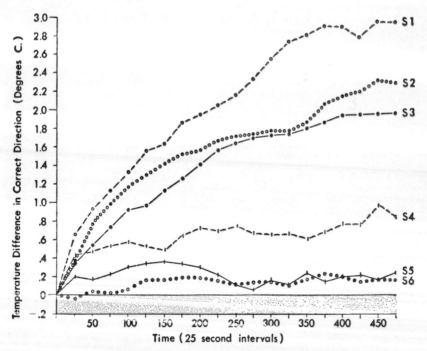

FIG. 1. Mean temperature difference in the correct (specified) direction for nine alternating trials over three sessions with feedback. (Each subject is shown separately (*N* = 6).)

six subjects combined were significant for each data point analyzed separately as well as for the overall t, which was 14.63 ($df = 5$, $p < .001$).

Table 1 also shows that Subject 1 produced maximum temperature differences as high as 5.6° centigrade in this part of the experiment, and the maximum of her average temperature difference was 2.96° centigrade. Subjects 2, 3, and 4, while producing smaller maximum temperature changes, were less variable in their performance than Subject 1. Across nine trials, average change from base temperature in the correct direction in one hand ranged from 0% to 10%. Changes from basal temperature were as high as 28% on individual trials.

Data from "right-hand warm" trials and "left-hand warm" trials were also analyzed separately. In this analysis the standard deviation was computed from the average of each of the 19 data points for all sessions combined so that $N = 19$ for each subject. The results are shown in Table 2. For left-hand warm trials, all subjects showed significant changes from zero in the correct direction beyond the .005 level of confidence. For right-hand warm trials, all showed significant changes from zero in the correct direction beyond the .0005 level of confidence except Subject 6, whose mean was .05 degrees centigrade in the direction opposite that requested.

When the differences attained in left-hand warm and right-hand warm trials were compared, the mean of the differences was .12, which is not significant. However, the overall

TABLE 2

AVERAGE TEMPERATURE CHANGE IN THE CORRECT DIRECTION FOR RIGHT-HAND WARM AND LEFT-HAND WARM TRIALS SEPARATELY

Subject	Trial					
	Left-hand warm			Right-hand warm		
	M	SD	t	M	SD	t
1	1.60	.87	8.05	2.53	.66	16.65
2	1.54	.46	14.72	1.64	.46	15.50
3	1.58	.50	13.65	1.32	.52	11.02
4	.61	.19	13.85	.70	.16	19.60
5	.14	.17	3.45	.32	.12	12.02
6	.25	.12	8.75	−.05	.09	−2.32

Note. With 18 df, $p < .05$ when $t = 1.73$ and $p < .01$ when $t = 2.55$ (one-tailed).

mean for the left-hand trials of .95 is significantly different from zero at the .025 level of confidence ($t = 3.34$, $df = 5$), and the mean of 1.07 for the right-hand trials is also signifi-

cantly different from zero at the .025 level ($t = 2.78$, $df = 5$).

When Subject 1 and Subject 2 were evaluated for six additional alternating trials in the temperature-controlled room without feedback, they performed even better than previously. The results are shown in Table 1 and Figure 2. In these trials, data were recorded at 60-second intervals for the same eight-minute trials as described previously. Subject 1 attained a maximum temperature difference of 9.2° centigrade on one trial and Subject 2 a maximum difference of 3.7° centigrade. The maximum of the mean temperature differences for the six trials was 4.92 for Subject 1 and 2.37 for Subject 2.

Response Patterns

To determine the response patterns of each subject, temperatures of the right and left hands were averaged for each of the 19 data points for "left-warm" and "right-warm" trials separately during the nine experimental trials. The results were graphed, and inspection of the objective data shows that different subjects used different response patterns to accomplish the results. These included making both hands colder (or warmer) but at different rates, holding one hand constant while raising or lowering the temperature of the other, or diverging the temperature of the two hands. This raises the possibility that different physiological processes may be involved in response patterns. It should be noted, also, that all subjects were able to change the temperatures of their hands significantly, but not always differentially.

Subjective Reports and Observations

One of the most notable aspects of this experiment was the apparent high degree of motivation and involvement of subjects. Appointments were all kept and on time. When the experiment was completed subjects held a surprise party for one experimenter who was leaving (a happening we suspect is rare in experimental psychology). All subjects reported the experiment to be a helpful and valuable experience to them, and subjects who achieved the least control spontaneously expressed a wish to have learned more.

All six subjects reported hallucinating the effect of changing skin temperatures at some times during the experiment. During training trials, subjects would report temperature

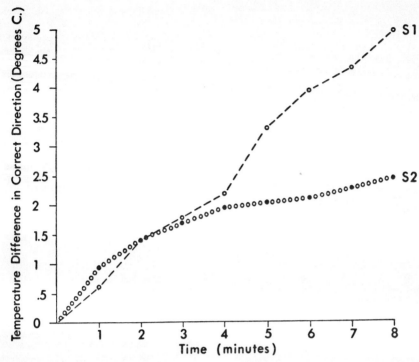

Fɪɢ. 2. Mean temperature difference in the correct (specified) direction for six alternating trials over two sessions without feedback. (Each subject is shown separately $(N = 2)$.)

changes occurring when objective polygraph data showed no changes. On a few occasions some subjects reported that the feedback tone changed in the appropriate direction when, in fact, it had not.

All subjects reported that hypnosis helped, but only Subject 6 felt that it was necessary. Subject 2 felt that some altered state of consciousness, but not necessarily hypnosis, was necessary.

There appeared some relationship between reported depth of hypnotic trance and the ability to control skin temperature. Asked to rate average depth of hypnotic trance on a 5-point scale from "awake" to "very deep," Subject 1 and Subject 2 reported "very deep" (depth well beyond that required to successfully complete all items on Form C of the Stanford Scale), Subject 3 reported "deep" (depth required to complete all items on Form C), Subject 4 reported "moderate" (depth required to complete most of the items on Form C), and Subject 5 reported "light" (depth required to complete a few items on Form C). The exception to this pattern is

Subject 6 who reported "very deep" along with Subject 1 and Subject 2.

Subjects were asked what they would say if they had to explain to someone else how they might control their skin temperature. Responses to this question were not consistent across subjects, and it is our impression that these written explanations were not particularly helpful in explaining what subjects did to produce the effect. However, the more successful subjects reported that they were able to communicate *with each other* concerning what they did and what they experienced (cf. Tart, 1972), although there is no independent evidence to support these reports.

DISCUSSION

The data from this experiment unequivocally demonstrate that some individuals are capable of achieving a high degree of voluntary control over the autonomic processes involved in peripheral skin temperature regulation. There were, however, significant individual differences in terms of ability of learn, rate of learning, and the magnitude of control that could be achieved. Further experimental work will be needed in order to determine the degree to which learning ability is related to physiological, motivational, and personality variables.

The data from the present experiment do not clarify the physiological mechanisms responsible for the control of skin temperature. However, following the completion of the experimental work described in this article, A. H. Sacks and E. Glenn Tickner of the Palo Alto Research Foundation provided apparatus and helped collect some preliminary data. During a separate special session, the temperature of Subject 1 was monitored as previously while blood flow was recorded over the volar digital artery (at the ring finger) using an ultrasonic flow meter and transcutaneous probe. When the subject decreased temperature in the monitored hand, blood flow was almost completely cut off except during the suppressed arterial pulse. When the subject increased temperature in the hand, an accelerated pulse and blood flow was detected. Since different subjects use different response patterns, the possibility remains that different physiological processes are involved across subjects.

This study also confounds the variables of hypnosis and auditory feedback so that it is not clear whether hypnosis is a necessary adjunct to learning or promotes the learning process. Maslach et al. (1972) and others indicate that the effects described can be demonstrated with hypnosis and without external feedback, and the data in this study provide strong support for their findings. Miller (1969) and others, on the other hand, suggest that autonomic control can be learned with feedback and without hypnosis. Our own view, as yet unsupported by experimental evidence, is that the *ability* to alter one's state of consciousness (Hilgard, 1969; Tart, 1972), together with associated motivational and training variables, will be among the more critical

variables in predicting the ability to control voluntarily autonomic processes, while hypnosis per se may not be necessary.

What seems clear is that some individuals can achieve a high degree of voluntary control over the autonomic processes involved in regulating peripheral skin temperature. The control appears to be of sufficient magnitude to make possible the therapeutic management of certain psychosomatic disorders, some circulatory disorders (e.g., Raynaud's disease, migraine headache), or other disorders that might be helped by localized changes in blood flow (e.g., burns, arthritis). As suggested by Miller (1969), the data increase the likelihood that at least some psychosomatic reactions are learned and can be modified.

REFERENCES

Chapman, L. F., Goodell, H., & Wolff, H. G. Increased inflamatory reaction induced by central nervous system activity. *Transactions of the Association of American Physicians*, 1959, 72, 84–109.

Green, E. E., Green, A. M., & Walters, E. D. *Progress of cybernetics: Proceedings of the International Congress of Cybernetics, London, 1969*. London: Gordon and Breach, 1970.

Hadfield, J. A. The influence of suggestion on body temperature. *Lancet*, 1920, 2, 68–69.

Hilgard, E. R. Altered states of awareness. *Journal of Nervous and Mental Disease*, 1969, 149, 68–79.

Luria, A. R. *The mind of a mnemonist*. New York: Discus Books, 1969.

Maslach, C., Marshall, G., & Zimbardo, P. Hypnotic control of peripheral skin temperature: A case report. *Psychophysiology*, 1972, 9, 600–605.

Miller, N. E. Learning of visceral and glandular responses. *Science*, 1969, 163, 434–445.

Tart, C. T. States of consciousness and state-specific sciences. *Science*, 1972, 176, 1203–1210.

Weitzenhoffer, A. M., & Hilgard, E. R. *Stanford Hypnotic Susceptibility Scale, Form C*. Palo Alto, Calif.: Consulting Psychologists Press, 1962.

(Received July 24, 1972)

Instrumental Conditioning of Large-Magnitude, Daily, 12-Hour Blood Pressure Elevations in the Baboon

2

Alan H. Harris, Willie J. Gilliam, Jack D. Findley and Joseph V. Brady

Abstract. *Blood pressure and heart rate were monitored continuously in four baboons during extended exposure to a daily 12-hour conditioning procedure providing food and shock-avoidance as contingent consequences of prespecified increases in diastolic blood pressure. Sustained and significant increases (30 to 40 mm-Hg) in both systolic and diastolic blood pressure were maintained throughout the daily 12-hour conditioning sessions, accompanied by elevated heart rates.*

Previous reports of instrumental blood pressure conditioning in laboratory animals and man have generally described cardiovascular changes limited, for the most part, in magnitude and duration. Typically, such conditioned blood pressure elevations in laboratory rats (1), squirrel monkeys (2), rhesus monkeys (3), and baboons (4) have been maintained for intervals limited to seconds or minutes, and, with few exceptions (5), only small-magnitude conditioned-pressure changes (less than 6 mm-Hg) have been described in human subjects (6). In addition, numerous theoretical and methodological questions have been raised concerning the role of "voluntary mediators" (for example, respiratory and skeletal responses) in the development and maintenance of such instrumental visceral-autonomic conditioning effects (7).

The present report describes sustained, large-magnitude elevations in blood pressure accompanied by elevated but progressively decreasing heart rates in baboons related to instrumental food-reward and shock-avoidance conditioning. Specifically, maintained elevations of 30 to 40 mm-Hg in both systolic and diastolic blood pressure were accompanied by elevated but decreasing heart rates during 12-hour conditioning sessions. Additionally, both blood pressure and heart rate were observed to decrease progressively during alternating 12-hour daily "rest" ("conditioning-off") intervals.

Four adult male dog-faced baboons (*Papio anubis*), each weighing approximately 35 lb (16 kg), served as subjects. Each animal was maintained in a primate restraining chair (8) housed in a sound-reducing experimental chamber provided with stimulus lights and an automatic food dispenser, as described in previous reports (4). Brief electric shocks (8 ma for 0.25 second) were administered through stainless steel electrodes applied with conducting paste to a shaved portion of the animal's tail. Each animal was surgically prepared (9) with two silicone-coated polyvinyl catheters, one implanted into the femoral artery to a point just above the level of the iliac bifurcation, and the other inserted into the vein and advanced to the inferior vena cava. The distal end of each catheter was tunneled under the skin, exited in the interscapular region, fitted with an 18-gauge Luer stud adapter, and connected to a Statham transducer (p23De) shock-mounted on the outside top of the experimental chamber. Patency of the catheter was maintained by continuous infusion of lightly heparinized saline (5000 USP units per liter) at a constant rate of approximately 4 ml/hour, and by a more rapid "flush" once each day. Periodic blood chemistry determinations of plasma sodium levels showed them to remain within the normal limits for the baboon (10) under these saline infusion conditions. Daily calibration of the system was accomplished without dismantling the components by integration of a mercury manometer through a series of three-way valves (11). Pressure signals from the transducer were amplified and displayed on an Offner polygraph (type R) which provided continuous heart rate and beat-by-beat blood pressure recordings. In addition, the pressure and rate signals were analyzed by an electronic averager (12) which provided on-line printout of heart rate (in beats per minute) and both systolic and diastolic blood pressure (in millimeters of mercury) over consecutive 40-minute intervals. Throughout the experiment, blood pres-

sure and heart rate were measured continuously, 24 hours each day, and adjustable meter relays integrated with the physiological recording system provided for selection of criterion diastolic blood pressure levels and automatic programming of contingent food and shock events. Two "feedback" lights, mounted in front of the animal, signaled when diastolic blood pressure levels were above or below the prescribed criterion.

The instrumental conditioning procedure required the animals to maintain prespecified diastolic blood pressure levels in order to obtain food and avoid shock. Five 1-g food pellets were delivered to the animal for every 10 minutes of accumulated time that the diastolic blood pressure remained above criterion. Conversely, the animal received a single shock for every 30 seconds that the diastolic blood pressure remained below the criterion level. Additionally, each food reward delivery reset the shock timer (thus providing an additional 30 seconds of accumulated shock-free time), and each occurrence of an electric shock reset the food timer (thus postponing the delivery of food for at least an additional 10 minutes of accumulated time). Initially, the criterion diastolic blood pressure was determined by the animal's pre-experimental resting baseline level (approximately 75 mm-Hg) with progressive increases programmed to occur at a rate approximating 4 mm-Hg per week over a period of 8 to 10 weeks. Within this 2- to 3-month interval, all four baboons attained diastolic blood pressure levels above 100 mm-Hg and maintained these elevated levels for more than 95 percent of each daily 12-hour conditioning-on period. During these daily conditioning sessions, the animals received, on the average, two

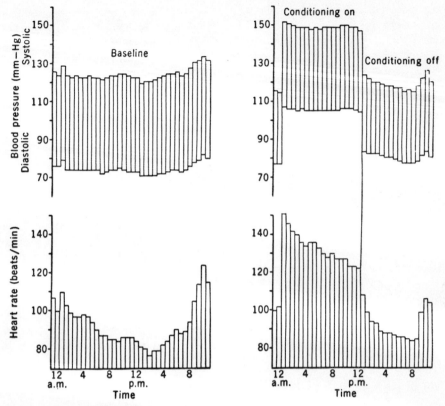

Fig. 1. Average blood pressure and heart rate values foi four baboons over consecutive 40-minute intervals during sixteen preexperimental baseline determinations (left panel) compared with sixteen 12-hour conditioning-on, 12-hour conditioning-off sessions (right panel).

electric shocks and 25 food pellets per hour.

Figure 1 compares the concurrent changes in blood pressure and heart rate during the 12-hour conditioning-on, 12-hour conditioning-off periods with the changes in blood pressure and heart rate during the preconditioning baseline period. The data plot in Fig. 1 is in the form of averages for three to five consecutive 24-hour experimental conditioning sessions (right panel) for each of the four baboons (that is, 16 total sessions) and three to five consecutive 24-hour preexperimental baseline sessions (left panel) for the same four animals before conditioning

(that is, 16 total sessions). This figure shows consecutive 40-minute-interval averages, and summarizes, in the right-hand panel, the stable response pattern which developed after the baboons had been exposed to at least 40 daily 12-hour conditioning sessions. Characteristically, sustained elevations of 30 mm-Hg or more in both systolic and diastolic blood pressure were maintained throughout the 12-hour conditioning-on period, accompanied by elevated but progressively decreasing heart rates over the course of the same 12-hour interval. During the ensuing 12-hour conditioning-off recovery period, heart rate continued to fall, and blood pressure re-

Table 1. Average heart rate (HR, in beats per minute) and both systolic (Sys) and diastolic (Dia) blood pressures (in millimeters of mercury) for each baboon during the baseline determinations compared with the 12-hour conditioning-on, 12-hour conditioning-off sessions. Listed are the mean, the standard error of the mean (S.E.M.), and the number (N) of 40-minute intervals in each sample. All cardiovascular values are averages of the last 6 hours of the conditioning-on period, and of the first 6 hours of the conditioning-off period, with baseline entries for the corresponding 6 to 12 p.m. and 12 to 6 a.m. time periods. The asterisks indicate cardiovascular values that are significantly different (P < .001) from both the corresponding baseline and the conditioning-off cardiovascular determinations.

Animal	Baseline 6 p.m. to 12 p.m.			Baseline 12 p.m. to 6 a.m.			Conditioning on 6 p.m. to 12 p.m.			Conditioning off 12 p.m. to 6 a.m.		
	Sys	Dia	HR	Sys	Dia	HR	Sys	Dia	HR	Sys	Dia	HR
Baboon 1												
Mean	127	77	108	120	69	96	146*	103*	134*	122	86	93
S.E.M.	0.9	0.9	2.0	0.8	0.9	1.1	0.5	0.2	1.8	0.6	0.6	1.5
N	36	36	36	36	36	36	36	36	36	36	36	36
Baboon 2												
Mean	130	74	75	135	77	81	149*	100*	144*	123	79	101
S.E.M.	0.9	0.8	0.8	1.3	1.0	2.4	0.2	0.1	3.1	0.6	0.4	2.1
N	36	36	36	36	36	36	36	36	36	36	36	36
Baboon 3												
Mean	123	76	96	119	74	88	161*	111*	121*	130	85	103
S.E.M.	0.6	0.5	0.7	0.6	0.6	1.0	0.4	0.3	2.4	0.7	0.5	1.6
N	27	27	27	27	27	27	45	45	45	45	45	45
Baboon 4												
Mean	114	67	63	116	68	63	140*	106*	105*	103	74	73
S.E.M.	0.5	0.6	0.5	0.9	1.0	0.9	0.5	0.3	1.6	0.5	0.4	1.9
N	45	45	72	45	45	72	27	27	27	27	27	27
Group												
Mean	123	73	85	123	72	82	149*	105*	126*	119	81	92
S.E.M.	0.7	0.7	1.0	0.9	0.9	1.4	0.4	0.2	2.2	0.6	0.5	1.8

turned to approximately basal levels (or slightly above) within 6 to 8 hours. In contrast, cardiovascular changes during the preexperimental baseline period, summarized in the left-hand panel of Fig. 1, show virtually no change in blood pressure (save the minimal diurnal variation) throughout the 24-hour interval, and only moderate fluctuations in heart rate.

Table 1 summarizes the results of an analysis of these changes testing the statistical significance of the differences in blood pressure and heart rate between the last nine 40-minute intervals (6 hours) of the conditioning-on periods and the first nine 40-minute intervals (6 hours) of the conditioning-off periods for each animal individually and for the group as a whole. In addition, Table 1 shows the statistical significance of the difference in blood pressure and heart rate between the last nine 40-minute conditioning-on periods (6 hours) and the nine 40-minute intervals representing an identical time span (that is, 6 p.m. to midnight) during the preexperimental baseline period for each animal individually and for the group as a whole. Highly significant ($P < .001$) differences are shown for all measures in both individual and group averages.

That these large-magnitude, sustained elevations in blood pressure are related directly and specifically to the programmed contingency requirements of the instrumental conditioning procedure is further confirmed by the results obtained with two additional baboons exposed to virtually identical experimental conditions with the exception that concurrent food-reward and shock-avoidance were made contingent upon *decreasing* diastolic blood pressure. Over extended intervals (6 months or more) of daily exposure to this instrumental procedure for lower-

ing blood pressure (involving electric shocks, food deprivation and reward, surgery and chronic catheterization, confinement and chair restraint) neither animal showed any change from baseline cardiovascular levels under the same general laboratory conditions obtaining for the four baboons which provide the basis for this report.

The results of this experiment show clearly that instrumental learning of cardiovascular responses can produce sustained large-magnitude changes in blood pressure which cannot be accounted for on the basis of short-term "voluntary mediators" (for example, the Valsalva maneuver) (3). All four baboons in this study showed daily elevations of 30 mm-Hg or more in both systolic and diastolic blood pressures and maintained such elevations for the entire 12-hour conditioning-on segment of each experimental session. These findings suggest the involvement of more durable adaptive mechanisms supporting the sustained pressure elevations, although the relative contributions of cardiac output and peripheral resistance to the establishment and maintenance of these hypertensive levels cannot be determined from the present data alone. In dogs anticipating (over a 15-hour interval) performance on a shock-avoidance procedure (13), and in rhesus monkeys during a 72-hour shock-avoidance procedure (14), similar blood pressure elevations have been reported, and concurrent measurements of cardiac output under such conditions (15) have revealed that the pressure elevations were determined by substantial increases in total peripheral resistance. Although the relationship of these sustained blood pressure elevations in the baboon to the circulatory changes characteristic of essential hypertension in humans (*16*) is far from clear, chronic exposure to aversive behavioral conditioning procedures has been reported to produce hypertensive patterns (*17*), with a bradycardia accompanying the chronic pressure elevations in at least some animals (*18*). The present findings with the baboon extend the range of potentially useful laboratory models for the analysis of environmental-behavioral influences upon the cardiovascular system, and call for further experimental scrutiny of the physiological mechanisms (for example, baroreceptor reflex) which mediate this significant alteration of the systemic circulation.

ALAN H. HARRIS, WILLIE J. GILLIAM
JACK D. FINDLEY, JOSEPH V. BRADY
*Department of Psychiatry and
Behavioral Sciences, Johns Hopkins
University School of Medicine,
Baltimore, Maryland 21205*

References and Notes

1. L. V. DiCara and N. E. Miller, *Psychosom. Med.* **30**, 489 (1968).
2. H. Benson, J. A. Herd, W. H. Morse, R. T. Kelleher, *Amer. J. Physiol.* **217**, 30 (1969).
3. L. A. Plumlee, *Psychophysiology* **4**, 507 (1968).
4. A. H. Harris, J. D. Findley, J. V. Brady, *Conditional Reflex* **6**, 215 (1971).
5. J. Brener and R. A. Kleinman, *Nature* **226**, 1063 (1970); H. Benson, D. Shapiro, B. Tursky, G. E. Schwartz, *Science* **173**, 740 (1971).
6. D. Shapiro, B. Tursky, E. Gershon, M. Stern, *Science* **163**, 588 (1969); D. Shapiro, B. Tursky, G. E. Schwartz, *Psychosom. Med.* **32**, 417 (1970); *Circ. Res.* **26** (Suppl. 1), 27 (1970); G. E. Schwartz, D. Shapiro, B. Tursky, *Psychosom. Med.* **33**, 57 (1971); G. E. Schwartz, *Science* **175**, 90 (1972); D. Shapiro, G. E. Schwartz, B. Tursky, *Psychophysiology* **9**, 296 (1972).
7. E. S. Katkin and E. N. Murray, *Psychol. Bull.* **70**, 52 (1968); A. Crider, G. Schwartz, S. Shnidman, *ibid.* **71**, 455 (1969); E. S. Katkin, E. N. Murray, R. Lachman, *ibid.*, p. 462.
8. J. D. Findley, W. W. Robinson, W. J. Gilliam, *J. Exp. Anal. Behav.* **15**, 69 (1971).
9. J. Perez-Cruet, L. Plumlee, J. E. Newton, *Proc. Symp. Bio-Med. Eng.* **1**, 383 (1966); D. Werdegar, D. G. Johnson, J. W. Mason, *J. Appl. Physiol.* **19**, 519 (1964).
10. A. De La Pena and J. W. Goldzieher, in *The Baboon in Medical Research*, Proceedings of the Second International Symposium on the Baboon and Its Uses as an Experimental Animal, H. Vagtborg, Ed. (Univ. of Texas Press, Austin, 1965), vol. 2, p. 379.
11. J. D. Findley, J. V. Brady, W. W. Robinson, W. J. Gilliam, *Commun. Behav. Biol.* **6**, 49 (1971).
12. M. E. T. Swinnen, *Proc. Annu. Conf. Eng. Med. Biol.* **10**, 18.4 (1968).
13. D. E. Anderson and J. V. Brady, *Psychosom. Med.* **35**, 4 (1973).
14. R. P. Forsyth, *Science* **173**, 546 (1971).
15. D. E. Anderson and J. Tosheff, *J. Appl. Physiol.* **34**, 650 (1973).
16. I. Page and J. W. McCubbin, in *Handbook of Physiology*, W. F. Hamilton, Ed. (American Physiological Soc., Washington, D.C., 1965), section 2, *Circulation*, vol. 3, pp. 2163–2208.
17. J. A. Herd, W. H. Morse, R. T. Kelleher, L. G. Jones, *Amer. J. Physiol.* **217**, 24 (1969).
18. R. P. Forsyth, *Psychosom. Med.* **31**, 300 (1969).
19. Supported by NIH grant HE-06945 and ONR subcontract N0014-70-C-0350.

5 June 1973

Large Magnitude Voluntary Heart Rate Changes

3

David T. Wells

ABSTRACT

An experiment was performed to demonstrate methods for enabling subjects (Ss) to produce large magnitude heart rate (HR) changes under conditions which include adequate controls for basal HR changes and elicitation of the HR response by breathing changes. The methods used were an attempt to optimize motivational, feedback, and practice variables. Of 9 Ss, 6 displayed mean HR increases ranging from 16.7 bpm to 35.2 bpm. The greatest mean HR decrease for any S was 3.1 bpm. Control procedures indicated that breathing changes accompanying large increases in HR were not sufficient to account for the magnitude of HR change.

DESCRIPTORS: Voluntary control, Operant control, Heart rate. (D. T. Wells)

In a detailed review and criticism of the literature, Katkin and Murray (1969) proposed that a distinction, originally made by Skinner (1938), between operant *conditioning* and operant (or voluntary) *control* of autonomic responses may help to clarify research objectives in this field. Thus, the researcher who is interested in *control* of autonomic functions may wish to detect mediating behavior, not to resolve the theoretical issue of whether the response is operant or elicited, but as an aid in making the control more efficient.

Examining the literature on voluntary control of heart rate (HR) in light of this distinction, Headrick, Feather, and Wells (1971) found three sources of difficulty in evaluating results for evidence of *control*. The first is that the use of the yoked-control procedure offers the same possibilities for spurious results in the demonstration of voluntary control as it does in the demonstration of operant conditioning (Church, 1964; Katkin & Murray, 1968). The second source of difficulty is that in studies where HR change has not been assessed relative to prestimulus level, ambiguity exists over whether observed differences in HR were the result of increases or decreases in rate, or both. The third source of difficulty is the relatively small magnitude of reported changes in HR, which may contribute to lack of consistency of results across studies, as well as making more difficult any examination of concomitant or mediating responses.

The present experiment was a direct outgrowth of critical comments by Headrick et al. (1971). Its purpose was not to demonstrate operant *conditioning* of HR (that is, not to show unelicited changes in HR); but rather to demonstrate methods for enabling Ss to produce large magnitude HR changes under volun-

This research was conducted at Duke University Medical Center under NIMH Grant 2 RO1-11549 to Ben W. Feather, M.D., Ph.D., for whose advice and encouragement the author is indebted. The author also wishes to thank Mr. Edward Walter for computer programming of statistical analyses and Mr. Joseph Burch for his assistance with the electronic equipment used in this study.

Address requests for reprints to: David T. Wells, Ph.D., Department of Psychiatry, Baltimore City Hospitals, 4940 Eastern Avenue, Baltimore, Maryland 21224.

tary *control*, given the specified conditions of the experiment. Use of the yoked-control design was avoided by having each S attempt both increases and decreases in HR. Changes in HR were measured relative to pretrial level, as in the Headrick et al. (1971) study.

An additional procedure in the present experiment was designed to contribute to methodology in evaluating concomitant responses. Most investigations have measured respiration as a possible source of eliciting stimulation for observed voluntary HR changes. Evaluation of this possible relationship has been made by testing whether there is statistically significant respiration change accompanying the HR change. However, changes in the two responses could equally well be viewed as parallel effects of some common cause. The present experiment incorporated procedures designed to provide a more adequate evaluation of the effects of respiration changes.

Method

Subjects

Two female and 7 male Ss, ranging in age from 18 to 21 yrs, participated in the experiment. All were university students. Eight Ss were selected from respondents to a newspaper advertisement. The other S was selected because he had shown large magnitude HR increase in a previous, single-session experiment (Headrick et al., 1971). He was run initially as a pilot S; but, since the procedures used were almost identical to those for the other Ss, his data are also presented in the results. None of the Ss had any medical disorder, and none were taking medication at the time of the experiment.

Apparatus

All physiological variables were recorded on a Grass Model 7 polygraph. Heartbeat was detected from electrodes applied to the chest for male Ss and over the shin and medial portion of the clavicle for female Ss. In both cases an indifferent electrode was applied over the mastoid process. The amplified signal from these electrodes was used to trigger a Grass Model 7 tachograph. Output voltage from the tachograph channel was used to provide feedback of HR to the S. The feedback apparatus was identical to that used in Experiment 2 of the study by Headrick et al. (1971). Briefly, tachograph output was displayed for the S during trials on a Simpson Model 29 DC microammeter. The meter was mounted behind a half-silvered mirror and was visible only when lights behind the mirror were turned on. Programming equipment counted number of heartbeats in each pretrial period and automatically adjusted the balance of the meter circuit so that the meter reading during a trial was at center scale when the S's HR was equal to his mean rate in the immediately preceding pretrial period. The gain of the meter circuit was set so that an increase of 40 bpm from pretrial mean resulted in a full-scale deflection to the right. A comparable decrease in rate resulted in a full-scale deflection to the left.

Respiratory flow was measured by means of a disposable-type oxygen mask specially adapted by fitting a piece of #500 copper mesh screen in the orifice of the mask. The entire respiratory flow passed through the screen, creating a pressure gradient across the screen proportional to direction and velocity of flow. The pressure gradient was measured with a Grass Model 5 pressure transducer connected to a DC preamplifier on the polygraph. Pen deflection was calibrated in terms of liter per min flow by standardization with a commercial flowmeter. Respiratory volume was calculated from the tracing by measuring the area under pen deflections with an Amsler Model 2002 planimeter.

The output from an electronic breathing simulator was delivered to the *S* through earphones, and the *S* matched his rate of respiration to this signal. The signal produced by this device was in the form of "white" noise whose frequency distribution and amplitude changes closely approximated the sounds of human breathing. Inspiration and expiration time, as well as pauses in mid-cycle and between cycles, could be adjusted independently. Careful adjustment of these parameters permitted a close approximation to the *S*'s normal breathing pattern.

The *S* sat in a semi-reclining position inside a sound-attenuated chamber and was observed over closed-circuit television.

Procedure

Selection of Subjects. When a prospective *S* telephoned in response to the advertisement, the experimenter (*E*) made every effort to discourage him from participating either for money ($2.00 per session) or out of mild curiosity. If the prospective *S* then agreed to come to the laboratory for an interview, he was given an orientation to the problem being studied. All the apparatus was shown and explained to him, and the exact procedures to be used were described. While 18 *S*s remained willing to be in the experiment, *E* selected on a subjective basis the 8 who seemed to have the greatest motivation and interest.

Experimental Procedures. Subjects participated in 13 experimental sessions, each lasting 1¼ to 1½ hrs. Each *S* had approximately 3 sessions per week. Only 11 of the 13 sessions were HR training sessions. Of the other 2, one (session 1) was devoted to giving the *S* practice in pacing respiration. In the other non-training session (session 8) *S* was instructed to breathe at varying depths, but constant rates, during 10 90-sec periods. Change in HR during these periods was measured, but not fed back to *S*. Instead, the signal from the respiration channel of the polygraph was displayed on the feedback meter, both to aid instructions on depth of respiration and to duplicate as closely as possible the stimulus conditions during HR training trials. *S*s were fully informed about what the meter display represented. They were instructed to increase respiratory depth during 3 of the 90-sec periods, decrease depth during 3 periods, and maintain a constant depth during 4 periods.

During the other 11 sessions (sessions 2 through 7 and 9 through 13) *S*s attempted to control HR during 90-sec trial periods. Of these sessions, the first (session 2), the middle (session 7), and the last (session 13) were no-feedback sessions. Feedback was withheld on all trials of these 3 sessions by disconnecting the meter circuit from the tachograph amplifier. The meter was lighted during these trials, but its reading stayed at center scale. The *S*s were informed of these conditions prior to each of the 3 sessions. During each of the 11 sessions of attempted HR control, 2 blocks of 10 trials each were presented, separated by a 5-min rest period during which *E* entered the chamber and allowed *S* to remove headphones and respiration mask. The *S* was to increase HR during one block of trials and decrease HR during the other. The order of increase and decrease blocks was alternated from session to session, starting with increase first on the first session.

Each session began with a rest period of approximately 15 min during which the breathing simulator was adjusted to *S*'s observed pattern of respiration. Each trial was preceded by a 30-sec pretrial period during which baseline HR was measured, but no stimuli were delivered to the *S*. The trial period started immediately following the pretrial period and consisted of the meter being illuminated for 90 sec. After a 10-sec delay following the end of the trial, a signal light informed the *S* that he could move and adjust his position in the chair if necessary. This movement period lasted 15 sec, and *S* was instructed that at all other times he was to remain as still as possible. After a pause of 10, 15, or 20 sec (presented in nonsystematic order) the pretrial period began.

Data Quantification and Analyses

Heart Rate. Mean HR was calculated for the various measurement periods from the polygraph charts by manually counting number of heartbeats in the period and dividing by the length of the period in minutes. The HR score for each trial period of attempted HR control or respiratory manipulation was expressed as the mean HR during the trial, minus the mean HR in the immediately preceding 30 sec.

In addition, a sample plot of HR change within trials was derived from the increase trials of *S* 6 on session 13. Pretrial, trial, and 10-sec posttrial intervals were divided into 5-sec periods. Mean HR for each 5-sec period of each trial was calculated from the cardiotachometer tracing by averaging the bpm values of all heart cycles whose duration lay at least 50% within that 5-sec period. Mean HR values for corresponding 5-sec periods were then averaged across the 10 trials.

The statistical significance of HR changes during training was initially tested by an analysis of covariance (Scheffe, 1959) with pretrial rate as the covariate. However, application of Hartley's test for homogeneity of variance (Winer, 1962) revealed that variance of scores was not the same from session to session for most of the *S*s. This finding was not changed for one *S* whose scores were inverted. Since unequal variances would violate one of the assumptions underlying the analysis of covariance, it was decided to use individual *t* tests on data within sessions. In order to reduce the number of tests performed, and thereby the probability of falsely rejecting some null hypothesis, only data from sessions 12 and 13 were tested. Sessions 12 and 13 were chosen to reflect the final level of performance with and without feedback, respectively. The *t* tests employed were derived from the analysis of covariance model[1] (Scheffe, 1959) and contained a correction for dependency of the scores on pretrial level. These tests were applied separately to each *S*'s data. Group data were not used for these tests, since the purpose of the experiment was to describe each *S*'s performance under the specified experimental conditions, rather than to draw inferences about populations from which these *S*s might be a sample.

Respiration. Inspiration volume was measured by planimeter method from polygraph tracings of respiratory flow. Total inspiration volume, in liters, was calculated for pretrial and trial periods of respiratory manipulation, of attempted HR increase on the session showing the greatest mean increase, and of attempted HR decrease on the session showing the greatest mean decrease. Amount of HR change associated with a given change in respiratory depth was compiled separately for each *S*. The mean change in HR and respiration was calculated for the 3 trials of instructed increase in respiratory depth. In some cases *S*s were not able to produce an overall decrease in respiratory depth during

[1] The author is indebted to Dr. David G. Herr for formulation of the statistical procedures used in this study.

all 3 of the trials where this was instructed. In such cases means of HR and respiratory changes were calculated for those trials which did show a decrease in respiratory depth.

Results

Heart Rate Change During Training

Fig. 1 presents mean changes from pretrial HR during both increase and decrease trials for each S, uncorrected for dependency on pretrial level. Increase performance for Ss 1, 2, and 3 remained below about 7 bpm for the entire experiment. The remaining Ss all reached a level of at least a 15 bpm increase from pretrial rates on one or more sessions. After achieving a mean increase of 16.7 bpm on session 10, S 4 withdrew from the experiment.

Two Ss (Ss 7 and 9) failed to show a mean decrease from pretrial rates on any session. Only on sessions 9 and 10 did S 5 show a mean decrease. The largest decrease shown by any S was 3.1 bpm for S 3 on session 11. In general, then, the decrease performance of these Ss can be characterized as minimal compared to increase performance and within the range of changes reported in previous experiments.

The results of the t tests showed that, with the exception of S 2, all Ss achieved a significant increase in HR on session 12 during increase trials ($p < .0083$). (Data from S 4's last session, session 10, were used for these tests.) During decrease trials, however, only Ss 2, 3, and 4 showed significant decreases in rate. Heart rate during decrease trials for S 7 was significantly higher than pretrial level. The t tests for the difference between changes on increase and decrease trials on session 12 were significant for all Ss.

The remaining t tests indicated that on session 13 increase performance without feedback continued to be significantly above pretrial rates for all but S 1. (Data for S 4 could not be tested, since he withdrew from the experiment following session 10.) Only S 3 maintained significant decreases in session 13. All but Ss 1 and 7 achieved significantly greater increases during increase trials than during decrease trials in session 13.

Fig. 2 shows the average HR response of S 6 during the 10 increase trials of session 13. This S's mean HR increase on session 13 was 23.2 bpm. His performance in this session was typical, both in terms of magnitude (see Fig. 1) and form of the response. The typical features of response form which Fig. 2 illustrates are a rapid initial rise in HR (almost 10 bpm within the first 5-sec period), a more prolonged second rise in rate, stable high rate during most of the rest of the trial, and rapid deceleration following trial offset.

Pretrial Heart Rate

Pretrial HR was examined for two reasons: (a) to determine whether Ss showed a consistent difference between HR prior to increase trials and HR prior to decrease trials and (b) to provide information on the amount of change in baseline HR, both across and within sessions. Five Ss had higher HRs prior to increase trials and 4 had higher HRs prior to decrease trials during sessions 2–5. During sessions 10–13 4 Ss were higher prior to increase trials and 5 were higher prior to decrease trials. A sign test (Siegel, 1956) indicated no significant difference in either comparison. Differences in rates prior to the two trial types were less than 3 bpm, except for S 2, whose HR averaged 4.4 bpm higher prior to increase trials during sessions 10–13.

HRs were slower during the second 10 than during the first 10 pretrial periods of a session, during both early and late sessions for all but one S (sign test, $p = .02$). Another feature of this data is the range of HR changes shown by different Ss, from virtually no change ($+0.25$) to a decline of 6.80 bpm. Pretrial HR within halves of sessions also was higher during early versus late sessions for all but one S (sign test, $p = .02$). The change in pretrial HR across sessions ranged from $+0.25$ to -6.85 bpm.

Heart Rate During Respiration Control Trials

Table 1 presents comparisons between HR and respiratory change during trial periods of respiratory manipulation on session 8 and during HR training trials. For each S showing relatively large magnitude HR increases (Ss 4–9), HR increase was greater during every HR training trial examined than it was during any of the periods of instructed deep breathing. Table 1 indicates that all but one of these Ss had a mean increase in depth of respiration at least as great during respiration control trials as during increase HR trials. Fig. 3 illustrates these data in the case of S 9. For Ss 1–3 during increase HR trials and all Ss during decrease trials the same sort of clear separation in amount of HR change with given changes in respiratory depth did not occur. Table 1 indicates that the effects on HR of changes in depth of respiration seem to be quite variable across Ss, particularly in the case of decreases in respiratory depth, but for the most part limited to HR changes of less than 10%.

Discussion

This experiment has succeeded in producing results which fulfill both of its primary objectives. First, it has demonstrated that HR can be brought under voluntary control by human Ss under restricted laboratory conditions which rule out elicitation of the HR response by exteroceptive stimulation. Measurement of HR changes during trials relative to a pretrial baseline constituted an automatic correction for adaptational effects. Using this method of measurement, only 3 of the Ss achieved a statistically significant decrease in HR on the final session with feedback. By contrast, all Ss achieved a statistically significant increase above pretrial rates on that session, and 6 of them showed a mean increase of more than 15 bpm.

It is interesting that performance at increasing HR was maintained, although for some Ss at a lower level, without feedback on the last session. If feedback of HR is considered the source of reinforcement for the response, the sessions without feedback can be considered extinction sessions. Two explanations might be offered for failure to extinguish the response on the last session. One is that 10 trials without feedback are not sufficient to extinguish the response, and with further no-feedback sessions extinction would be more complete. Another explanation is that Ss developed a sensitivity to internal sources of feedback and were able to rely on these sources in the absence of external feedback from the meter. Although voluntary control of HR in the absence of external feedback has been reported before (Brener, Kleinman, & Goesling, 1969), a more extended series of extinction trials in future research would provide needed information for further defining the characteristics of responses under these conditions.

The experiment has fulfilled its second objective by demonstrating an improved method for the assessment of possible elicitation of the HR response by a preceding response ("mediation"). By showing that the increases in respiratory

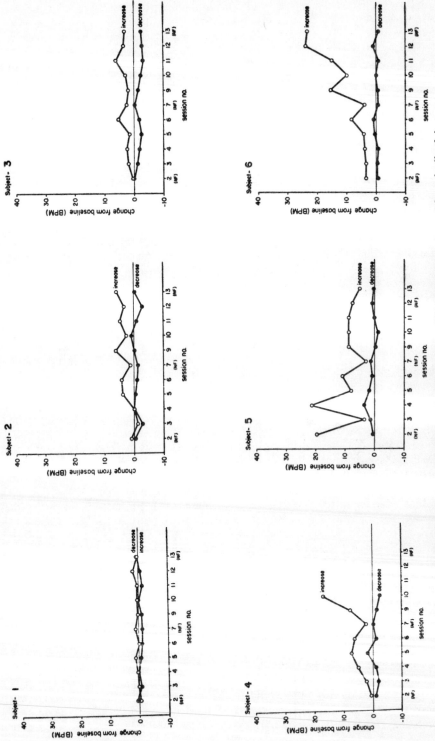

Fig. 1. Mean change from pretrial heart rate across sessions. (NF indicates sessions with no feedback.)

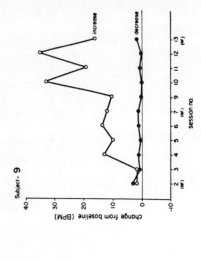

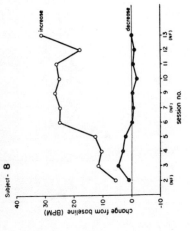

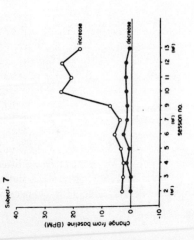

Fig. 1.—*Cont.*

TABLE 1

Heart rate response versus changes in respiratory depth

Subj.	Control Trials With Increased Respiratory Depth		Increase HR Trials		Control Trials With Decreased Respiratory Depth		Decrease HR Trials	
	% Change in Resp.	% Change in HR	% Change in Resp.	% Change in HR	% Change in Resp.	% Change in HR	% Change in Resp.	% Change in HR
1	+49.7	+1.6 (+0.9)	+14.5	+2.9 (+1.7)	−5.9	−1.3(−0.7)	−4.1	−1.9(−1.3)
2	+88.1	+3.0 (+2.2)	+64.4	+9.9 (+6.1)	−2.4	+5.9(+4.0)	−2.5	−3.6(−2.9)
3	+135.6	+21.5(+10.2)	+12.2	+11.8 (+6.3)	−40.8	−6.4(−3.1)	−10.4	−4.5(−3.1)
4	+53.1	+2.3 (+1.6)	+51.8	+23.0(+16.7)	−30.2	−1.6(−0.9)	−9.4	−3.4(−2.6)
5	+325.2	+6.8 (+4.5)	+78.6	+29.1(+21.3)	—	—	−8.7	−1.5(−1.1)
6	+148.5	+5.5 (+2.9)	+86.0	+39.1(+23.2)	−40.2	−1.7(−0.9)	+6.4	−1.2(−0.7)
7	+154.7	+5.9 (+3.3)	+108.0	+39.2(+24.7)	—	—	+12.9	+1.3(+0.1)
8	+73.5	+23.2(+13.3)	+158.4	+58.2(+31.0)	−22.2	−0.8(−0.4)	+0.4	−3.0(−1.8)
9	+101.6	+4.7 (+3.1)	+75.5	+51.4(+35.2)	−32.1	+0.7(+0.3)	+5.1	+0.2(+0.1)

Note.—Numbers in parentheses are the bpm equivalents of percentage changes.

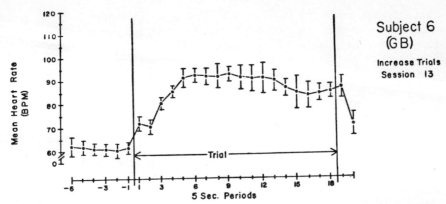

Fig. 2. Heart rate responses of *S* 6 on increase trials of session 13. Each of the connected points represents the mean value for 10 trials. Vertical lines mark one standard deviation above and below the mean.

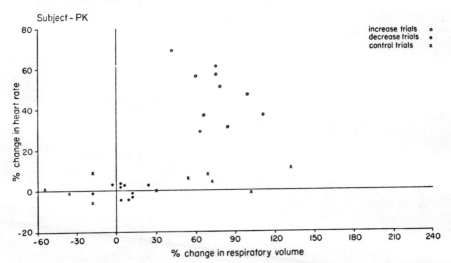

Fig. 3. Change in heart rate as a function of change in depth of respiration for *S* 9. Data are from increase trials on session 12 and decrease trials on session 10.

depth which accompanied large-magnitude HR increases were not of sufficient magnitude to elicit the HR change in themselves, respiratory behavior was ruled out as a sufficient source of HR increases for 5 of the 6 most successful *S*s. The systematic application of this method in future research could answer the same questions about other responses which are suspected of eliciting the HR change.

The importance of attention to changes in basal HR is indicated by data from the present study showing a consistent tendency for pretrial HR to decline both across and within sessions and a considerable between-*S* variability in the magnitude of decline. Failure to adequately assess decline in baseline HR could result in overestimation of HR decreases due to voluntary control. In addition, between-*S* variability in amount of decline in pretrial HR supports the notion that within-*S* controls are the most appropriate for assessment of changes in baseline HR.

While control procedures indicated that the degree of change in depth of respiration was not sufficient by itself to cause such large increases in HR, the presence of breathing changes during trials with large-magnitude HR increases raises questions about the specificity of the HR response. It is obvious that, unlike the findings with rats (Miller & Banuazizi, 1968), the responses of subjects in the present experiment were not limited to changes in HR. While respiration increases were not sufficient to raise HR, they may have been necessary. The limits of specificity of the HR response in human Ss is an important area for future research, in part because such investigations could provide clues to the nature of the underlying physiological mechanisms involved. The methods developed in the present experiment should prove useful in studies of concomitant responses, since large magnitude changes in HR should lead to more easily detectable changes in associated responses.

In addition, future research should confirm the generality of the present findings in different S populations. One limiting factor of such research is that in order to ensure high motivation a certain amount of selection of Ss is necessary. It is not likely that college psychology students fulfilling mandatory subject requirements will have as great motivation for success in changing HR as did the Ss in this experiment.

REFERENCES

Brener, J., Kleinman, R., & Goesling, W. The effects of different exposures to augmented sensory feedback on the control of heart rate. *Psychophysiology*, 1969, *5*, 510–516.

Church. R. M. Systematic effect of random error in the yoked control design. *Psychological Bulletin*, 1964, *62*, 122–131.

Headrick, M. V., Feather, B. W., & Wells, D. T. Unidirectional and large magnitude heart rate changes with augmented sensory feedback. *Psychophysiology*, 1971, *8*, 132–142.

Katkin, E. S., & Murray, E. N. Instrumental conditioning of autonomically mediated behavior: Theoretical and methodological issues. *Psychological Bulletin*, 1969, *70*, 52–68.

Miller, N. E., & Banuazizi, A. Instrumental learning by curarized rats of a specific visceral response, intestinal or cardiac. *Journal of Comparative & Physiological Psychology*, 1968. *66*, 8–12.

Scheffe, H. *The analysis of variance.* New York: John Wiley & Sons, 1959.

Siegel, S. *Nonparametric statistics for the behavioral sciences.* New York: McGraw-Hill, 1956.

Skinner, B. F. *The behavior of organisms: An experimental analysis.* New York: Appleton-Century, 1938.

Winer, B. J. *Statistical principles in experimental design.* New York: McGraw-Hill, 1962.

Effect of Immunosympathectomy
on Operant Heart Rate Conditioning in the
Curarized Rat

4

E. W. Thornton and C. Van-Toller

THORNTON, E. W. AND C. VAN-TOLLER. *Effect of immunosympathectomy on operant heart rate conditioning in the curarised rat.* PHYSIOL. BEHAV. 10(2) 197–201, 1973.– Attempts were made to shape increases in heart rate in immunosympathectomised and control animals using an operant schedule involving negative reinforcement. Although all the animals showed a consistent mild tachycardia to the shock reinforcer throughout training, the results indicated that the immunosympathectomised rats were unable to maintain the high levels of heart rate required by the schedule. In contrast, increases in heart rate were successfully shaped in control animals.

Immunosympathectomy   Heart rate   Conditioning   Curare

LEVI-MONTALCINI and her co-workers [12, 13, 15] have described a nerve growth factor antiserum which produces hypotrophy in the sympathetic nervous system. Since Adolph [1] had demonstrated that the control of heart rate in small mammals is sympathetically dominant, it would follow that rodents who have been subjected to immuno-sympathectomy should reveal differences in their cardiac rates. Brody [4] and Hofer, Engel and Weiner [10], using rats, and Wenzel, Carson and Chase [23], using mice have shown immunosympathectomy to have little effect on baseline heart rates. However, Wenzel [22] has reported that Carson [6] found immunosympathectomised mice had lower heart rate baselines than controls. Using a telemetry device, Carson examined the heart rate response of mice in a number of behavioural tests. She found that, although similar levels of tachycardia to stimuli were seen in both the immunosympathectomised and control mice, these increases in heart rate were maintained for much briefer periods in the experimental animals.

In a number of recent investigations of cardiac functions [7, 8, 16] considerable success has been obtained in demonstrating the effects of operant contingencies for conditioning heart rate changes in deeply curarised animals. Unfortunately there has been little systematic investigation of the mechanisms underlying these changes. However,

[1] This experiment is part of an unpublished Ph.D. thesis submitted to the University of Durham, 1971.
[2] Present address: Department of Psychology, University of Liverpool, Liverpool, L69 3BX, England.

DiCara and Stone [9] have reported that operant increases in heart rate in the curarised rat are a result of increased sympathetic activity. It would be of value, therefore, to determine if it is possible to operantly shape heart-rate increases in immunosympathectomised animals.

METHOD

Animals

A litter of twelve animals was obtained from a multiparous female taken from a strain of hooded rats maintained in the Department of Psychology, University of Durham. A split litter design was used with half the neonates receiving NGF antiserum and the other half normal horse serum. Sera used in this study were purchased from the Wellcome Research Laboratories (Beckenham, Kent, England). Preliminary studies had shown that, unlike mice, large amounts of the expensive NGF antiserum were required to produce substantial hypertrophy of the sympathetic nervous system in rats. This factor restricted the number of animals that could be used. Using a standard technique [18, 20] the immunosympathectomised rats (IS) were injected with 0.1 ml of a double strength antiserum and the control animals with an equivalent amount of a normal horse serum (NHS). Injections were given daily for eleven days postpartum. The litter was weaned after 28 days and the animals separated into individual cages. The experiment was started when the animals were approximately two months old.

Apparatus

During heart rate training procedures, the animal was situated in a sound attenuating chamber 40 cm wide, 45 cm high and 32 cm deep. The enclosure was fitted with a 60 W lamp, situated 15 cm above the rat, which served as a discriminative stimulus. Shock was applied via two wires wrapped around the tail. A Grason Stadler shock generator (Model E106 4GS) was set to deliver fixed pulses of 0.1 sec at an intensity of 0.5 mA.

Throughout the experiment aritficial ventilation was maintained from a small animal respirator (E & M Instruments, Houston, Texas). Connections to the animal inside the chamber were made via tubing and a snout mask. The procedure has been described by Trowill [19] and Thornton [18].

The electrodes used for recording the heart rate were stainless steel needles inserted subdermally on either side of the thorax. The indifferent electrode was a hypodermic needle inserted into the peritoneal cavity. A connection from this needle to the outside of the chamber by polythylene tubing allowed additional doses of the drug to be administered without distrubance to the rat during training.

The EKG output from an Alvar electroencephalograph was taken from the terminal stage of the power amplifier and passed through a sensitive electronic pulse former whose final stage operated a reed relay. Adjustments were made so that the reed relay was just operated by the QRS wave of the EKG signal. The pulse from the electronic pulse former operated the criterion and counter circuitry. A simultaneous cardiotachometer recording was obtained from a Beckman (Type RP) Dynograph.

Procedure

The rat was injected I.P. with 0.6 mg/Kg of d-tubo-curarine chloride. In preliminary studies it had been found that this dose was sufficient to completely suppress EMG activity in the gastrocnemius muscle if supplemented with additional doses of 0.06 mg/Kg injected through the indifferent electrode every six min throughout the experimental period. When the rat became flaccid and showed signs of respiratory failure, it was placed on its side and fitted into the snout mask. Artificial ventilation was applied at 70 c/min with a peak pressure of 14 cm of water. The temperature of the enclosure was maintained at approximately 30°C. Electrodes for recording heart rate were inserted under xylocaine anaesthesia. The shock electrodes were then attached to the tail and the chamber closed. A period of 30 min was allowed for the heart rate to stablise, and to enable an appropriate criterion level to be selected such that it would be attained on about 40 percent of the sampling periods.

The method and circuit for determining whether the heart rate of an animal was above or below a certain criterion level was based on the procedure described by Trowill [19]. In essence, the circuit determined whether a sample number of heart beats occurred in a faster or slower time than predicted if the heart rate was steady at the given criterion level. Samples were taken over intervals ranging from 1.7–2.3 secs.

On any operant trial, if the criterion level was attained within five sec, the light went out and no shock was delivered. However, if the criterion level had not been attained within the period of five sec, then a 0.1 sec pulse of shock was programmed to be delivered. Similar shocks were delivered if successive samples of heart rate indicated that the criterion level had not been reached. Thus, pulsed shock was delivered at the end of each sample until the criterion level was attained. When the criterion level was reached, the light went off and the trial terminated. Throughout training, the last trial in every block of trials was an operant test trial in which the light came on for five sec but the criterion circuitry was inactivated. This trial allowed the determination of the mean heart rate during five sec of the operant stimulus in the absence of contamination by shock presentation or light termination. A five sec blank trial was incorporated into the training schedule. During this blank trial no stimulus was presented but the number of heart beats was recorded.

The operant training schedule was programmed to comprise of eight blocks of thirty trials, consisting of ten operant and twenty blank trials. The end of each block of trials was marked by a single operant test trial. Trials were presented with a fixed intertrial interval of 20 sec. Within any block, each trial occurred in a predetermined random manner with the constraint that no more than two operant trials occurred consecutively and, that no more than five blank trials separated any two operant trials. The sequence of trials within each block of the training schedule was consistent and identical for all the animals.

If, during training, the animal successfully avoided shock on four consecutive operant trials, the criterion was made more difficult (by approximately 2 or 3 percent). If the combined number of shocks received on two consecutive operant trials was greater than 20 pulses, then the criterion level was reduced by an equivalent amount. When the schedule had been completed, the programming apparatus was turned off and no further injections were administered. Initial studies [18] had shown this particular schedule to be successful in shaping heart rate changes in normal rats.

The basic design of the experiment consisted of two treatment groups of four animals shaped for increases in heart rate: IS increase group and NHS increase group. No tendency had been found for the heart rates of normal animals to change under the baseline conditions of curarisation and artificial ventilation. However, controls were necessary to confirm that the aversive training schedule in conjunction with baseline procedures did not increase heart rates in the treatment increase groups regardless of the specific training schedule in effect. Thus, as a minimal control for such tendencies, two IS and two NHS rats were shaped for decreases in rat.

Physiological Measurements

Four weeks after operant training, animals were weighed and killed over ether. The cervical and thoracic ganglia were dissected out cleaned of fat and connective tissue and weighed. A similar procedure was used with the adrenals.

RESULTS

The range of heart rates of both the immunosympath-ectomised (IS = 457.2 ± 20.2 beats per min) and control (NHS = 454.2 ± 57.0 beats per min) animals were large and

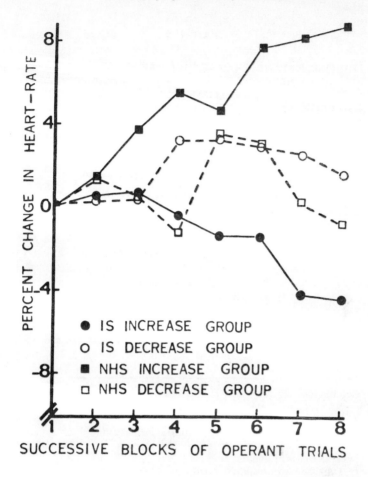

FIG. 1. Mean heart rate changes for each group over successive
blocks of trials.

showed a number of overlaps. Consequently, no evidence
was obtained to support a finding of lower resting rates in
IS animals during the baseline conditions of curarisation
and artificial ventilation.

An early study [7] had shown good evidence for
discrimination in operant heart rate changes between
reinforced and non reinforced trials. However, other studies
[16] have not consistently obtained the same positive
result. In the present experiment, no evidence was found
for any discrimination in heart rate responses between
operant test and blank trials during the training schedule.
As a consequence, it was decided to analyse the results in
eight blocks of operant test trials.

The group mean changes in heart rate over the blocks of
trials for both groups of IS and NHS animals are presented
in Fig. 1. The graph shows little evidence for success in
shaping increases in the heart rate of IS animals and,

TABLE 1

THE PERCENTAGE CHANGE IN HEART RATE OVER TRAIN-
ING ATTAINED BY EACH IMMUNOSYMPATHECTOMISED
AND CONTROL ANIMAL, TOGETHER WITH THE FREQUENCY
AND PROBABILITY OF RECEIVING SHOCKS DURING TRAIN-
ING BY THAT ANIMAL

	NHS Increase Group				IS Increase Group		
S	A	B	C	S	A	B	C
1	16.3	12.1	3.9	1	-3.4	20.8	4.1
2	1.6	20	2.7	2	-0.3	20.3	4.3
3	8.1	16.6	3.5	3	-12.8	24	3.4
4	8.6	17.4	3.5	4	-1	19.9	4.2
	Decrease Group				Decrease Group		
5	-2.7	15.6	4.3	5	0.6	15.4	3
6	1.2	19.3	4.1	6	3	21	3.8

Column headings:
   S = Animal number.
   A = Percentage change in heart rate over training attained by
each animal. Negative numbers indicate decrease in rate.
   B = The mean number of shocks received per block of ten
operant trials throughout training.
   C = The mean number of trials per block of ten operant trials on
which a shock was received during training.

paradoxically, the heart rate of these animals shows an
apparent decrease. In contrast, shaped heart rate increases
were found in NHS rats. An analysis of variance for the
data from the two treatment groups of animals shaped for
increases in rate revealed a significant interaction ($F = 5.39$;
$p < 0.001$) between the two groups over the blocks of trials.
A subsequent trend analysis revealed a significant linear
component ($F = 5.99$; $p < 0.05$) which accounted for 89.9
percent of the interaction. Calculation of the regression line
for the combined data from both the NHS and IS increase
groups was significant ($F = 9.44$; df 1.60; $p < 0.01$).
Determination of the regression lines for each of the groups
separately, revealed the increasing slope for the NHS
animals to be different from zero ($F = 4.75$; df 1.30;
$p < 0.05$). The decreasing change in rate of the IS animals
was also significantly different from zero ($F = 8.23$; df
1.30; $p < 0.01$). Thus there was a real increase in heart rate
in NHS animals shaped for that response and a paradoxical
but significant, decrease in heart rate of IS animals shaped
for increases in rate.

The mean number of shocks received by each animal per block of training trials is shown in Table 1. The small difference in the number of shocks received by IS animals shaped for increases in rate compared to the similar group of NHS animals was not significant. Moreover, there was no significant difference between the two groups in the mean number of trials per block of trials in which a shock was received. The absolute value of this parameter for each animal is also presented in Table 1. The results confirm that the difference in heart rate responses between increase groups of NHS and IS animals was not a consequence of differences in the frequency or probability of receiving shock during the training period.

The difference between the groups would not appear to be a consequence of the tendency for either the heart rate of NHS animals to increase, or the rate of IS animals to decrease regardless of the training contingencies in effect, since such response tendencies were not evident in the minimal control animals shaped for decreases in rate.

The heart rate change over the training period of each rat is given in Table 1. The mean change in the rate of NHS animals shaped for increases was from 472–512 beats per min. Paradoxically, the group mean decrease in rate for the equivalent group of IS animals was from 468–447 beats per min. In all cases where there was a change in rate greater than one percent there was no overlap in heart rate between the first and last block of training trials. The changes were, therefore, reliable and not produced as a consequence of increased heart rate variability over the training period.

The continuous shifting of criterion level required to shape heart rate changes precluded detailed analysis of any tendency, which might have occurred for the NHS animals to escape from shock more quickly than the IS animals. However, the mean number of shocks received in each trial in which at least one shock was received was used as an index for such a tendency. A comparison of the difference in this index between the second and last block of training trials for each animal revealed the group means for the NHS increase groups to be 6.25 and 4.68 respectively. This difference was not significant ($t = 0.96$; df 6). The equivalent values for the IS animals in the increase group were 5.15 and 6.1 and, again, the difference was not significant ($t = 0.79$; df 4). The second block of trials was chosen in preference to the first because of the variability in this particular index of shock escape produced by the initial setting of the criterion level during the first block of trials.

The body of weight of each animal at the time of dissection, together with the weight of the two adrenal glands and the combined weight of the four sympathetic ganglia is presented in Table 2. The weights of the ganglia of IS animals were considerably, and significantly, lower

TABLE 2

	Body Wt. (g)	Combined ganglia Weight in mg.	Combined Adrenal Weight in mg.
NHS N = 6	279 ± 67.4	1.29 ± 0.24	6.48 ± 0.53
IS N = 6	271 ± 60.5	0.42 ± 0.18	6.40 ± 0.36

The body weight and the tissue weight of adrenal glands and sympathetic ganglia dissected out from each immunosympathetomised and control rat. The adrenal weight is the combined weight of the two glands. The weight of the ganglia is the combined weight of the two cervical and two thoracic sympathetic ganglia.

than those of the NHS controls. However, in accord with other studies, there were no differences between the weights of the adrenal glands from IS and control animals.

DISCUSSION

It is clear from the results that immunosympathectomy has a profound effect on the success in shaping increases in baseline heart rate with the operant schedule used in this experiment.

In an early paper on operant heart rate conditioning using dogs, Black [2] was unable to show changes in rate in deeply curarised animals, although showing convincing results with animals curarised sufficiently to suppress overt but not covert muscle activity. He concluded that at high dose levels d-tubocurarine produces blockage at the paravertebral ganglia and there is evidence which supports his view [3]. The results of the present experiment conflict somewhat with Black's conclusion and this emphasises the probable species differences in the drug effect and therefore poses problems for the use of curariform drugs in studies of autonomic conditioning.

Although it was impossible to shape steady increases in heart rate in immunosympathectomised rats, the cardiotachometer recordings showed that all animals gave a consistent mild tachycardia to shock during training. A number of studies [14,21] have shown depletion in levels of catecholamines in sympathetically innervated organs of immunosympathectomised animals. However, other studies [5,17] have obtained some evidence for compensating sources of catecholamines in immunosympathectomised rats. This further evidence would support Adolph's [1] view of the rat as a sympathetically dominant animal.

It is concluded that immunosympathectomised rats were able to produce phasic increases in heart rate to shock, but were unable to maintain their heart rate at the high levels required by the operant schedule used in this experiment. This finding is similar to that of Carson [6] arising from her studies on the telemetered heart rate responses of immunosympathetomised mice.

Although the absence of heart rate increases in IS animals was predicted, the significant decrease in heart rate of the IS animals during training when operant contingencies for shaping increases in heart rate were in effect, was unexpected. A number of unpublished studies [18] have suggested that the combination of the operant schedule and curarisation procedures used in this study are stressful to the rat, resulting in increased output from the sympathetic nervous system and the adrenal medulla. Indeed, it has been suggested by Koelle [11] that curare itself produces an increase in sympathic activity. It may be that the requirement of maintaining high levels of heart rate by the operant schedule for increasing rates depletes compensating sources of catecholamines, thus leading to an overall decrease in baseline rate.

REFERENCES

1. Adolph, E. F. Ranges of heart rates and their regulation at various ages (rat). *Am. J. Physiol.* 212: 595–602, 1967.
2. Black, A. H. Operant conditioning of heart-rate under curare. Technical Report No. 12: Department of Psychology, McMaster University, Ontario Canada.
3. Bovet, D., F. Bovet-Nitti and G. B. Marini Bettolo. *Curare and Curare-like Agents.* Amsterdam: Elsevier, 1959.
4. Brody, M. J. Cardiovascular responses following immunological sympathectomy. *Circulation Res.* 15: 161–167, 1964.

5. Carpi, A. and A. Oliverio. Urinary excretion of catecholamines in the immunosympathectomised rat. Balance phenomen between adrenergic and noradrengergic systems. *Int. J. Neuropharmac.* **3**: 427–431, 1964.
6. Carson, V. G. The effects of immunosympathectony and medullectomy on telemetered heart-rate and foot impedance in mice. Unpublished Ph.D. thesis, University of California, 1970.
7. DiCara, L. V. and N. E. Miller. Changes in heart rate instrumentally learned by curarized rats as avoidance responses. *J. comp. physiol. Psychol.* **65**: 8–12, 1968.
8. Dicara, L. V., and J. M. Weiss. Effect of heart-rate learning under curare on subsequent non-curarised avoidance learning. *J. comp. physiol. Psychol.* **69**: 368–375, 1969.
9. Dicara, L. V., and E. A. Stone. Effect of instrumental heart-rate training on rat cardiac and brain catecholamines. *Psychosom. Med.* **32**: 359–368, 1970.
10. Hofer, M. A., M. Engel, and H. Weiner. Development of cardiac rate regulation and activity after neonatal immunosympathectomy. *Communs behav. Biol.* **6**: 59–62, 1970.
11. Koelle, G. B. Neuromuscular blocking agents. In: *Pharmacological Basis of Therapeutics,* edited by L. S. Goodman and A. Gilman. New York: Macmillan, 1965.
12. Levi-Montalcini, R. and B. Booker. Destruction of the sympathetic ganglia in mammals by an antiserum to a nerve-growth protein. *Proc. natn. Acad. Sci.,* **46**: 384–391, 1960.
13. Levi-Montalcini, R. Growth control of nerve cells by a protein factor and its antiserum. *Science* **143**: 105–110, 1964.
14. Levi-Montalcini, R. and P. U. Angeletti. Noradrenaline and monaminoxidase content in immunosympathectomised animals. *Int. J. Neuropharmac.* **1**: 161–164, 1962.
15. Levi-Montalcini, R. and P. U. Angeletti. Immunosympathectomy. *Pharmac. Rev.* **18**: 619–628, 1966.
16. Miller, N. E. and Dicara, L. V. Instrumental learning of heart-rate changes in curarised rats: shaping of specifity to discriminative stimulus. *J. comp. physiol. Psychol.* **63**: 12–19, 1967.
17. Schonbaum, E., G. E. Johnson and E. A. Sellars. Acclimatisation to cold and noradrenaline effects of immunosympathectomy. *Am. J. Physiol.* **211**: 647–650, 1966.
18. Thornton, E. W. Operant heart-rate conditioning in the curarised rat. Unpublished Ph.D. thesis, University of Durham, England, 1971.
19. Trowill, J. A. Instrumental conditioning of the heart-rate in the curarised rat. *J. comp. physiol. Psychol.* **63**: 7–11, 1967.
20. Van-Toller, C. Immunosympathectomy and open field behaviour in in male mice. *Physiol and Behav.* **3**: 1–4, 1968.
21. Visscher, M. B., Lee, Y.C.P., and Azuma, T. Catecholamines in organs of immunosympathectomised mice. *Proc. Soc. exp. Biol. Med.* **119**: 1232–1234, 1965.
22. Wenzel, B. M. Immunosympathectomy and Behaviour. In: *Immunosympathectomy,* edited by G. Steiner and E. Schonbaum. Elsevier: in press.
23. Wenzel, B. M., V. G. Carson, and K. Chase. Cardiac responses of immunosympathectomised mice. *Percept. Mot. Skills.* **23**: 1009–1010, 1966.

Operant Conditioning of Heart Rate Changes in the Functionally Decorticate Curarized Rat

5

E. W. Thornton and C. Van-Toller

THORNTON, E. W. AND C. VAN-TOLLER. *Operant conditioning of heart-rate changes in the functionally decorticate curarised rat.* PHYSIOL. BEHAV. 10(6) 983–988, 1973.– Using an operant schedule involving negative reinforcement, attempts were made to shape heart-rate changes in curarised rats whose cortical activity had been eliminated by spreading depression. Despite the presence of unconditioned cardiac responses to stimulus presentations during training, and in contrast to controls, appropriate changes were not found for the experimental groups. It is concluded that the results support an earlier theory that the cortex is essential for operant learning.

Heart-rate   Operant conditioning   Curare   Spreading depression

---

ALTHOUGH a number of studies have successfully demonstrated conditioning of heart-rate changes in curarised animals by operant techniques, there have been few investigations of the peripheral or central physiological mechanisms underlying response changes.

It has been reported [16, 18, 19] that the acquisition and maintenance of operantly conditioned skeletal responses is dependent on an intact cerebral cortex. In contrast, surgical decortication appears to have little effect on the acquisition and maintenance of classically conditioned cardiac responses [1,16]. Partially on the basis of such studies, Russell [16, 19, 20] has argued that operant conditioning is crucially dependent on cortical processes, whilst the attentional components, if not the significance evaluation components, of classical conditioning are not so dependent.

The most convincing evidence suggesting a distinction of neuroanatomical locus for different learning processes, per se, rather than in differences in the type of response output required, has been provided by the study of DiCara, Braun and Pappas [4], which demonstrated that surgical removal of over 90 percent of the neocortex eliminated the ability

[1]This experiment is part of an unpublished Ph. D. thesis submitted to the University of Durham, 1971. Present address: Department of Psychology, University of Liverpool, P. O. Box 147, Liverpool, L69 3BX, England.

of curarised rats to acquire an operantly conditioned cardiac response, whilst unaffecting the classical conditioning of a heart-rate response to the same stimuli.

However, it has been pointed out, [19] that studies involving surgical removal of the neocortex are confounded by the problem of diaschisis. Moreover, the long period of postoperative recovery that is required after surgical decortication may allow compensatory changes to occur before the testing for learning ability is carried out. An alternative procedure, is the utilization of Leáo's [12] technique of producing a functional decortication by spreading cortical depression (SCD).

The aim of the present study was to determine if a functional decortication produced by SCD specifically affected the ability to shape heart-rate changes in the rat by operant conditioning techniques. Although SCD has been shown to severely affect conditioning of skeletal responses [19,21], the few studies which have determined its consequences on the ability to condition responses of the autonomic nervous system, have involved only classical conditioning. Mogenson and Peterson [15] demonstrated that a classically conditioned heart-rate response was unimpaired by bilateral SCD whilst Burgoyne, Pote and Freedman [3] have claimed to show the stable acquisition of a classically conditioned cardiac acceleration in the rat under SCD. The effects of SCD on classically conditioned heart-rate changes appear to parallel those produced by surgical lesions.

EXPERIMENT 1

Method

Animals. Sixteen hooded rats were obtained from two litters of females maintained in the Department of Psychology, University of Durham. Each rat was isolated after weaning and used for the operant procedures when weighing between 210–300 g. Owing to an apparatus failure no data were collected for one animal.

Operative procedure. A chronic preparation similar to that suggested by Schnedier and Behar [22], was used to administer the potassium chloride solution to produce the SCD. The operative procedure was carried out under

After an adaptation period of 30 min to allow the heart-rate to stabilise, the operant training was started. Within a bidirectional design, an avoidance schedule was employed in which half the animals avoided or escaped from a mild electric shock by increases in heart-rate to a criterion level, and half by decreases in rate. A shaping procedure was used such that the criterion levels were successively changed by 2 percent if the animal was consistently avoiding shock. An initial criterion level was selected at the end of this period such that the level was attained on about 40 percent of the sampling periods.

The method and circuit for determining whether the heart-rate was above or below a certain criterion level rate was based on the procedure described by Trowill [25]. In essence, the circuit determined whether a sample number of heart-beats occurred in a faster or slower time than predicted if the heart-rate was steady at a given criterion level. Because of the specific electronic circuit used in making this comparison, it was necessary to sample the heart-rate over intervals ranging from 1.7–2.3 sec [24,25].

On any operant trial, if the criterion level was attained within five sec, the light went out and no shcok was delivered. However, if the criterion level had not been attained within the period of five sec, then a 0.1 sec pulse of shock was programmed to be delivered. Similar shocks were delivered if successive samples of heart-rate indicated that the criterion level had not been reached. Thus, pulsed shock was delivered at the end of each sample until the criterion level was attained. When the criterion level was reached, the light went off and the trial terminated. Throughout training, the last trial in every block of trials was an operant trial test in which the light came on for five sec but the criterion circuitry was inactivated. This trial allowed the determination of the mean heart-rate during five sec of the operant stimulus in the absence of contamination by shock presentation or light termination.

A five sec blank trial was incorporated into the training schedule. During this blank trial no stimulus was presented but the number of heart beats was recorded.

The operant training schedule was programmed to comprise of eight blocks of thirty trials, consisting of ten operant and twenty blank trials. The end of each block of trials was marked by a single operant test trial. Trials were presented with a fixed intertrial-interval of twenty sec. Within any block, each trial occurred in a predetermined random manner with the constraint that no more than two operant trials occurred consecutively and, that no more than five blank trials separated any two operant trials. The sequence of trials within each block of the training schedule was consistent and identical for all the animals.

If, during training, the animal successfully avoided shock on four consecutive operant trials, the criterion was made more difficult (by approximatley 2 or 3 percent). If the combined number of shocks received on two consecutive operant trials was greater than 20 pulses, then the criterion level was reduced by an equivalent amount.

Results

The baseline heart-rates at the end of the thirty min

adaptation period showed no significant difference between the increase and decrease groups ($t = 1.11$, $df = 13$). There were also no differences in heart-rate between operant test and blank trials for any animal during the training period. Nembutal anaesthesia. A midline incision was made along the scalp and, after scraping the periosteum from the surface of the skull, a circular fenestra 4 mm dia. was trephined into each side of the skull to expose the cerebral hemispheres, taking care not to damage the dura mater. Each fenestra was situated midway in the parietal bone about 4 mm caudal to the coronal suture and with their closest edges 1 mm from the midsagittal plane. A perspex cannula 11 mm dia. was located over the fenestrae by means of stainless steel wire through small holes drilled in the flange around the top of the cannula. The cannula was plugged with a sterile cotton wool pad soaked in isotonic saline and capped. A subcutaneous injection of penicillin was given after the operation. The saline pads were changed daily under mild ether anaesthsia.

Procedure for producing cortical depression. Four days after the operative procedure, the rat was briefly anaesthetised with ether, the saline pad removed and filter paper soaked in a 25% solution of potassium chloride placed on the exposed surface of the dura. A pad of cotton wool moistened in potassium chloride was inserted into the cannula which was then capped.

The EEG of the experimental rats was not monitored either before, or during, the heart-rate training procedures. However, the effectiveness of these procedures in producing cortical depression was determined in a preliminary study [23] using six nonexperimental animals. In these animals, EEG recordings were obtained from electrodes attached to the skull over the frontal lobes. The recordings were taken under mild ether anaesthesia during three sessions, at half hour intervals both before and after application of potassium chloride to the dura. Suppression of EEG traces were obtained for periods of at least two hours. Paw placing reflexes were observed during periods between recordings.

Apparatus for operant conditioning of heart-rate changes. The apparatus and procedures for the curarisation and artifcial ventilation of the curarised rat have been described previously [10,23]. During heart-rate training procedures, the rat was situated in a sound attenuating chamber. The enclosure was fitted with a 60 watt lamp situated 15 cm above the animals, which served as a discriminative stimulus. Stainless steel needle electrodes, inserted subdermally on either side of the thorax, were used to record heart-rate. The indifferent electrode was a hypodermic needle inserted into the peritoneal cavity. A connection from this to the outside of the chamber allowed additional doses of *d*-tubocurarine to be administered to the animal during training in order to maintain a flaccid musculature [23].

The EKG output was electronically formed such that only the QRS wave of the signal operated the criterion and counter circuitry. A simultaneous cardiotachometer recording was obtained on a Beckman (Type RP) Dynograph.

Procedure for operant conditioning of heart-rate changes. Whilst initiating spreading depression under mild ether anaesthesia, the rat was injected with 0.6 mg/kg of *d*-tubocurarine chloride. When the rat showed signs of respiratory failure it was artificially ventilated with a small animal respirator (a ventilation rate of 70c/min, 1:1 inspiration − expiration ratio, with a peak pressure of 14 cm of water was used for all animals). After topical application of xylocaine, the electrodes for recording heart-rate were inserted, and the wire for the delivery of shock attached to the tail. The chamber was then closed.

Thus, there was no evidence to suggest a discrimination of heart-rate changes to the light stimulus. This result is in contrast to early studies [5,14] which provided positive evidence for discrimination learning of operantly conditioned cardiac responses. However, results have not been unequivocal. DiCara and Miller [6] were unable to demonstrate discrimination of operantly conditioned vasomotor responses in curarised rats. Also, DiCara and Stone [9] found no differences between test and blank trials in curarised rats shaped specifically for increases in rate. Studies on the transfer of operant heart-rate changes from curarised to noncurarised state and vice versa [7,8] have also been unable to consistently demonstrate discrimination of operantly conditioned heart-rate changes. Inconsistencies in the demonstration of discrimination learning may have been produced as a consequence of making reinforcement contingent on the average number of beats occurring in a given time sample. For example, it is difficult to specify what response change is being reinforced: it could be a change in one single interbeat interval, or smaller changes in most of the interbeat invervals. The latter, combined with an aversive schedule which may be stressful [23,24] would not be conducive for discrimination of operant heart-rate changes. The bidirectional design used in these experiments, however, focuses on the differences in rates obtained between rats shaped for increases or decreases in rate rather than on absolute rates or discrimination learning. Because of the lack of evidence for discrimination of heart-rate changes between the operant and blank trials, the results were analysed in terms of the eight blocks of operant test trials.

Figure 1 presents the mean heart-rate changes of the two groups of rats over each block of training trials. An analysis of variance of the data used to compile the figure, using an

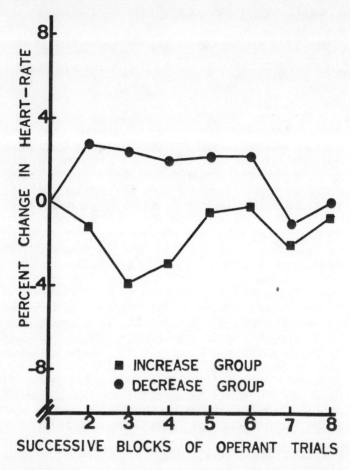

FIG. 1. Mean heart-rate changes for each group of functionally
decorticate animals over successive blocks of operant trials.

unweighted mean solution for the unequal groups, showed
no significant interaction between group heart-rate changes
over the blocks of trials. The percent change in heart-rate of
each rat between the first and last operant test trial is
shown in Column B of Table 1. No difference was evident
between the two groups in such percent heart-rate changes
($t = 0.22$, $df = 13$).

The absence of differential changes in heart-rate was
found despite a significant difference between the groups in
the mean number of shocks they received per block of
operant trials ($t = 3.2$, $df = 13$; $p < 0.01$). The absolute
values of this parameter of shock frequency are presented
in Column B of Table 1. There was also a significant
tendency for the rats shaped for increases in heart-rate to
escape from shock more quickly than rats shaped for
decreases. The mean number of shocks received on each
trial in which at least one shock was delivered was utilised

TABLE 1

THE PERCENTAGE CHANGE IN HEART-RATE OVER
TRAINING ATTAINED BY EACH FUNCTIONALLY DECORTI-
CATE, CURARISED RAT, TOGETHER WITH THE FREQUENCY
AND PROBABILITY OF RECEIVING SHOCKS DURING
TRAINING BY THAT ANIMAL

Increase Group			Decrease Group		
A	B	C	A	B	C
2.1	23.9	4.7	4.3	18.4	4.3
11.5	12.6	3.3	−7.4	28.4	10.1
0	20.3	5.4	4.9	25.4	5.7
−5.5	10.5	2.0	−1.5	23.6	6.2
−1.7	18.4	4.3	0	23.5	5.6
−1.5	11.1	2.5	2	21.3	6.2
−6.9	14.3	2.5	−1.4	19	4.3
−1.6	15.6	4.3			

A = Percentage change in heart-rate over training trials. Negative numbers indicate a decrease in rate.

B = The mean number of shocks received per block of ten operant trials throughout training.

C = The mean number of shocks received per operant trial on which at least one shock was received, throughout training.

as an index of this tendency. Values of this index for each animal are presented in Column C of Table 1. Analysis gave a value of $t = 2.82$, $df = 13$; $p<0.02$. The continuous shifting of the criterion level was effective to the extent that there was no tendency for the index of shock escape to change over training for animals in either the increase group ($t = 1.25$, $df = 14$) or the decrease group ($t = 0.63$, $df = 12$). The differences in shock frequency and escape latency between the two groups appeared to be a consequence of the unconditioned response to the shock rather than a function of learning. As can be seen in Fig. 2, the effect of the first shock on any operant trial for every animal was a mild tachycardia, the response becoming more unstable as further shocks were received.

It would seem that the results of the experiment demonstrate that a functionally decorticate, curarised rat is unable to show acquisition of operant changes in heart-rate. This conclusion was supported by a second study which indicated that the heart-rate changes were unlikely to have been produced by unconditioned shock effects, or the

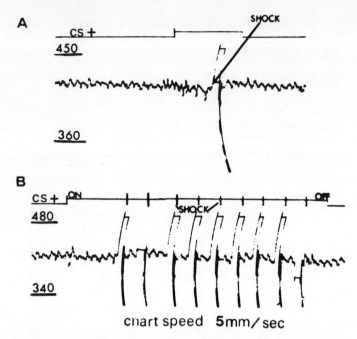

FIG. 2. Cardiotachometer tracings obtained from two rats during operant heart-rate training. Trace A: The rat is being shaped for heart-rate increases. The criterion level for an avoidance response is not attained and a pulse of shock is received. A mild tachycardiac response is evident after the shock and the criterion level is attained on the first sampling period following shock delivery. Trace B: The rat is being shaped for heart-rate decreases. Again, a criterion level for an avoidance response is not attained. The first shock pulse again produces a mild tachycardia. This response is inappropriate for shock escape; the criterion level is not attained during the following sample, and a shock pulse follows. As more shock pulses are received the tachycardiac response to shock ceases to occur and, after nine shock pulses, the heart-rate has decreased sufficiently for the criterion level to be attained.

operative procedures required to initiate spreading depression.

EXPERIMENT 2

The same operant schedules as those of the previous experiment were used to shape either increases or decreases in the heart-rates of sham operated rats with a functional intact cortex. The sham operative procedure did not involve exposure of the dura since this may in itself produce cortical depression.

Experimental evidence suggests that unconditioned heart-rate responses are unaffected by SCD [15]. Since these same unconditioned responses were hypothesised to produce the differences in shock parameters in the previous experiment, then similar differences in shock parameters should be evident in the two groups of sham-operated rats. However, in the sham-operates, differences in heart-rates between the groups should occur as a consequence of the operant schedules.

Method

Animals. A litter of ten hooded rats was obtained from one female. The animals were used for the experiment when weighing between 210 and 250 g.

Operative procedure. A 2 cm sagittal incision was made in the scalp under Nembutal anaesthesia and the periosteum scraped from the surface of the skull. The wound was then closed and the animal given a subcutaneous injection of penicillin.

Procedure for operant conditioning of heart-rate changes. The procedures for curarisation, artificial ventilation and operant training were exactly the same as those employed for the cortically depressed rats. Five animals were shaped for heart-rate decreases and five for heart-rate increases.

Results

There was considerable overlap in the baseline heart-rate of rats in both the increase (473.3 ± 25.2 beats per min) and decreases (454.8 ± 56.2 beats per min) groups prior to operant training. Thus, as in the previous experiment, there was no significant difference in the heart-rates of the two groups at the end of the adaption period ($t = 1.01$, $df = 8$). Again, no differences were observed in the heart-rate responses of any animal between operant and blank trials, and the results were analysed in terms of eight blocks of operant test trials.

The percent change in heart-rate of each animal between the first and last block of trials is presented in Column A of Table 2. The group mean changes in heart-rate over the training period are shown in Fig. 3. The graph suggests a divergence in the group mean heart-rate changes over the training period; the change for each group being in the direction appropriate to the specific schedule used. An analysis of variance of the data used to compile the graphs showed a signficant interaction ($F = 3.23$, $df = 7.56$ $p<0.01$) between heart-rate changes of the two groups over the blocks of trials. An analysis of the interaction showed that a large (80.9 percent), though not quite significant ($F = 4.09$, $df = 1.8$), proportion was accounted for by a linear component. An extension of the analysis of variance, described by Brownlee [2] was used to determine whether the difference between the slopes was significant, and whether each slope was significantly different from zero. The procedure involved calculation of regression lines using the data from both groups. The significant improvement ($F = 7.05$, $df = 1.80$; $p<0.01$) obtained in using the separate

TABLE 2

THE PERCENTAGE CHANGE IN HEART-RATE OVER TRAIN-
ING ATTAINED BY EACH SHAM-OPERATED ANIMAL,
TOGETHER WITH THE FREQUENCY WITH WHICH SHOCKS
WERE RECEIVED DURING TRAINING BY THAT ANIMAL

Increase Group			Decrease Group		
A	B	C	A	B	C
10.3	11	3.5	5.3	20.3	6.8
−1.5	15.4	3.1	−6.4	27.7	8.7
17.7	17.6	5.1	−1.5	25.6	8.1
3.3	16.4	4.6	−12.4	22.8	3.8
17.8	12.8	2.3	−5	23.4	6.8

A = Percentage change in heart-rate over training trials. Negative
numbers indicate a decrease in rate.

B = The mean number of shocks received per block of ten
operant trials throughout training.

C = The mean number of shocks received per operant trial on
which at least one shock was received, throughout training.

rather than combined regression lines is used to indicate a
difference between the slopes. However, neither the slope
for the increase group (F = 3.87, $df = 1.38$), nor for the
decrease group (F = 3.17, $df = 1.38$) was significantly
different from zero, although the slopes were clearly in the
appropriate direction.

Although the heart-rate changes were very different
from those obtained in the functional decorticate rats,
analysis of data on shock frequency (Column B, Table 2),
and shock escape (Column C, Table 2) revealed essentially
similar results. Thus, the mean number of shocks received
per block of operant trials by animals in the decrease group
was significantly greater than the number received by
animals in the increase group (F = 5.35, $df = 8; p < 0.001$).
Using the same index as in the previous experiment,
analysis revealed a significant difference between the two
groups in the latency of escape from shock ($t = 2.96, df =
8; p < 0.02$). There was no tendency for the animals in
either the increase ($t = 0.15, df = 8$) or the decrease ($t = 0$)
group to escape from shock more of less quickly between
the beginning and end of training.

As far as the index of shock escape was concerned, the
beginning of training was taken from the second rather than
the first block of trails. This was because of the variability
in the index during the first block of trials as a consequence
of the initial setting of the criterion level.

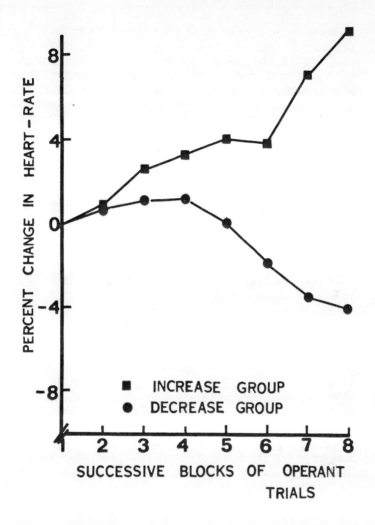

FIG. 3. Mean heart-rate changes for each group of sham operated animals over successive blocks of operant trials.

DISCUSSION

The results of these experiments show that little differential change in heart-rate was produced between the two groups of functionally decorticate rats shaped for either increases or decreases in rate. The differences between the groups in frequency and probability of receiving shock, which confounds the bidirectional design, seems to have arisen as a direct consequence of the unconditioned effects of shock on heart-rate. Since similar differences in shock parameters were found between the two groups in both experiments, and yet a divergence in heart-rate found only in the sham operated animals. It is unlikely that the differential heart-rate changes were due to sensitisation effects to shock.

On a subsequent occasion [23] additional evidence was obtained to support this conclusion. A yoked control for each rat in the second experiment was curarised and artifically ventilated in the same apparatus as the experimental animal. Presentations of trials and of light and shock were determined from a recording of the same presentations to its paired experimental animal and were independent of its own heart-rate. The results showed no differences in the heart-rates of yoked controls for rats in the increase groups and the heart-rates of the controls for rats in the decrease group, either at the beginning ($t = 0.38, df = 8$), or end ($t = 0.15, df = 8$) of training.

It is not clear why the experiments of Miller and associates, which utilise the same procedures and design, have not reported similar confounding differences in shock parameters as a consequence of unconditioned responses in heart-rate. Such confounding effects would seem to be best overcome by use of a time out procedure after each reinforcement as suggested by Hothersall and Brener [11].

The operant contingencies used did produce a significant difference in heart-rate changes between the increase and decrease groups of rats with a functional, intact cortex. However, the changes for each group were not significantly different from zero. It is noteworthy that Miller [13] has recently reported that the shaping of heart-rate changes in curarised rats in his laboratories has produced considerably smaller changes than reported in his earlier experiments.

No attempt was made in the present study to determine if the attentional components of classical conditioning, as measured by heart-rate changes, were unaffected by SCD. However, the results do clearly suggest that the acquisition of operant changes in heart-rate does depend on cortical processes and thus lends support to the study of DiCara *et al.* [4]. These studies together provide important data related to the determination of the neuroanatomical basis of learning by supporting the dependence of operant conditioning on cortical processes. A criticism of experiments supporting this proposition has been that a surgical or functional decortication may produce a decrement in operant behaviour through impairment of the response in question rather than on the learning process per se. However, Russell [21] has made this criticism unlikely, and the present study also provides additional support against the motor deficit viewpoint in that the response mechanisms involved are most likely controlled at the subcortical level. However, it has yet to be determined whether operant changes in heart-rate are mediated by cortical motor, or possibly cardiac, control mechanisms [17].

REFERENCES

1. Bloch, S. and I. Lagarrigue. Cardiac and simple avoidance learning in neodecorticate rats. *Physiol. Behav.* **3**: 305–308, 1968.
2. Brownlee, K. A. Industrial experimentation. Directorate of Royal Ordnance Factories, Ministry of Supply, H.M.S.O., 1948.
3. Burgoyne, L., R. Pote and N. Freedman. Conditioned cardiac acceleration under cortical depression. *Psychon. Sci.* **9**: 417–418, 1967.
4. Dicara, L. V., J. J. Braun and B. A. Pappas. Classical conditioning and instrumental learning of cardiac and gastrointestinal responses following removal of neocortex in the rat. *J. comp. physiol. Psychol.* **73**: 208–216, 1970.
5. Dicara, L. V. and N. E. Miller. Changes in heart-rate instrumentally learned by curarised rats as avoidance responses. *J. comp. physiol.. Psychol.* **65**: 8–12, 1968.
6. Dicara, L. V. and N. E. Miller. Instrumental learning of vasomotor responses by rats: Learning to respond differentially in the two ears. *Science* **159**: 1485–1486, 1968.
7. Dicara, L. V. and N. E. Miller. Transfer of instrumentally learned heart-rate changes from curarised to non-curarised state: Implications for a mediational hypothesis. *J. comp. physiol. Psychol.* **68**: 159–163, 1969.
8. Dicara, L. V. and N. E. Miller. Heart-rate learning in the non-curarised state, transfer to the curarised state, and subsequent retraining in the non-curarised state. *Physiol. Behav.* **4**: 621–624, 1969.
9. Dicara, L. V. and E. A. Stone. Effect of instrumental heart-rate training on rat cardiac and brain catecholamines. *Psychosom. Med.* **32**: 359–368, 1970.
10. Hahn, W. W. Apparatus and technique for work with the curarised rat. *Psychophysiology* **7**: 283–286, 1970.
11. Hothersall, D. and J. Brener. Operant conditioning of changes in heart-rate in curarised rats. *J. comp. physiol. Psychol.* **68**: 338–343, 1969.
12. Leão, A. A. P. Spreading depression of activity in the cerebral cortex. *J. Neurophysiol.* **7**: 359–390, 1944.
19. Russell, I. S. Neurological basis of complex learning. *Br. med. Bull.* **27**: 278–285, 1971.
20. Russell, I. S., D. Kleinman, H. C. Plotkin and R. B. Ross. The role of the cortex in acquisition and retention of a classically conditioned passive avoidance response. *Physiol Behav.* **4**: 575–581, 1969.
21. Russell, I. S., H. C. Plotkin and D. Kleinman. Cortical depression and the problem of motor impairment. *Physiol. Behav.* **3**: 849–855, 1968.
22. Schneider, A. M. and M. Behar. A chronic preparation for spreading cortical depression. *J. exp. Analysis Behav.* **7**: 350, 1964.
23. Thornton, E. W. *Operant Heart-rate Conditioning in the Curarised Rat.* Unpublished Ph. D. thesis. University of Durham, England, 1971.
24. Thornton, E. W. and C. Van-Toller. Effect of immunosympathectomy on operant heart-rate conditioning in the curarised rat. *Physiol. Behav.* **10**: 197–202, 1973.

25. Trowill, J. A. Instrumental conditioning of the heart-rate in the curarised rat. *J. comp. physiol. Psychol.* 63: 7–11, 1967.
13. Miller, N. E. Two psychosomatic effects of learning. Internationl Congress of Psychology, Tokyo, 1972. Abstract guide, p. 67.
14. Miller, N. E. and L. V. Dicara. Instrumental learning of heart-rate changes in curarised rats: Shaping and specificity to discriminative stimulus. *J. comp. physiol.. Psychol.* 63: 12–19, 1967.
15. Mogenson, G. J. and R. J. Peterson. Effects of cortical spreading depression on cardiac and somatomotor conditioned responses. *Can. J. Physiol. Pharmac.* 44: 39–45, 1966.
16. Oakley, D. A. and I. S. Russell. Neocortical lesions and Pavlovian conditioning. *Physiol. Behav.* 8: 915–926, 1972.
17. Obrist, P. A., R. A. Webb, J. R. Sutterer, and J. L. Howard. The cardiac somatic relationship: Some reformulations. *Psychophysiology* 6: 569–585, 1970.
18. Pinto Hamuy, T., H. G. Santibanez and A. Rojas. Learning and retention of a visual conditioned response in neodecorticate rats. *J. comp. physiol. Psychol.* 56: 19–24, 1963.

Muscle Tension in Human Operant **6**
Heart Rate Conditioning

Robert Belmaker, Eugenia Proctor,
and Ben W. Feather

Abstract—The physiological mechanism involved in human operant heart rate conditioning is not known. If skeletal muscle tension is a mediator, it should be possible to generate significant heart rate increases by inconspicuous voluntary muscle tension. Eleven subjects were instructed to generate inconspicuous muscle tension for 90-second periods. No gross muscle movements were observed, but average heart rate during the trials was over 13 beats-per-minute greater than pre-trial base lines. Respiratory pattern changes and surface electromyogram changes did not reliably correlate with heart rate increases. Inconspicuous muscle tension could be a mediator in human operant heart rate conditioning, and cannot be ruled out by absence of change in respiratory pattern or electromyogram.

VARIOUS INVESTIGATORS have reported successful operant conditioning of human heart rate (Brener and Hothersall, 1967; Engel and Chism, 1967; Engel and Hansen, 1966; Headrick, Feather and Wells, 1971; Shapiro *et al.*, 1970). The physiological mechanism of these reported heart rate (HR) changes is poorly understood. Animal experiments (Miller and DiCara, 1967) in which the skeletal musculature was paralyzed by curare have demonstrated that the autonomic nervous system itself may be modified by operant learning. It is as yet unknown, however, whether direct modification of

* Department of Psychology, Duke University, Durham, N. C.

† Present address: Butler Hospital, Providence, R. I.

Supported by NIMH Grant 5 K02 MH 19523 and NIMH Grant 2 R01 MH 11549 to Dr. Ben W. Feather.

Address reprint requests to: Dr. Robert Belmaker, P. O. Box 3316, Duke University Medical Center, Durham, N. C. 27710.

the autonomic nervous system plays a significant role in human operant HR conditioning.

Recent workers have exerted increasing amounts of effort to monitor skeletal responses during human HR conditioning. Brener and Hothersall (1967) demonstrated HR control under conditions of paced respiratory rate and fixed respiratory amplitude. They state, however, that "the possibility that the observed cardiac control was mediated by learned changes in muscle tension remains a problem worthy of empirical investigation (p. 6)." In order to investigate muscle tension as a possible mediator in operant HR conditioning, one must determine if the effects of inconspicuous muscle tension on HR are large enough to compare with conditioned HR changes. Then one must evaluate measures of skeletal activity to determine if they detect changes of the magnitude necessary to cause reported HR increases. The purpose of this experiment is to measure HR changes that result from muscle tension, and to determine if such muscle tension can be hidden from two conventional measures of skeletal activity, the electromyogram (EMG) and the respiratory pattern.

Methods

The subjects (Ss) were 11 healthy young men. Recordings were taken in a well-lit, sound-attenuated IAC chamber while Ss reclined in a comfortable chair. Each S had two pairs of Industrial Medical Instruments fluid electrodes placed on his chest. One pair of electrodes was placed transthoracically, approximately 5 cm below and 5 cm lateral to each nipple. The second pair of electrodes was placed approximately 5 cm below the left nipple, 1 cm apart. Both electrode pairs were connected to a Grass Model 7 Polygraph and each channel was observed for high-frequency (EMG) activity. In addition the transthoracic electrodes' channel triggered a cardiotachograph channel on the Grass Polygraph.

Respiratory rate and amplitude were monitored by use of a pneumotachograph. This consisted of an adjustable clear plastic face mask with a small grid opening and a separate connection via tubing to a Grass PT5 transducer. Respiratory rate was paced by use of electronically simulated inspiratory and expiratory sounds conveyed to the S through earphones. Length of inspiration, expiration, and the pauses before each were independently adjusted to the S's comfort. Each S was monitored on closed-circuit television and by a microphone in the chamber.

On arrival each S was told that he was one of a control group for experiments on autonomic activity and muscle tension. The purposes of the electrodes were explained, and the S was then allowed to acclimate to the face mask and to paced breathing. The S was then told that each trial of muscle tension would last 90 seconds. He was requested to keep his breathing as constant as possible while waiting for a trial, during a trial, and immediately after a trial. The trials were signalled by a white light that came on immediately in front of the S and remained on for 90 seconds. Each S was told to tense immediately on seeing the light and to relax immediately on the light's disappearance.

Each of the six Ss of Instruction Group A was told to "tense the chest muscles, as if a heavy pile of sand were on the chest and it were difficult to breathe." In addition, each S of Group A was told to "breathe as if he were breathing through a small tube with great resistance, or as if he had an obstruction in the larynx." Each of the five Ss of Instruction Group B was told to "tense the diaphragm and upper abdominal muscles, as if expecting a blow." In order to give an example of such tension, each S of Group B was then asked to reproduce the tension felt during this maneuver, but to try to maintain a normal breathing pattern.

Individuals of both groups were instructed further as needed after each 90-second trial of muscle tension. If there were respiratory changes in a particular trial, the S was told so and was asked to keep respirations during the next trial closer to his resting pattern. If there was high-frequency (EMG) activity detected by the chest wall electrodes during a trial, the S was told after the trial to "keep the tension inside the chest and not to allow muscle trembling." If HR did not increase during a trial, the S was told to "tense harder" on the next trial. If HR increased only in one phase of respiration, the S was told to "keep the tension equal throughout the respiratory cycle." If any movement or postural change was noted on television, the S was told to eliminate this. In short, a shaping procedure was attempted that rewarded HR increases and punished respiratory changes, detectable EMG activity, or gross movement.

Each S received at least 4 pre-trial–trial sequences.‡ Each pre-trial–trial sequence consisted of a 30-second pre-trial immediately followed by a 90-second trial. The S was unaware of the pre-trial

---

‡ S A2 became anxious about his mask and did not complete the fourth trial. The recordings for his third trial are included instead.

TABLE 1. HR Increases (BPM)

S	Trial 1	Trial 2	Trial 3	Trial 4	Mean
Group A					
1	16.0	16.7	13.3	16.7	15.7
2	0.7	22.0	30.0	–	17.6
3	6.0	2.7	2.0	16.0	6.7
4	31.3	12.0	20.7	17.3	20.3
5	8.7	15.3	17.3	13.3	13.6
6	−2.0	14.0	5.3	8.7	6.5
Mean	10.1	13.8	14.8	14.4	13.4
Group B					
1	2.0	3.3	16.7	10.7	8.2
2	2.0	9.3	8.7	10.0	7.5
3	12.0	20.7	36.0	24.7	23.4
4	16.7	12.7	18.7	15.3	15.8
5	12.0	16.0	5.3	12.0	11.3
Mean	8.9	12.4	17.1	14.5	13.2

period, and the trial period was signalled by the white light in view of the S. Heart beats were electronically counted during each pre-trial and trial period. The interval between pre-trial–trial sequences varied from 2 to 8 minutes. After completion of instructions to the S, programming apparatus initiated the next trial sequence after a variable delay.

Results

HR increases were calculated for each trial by subtracting the average HR of the pre-trial period from the average HR of the trial period. These results are presented in Table 1. Every S achieved HR increases of 10 beats-per-minute (BPM) or greater during at least one of the 4 trials, and some achieved this on the first trial. The mean HR increase for the four trials was 13.3 BPM, and the mean HR increase for the fourth trial was 14.4 BPM. Since there was no significant difference between the mean HR increases of Group A and Group B, the two groups will be considered together below.

Increased respiratory amplitude and increased frequency of respiratory irregularities were noted in most Ss during early experimental trials. However, these tended to decrease with further instructions. Pre-trial and trial respiratory patterns are shown for

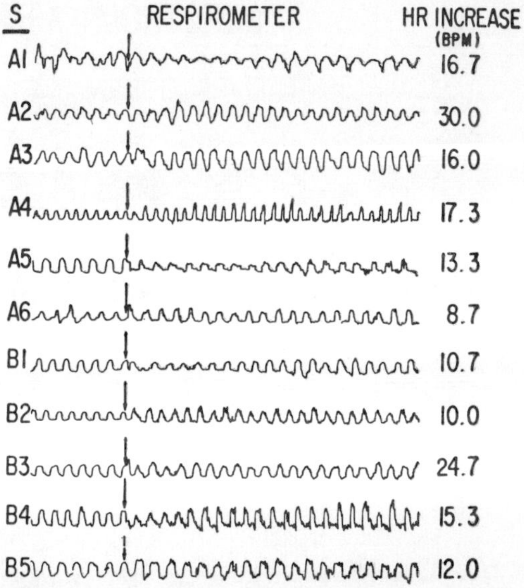

FIG. 1. Respiratory patterns during inconspicuous muscle tension. Beginning of trial is noted by arrow. HR increases for each trial is presented to the right of respiratory pattern.

the fourth trial for each S in Figure 1.‡ Two observers ignorant of the Ss HR increases were asked to rank-order the respiratory patterns in Figure 1 for differences between the pre-trial and trial periods, including amplitude, irregularities between cycles, and irregularities within each cycle. A Spearman rank correlation coefficient (Hays, 1963) was used to analyze the correlation between ranked HR increases and ranked respiratory pattern changes. The rank correlations were not significant ($r_s = .055$, and $r_s = .146$) though the observers' ranks correlated well ($r_s = .964$).

High-frequency activity in the chest wall electrodes (EMG) occurred in a variable way during the trials but did decrease with instructions. Pre-trial and trial EMG for the fourth trial is shown in Figure 2 for each S.‡ For each S the pair of electrodes that detected *most* high-frequency activity is pictured. Two observers ignorant of the Ss HR increases were asked to rank-order the EMG patterns in Figure 2 for differences in high-frequency activity between the pre-trial and trial periods. A Spearman rank correlation coefficient was used to analyze the correlation between ranked HR increases and ranked EMG changes. The rank correlations were not significant ($r_s = -.391$, and $r_s = -.409$) though the observers' ranks correlated well ($r_s = .991$).

Discussion

Instructions to tense chest muscles can cause HR changes averaging 13–14 BPM. Such HR changes are evident even though

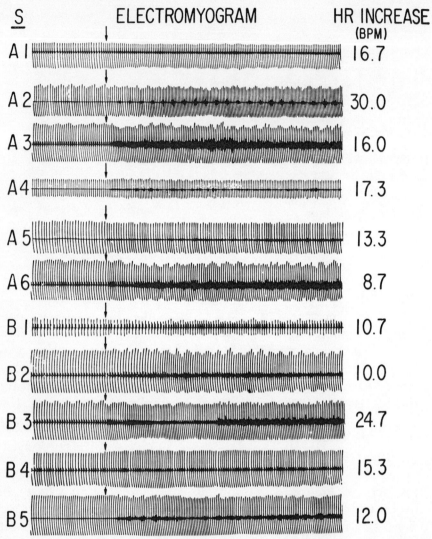

FIG. 2. EMG patterns during inconspicuous muscle tension. Beginning of trial is noted by arrow. HR increase for each trial is presented to the right of EMG pattern.

there are no reliable changes of respiratory pattern or surface EMG. The surface EMG reflects activity in a limited area of the body only. Even if muscle tension is encouraged in the specific area of the detecting electrodes, as in this experiment where the chest was the presumed site of tension and also of the electrodes, the muscle tension may be too deep for detection with surface electrodes (Basmajian, 1967).

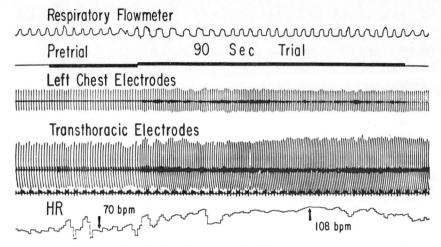

Fɪɢ. 3. Sample pre-trial–trial sequence.

One early study of the effect of sustained isometric tension on HR was done by Peters and Gantt (1953). They had Ss attempt to maintain maximal or one-sixth maximal tension on a hand dynamometer. During 30 seconds of maximal exertion the HR averaged 27 BPM greater than pre-trial level. During the first 30 seconds of two minutes of one-sixth maximal exertion the average HR was 8 BPM greater than the pre-trial level. The rate of increase was also much greater with maximal exertion; HR accelerated within the first second of exertion. The HR rapidly dropped to resting levels following cessation of effort.

Lind, Taylor, Humphreys, Kennelly and Donald (1964) also explored the cardiovascular effects of isometric contractions. They had four Ss grip a hand dynamometer with 10, 20 and 50 per cent of the maximal voluntary contraction. With 20 per cent maximal voluntary contraction the Ss' average HR had increased from 71 BPM to 80 BPM at the end of one minute. With 50 per cent of maximal voluntary contraction the average HR had increased 34 BPM at the end of 30 seconds. Decreases of HR to resting levels occurred within seconds after cessation of isometric tension. Lind and McNichol (1967) explored the cardiovascular response to isometric tension in various muscle groups and found that the quantity of cardiovascular response seems to be proportional to the percentage of maximal contraction and not to the size of the muscle groups involved or to the absolute force exerted. When strongly contracted, relatively small muscles can generate a significant HR increase.

An approach to the mechanism of operant HR changes in humans might be sought in a closer investigation of HR decreases with operant conditioning. Muscle tension changes may *not* be able to account for any large HR decreases from base line. However, operantly conditioned HR decreases have yet to be convincingly demonstrated in humans. None of the reported studies was sufficiently controlled for the adaptational slowing of HR during the course of an experiment. This adaptational slowing can be quite significant, as exemplified in the data that Brener (1966) presented on the HR of control Ss after a preliminary 20-minute rest period was over. These yoked control Ss received considerable noise and electric shock. Yet average HR, calculated from pre-experimental and end-experimental interbeat data that Brener presents, declined almost 6 BPM during the 45 minute experiment. This adaptation occurred *after* a 20-minute rest period.

Engel and Hansen (1966) reported operant HR slowing in humans. They allowed Ss to rest for 30 minutes and then gave beat-by-beat reinforcement for HR slowing. There were 10 Ss, with yoked controls for 5 of them. The mean change in HR of the experimental Ss was −0.5 BPM. The yoked controls showed a mean increase of 5.6 BPM. In view of the persistent difficulties of the yoked control design (Church, 1964) the significant HR speeding of the yoked controls does not justify interpreting the behavior of the experimental Ss as slowing. Levene, Engel and Pearson (1968) allowed Ss to rest for 30 minutes and then gave beat-by-beat reinforcement for HR speeding or slowing during alternating periods of one minute each. The mean decrease during HR slowing periods was −1.6 BPM, which could be due to adaptation. Brener and Hothersall (1967) used no rest period before beginning alternating trials of HR increase and decrease, and thus considerable adaptation of HR may have occurred.

Since contraction of a small muscle anywhere in the body can cause HR increases, it becomes difficult indeed to investigate muscle tension as a mediator of operant HR changes. Needle electromyography, which can measure deep muscle activity, would have to be done simultaneously in numerous sites in order to evaluate changes in overall muscle tension in the body. Perhaps sensitive measurement of total oxygen consumption during HR increases could give information on the extent of overall muscle tension and arousal that occurs with HR increases. No available technique short of using curare-like drugs would allow us to eliminate skeletal activity in a normal organism, and curarization is too traumatic to be used repeatedly with human subjects.

It is possible that operant conditioning of human HR is merely a slower form of the procedure used here to produce HR increases with inconspicuous muscle tension. Certainly most experiments in operant conditioning of human HR reward changes in HR by use of a feedback technique, while giving instructions that discourage overt breathing changes or body movement (Brener and Hothersall, 1967; Levene, Engel and Pearson, 1968; Headrick, Feather and Wells, 1971; Shapiro *et al.*, 1970). The magnitude of operantly conditioned HR changes is comparable to that produced here by inconspicuous muscle tension: Engel and Chism (1967) reported a 3 BPM increase; Levene, Engel and Pearson (1968) reported a 6.4 BPM difference between increase and decrease trials on the average; Brener and Hothersall (1967) reported a 13 BPM difference between final increase and decrease trials without paced respiration; Shapiro *et al.*, (1970) reported a 6 BPM average difference between their increase and decrease groups on the final trial; Headrick, Feather and Wells (1971) reported one S who achieved HR increases of 30 BPM (compare S A2 in Table 1).

Smith (1967) argues that autonomic conditioning is trivial if it is mediated by learned changes in respiration or muscle tension. We see no reason to denigrate as "trivial" any means of control over nature merely because of its mechanism of mediation. It is true, however, that if control over HR is the desired goal, it may be more efficient to tell a S to voluntarily tense his muscles rather than to reinforce HR changes beat-by-beat in a tedious operant paradigm. Each time the operant conditioning paradigm demonstrates control over an autonomic nervous system function in humans, one might ask if the same control cannot be achieved more efficiently by voluntary use of the skeletal nervous system.

There is another crucial reason for continuing to ask what mediates operant HR conditioning in humans, even if the mediator is an extremely elusive entity experimentally. The autonomic nervous system tends to function tonically, with an operant level of firing to each effector organ. The skeletal nervous system tends to function episodically, with little tonic activity to most organs. Thus direct operant conditioning of the autonomic nervous system might be expected to persist, whereas skeletally mediated changes may fatigue rapidly outside the laboratory. Instrumental approaches to the treatment of psychosomatic disorders might be grounded better on direct operant conditioning of the autonomic nervous system, such as has been demonstrated to be possible in animals (Miller and DiCara, 1967). However, such direct operant autonomic conditioning may be difficult, if not impossible, to obtain in human subjects. The roles played by various mechanisms in human operant HR conditioning should be investigated, because it may be necessary to isolate one therapeutically practical mechanism that could then be refined.

Acknowledgment

The assistance and advice of Dr. John Salzano, Dr. John B. Nowlin, and Dr. David T. Wells are gratefully acknowledged.

References

Basmajian, J. V.: *Muscles Alive: Their Function Revealed by Electromyography.* Baltimore, Williams & Wilkins, 1967.

Black, A. H.: Transfer following operant conditioning in the curarized dog. *Science,* 155:201-203, 1967.

Brener. J.: Heart rate as an avoidance response. *Psychol. Rec.,* 16:329-336, 1966.

Brener, J., and Hothersall, D.: Paced respiration and heart rate control. *Psychophysiology,* 4:1-6, 1967.

Church, R. M.: Systematic effect of random error in the yoked control design. *Psychol, Bull.,* 62:122-131, 1964.

DiCara, L. V., and Miller, N. E.: Instrumental learning of systolic blood pressure responses by curarized rats: Dissociation of cardiac and vascular changes: *Psychosom. Med.,* 30:489-494, 1968.

Donald, K. W., Lind, A. R., McNichol, G. W., Humphreys, P. W., Taylor, S. H., and Staunton. H. P.: Cardiovascular responses to sustained (static) contractions. *Circ. Res.,* 20: Supplement 1, 15-20, 1967.

Engel, B. T., and Chism, R. A.: Operant conditioning of heart rate speeding. *Psychophysiology,* 3:418-426, 1967.

Engel, B. T., and Hansen, S. P.: Operant conditioning of heart rate slowing. *Psychophysiology,* 3:176-187, 1966.

Grossman, W. I. and Weiner, H.: Some factors affecting the reliability of surface electromyography. *Psychosom. Med.,* 28:78-83, 1966.

Hays, W. L.: *Statistics for Psychologists.* New York, Holt, Rinehart, & Winston, 1963.

Headrick, M. W., Feather, B. W., and Wells, D. T.: Unidirectional and large magnitude heart rate changes with augmented sensory feedback. *Psychophysiology,* 8:132-142, 1971.

Katkin, E. S., and Murray, E. N.: Instrumental conditioning of autonomically mediated behavior: Theoretical and methodological issues. *Psychol. Bull.,* 70: 52-68, 1968.

Levene, H. L., Engel, B. T., and Pearson, J. A.: Differential operant conditioning of heart rate. *Psychosom. Med.,* 30:837-844, 1968.

Lind, A. R. and McNichol, G. W.: Circulatory responses to sustained hand-grip contractions performed during other exercise, both rhythmic and static. *J. Physiol.*, **192**:595-607,1967.

Lind, A. R., Taylor, S. H., Humphreys, P. W., Kennelly, B. M., and Donald, K. W.: The circulatory effects of sustained voluntary muscle contraction. *Clin. Sci.*, **27**:229-244, 1964.

Miller, N. E.: Learning of visceral and glandular responses. *Science*, **163**:434-445, 1969.

Miller, N. E., and DiCara, L. V.: Instrumental learning of heart rate changes in curarized rats: Shaping, and specificity to discriminative stimulus. *J. Comp. Physiol. Psychol.*, **63**:12-19, 1967.

Murray, E. N., and Katkin, E. S.: Comment on two recent reports of operant heart rate conditioning. *Psychophysiology*, **5**:192-195, 1968.

Peters, J. E., and Gantt, W. H.: Effect of graded degrees of muscular exertion on human heart rate and the role of muscular exertion in cardiac conditioned reflexes. *J. Gen. Psychol.*, **49**:31-43, 1953.

Shapiro, D., Tursky, B., and Schwartz, A. M.: Differentiation of heart rate and systolic blood pressure in man by operant conditioning. *Psychom. Med.*, **32**:417-423, 1970.

Smith, K.: Conditioning as an artifact. In G. A. Kimble (Ed.): *Foundations of Conditioning and Learning*. New York, Appleton-Century-Crofts, 1967.

The Effects of Immediate Feedback 7
Upon Voluntary Control of Salivary Rate

David T. Wells, Ben W. Feather,
and Mary W. Headrick

ABSTRACT

Thirteen human subjects (Ss) were given immediate auditory feedback concerning their salivary rates and were asked both to increase and to decrease their rates during a series of 30-sec trials. Significant decreases, but not increases, in salivary rate were obtained relative to baseline. During the second half of the experiment, when feedback was omitted until the end of each trial, Ss maintained significant differential response rates between increase and decrease trials, but the reliability of decreases from expected baseline was reduced. Thirteen control Ss, who received feedback only at the end of each trial during both halves of the experiment, were unable to alter their rates during either half. Salivation on increase and decrease trials was not systematically correlated with changes in either heart rate or breathing rate in the immediate feedback group.

DESCRIPTORS: Voluntary control, Instrumental autonomic conditioning, Salivation. (D. T. Wells)

Although evidence based upon animal studies strongly supports the notion that responses mediated by the autonomic nervous system (ANS) are modifiable by instrumental conditioning procedures (Miller, 1969), several features of instrumentally controlled ANS responses in humans need further clarification. First, the specific effect of reinforcement upon change in human ANS responses has not been clearly demonstrated in experiments which control for differences in base level, general arousal, or motivation. Second, there is some evidence that increases and decreases in the activity of ANS response systems are not equally modifiable by instrumental procedures. Specifically, heart rate (HR) increases appear to be learned more easily than HR decreases (Levene, Engel, & Pearson, 1968; Headrick, Feather, & Wells, 1971; Wells, 1973). The generality of this finding needs verification in other ANS response systems, since differential conditionability would affect hypotheses concerning mechanisms involved in instrumental control of ANS responses. Finally, the extent to which modified response patterns are maintained in humans when reinforcement is delayed or withheld has received only minimal attention (Brener, Kleinman, & Goesling, 1969).

This research was supported by NIMH PHS Grant MH 08394-05, NIMH Grant 5 KO2 MH 19523, and NIMH Grant 2 RO1 MH 1159.

Address requests for reprints to: David T. Wells, Ph.D., Department of Psychiatry, Baltimore City Hospitals, 4940 Eastern Avenue, Baltimore, Maryland 21224.

Evidence concerning retention is not only of theoretical importance, but is basic to the possibility of therapeutic applications of instrumental ANS conditioning to psychosomatic disorders.

Although instrumental conditioning of cardiac, electrodermal, and electrocortical responses in humans has received considerable attention, only four studies of instrumental salivary conditioning have been reported using either humans or animals. The results of these studies are ambiguous due to inadequate control of factors such as general arousal and skeletal movement. The difficulty posed by concomitant changes in general arousal and salivation is evident in the report by Miller and Carmona (1967), in which momentary increases or decreases in salivary rate of thirsty dogs were rewarded with water. While highly reliable bidirectional changes in salivary rate were demonstrated, these changes were highly correlated with changes in HR, breathing, and electroencephalographic (EEG) measures. Miller and Carmona noted the drowsy state of the dogs rewarded for decreases and, on the basis of evidence in humans that salivary rate is decreased during sleep (Scott, Wells, Delse, & Feather, 1968), it seems likely that the dogs were learning to change their general state of alertness rather than salivary rate specifically.

Methodological problems also limit the conclusiveness of the three studies which have reported successful instrumental control of salivation in humans. Brown and Katz (1967) obtained increases in spontaneous acceleration of salivary rate using contingent monetary reward. Unfortunately, no objective method was used to detect swallowing and other movements which are known to produce momentary increases in salivation (Feather & Wells, 1966), and no attempt was made to condition salivary decreases. Frezza and Holland (1971) had subjects (Ss) alternate between periods of continuous reinforcement (advancing a counter at each drop of saliva) and reinforcement for zero responding. The authors detected evidence of conditioning in 3 of the 4 Ss in the experiment. Unfortunately only a sample of this data from one S was presented, and it is impossible to evaluate the significance of the results. Additionally, the authors stated that their method of measuring swallows (microswitch contacting the neck) was not satisfactory.

Delse and Feather (1968) controlled for mouth movements by eliminating trials in which submental electromyographic (EMG) measures indicated muscle activity in the mouth region. These investigators demonstrated significant differences in salivary rate between increase and decrease trials in a group of Ss receiving feedback as compared with a group receiving no feedback from salivary rate. The results of this study are not conclusive, however, since no estimate of baseline salivary rate was recorded and it is not possible to determine whether the significant effects represent differences in baseline or in changes from baseline as a function of feedback. It is also possible that the between-group differences in salivary rate were due to differences in arousal produced by the presence and absence of feedback in the respective groups. There was some indication from post-experiment interviews that Ss in the no-feedback group had difficulty maintaining interest and tended to become drowsy during the experiment.

The present study was designed to improve the method and extend the findings of Delse and Feather (1968) by including an estimate of baseline salivation and by comparing groups of Ss who were comparably motivated. Specifically, the present study is concerned with (a) the influence of immediate feedback upon changes in salivary rate from an expected baseline; (b) the bidirectional conditionability of salivary rate changes; (c) the retention of responses learned with immediate feedback when feedback is withheld until the end of each trial; and (d) the concomitant changes in breathing and HR which may be correlated with modified salivary response patterns.

Method

Subjects

A total of 36 undergraduate psychology students served as Ss to fulfill experimental participation requirements. Ss were randomly assigned to either a group for which feedback was immediate (IF) or to a group for which feedback was withheld until the end of each trial (WF). Randomization was restricted such that each group had an equal number of males and females. Four Ss were discarded from each group due to movement and/or recording artifacts. One additional S was deleted from the IF group as an outlier on the basis of a test for extreme scores (Natrella, 1963) and one randomly selected S was deleted from the control group, leaving a total of 13 Ss in each group.

Apparatus

Saliva was collected from the right parotid gland by means of a double-chambered Lucite capsule placed over Stensen's duct and held by suction applied to the outer chamber. Pressure in the collection chamber of the capsule was essentially at atmospheric level. Salivary rate was obtained by means of a high-resolution, liquid-displacement sialometer with a drop size of 480 per cubic centimeter (cc). This system has been described in detail elsewhere (Feather & Wells, 1966). A photoelectric drop-counting system coupled with a Grass Model 7 polygraph amplifier provided a continuous record of salivation. Output from the polygraph amplifier for salivation provided relay closures for each drop, which incremented printing counters and allowed the presentation of feedback immediately contingent upon each drop of saliva. This feedback consisted of a 0.2-sec, 1000 Hz tone burst presented through earphones at approximately 60 dB (re 0.0002 dynes per cm^2). Electrocardiogram was obtained from Grass EEG electrodes placed one on each wrist, and submental EMG from two silver disc electrodes of 1.5 cm diameter placed 1 cm on either side of the midline of the submental region. A ground electrode was placed on the right mastoid process. Breathing rate and amplitude were monitored using an air-filled rubber tube encircling the chest below the sternum and coupled to a Grass PT5 pressure transducer. Instructions and other communication between the experimenter and S were presented through earphones. All stimuli were controlled automatically by electronic programming equipment located outside the sound-attenuated experimental chamber (Industrial Acoustics Corporation). All physiological measures and stimuli were recorded on a Grass Model 7 polygraph.

Signals to S indicating increase or decrease trial periods, periods when swallowing was permitted, and the occurrence of a swallow during trial periods were provided by a sign board measuring 2 ft (60.5 cm) on a side, mounted 5 ft (151.3 cm) above the floor of the chamber approximately 6 ft (181.5 cm) in front of S's head. The face of the sign board was constructed of translucent white Lucite with messages printed in block letters behind this face. The messages could be individually illuminated by lights mounted behind the Lucite panel. The messages read "OK TO SWALLOW," "INCREASE," and "DECREASE." A separate light with a 0.5-in. (13-mm) red lens was mounted at the bottom edge of the sign board to signal the occurrence of a swallow.

Procedure

The experiment consisted of two halves, separated by a 5-min rest period. During this rest period E entered the chamber, removed headphones and salivary capsule, gave S instructions for the second half of the experiment, then replaced capsule and headphones. During each half there were 6 trials on which Ss were to increase salivary rate (Increase trials), 6 trials on which they were to decrease salivary rate (Decrease trials), and 6 "blank" trials (Baseline trials) on which they made no attempt to alter salivary rate. Baseline trials were interspersed between pairs of nonregularly ordered Increase and Decrease trials. The order of trial presentation was restricted such that no more than 2 trials of the same type occurred sequentially.

The sequence of events at each trial consisted of (a) the application of 2 cc of 0.15% acetic acid through tubing attached to the capsule; (b) a 30-sec period during which Ss were instructed by a sign that they could swallow and move their mouths; (c) a post-movement period during which salivary rate was monitored until the first incidence of a 3-sec delay between drops; and, following immediately, (d) the 30-sec trial period, during which a sign was lighted and immediate feedback, when appropriate, was presented on Increase and Decrease trials. On Baseline trials the sign and feedback were not presented and Ss received no stimuli subsequent to the offset of the swallow sign. Ss were informed by a red light when swallowing movements were detected during a trial. The interval between the end of the 30-sec trial period and the next application of acid was 5 sec. The rate-dependent initiation of feedback periods and inclusion of Baseline trials were employed to provide identical salivary rates at the onset of measurement periods.[1]

During the first half of the experiment Ss in the IF group received a brief tone through earphones at each drop of saliva secreted during Increase and Decrease trials. Ss in the WF group were informed over the intercom by the experimenter at the end of the 30-sec period of the total number of drops secreted during that trial. No feedback was given to either group on Baseline trials. During the second half of the experiment Ss in both groups received feedback in the same manner as the WF Ss had during the first half.

Ss were seated in a semi-reclining position and all recording devices were explained briefly as they were attached. Each S was instructed to attempt either to increase or decrease his salivary rate on successive trials depending upon which of two signs in front of him was lighted. Each S in the IF group was informed that changes in the rate at which the tone bursts occurred would indicate changes in his salivary rate. Ss in both groups were cautioned to swallow and move their mouths only when the "OK TO SWALLOW" sign was lighted, and that they would be reminded by the red signal light of swallows occurring during a trial period. They were told to alter salivary rate by purely "mental effort"; no other instructions were given as to how they should deal with the task.

---

[1] It should be noted that the response measured on baseline trails does not represent a spontaneous baseline, but rather is the expected response rate following acid stimulation.

Data Quantification and Analyses

The total number of drops of saliva secreted during each 3-sec interval of the 30-sec measurement period of all Increase, Decrease, and Baseline trials constituted the basic datum. Trials upon which mouth movement was indicated by EMG recordings were discarded. If 3 or more trials of a single type in either half of the experiment were discarded, the S was eliminated from the study. Salivary rate scores were averaged for each S into 2 blocks of 5 3-sec periods for Increase, Decrease, and Baseline trials for each half of the experiment. Multivariate analyses of variance were performed on the data (Starmer & Grizzle, 1968). The 2 15-sec periods within each of the three types of trials during each half of the experiment constituted the 12-element vector of each S in the two-group model. Each of the nine multivariate tests performed yielded exact likelihood ratio Fs as well as univariate F ratios for each element in the contrast. Univariate contrasts were performed within each half of the experiment to test differences between specific elements. Since a total of 36 univariate contrasts were made for each half of the experiment, some adjustment of the confidence levels of individual probability statments is appropriate. On the basis of the relatively conservative Bonferroni t statistic (Miller, 1966), the probability of a Type 1 error occurring anywhere among the 36 tests is less than .05 for F ratios equal to or greater than 13.03 and less than .01 for F ratios equal to or greater than 18.49. The probabilities reported are for individual tests, since there is no established method of adjusting individual probabilities directly within the multivariate contrast model.

The total number of heart bearts and breathing cycles completed within each 30-sec measurement period on Increase and Decrease trials was correlated within trial types for the first half of the experiment with the total number of drops of saliva secreted during that period. Correlations were computed separately for each S in the IF group.

Results

Salivation

The effects upon salivary rate of immediate feedback employed during the first half of the experiment are shown in Fig 1. It can be seen that, in the IF group, salivary rate was higher on Increase and lower on Decrease trials than on Baseline trials ($\bar{X} = 1.53$, 1.17, and 1.40 cc $\times 10^{-2}$, respectively). In contrast, changes in salivary rate in the WF group were negligible, with responses on both Increase and Decrease trials being slightly below baseline trials.

Separate analyses of responses of the IF and WF groups were performed to assess the respective reliabilities of increases and decreases from Baseline trials in each group. For the WF group, performance on Increase and Decrease trials failed to differ significantly either from Baseline trials or from each other at any point during the first half of the experiment. In contrast, reliable overall decreases relative to Baseline trials were found in the IF group ($F = 8.30$, $p < .008$, $df = 1/24$). Separate contrasts of Decrease with Baseline trials for each 15-sec period revealed that decreases were not significant during the first 15-sec period, but were highly reliable during the second 15-sec period ($F = 15.00$, $p < .001$, $df = 1/24$). The difference in performance between Increase and Decrease trials was significant overall and in both 15-sec periods ($F = 15.22$, $p < .001$; $F = 9.36$,

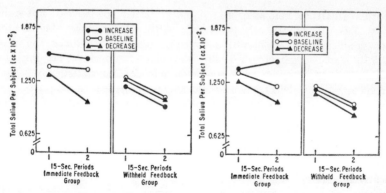

Fig. 1. Salivary rates of *S*s on Increase, Decrease, and Baseline trials during the first half of the experiment when feedback was either given immediately (IF group) or was withheld until the end of each trial (WF group).

Fig. 2. Salivary rates of *S*s on Increase, Decrease, and Baseline trials during the second half of the experiment when feedback was withheld until the end of each trial for all *S*s.

$p < .005$; $F = 15.07$, $p < .001$, $df = 1/24$, respectively). The increases apparent in Fig. 1 for the IF group failed to reach statistical significance. In summary, reliable decreases, but not increases in salivary rate were obtained only with immediate feedback.

Multivariate analyses of variance of responses in the first half of the experiment showed that the IF and WF groups differed significantly in their overall responses across Increase, Decrease, and Baseline trials ($F = 5.57$, $p < .01$, $df = 2/23$). Across the entire 30-sec period the IF group showed significantly greater differential response between Increase and Decrease trials than the WF group ($F = 11.62$, $p < .002$, $df = 1/24$) and a marginally greater response when Increase and Decrease trials were each contrasted with Baseline trials ($F = 4.28$, $p < .04$; $F = 3.60$, $p < .06$, $df = 1/24$, respectively). Separate tests of performance during each 15-sec measurement period showed greater differential response between Increase and Decrease trials in the IF group during both 15-sec periods ($F = 8.85$, $p < .006$; $F = 10.33$, $p < .003$, $df = 1/24$, respectively) and greater decreases relative to Baseline trials during the second 15-sec period ($F = 6.40$, $p < .01$, $df = 1/24$). In addition, the change in magnitude of decreases from Baseline between the first and second 15-sec periods was relatively greater in the IF than WF group ($F = 6.25$, $p < .01$, $df = 1/24$).

Data from the second half of the experiment were examined to determine the extent to which response patterns established with immediate feedback were retained when feedback was delayed. It can be seen in Fig. 2 that salivary rate was, again, higher on Increase and lower on Decrease trials than on Baseline trials ($\bar{X} = 1.46$, 1.15, and 1.29 cc $\times$ 10^{-2}, respectively) in the IF group. Responses in the WF group showed no differential trends. The reliable group differences found in the first half of the experiment were not found during the second half; however, separate analyses of responses in the IF and WF groups indicated that the performance of the IF group was influenced by the brief training with immediate feedback, whereas no significant effects were found in the WF group. Specifically, in the IF group, the difference between Increase and Decrease trials was reliable overall ($F = 7.02$, $p < .01$, $df = 1/24$)

and this difference increased in reliability during the second 15-sec period ($F = 7.77$, $p < .009$, $df = 1/24$). Although responses tended toward a non-significant increase in variability when immediate feedback was withheld, the pattern of changes obtained with immediate feedback persisted with some reliability. Overall multivariate contrasts indicated no statistically significant differences between the first and second halves of the experiment in the pattern of responses across groups, trial types, or 15-sec periods.

Heart Rate and Breathing

In order to determine if changes in salivary rate were part of a more general response pattern, correlations were computed between salivary rate and both HR and breathing rate. Using data from the first half of the experiment, a correlation was computed for each S in the IF group between total number of drops in each Increase trial and the corresponding totals of heart beats and breathing cycles. The same two correlations were computed for Decrease trials, yielding four correlations for each S. For each of the four sets of correlations the hypothesis was tested that the number of positive and negative correlations was equal. T tests using the normal approximation to the binomial showed no tendency in any of the four sets of correlations for either positive or negative correlations to predominate.

Discussion

The results of the present experiment have demonstrated that human Ss, when given immediate feedback, can significantly decrease, but not increase, salivary rates relative to an expected baseline. Withholding of feedback until the end of a 30-sec trial period was sufficient to prevent any significant alterations in salivary rate. Training with immediate feedback enabled Ss in the IF group to continue to display changes in salivary rate when feedback was withheld until the end of the trial. Some diminution of this ability was apparent, however, from the fact that in the second half of the experiment IF Ss showed differences between Increase and Decrease trials, but not between either Increase or Decrease and Baseline trials. Correlations between salivary rate and HR and breathing rate failed to provide evidence that changes in salivary rate were part of a more general physiological response pattern.

While the present results indicate that immediate reinforcement is critical during initial learning, there is some evidence to indicate that it is less critical once a response is well established (Wells, 1973; Levene et al., 1968). The effects observed in the present study suggest that it is the timing, rather than the information content of feedback, that is critical, since the feedback given to the WF group provided almost the same total information concerning the "correctness" of responses as did the immediate feedback. This finding is consistent with general learning theory based upon both classical and instrumental paradigms. In the case of instrumental ANS conditioning, the function of immediate feedback may be to augment naturally occurring feedback (Brener & Hothersall, 1966).

Immediate feedback does not seem to be a sufficient condition for the learning of salivary increases, at least not with brief training periods. The presence of reliable decreases, but not increases, in salivation supports the findings from previous investigations with HR in which increases were learned more easily than decreases (Levene et al., 1968; Engel & Chism, 1967), decreases failed to occur with brief training (Headrick et al., 1970), or in which large-magnitude HR increases were produced with extended training, while large-magnitude HR decreases failed to occur with similar training (Headrick et al., 1970; Wells, 1973).

One hypothesis concerning the unidirectional conditionability of ANS mediated responses is that, in intact humans, these responses are physiologically more reactive in one direction than the other to external contingencies. On the basis of previous HR data and the present study, it seems justifiable to speculate that, at least in these response systems, sympathetic-like responses, i.e., HR increases and salivary decreases, are more easily conditionable than parasympathetic-like responses. It is difficult to evaluate this hypothesis on the basis of existing human HR data since skeletal muscle activity could be responsible for the observed increases in HR. The present data provide more straightforward evidence of unidirectional conditionability since muscle activity produces salivary increases rather than decreases (Feather & Wells, 1966), and no relation was found between salivary rate and indices of general arousal.

It does not appear to be a question of whether bidirectional changes can be produced under special circumstances, since there is some evidence that response changes in the direction of sympathetic hypoactivation can be produced in humans who have atypically high sympathetic-like baseline activity (Engel & Melmon, 1968). Rather, it is of etiological interest whether unidirectional change is the typical response to external contingencies and of methodological interest to those concerned with modifying ANS mediated responses.

The present study provides some evidence that instrumentally established ANS responses are retained when immediate feedback is withheld and the results are consistent with those reported by Brener et al. (1969), Levene et al. (1968), and Wells (1973). In view of the small number of training trials with immediate feedback and the relative novelty of the response, it is not too surprising that retention was relatively unstable. The data add generality to the previous findings with HR, however, and indicate that further examination of the necessary and sufficient conditions for maintenance of instrumentally controlled ANS responses be undertaken.

REFERENCES

Brener, J., & Hothersall, D. Heart rate control under conditions of augmented sensory feedback. *Psychophysiology*, 1966, *3*, 23–28.

Brener, J., Kleinman, R. A., & Goesling, W. J. The effects of different exposure to augmented sensory feedback on the control of heart rate. *Psychophysiology*, 1969, *5*, 510–516.

Brown, C. C., & Katz, R. A. Operant salivary conditioning in man. *Psychophysiology*, 1967, *4*, 156–160.

Delse, F. C., & Feather, B. W. The effect of augmented sensory feedback on the control of salivation. *Psychophysiology*, 1968, *5*, 15–21.

Engel, B. T., & Chism, R. A. Operant conditioning of heart rate speeding. *Psychophysiology*, 1967, *3*, 418–426.

Engel, B. T., & Melmon, L. Operant conditioning of heart rate in patients with cardiac arrhythmias. *Conditional Reflex*, 1968, *3*, 130. (Abstract)

Feather, B. W., & Wells, D. T. Effects of concurrent motor activity of the unconditioned salivary reflex. *Psychophysiology*, 1966, *2*, 338–343.

Frezza, D. A., & Holland, J. G. Operant conditioning of the human salivary response. *Psychophysiology*, 1971, *8*, 581–587.

Headrick, M. W., Feather, B. W., & Wells, D. T. Unidirectional and large magnitude heart rate changes with augmented sensory feedback. *Psychophysiology*, 1971, *8*, 132–142.

Levene, H. I., Engel, B. T., & Pearson, J. A. Differential operant conditioning of heart rate. *Psychosomatic Medicine*, 1968, *30*, 837–845.

Miller, N. E. Learning of visceral and glandular responses. *Science*, 1969, *163*, 434–445.

Miller, N. E., & Carmona, A. Modification of a visceral response, salivation in thirsty dogs, by instrumental training with water reward. *Journal of Comparative & Physiological Psychology*, 1967, *63*, 1–6.

Miller, R. G. *Simultaneous statistical inference*. New York: McGraw-Hill, 1966.

Natrella. M. G. *Experimental statistics. National Bureau of Standards Handbook No. 1*, 1963.

Scott, J., Wells, D. T., Delse, F. C., & Feather, B. W. Salivation during sleep in humans. *Psychophysiology*, 1968, *4*, 363. (Abstract)

Starmer, C. F., & Grizzle, J. E. *A computer program for analysis of data by general linear models*. Institute of Statistics Mimeo Series, No. 560, University of North Carolina, 1968.

Wells, D. T. Large magnitude voluntary heart rate changes. *Psychophysiology*, 1973, *10*, 260–269.

II

EVOKED POTENTIALS
AND MOTOR UNITS

Operant-Controlled Evoked 8

Responses: Discrimination of Conditioned

and Normally Occurring Components

J. Peter Rosenfeld and Bruce E. Hetzler

Abstract. *Rats were rewarded for signaling large and small sensory evoked components with appropriate bar presses. Most rats operantly generated large components and correctly signaled only these. Two rats correctly signaled successful and unsuccessful attempts to generate large waves. One rat discriminated component amplitudes without operantly attempting to generate specific wave types.*

Operant conditioning of sensory evoked components has been frequently reported (1, 2). The phenomenon in humans and subhumans is not trivially mediated by changes in receptor orientation or by execution of discrete skeletal responses (1, 2). It has been assumed that organisms control their neural activity by learning to discriminate and generate familiar psychological states whose neural correlates are the reinforcement-specified changes (1). Such a view suggests that organisms should be able to discriminate differences in a conditionable neural parameter, since operant conditioning of the neural event hypothetically proceeds by the organism's first learning to discriminate the reinforced event from other events. We explored this possibility by reinforcing rats for correctly signaling the size of a flash-evoked cortical component with an appropriate bar press.

It was found that such discrimination behavior can be acquired, although rarely in the absence of attempts by the animals to generate particular kinds of evoked potentials.

Discrimination of neural events has been previously reported (3). In this work, humans were trained to discriminate the presence and absence of certain electroencephalographic (EEG) frequencies. Although evoked components are more phasic than are EEG epochs, our results may be related to the EEG data in that phasic evoked components may be mediated by tonic states (2).

Ten male albino rats were implanted surgically with standard long-term recording plugs; nine rats survived all procedures. Evoked potentials were bipolarly recorded from a screw over the visual cortex and from a Nichrome wire 1.5 mm beneath the cortical surface underlying the screw. Potentials were amplified by a modified Tektronix 122 preamplifier with filters set to pass signals between 0.8 and 250 hertz. Signals were then led to an analog-to-digital converter of a PDP8L computer. Rewards consisted of 400-msec 60-hertz stimulations of the medial forebrain bundle. [Before any other training, the stimulation was confirmed as rewarding in a two-way approach-avoid box. (4)]. The animals were initially trained to press either of two bars protruding from one wall of an operant chamber for continuous reinforcement. Electrical circuitry prevented the development of bar preferences because reinforcement was delivered in initial training by a capacitative one-shot circuit that failed to operate after five or six rapid presses of one bar in succession. This training was then replaced by a computer-controlled, signaled, fixed-interval operant procedure in which the simultaneous onset of houselights and a constant-intensity 10-μsec stroboscopic flash (evoking stimulus) cued the animal that the bars were activated. The flash unit was mounted in the wall of the operant chamber perpendicular to the wall containing the operant bars. The houselight was overhead. A press of either bar in the next 3 seconds resulted in a single 400-msec brain stimulation reward. The bars were so spaced that they could not both be pressed at once. Houselights were turned off by the first bar press or by computer 3 seconds after their onset. Intervals between flashes (trials) were 4.5 seconds. The flash-evoked potentials obtained during a week of this training were collected to yield a median criterion segment for each rat, based on 3500 samples. A 30-msec segment of the surface-negative component, centered at 130 msec after the strobe flash stimulus, was averaged by computer on each trial to yield the criterion segment for the trial. Computer resolution was 1 msec per word.

Henceforth, evoked component criterion segments exceeding the median are called positive waves (WP), and those below are called negative waves (WN). The final paradigm required rats to press one bar (B1) if a WP occurred on a given trial, or the other bar (B2) if WN occurred. Either correct press is called a hit; hitP means WP was correctly signaled; hitN means WN was correctly signaled. Miss trials, WPB2 or WNB1, were punished with nonreinforcement and a 5-second delay before onset of the next trial. For half the rats, a bar on the rat's left as he faced the bar-containing chamber wall was called B1 and the other bar (on his right) was called B2. The definitions were reversed for the remaining animals. Failures to press either bar occurred in less than 5 percent of all trials and are neglected. Before the final paradigm was instituted, waves were monitored during a further 5-day baseline period to verify that a priori probabilities for the following were each near their chance expected values of .5: hits, WP, WN, B1, B2, correctly signaled WP, and correctly signaled WN. All of these values were between 44 and 58 percent in the baseline period. In all phases of training, rats were given 500 trials per day. The final training phase of discrimination lasted 21 days.

A two-tailed, within-subject t-test was done to test the significance of the difference between the mean percentage of hits during the 5 days of the baseline period (48 percent) and during the last 5 days of training (61 percent). The training effect was significant ($t = 4.2$, $P < .01$). Close analysis of individual data between and within days, however, showed that only one of the animals learned the discrimination without attempting to selectively generate WP or WN. One animal

Fig. 1. Within-day data illustrating differing response styles in the last phase of training period. Each pair of panels represents data for 1 day. Percentage data are given for the following: hits, correctly signaled waves of both kinds, positive and negative; (hits P)/WP, positive waves correctly signaled; (hits N)/WN, correctly signaled negative waves; WP, positive waves; and bar 1, presses of bar to correctly signal a WP. (A to D) Pure amplitude discrimination without conditioning is illustrated. Both kinds of waves are correctly signaled more often than the 50 percent chance level, but WP responses remain around the chance level. (E and F) Discrimination of successful and unsuccessful attempts to produce WP is illustrated. Signaled events of both kinds are above the chance level but WP is likewise elevated.

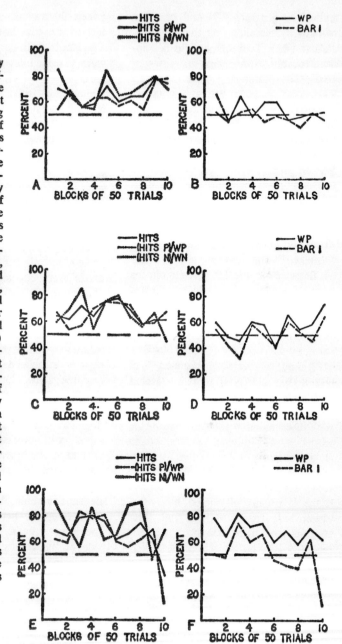

learned to generate WN and obtained rewards by remaining on the appropriate bar (B2). Two animals did not appear to show appreciable increases in hits. The remaining five animals learned to generate WP and obtained rewards by remaining on the appropriate B1 bar. However, two animals, following simple conditioning, also learned to signal failures to produce WP on given trials. Thus, they learned to discriminate their successes and failures. These conclusions are based on the kind of data shown in Fig. 1. Figure 1, A to D, is based on representative days of pure discrimination performance. The percentage of WP oscillates about the 50 percent chance level through the day, which indicates that the animal was not tending to generate either WP or WN. At the same time, the percentages of hits, of correctly signaled WP [$100 \times$ (hits P)/ WP], and of correctly signaled WN [$100 \times$ (hits N)/WN] remain elevated well above chance levels. Careful visual monitoring of the rat's behavior during such discrimination showed that during sequences of consecutive hits, which at times were 12 in number, the rat never pressed one or the other of the bars in more than four consecutive trials. It usually alternated busily between bars from trial to trial. This suggests that there was no systematic tendency for clusters of WP or of WN to occur, and, further, that consistent receptor orientations could not develop. For animals that first learned to produce WP and then learned to signal successes and failures in attempts to generate WP, representative data are shown in Fig. 1, E and F. These rats consistently tended to produce WP but consistently correctly signaled the less frequently occurring WN as well as WP, so that correctly signaled WP and correctly signaled WN remained be-

tween 60 and 80 percent during the last asymptotic days of their training. The less frequently occurring WN trials were usually interspersed between WP sequences; WN clusters were atypical. Animals classified as exclusive WP operant conditioners gave 75 to 95 percent B1 responses and showed 60 to 80 percent WP throughout. Although 80 to 90 percent of WP were often correctly signaled, only 10 to 30 percent of WN were correctly signaled. These two curves were usually mirror images over trials, what one would expect of animals that predominantly generate WP and press B1. As expected, records for the sole WN generator were opposite to those of WP generators.

Figure 2 shows averaged evoked WP responses and criterion segment distributions in baseline and training periods associated with the different response styles. Dramatic changes in distribution parameters were associated with (i) exclusive operant WP production, (ii) WP production with correct signaling of successes and failures, and (iii) exclusive operant WN production. In contrast, for the pure discriminator, baseline and training distributions can be superimposed. We found a significant difference between the means of the most extreme values on the WP side of the criterion segment distribution in the baseline period as compared to the same measure on the best WP production day for all WP producers ($t = 2.9$, $P < .05$; two-tailed t-test). The same t-test done on extreme values at the WN end of the distributions was also significant ($t = 3.31$, $P < .05$). We also noted some tendency for a skew reversal of the criterion segment distributions between baseline and conditioning (Fig. 2, B and C), but this was not apparent in all rats.

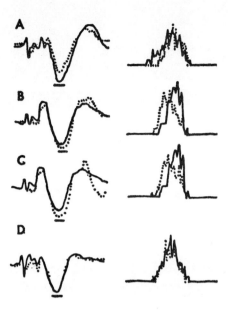

Fig. 2. Average evoked potentials within WP category (left column) and criterion segment amplitude distributions (right column) superimposed on baseline data (solid curves) and training data (dotted curves) associated with different response styles. Data are X-Y plotter outputs for (A) simple WN production conditioning; (B) simple WP production conditioning; (C) WP conditioning with correct signaling of failures and successes; and (D) pure discrimination. The WP tends to become more positive in simple and signaled WP conditioning and less positive in WN conditioning. In discrimination, relatively fewer changes are evident in superimposed waves and in superimposed distributions. Each training curve shown is data for a single day when performance best satisfied the training criteria for the particular response mode. Baseline curves are data for a day randomly selected from each animal's set of five baseline days. Average evoked potentials were usually in the range of 100 to 150 μv measured from the baseline before evoked activity to the down-going peak of the criterion segment. The bars below waves denote the 30-msec criterion segments. For amplitude distributions, the WP direction is to the left and each sequence of four raw data points is represented by one average point.

We interpret these data as suggesting that operantly conditioned neural activity may not represent processes that typically occur during the baseline situation in normal animals. That is, a conditioned increase in evoked component amplitude may not represent the same information that spontaneous occurrences of enhanced amplitude represent in naive subjects. This view is suggested by the alterations of neural distribution parameters seen in the conditioned WP producers in this study. A previous study from this laboratory noted the emergence of correlations between activities in trained and untrained cortical loci in conditioning (2). Such results also suggest the development of processes in conditioning which do not exist in the naive subject in baseline periods.

The one animal that successfully discriminated amplitude in the absence of evidence for conditioning was, we feel, learning to discriminate states normally occurring during the baseline period, since its baseline distribution parameters did not change during training. The rats that learned to discriminate successes and failures at generating conditioned amplitudes seemed to be special cases of simple conditioners in that the neural distribution parameters of both response styles showed similar changes between baseline and training.

The fact that the neural concomitants of pure neural discrimination behavior appeared so different from the characteristics of simple or signaled conditioning suggests that operant conditioning of neural events does not proceed simply by the animal's learning to discriminate and then selectively generating states that commonly occur in the baseline situation. We are not necessarily suggesting that the state (or states) mediating neural conditioning are unphysiological or that they have never or rarely occurred previously in the rat's life. Many different conditions may result in altered evoked potentials. Such conditions include arousal, sleep, attention, distraction, pharmacological intervention, brain stimulation, and so forth. The data do suggest, however, that the mediating states do not commonly occur during operationally defined baseline periods and that, therefore, the conditioning process does not involve selection of a baseline state for production. It follows that the neural processes activated during conditioning represent a distinctive set of states. Thus, the conditioning technique may not be an appropriate way of isolating for study a process that is occasionally observed in a baseline period. These implications, on the one hand, restrict the applicability of operant neural conditioning for the purpose of direct study of normal psychology and physiology. On the other hand, the intriguing possibility remains that neural conditioning methods may allow experimental isolation of unusual or even otherwise unobservable patterns of novel behavior or cognition of potentially adaptive value.

J. PETER ROSENFELD
BRUCE E. HETZLER
*Cresap Laboratory of Neuroscience
and Behavior, Psychology Department,
Northwestern University,
Evanston, Illinois 60201*

References and Notes

1. S. S. Fox and A. P. Rudell, *Science* **162**, 1299 (1968); *J. Neurophysiol.* **33**, 548 (1970); A. P. Rudell and S. S. Fox, *ibid.* **35**, 892 (1972); J. P. Rosenfeld, A. P. Rudell, S. S. Fox, *Science* **165**, 821 (1969).
2. J. P. Rosenfeld and R. Owen, *Physiol. Behav.* **9**, 851 (1972).
3. J. Kamiya, in *Altered States of Consciousness*, C. T. Tart, Ed. (Wiley, New York, 1969), pp. 519–529.
4. J. P. Rosenfeld, T. Bieneman, R. Cohen, A. Routtenberg, *Physiol. Behav.* **9**, 527 (1972).
5. Supported by NIH grants 5-550-5RR07028 and FR7028-05 to Northwestern University (J.P.R.).

13 February 1973; revised 21 May 1973   ∎

Instrumental Conditioning of Photic Evoked Potentials: Mechanisms and Properties of Late Component Modification

9

J. Peter Rosenfeld and Robert L. Owen

ROSENFELD, J. P. AND R. L. OWEN. *Instrumental conditioning of photic evoked potentials: mechanisms and properties of late component modification.* PHYSIOL. BEHAV. 9(5) 851–858, 1972.—Instrumental conditioning of late components of photic evoked potentials in cats was demonstrated using both random and regular interflash intervals. Cats performed equally well under both conditions. During conditioning, it was observed that cortical recordings from sites other than those to which the reinforcement contingency was applied showed systematic changes.

Photic evoked potentials   Instrumental conditioning

INSTRUMENTAL conditioning of neural activity is a potentially valuable technique for the neurosciences [4, 8]. The present experiments were designed to examine some fundamental properties of photic evoked potential conditioning. The first question is whether the organism generates criterion evoked components via the execution of discrete (phasic) behavioral or autonomic responses (whose central efferent drive or feedback would constitute the criterion component), or whether the animal generates a tonic cortical state existing in advance of the evoking stimulus and which is not associated with any particular skeletal response. Previous evoked potential conditioning studies have employed regular interstimulus intervals [9, 10, 12]. The latencies of conditioned components were sometimes chosen to be early enough to disallow the possibility that the evoking stimulus signalled the animal to perform a discrete response. However a regular interstimulus interval can produce temporally conditioned behavioral responses with potentially mediating neural correlates. The use of paralyzing agents does not rule out discrete responses of the autonomic nervous system as

---

[1] Supported by NIH grants No. 5-50-5RR07028 and FR 7028-05 to Northwestern University (JPR).

Reprinted with permission of Brain Research Publications from *Physiology and Behavior*, Vol. 9, 1972, 851-858.

possible mediators. The peripheral effects of this system are readily conditioned in the curarized rat [6]. It seemed to us that a reasonable method of confirming the tonic state hypothesis of evoked potential conditioning was to demonstrate the instrumental control of 10 msec component segments evoked by stimuli presented at random intervals.

Secondly, we studied effects of conditioning a given cortical site on acitivity at other cortical sites. The implication of findings that widespread modification of cortical acitivity results from instrumentally conditioning a small tissue volume may be relevant to controlling peripheral or psychological activities involving massive cerebral participation. In any case, knowledge of degree of spread of conditioning effects may cast new light on mechanism(s) of the neural conditioning phenomenon. Also, to the extent that neural conditioning involves cortical events which may be related to conventional learning, the electrophysiological events accompanying neural learning may be relevant to the physiology of behavioral learning.

Finally, we investigated a limitation on conditionability of cortical potentials by attempting and partially failing to condition slow components using an amplifier with restricted low frequency bandpasss.

METHOD

Surgery, Recording, Stimuli and Reinforcers

Five cats were implanted with standard chronic recording sockets mounted in dental acrylic fastened to skull. Each cortical bipolar electrode pair consisted of a stainless steel screw driven to rest upon dura and a 250 μ nichrome wire driven at an angle from a skull hole lateral to the screw to a point 2 mm below the center of the screw. The tip of the otherwise insulated wire was bare and scraped ½ mm from the tip. Recording was always differential from screw to wire (with a screw in frontal sinus serving as animal ground point) at to-be-trained and collaterally monitored sites. On some occasions, localization studies required monopolar (but differential) recording between either element of the surface to depths bipolar pair and a frontal sinus screw serving as distant, indifferent reference, with another sinus screw grounded.

The trained site leads, via a 14 pin Winchester plug, were led to an FET impedance matching amplifier which defeated cable artifact [13]. (The device had a flat frequency response from DC to 50 KHz.) The outputs of the FET and of the collateral site were led via Microdot cable to Tektronix 122 preamplifiers. In one experiment, these amplifiers had frequency responses 3 db down at 12 and 300 Hz. This low-end attenuation was unintentional and occurred due to modification of the amplifiers to achieve higher gain than that with which they are provided in the commercially available models. The experiment was under way before the defects were noted. The problem was rectified in the second experiment in which filter settings were 0.8 Hz to 250 Hz. Gain settings varied among cats from 4000 to 10,000. The outputs of the amplifiers were led to 2 of the analog-to-digital converter channels of a PDP8L computer which controlled all experiments. Potentials were either photographed or hand traced from the computer scope display.

Photic flash stimuli were provided by a strobe unit. Reinforcement consisted of 0.45 cc milk pumped under 35 lb pressure through a chronically implanted cannula from skull surface to roof of mouth. Cats were maintained at 85% normal weight.

Procedure

The trained site potentials were monitored for two weeks so as to determine the mean value over trials and standard deviation of a 10 msec segment of evoked potential. The first point of the segment had a latency of 155 msec. The segments averaged were each averages of the 10 voltage values occurring on each trial at each time point in the 10 msec segment; (the computer resolution was 1 msec/word). Segments, however, will hereafter be referred to as if they were unitary. The training procedure involved reinforcing the animal for segment values of 1 standard deviation (SD) from the pretraining mean. Assuming a normal distribution of segment amplitudes, the pretraining or chance probability of such criterion responses is 0.16. The theoretical probabilities were empirically confirmed by observing potentials for two further weeks during which milk was delivered noncontingently in 16% of the daily baseline trials while the computer kept a record of reinforceable responses (had the contingency been in effect). The reinforcement contingencies were then imposed. Although it obtained that a random versus a regular interflash interval had no effect on the pretraining segment means, half of the baseline samples were collected under each condition since the animals were to be trained under each.

Two of the five animals began training under a regular interflash interval of 3 sec. After reaching what the investigators judged to be a stable level of percent criterion responses (at least five days at asymptote ±10%), the cats were switched to the random interflash interval condition. In one case, during the second experiment a cat was reversed after one day at 74% criterion responses preceded by 5 days at about 50% criterion responses. This animal had several incidents of urinary retention requiring catheterization. His performance (which from experience we doubted he would exceed) and his precarious life expectancy prompted us to reverse him to the random condition as soon as possible. The other 3 cats were started with the random interflash interval and switched to the regular condition after stable performance in the random condition. One random starter was required to generate surface positivity (+1SD) and the other surface negativity (−1SD); one regular starter was required to produce surface positivity, the other two, surface negativity. As a further, within-subject control for noncontingent effects of reinforcement (see [8, 9]) all cats were required to reverse polarity (e.g. negativity to positivity or vice versa) under the random condition (only) following achievement of asymptote for at least 5 days each under the sequential random and regular conditions of their first polarity tasks. Early training and baseline days consisted of 1000 trials per cat; at asymptote, only 500 trials per cat per day were given.

The random interflash interval was obtained by calling a pseudo-random number generator routine and converting the number produced on each trial to msec. Random interflash intervals varied between 2 and 4.047 sec. The distribution of intervals, we empirically verified, was approximately rectilinear with a mean of about 3 sec. The regular interval used was 3 sec.

During all phases of the experiments, the end of a day's run for each cat would terminate with printed and displayed computer outputs. For the trained site, all potentials of rewarded trials (hits) were separately averaged and displayed. All (miss) trials were likewise averaged and displayed. For collateral sites, all potentials occurring simultaneously with hits at the rewarded sites would be separately averaged and displayed and likewise with potentials at collateral loci associated with misses at the trained site. Such displays were hand traced. All collateral sites were sampled at least once under baseline and all training conditions. The printed outputs included total number of hits, average voltage of the evaluated segment, mean interflash interval preceding hit trials, and same for miss trials, and SD of the evaluated or criterion segment. The computer also displayed single sweeps of both trained and collateral sites in the interflash interval. An option in the program enabled us to have a printout on each trial of the interflash interval preceding the trial. From this we could derive the distributions of intervals for hits and misses separately. (This was of interest during random conditions only.)

The procedures were followed twice; once with low-end attenuated amplifiers (Experiment 1) and again with restored frequency response (Experiment 2; see paragraph on recording, above.)

Trained sites in all cats in both experiments were in secondary visual cortex (VII). Collateral sites in all cats included the secondary visual cortex contralateral to the trained site, the contralateral primary visual cortex (VI) and the ipsilateral primary visual cortex. In three animals. collateral sites were additionally in the lateral geniculates, bilaterally. (Stereotaxic coordinates used for VI were AP: -4, L: 4; for VII the coordinates were AP: +8, L: 2).

RESULTS

Experiment 1

With filters on recording amplifiers set to block passage of lower frequencies (0–12 Hz) in evoked potentials, the attempt to instrumentally condition the cirterion segment at 155–165 msec of the photic evoked potential failed in three of five cats. In these three animals, the percentage of successful responses with reinforcement contingencies in effect was never above 18% for any 5 days sequence of training days regardless of polarity specified or interflash interval (IFI) condition. Each polarity - IFI combination was in effect for 30 days before another combination was attempted. When all such attempts failed, criterions were lowered so as to shape the animals' performance gradually. None of these manipulations had any effect in the three unsuccessful cats.

The two successful animals' learning curves were similar in shape and levels reached to learning curves reported in previous studies of this kind [8, 9, 10]. Baseline means were 17.1% and 15.2% criterion responses in these animals, and the means of the last 5 days of all IFI-polarity training combinations were 38.2% and 44.8% criterion responses.

In these cats, there was no apparent effect on the course of learning due to the change from a random to a regular or from a regular to a random IFI condition. Figure 1a illustrates the course of learning in one of these animals. The learning curve does not show a discontinuity between regular and random conditions. It is also seen that when the reinforcement contingency changed from negativity to positivity, there was a signifigant drop (in percent criterion responses) followed by a recovery; this indicates the expected extinction of the negativity response and the learning of positivity. In the other successful cat (whose data is not shown) the course of learning was similar. This other cat was initially trained with a random interflash interval.

It might have been possible that animals trained with a random IFI could have been generating respectable percentages overall by generating successful responses only following a particular class of IFIs. This was not the case: on a day of training on random IFI for the cat whose data is shown in Fig 1a, we output each IFI during 400 trials and sorted IFIs preceding unsuccessful and successful trials into 5 categories; I. 2009–2399 msec II. 2400–2799 msec III, 2800–3199 msec IV. 3200–3599 msec V. 3600–3999 msec. The percentages of successful responses in each interval category were I: 39.6 II. 35.4 III. 37.4 IV. 40.5 V. 37.5. In the other cat, the same operations yielded I. 40.9 II. 42.7 III. 44.7 IV. 39.9 V. 43.0. These percentages are (within each cat) quite similar; no interval is favored. This kind of data is supported by inspection of a typically occuring sequence of 12 successive intervals, each preceding a criterion response; (e.g. the cat on random IFI generated 12 hits in a row). The interval lengths were 3643, 2885, 3788, 3738, 3503, 2542, 2991, 2042, 2546, 3870, 3189, and 3563 msec. These intervals are well distributed along the interval range used and yet each is followed by a successful brain response. In this experiment, successful responding in no way depended upon information provided by a regular IFI.

In an attempt to account for the 3 failures in this experiment, single sweeps were carefully studied. We noted an obvious difference between the single responses of successful versus unsuccessful cats. Figure 2a shows a typical single sweep from an unsuccessful cat photographed during the second month of our futile attempt to train him. It is seen that in the latter ¾ of the epoch (where the criterion segment falls) there is very little high amplitude activity of high frequency. (This animal was successfully trained in Experiment 2. With the low end of the frequency range restored, large slow waves were obvious in the latter part of the recording epoch as is seen in Fig. 3d, 3h, and 3 l). Figure 2b is a single sweep from a successful animal

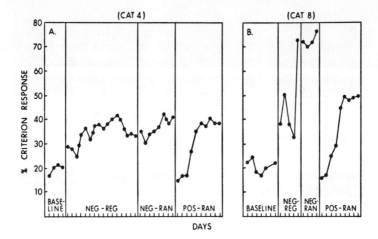

FIG. 1. Percent criterion responses as a function of training days under the various treatment combinations used in the experiment. BASELINE = noncontingent reinforcement period. NEG = animal rewarded for increased surface negativity of criterion component. POS = animal rewarded for more positive criterion components. REG = regular interflash interval. RAN = random interflash interval. (a) A representative cat in Experiment 1. (b) A representative cat in Experiment 2. This animal shows rapid acquisition in Experiment 2 although he failed to learn in Experiment 1 after 72 days of training.

photographed during the baseline period. It is clear in this figure that there is high amplitude, high frequency activity in the latter part of the epoch. The figures are quite typical of learners and nonlearners in Experiment 1. The limited data set presented suggests that if an animal must generate criterion responses of high frequency (when low frequencies are attenuated electronically) the animal cannot master the task if there is low incidence of higher frequency activity in the criterion segment region of the evoked potential.

Experiment 2

With recording amplifiers set to pass signals between 0.8 and 250 Hz, the original 5 animals were retrained. The to be trained sites were changed in the two successful cats of Experiment 1 to the secondary visual cortex which was a contralateral collateral site in the first experiment. New criteria were calculated and new baseline data were collected. Experiment 2 followed the end of Experiment 1 by 2 months.

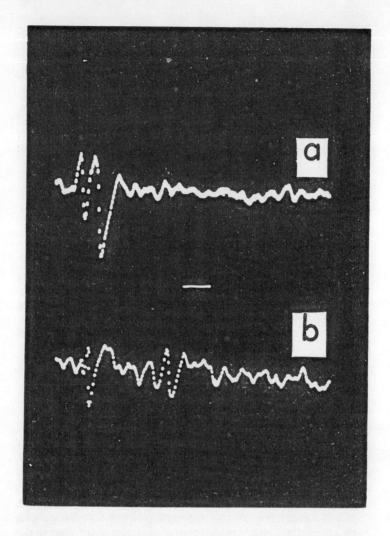

FIG. 2. Two typical single sweeps from an unsuccessful (a) cat and from a successful (b) cat in Experiment 1. The criterion segment is the central 1/3 of the indicated horizontal line. Epoch = 300 msec; surface positivity is down. The peak-to-peak amplitude of (a) is 140 μV.

In our second experiment, 4 of the 5 animals were successfully conditioned. A nonlearner from Experiment 1 was the sole nonlearner in Experiment 2, but 2 of the nonlearners in Experiment 1 rapidly acquired each task in Experiment 2 under all polarity-IFI treatment combinations, as did the 2 successful animals of Experiment 1. Table 1 gives the percentages of criterion responses achieved on the last day in each training condition for each cat. (These last days were chosen before the data were collected on the basis of our completion of the collateral site data collection in each cat.) The one nonlearner in both experiments was Cat 6 (see Table 1). All other cats at least doubled baseline (chance) performance levels in all conditions.

Figure 1b shows the course of learning in the remarkably performing Cat 8. As in Experiment 1, the transition from regular to random IFI is quite smooth. (The cat was reversed to random IFI after only 1 day at high level performance under regular IFI for reasons given in the Method section.) This was the case for the other animals as well, although they did not reach the high levels attained by Cat 8. We output distributions of numbers of occurrences of criterion responses in each interval category under random IFI, (as was described in Experiment 1, Results section). In each successful cat, such distributions were rectangular as in Experiment 1. IFIs associated with hit sequences were also output in Experiment 2. It is noted that the evoked responses associated with these sequences were all completely superimposable in the primary complex and usually similar in the region of the criterion segment at 155–165 msec. The responses were all above criterion in the criterion segment (as they were all successful) although following the criterion segment, the components generated were sometimes variable in peak latency. They were never more than 20 msec different in latency from one trial to the next although the associated successive random IFIs were usually 200–1000 msec different (see Fig. 4). The amount of latency variability obtained with the regular IFI was no different than that seen with random IFI. In such sequences of criterion responses, there was never any relationship between criterion component peak latency and preceding IFI. It is noted that Cat 8 could not have achieved the high levels he obtained by favoring particular classes of interval durations since all durations were equally probable.

It is noted in Table 1 that negativity training yielded higher percentages of criterion responses than did positivity training. Such has been reported before [9, 10, 15] with monopolar recordings.

We observed each cat in the recording box through a wide angle peep-hole lens during all phases of training. As has been reported previously [9, 10, 15] no consistent behavior or orientation to the light source could be identified as a correlate of the criterion evoked potential under any treatment combination, between or within animals.

Conditioning Effects on Other Sites; Localization Studies with Monopolar Recordings

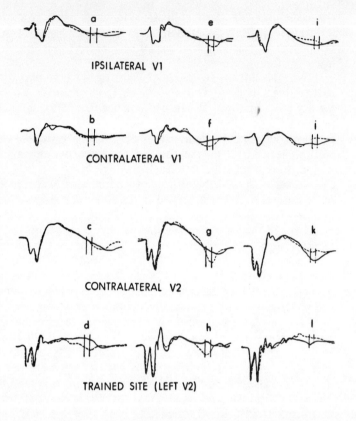

FIG. 3. Superimposed sorted average evoked potentials from Cat 8 in all phases of Experiment 2. The top 3 rows are from cortical collateral sites as indicated. The solid line traces represent averages of all collaterally recorded potentials simultaneous with misses at the trained site. The dashed line traces are averages of potentials recorded from collateral sites during hits at the trained site. The bottom row shows traces from the trained site; the solid line traces are averages of misses; the dashed line traces are averages of hits. Criterion segments are indicated with vertical lines. The segments begin 165 msec after trace origin which is 10 msec prior to stimulus onset. The right column shows averages recorded during positivity training under random interflash interval. The middle column has traces taken during negativity training under a random interflash interval. The left column represents baseline data sorted with the negativity reinforcement contingency. Surface positivity is up. The averages were hand traced from computer displays.

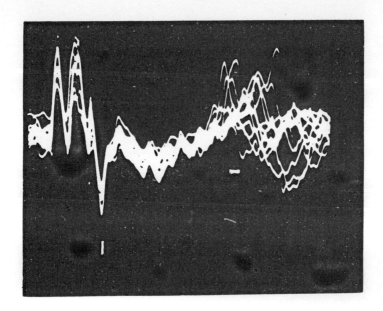

FIG. 4. A sequency of 13 consecutive hits from a training site. The traces are superimposable from the down going (surface positive) peak indicated to the criterion segment (indicated with horizontal bar).

In both experiments, each single trial potential recorded at collateral sites was sorted into 2 average evoked potential buffers on the basis of whether or not the collateral potential was simultaneous with a criterion response in the trained site. Trained site potentials were sorted into hit and miss averages. Sorting was done in all training phases. In the baseline data collection phase, sorting was also done, although the cats received noncontingent reinforcement. Random and regular IFI conditions are not separately considered since the two conditions had no differential effects in the present study. It is noted that the operations of the sorting procedure require that the sorted pair of averaged evoked potentials from the trained site differ by a finite voltage during the criterion time segment. This difference need not be large nor is the criterion segment the only time locus where sorted pair members may differ. A collateral sorted pair need not show any differences.

Figure 3 shows sorted pairs for the trained site and three collateral sites during the baseline, negativity training, and positivity training phases of Experiment 2 for Cat 8. Except as noted below, the figure is representative of the results for all cats. The salient features of Fig. 3 are:

TABLE 1

TREATMENT COMBINATIONS IN ORDERS GIVEN

	Baseline	(1)	(2)	(3)	(4)
CAT 4 (Male)	14.1	REG NEG 41.0	RAN NEG 40.2	RAN POS 36.7	——
CAT 5 (Female)	9.9	RAN NEG 35.5	REG NEG 38.2	RAN POS 29.1	——
CAT 6 (Female)	18.7	RAN POS 14.2	REG POS 12.7	RAN NEG 10.0	REG NEG 12.9
CAT 8 (Male)	21.9	REG NEG 72.2	RAN NEG 76.4	RAN POS 50.0	——
CAT 9 (Female)	14.0	REG POS 30.1	RAN POS 29.1	RAN NEG 32.7	

Percent criterion responses on the last day of each specified treatment combination for training phases. Baseline values are the means for entire baseline periods.

(Fig. 1 defines the pneumonic terms.)

(1) During the baseline phase, the trained site sorted pair members (Fig. 3d) differ during the criterion segment and elsewhere, although the differences are greatest in the criterion segment region. The cortical collateral site pairs (Fig. 3a, 3c) show slight differences all along the epoch; time segments in which the differences are maximal do not correspond to the time of the criterion segment at the trained site. For some collateral pairs in some cats, the traces were essentially superimposable.

(2) During negativity training, a unique and well localized segment of difference appears in the trained site sorted pair (Fig. 3h). It is wider than the criterion segment,

but it is centered about this axis. The other portions of the epoch contain essentially superimposable waveforms. Likewise during negativity training, the collateral cortical sorted pair members differ at unique time segments which are centered at or very near to being centered at the criterion segment axis, (Fig. 3e, 3f, 3g). The difference segments in trained and collateral site pairs always overlap appreciably in time. Other portions of the epoch for collateral pairs show essentially superimposable waves. Differences in cortical collateral sorted pairs correspond in time and with respect to polarity to differences between sorted pairs from training sites.

(3) During positivity training, results are the same as was described for negativity training except that the segment of maximum difference in the trained sorted pair (Fig. 3l) is longer, although still centered about the criterion segment. Difference segments in collateral pairs are likewise of longer duration in positivity training.

(4) The lateral geniculate collateral potentials (in the cats which had such placements) were unaffected by sorting; that is, sorted geniculate pairs were always virtually superimposable in all phases of the experiment. Similar results were reported by Rudell [8, 15].

Attention is called to the fact that although collateral pairs showed difference segments obviously related to the training effects on the trained site, the segment of maximum difference in some collateral pairs did not typically overlap perfectly in time the segment of max-imum difference in the trained site sorted pair, as is evident in the comparison of Fig. 3g and 3h. Roughly half the difference segments in collateral pairs on all cats showed a slight lag as was just described, with the remaining collateral pairs having difference segments virtually identical in time to difference segments in trained pairs, (as is the case for Fig. 3e, 3f, and 3k). This observation is relevant to the possibility that effects observed at other cortical sites during training were merely distance recordings of activity at the training site. This possibility is remote for two reasons. First of all, distance recordings would have shown consistent time relationships to the source; this was not the case. In Cat 8, for example, the segment of difference in the sorted pair from contralateral secondary visual cortex slightly lags the segment of difference in the trained sorted pair (Fig. 3g and 3h), whereas in Cat 5, the contralateral pair difference leads. In some cats, we recorded the same collateral site on more than one occasion. The sorted segments of difference were always near or at the criterion segment of the trained site, but within the animal, the collateral segment of difference did not typically have the same time relations with the criterion segment from one replication to the next. These findings on average evoked potentials are quite consistent with our observations of single sweeps from simultaneously recorded trained and collateral sites during training. It was sometimes possible to see a criterion component appear in the trained site at the same time as a similarly oriented component appeared in the collateral site, but about 20% of the sweeps we observed suggested trial-wise independence of trained and collateral sites: during such sweeps an obvious criterion component appeared in the trained site while the collateral potential remained flat. On other trials, the trained site component remained small in the criterion segment whereas the collateral potential contained what would have been a criterion response at that site had the reinforcement contingency been in effect there (Fig. 5). Thus there was correlation of all averaged but not of all individual segments of difference between trained and collateral potentials.

Although the data just described suggests that collateral segments of difference are not simply due to distance recordings of the trained site, it does not necessarily follow that differences between collateral potentials associated with hits and collateral potentials associated with misses are of local origin, e.g., due to source and sink configurations at the collateral site. We attempted to investigate the question of local origins with monopolar recordings from each element of the bipolar electrodes. We could not obtain distinct polarity reversals in the evoked potentials of our animals. (Postmortem examination of one cat made it apparent that the surface screws of the bipolar electrodes had been driven too far below the under surface of the skull causing dimples on the cortical surface to appear. Such disfigurations probably distorted the normal potential fields of the cortex.) The question of local origins remains open.

DISCUSSION

Mediation of Conditioned Neural Events by a Tonic State

Instrumental conditioning of neural events has now been reported by several investigators [4]. Most of the reports have described conditioned modification of self-paced activity. Animals have been trained to alter (1) the amount of alpha [5] or theta [3, 4] or other rhythms [16] present in spontaneous EEG or (2) the magnitude of neural measures (in motor and sensorimotor structures) correlated with voluntary motor behavior [7, 13]. In the latter case it is obvious that animals control the timing of emitted neural activity. In the case of spontaneous EEG phenomena, while some of the paradigms used have involved cues presented to animals for the purpose of informing them that a criterion period has begun, the animals were free to generate reinforceable neural events at any time during the criterion period.

However, in the paradigm used in this report, the time of the reinforceable neural event is part of the neural reinforcement contingency. The animals are rewarded for altering the amplitude of a specific (10 msec) segment of an elicited response. This contingency requires that animals alter a certain set of synaptic activation patterns whose integral is the evoked component in which the criterion segment is localized. Despite the fact that the potentials are recorded from a sensory cortex, it remains possible that criterion responses in previous reports [8, 9, 10, 12, 14, 15] could somehow have been associated with overt and discrete motor acts. For example, an animal could learn to flex some muscle, feedback from which could diffusely influence the synaptic organization producing the criterion component via somatosensory input to ascending reticular

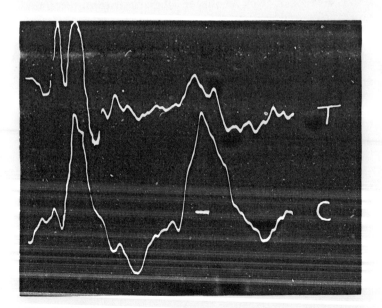

FIG. 5. Simultaneously recorded single sweeps from training (T) and collateral (C) sites. Criterion segment is indicated with a horizontal line. Note that hit in C is simultaneous with a miss in T; (see text). The collateral site is a contralateral VII locus.

systems. Such a mechanism would require, however, that an animal be able to timelock the discrete motor act to the criterion segment. This implies that the animal must have information about the time of the criterion segment. In the evoked potential conditioning paradigm, such information can be provided in only two ways: (1) by a regular interstimulus interval, (2) by the stimulus itself.

The first possibility has been eleminated in the present results. Animals were conditioned with evoking stimuli presented at random intervals and showed no effects of being switched from the regular to the random IFI condition. The second possibility implies that the animal can react to the stimulus in time to execute a discrete act mediating a criterion response. Rudell and Fox [14] reported the instrumental modification of the primary photic cortical evoked response. The latency of this component (20 msec) is obviously less than reaction time. While the study involved a regular interstimulus interval, it clearly demonstrated that instrumental conditioned evoked responses are producible without information provided by the stimulus itself. The present study specified a later criterion segment at 155–165 msec following the stimulus. It is conceivable that cats could have reaction times of this order. Feedback from an alleged mediating motor response, however, would add more time. Moreover, two features of Fig. 4 argue against the possibility that in the absence of a regular interstimulus interval, the stimulus itself provides timing information to which an animal may react. First, although the criterion segment begins at 155 msec, it is obvious that the criterion component begins much earlier; the waves in Fig. 4 start going more negative at about 100 msec. Secondly, the superimposability of the potentials between 100 and 150 msec does not support the notion that they are correlates of discrete motor reactions, whose onsets would show a latency distribution with greater variability.

The results support a tonic mediation hypothesis. The subject generates a state (whose duration may be as long as a sequence of successive hits) which presets the excitabilities of synapses generating the criterion component before the stimulus is presented. The stimulus serves merely to probe those excitabilities when it arrives. It is perfectly analogous to a test stimulus in the conditioning-test situation. This hypothesis does not rule out motor behavior in general, but only discrete motor responses as mediators of discrete criterion components. It may be that ongoing feedback from the constellation of motor responses that we sometimes observe during training sessions does, in fact, provide a background cortical excitability level capable of yielding criterion responses. This background however would still constitute a tonic influence.

Changes at Other Cortical Sites Associated with Conditioned Modification of Activity at a Specified Site

In a previous study of evoked response conditioning, Rudell [8, 15] recorded and sorted collateral activity using sorting operations identical to those used here. This work employed collateral sites in the lateral geniculate and in the midbrain reticular formation. The subcortical sites did not show activity related to the cortical trained site. (We confirmed this finding for the lateral geniculate.) These results supported Rudell's notion that the conditioned state did not depend upon direct or indirect sensory projections. A monopolarly recorded collateral site in primary visual cortex did reflect trained site activity in the training phase of Rudell's experiments, but there were no data collected pertaining to related collateral activity in the naive (untrained) animal. The presently reported study formally pursued the question of collateral cortical activity related to training of a given site.

It was found that differences between successive evoked potentials recorded from a given site in secondary visual cortex were not paralleled by related changes in evoked potentials taken from other visual cortical sites in the naive cat. When training procedures produced changes in designated criterion segments in potentials recorded from sites at which the reinforcement contingencies operated, the conditioned changes were followed by changes in average responses at other sites.

Although attempts at electrophysiological localization of criterion responses at trained and collateral sites yielded unclear results, there was ample reason to believe that the criterion response generalization seen at collateral sites was not due to distance recordings of processes at the trained site. First, simultaneous single responses from trained and collateral sites were not always superimposable at the criterion segment latency. More importantly, the resemblance of trained and collateral site criterion segments obtained only in training, although the sorting operations employed to illustrate the resemblance were identical during baseline and training phases. Distance recordings of large negative or positive amplitudes would have occurred in the baseline phase as well as in training. Finally, within and between cats, the time relations of difference segments in trained sorted pair averages and in particular collateral sorted pair averages were not the same. If the resemblance of a given collateral sorted pair and the trained sorted pair was due to distance recording from a fixed source, then if on a given set of trials the average collateral pair segment of difference lagged the trained pair segment, this same time relation should have obtained on replication; it did not.

The results suggest that large areas of cortex show changes related to the reinforcement contingency defined presumably for the trained site. That relationships between evoked potentials in several cortical areas appear only in training suggests that the training procedure leads to new cortical processes, that is, processes which are not active in the naive animal. Perhaps the widespread changes observed are related to learning mechanisms subserving the learning of any responses. Indeed, recent neural correlates of behavioral learning studies have reported emergent relations between activity in different structures [11] during learning or between single cells during performance of new, psychologically significant tasks [1]. In the present context, however, it seems intuitively obvious that since the emergent relations between brain waves are described in terms of the response parameters, (amplitudes of components at the criterion segment latency), the processes represented here by the emergent cortical relations must relate to response mechanisms. In any case, our data suggest that a criterion response in the naive animal may not represent the same events as it does in the trained animal.

1. Adey, W. R. Intrinsic organization of cerebral tissue in alerting, orienting, and discriminative responses. In: *The Neuroscience: A study program*, edited by B. C. Quarton, T. Melnechuk, and F. O. Schmitt. New York: Rockefeller University Press, 1967.
2. Beck, E. C. and R. W. Doty. Conditioned flexion reflexes acquired during combined catelepsy and de-efferentiation. *J. comp. physiol. Psychol.* 50: 211, 1957.
3. Black, A. H. The direct control of neural processes by reward and punishment. *Am. Scient.* 59: 236–245, 1971.
4. Black, A. H. The operant conditioning of central nervous system activity. In: *The Psychology of Learning and Motivation, Vol. 6*, edited by G. H. Bower. New York: Academic Press, in press, 1972.
5. Carmona, A. Trial and error learning of cortical EEG activity. Doctoral dissertation, Yale University, New Haven, Connecticut: 1967.
6. DiCara, L. V. Plasticity in the autonomic nervous system: Instrumental learning of visceral and glandular responses. In: *The Neurosciences Second Study Program*, edited by F. O. Schmitt. New York: Rockefeller University Press, 1970.

7. Fetz, E. E. and D. V. Finocchio. Operant conditioning of specific patterns of neural and muscular activity. *Science* 174: 431–435, 1971.

8. Fox, S. S. Evoked potential, coding, and behavior. In: *The Neurosciences Second Study Program*, edited by F. O. Schmitt. New York: Rockfeller University Press, 1970.

9. Fox, S. S. and A. P. Rudell. Operant controlled neural event: Formal and systematic approach to electrical coding of behavior in brain. *Science* 162: 1299–1302, 1968.

10. Fox, S. S. and A. P. Rudell. The operant controlled neural event: Functional independence in behavioral coding by early and late components of the visual cortical evoked response in cats. *J. Neurophysiol.* 33: 548–561, 1970.

11. John, E. R. *Mechanisms of Memory.* New York: Academic Press, 1967.

12. Rosenfeld, J. P., A. P. Rudell and S. S. Fox. Operant control of neural events in humans. *Science* 165: 821–823, 1969.

13. Rosenfeld, J. P. and S. S. Fox. Operant control of brain potential evoked by a behavior. *Physiol. Behav.* 7: 489–494, 1971.

14. Rudell, A. P. and S. S. Fox. The operant conditioning of early and late components in the visual evoked potential. *Fed. Proc.* 29: 590, 1970 (abstract).

15. Rudell, A. P. The operant conditioning of primary and secondary components in the visual evoked potential with measurement of collateral neural and behavioral activity. Doctoral dissertation, University of Iowa, Iowa City, Iowa, 1970.

16. Wyrwicka, W. and M. B. Sterman. Instrumental conditioning of sensorimotor cortex EEG spindles in the waking cat. *Physiol. Behav.* 3: 703–707, 1968.

Operantly Conditioned Patterns 10 of Precentral Unit Activity and Correlated Responses in Adjacent Cells and Contralateral Muscles

Eberhard E. Fetz and Mary Ann Baker

THE ABILITY to record activity of single neurons in awake, behaving animals allows us to investigate the relationships between neuronal firing and voluntary motor activity, conditioning, and other behavioral functions of the nervous system. By appropriate training procedures experimenters have controlled the behavior of the animal and elicited specific response patterns designed to test the function of the cells investigated. For example, a simple reaction-time paradigm has been used to study the temporal sequence of neural events preceding a voluntary movement. Subjects were trained to emit a specific motor response as quickly as possible after a visual or auditory cue. With sufficient training the responses recurred in a repeatable sequence and one could examine the activity in various neural centers during the 150–200 msec between stimulus and response for evidence of their functional relation to the movement. Under these conditions Evarts (5) and Luschei et al. (15) found that many precentral "motor" cortex cells in the monkey changed their discharge patterns 50–100 msec before the first electromyographic activity in muscles of the responding limb. A second approach used to study the function of specific cells involves training a set of responses which directly test the hypothesized function of the central cells. To determine whether the activity of precentral pyramidal tract (PT) cells was more strongly correlated with the position of a limb or the force required to move it, Evarts (6, 7) and Humphrey et al. (14) trained monkeys to perform movements in which these parameters could be independently varied. When the monkey moved a lever through the same displacement, but against different loads, these experimenters found that precentral unit activity was more closely correlated with force or its derivative than with position.

In both of these approaches the animal was trained to perform a specific pattern of muscular responses to which cell activity could be related. We have investigated an alternate strategy for studying neuronal function in which the animal was trained to generate bursts of activity in precentral cells and the correlated motor activity was observed. In this approach the reinforced response was a pattern of central neuron activity, and the correlated motor activity was allowed to occur under relatively unrestrained conditions. Our hypothesis was that if a cell in the precentral motor cortex were involved in a specific movement, this movement might be emitted with conditioned bursts of activity in the cell.

Since Olds (17–19) first investigated operant conditioning of neural activity in rats, an increasing number of studies have employed the technique of making operant reinforcement contingent on patterns of central neural activity (3, 4, 8, 10, 11, 25, 26). This paper concerns the techniques and consequences of operantly conditioning patterns of activity of single precentral neurons in monkeys. The first sections describe changes in firing rates obtained by reinforcing transient increases or decreases in unit activity; the second part examines the degree to which activity of adjacent cortical units was correlated with activity of the

Received for publication May 22, 1972.

Reprinted by permission of The American Physiological Society from the *Journal of Neurophysiology*, Vol. XXXVI, March 1973, No. 2, 179-204.

reinforced unit and the degree to which adjacent units could be independently conditioned. The final sections describe the movements associated with operantly reinforced bursts of specific cells, as determined by visual observation of gross behavior and by recording EMG activity of contralateral limb muscles.

METHODS

Six monkeys (*Macaca mulatta*) weighing 3–5 kg were used. During recording and training sessions monkeys sat in primate restraint chairs which allow relatively free movement of arms and legs. Extracellular unit recordings were made with tungsten microelectrodes insulated with Isonel 31. Electrodes were advanced with a remotely controlled hydraulic microdrive (Trent Wells) fastened to a stainless steel bone-fixed adapter permanently implanted over precentral arm or leg cortex. The adapter was sealed with a thin sheet of Silastic rubber (Dow Corning) to protect dura and retard infections. Early adapters allowed exploration of a circular region of cortex 5 mm in diameter; subsequent adapters allowed recording within a 20-mm-diameter circle. In the latter the Silastic membrane was held in a threaded center ring, which could be removed to treat any infection or permit surgical removal of extradural scar tissue. Recording sites were histologically confirmed to be in area 4 of the precentral gyrus.

In four monkeys electromyographic (EMG) electrodes were chronically implanted in flexors and extensors of the ankle and knee contralateral to the cortical recording site. Each electrode set consisted of a pair of nylon-insulated stranded stainless steel wires (Bergen Wire Rope Co., Lodi, N.J.) bared at the tip and sutured into the muscles with tip separations of 5–20 mm. The ends of the wires led subcutaneously to a connector cemented to the skull. Four monkeys had a bipolar stimulating electrode chronically implanted in the pyramidal tract (PT); no consistent difference was found between PT and non-PT precentral units with respect to conditionability.

In these experiments we tended to sample units with large action potentials and some degree of fluctuating "spontaneous" activity. The larger units provided prolonged stability during relatively unrestricted limb movements. To assure that only one and the same unit was monitored throughout the session we displayed its action potentials on an oscilloscope beam triggered from the rising edge of the waveform, with the sweep set fast enough to display the entire action potential over the whole screen.

Under these conditions two or more units could be readily distinguished on the basis of differing time courses of their action potentials. To further assure that a training session involved only one cell, we recorded 1-msec voltage pulses triggered from the unit on a second channel of the magnetic tape recorder. To verify that these pulses were associated with only one unit throughout the session, we played the tape backward and examined the data channel on an oscilloscope sweep triggered from the leading edge of the 1-msec voltage pulses. This produced a time-reversed display of the entire action potential which had triggered each pulse; any records in which the pulses were associated with more than one action potential waveform were discarded.

Most cells were characterized with respect to their responses to passive joint movements and gentle stimulation of the skin (1, 9, 24). Under these conditions the monkey was reinforced for passively allowing such manipulations without struggling.

Unit activity was continually monitored and appropriately reinforced with an electronic "activity integrator" (AI) (Fig. 1), consisting of a parallel RC integrator with a variable passive decay and a "reinforcement level" for triggering the feeder. To reinforce high rates of unit activity, the AI integrated rectangular voltage pulses triggered from the unit's action potentials. Each pulse drove the integrator voltage toward the reinforcement level (T) by a constant small increment (h); in the absence of cell activity the voltage decayed exponentially toward zero with a time constant $\tau = RC$. Thus, the integrator voltage was roughly proportional to the firing rate of the cell. The time constant τ (usually 50–100 msec) and the voltage step h (usually 0.05–0.5 T) were adjusted for each cell so that the average firing rate sustained the integrator voltage at some value below the reinforcement level. Occasional bursts of sufficiently high frequency activity brought the integrator voltage to reinforcement level, which triggered the feeder and reset the integrator voltage to zero for 100 msec or less. In practice the reinforcement level T was held constant at 2 v (via a Digibit Schmitt trigger) and the height of the 0.1-msec voltage pulses was varied; as cell firing rates increased the pulses were reduced, so that on the average the integrator voltage continued to fluctuate below reinforcement level and only the highest frequency bursts were reinforced. If cell firing rates dropped for more than 30 sec, we increased the pulse height to again reinforce peak rates. Thus, during reinforcement periods we continually adjusted the ratio of reinforcement

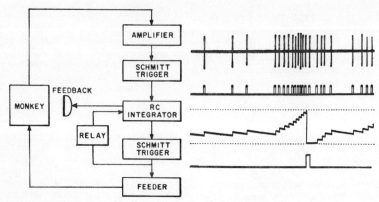

FIG. 1. Activity integrator used to reinforce operant bursts of unit activity. Components of the circuit are schematized at left and typical voltage signals shown at right. The first Schmitt trigger converted unit action potentials to voltage pulses, which were temporally integrated in a parallel RC circuit with a passive decay of 50–100 msec. The second Schmitt trigger set a reinforcement level (upper dashed line) on the integrator voltage at which the feeder was triggered and the integrator reset to zero (lower dashed line) by a relay. "Feedback" indicates a meter facing the monkey; meter deflection was proportional to the integrator voltage. Sweep duration = 2 sec.

level to step height (T/h), attempting to keep the reinforcement frequency between 5 and 15 reinforcements per minute.

To reinforce low rates of activity two inputs to the AI were summed: one contributed positive voltage pulses from a pulse generator, which continuously drove the integrator level toward T; the second added negative voltage pulses triggered from the unit, which drove the integrator level away from T. The relative contributions of these two inputs were balanced so that on the average the AI level fluctuated at some value below T. Pauses in cell activity allowed the multivibrator pulses to drive the AI level toward the reinforcement level; high rates of unit activity drove the AI away from T and withheld reinforcement.

During training sessions the monkey sat in a primate restraint chair placed inside a dimly illuminated sound-attenuating chamber (IAC 400). The first monkey was free to move his head; this animal was reinforced with 190-mg banana-flavored pellets delivered to a food cup sufficiently close to his mouth to allow the pellets to be licked up. The five subsequent monkeys had their heads restrained during experimental sessions and were reinforced with 1–2 ml apple juice delivered directly into the mouth. This improved recording stability by preventing sudden head movements and abolishing artifacts associated with chewing.

In addition to food reinforcement monkeys received visual feedback in the form of an illuminated meter, whose pointer deflection was proportional to the AI voltage. The extreme

rightward position of the pointer corresponded to reinforcement level; thus, the meter continually indicated the degree to which the monkey's pattern of cell activity approximated criteria for reinforcement. Illumination and activation of the meter occurred only during reinforcement periods and could eventually become a discriminative stimulus for reinforcement. Since extreme deflection of the meter pointer to the right was consistently associated with delivery of food, any meter deflection toward the right could become a secondary reinforcer for activity which produced such deflections. In a few initial experiments we used auditory feedback, consisting of an audible click for each unit spike (8); thus, high rates of clicking could become discriminative for reinforcement. However, this mode of feedback was abandoned in favor of the meter because: 1) discrete clicks might generate auditory responses in the unit (8); 2) meter deflections were automatically scaled relative to a consistent reinforcement level, whereas click rates were always proportional to absolute firing rates; and 3) the meter could continue to provide feedback during reinforcement of differential patterns of activity in more than one element (10).

After isolating a unit we first recorded its preconditioning pattern of activity during a 9- to 30-min preconditioning period before any reinforcement or feedback was introduced. During the subsequent conditioning period the meter was illuminated and activated, and appropriate patterns of cell activity were reinforced. Most of the cells reported here underwent "differential reinforcement of high rates" (DRH) in which the highest frequency bursts of cell activity were reinforced. A few cells underwent "differential reinforcement of zero activity" (DRO) in which suppression of cell activity was reinforced. The reinforcement period was usually continued until unit firing rates had reached a new plateau level for at least 6 min; then an extinction period (S$^\Delta$) was introduced, in which reinforcement was withheld and the meter shut off. This extinction period usually lasted 6 min and was generally followed by a series of reinforcement periods (DRH-2, DRH-3, . . .) alternating with extinction periods (S$^\Delta$-2, S$^\Delta$-3, . . .) for the remainder of the session.

In 20 of the sessions we attempted to record the activity of two cortical units simultaneously, by positioning the electrode so that two action potentials were separable on the basis of clear and consistent differences in spike height and shape. Using two Schmitt triggers and an anti-coincidence circuit, we generated and recorded two separate pulse trains corresponding to the "large" and "small" unit. (Note: the terms large and small refer to the relative heights of the units' action potentials and not necessarily to their anatomical dimensions.) Subsequent examination of the action potentials, which had triggered the small unit pulses (by playing the tape backward), revealed that in 10 sessions more than one type of action potential had reached the voltage window for triggering these pulses. Only the 10 remaining sessions, in which both units were reliably isolated throughout the session, are considered here. In nine of these sessions the initial schedule reinforced high rates of the large unit with no contingency on the small; in some sessions the small unit rate was also included in the reinforcement contingency. In several sessions we reinforced a differential pattern of activity in large and small units. For example, we could reinforce increased firing of the large cell and simultaneous suppression of the small cell (DRH:L/DRO:S) by using pulses from the large unit to drive the AI toward reinforcement level and pulses from the small unit to drive the AI away from reinforcement level.

In order to characterize the possible motor activity associated with reinforced bursts of cortical unit activity we visually observed the monkey's behavior and monitored EMG activity of the contralateral limb. In early experiments visual observation was not possible without opening the door to the IAC booth and risking disruption of the monkey's behavior; since these initial experiments were designed to investigate the effects of the behavioral procedures on unit rates, such disruptions were avoided. In later experiments a closed-circuit TV system allowed observations of the monkey's movements without introducing distracting stimuli.

A seven-channel FM tape system recorded *1*) unit activity from the microelectrode; *2*) 1-msec pulses triggered from the unit(s); *3*) a "trigger pulse" 1 sec after each reinforced response—i.e., after each feeder discharge; *4*) EMG activity of two to four muscles of the contralateral leg; and *5*) voice. For each session we analyzed and displayed data in two forms. Unit activity was graphed on a session average, which plotted average firing rates over successive 1-min intervals throughout the sessions (Figs. 2*B*, 4, 5, 6*A*, 9). We also computed the average patterns of unit and muscle activity associated with the reinforced responses on a response average. This was computed by playing the tape recorder backward, triggering a Nuclear Chicago data retrieval computer from the delayed trigger pulses, and computing time histograms of unit activity and transient averages of full-wave rectified EMG activity over the 2-sec intervals around each response. The response averages showed both the mean "reinforced pattern" in the unit(s) whose activity was reinforced and the "correlated pattern" in units and muscles which did not enter into the reinforcement contingency.

RESULTS

Figure 2 illustrates the main features of a typical DRH conditioning session. The session average (Fig. 2*B*) shows the mean firing rate of the unit in successive 1-min intervals throughout the session. During the 12-min preconditioning period unit firing rates remained approximately steady at 2.8 ± 0.9 impulses/sec (mean ± standard deviation). With the beginning of the first reinforcement period (DRH-1) the monkey began to increase the firing rate of the cell by increasing both the number of bursts per minute and the maximum frequency of cell firing during each burst. As unit bursts became more intense, we continually reduced the size of the pulses to the AI, to keep the reinforcement rate approximately steady between 11 and 20/min. After about 4 min, unit activity reached a new plateau level of 15.4 ± 4.6 impulses/sec. Under extinction conditions (S$^\Delta$–1), rates quickly dropped again to lower levels. During subsequent reinforcement periods (DRH-2, DRH-3), the monkey readily increased firing rates again.

The pattern of cell activity over each period of the session is summarized by the

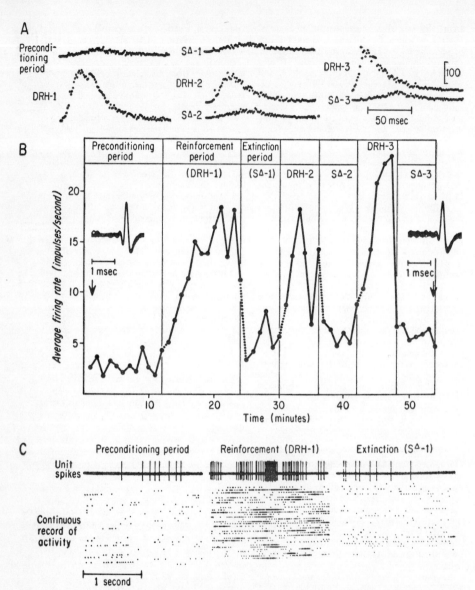

FIG. 2. A typical unit-reinforcement session. The session average (*B*) plots 1-min averages of firing rate under different behavioral conditions: preconditioning period, differential reinforcement of high rates (DRH), and extinction (S△). Insets show several superimposed action potentials of cell recorded during first and last minutes of session (arrows). *A*: interspike-interval histograms compiled over the indicated periods. Each dot represents a 1.25 msec time bin, and vertical calibration bar represents 100 counts. *C*: samples of cell activity taken from first three periods. Dot rasters show one continuous minute of activity in 30 successive 2-sec sweeps. Session S:2/24/69.

interspike-interval histograms in Fig. 2*A*, which plot the relative number of intervals between 0 and 125 msec occurring during the designated periods. The distribution of intervals during the preconditioning period and extinction periods was approximately the same: a shallow peak at 50 msec indicates the most common interval, with shorter and longer intervals broadly distributed around this peak. In contrast, during DRH periods the operant bursts contributed many more shorter intervals, resulting in a higher peak at about 25 msec.

The actual firing pattern of this cell is illustrated in Fig. 2*C;* the dot rasters show continuous 1-min samples of activity from the first three periods. The preconditioning period was characterized by sporadic cell firing, punctuated by occasional weak bursts. In contrast, at the end of the first DRH period the monkey was repeatedly firing the cell in prolonged high-frequency "operant bursts." Under extinction conditions, cell activity returned to a more sporadic pattern of firing, resembling the preconditioning pattern.

Typical examples of operant bursts obtained by these techniques in three different monkeys are illustrated in Fig. 3. The dot rasters show successive operant bursts which triggered the feeder, aligned at the feeder discharge point in the center of each sweep. Below each dot raster is a time histogram of unit activity computed over 100–200 successive bursts. These response averages show that peak firing rates attained during these bursts were 60–80 impulses/sec. Typically, cell activity began to increase 300–700 msec before the peak and dropped somewhat more rapidly thereafter. Thus, most of the cell activity in the operant bursts preceded feeder discharge. If any cell had been activated subsequent to feeder discharge, its response average would show an increase in firing after the feeder discharge. None of the cells in this study showed any such increase in rate immediately following the feeder discharge. However, in one monkey, whose head was unrestrained, several units showed periods of suppression beginning

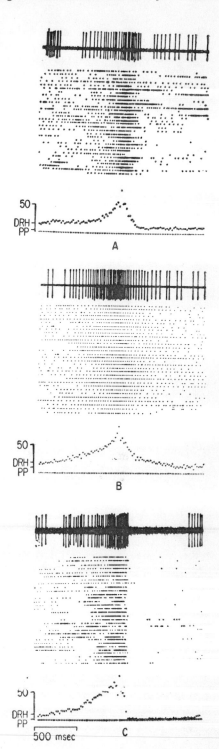

FIG. 3. Operant bursts of cell activity during DRH periods from three different monkeys. Top: sample of original action potentials; middle: dot rasters of successive bursts; bottom: time histograms computed over specified number of bursts. All traces are aligned around the time of feeder discharge, indicated by the peak of the time histogram. Height of vertical bars on averages indicates 50/sec firing rate; marks indicate mean rates during preconditioning (PP) and DRH periods for each unit. *A*: session S:2/24/69; number of bursts on average = 200. *B*: session R:3/13/69; N = 100. *C*: session E: 6/15/68; N = 100.

80–100 msec after feeder discharge and lasting 800–1,200 msec (Fig. 3C); such suppression was probably related to movements associated with feeding, since it was not seen in the same cell when feeder discharge was prevented.

Note that the mean firing rates during the operant bursts in the response average are higher than mean firing rates averaged over successive 1-min intervals in the session average. In Fig. 2 the 1-min average rate of the unit varied between 13 and 18/sec toward the end of DRH-1, while the response average in Fig. 3A shows that this unit actually attained peak rates of 50/sec during the operant bursts. The response average reflects higher rates because it was computed over those 2-sec intervals in which burst rates reached levels sufficiently high to trigger the feeder. Such periods represent 20–50% of the time included in the 1-min averages. To facilitate comparison, the calibration bars beside the response averages in Fig. 3 indicate the overall mean firing rates of these units during DRH and preconditioning periods.

Summary of unit conditioning sessions

With the six monkeys included in this report we attempted operant conditioning of high rates on a total of 75 precentral units. Table 1 summarizes the results from the 33 units that met the following criteria: they remained well isolated and uninjured throughout a session involving one or more DRH and extinction periods and showed clear increases in activity with reinforcement. Of the remaining 42 sessions, 23 were either terminated or subsequently rejected because unit isolation was lost (18 sessions) or the cell showed signs of injury (5 sessions), and 18 were training sessions which produced no clear increase in unit activity. The "training sessions" were either the initial sessions with that monkey (14 sessions) or sessions which followed a lapse of 1–12 months since the previous successful conditioning session (4 sessions). Completely naive animals usually required 2–8 training sessions before they could reliably increase the firing rates of newly isolated units. However, two monkeys given some preliminary experience with the feeder and feedback (i.e., "magazine training") were able to increase the activity of a unit during their first conditioning session. In general, the monkeys' ability to increase the activity of newly isolated cells quickly and reliably and to sustain the increase throughout DRH improved with experience. (Only one session (C:12/8/68) produced no increase with reinforcement although the monkey had driven rates up previously; this unit had an unusually low preconditioning rate (0.65 ± 0.69/sec.) and was abandoned after it showed no increase after 18 min of DRH.)

The results of DRH conditioning sessions are summarized in Table 1, which shows the total time each unit was observed before conditioning (preconditioning period), during reinforcement for high rates (DRH), and during extinction (S$^\Delta$). The average firing rate of each unit and the standard deviation of 1-min counts are given for each condition. Typically, a session consisted of several DRH periods of 6–15 min, alternating with extinction periods of comparable length. For the 33 units in Table 1 the number of DRH periods (and of extinction periods) per session ranged from 1 to 12 with a mean of 4.

It usually took several minutes at the beginning of the first DRH period to increase the cell's firing rate to a higher terminal plateau value (e.g., the first 4 min of DRH-1 in Fig. 2); occasionally subsequent DRH periods also began with low firing rates (e.g., the first minute of DRH-2 and of DRH-3 in Fig. 2). Such low rates at the beginning of DRH periods can be attributed to the fact that the monkey had to learn the appropriate responses to increase the firing rate of each new unit. Accordingly, the number of minutes required at the beginning of a DRH period to reach the terminal plateau level of firing was defined as the "acquisition time"; the remainder of the period was designated "terminal time." Total acquisition times for sessions in Table 1 ranged from 28 min for some sessions to 1 min or less for others, with a mean of 6.5 min for all 33 sessions. The DRH average rate and standard deviation in Table 1 were computed for the entire terminal time for each session.

For most units in Table 1 the average firing rate during extinction was within 1

TABLE 1. *Summary of DRH conditioning sessions using single units*

Unit	Preconditioning Period			DRH				Extinction			% Incr
	Time	Av rate	SD	Aq time	Term time	Av rate	SD	Time	Av rate	SD	
E: 6/ 7/68	15	40.2	6.83	0	15	59.2	8.91	13	40.7	5.0	47.1
E: 6/15/68	15	1.76	1.75	2	31	11.1	2.85	18	3.8	2.78	528.4
E: 6/27/68	18	14.0	3.40	3	18	35.8	8.77	21	14.3	5.84	155.7
B: 10/18/68	12	10.1	4.03	4	14	21.4	3.06	36	11.0	4.14	111.6
B: 10/21/68	15	20.5	2.38	1	25	26.1	2.63	24	19.4	2.92	27.3
B: 10/23/68	21	10.8	3.76	5	10	23.0	2.74	13	12.3	5.56	112.9
B: 10/31/68	10	12.2	1.88	3	22	28.9	5.20	20	24.2	3.26	136.7
C: 11/22/68	12	6.88	5.79	28	20	13.3	3.75	48	4.86	3.19	93.9
C: 11/23/68	10	18.7	9.30	1	47	21.8	6.08	54	6.37	3.47	16.8
C: 11/27/68	16	22.6	5.61	19	29	40.0	6.33	58	26.6	4.21	77.3
C: 12/ 4/68	12	8.69	2.73	2	16	40.1	5.46	17	11.0	9.03	361.5
C: 12/ 6/68	12	13.8	5.25	4	14	29.5	2.88	23	11.4	6.73	113.6
C: 1/10/69	12	15.3	2.77	8	16	30.5	8.67	24	17.3	3.97	99.9
C: 1/17/69	18	20.5	8.77	1	28	38.7	6.28	30	24.6	4.26	89.0
C: 1/31/69	12	32.9	1.96	25	18	45.2	5.13	30	30.4	3.82	37.6
S: 2/ 9/69	5	7.67	2.80	7	44	13.7	2.93	18	6.87	2.66	79.0
S: 2/10/69	17	25.7	7.12	5	19	39.1	6.05	24	23.9	3.29	52.0
S: 2/19/69	11	15.6	4.04	4	30	23.2	7.36	12	13.4	4.92	48.6
S: 2/21/69	12	15.5	7.50	10	29	24.6	3.41	24	18.1	4.01	59.1
S: 2/24/69	12	2.79	0.89	6	18	15.4	4.61	18	5.85	1.38	450.5
R: 2/28/69	18	11.7	3.58	0	78	17.0	4.13	75	14.2	3.37	45.1
R: 3/ 3/69	12	15.9	4.65	8	48	26.2	2.51	43	17.1	4.40	64.8
R: 3/ 4/69	12	6.72	2.54	1	35	12.4	2.44	27	8.46	2.52	83.9
R: 3/ 5/69	15	13.2	1.86	4	38	18.0	1.86	24	13.3	2.55	36.6
R: 3/11/69	11	8.27	6.40	9	62	16.3	6.48	46	7.63	6.08	97.6
R: 3/12/69	12	10.4	4.15	4	17	18.1	4.16	18	3.77	3.67	74.0
R: 3/13/69	12	10.9	4.66	7	35	19.5	2.77	27	11.6	3.98	79.1
R: 3/14/69	12	2.67	0.86	3	31	7.94	4.88	18	3.38	1.19	197.4
R: 3/15/69	12	5.10	3.15	3	9	14.3	2.63	18	2.72	1.55	180.6
R: 4/26/69	12	13.4	1.11	3	6	19.7	6.42	6	13.0	1.70	47.9
R: 5/15/69	14	9.46	3.28	11	53	19.7	4.77	39	7.33	3.81	108.1
M: 5/30/69	21	13.2	4.53	6	69	29.2	6.97	77	16.4	5.02	122.0
M: 7/10/70	25	6.74	4.32	19	32	35.0	8.48	16	8.54	4.94	418.6
Mean	14.3	13.4	4.05	6.54	29.6	25.3	4.90	29.1	13.8	3.92	128.9

Average and standard deviations of unit firing rates before, during, and after reinforcement for high rates. Each session is identified by monkey and date. Entries give total time (min), overall average firing rates (impulses/sec), and standard deviations of 1-min samples of rates under each behavioral condition: preconditioning period, DRH period(s), and extinction period(s). All DRH periods of a given session were summed together, as were all extinction periods. Means at bottom give values for all 33 sessions.

standard deviation of the preconditioning rate. The overall mean preconditioning rate for all 33 cells (13.4 ± 4.1 impulses/sec) was comparable to the overall mean extinction rate (13.8 ± 3.9 impulses/sec), and both were significantly exceeded by the mean DRH rate (25.3 ± 4.9 impulses/sec). For each session we computed the "percent increase" in rate defined as 100 × (DRH rate − preconditioning rate)/preconditioning rate. The percent increase ranged from 16.8 to 528%, with a mean of 129% for all

cells. In a few sessions the percent increase over preconditioning rates was relatively low, although the percent increase computed with respect to extinction rates would have been considerably higher; this occurred when extinction rates dropped significantly below preconditioning rates. For example, in session C:11/23/68 the DRH rate was only 16.8% above preconditioning rates, but 242% above extinction rates.

For the cells of Table 1 the percent increase was significantly related to the pre-conditioning rate. Units with lowest pre-conditioning rates tended to have the highest percent increase, and vice versa. Units with low preconditioning rates also tended to have high coefficients of variation, where coefficient of variation equals standard deviation/mean.

Under DRH conditions, three types of changes in firing patterns could contribute to increases in average rate: *1*) operant bursts of unit activity recurred more frequently, *2*) the number of impulses per burst increased due to higher frequency and/or longer burst discharges, and *3*) the interburst firing rate often increased over preconditioning rates. Since it was difficult to obtain independent measures of these three factors, their relative contributions to increased rates could not be satisfactorily quantified.

Correlation between firing rate and reinforcement

A number of control sessions were designed to test whether food delivery and feedback alone were sufficient to increase firing rates. They were not sufficient for naive animals, since initial training sessions did not produce such increases. However, in experienced animals the mere presentation of food and feedback might occasion generalized motor activity which could be effective in increasing rates of many motor cortex cells. To test this possibility, the correlation between reinforcement and firing rates was frequently changed by presenting reinforcement independently of the unit's activity. By playing back a tape recording of a DRH period from a previous session to trigger the feeder and deflect the meter, these stimuli were presented randomly with respect to the monitored cell, and the animal served as his own "yoked control." Under these conditions no increases in firing rate were obtained. An example of such a session is shown in Fig. 2 of ref 8.

Even in sessions in which reinforcement of bursts had already produced higher firing rates, a change in the temporal correlation between cell activity and reinforcement abolished the effectiveness of the reinforcement to sustain high rates. Figure 4 shows a session in which reinforcement

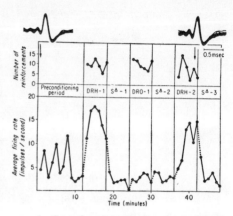

FIG. 4. Control session showing that reinforcement must be correlated with bursts to increase firing rate of unit. The number of reinforcements delivered are plotted at top. When reinforcement was delivered for bursts of unit activity (DRH-1 and DRH-2) average rates increased; when reinforcement was delivered at the same rate but during cell inactivity (DRO) rates did not increase. Insets at top: superimposed action potentials of cell from $t = 1$ and $t = 41$. Session R:3/15/69.

was correlated with bursts in DRH-1, producing increased firing rates. During the DRO-1 period food was delivered whenever the cell was relatively inactive; under these conditions reinforcement did not produce an increase in cell firing, even though the frequency of food delivery was approximately the same as during DRH-1. The subsequent DRH-2 period again demonstrated that a correlation between reinforcement and high rates of unit activity was necessary to produce an increase.

By differentially reinforcing low rates of unit activity (DRO) it was possible to condition monkeys to suppress cell firing below preconditioning and extinction levels. All monkeys were initially trained on DRH schedules, and usually required several periods of DRO training before successfully reducing cell activity. (The session in Fig. 4 was this monkey's first exposure to DRO and did not produce rates below S^Δ rates.) Figure 5 illustrates a session in which another monkey increased cell rates during a DRH period and decreased activity of the same cell under DRO conditions. The dot rasters below the graph illustrate 1-min samples of activity during the designated periods. Mean terminal rates under DRH

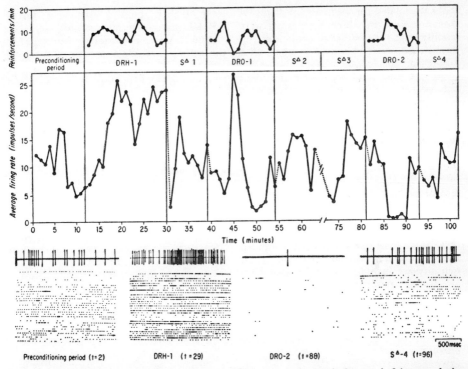

FIG. 5. Conditioning of high and low firing rates of the same unit. Graph shows unit firing rate during reinforcement of high (DRH-1) and low (DRO-1, DRO-2) rates, with the number of reinforcements during each period plotted at the top. Bottom: samples of spike data and dot rasters of cell activity sampled at indicated times. Dot rasters show one continuous minute of activity in 30 successive 1-sec sweeps. (The omitted portion of the graph contained an attempted DRH period in which the feeder failed and was repaired.) Session B:10/18/68.

conditions (21.4 ± 3.1 impulses/sec) were approximately twice the mean preconditioning rate (10.1 ± 4.0 impulses/sec) and average S^Δ rate (11.0 ± 4.1 impulses/sec). During the first DRO period activity dropped initially, but then reverted to high-frequency bursts $(44 \leqslant t \leqslant 48)$. This increased activity was inappropriate for the schedule, but explainable in light of the animal's previous reinforcement history on DRH. Eventually, he suppressed rates to an average of 2.7/sec for a 4-min interval $(48 \leqslant t \leqslant 52)$. A second DRO period produced more convincing suppression of cell activity; after the first 4 min the monkey kept unit activity at an average of 0.00 ± 0.26/sec for a continuous 5 min interval $(85 \leqslant t \leqslant 90)$. In this session suppression of cell activity was not sustained throughout the DRO periods; however, this was

the first session in which this monkey had been exposed to a DRO schedule.

Reinforcement rates are shown at the top of Fig. 5. Since approximately equal reinforcement frequencies sustained high rates during DRH and low rates during DRO, the crucial factor was evidently the correlation between reinforcement and firing rates, not the reinforcement per se.

Activity of units adjacent to reinforced unit

In order to investigate the degree to which other cortical neurons were coactivated during operant bursts of the reinforced unit we often attempted to record activity of two units simultaneously. In the deeper layers of precentral cortex (probably layer 5) we could often position the microelectrode such that two action potentials could be isolated for prolonged periods. Of the 10 sessions in which both units were reliably isolated without contamination throughout several periods, 9 began with DRH:L periods in which only bursts of the large unit were reinforced, with the small unit activity not included in the reinforcement contingency.

Table 2 summarizes the overall changes in firing rates for large and small units during the different behavioral periods of these 9 double-unit sessions. The percent increase in firing rates was computed with respect to preconditioning rates for both units. As indicated by the table, the rate increases of the reinforced unit (L) during DRH:L were typically accompanied by some rate increases of the neighboring unreinforced unit (S); in only one session did the mean rate of the small unit decrease slightly. In four sessions, including all three with *monkey C*, the unreinforced unit showed an even higher percent increase during DRH:L than the reinforced unit.

As with single-unit sessions, we examined the activities of large and small units on two levels of temporal resolution, the session average and the response average. The session averages revealed the degree to which the rates of the two units tended to fluctuate together in successive minutes within each period and between different behavioral periods. We found that those units whose rates tended to show correlated fluctuations in successive 1-min intervals in any one period also displayed correlated increases during DRH periods relative to extinction periods. All pairs of cells that showed correlated firing rates in the session average were positively correlated—i.e., their rates tended to increase and decrease together rather than reciprocally.

In order to quantify the degree of correlation between each pair of cells we rated

TABLE 2.   *Comparison of large- and small-unit rates with conditioned increases of large-unit rate*

		Precond Period		DRH:L		Extinction		% Incr	Correlation Rating	
Session		T	Rate	T	Rate	T	Rate		Sess Av	Resp Av
B: 10/21/68	L	15	20.5	14	25.8	12	20.3	25.9	2	0
	S	15	19.0	14	17.8	12	18.1	−6.3		
B: 10/23/68	L	21	10.8	10	23.0	13	12.3	112.9	2	0
	S	21	15.4	10	20.5	13	17.5	33.1		
C: 12/ 6/68	L	12	13.8	14	29.5	23	11.4	113.6	3	1
	S	12	15.9	14	40.5	23	20.1	154.7		
C: 1/10/69	L	12	15.3	16	30.5	24	17.3	99.9	3	2
	S	12	3.4	16	28.2	24	7.6	729.4		
C: 1/17/69	L	18	20.5	28	38.7	30	24.6	89.0	3	2
	S	18	7.7	28	22.7	30	13.1	194.8		
R: 3/ 3/69	L	12	15.6	48	26.2	43	17.1	64.8	1	2
	S	12	9.1	48	17.9	43	15.9	96.7		
R: 3/ 4/69	L	12	6.7	35	12.4	27	8.5	83.9	3	3
	S	12	7.1	35	11.3	27	6.1	59.2		
R: 3/13/69	L	12	10.9	35	19.5	27	11.6	79.1	2	1
	S	12	6.7	35	10.8	27	4.8	61.2		
R: 3/14/69	L	12	2.7	31	7.9	18	3.4	197.4	2	2
	S	12	8.0	31	18.8	18	9.5	135.0		

In each session two units were recorded with the microelectrode; the large (L) was reinforced for high rates, while the smaller (S) was not reinforced. Columns as in Table 1. DRH:L time and rates represent terminal time for large unit. Percent increase of DRH:L rates over preconditioning rates is given for both units. The correlation rating represents an estimated scaling of the degree to which units fluctuated together in successive minutes of the session (session average) and during the 2-sec periods around operant bursts of large unit (response average). We distinguished four degrees of correlation: 0 = none, 1 = weak, 2 = moderate, and 3 = strong.

the correlation of each pair on a subjective scale from none to strong (Table 2). All nine pairs of cells showed some degree of correlation in the session average; the correlation was judged "strong" for four pairs, "moderate" for four pairs, and "weak" for one. For the most highly correlated pair (Fig. 6A) the fluctuations in firing rates during successive minutes were exceptionally large, and the rates of the two units tended to be positively correlated during most periods (e.g., DRH-3). Furthermore, the increased firing rates of the reinforced unit during DRH periods were accompanied by an overall increase in rate of the small unit. In other sessions the two adjacent units fired relatively independently (Fig. 9).

To determine whether operant bursts of the reinforced unit were accompanied by a correlated pattern of activity in the adjacent unreinforced unit, we examined the response averages for each pair. As with the session averages, we subjectively rated the intensity of any correlated fluctuations of the small unit (Table 2). Most unit pairs exhibited some degree of correlated activity in the response average. We found three main types of correlated patterns in the small unit: in four cases the small unit fired in a simple burst pattern, similar in configuration to the operant burst of the reinforced unit; in three cases the small unit exhibited a more complex pattern of activity, involving suppression as well as facilitation; in two cases the small unit showed no modulation in rate during bursts of the large. (One additional example of the latter case was the session in Fig. 9, which was excluded from Table 2 because it began with a differential schedule.) The stability of these correlated patterns was tested by computing the response averages during different DRH periods of the session. Usually the average correlated pattern of the small unit was the same shape in all DRH periods; sometimes the amplitude changed, but usually in proportion to the amplitude of the operant bursts.

The unit pair illustrated in Fig. 6 was highly correlated in the response average as well as the session average. The correlated pattern of the small unit was a burst quite similar in shape and intensity to the operant bursts of the large unit (Fig. 6B). Examination of individual bursts in the dot raster verifies that the units tended to burst together in individual trials, with the small cell often becoming active slightly before the large. (These bursts were repeatedly associated with a visible twitch of the contralateral ankle, and both units could be driven by passive dorsiflexion of the ankle.)

The remaining unit pairs were less strongly correlated on the level of the response average. Figure 7B illustrates another pair for which the correlated pattern was a simple burst of the small unit. In this case the peak of the small-unit burst occurred 200 msec after the peak of the large-unit activity; this temporal relationship was the same in each of the three DRH periods of this session. Figure 7A shows a pair for which the firing rate of the small unit did not fluctuate during the operant bursts of the large unit. Figure 7C illustrates one of the three pairs with a complex correlated pattern; operant bursts of the large cell were preceded by suppression of the small unit, followed by weak facilitation. The converse biphasic sequence, activation followed by suppression, was also observed (session C:12/6/69, not illustrated). In both of these cases the large and small units responded to the same passive joint movements. The third complex correlated pattern of small-unit activity was a "triphasic" pattern (Fig. 7D): the first peak in small-cell activity coincided with the peak of the operant burst; this was followed by a suppression 80 msec later and a second peak 200 msec later. Although this pattern is most clearly illustrated by the overall average of 500 bursts compiled over five DRH periods, the same pattern was evident in the averages of 100 bursts each, compiled during each of the individual DRH periods. In this case the stability of the correlated pattern is particularly remarkable in view of the fact that the visually observed motor activity associated with the operant unit bursts was quite generalized.

Differential conditioning of adjacent cortical cells

The degree to which adjacent cortical cells might be independently controlled was tested in six sessions in which the firing rate of the small cell was included in the rein-

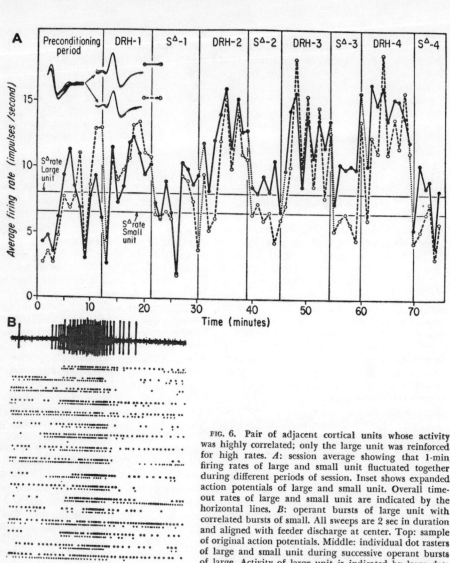

FIG. 6. Pair of adjacent cortical units whose activity was highly correlated; only the large unit was reinforced for high rates. *A*: session average showing that 1-min firing rates of large and small unit fluctuated together during different periods of session. Inset shows expanded action potentials of large and small unit. Overall time-out rates of large and small unit are indicated by the horizontal lines. *B*: operant bursts of large unit with correlated bursts of small. All sweeps are 2 sec in duration and aligned with feeder discharge at center. Top: sample of original action potentials. Middle: individual dot rasters of large and small unit during successive operant bursts of large. Activity of large unit is indicated by large dots in top trace of each pair; simultaneous activity of small unit is given by small dots in lower trace of each pair. Bottom: response average for large and small unit (upper and lower histograms, respectively) computed over 200 operant bursts. Vertical bars represent 50 impulses/sec. Session R:3/4/69.

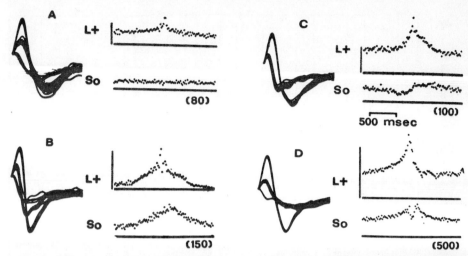

FIG. 7. Action potentials and response averages for unit pairs during reinforcement of operant bursts of large unit. Sweeps showing expanded action potentials (left side of each set) were triggered at "noise level." Response averages (right) gave time histograms of large unit activity, which was reinforced (L+), and simultaneous small-unit activity, which was not reinforced (So). Number of samples in each set of response averages is shown in parentheses. Vertical bars indicate 50/sec firing rate for both large and small unit of each set. *A*: session B:10/21/68; *B*: session R:3/14/69; *C*: session C:1/17/69; *D*: session R:3/3/69.

forcement contingency. Two of these sessions were subsequently discarded because isolation of the small unit was lost. One session (B:10/23/68) involved simple DRH of small-unit rates with no contingency on the large (DRH:S); this schedule was imposed after the large cell had already been reinforced for high rates (DRH:L). Although the two units fluctuated together in successive 1-min average rates, the response averages revealed that the bursts of the large cell were unaccompanied by consistent correlated fluctuations in small cell rate, and vice versa.

In three sessions the reinforcement contingency involved differential control of the firing rates of both cells, i.e., the monkey was rewarded for increasing the firing rate of one cell and simultaneously suppressing firing of the other. In one such session (Fig. 8) we first reinforced high rates of the large cell in four separate DRH:L periods. The session average showed that the small unit was moderately correlated with the large; its overall rate increased with the large unit during the DRH:L periods. Figure 8*A* plots the mean firing rates of these units averaged over each behavioral period. In the response averages (Fig. 8*B*) the small unit ex-

hibited a weak correlated burst pattern during the operant bursts of the large. In the fourth DRH:L period we introduced the additional condition that the small-unit rates be decreased during the bursts of the large (DRH:L/DRO:S). This produced a change in the rewarded direction; comparing mean rates on the differential schedule with mean rates on all preceding DRH:L periods shows that the differential schedule produced a drop in the small-unit rate with little change in the large-unit rate. The mean firing rate of the small unit during the entire differential period (5.5/sec) was 54% of its mean rate during all DRH:L periods (10.3/sec). By comparison, the mean rate of the large unit during the differential period (19.3/sec) was 105% of its rate during all previous DRH:L periods (18.5/sec). The response averages computed during the DRH:L/DRO:S period (Fig. 8*B*) also show a shift in the reinforced direction: the correlated pattern of small-unit activity associated with operant bursts of the large was a suppression of firing during the differential period. In this session a cell pair whose firing was correlated during a simple DRH:L schedule could also be dissociated on a differential schedule.

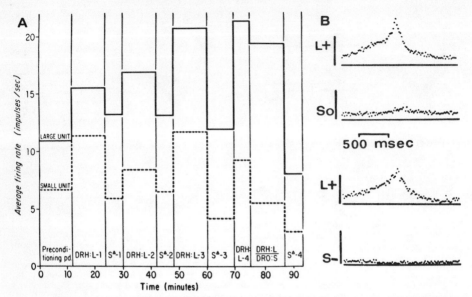

FIG. 8. Differential conditioning of two adjacent units. The bar graph (*A*) plots the mean firing rates of the large and small unit averaged over each behavioral period. During the first four reinforcement periods high rates of the large unit were reinforced without any contingency on the small unit rate (DRH:L). At *t* = 75 we differentially reinforced high rates of large unit and simultaneous low rates of small (DRH:L/DRO:S). The response averages at right (*B*) show time histograms of large (L) and small (S) unit rates computed for each reinforced pattern and aligned around the feeder discharge. Each set consists of 100 responses and bars calibrate 50/sec. Session R:3/13/69.

More dramatic evidence of differential control of adjacent cortical cells is provided by the session illustrated in Fig. 9. The first contingency reinforced high rates of activity in the small unit and low rates in the large (DRH:S/DRO:L). The session average shows that the small-unit rate almost doubled, while the large-unit rate remained approximately at preconditioning levels. The response averages for this period (Fig. 9, bottom) show that operant bursts of the small unit were not accompanied by a clear correlated pattern in the large unit, although the tonic rates of both cells increased over preconditioning levels. During the subsequent S^Δ period the rates of both cells dropped toward their mean extinction levels, indicated by the horizontal lines. In the second reinforcement period the differential schedule reinforced increases in large-unit rates and decreases in small-unit rates (DRH:L/DRO:S); the session average shows a 69% increase in large-unit rates, with a lesser increase (34%) in small-unit rate. The response average for this period

reveals the higher tonic rate of the large cell during this period as compared with the preconditioning period, and shows that the operant bursts of the large unit were not accompanied by any strong correlated pattern in the small unit. During the subsequent S^Δ period firing rates of both units returned to their extinction levels. The next schedule (DRO:L) reinforced only suppression of the large-unit rates, with no contingency on the small-unit rate. At first the monkey increased large-unit rates, as would have been appropriate in the previous reinforcement period, but after 15 min he suppressed the firing rate of the large unit to a mean level of 17.5/sec over the final 13 min of this period (55% of extinction rates). During this time the small-unit rate remained relatively unchanged compared with its extinction rate. Response averages computed around the reinforced pauses in large-unit activity during this DRO:L period indicate that the large unit was inactive for 100 msec before feeder discharge, and otherwise fired at a very low

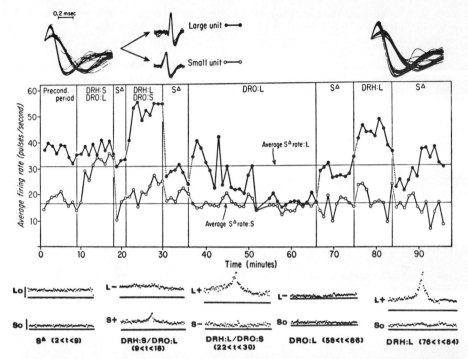

FIG. 9. Differential conditioning of two independent cortical units. Insets at top illustrate superimposed action potentials of large and small units from beginning and end of session. The graph plots 1-min firing rates for both units under different behavioral schedules (see text), and shows mean time-out rates of large and small unit. Response averages (bottom) give time histograms of large (L) and small (S) unit rates for each specified period, aligned around the feeder discharge. Each set includes 60 responses obtained during the time interval given in parentheses, except L+/S−, which includes 30 responses. Vertical bars calibrate 50/sec firing rate for all sets; duration of response averages is 2 sec. Session B:10/25/68. (Note: several hours before this session the monkey had been exposed to another differential training session in which isolation of the small unit was lost; the prior session included 32 min on a differential schedule, and terminated 1 hr before this session began. This previous exposure to the differential schedule may explain the unusually rapid acquisition of responses in this session.)

rate during the 2-sec analysis interval. The correlated pattern of small-unit activity shows only a slight decrease in overall rate, but exhibits no clear correlated fluctuation. With the return to S^Δ conditions the rate of the large cell immediately reverted to its extinction level, confirming that the preceding suppression was sustained by the reinforcement. The final reinforcement schedule (DRH:L) rewarded bursts of activity in the large unit, with no contingency on the small. The session average shows that the large-unit rate increased significantly (37%) with no sustained increase in the small-unit rate. In the response average of this period the intense operant bursts of the large unit

were not accompanied by a clear correlated pattern in the small unit, even though the latter was not included in the reinforcement contingency.

This session provides a convincing example of two adjacent units whose rates could be independently controlled. The initial differential conditioning periods demonstrate that either the large or small unit could be made to increase in rate without comparable increases in the other. Furthermore, even when the small-unit rate was not included in the reinforcement contingency, the rate of the large unit was increased and suppressed without comparable changes in the rate of the neighboring small unit. This relative independence appeared not only in the successive 1-min rates of the session average, but also on the more sensitive level of the response averages.

Visually observed movements associated with operant bursts

In some sessions the monkey's activity was visually observed during DRH periods to see whether specific movements were associated with operant bursts of the conditioned unit. Most monkeys sat in a primate chair with head restrained, allowing relatively free movements of arms and legs. Under these conditions, movements associated with operant bursts of different precentral units fell into three broad classes: specific, variable, and none. *1*) Specific movements such as flexion or extension of one or more joints were sometimes observed to be repeatedly emitted with each operant burst. In several cases such movements were initially part of more general and variable motor activity at the beginning of DRH, involving moderately large excursions of the limb and movement of several joints. After 10–20 min of DRH conditioning, many components of this motor activity gradually dropped out, until each burst was associated with a specific, discrete movement, often involving slight excursions of a single joint. *2*) In other sessions operant bursts of the reinforced cell were associated with variable movements throughout the session. In these instances no single movement occurred consistently with successive unit bursts; instead, bursts seemed to be associated with a variety of motor responses. *3*) In several cases the reinforced unit bursts were emitted with no observable movement. In such sessions the beginning of the DRH period sometimes occasioned very little or no motor activity and the monkey fired the cell in bursts while sitting quite still.

Although visual observations are qualitative, they permit several general conclusions: gross motor activity was observed with most, but not all, precentral units whose activity was conditioned. Such movements were generally not the same from one cell to the next; the activity associated with bursts of one unit could be quite different from that emitted with the next unit. In an attempt to obtain a more quantitative measure of muscle activity, we recorded electromyographic (EMG) activity with many of these cells.

Electromyographic activity correlated with operant bursts

In 15 sessions we recorded the EMG activity of two to four contralateral leg muscles, including flexors and extensors of the ankle (tibialis anterior and gastrocnemius) and of the knee (hamstring and quadriceps). Subcutaneously implanted EMG leads did not appear to interfere with movements of the leg, nor did movements generate electrical artifacts. In most sessions some EMG activity accompanied the operant bursts of the reinforced unit, but from one burst to the next the amount of correlated activity in a given muscle could vary. Since the exact temporal relationships between unit and muscle activity were hard to estimate reliably from inspection of individual trials, we averaged the rectified EMG activity over the 2-sec intervals surrounding the operant bursts. Such response averages revealed that the typical average EMG pattern correlated with the average operant unit burst consisted of a simple burst of EMG activity in most or all muscles recorded. Response averages never showed a consistent suppression of EMG activity correlated with unit bursts. With few exceptions, the correlated EMG pattern had a simple monophasic shape broadly coincident with the operant unit burst (Fig. 10).

We examined the amplitude and duration of the average EMG bursts and the latency of the peak EMG activity relative to the peak of the operant unit burst. The stability of these parameters was estimated by comparing averages over a given number of bursts (usually 50 or 100) during different portions of the session. Although the absolute amplitude of the average EMG burst of a given muscle could vary from one DRH period to another (as could the size of the average operant burst), the relative amplitudes of EMGs in different muscles were usually consistent through the session. That is, the rank order of most to least active muscle was usually the same for all

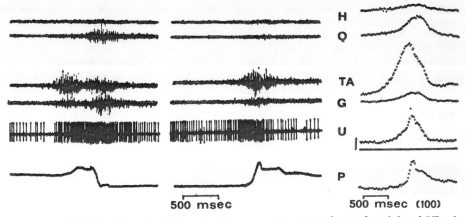

FIG. 10. Relationship of muscle activity and ankle movement to operant bursts of a reinforced PT unit. Two trials are shown at left and response average over 100 bursts is shown at right. From top, EMG of hamstrings (H), quadriceps (Q), tibialis anticus (TA), and gastrocnemius (G); unit spikes (U) and ankle position (P). Dorsiflexion is up on position trace. In this case the foot was placed in a cast hinged at the ankle, but the average EMG bursts are typical of patterns seen with unrestricted movement. Vertical bar calibrates 50 impulses/sec. Session M:5/30/69.

DRH periods with a given unit; however, this rank order could be different for other units. For the unit in Fig. 10, the most active muscle was tibialis and least active was hamstring.

In most cases the response averages were representative of patterns seen in individual trials. In a few instances in which the response averages indicated an increase in several muscles, examination of individual trials revealed that with successive bursts either one muscle or its antagonist was predominantly active, but the two were not consistently coactivated. Under such circumstances, the sum over many trials showed an average increase in activity of several muscles. Figure 10 illustrates one such example. After six DRH periods with the legs and feet unrestrained, it appeared that operant unit bursts were associated with dorsiflexion of the ankle. In order to document this movement we placed the foot in a cast hinged at the ankle through a potentiometer, and continued to reinforce bursts of unit activity. The most common response was in fact dorsiflexion of the foot, but about one-third of the unit bursts were associated with plantar flexion. The sum over these alternating movements shows that all muscles underwent some increase in activity in relation to the average unit burst.

For a given cell the duration of the average EMG bursts could be either longer or shorter than the duration of operant unit bursts, and was consistently so throughout the session. Although the average EMG and operant unit bursts broadly overlapped in time, a latency difference between peak unit activity and peak EMG activity could be measured on the response averages to 20-msec resolution. For a particular unit the relative timing of peak unit activity and peak EMG activity was consistent through all periods of the session, although the exact value of the latency difference might vary. Furthermore, when peak unit activity preceded or followed peak muscle activity, it did so for all correlated muscles. For 7 of the 11 precentral cells analyzed, peak unit activity preceded peak muscle activity; in two cases the unit and muscle peaks coincided, and in two cases peak unit activity followed peak muscle activity. Whether the peak unit activity preceded or followed the peak EMG activity would indicate whether the cell tended to fire predominantly before or after any correlated peripheral motor response. Any unit which the monkey activated by stimulating peripheral receptors might be expected to reach peak activity after the EMG activity. In fact, we found that although most cells responded to passive joint movements, the operant bursts usually reached their peak before the correlated EMG activity.

Sensory responses of precentral units

In the course of these studies we tested the responses of 233 precentral units to passive stimulation of the peripheral receptors (9). Most cells were excited clearly and repeatedly by passive movements of one or more joints of the contralateral leg. A few units responded to cutaneous stimulation such as brushing hairs or touching skin over specific regions of the body, and some units did not respond to any stimulation. The response of a given unit to a specific set of stimuli could be demonstrated repeatedly over many hours, and occurred without overt resistance or recorded EMG activity. These observations suggest that the sensory input to precentral cells previously documented in anesthetized monkeys (1, 24) and recently reported in humans (12) may also be demonstrated in alert monkeys, and may be used to characterize these units.

The fact that most precentral units could be activated by peripheral stimulation suggests that the monkeys might have generated operant bursts through movements which stimulated appropriate peripheral receptors. Such movements would presumably involve muscle activity which would precede the consequent unit response. In most cases, however, we found peak unit activity preceding peak muscle activity, even though many of the same units could be driven by passive joint movements. One cell, which responded to brushing hairs, reached peak firing rates 40–80 msec before peak muscle activity. These observations are consistent with more recent studies in which we reinforced specific movements, and suggest that although precentral cells may respond to peripheral stimulation under passive conditions, they can also be activated through central pathways before any correlated motor responses. The degree to which operant bursts may be sustained by sensory feedback from peripheral receptors remains to be more directly investigated.

We reviewed our results to determine whether the passive movements which drove a precentral unit were related in a consistent manner to the active movements which accompanied the operant bursts. From the limited number of cells for which the active movements were adequately characterized, we can only conclude that there is no simple relation for all or even most cells. Of the units responding to passive joint movement in one direction, the operant bursts were associated with active movements in the same direction for some units, and in the opposite direction for others. Some units, such as the one in Fig. 10, responded to passively moving a joint in both directions and fired during active movements of that joint in either direction. Some precentral units could not be driven by passive stimulation, but fired before (S:2/21/69) or after (R:3/13/69) a motor response. More recently we have found precentral units which responded to passive stimulation, but whose operant bursts were not associated with any measured muscle activity. Thus, almost every type of relation between a unit's sensory input and its burst-correlated motor response seems possible; a more comprehensive study would be necessary to determine whether any specific relations predominate.

Among the pairs of adjacent cortical cells, we noted that the units with the highest degree of correlation in firing rates tended to respond to the same passive movements. For example, the pair in Fig. 6 (R:3/4/69) was highly correlated in both session and response averages, and both units were driven readily by passive ankle dorsiflexion. Similarly, the two correlated units in Fig. 7C (C:1/17/69) both responded to knee extension and ankle dorsiflexion. When one of two adjacent units responded to movement of a different joint or was unresponsive (B:10/21/68), the correlation in firing rates tended to be weaker. A notable exception was the pair in Fig. 9 (B:10/25/68), which fired relatively independently in both session and response averages, although both units could be driven by passive knee extension.

DISCUSSION

In these experiments we investigated the behavioral conditions under which monkeys could be operantly conditioned to control the activity of single precentral cortex units. In most sessions the reinforced response pattern was a high-frequency burst of unit activity, called an operant burst, which experienced monkeys readily learned to produce in newly isolated cells during reinforcement (DRH) periods. During these DRH periods the monkeys increased the mean firing rate of the units, *1*) by producing operant bursts more frequently and *2*) by increasing the intensity of such bursts; usually they *3*) increased the interburst firing rate as well. That these were "voluntary" responses sustained by reinforcement is indicated by the fact that under extinction conditions firing rates typically returned to preconditioning levels in less than 1 min.

Various lines of evidence indicate that these bursts were true operant responses, not simply increases in activity directly evoked by delivery of food. Comparable increases in cell activity did not occur in naive monkeys when food was delivered, nor in experienced monkeys when reinforcement was not correlated with high rates. If the increase in cell activity had occurred predominantly as a direct consequence of food delivery, such as unit activity associated with consumption of the pellet or fruit juice, the response averages would have shown the greatest amount of unit activity occurring just after the feeder discharge. This was not observed for the cells in this study, which were recorded in leg or arm area of precentral cortex. Instead, most of these units underwent the greatest increase in activity prior to feeder discharge (Fig. 3), indicating that the bursts were true operant responses generated by the monkey, not direct consequences of food delivery or concomitants of feeding behavior.

One might suppose that experienced monkeys could simply learn to increase motor activity in general during DRH periods, so as to activate many precentral cells indiscriminately. Even in sessions in which the monkey's motor and EMG activity were not directly observed, behavioral evidence suggested that reinforcement alone did not sustain generalized motor activity. When reinforcement was delivered randomly with respect to unit bursts, there was no increase in rates (8). Furthermore, in session R:3/15/69 (Fig. 4) the monkey had already in-

creased activity of the monitored cell during an initial DRH period; when the correlation between reinforcement and unit rates was changed, the same rate of juice delivery did not sustain high firing rates. Finally, in sessions with successful DRO periods, activity of a given unit could be suppressed as well as increased (Figs. 5, 9), indicating that the critical variable in the behavioral effect of reinforcement was its correlation with specific changes in unit activity, not its mere presentation.

Some have suggested that monkeys might learn to generate bursts of cortical unit activity by transiently increasing intracranial pressure by the Valsalva maneuver (attempted expiration against closed glottis). The resultant displacement of cortical tissue could move the cell against the microelectrode, producing an injury discharge. While we have not measured intracranial pressure directly, we consider this explanation to be unlikely for several reasons: *1*) the height of the action potentials invariably remained constant during the operant bursts (Figs. 3, 6*B*, 10); *2*) we usually confirmed that the electrode could pass the cell without increasing its activity; *3*) on DRO schedules monkeys could also decrease unit activity (Figs. 5, 9); and *4*) on differential schedules the monkeys could control rates of two units independently (Figs. 8, 9). These observations seem easier to explain on the basis of synaptic control than by the Valsalva maneuver.

Although delivery of reinforcement was made contingent on the activity of a single cortical unit, that unit was obviously not the only one whose activity changed. With operant bursts, one can argue a priori that there should be some correlated activity in other cells and probably in muscles. At the least one would expect those cells involved in controlling the reinforced unit to undergo correlated changes in firing rate. In addition one might expect to see concomitant activity in other neurons and muscles involved in a wider correlated response pattern, of which the operant unit burst may be a part. In fact, we found that adjacent cortical cells and contralateral muscles were often coactivated with operant bursts. The nature of this correlated activity and its relation to the reinforced unit bursts was investigated by examining burst-correlated patterns of activity in adjacent units and contralateral muscles in the response averages and by visually observing movements associated with operant bursts.

When the activity of two adjacent cortical cells was simultaneously monitored, the rates of the two units often fluctuated together during successive minutes of the session (Fig. 6A), and the overall increases in rate of the reinforced unit during DRH periods were usually associated with increases in mean firing rate of the neighboring cell (Table 2). On the other hand, some unit pairs exhibited relatively independent rates in the session average (Fig. 9). On a finer level of temporal resolution, the response averages showed that in most cases during operant bursts of the reinforced unit the neighboring cell underwent some correlated fluctuation in rate, either a simple burst or a more complex pattern (Figs. 6B, 7, 8). The fact that some adjacent cortical units showed correlated changes in activity is perhaps not surprising considering the high probability that neighboring cells would share common neural circuits and might be involved in the same motor responses (24). However, less than half of the unit pairs that we observed showed a similar burst pattern in both units during operant bursts of the reinforced unit. More often, the firing patterns of the two units were dissimilar during the operant bursts (Fig. 7C, D) and sometimes there was no change in pattern of the unreinforced unit (Figs. 7A, 9). Thus, even neighboring cells separated by no more than a few hundred microns may exhibit quite independent activities.

Since any influence of the motor cortex on movements would ultimately involve the correlated output of many thousands of neurons, the relationship between activity in different precentral cells is of considerable interest. As Humphrey et al. (14) have suggested, the "temporal relations between the spike trains of separate cortical cells may be a significant variable in the control of movement . . ."; they found that the accuracy with which various measures of motor performance could be predicted from precentral spike trains increased in proportion to the number of independent spike trains used. When we tested the stability of observed correlations in activities of adjacent units by including both in the reinforcement contingency, the correlations between neighboring precentral units could be readily modified. The pair in Fig. 8 was weakly correlated when only operant bursts of the large unit were reinforced; however, when the contingency included simultaneous suppression of small-unit rates, the monkey quickly shifted to the appropriate pattern. Such flexibility is hardly surprising in view of the demonstrations that adjacent motor units of the same muscle may be independently controlled (2, 13). Evarts (6) has also noted that correlations between adjacent precentral units may vary under different behavioral conditions; our observations confirm this and lead us to conclude that operant control of correlations is feasible and may prove useful in testing the functional role of this variable.

We investigated the motor activity associated with operant bursts by visually observing movements and by examining response averages of EMG activity. Both methods indicated that different precentral units could be associated with different motor responses. With some units the monkey emitted variable and generalized movements throughout the session. Often, unit bursts were associated with some specific movements of one or two joints of the contralateral limb. In a few sessions the monkey repeatedly drove the unit in bursts without any visible movements. Examples of each type of associated movement were found for cells in the same cortical area in a given monkey. Different cells in the same area could be associated with specific movements of different joints or could involve different movements of the same joint. These observations suggest that the monkey did not simply adopt the strategy of producing a single generalized motor pattern which was effective in activating all recorded precentral units.

Patterns of correlated EMG activity could also be different from one cell to the next. As noted with observed movements, different cells exhibited different degrees of variability in correlated EMG patterns from one burst to the next. Averaging over many bursts provided a more stable measure of correlated EMG patterns; for a given unit, response averages compiled in various periods were usually consistent in showing the same rank order of muscles activated and the same relative timing of peak unit and peak EMG activity. These variables could be different, however, for another unit in the same cortical area. Some precentral units have now been observed for which operant bursts were not accompanied by any recorded EMG activity. Again, such observations support the conclusion that different movements may accompany operant bursts of different precentral cells.

It would be useful to contrast our approach for investigating the relation of motor cortex cells to movements with the strategy of reinforcing specific motor responses (5–7, 14–16, 22). In the latter approach monkeys were trained to make certain movements—e.g., flexion and extension of a joint—and precentral unit activity was related to the position and force trajectories of the responding limb. In contrast, our approach has been to reinforce activity of specific precentral cells and observe correlated movements under relatively unrestricted conditions. Each approach offers certain advantages and suffers limitations. Studying a simple, repeatable response pattern with quantifiable mechanical parameters provides distinct advantages in investigating relationships between precentral cell activity and net force and position. As Evarts (7) has pointed out, however, documenting the relation of precentral motor cortex cells to one specific movement is analogous to documenting the relation of postcentral "sensory" cortex cells to one specific stimulus. In each case some cortical units may be directly related to the peripheral event (movement or stimulus), others will be peripherally related, and the remainder unrelated. The strategy of finding those peripheral events which are optimally associated with each unit is relatively simple in the sensory system: one determines the modalities and receptive fields of those stimuli which most effectively drive the postcentral cell. The motor analogue of this procedure would be to elicit that motor pattern with which a given precentral cell may be most strongly correlated. We have

investigated this possibility by reinforcing bursts of activity for each unit and looking for correlated movements. With the animal's limbs and trunk relatively unrestrained he was free to make whatever limb movements might be associated with operant bursts, whether they involved one particular joint or not.

In experiments employing a specific trained movement, a considerable proportion of precentral units was found unrelated to the movement. Whether such cells are related to another movement or are not related to any may be determined by examining their relation to an exhaustive repertoire of movements (7), or more simply by reinforcing the cell directly. In the present study experienced monkeys could fire virtually every isolated precentral unit in bursts, and most units were associated with some specifiable motor responses.

A severe limitation of our approach is the degree of precision with which any concomitant motor response could be documented. While visual observation provided a convenient first-order indication of associated movements, such observations are too subjective and unquantifiable to allow precise correlations. With relatively free movements of the limbs, neither force nor position could be easily measured. In hopes of obtaining more quantitative measures of muscle activity with which precentral unit activity could be correlated, we recorded the EMG activity of representative muscles of the contralateral limb. Under conditions of free movements, however, patterns of EMG activity were not always consistently correlated with successive bursts of a given precentral unit. This contrasts with results obtained under more controlled behavioral conditions, such as well-trained stereotyped movements (5–7, 14–16) or isometric muscle activity (10); under these circumstances EMG patterns and unit-muscle correlations may be considerably more repeatable over successive responses. By averaging over a number of operant bursts we found that averaged muscle patterns did show more consistent relation to the operant bursts, but such responses often involved many muscles.

A second limitation common to all

chronic unit experiments concerns the conclusions one can draw from observation of correlated events concerning functional relations. Even when a specific movement is repeatedly associated with operant bursts of a given unit, a variety of functional relations between cell and muscle activity are logically possible. The existence of functional connections between some precentral cells and motoneurons has been amply demonstrated by experiments showing that activity of the former may generate synaptic potentials in the latter, either directly or indirectly (20, 21, 23). Such functional connections may be strong or weak, depending on whether the cortically generated synaptic potentials represent a greater or lesser fraction of the total synaptic depolarization needed to fire the motoneuron. In chronic recording experiments, the basic observable was a temporal correlation between unit and muscle activity—i.e., the degree to which their activity was modulated together. This temporal correlation could also be strong or weak, depending on whether the two were consistently activated together or tended to fire more independently. One might assume that strong functional connections would produce strong temporal correlations. Such is the case in the extreme example of the connection between motoneuron and muscle fiber, in which the former always produces a sufficiently strong depolarization in the latter to generate contraction; under such circumstances the activity of the two elements is invariably correlated. The functional connection between precentral cells and motoneurons is known to be considerably weaker, even in the optimal anatomic case when the former have direct synapses on the latter. Other synaptic influences converging on the motoneuron may be just as potent and could, in principle, override the synaptic effect of a given precentral cell. The degree to which these other influences on the motoneuron act independently of the precentral cells would be reflected in the degree to which the correlations between precentral cell and muscle activity vary from one response to the next. While such variations are relatively small when stereotyped, overtrained movements are employed, they are considerably greater when only the unit is reinforced and movements are unrestricted. The observed variability in unit-muscle correlations under free conditions suggests that an individual precentral cell may act quite independently of other systems controlling motoneuron activity. In the likelihood that some of these cells did have synaptic connections with motoneurons of recorded muscles, the variability of the correlations would suggest that one may have functional connections without consistent temporal correlations (see also ref 10).

The converse condition, i.e., temporal correlations without functional connections, is also possible. It may be that the unit whose activity is correlated with muscle activity has no synaptic influence—either direct or relayed—on the relevant motoneurons. Such a spurious correlation would be sustained as long as the two elements are coactivated. However, if two correlated responses are functionally independent and only one continues to be reinforced, the other may eventually drop out. This was observed in some sessions with prolonged or repeated DRH periods; after 10–30 min of DRH we often saw many components of the associated motor response drop out. Presumably, the rate at which such functionally independent components of a response pattern drop out depends on their variability; the more they fluctuate from one reinforced trial to the next, the weaker the correlation between them and the reinforcement. Thus, they would be less likely to be sustained by reinforcement and more likely to drop out. This method of eliminating components of the total response pattern, which are functionally independent of the reinforced pattern but initially correlated with it, would be least effective for those components with the strongest correlation.

A more direct test of the stability of an observed temporal correlation between two responses is to bring both into the reinforcement contingency. In more recent studies isometric EMG activity of individual muscles could be included with the precentral unit activity as part of the reinforced pattern (10). In these studies units were found whose activity consistently preceded activation of a given muscle when either the muscle or unit alone was reinforced, or when movement involving activation of the muscle was reinforced. When such correlated unit and muscle(s) were simultaneously included in the reinforcement contingency and their dissociation was reinforced, the monkey readily produced operant unit bursts without any recorded muscle activity. These observations confirm the flexibility of temporal correlations between single precentral units and contralateral muscles. However, they cannot decide the issue of functional connections, since they are compatible both with absence of functional connections as well as with presence of functional connections which are overridden by other descending influences on motoneurons.

While observations of temporal correlations may not permit definitive conclusions concerning specific functional relations, the technique of reinforcing central unit activity promises to be a useful approach to investigating neural functions. It provides a direct method of controlling the activity of specific cells and of eliciting correlated behavioral responses.

SUMMARY

Activity patterns of single precentral units were operantly reinforced in six awake, chaired monkeys (*Macaca mulatta*). Training sessions consisted of *1*) a preconditioning period in which firing rates were monitored before any reinforcement was introduced, *2*) reinforcement periods in which the monkey was rewarded with fruit juice for transient increases in rates (DRH) or transient decreases in rates (DRO), and *3*) extinction periods in which reinforcement and feedback were withdrawn. During reinforcement periods a meter facing the monkey was illuminated and its needle deflections indicated the degree to which the monkey's response pattern met criteria for reinforcement. After several training sessions monkeys learned to increase firing rates of newly isolated cells in operant bursts under DRH conditions and suppressed rates of some of the same units under DRO conditions. Responses were emitted more frequently only when reinforcement was contingent on the occurrence of the response, but not when reinforcement was randomly presented.

When units adjacent to the reinforced unit were simultaneously monitored some were found to fluctuate with the reinforced unit, both during successive minutes of the session (session average) and during the 2-sec periods around the reinforced operant burst (response average). Other adjacent units fired independently of the operant bursts of the reinforced unit. When activity of both units was included in the reinforcement contingency, monkeys learned to generate differential patterns of activity.

When movements associated with operant bursts were visually observed we found that they fell into three classes: variable movements, which differed significantly from one operant burst to the next; specific movements, involving repeated excursions of a given joint or joints; and no movements. Sometimes burst-associated movements were initially generalized and variable, but became more specific after several DRH periods.

When EMG activity was recorded from contralateral limb muscles, we found that operant bursts of most units were accompanied by some EMG activity; for many units concomitant EMG activity was relatively variable from burst to burst; for others EMG patterns were quite repeatable. Response averages of rectified EMG activity revealed an average increase of activity in most muscles, in a burst pattern whose peak could precede or follow the peak of the operant burst by up to 300 msec. For a given unit such response averages were consistent from one DRH period to the next in the relative degree to which individual muscles were activated, and in relative timing of peak unit and peak muscle activity.

Most precentral units showed a consistent excitatory response to phasic passive movements of one or more joints of the contralateral limb in the absence of any recorded EMG activity. From one unit to the next these passive responses did not seem to have any consistent relation to the active movements accompanying the operant bursts, although frequently both active and passive movements involved the same joint.

Operant conditioning of central unit activity may prove to be a useful technique for eliciting correlated behavioral responses in which the unit may play a functional role. However, observation of a temporal correlation is neither necessary nor sufficient evidence to establish a functional connection since either can logically occur without the other.

NOTE ADDED IN PROOF:

Recently Dr. David E. Hiatt (*Investigations of Operant Conditioning of Single Unit Activity in the Rat Brain* (Ph.D. thesis), Pasadena: California Institute of Technology, 1972) reported many similar observations for five different brain areas of the rat. Associated with conditioned increases in firing rates, Hiatt also observed correlated increases in control cells and in motor activity. Paralyzing rats with gallamine triethiodide abolished conditioned increases in all areas except brain stem.

ACKNOWLEDGMENTS

We gratefully acknowledge Dr. Erich Luschei's helpful suggestions concerning chronic recording techniques and Ms. Susan Barrow's invaluable assistance during initial experiments. We thank Dr. Dom V. Finocchio for helpful discussions concerning behavioral techniques, Ms. Barbara Klompus for computing innumerable averages, and Mr. Francis Spelman for assisting with the electronic instrumentation.

This work was supported by National Institutes of Health Grants RR 00166 and NB 00396, and Public Health Service Grant 5 T1 NB 5082-13.

E. E. Fetz is a recipient of National Institute of Neurological Diseases and Stroke Teacher-Investigator Award (2 F11 NS 11, 027-02 NSRB). He is now also with the Dept. of Neurological Surgery, University of Washington.

M. A. Baker was supported by a postdoctoral fellowship from the Bank of America Giannini Foundation. Her present address: Dept. of Physiology, University of Southern California School of Medicine, Los Angeles, Calif. 90033.

REFERENCES

1. ALBE FESSARD, D. AND LIEBESKIND, J. Origine des messages somatosensitifs activant les cellules du cortex motur ches le singe. *Exptl. Brain Res.* 1: 127–146, 1966.
2. BASMAJIAN, J. V. *Muscles Alive.* Baltimore: Williams & Wilkins, 1967.
3. BLACK, A. H. The operant conditioning of central nervous system electrical activity. In: *The Psychology of Learning and Motivation*, edited by G. H. Bower. New York: Academic, Vol. 6. In press.
4. CHASE, M. H. AND HARPER, R. M. Somatomotor and visceromotor correlates of operantly conditioned 12-14 c/sec sensorimotor cortical activity. *Electroencephalog. Clin. Neurophysiol.* 31: 85–92, 1971.
5. EVARTS, E. V. Pyramidal tract activity associated with a conditioned hand movement in the monkey. *I. Neurophysiol.* 29: 1011–1027, 1966.
6. EVARTS, E. V. Representation of movements and muscles by pyramidal tract neurons of the precentral motor cortex. In: *Neurophysiological Basis of Normal and Abnormal Motor Control*, edited by M. D. Yahr and D. P. Purpura. Hewlett, N.Y.: Raven, 1967.
7. EVARTS, E. V. Relation of pyramidal tract activity to force exerted during voluntary movement. *J. Neurophysiol.* 31: 14–27, 1968.
8. FETZ, E. E. Operant conditioning of cortical unit activity. *Science* 163: 955–957, 1969.
9. FETZ, E. E. AND BAKER, M. A. Response properties of precentral neurons in awake monkeys. *Physiologist* 12: 223, 1969.
10. FETZ, E. E. AND FINOCCHIO, D. V. Operant conditioning of specific patterns of neural and muscular activity. *Science* 174: 431–435, 1971.
11. FOX, S. S. AND RUDELL, A. P. Operant controlled neural event: functional independence in behavioral coding by early and late components

of visual cortical evoked response in cats. *J. Neurophysiol.* 33: 548–561, 1970.
12. GOLDRING, S. AND RATCHESON, R. Human motor cortex: sensory input data from single neuron recording. *Science* 175: 1493–1495, 1972.
13. HARRISON, V. F. AND MORTENSEN, O. A. Identification and voluntary control of single motor unit activity in the tibialis anterior muscle. *Anat. Record* 144: 109–116, 1962.
14. HUMPHREY, D. R., SCHMIDT, E. M., AND THOMPSON, W. D. Predicting measures of motor performance from multiple cortical spike trains. *Science* 170: 758–762, 1970.
15. LUSCHEI, E. S., GARTHWAITE, C. R., AND ARMSTRONG, M. E. Relationship of firing patterns of units in face area of monkey precentral cortex to conditioned jaw movements. *J. Neurophysiol.* 34: 552–561, 1971.
16. LUSCHEI, E. S., JOHNSON, R. A., AND GLICKSTEIN, M. Response of neurons in the motor cortex during performance of a simple repetitive arm movement. *Nature, London* 217: 190–191, 1968.
17. OLDS, J. Operant conditioning of single unit responses. *Intern. Congr. Physiol. Sci., 23rd, Tokyo, 1965*, p. 372–380.
18. OLDS, J. The limbic system and behavioral reinforcement. In: *Structure and Function of the Limbic System*, edited by W. R. Adey and T. Tokizane. Amsterdam: Elsevier, 1967.
19. OLDS, J. AND OLDS, M. E. Interference and learning in paleocortical systems. In: *Brain Mechanisms and Learning*, edited by J. F. Delafresnaye. Oxford: Blackwell, 1961.
20. PHILLIPS, C. G. AND PORTER, R. The pyramidal projection to motoneurons of some muscle groups of the baboon's forelimb. In: *Physiology of Spinal Neurons*, edited by J. C. Eccles and J. P. Schade. Amsterdam: Elsevier, 1964.

21. PORTER, R. Early facilitation at corticomotoneuronal synapses. *J. Physiol., London* 207: 733–745, 1970.

22. PORTER, R., LEWIS, M., AND HORNE, M. Analysis of patterns of natural activity of neurones in the precentral gyrus of conscious monkeys. *Brain Res.* 34: 99–113, 1971.

23. PRESTON, J. B. AND WHITLOCK, D. G. Intracellular potentials recorded from motoneurons following precentral gyrus stimulation in primates. *J. Neurophysiol.* 24: 91–100, 1961.

24. ROSEN, I. AND ASANUMA, H. Peripheral afferent inputs to the forelimb area of the monkey motor cortex: input-output relations. *Exptl. Brain Res.* 14: 257–273, 1972.

25. ROSENFELD, J. P. *Operant Control of a Neural Event Evoked by a Stereotyped Behavior* (Ph.D. Thesis). Iowa City: University of Iowa, 1971.

26. WYRWICKA, W. AND STERMAN, M. B. Instrumental conditioning of sensorimotor cortex EEG spindles in the waking cat. *Physiol. Behav.* 3: 703–707, 1968.

Auditory Feedback
and Conditioning of the Single Motor Unit

Bruce C. Leibrecht, Andree J. Lloyd,
and Sadie Pounder

ABSTRACT

The effects of direct auditory feedback of the electromyogram (EMG) on learn-ing to control a single motor unit (SMU) were investigated. Seventeen human subjects were injected with bipolar fine-wire electrodes into the tibialis anterior muscle. A trial light indicated the onset of a trial. If the subject activated an SMU, a correct light appeared. A non-SMU response was followed by an incorrect light. All subjects received an initial training series with auditory EMG feedback followed by a retest at 2 weeks without EMG feedback. Speed of initial learning was sub-stantially improved by direct EMG feedback. The nature and amount of learning, including the ability to use proprioceptive cues in controlling an SMU, were not affected, nor was retention of learning.

DESCRIPTORS: Motor unit training, Motor skills, Electromyography, Biofeed-back, Motor performance.

Lloyd and Leibrecht (1971) have recently introduced a technique which allows examination of the learning process that emerges during single motor unit train-ing. Their results demonstrated that subjects can learn to control a single motor unit (SMU) without direct feedback of their electromyographic (EMG) activ-ity. However, learning in the absence of EMG feedback often required lengthy training sessions, with nearly 25% of the subjects failing to reach criterion after 3 hours of training. The present study was undertaken to assess the effects of adding auditory feedback of the EMG to the basic procedure used by Lloyd and Leibrecht (1971). Such a modification might lead to quantitative or qualitative changes in performance, or possibly both.

Most previous investigations of SMU training have provided visual and/or auditory feedback of the EMG activity. However, very little is known about the effects of such feedback. Basmajian, Baeza, and Fabrigar (1965) and Carlsöö and Edfeldt (1963) demonstrated that maintenance of established control of an

Address requests for reprints to: Bruce C. Leibrecht, Experimental Psychology Division, US Army Medical Research Laboratory, Ft. Knox, Kentucky 40121.

SMU was substantially easier with auditory and/or visual EMG feedback than without such feedback. Carlsöö and Edfeldt (1963) also compared auditory vs visual feedback and found that auditory feedback produced better performance than did visual feedback. This finding has been supported by the informal observations of Harrison and Mortensen (1962) and Wagman, Pierce, and Burger (1965). In addition, Carlsöö and Edfeldt's (1963) results suggested that isolation of an SMU occurred more quickly with only auditory than with both auditory and visual feedback, although SMU activity was maintained longer when both forms of augmented feedback were provided.

The present study was designed to answer two basic questions. What changes occur in the learning curve during acquisition of SMU control when auditory feedback of the EMG is added? And how does augmented feedback affect retention of the learned skill? Accordingly, the present experiment used the same training procedures and performance criteria as did Lloyd and Leibrecht (1971). However, continuous auditory feedback of the EMG was introduced during the initial training phase.

Method

Subjects

The Ss consisted of 17 male volunteers ranging in age from 17 to 23 yrs. None had any known muscle abnormality, and none had participated previously in a similar experiment.

Apparatus

The apparatus, which was the same as that used by Lloyd and Leibrecht (1971), was positioned in an electrically shielded room. A padded reclining chair provided support for the entire body. Bipolar fine-wire electrodes for intramuscular electromyographic (EMG) recordings were made from 25μ Teflon-coated platinum-iridium wire, with $\frac{1}{2}$-in., 27-ga. hypodermic needles serving as carrier vehicles for insertion (for details, see Basmajian & Stecko, 1962).

The EMG signals were first passed through a low-level amplifier and then fed simultaneously into a cathode ray oscilloscope and through an ultralinear audio monitor into a headphone or speaker. The face of the oscilloscope was visible only to the experimenter. Thus, while only auditory feedback of the EMG could be provided to the S when desired, both auditory and visual displays of the EMG were available to the experimenter. A panel of three lights, signalling trial onset and duration, correct response and incorrect response, provided the S information about his performance.

Procedure

The basic procedure, detailed by Lloyd and Leibrecht (1971), will be outlined briefly. A group demonstration of SMU isolation and control preceded the start of the experiment. Following the injection of electrodes into the right tibialis anterior muscle, the S was instructed to attempt to activate an SMU as long as the trial duration light was on. In the event of an incorrect response, i.e., no EMG response within 5 sec or more than one motor unit in the EMG, the experimenter terminated the trial by activating the incorrect light. If an SMU appeared within the first 5 sec of a trial, the experimenter turned on the correct light and kept it on as long as an SMU was present. Onset of the correct light extended the total trial duration to 10 sec.

A maximum of 500 trials was administered in 5 sessions, with an intertrial interval of approximately 15 sec and an intersession interval of 30 min. Feedback of the EMG was continuously available through the speaker during each session. The S was run to a performance criterion of 5 successive trials in which continuous activation of an SMU occurred for at least 5 sec.

The same procedure, except without auditory EMG feedback, was repeated for all Ss approximately 14 days later. A new set of electrodes was implanted in relatively the same position as the original set.

Results

Percent correct scores were obtained for each S in successive blocks of 10 trials. Once an individual attained criterion, a score of 100% correct was assigned to the remaining trial blocks. An additional measure of performance was obtained by determining the length of time a correct response was maintained for each trial block. Upon reaching criterion, an individual's score for the remaining trial blocks was determined by computing the mean response time of the 5 criterion trials and multiplying by 10. The present data were organized so as to be directly comparable with the results of the Lloyd and Leibrecht (1971) study, subjects for which were drawn from essentially the same population according to the same criteria. The demographic comparability of the two groups was established by determining that IQ, age, and educational level were statistically comparable. Wherever comparisons are made, the earlier study will be referred to as Group 1, while the present study will be referred to as Group 2.

Mean percent correct responses are presented in Fig. 1. Analysis of variance of the data from the initial test alone indicated that significant learning occurred across the 10-trial blocks ($F = 10.79$, $df = 9/288$, $p < .001$) and across the 5 sessions ($F = 21.39$, $df = 4/128$, $p < .01$). The difference between Groups 1 and 2 was highly significant ($F = 25.97$, $df = 1/32$, $p < .001$). The trial blocks × sessions interaction was significant ($F = 3.53$, $df = 36/1152$, $p < .001$), as was the interaction of sessions × groups ($F = 8.87$, $df = 4/128$, $p < .001$).

Mean response times are presented in Fig. 2. Analysis of variance of the initial test data yielded a pattern of results similar to that found for percent correct data. There were significant effects due to trial blocks ($F = 20.71$, $df = 9/288$, $p < .001$), sessions ($F = 23.05$, $df = 4/128$, $p < .001$), and groups ($F = 22.19$, $df = 1/32$, $p < .001$). The interaction of trial blocks × sessions was significant ($F = 5.67$, $df = 36/1152$, $p < .001$), as was the sessions × groups interaction ($F = 6.96$, $df = 4/128$, $p < .001$).

As a measure of speed of learning on the initial training series, trials to criterion scores were examined for the two groups. Group 1 required an average of 256.7 trials to reach criterion in the initial series, while the mean for Group 2 was 42.1 ($t = 4.97$, $df = 32$, $p < .001$). In addition, whereas 4 of the 17 Ss in Group 1 failed to obtain criterion within 500 trials, all Ss in Group 2 reached criterion within 5 to 228 trials.

Percent correct scores for the retest series (see Fig. 1 for mean curves) were subjected to analysis of variance. Significant improvement in performance oc-

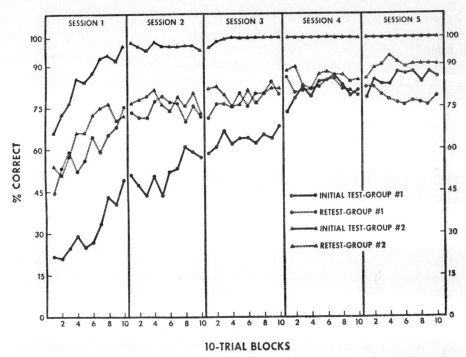

Fig. 1. Mean percent correct response of successive 10 trial blocks for the initial and retest series of both groups.

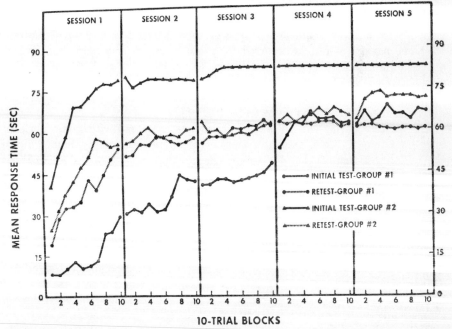

Fig. 2. Mean response time of successive 10 trial blocks for the initial and retest series of both groups.

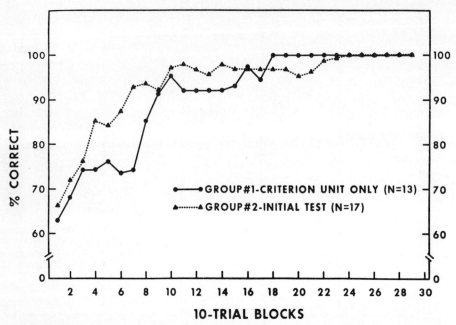

Fig. 3. Mean percent correct response of successive 10 trial blocks in the initial series following first appearance of the criterion SMU for Group 1 and in the first 3 sessions of the initial series for Group 2.

curred across trial blocks ($F = 2.83$, $df = 9/288$, $p < .005$) and across sessions ($F = 13.80$, $df = 4/128$, $p < .001$). However, there were no significant effects due to groups nor to any interaction involving groups. The trial blocks × sessions interaction was significant ($F = 2.84$, $df = 36/1152$, $p < .001$). Essentially the same pattern of results occurred for retest response time data (see Fig. 2), with significant effects due to trial blocks ($F = 15.07$, $df = 9/288$, $p < .001$), sessions ($F = 16.74$, $df = 4/128$, $p < .001$), and the trial blocks × sessions interaction ($F = 5.86$, $df = 36/1152$, $p < .001$). There was no significant difference between the two groups ($p > .10$).

Performance during the initial test series was compared with retest performance for Group 2. Mean percent correct scores were significantly higher during the initial test than during the retest ($F = 7.08$, $df = 1/16$, $p < .025$). In addition to the significant main effects of trial blocks and sessions, the trial blocks × sessions interaction was significant ($F = 5.60$, $df = 36/576$, $p < .001$). This same pattern of results occurred among response time data.

Since Ss were free to switch from one SMU to another during training, the number of SMUs used in each series was examined. In the initial test Ss in Group 1 used a median of 3 SMUs (range, 1–8), as compared with a median of 1 SMU for Group 2 (range, 1–3). The difference between these medians was significant (Mann-Whitney $U = 61.5$, $p < .01$). In addition, Group 2 used a median of 2 SMUs (range, 1–8) during the retest, which was significantly higher than the same group's median on the initial test (Wilcoxon signed-ranks test, $p < .01$).

Because of the difference between groups in the number of SMUs used in the initial test, a comparison was made between the performance of Group 1 following the first appearance of the SMU with which criterion was reached and the initial test performance of Group 2. Such a comparison focused, for both groups, on that stage of training involving principally the criterion SMU, when minimal switching from one unit to another occurred. In Group 1 only the 13 *S*s who reached criterion within 500 trials could be included. For these *S*s, the first trial on which the criterion SMU appeared became, in effect, Trial 1. For Group 2, data from the entire first 3 sessions were included, since only 2 *S*s in this group started with an SMU other than the criterion unit. The results of the comparison are presented in Fig. 3. Analysis of variance revealed no differences between the curves for the two groups.

Discussion

Auditory feedback of the EMG had substantial effects on initial acquisition of SMU control. These effects were immediate, with Group 2 beginning at a performance level of 66% correct while Group 1 started at 21%. The rate of improvement was significantly faster for Group 2 than for Group 1, at least among response time data, which showed a steep rise in the first half of Session 1 for Group 2. Comparable results have been reported by Hefferline, Keenan, and Harford (1959) during operant conditioning of a covert thumb-twitch. As a result of the higher initial level and differential rate of improvement, Group 2 reached asymptote much earlier than did Group 1. Performance for Group 2 had leveled off by the end of Session 1, while asymptote did not occur for Group 1 until Session 4. This pattern was also reflected in trials to criterion scores, with Group 1 requiring, on the average, six times as many trials as did Group 2 to reach criterion.

Performance on the retest with no auditory feedback for either group revealed that, following a 2 week interval, all differences between the two groups had disappeared. This suggests that retention of learning was independent of feedback conditions during original training. It may seem contradictory that the performance of Group 2 was poorer on the retest than on the initial test. However, this was clearly due to withholding auditory feedback in the retest. *S*s in Group 2 performed no differently during the retest than did their counterparts in Group 1, whose performance on the retest was significantly better than on the initial test (Lloyd & Leibrecht, 1971). On the retest, then, Group 2 performed not like naive *S*s but, rather, like *S*s who had received previous training with no auditory feedback. It thus seems clear that both groups learned the same amount during the initial series. Augmented feedback produced only quantitative differences in learning, principally in the form of faster learning. This is perhaps not surprising, since the same performance criterion was applied in both conditions. It does, however, establish the criterion employed as a stable measure of performance which is unaffected by differential feedback conditions. It also establishes that availability of auditory feedback did not appreciably affect the degree to which *S*s learned to use proprioceptive cues in acquiring control of an SMU. Both groups performed nearly identically when relearning with only proprioceptive cues plus the lights.

The latter conclusion regarding the use of proprioceptive cues is supported by informal observations and comments. When asked what strategies they found successful in activating an SMU, Ss in the present study most frequently reported slight flexion of the toes or foot, weak contraction or tightening of the tibialis anterior muscle, or reliance on cutaneous pressure sensations of the foot or ankle. Many Ss appeared to be unaware of the proprioceptive cues involved until queried, a finding which has been reported in other situations involving covert responses (Hefferline, 1958). Basically the same patterns were observed in the earlier study by Lloyd and Leibrecht (1971), where auditory feedback of the EMG was unavailable. The auditory feedback provided in the present study, therefore, did not appear to mask or replace the normal proprioceptive cues. It seems likely, rather, that the information derived from the auditory display of the EMG served to greatly augment that available through proprioceptive channels. A similar interpretation of the effects of augmented feedback has been proposed by Hefferline et al. (1959). The auditory information was more differentiated, perhaps allowing the S to make better use of the proprioceptive information. That is, auditory feedback informed the S not only of whether his current attempt was correct or incorrect, but, if incorrect, in what direction he was erring and by how much. In addition, the auditory feedback was instantaneous, whereas the lights signalling a correct or incorrect response provided feedback which was delayed by the experimenter's reaction time. The deleterious effects of delayed feedback have been well documented and may account for some of the differences in the performance of the two groups.

More definitive information on the role played by auditory feedback was provided by the examination of performance following the first appearance of the criterion SMU in the initial series (Fig. 3). This examination was prompted by the finding that Ss without auditory feedback available used significantly more SMUs during the course of training. When this difference was taken into account by looking principally at the criterion SMU, there were no differences between the two conditions. That is, most, if not all, of the performance differences between the two groups occurred prior to the first appearance of the SMU with which criterion was reached. This fits well with Lloyd and Leibrecht's (1971) suggestion that the early stages of SMU training involve trial and error behavior which leads to selection of the SMU most easily controlled. It would appear that auditory feedback greatly sped up or eliminated this process, since only 2 Ss in Group 2 used more than one SMU during initial training. Auditory feedback had no significant influence on performance once the criterion SMU had been selected.

The effects of auditory feedback of the EMG on acquisition of SMU control can be summarized as follows. Augmented feedback produced only quantitative changes in learning, speed of learning being six times faster with such feedback present. This improved speed of learning resulted from a shortening or elimination of the initial search process which led to selection of an easily controlled SMU. Once the search phase was complete, the influence of auditory feedback was minimal. The nature and amount of learning, including the ability to use proprioceptive cues in controlling an SMU, were not affected, nor was retention of learning. The addition of auditory EMG feedback to the procedure established by Lloyd and Leibrecht (1971), therefore, appears to be a convenient means of providing a less time-consuming paradigm without modifying the basic nature of the learning process.

REFERENCES

Basmajian, J. V., Baeza, M., & Fabrigar, C. Conscious control and training of individual spinal motor neurons in normal human subjects. *Journal of New Drugs,* 1965, *5,* 78–85.

Basmajian, J. V., & Stecko, G. A new bipolar electrode for electromyography. *Journal of Applied Physiology,* 1962, *17,* 849.

Carlsöö, S., & Edfeldt, A. W. Attempts at muscle control with visual and auditory impulses as auxiliary stimuli. *Scandinavian Journal of Psychology,* 1963, *4,* 231–235.

Hefferline, R. F. The role of proprioception in the control of behavior. *Transactions of the New York Academy of Sciences,* 1958, *20,* 739–764.

Hefferline, R. F., Keenan, B., & Harford, R. A. Escape and avoidance conditioning in human subjects without their observation of the response. *Science,* 1959, *130,* 1338–1339.

Harrison, V. F., & Mortensen, O. A. Identification and voluntary control of single motor unit activity in the tibialis anterior muscle. *Anatomical Record,* 1962, *144,* 109–116.

Lloyd, A. J., & Leibrecht, B. C. Conditioning of a single motor unit. *Journal of Experimental Psychology,* 1971, *88,* 391–395.

Wagman, I. H., Pierce, D. S., & Burger, R. E. Proprioceptive influence in volitional control of individual motor units. *Nature,* 1965, *207,* 957–958.

Instrumental Learning Without 12
Proprioceptive Feedback

Inessa B. Koslovskaya, Robert P. Vertes,
and Neal E. Miller

KOSLOVSKAYA, I. B., R. P. VERTES, AND N. E. MILLER. *Instrumental learning without proprioceptive feedback.*
PHYSIOL. BEHAV.10(1) 101–107, 1973. A preliminary technique was developed for studying instrumental motor nerve
conditioning in paralyzed animals. Twelve rats completely paralyzed by d-tubocuarine were trained to change the level of
motor nerve activity while the integrated neurogram served as the motor output. All rats demonstrated the ability to
increase nerve activity when increases were reinforced by electrical stimulation of the brain. Three out of four rats were
able to adjust the level of neural firing to alternating increases and decreases in the criteria for reward. And three out of
four rats showed the ability to produce more activity in the nerve of one leg than in that of the other when a difference in
a specific direction was rewarded.

Motor learning   Curarized animal   Proprioceptive feedback   Instrumental conditioning

THESE experiments were part of a series aimed at testing
the learning ability of the motor system of the skeletal
muscles in the complete absence of kinesthetic feedback.

This problem has been studied for more than 75 years,
starting with the classical experiments of Mott and
Sherrington in 1895 [16]. The results of experiments on
this problem are, however, quite contradictory. In complete
agreement with clinical observations on the necessity of
somatic sensation for the performance of voluntary movements, most of the early studies [2, 12, 16, 20] have shown
that deafferentation renders animals incapable of purposeful movements.

However, in the experiments with monkeys in which the
healthy limb was restricted, the animals were quite capable
of complicated purposeful movements with the
deafferented limb [17]. This observation was supported by
the results of behavioral conditioning experiments performed more recently [7, 9, 19, 21, 22]. In these
experiments, animals given instrumental training were
capable of retaining old habits and even of learning new
motor responses with the deafferented limbs.

[1] Supported by USPHS Research Grant MH 13189.
[2] Exchange Fellow of the Academy of Sciences of USSR, Moscow.
[3] Requests for reprints should be addressed to R. P. Vertes, The Rockefeller University, New York, N. Y. 10021, U.S.A.

In our previous experiments [10, 11] after complete deafferentation of the forelimb, dogs were capable of learning to avoid electric shock by flexing the unseen, deafferented limb; they were not, however, able to learn a sustained avoidance reaction: to hold the limb lifted for a required period of time [11].

However, even in the case of broad deafferentation, there always remains the chance of incomplete blockade or the possibility of utilizing, during learning, information coming through indirect afferent channels, such as those controlling posture and equilibrium.

To eliminate afferent feedback completely, we chose a curarized preparation in which the required response was a change of activity in a peripheral nerve (sciatic) recorded from electrodes hooked around the nerve. Because of the neuromuscular block produced by the curare, this response could in no way affect the skeletal musculature and hence influence the afferent flow of information.

Other investigators using similar preparations have again provided us with conflicting results. Classical conditioning was detected during paralysis caused by crushing the anterior nerve roots [13] and during bulbocapnotic catatonia [1]. In animals paralyzed by *d*-tubocurarine, training during paralysis influenced instrumental responses elicited subsequently in the nonparalyzed state [3, 4, 18]. The negative results obtained in analogous experiments [8, 15] were probably inconclusive because of possible anesthetic effects of the old type of curare that was used.

Gama efferent neurons recorded at the ventral root were classically conditioned in animals under Flaxedil by Buchwald *et al.* [5]. These same researchers later demonstrated that animals subjected to a classical conditioning procedure under Flaxedil showed a much greater propensity to develop a conditioned flexion response in the normal state than animals that were not so pretrained [6].

It has yet to be shown that the instrumental learning (operant conditioning) of a motor nerve response can develop in an animal completely devoid of afferent feedback. If such learning can be demonstrated, the question remains whether the neurons involved are alpha or gamma. If they are alpha motor neurons, then those neurons responsible for movement per se can be operantly conditioned without proprioceptive feedback. If they are gamma motor neurons, then those neurons that prepare and facilitate movement are capable of operant learning under conditions of paralysis, neurons which under similar conditions of paralysis have been classically conditioned [5].

In this paper, we present the results of experiments in which electrical stimulation of the brain (ESB) was used as a reward for changing the rate of firing of the sciatic nerves of animals paralyzed by d-tubocurarine.

GENERAL METHOD

Animals

The animals were 12 adult male albino Sprague-Dawley rats, weighing approximately 350 g. Each animal was stereotaxically implanted with bipolar electrodes in the posterior region of the lateral hypothalamus with flat skull coordinates of 2.5 mm posterior to bregma, 1.5 mm lateral to it and 9.0 mm vertical to the surface of the skull. All animals showed a stable rate of performance (more than 300 responses in 30 min) when pretested for reward in a bar-pressing situation.

Apparatus

Tests for the reinforcing effects of brain stimulation were given in a clear plastic box, 12 in. x 10 in. x 16 in., with a lever elevated 1.5 in. above the floor. The reinforcing stimulus consisted of a train of 0.2 msec square wave pulses delivered at 100 pulses/sec from a Grass stimulator (Model S4) with a Grass stimulus isolation unit (Model SIU-4B) in series. The current, which ranged from 20–100 μA, was adjusted for each rat to a level which produced a strong reward. It remained on as long as the rat held the bar down; in this area the initial effects of stimulation are rewarding, but prolonged ones are aversive.

During sessions under d-tubocurarine, the animal's respiration was maintained artificially by means of a small animal respirator (E. & M. Instrument Co., Model V5KG) at a fixed rate of 70 inspiration-expiration breaths per min and at a pressure of 15–20 cc of water. The neurograms from the common peroneal and sometimes from the tibial nerves were recorded bipolarly by platinum hook electrodes on which the nerves rested. A Tektronix low-level amplifier (Type 122) was used to amplify the signal 100 times. From the preamplifier the signal was simultaneously relayed to a Tektronix 502 dual beam oscilloscope, to provide the recording of raw nerve activity, and to an integrator channel (Model 753A) of a Grass polygraph (Model 7), to display the average value of nerve activity for an integration time of 200 msec. The level of averaged nerve activity taken from the output of the driver amplifier served as the response which triggered the reinforcement circuit composed of a Schmitt trigger and standard relay equipment programmed so that a set level of activity could be determined and reinforced. As long as the level of the integrated neurogram exceeded the criterion level, ESB was delivered to the animal. The EMG was recorded with needle electrodes placed into the biceps and triceps of the animal's left forelimb. Body temperature was continuously monitored by means of a Telethermometer (Yellowsprings Instrument Co.). In complete agreement with Miller and DiCara [14], we found that a constant heart rate (420–450 beats per min) and a constant high temperature (not less than 38°C) were most reliable signs of a good condition in the preparation.

Procedure

On the day before the recording session, the rat was anesthetized with Nembutal. His hind limbs were opened and both sciatic nerves and their main branches (common peroneal and tibial nerves) were freed from the surrounding tissues so as to make them accessible for recording (Fig. 1). After the surgery, the edges of the skin were clamped together.

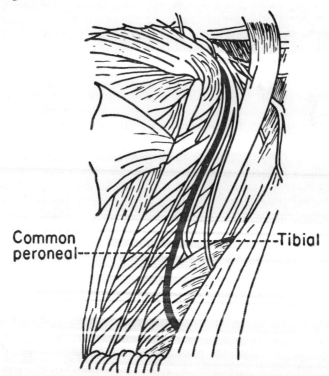

FIG. 1. A. Lateral aspect of the left thigh dissected to show the common peroneal and tibial nerves, from which the recordings were made. Taken from *The Anatomy of the Rat* by E. C. Greene (1959).

On the day of the recording session the animals were retested in the bar-pressing situation to determine that the previous day's operation had not had any adverse effect on posterior limb movement (i.e., damage to the sciatic nerve) and that the rewarding properties of the ESB remained intact. If no adverse effect was observed, the experiment was begun. The subjects were injected intraperitoneally with 0.3 to 0.4 ml of a 3 mg/ml solution of d-tubocurarine chloride (Squibb), sufficient to maintain complete paralysis of the rat for approximately 1 hr. Subsequent doses of 0.2 ml were given every 30 min.

The animals were fitted with a small face mask that was connected to the respirator as described in Miller and DiCara [14]. Heart and EMG electrodes and the rectal thermometer were inserted. After all measures (heart rate, respiration, temperature) indicated that the animals were in good condition, the skin and tissue around the wounds were injected with Xylocaine, and the nerves were reexposed and placed on the platinum electrodes. Skin around the nerve was lifted up and clamped to a metal ring to form a cavity that was filled with warm mineral oil to protect the nerve.

After these preparations were completed, the animals were given 30–40 min of rest. At the end of the rest period a neurogram of very low amplitude (not exceeding 5–10 μV) was usually recorded with spontaneous bursts of 10–15 μV in amplitude, as illustrated respectively by traces A and B in Fig. 2, lasting 5–20 sec and occurring with a frequency of 1–4 bursts per min. However, if rats were suddenly aroused by approach, touch, bright light, or loud noise, high amplitude activity of 30–40 μV occurred and lasted 2–3 sec.

The first part of every experiment consisted in the shaping of the response to increase the magnitude of spontaneous nerve activity. The shaping was accomplished by first rewarding spontaneous bursts of low amplitude and then demanding bursts of ever increasing amplitude. In animals in which spontaneous bursts did not occur, activity initially aroused by touch or noise was rewarded until spontaneous bursts did occur. Shaping was continued until the subject was able by itself to maintain self-stimulation rates, producing bursts of the amplitude required by the criterion. During shaping, the magnitude of the bursts usually was increased by 2.5–3 times, reaching 35–40 μV; however, in some preparations it could be brought up to 75 μV (traces C and D of Fig. 2). After shaping, the criteria for reward were changed in a way corresponding to the conditions of Experiments 1, 2, and 3 which involved, respectively, training to a certain level, training to different levels, or training to different levels of activity in the nerves of the two sides. Student's *t*-test was used for all analyses of data.

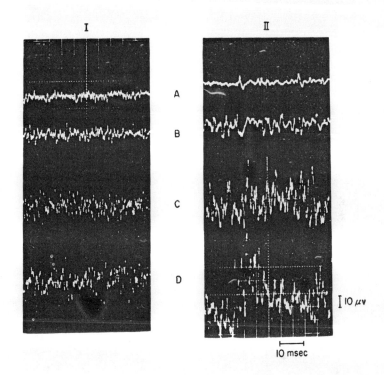

FIG. 2. Neurograms of the peroneal nerves of two curarized rats at different states of the experiments. A and B show the neurograms at the beginning of training; C and D represent activity at the middle and the end of training.

EXPERIMENT 1: INCREASE IN LEVEL

In this experiment, four rats were trained to increase their level of activity. Similar training was also given to the rats in Experiments 2 and 3 during the first, or shaping, part of those experiments.

Special Procedure

The procedure consisted of the following periods: 20–30 min of training; 10–15 min of extinction, during which bursts of neural activity were no longer followed by ESB; and a final 15–20 min of retraining with reward for high neural activity.

The activity of the sciatic nerve during every fifth min of each of the intervals mentioned above was analyzed to determine the frequency of occurrence of criterion response (causing ESB to be delivered) per min, the average length of time between two successive criterion responses, and the duration of each criterion response. When the record was not quite 20 min long, every fourth min was analyzed in order to yield a total of 4 points.

Results

The results of the experiment showed that all the rats, when rewarded by ESB for as long as they remained above the criterion, were able in the paralyzed state to produce rhythmical bursts of nerve activity of a relatively standard length and amplitude, as illustrated during the twenty-first min of training in Fig. 3. The frequency and duration of the bursts varied from rat to rat, just as did the frequency and duration of holding down the bar by the free moving rats. However, two main patterns of response could be distinguished in the neurograms of the paralyzed rats: a low frequency pattern of 5–6 bursts per min with each burst lasting 2–3 sec, and a high frequency pattern of 25–37 bursts per min with each burst lasting only 0.2–0.8 sec. Usually these two parameters of performance were negatively correlated.

During extinction periods, when ESB was omitted, intervals between bursts progressively lengthened, the amplitude of the bursts decreased, and the overall neurogram activity returned to the pretraining level, as shown in the last sequence of Fig. 3.

Results of the various procedures are summarized in histogram form in Fig. 4, which shows the clear-cut differences in the amount of time the neurogram activity was above the criterion level in the different parts of the experiment. When high amplitude activity was reinforced (during the periods of initial training and of retraining after extinction), each of the animals displayed significant increases in the overall duration of activity above the criterion level ($p < 0.001$ for rats 2.13, 2.24, 2.28 and < 0.01 for rat 2.29). During the extinction period, when ESB was omitted, the duration of such activity declined below that at the end of training ($p < 0.001$). To reinstate learning, two out of four rats needed to be reshaped by reinforcing responses evoked by touch or noise. All of them showed reliable increases ($p < 0.01$).

That the foregoing results represent true learning is demonstrated by controls inherent in the following two additional experiments.

EXPERIMENT 2: DIFFERENT LEVELS

The purpose of this experiment was to study the ability of the paralyzed rats to change the amplitude of their neurograms appropriately as the criterion was shifted to different low and high levels.

Special Procedure

Four additional rats were first shaped to perform at a high level by the procedures that have already been described in GENERAL METHOD. Then they were given training consisting of four or more alternating periods of reward for low, high, low, and high levels of activity. Each change to a new level was performed gradually and reward was administered immediately upon achievement of the criterion level of activity.

Results

One of the rats failed to learn. The results of the three rats who did succeed in the different levels procedure are summarized in Fig. 5. It can be seen that in each case an increase or a decrease in the criterion level produced a corresponding, significant change in neural activity. This result controls for any general activating effect of the ESB which could conceivably account for an increase in neural activity during training but scarcely for one that was larger when the criterion for reward was made more difficult and smaller when it was made easier.

Further analysis of the performance showed that the different paralyzed rats solved the task in different ways. Rat 5.23 responded to changes in the required level by a shift in the absolute magnitude of each specific response, from 15 μV when exposed to a low-level criterion to almost 100 μV when a high-level criterion was introduced ($p > 0.001$). Rat 6.23 gave, under each condition, a rather standard size of response, changing mainly the baseline level of activity so that under the demands of a high criterion the standard sized response still could reach it ($p < 0.001$). Rat 5.22 changed his baseline in response to the first increase required ($p < 0.001$), but with further increase in criterion also changed the magnitude of response ($p < 0.001$).

With the increase in the magnitude of the responses, their duration usually also increased and their frequency decreased. With increase only in magnitude, as in Rat 5.23, one might say that the rat had merely learned to keep increasing his level of neural activity until he achieved the criterion with the ESB terminating further increases, much

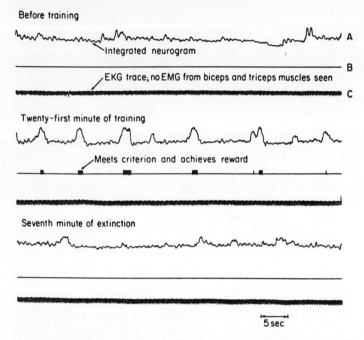

Before training

Integrated neurogram

EKG trace; no EMG from biceps and triceps muscles seen

Twenty-first minute of training

Meets criterion and achieves reward

Seventh minute of extinction

5 sec

FIG. 3. Sample records of integrated neurogram of rat No. 2.27. Three sample min illustrate different stages of learning: before training, the twenty-first min of training; and the seventh min of extinction. Trace A shows the integrated neurogram. Trace B marks the time of activity above the criteria and, hence, reward. Trace C records ECG and EMG. Notice the absence of EMG activity due to the curarization.

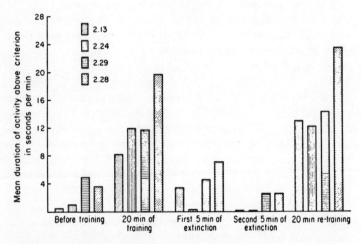

FIG. 4. Mean durations of the activity above criteria at different periods of experiments. Column 1, 2, 3, 4 represent the activity of different rats.

A

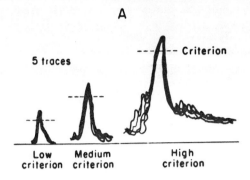

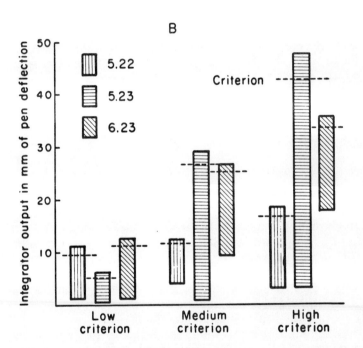

FIG. 5. A. Superimposed traces of 5 successive bursts of an integrated neurogram of Rat 5.23 during low, medium, and high criterion intervals. The solid and broken lines indicate, respectively, the levels of baseline activity and of criterion. B. Mean amplitudes of integrated bursts of three successful rats during low, medium, and high criterion intervals, shown in mm of pen deflection. The tops of histograms represent peak value of bursts; the bottoms reflect changes in baseline activity. 5 mm of pen deflection correspond to 10 μV changes in the neurogram.

as a person might pull harder and harder at a sticking door until it opened. Or perhaps the rat even had an innate tendency to perform in this way once he had learned to fire his nerve in order to secure reward. But the two cases in which the baseline changed must have involved, in addition to this, some real memory traces because the changed activity induced by the changed criterion persisted between bursts, when the ESB was not present as an immediate cue.

EXPERIMENT 3: DIFFERENTIAL RESPONSE IN TWO NERVES

In the preceding experiments the curarized rats showed a high synchrony of the activity of the nerves to the two legs, which suggests that a general, nonspecific activation, perhaps a struggling response, had been learned. The purpose of this experiment was to study the ability of the paralyzed animals to learn specific differential activity in the two nerves.

Special Procedure

The outputs of the integrated activity from the symmetrical nerves on the two sides were recorded separately as usual but also put into a bridge circuit which, in turn, yielded an output proportional to the algebraic difference between the two activities. This differential output with appropriate sign (indicating which of the two nerves had to be the more active) was used to activate a Schmitt trigger when the difference in the appropriate direction reached a criterion magnitude.

Four additional rats were used in this series. Gains in the two recording channels were adjusted to yield approximately equal signals from the two nerves. The training to differential levels of response by the two nerves started, after completion of the usual period of shaping described in GENERAL METHOD, with rewarding of small spontaneous differences in the direction of the nerve that had not been rewarded during this initial shaping. As the rat learned, the criterion was gradually increased, until greater differences in the correct direction were achieved.

After the rats had learned to respond with greater activity in the selected nerve, reversal training was given in the same way, to show the rat's ability to learn a greater activity in the opposite nerve.

Results

One of the four rats failed to learn a differential response. The other three paralyzed rats demonstrated a highly reliable ability to learn to differentiate the activity of the two nerves when rewarded for doing so. This differential learning is an additional control for any sensitizing or generally activating effects of the brain stimulation used as a reward.

Figure 6 shows the process of initial and reversal training for rat 3.28. The record displays superimposed traces of the integrated responses from each of the two nerves during each of the specified minutes of training. As illustrated on the left, during initial training the increase in differences between the two sides was achieved by this rat mainly by suppressing the activity of the nonrewarded nerve without changing the activity of the rewarded one. However, when the reversal procedure was introduced, as shown on the right side of Fig. 6, the behavior in the previously inhibited nerve increased while that in the previously rewarded one gradually decreased.

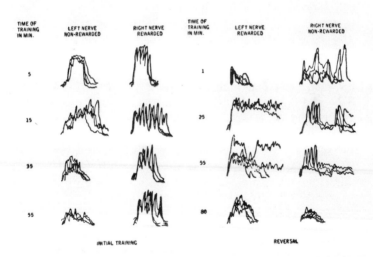

FIG. 6. Superimposed traces of 5 successive bursts of an integrated neurogram of the right and left peroneal nerves of the rat at the end of 4 successive intervals of training to differentiate activities of the two sides. The left side of the figure shows the initial training when the difference favoring the activity of the right nerve was rewarded. The right side of the figure demonstrates the effects of reversal training.

The results on all of the rats used in this experiment are summarized in Fig. 7. As illustrated in Part A, which represents the averages of the ratio of activity of the two nerves during initial and reversal training periods, at the beginning of training the ratio of the activity of the rewarded to the nonrewarded nerve was approximately 1 but with training it increased to approximately 3. During reversal training the ratio of the activity of the same two nerves rapidly dropped to approximately 1 and then gradually decreased to zero, as their roles were reversed.

Part B of Fig. 7 shows the average activity of each nerve for each of the four rats during the five successive stages of training, the first three of which were original training and the last two reversal training. It clearly shows that in a 40–50 min period of initial training, each of the rats would clearly suppress the activity on the nonreinforced nerve without to a great extent changing the activity of the reinforced side, which slightly increased in the neurogram of Rat 3.27, did not change in Rat 3.21, and even slightly decreased in Rats 3.07 and 3.28. However, when the reversal procedure was tested, the activity of the previously suppressed nerve increased, reaching the pretraining level in Rat 3.27 and even exceeding it in Rats 3.21 and 3.28 The activity of the nonrewarded nerves in Rats 3.21, 3.27 and 3.28 gradually decreased so that there was a clear-cut difference in the activity at the end of the original training between rewarded and nonrewarded nerves in Rats 3.28, 3.27 and 3.21 ($p < 0.001$ in each case), which was reversed at the end of reversal training ($p < 0.001$, < 0.01 and n.s. respectively). Rat 3.07 always gave a larger response with the right than with the left nerve and hence failed to show clear-cut evidence of learning a differential response.

GENERAL DISCUSSION

The results of our experiments showed that the complete block of kinesthetic feedback does not eliminate the ability for instrumental learning by motor neurons. Twelve rats trained while paralyzed by d-tubocurarine increased the amplitude of their neurograms when increases were rewarded by electrical stimulation of the brain.

In experiments involving additional training, three out of four rats were able to adjust the level of neural firing to alternating increases and decreases in the level of the criterion for reward. Finally, three out of four rats showed the ability to learn to produce more activity in one nerve

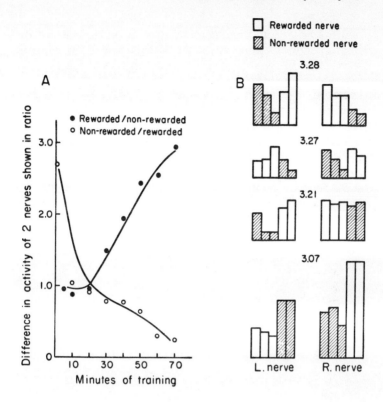

FIG. 7. A. Mean ratio of the burst activity of the rewarded nerves versus nonrewarded during differential training as a function of training time averaged for 4 experimental rats. The initial training is represented by closed circles, the reversal by opened circles. The area covered by activity above the baseline (like that represented in Figs. 5A and 6) was counted in mm^2 per min, indicated on the ordinate. B. Mean burst activity per min of 4 experimental rats during differential training averaged for 5 min of each of the represented periods of initial and reversal training. Rewarded nerves are indicated by white, non rewarded by black. Heights of histograms show the value of the burst activity counted, as in the previous figure, in mm^2 per min.

than in the other when a difference in a specific direction was reinforced.

So our results agree with those of previous investigators who, using instrumental procedures, have demonstrated learning ability under the somewhat less rigorous conditions of removing the kinesthetic feedback by deafferentation [2, 11, 19, 21, 22]. Using a classical conditioning procedure, Buchwald *et al.* [5, 6] secured conditioning of gamma neurons in deeply paralyzed animals. It is possible that our instrumental learning involved fibers from such neurons. Further work will be needed to determine which types of fibers were involved in our case. In experiments soon to be reported, we found that we could produce only transient classical conditioning, which might be interpreted as no stable learning at all, at the deep level of paralysis that we used in the present study, but that as soon as the level of paralysis was reduced to the point where EMG activity began to appear, consistent classical conditioning could be secured. This result raises the possibility that our technique was recording the activity of alpha fibers which can be trained by instrumental but not by classical conditioning techniques.

REFERENCES

1. Beck, E. C. and R. W. Doty. Conditioned reflexes acquired during combined catelepsy and deafferentation. *J. comp. physiol. Psychol.* 50: 211–216, 1957.
2. Biekel, A. Untersuchungen über den Mechanismus der nervosen Bewegung Regulation. *Pflügers Arch.* 67: 299–344, 1897.
3. Black, A. H. The extinction of avoidance responses under curare. *J. comp. physiol. Psychol.* 51: 519–524, 1958.
4. Black, A. H. Transfer following operant conditioning in the curarized dog. *Science* 155: 201–203, 1967.
5. Buchwald, J. and E. Eldred. Conditioned responses in the gamma efferent system. *J. nerv. ment. Dis.* 132: 146–152, 1961.
6. Buchwald, J. S., M. Standish, E. Eldred and E. S. Halas. Contribution of muscle spindle circuits to learning as suggested by training under Flaxedil. *Electroenceph. clin. Neurophysiol.* 16: 582–594, 1964.
7. Gorska, T. and E. Yankowska. The effect of deafferentation on instrumental (type II) conditioned reflexes in dogs. *Acta Biol. Exp.* 21: 219–234, 1961.
8. Harlow, H. F. and R. Stagner. Effect of complete striate muscle paralysis upon the learning process. *J. exp. Psychol.* 16: 283–294, 1933.
9. Knapp, H. D., E. Taub and A. J. Berman. Movements in monkeys with deafferented forelimbs. *Expl. Neurol.* 7: 303–315, 1963.
10. Koslovskaya, I. B., R. L. Gasanova and N. G. Ivanova. The functional organization of complex forms of avoidance reflexes. *Proc. XVIII Int. Congr. Psychol. Moscow, 1966* , pp. 118–122.
11. Koslovskaya, I. B., A. V. Ovsjannikoff and R. L. Gasanova. Avoidance conditioning after deafferentation of the operant limb. *Proc. XXI Meeting on the Problem of Higher Nervous Activity, Leningrad, 1966*, pp. 149–150.

12. Lassek, A. M. Inactivation of voluntary motor function following rhizotomy. *J. Neuropath. exp. Neurol.* **12:** 83–87, 1953.
13. Light, J. S. and W. H. Gantt. Essential part of reflex arc for establishment of conditioned reflex. *J. comp. Psychol.* **21:** 19–36, 1936.
14. Miller, N. E. and L. V. DiCara. Instrumental learning of heart rate changes in curarized rats. *J. comp. physiol. Psychol.* **63:** 12–19, 1967.
15. Morgan, C. T. The psychophysiology of learning. In: *Handbook of Experimental Psychology,* edited by S. S. Stevens. New York: Wiley, 1951, pp. 770–772.
16. Mott, F. W. and C. S. Sherrington. Experiments upon influence of sensory nerves upon movement and nutrition of the limbs. *Proc. R. Soc. Lond.,* 57: 481–488, 1895.
17. Munk, H. *Über die Funktionen von Hirn und Rüchenmark.* Berlin, 1909.
18. Solomon, R. L. and L. H. Turner. Discriminative classical conditioning in dogs paralyzed by curare can later control discriminative avoidance response in the normal state. *Psychol. Rev.* 69: 202–219, 1962.
19. Taub, E., R. C. Bacon and A. J. Berman. Acquisition of a trace-conditioned avoidance response after deafferentation of the responding limb. *J. comp. physiol. Psychol.* 59: 275–279, 1965.
20. Twitchell, T. E. Sensory factor in purposive movements. *J. Neurophysiol.* 17: 239–254, 1954.
21. Yankowska, E. Ruchowe instrumentalne odruchy warunkowe deafferentowaney konezyny u kotow. *Acta physiol. Pol. (Warszawa)* 8: 360–366, 1957.
22. Yankowska, E. Instrumental scratch reflex of the deafferented limb in cats and rats. *Acta Biol. exp. (Warszawa)* 19: 233–242, 1959.

ELECTROENCEPHALOGRAPHIC CONTROL

Visual Effects on Alpha 13
Feedback Training

David A. Paskewitz and Martin T. Orne

Abstract. *Presenting an audible indication of subjects' electroencephalographic alpha activity under conditions of dim ambient illumination led to systematic increases in alpha density, while in total darkness the same procedure did not. These results support the view that feedback training can be clearly demonstrated only when factors leading to a suppression of alpha activity are present in the environment.*

Much of the current interest in electroencephalographic (EEG) alpha activity centers around the apparent ability of individuals to learn volitional augmentation of alpha densities in their EEG. Kamiya (1) and Mulholland (2) have independently demonstrated that providing a subject with feedback concerning the presence or absence of his own EEG alpha activity makes it possible for him to alter the amount of such activity seen in the record. In addition, it has been suggested that volitional increases in alpha density lead to changes in subjective mood (3, 4), and it has even been proposed that feedback techniques may be useful as a means of "mapping the subjective space of consciousness" (5).

The effects of feedback training usually have been demonstrated in one of two ways, both of which contain inherent methodological shortcomings. The first procedure involves comparing periods during which subjects are instructed to maximize alpha density with similar periods when they are instructed to minimize density. Although it is easy to demonstrate differences between periods when subjects are instructed to produce alpha activity and periods when they are instructed to block it, such differences rarely reflect symmetrical increases and decreases. Usually subjects learn to block alpha activity volitionally within one or two trials, and impressive differences with this procedure tend to be the result of unidirectional rather than bidirectional control.

The second procedure involves comparing initial baseline levels with the higher densities seen after training. Such a comparison more appropriately

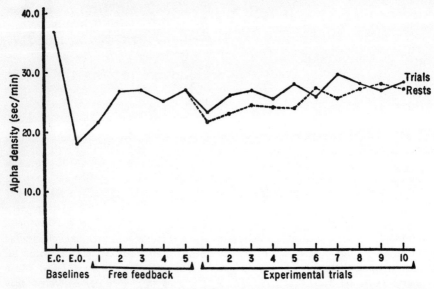

Fig. 1. Average alpha densities for several segments of the first day with total darkness. All points are averaged over nine subjects, with eyes-closed (*E.C.*) and eyes-open (*E.O.*) baselines averaged over 3 minutes and trials averaged over 2 minutes. The alpha density is expressed as the number of seconds that alpha activity is present in the EEG per minute.

of these effects is different from what is usually described in alpha feedback training. It furthermore appears that subjects had approached their asymptotic density during the initial orientation period. The subjects exhibit a non-significant maximum further increase of 7.2 percent from their highest single minute during the orientation period to the highest density reached during any of the ten trials where subjects were instructed to maximize alpha density ($t = 1.81$, $P > .10$). Although in the group data the resting levels tended to be below trial levels, these differences were not significant.

Within the first session, subjects' highest trial densities were significantly lower than their initial eyes-closed baseline densities ($t = 2.46$, $P < .05$). When both trial and resting averages are examined for all six sessions, with an analysis of variance repeated measures design, none of the differences are significant (trials: $F = 0.19$, $P > .20$; rest: $F = 0.05$, $P > .20$), and the largest difference between any two trial averages is only about 4 seconds of alpha activity in a minute. The trial average for the sixth session was not greater than the level of alpha density reached during the third minute of the orientation feedback period ($t = 0.35$, $P > .20$).

These findings contrast with data reported by others, which imply large increases in alpha density as a consequence of alpha feedback training. We had previously proposed that subjects in the alpha feedback situation are involved in overcoming factors which normally exert an inhibitory influence on alpha activity (7), and we reasoned, therefore, that the lack of consistent increases beyond 2 minutes in our subjects when run in total darkness may well have stemmed from the relative absence of inhibitory stimuli in the situation, especially visual stimuli which addresses the question whether individuals can learn to augment their level of alpha activity significantly. It then, however, becomes crucial to specify the nature of the baseline level from which increases can be measured. Novelty and apprehension are known to depress the subject's initial alpha density during baseline determination, but as factors such as these dissipate, one tends to see a spontaneously rising baseline. To attempt to follow such a rising baseline, however, through the use of resting periods, interspersed throughout the training sessions as "floating" baselines, does not permit separation of the effects of feedback training from those increases which are due to changes in arousal or motivation; for the subject, definition of a period as a rest period produces changes in both motivation and arousal.

The present report is intended to help clarify the circumstances under which subjects are able to learn to augment alpha density and shed light on some of the possible mechanisms involved. Specifically, we were concerned with determining whether subjects could learn to significantly exceed the alpha density of their own baseline obtained under optimal circumstances. Because of the known overriding influence of visual stimulation on alpha activity (2), the first study was conducted in total darkness, although to lessen the likelihood of their falling asleep subjects were instructed to keep their eyes open throughout the experiment. Prior to the actual experiment, every effort was made to reassure the subjects and make certain that they were comfortable and understood the equipment and procedures. Nine paid volunteer college students served as subjects, and were recruited for an experiment in "the control of physiological responses." The subjects were given six training ses-

sions, approximately 1 week apart. The monopolar occipital (O_2) to right mastoid EEG signals were recorded on a Beckman polygraph and filtered with step-function cutoffs at 8 and 12 hz (6). Although the amplitude levels necessary to trigger the feedback stimulus were set in discrete 5-μv steps from 10 to 25 μv for a given subject, depending on initial levels of alpha density, the data used in this report were collected by using an invariant threshold of 15 μv for all subjects. Each session consisted of (i) two 3-minute baseline periods, (ii) a 5-minute orientation period during which feedback was provided and subjects were encouraged to experiment, and (iii) ten trials of 2 minutes each, alternated with 1-minute rest periods. The presence of alpha activity raised the pitch of a feedback stimulus tone from 280 to 360 cycles per second, and activated a clock, the output of which recorded alpha density in seconds per minute. The subjects were instructed that during the trials they should keep the higher (alpha) tone on as much of the time as possible. The absence of any tone served to signal a rest period. At the beginning of each rest period a digital display was illuminated briefly to give the subject a cumulative total of his alpha activity for each trial, and the subject was required to repeat the total out loud.

An examination of the results for the first session, as shown in Fig. 1, reveals that although subjects' initially high alpha activity was decreased markedly by opening their eyes in total darkness, they had recovered much of this drop by the middle of the initial 5-minute orientation period when the feedback tones were first available to the subjects. These increases occurred within 2 or 3 minutes, without volitional effort. Whether they represent true learning or adaptation is unclear, but the rapidity

Mulholland and Peper have emphasized as primary influences on alpha activity (*2, 8*). Another group of seven subjects was therefore placed in the same training situation with auditory feedback and exposed to the identical procedure used with the previous group, adding only the presence of dim ambient light.

The results for these subjects are shown in Fig. 2A. With this new group, the same drop from eyes-closed to eyes-open baseline is evident. The recovery during the free orientation period preceding the trials is not, however, as great as that seen in darkness. Unlike the earlier group, this second group tested in ambient light exhibited alpha activity during trial periods which was significantly higher than that seen during resting periods ($t = 4.33$, $P < .01$) and, furthermore, densities increased beyond the orientation period, as evidenced in a significant 96.8 percent increase in densities from the highest minute during the free orientation period to a subject's highest trial density ($t = 4.06$, $P < .01$).

Figure 2A resembles some of the reported findings (*1, 3, 9*), showing clearcut increases in alpha density with training. These data would, of course, be even more impressive if the initial eyes-closed baseline were not included in the graph. Most previous reports on the effects of alpha feedback have shown little in the way of such a baseline, and have not considered the possible effects of ambient light.

The significance of the presence of light is seen most clearly by comparing the absence of continuing augmentation in the original group of subjects, run for six sessions in total darkness, with the same group's response during a single session in the presence of dim ambient light. Eight of the original nine subjects were presented with the identical auditory feedback procedure they had previously experienced, with only dim ambient light added. The results for this original group, during their seventh session, the first session with light in the room, are shown in Fig. 2B. Recovery from the initial drop takes place slowly, and a significant increase of 55.7 percent was evident from subjects' highest minute during the orientation period to their highest trial density ($t = 3.04$, $P < .02$). The difference between trial and resting averages was significant ($t = 2.47$, $P < .05$).

Tests between the results of the first session in total darkness and the subsequent session with dim ambient light indicate that the session with light for those same subjects was significantly different, both in trial averages ($t = 9.11$, $P < .001$) and resting averages ($t = 5.57$, $P < .001$), from their performance in darkness. The session with light for the independent group of subjects also differed significantly from the session in total darkness, both in trial averages ($t = 1.96$, $P < .10$) and resting averages ($t = 2.64$, $P < .05$). No significant differences exist between the two sessions with light.

Though there may have been some effects of alpha feedback training for six sessions in the dark, the data appear to indicate that the response of the two groups of subjects to alpha feedback training is more alike in the presence of light than the responses of one of those groups with and without the presence of dim light.

The significant differences in the relative level of resting alpha densities between light and dark conditions are probably a function of the fact that light allows the subject to engage in visual scanning during the resting periods, in contrast to the limited scanning possible in total darkness. These results help to explain the discrepancy between Kamiya's findings (*1*), which showed resting periods at about the same level as during the trial periods, and Brown's

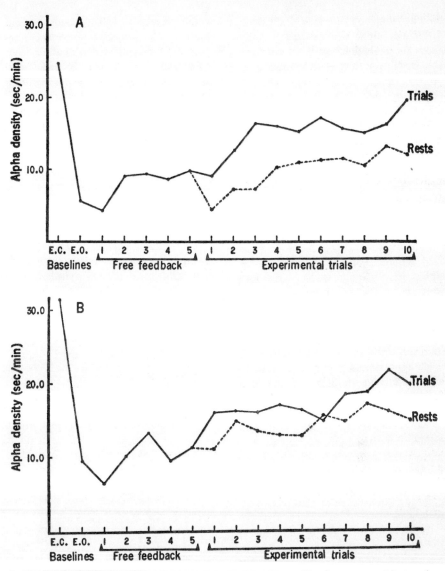

Fig. 2. (A) Average alpha densities for the first day with the seven subjects who began with dim light. (B) Average alpha densities for the seventh day with eight subjects from the original group, their first day with dim light. In both cases, eyes-closed (*E.C.*) and eyes-open (*E.O.*) baselines are averaged over 3 minutes, the free feedback period over 5 minutes, and individual trials over 2 minutes.

results (3), where subjects exhibited resting levels significantly lower than those seen during feedback. Kamiya used an auditory feedback stimulus, and usually had subjects close their eyes. Brown, in contrast, used a visual stimulus, a procedure which necessitated the subjects' keeping their eyes open in a lighted room.

The popular view that alpha feedback

training somehow permits individuals to increase alpha densities significantly above those obtained during a comfortable baseline with eyes closed in a nondrowsy, relaxed state cannot be supported by our data. Indeed, despite many training sessions, we have failed to note any individuals whose capacities for producing alpha activity were altered by the feedback procedure. What does seem clear, however, is that alpha feedback training can lead to large and significant changes in alpha densities when conditions have lowered alpha density below the levels seen spontaneously under optimal conditions. Subjects can acquire volitional control over alpha activity only under conditions which normally lead to decreased densities. Thus, during the initial orientation in the dark, when subjects experiment, but are not especially set to increase alpha density, they achieve a level approximating the level reached with additional training. In the light condition, however, there are marked volitional increases. In spite of these increases, however, in the three procedures reported here, as well as during a number of other procedures run in our laboratory, we have not seen alpha densities beyond an individual's initially demonstrated normal physiological range.

While ambient light is sufficient in the present studies to act as a suppressing stimulus, it is likely that other stimuli such as anxiety or physical stress may, in some circumstances, also lead to suppression which persists. Although no increases in alpha density are seen when the situation presents few suppressing stimuli, alpha feedback training may enable a subject to overcome suppressing effects when they are present. The subjective experiences reported to be associated with alpha feedback training (*3, 4*) may be understood as a consequence of acquiring skill in disregarding stimuli in the external and, perhaps, internal environment which would ordinarily inhibit alpha activity. Increased alpha densities, then, may best be viewed not as an end in themselves, but as one convenient index of a subject's ability to acquire this skill.

DAVID A. PASKEWITZ
MARTIN T. ORNE
Unit for Experimental Psychiatry,
Institute of the Pennsylvania Hospital,
and *University of Pennsylvania,*
111 North 49 Street,
Philadelphia 19139

References and Notes

1. J. Kamiya, in *Altered States of Consciousness: A Book of Readings*, C. T. Tart, Ed. (Wiley, New York, 1969), p. 507.
2. T. Mulholland, *Activ. Nerv. Super.* **10**, 410 (1968).
3. B. B. Brown, *Psychophysiology* **6**, 442 (1970).
4. D. P. Nowlis and J. Kamiya, *ibid.*, p. 476.
5. J. Stoyva and J. Kamiya, *Psychol. Rev.* **75**, 192 (1968).
6. D. A. Paskewitz, *Psychophysiology* **8**, 107 (1971).
7. ———, J. J. Lynch, M. T. Orne, J. G. Costello, *ibid.* **6**, 637 (1970); J. J. Lynch and D. A. Paskewitz, *J. Nerv. Ment. Dis.* **153**, 205 (1971).
8. T. Mulholland and E. Peper, *Psychophysiology* **8**, 556 (1971).
9. J. T. Hart, *ibid.* **4**, 506 (1968).
10. We thank our colleagues H. D. Cohen, M. R. Cook, F. J. Evans, C. Graham, R. Hufgard, F. Mural, E. C. Orne, S. F. Pilato, J. W. Powell, L. L. Pyles, and D. S. Roby for comments, criticisms, and technical assistance during the course of this research and the preparation of this report. The research reported here was supported in part by the Advanced Projects Agency of the Department of Defense and was monitored by the Office of Naval Research under contract N00014-70-C-0350 to the San Diego State College Foundation. Reprint requests should be sent to M.T.O.

15 January 1973; revised 18 April 1973　∎

Alpha Rhythm Percentage 14
Maintained During 4- and 12- Hour
Feedback Periods

Quentin R. Regestein, Vernon Pegram, Brigitte Cook, and Doris Bradley

This experiment used Kamiya's feedback method (1) to induce electroencephelographic (EEG) alpha rhythm in experimental subjects. We first selected naturally high alpha subjects from a five hour conditioning procedure and subsequently reinforced high and then low amounts of alpha rhythm in them during two separate 12-hour periods. We had no idea whether the production and maintenance of either alpha rhythm or nonalpha EEG activity over such a prolonged period was possible, or which of these functions might prove more difficult for high alpha subjects. Therefore, the purpose of this study was to determine, amongst selected high alpha subjects, how much alpha time they could produce during extended conditioning sessions and to observe the effects of maintaining either alpha or nonalpha EEG activity.

METHODS

Thirty-one subjects were secured through a newspaper advertisement and word of mouth. The respondents were instructed to eat a large breakfast, to have no oily preparations on their scalps, to arrive promptly at 8:15 A.M., and they were told that the whole procedure would take 5 hours. The subjects were paid $2.50 for each hour they could produce alpha (alpha hour). Nine of the subjects were not paid in order to determine the relative reinforcing property of monetary reward.

*Peter Bent Brigham Hospital, Boston.

†Neurosciences Program, University of Alabama Medical School, Birmingham.

‡6571st Aeromedical Research Laboratory Holloman Air Force Base, New Mexico.

This study was conducted at the 6571st Aeromedical Research Laboratory, Holloman Air Force Base, New Mexico.

Received for publication April 3, 1972, final version received August 10, 1972.

Address for reprint requests: Quentin R. Regestein, M.D., Peter Bent Brigham Hospital, 721 Huntington Avenue, Boston, Massachusetts, 02115.

From the original pool of 31 subjects, 7 of the highest alpha producers were selected for a second phase of the experiment which required two 12 hour sessions of biofeedback conditioning. They were rewarded at $5–10 per alpha hour, depending on our budget. This study was part of a sleep experiment, to be reported subsequently, which required all subjects to sleep 5 nights in the laboratory and maintain their normal daily schedules except between the 4th and 5th night when they were required to spend 12 hours (8:00 A.M.–8:00 P.M.) producing alpha. After a two week period these same subjects were asked to return to the lab under the same experimental conditions and were then paid for producing nonalpha hours as a control for the 12 hours of confinement. Because the period between the initial 5-hour session and the subsequent 12-hour session took longer than the time many of our transient subjects stayed in the area, two subjects lack the 5-hour session, and the subject with the highest alpha index lacks the 12-hour control (non-alpha) period.

During the conditioning of alpha each subject was wired with Beckman bipotential microelectrodes attached in bipolar parietal-occipital pairs, P3–O1 and P4–O2, and a ground electrode placed between a bifrontal pair, which were used to determine eye

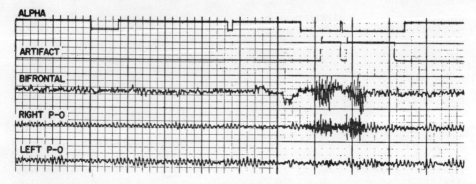

Fig. 1. The top trace is the alpha detector, with a downward deflection indicating the nonalpha condition. This condition can exist when the subject stops alpha production, as on the left and middle portions of this recording, and in an artifact condition as seen on the right side of this recording. The bifrontal leads are used to indicate movement artifact, and the parietal-occipital (P-O) pairs are used to determine the presence or absence of alpha.

movements. During the biofeedback experiments, EEG signals were taken from one of the P–0 lead pairs and frontal pairs and transmitted via a Signatron telemetry unit to a band pass filter set in the 8–13-Hz range and then to an alpha detector. This device consisted of a twin tee type 8–13-Hz band pass filter with a center frequency of 9.5 Hz, in combination with an envelope detector, consisting of a half-wave rectifier and an RC filter. The resulting signal fed a threshold detector with preset hysteresis. This circuit output was recorded as an on-off square-wave trace on one Grass channel, according to when activity in this range exceeded the preset level.

This level correlated with the alpha rhythm as determined by the investigator visually scanning the EEG, and was controlled by a gain adjustment on the subcarrier discriminator. At the beginning of any conditioning trial, the operator would simply note when alpha rhythm appeared on the EEG, and set the discriminator gain such that the detector output correlated with alpha activity. One setting was sufficient for the whole trial. An example of detector output is seen in Figure 1, where an approximately 0.4 second lag period lies between the appearance and disappearance of the alpha rhythm and the turning on and off of the alpha detector. Calibration on 6 subjects revealed that the operator set the alpha-detector such that it turned on at a mean level of 28.8 microvolts (SD = 2.15) and that the circuit dropped out below a threshold mean of 14.2 microvolts (SD = 1.81). Some subjects produced alpha at two distinct amplitudes, in which case the gain was adjusted so that only the high-amplitude rhythm was detected. The device dependably monitored the alpha activity as it appeared to the observers.

In addition, an "artifact detector" shut down the alpha detector when a given level of EEG activity was exceeded, to prevent crediting the subject for any 8–13 cps activity in noisy artifact. The artifact detector was hooked to the noisiest of the three channels, and its influence may be noted in Figure 1, where it caused the alpha detector to disregard alpha rhythm which intermingled with artifact. The subject therefore was actually rewarded for an "alpha and no artifact" condition. On the bifrontal leads the artifact detector was triggered by eye movements, and therefore the subjects rapidly learned to remain still. All the subjects seemed motivated to produce alpha rhythm, since they kept the artifact detector off except for occasional .1 to .5 second periods for eye movement, or 1–5 second periods for swallowing or readjusting their position, e.g. moving from lying to sitting position.

The output of the alpha detector was connected through a signal generator to a loud speaker, which generated a low-intensity 200-Hz tone when the subject produced alpha. Some of our subjects, chosen by the flip of a coin, heard the tone only when they did not produce alpha, and subsequent analysis of data revealed no significant difference between their mean performance and that of the others. Once either "on" or "off" mode was determined for a subject, he remained with his assigned mode throughout all sessions.

During the experiment, subjects remained in an 8′ × 10′ quiet, well-ventilated, dimly-lit room. For the first half hour, the subjects were simply told to lie quietly, and a baseline index of alpha percentage was determined. This index consisted of the time the counter detected alpha divided by the total experimental time, and expressed as a percentage. The exclusion of both the alpha falling below the voltage criterion and whatever alpha was present during the brief artifact periods made for a conservatively low estimate.

During the second half hour, the subject was introduced to the tone, and told to try to keep the tone on (or off, as mentioned, for one subgroup), and that being calm with eyes closed would help. After this second half hour, the subject was told that over the next 4 hours he should keep trying to control the tone.

The seven highest alpha subjects were returned to the experimental room for one twelve-hour period during which controlling the tone for payment required alpha maintenance, and another paid twelve-hour period requiring nonalpha maintenance. The order of these two programs presentations was random and the periods at least one week apart.

Since telemetry was used, the experimental conditions were in effect during the entire 12 hours, such that the subject was monitored during infrequent trips to the toilet or while eating food which was brought in; these were mostly counted as nonalpha. Comparisons of alpha percentages were made by t-tests.

The subjects were interviewed immediately after the experiment and asked how they felt and how they best controlled the feedback tone.

RESULTS

The 31 subjects produced a mean alpha percentage of 51.3% (SD = 24.8) over the 4 hour test period. Figure 2 shows a plot of the mean performance and the individual percentages are recorded in Table 1. Figure 2 also shows that after a 30-minute practice session the subjects began with

near-maximal rates; presumably as soon as they shut their eyes, and their performance remained fairly constant during the next 4 hours with the highest alpha output occurring toward the end of the conditioning period.

T-tests disclosed that, for the 4 hour subjects, there was no difference between the mean performance of the first two trial blocks after the practice period (57%, SD = 30%) and the practice period itself (49%, SD = 30%, p = 0.18). Furthermore, the subjects produced no more alpha rhythm during the last 4 blocks compared with the first 4 blocks of the performance period. These similarities, plus the fluctuating course of the performance curve, would indicate that spontaneous productions of alpha were probably more important to overall alpha performance than any effect of learning over the 4-hour period.

The results for the 12-hour alpha experiments are shown in Table 2 along with the 4 hour averages. When the performance from the 4- and 12-hour alpha reinforcement experiment was compared there was a high rank-order correlation (rho = 0.95, N = 5, p < 0.01),

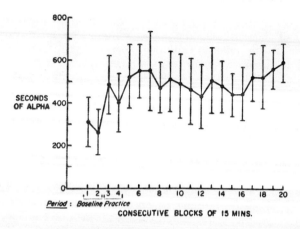

ALPHA TIME OVER 5 HOURS
IN 21 UNTRAINED SUBJECTS - Mean ± S.D.

Fig. 2. The average alpha maintenance (in seconds/15 min) for 31 subjects is plotted across the experimental conditions (30-minute baseline, 30-minute practice and 4 hours of uninterrupted biofeedback). The horizontal bars represent one standard deviation around that mean.

TABLE 1   Mean Alpha Percentage over 4 Hours

Age	Female Mean Alpha (%)	S.D. (%)	Age	Male Mean Alpha (%)	S.D. (%)
24	90.7	1.5	26	92.5	0.45
36	79.8	8.0[a]	26	87.7	8.0
21	74.6	3.9	21	81.8	1.1
23	66.9	2.3	19	80.2	1.0
28	59.3	4.3	32	77.6	10.6[a]
36	57.0	8.0	20	66.5	7.9[a]
27	52.3	5.9	26	60.3	6.8
28	52.2	2.4	21	54.3	5.6
19	43.1	6.0	35	51.8	3.4
36	39.7	2.2	22	48.8	3.3
18	39.6	6.5	28	45.6	7.2
50	27.9	6.0	25	35.1	3.5[a]
18	24.7	4.4	23	20.7	5.1[a]
18	24.0	5.6			
18	20.4	6.5			
52	20.1	5.6[a]			
36	13.7	1.5[a]			
31	1.0	2.2			

$\bar{x}$ = 43.7 (24.8) $\bar{x}$ = 61.8 (21.6)

Combined Mean = 51.3 (24.8)

[a]Based on 4 1-hour values; otherwise on 16 15-minute values.

indicating that subjects who can produce high percentages of alpha time initially will subsequently maintain the same position relative to the others. Thus one may reliably predict 12-hour performance from the shorter procedure.

Tables 3 (a) and 3(b) show the production of alpha under the two reinforcement conditions and demonstrates the wide variability which our subjects exhibited on an hourly basis, as well as the interesting variability between subjects. This variability is also reflected in the large standard deviations seen in Figures 2 and 3.

The group means of the 12-hour conditioning sessions are shown in Figure 3 and show that the high alpha subjects produced an average of 70.3 percent alpha rhythm when it was rewarded; and an average of 11.3 percent alpha when nonalpha or desynchrony was rewarded. These results demonstrate very clearly that the alpha rhythm can be produced and maintained for long periods of time

without apparent fatigue. In fact the two subjects who average over 90% mean alpha time for the 12-hour experiment expressed concern during the twelfth hour that they could not shut off the alpha feed-back tone. The first, a neurophysiologist, kept purposely opening his eyes to reassure himself that he could still desynchronize his brain waves. The second, a psychologist, feared that his mind had been affected and looked at the room light frequently during the twelfth hour to elicit a normal feedback response. These examples illustrate how easily high-alpha subjects can maintain virtually continuous alpha rhythm.

Despite the correlation between 4-hour and 12-hour alpha performance, there was no correlation between 12-hour alpha maintenance and 12-hour nonalpha maintenance, demonstrating an absence of any natural tendency for alpha rhythm to selectively assert itself amongst those subjects who can produce great amounts of it at will. In fact, two subjects perform-

TABLE 2   Mean Alpha Percentage Time for 7 Subjects

Sex	Subject	4-Hour experiment	12-Hour alpha	12-Hour nonalpha
M	1	92.5	91.4	—
F	2	79.8	55.1	5.5
M	3	81.8	71.8	26.8
M	4	87.7	90.6	7.5
M	5	74.6	47.6	11.3
M	6	—	77.3	3.9
M	7	—	58.3	12.9
Mean =		83.3	70.3	11.3
SD =		6.6	17.3	8.3

TABLE 3 (a)   Seconds of Alpha Rhythm per Subject, per Hour
When the Alpha Frequency was Reinforced

	Subject Number							
Hour	1	2	3	4	5	6	x	SD
1	518	3005	3433	2336	2382	2715	2398	1008
2	1211	2779	3497	934	2374	2891	2281	1006
3	480	2360	3413	1043	2866	2681	2140	1136
4	1757	1641	3201	1980	2650	1798	2171	619
5	2230	2106	3439	383	2040	954	1859	1070
6	2123	2604	3406	1797	2765	750	2241	916
7	3041	2809	3310	1632	1889	2079	2460	684
8	2130	3204	3280	2560	2306	1352	2473	720
9	2546	2270	3070	2584	2600	2380	2575	275
10	2327	2984	3093	2704	2987	1848	2657	484
11	2376	2478	3053	2516	2804	3002	2705	288
12	3064	2770	2934	104	3010	2763	2441	1152

mean $\bar{x}$ = 2367 (241)

ing comparably at the alpha task, at 77.3% and 71.8% for 12 hours, turned in the best and the worst nonalpha performance, respectively. Control of nonalpha would therefore seem independent from control of alpha rhythms.

Further data, obtained through interviews, pertained to the manner in which the subjects varied in their methods for producing alpha. These comments are catalogued in Table 4.

DISCUSSION

The performance of our seven high-alpha experimental subjects demonstrates that individuals may produce relatively high percentages of alpha rhythm for 12 hours. Kamiya (2) mentions two subjects

run for 20 hours, with a performance of 85% for one of them. Results for the other are not stated. The exact conditions and the criteria for the subject's performance are unclear in this discursive report, but our highest 12-hour alpha subject confirms Kamiya's finding of a very high alpha performance level. Kamiya also finds that most subjects show an inherent capacity to increase or suppress alpha percent at will. Our experiment did not directly add to Kamiya's finding, but a number of rather unexpected findings certainly pointed to an amazing flexibility associated with the production of alpha. For example, as previously mentioned, it apparently made no difference to our subjects whether they were paid or not, or whether they had the tone associated with alpha or not.

**TABLE 3 (b)   Seconds of Alpha Rhythm per Subject, per Hour
When the Non-alpha Condition Was Reinforced**

| Hour | Subject Number | | | | | | $\bar{x}$ | SD |
	1	2	3	4	5	6		
1	85	550	249	659	68	311	320	242
2	210	577	82	1119	294	307	415	383
3	200	966	151	700	127	384	421	342
4	339	690	79	1014	34	166	387	389
5	460	827	119	403	346	324	413	234
6	527	1113	181	215	1085	295	403	428
7	781	1333	92	329	261	208	501	471
8	1103	697	76	45	0	609	422	450
9	121	561	161	230	1	155	205	190
10	280	2017	625	10	337	300	595	723
11	439	1094	761	20	108	326	458	407
12	198	1146	639	32	30	152	367	443

mean $\bar{x}$ = 409 (94)

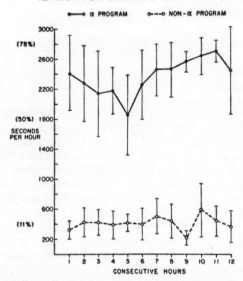

12 HOUR PERFORMANCE - Mean ± S.D. (n=6)

●——● α PROGRAM   ○– –○ NON-α PROGRAM

Fig. 3. A plot of the mean and standard deviation of alpha maintenance for subjects under two experimental
conditions; reinforced for maintaining alpha, and reinforced for maintaining nonalpha. The same
subjects were used in both conditions and were selected on their ability to maintain high levels of
alpha.

TABLE 4   Techniques for Alpha Maintenance

Subject	Feeling and Behavior	Method for Controlling Tone
1	Bored "Dazed" smoked cigarettes	Eyes closed or open but not focusing on anything, staring straight ahead, could think about anything
2	Bored	Daydreamed of pleasant subjects, "getting my mind in a certain state," no rapid movements or mental work
3	"Weak" bored annoyed with tone	Trying to be "drowsy," eyes closed or open but not focused
4	As if he had slept a long time	Lying quietly
5	Could sit	Not moving
6	Could write slowly but not think	Eyes could open "gently" towards end of session, first left eye, then both
7	Could pace about slowly; could gradually sing if he began slowly. Upon termination, felt need to run around building	Towards end, tone got automatic, controlled without effort

Our high-alpha population found alpha easier to produce with practice, but unlike Kamiya's subjects, did not use their new skill to significantly improve performance. Rather, they chose to take liberties with the state of motor and visual inhibition which was strictly required to produce alpha during earlier trials. This habituation to alpha-blocking over time has been observed by others (3). As alpha rhythm seems connected with inhibitory processes (4,5), these conditions of continual high alpha rhythm may have further raised the threshold of blocking to various stimuli, allowing our subjects a wider behavioral freedom that could remain consistent with the desired alpha pattern.

In contrast to the increasing ease which our subjects found in producing alpha rhythm, they complained that maintaining nonalpha became more difficult during the 12-hour attempt. Perhaps this is reflected in the increased variation of nonalpha performances shown during the last six hours in Figure 3. Interestingly, while the subjects found maintaining nonalpha increasingly difficult over the 12-hour period, they asserted that producing alpha over the same time period was even more stressful.

Given the subjective boredom of our prolonged alpha subjects, we disagree with the numerous advertisements for alpha-rhythm feedback machines now appearing in the popular press and elsewhere, which suggest that much time spent in alpha rhythm will psychologically benefit the purchaser of these devices. Also, as discussed by Tart (6), Zen and Yoga meditators may produce high amounts of alpha rhythm, but a high alpha index does not render one an Eastern meditator.

SUMMARY

Thirty-one male and female newspaper advertisement respondents, aged 17 to 52, participated in a five-hour alpha feedback experiment. After a half-hour baseline period and a half-hour practice period, 22 of them were paid $2.50 for each hour they produced alpha rhythm, and nine were not paid in order to determine the relative reinforcing property of monetary reward. Their performance waxed and waned over the four-hour conditioning session with alternating interest and boredom. They produced an average of 51% alpha time (SD = 25%), and there was no difference between paid and unpaid subjects.

The seven highest subjects emerging from this experiment (mean alpha = 83%)

were placed in a 12-hour paid alpha feedback condition and a 12-hour paid nonalpha feedback condition on two separate days, at least one week apart. They produced a mean alpha performance of 70% during the alpha and 11% during the nonalpha conditions. Alpha rhythm became easier for the subjects to produce over the 12 hours of alpha production, whereas maintaining nonalpha became increasingly difficult during the 12 hour period.

We wish to thank Dr. Benjamin Murawski for his helpful critiques of the text.

REFERENCES

1. Kamiya, J: Conscious control of brain waves. Psychology Today 1:56–60, 1968
2. Kamiya, J: Operant control of the EEG alpha rhythm and some of its reported effects on consciousness. Altered States of Consciousness. Edited by CT Tart. New York, Wiley and Sons, 1969, Chapter 35
3. Fenton, GW and Scotton, L: Personality and the alpha rhythm. Brit J Psychiat 113:1283–1289, 1967
4. Heinemann, LG and Emrigh, H: Alpha activity during inhibitory brain processes. Psychophysiology 7:442–450, 1971
5. Simonov, PV: Basic (alpha) EEG rhythm as electrographic manifestation of preventive inhibition of brain structures. Prog Brain Res 22:138–147, 1968
6. Tart, CT: Altered States of Consciousness. New York, Wiley and Sons, 1969, p. 486

Relative Independence 15

of Conditioned EEG Changes from Cardiac

and Respiratory Activity

Jackson Beatty and Charles Kornfeld

BEATTY, J. AND C. KORNFELD. *Relative independence of conditioned EEG changes from cardiac and respiratory activity.* PHYSIOL. BEHAV. 9(5) 733–736, 1972.– To investigate the system specificity of learned changes in EEG spectra in man and to rule out the possibility that changes in cardiac or respiratory activity mediate the observed central nervous system changes, 14 subjects were trained to produce occipital alpha and beta frequency activity differentially. Standard operant methods, including a discriminative stimulus, were used. Heart and respiration rates were recorded simultaneously. Subjects showed discriminant control of the EEG spectra, but no significant changes were found in either heart or respiratory systems. Our data indicate that conditioned changes in the EEG spectra are not mediated by shifts in either heart or respiration rates. Instead they suggest that the EEG generating system is relatively independent of the brain systems controlling respiration and heart function.

EEG   Alpha rhythm   Operant control   Biofeedback   Heart rate   Respiration

ONE OF the more puzzling issues arising from the operant control of central and autonomic nervous system functions is that of the apparent specificity of the conditioned changes, in the presence of more general behavioral and physiological effects. This problem is most elegantly posed by the work of DiCara and Miller in their studies of conditioned autonomic changes in animals. In previous papers these authors report that heart rate may be conditioned independently of skeletal muscle activity, intestinal contractions and blood pressure, with respiration held constant [14]. Similarly changes in urine formation, produced by altering renal blood flow, may be conditioned independently of heart rate or blood pressure [15]. Even differential control of vasomotor activity has been shown in the pinnae of the rat's ears [5]. These and similar data indicating the specificity of the learned autonomic response have been reported for various organ systems and are reviewed elsewhere by Miller [13]. Evidence for specificity is interesting in the context of other data, which indicate that such learned changes may have very general behavioral effects. DiCara and Weiss [7] report that prior heart rate conditioning differentially affects a rat's ability to learn an escape task, which the authors argue is the result of changes

[1] This research was supported by the advanced Projects Research Agency of the Department of Defense and was monitored by the Office of Naval Research under Contract N00014-70-C-0350 to the San Deigo State College Foundation.
[2] The authors wish to thank Carl Figueroa and Karen Sabovich for their help in the execution of this study and the analysis of the data used in this paper.

in emotional responsivity. Other very general effects of heart rate conditioning, such as differential shifts in brain norepinephrine, have been reported in animals [6].

The present study was designed to investigate the question of response specificity in a somewhat different context. We have previously reported a series of studies [1, 2, 3] confirming and extending the work of other investigators [4, 17] in which operantly conditioned changes in human central nervous system activity (EEG) were examined. The patterns of EEG activity for which we have demonstrated discriminant control (alpha frequency synchrony and desynchrony) are classically associated with changes in arousal [12]. Since shifts of arousal normally include visceral components [19], such conditioned changes might be expected to involve autonomic functions also. Further, it is conceivable that the observed CNS changes might even be mediated by alterations of autonomic or respiratory function.

To begin our investigation of these questions in man, the following simple experiment was performed. Subjects were trained as in our previous experiments [1, 3] to produce discriminant control of the occipital EEG spectra, while heart and respiration rates were concurrently measured. Heart rate was chosen since it is the single major index of cardiac function which is easily measurable in human subjects. Respiration rates were obtained because respiration seemed a likely covariate of conditioned EEG synchrony and desynchrony. Moreover, respiration is a skeletal response which could conceivably serve as a skeletal mediator for the EEG changes produced by our subjects.

METHOD

Fourteen undergraduate students served as subjects in order to partially satisfy the requirements of an introductory psychology course. Subjects were assigned to this experiment without prior knowledge of its exact nature. This procedure was thought to minimize problems stemming from the self-selection of subjects. Subjects who did not need full course credit were paid comparably.

Occipital EEG was recorded from position O_Z of the 10–20 system [10] referred to the right earlobe. The subject's left earlobe was grounded. The EEG was first amplified by a Grass P-15 amplifier and then by a series of integrated circuit amplifiers with active filters. The frequency response of the total system was essentially flat between 2 and 20 Hz, with 1/2 amplitude attenuation at 0.6 and 32 Hz. This signal was monitored for artifacts on an ocilloscope and a paper recorder was available at the analog/digital converter of the computer.

A Beckman Type R Dynograph was used, with appropriate transducers and couplers, to record the autonomic measures. Heart pulses were obtained with a reflected light plethysmograph on the index finger of the right hand. The respiratory cycle was recorded with a strain gauge belt around the chest of the subject.

The subjects were first told that they were participating in a study of brain wave and autonomic activity. After the recording electrodes were attached, subjects were seated in an electrically shielded room with a low level of ambient lighting. The autonomic measures were explained and the subjects were assured that they would not be shocked. They were asked to keep their eyes open and refrain from moving for a 300-sec period, during which the computer calculated the baseline spectra of their EEG. Baseline heart rate and respiration were also recorded. Subjects were then instructed as to the nature of their task, in words similar to the following: "While you have been sitting here, the computer has made a number of measurements of your EEG activity. You now have the opportunity to learn to control your own brain waves. The EEG is a complex waveform which may be thought to show many different patterns. From all these patterns we have arbitrarily selected two for today's study. Each second the computer will sample your EEG, looking for one of the two selected wave patterns. Before each trial, I will tell you which of the two patterns will be reinforced. Also, Light 1, which you see before you, signifies that the computer is reinforcing Pattern 1, and Light 2 means Pattern 2. When Light 3 is on, you may rest. During each trial when the appropriate pattern occurs the loudness of the background tone will be increased for 1 sec. Your job is to learn to produce the kinds of wave patterns which will keep the tone on. If you succeed in doubling either kind of EEG activity from your baseline level, you will receive an extra hour of experimental credit. If you double both, you will receive 2 free hours of credit. As before, keep your eyes open and refrain from moving."

The 14 subjects were then given 4 blocks of EEG training. Each block consisted of two 200-sec trials randomly ordered. In one trial an alpha frequency criterion was used for reinforcement. In the other, the subject was reinforced for producing occipital desynchronization. Between blocks, the room lights were turned on and the experimenters talked with the subject for at least 1 min about irrelevant matters. This procedure was used to counteract a growing sleepiness which subjects in psychological experiments often experience. At no time was mention made of alpha waves, desynchronization, relaxation procedures or similar topics.

With the exception of the recording of the cardiac and respiratory data, the experiment was run under computer control. During each trial and the baseline period, the EEG was sampled each second for one complete wave, referenced to 0 potential and beginning with a positive deflection. The period of this wave was then measured and classified by the method of Legewie and Probst [11] as a single wave at X Hz. This probability measure converges upon the estimate of the power spectrum as computed by standard spectral methods [20]. If the wave was within the criterion frequency band (8−12 Hz for alpha, 13 Hz or more for beta), the intensity of a quiet 400-Hz tone was augmented for 1 sec. During that second, the sampling and measurement procedure was repeated and, if that wave was also within the criterion bounds, the tone intensity remained high for another second. After each trial, the probability of encountering a wave at each frequency was printed. Heart rate and respiration rate were calculated from the paper record after the experiment was completed. Both rates were obtained by counting the total number of beats or breaths, over each 200-sec trial, from which the average rates per min were computed.

RESULTS AND DISCUSSION

Figure 1 summarizes the results obtained in the present experiment. Each graph in the figure shows the mean value of the measured parameter (probability of alpha and beta activity, heart and respiration rates) for each kind of trial (alpha or beta reinforcement) in each of the four trial blocks. Thus Fig. 1 A gives the probability of obtaining an alpha wave during alpha reinforcement (indicated by circles) and beta reinforcement (shown as squares). Our subjects clearly show discriminative control of their occipital EEG spectra throughout the experiment. The mean probability of observing an alpha wave is higher on the alpha reinforcement trial for each and every trial block. This conclusion is supported by an analysis of variance (ANOVA) on these probabilities, in which the main effect of reinforcement contingency is significant ($F=7.76$; 1,13 df; $p<0.025$). The small upward drift of the alpha probabilities over trials is also significant ($F=6.48$; 3,39 df, $p<0.025$). This latter estimate may be spuriously large since the univariate ANOVA is biased toward overestimating the significance level of data based upon multiple repeated measures, if the correlations between these measures are

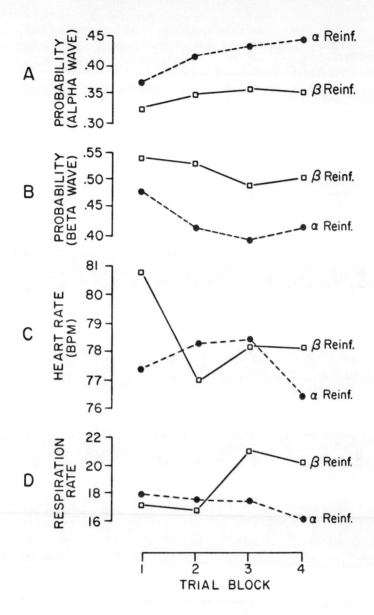

FIG. 1. Mean probability of an alpha wave (Fig. 1 A). mean probability of a beta wave (1 B), mean heart rate (1 C), and mean respiration rate (1 D) by reinforcement contingency and trial blocks. Broken lines signify alpha reinforcement and solid lines, beta. The separation of these curves in 1 A and 1 B is taken as evidence for discriminative control of EEG spectra. The absence of such a pattern in the heart or respiration rate data indicates the relative independence of these systems from the brain processes controlling occipital EEG synchrony. See text for a discussion of these data.

not equal. To guard against this possibility, the Geisser-Greenhouse conservative F-test [8], which assumes the worst case of unequal correlation, was also used to estimate the minimal level of significance of the effect of trials. This effect remains significant with $p < 0.025$. We attribute this drift in the alpha wave probabilities to a growing sleepiness or relaxation over the course of the experiment, which was not relieved by the conversations with the experimenter. Because of the extra sensors needed to measure heart rate and respiration, the subject was not able to leave the experimental chamber between trial blocks as in previous studies [1, 2, 3]. Previously reported data [2] show that there is no drift in the alpha probabilities over trials in no-treatment control subjects who simply sit in the experimental room with their EEGs monitored without reinforcement or task instructions but are removed at the appropriate intervals between trial blocks.

We believe that the drift of these probabilities over trials, which we tentatively attribute to a procedural change, may partially account for another difference in the pattern of results in the present study. No significant interaction between trials and contingency was seen (F=0.53; 3,11 df; N.S.), whereas this interaction was a constant feature of the data in our earlier reports.

An examination of the beta wave probabilities (shown in Fig. 1 B) supports the simple conclusion that our subjects may exert discriminative control of occipital cortex desynchronization. The mean probability of beta frequency activity is higher during beta contingent reinforcement for each and every trial block. This effect appears reliable (F=7.33; 1,13 df; $p < 0.025$).

The univariate ANOVA provides no clear answer to the question of significant drift in the beta wave probabilities. The effect of trials is significant by the conventional ANOVA (F=4.39; 3,39 df; $p < 0.01$) but not when the Geisser-Greenhouse test is applied (F=4.39; 1,13 df; N.S.). For that reason a multivariate statistic, Hotelling's T^2 [16] was computed to estimate this probability more accurately. By this test, the shift in beta probabilities over trials is not significant (F=2.46; 3.11 df; N.S.). There is also no significant interaction of reinforcement contingency and trials (F=1.20; 3,11 df; N.S.).

The EEG data thus suggest that our subjects show discriminative control of those parameters of the occipital EEG which are used as the criteria for reinforcement. Do other body systems show a similar pattern of response? If these effects are mediated by changes in heart rate or respiration, then a similar significant pattern in the means of these variables should be observed over trials and reinforcement contingencies. This is not the case. If the control of the conditioned cortical responses is not specific, then a similar but weaker patterning of means might be seen in the heart and respiration data. No such pattern is obvious.

Something, however, may be learned from examination of these data. The only effect in either the heart or respiration data approaching significance is the interaction of reinforcement contingency and trials for heart rate (using Hotelling's T^2, F=2.81; 3,11 df; $0.10 > p < 0.05$). The mean heart rates by trial block and contingency are shown in Fig. 1 C. It appears that there may be a rather large difference in heart rate between the reinforcement contingencies on the first trial which disappears with time. Indeed, the chance probability of the obtained order of means in the first trial block is rather low ($p < 0.01$) by a sign test [18]. This effect may be the transient correlation between heart rate and EEG alpha activity which Hord and Barber [9] have observed "during certain, as yet unspecifiable, periods" (p. 153). This is suggestive of the results previously reported by Miller and DiCara for a number of response systems [13]. Initially, specificity may be weak. Many autonomic changes besides that being reinforced occur early in training. With increased practice, however, the control of the conditioned behavior becomes much more specific and partially correlated responses drop out of the controlled behavior pattern. The topography of the response becomes differentiated in the course of training. A similar effect might exist in the present experiment [2].

Figure 1 D suggests that our subjects did not use changes in respiration to mediate the control of EEG activity. The effects of trials do not help contingency nor does their interaction approach significance. The elevation of mean respiration rate in the final two beta reinforcement trials deserves comment. One subject hyperventilated on those trials. The contribution of this subject to the means is rather large since he changed his respiration rate from 17 on the second beta reinforcement trial to 78 on the third. If this subject's data are removed, then the group means for the third and fourth trial blocks are approximately the same as those seen in the first two blocks. An ANOVA on the data with this subject removed also shows no effects even approaching significance.

We believe that our data indicate that conditioned changes in the spectra of the occipital EEG in man are not mediated by shifts in either heart or respiration rates. In addition, the learned control of EEG spectra is specific and is not accompanied by changes in either of the other responses measured, with the possible exception of very early training effects on heart rate. Together, this suggests that the EEG generating system is relatively independent of the brain systems controlling respiration and heart function in man.

REFERENCES

1. Beatty, J. T. Effects of initial alpha wave abundance and operant training procedures on occipital alpha and beta activity. *Psychonom. Sci.* 23: 197–199, 1971.

2. Beatty, J. T. Similar effects of feedback signals and instructional information on EEG activity. *Physiol. Behav.* in press, 1973.

3. Beatty, J. T. and C. M. Kornfeld. The relative independence of cognitive and visual determinants of cortical synchrony, in preparation, 1972.

4. Brown, B. B. Recognition of aspects of consciousness through association with EEG alpha activity represented by a light signal. *Psychophysiology* 6: 442–452, 1970.

5. DiCara, L. and N. Miller, Instrumental learning of vasomotor responses by rats: Learning to respond differentially in the two ears. *Science* 159: 1485–1486, 1968.

6. DiCara, L. V. and E. A. Stone. Effect of instrumental heart-rate training on rat cardiac and brain catecholamines. *Psychosom. Med.* 32: 359–368, 1970.

7. DiCara, L. and J. M. Weiss. Effect of heart-rate learning under curare and subsequent noncurarized avoidance learning. *J. comp. physiol. Psychol.* 69: 368–374, 1969.

8. Geisser, S. and S. W. Greenhouse. An extension of Box's results on the use of the F distribution in multivariate analysis. *Ann Math. Stat.* 29: 885–891, 1958.

9. Hord, D. and J. Barber. Alpha control: Effectiveness of two kinds of feedback. *Psychonom. Sci.* 25: 151–154, 1971.

10. Jasper, H. H. The ten-twenty electrode system of the International Federation. *Electroencephal. clin. Neurophysiol.* 10: 371–375, 1958.

11. Legewie, H. and W. Probst. On-line analysis of EEG with a small computer (period-amplitude analysis). *Electroencephal. clin. Neurophysiol.* 27: 533–536, 1969.

12. Lindsley, D. B. Attention, consciousness, sleep and wakefulness. *Handbook of Physiology*, Section I, Vol. 3, edited by J. Field. 1553–1593, 1960.

13. Miller, N. Learning of visceral and glandular responses. *Science* 163: 434–445, 1969.

14. Miller, N. and A. Banuazizi. Instrumental learning by curarized rats of a specific visceral response, intestinal or cardiac. *J. comp. physiol. Psychol.* 65: 1–7, 1968.

15. Miller, N. and L. DiCara. Instrumental learning of urine formation by rats; changes in renal blood flow. *Am. J. Physiol.* 215: 677–683, 1968.

16. Morrison, D. F. *Multivariate Statistical Methods*, New York: McGraw-Hill, 1967.

17. Nowlis, D. P. and J. Kamiya. The control electroencephalographic alpha rhythms through auditory feedback and associated mental activity. *Psychophysiology* **6**: 476–484, 1970.
18. Siegel, S. *Nonparametric Statistics for the Behavioral Sciences* New York: McGraw-Hill, 1956.
19. Sokolov, E. N. *Perception and the Conditioned Reflex*. New York: Macmillan, 1963.
20. Stark, L. Comments in: *Attention in Neurophysiology*, edited by C. R. Evans and T. B. Mulholland. New York: Appleton-Century-Crofts, 1969, 162–163.

Objective EEG Methods for 16
Studying Covert Shifts of Visual Attention

Thomas Mulholland

I. INTRODUCTION

Clinical neurophysiology, emphasizing studies of humans, managed to preserve many mentalistic concepts during the purge of those ideas from psychology by the arch-behaviorists. However, preservation is not development and old-fashioned concepts such as attention, volition, and mental imagery lagged behind the development of the main body of ideas in neurophysiology and behavioristic psychology.

More recently, mentalistic concepts have become respectable in contemporary psychology. With this new acceptance has come a new criticism of the use of those concepts as explanatory principles in neurophysiology and neuropsychology. The history of the concept of attention in electro-

[1] The work in this paper was supported in its entirety by the Veteran's Administration, RCS 15-4, Program 01/5890.1/69-09.

encephalography is a good example of these trends (Evans & Mulholland, 1969).

Attention has been an important concept in EEG since the early work of Berger (1930). Though researchers in the 1930s and 1940s, especially Adrian (Adrian & Matthews, 1934; Adrian, 1943) linked changes in the EEG occipital alpha to vision and visual control processes, this emphasis gave way to the concept of "visual attention" or simply "attention" (Mulholland, 1969). Attention in EEG was never clearly defined, yet it proved to be a remarkably durable explanatory concept.

For many researchers the outcome was a disenchantment with *any* psychological concept in neurophysiology, and a rejection of the EEG as an index of anything psychological except as a consequence of gross brain pathology or epilepsy. This contrasts with the current wave of enthusiastic faddism and exorbitant claims for alpha in relation to states of mind and alleged mental powers by nonscientific "alpha" pop groups (Mulholland, 1971). My attitude toward the alpha rhythms is between such extremes of scientific pessimism and popular optimism.

I will begin with a brief statement of the classical assumptions about the response of the occipital alpha rhythms to visual stimulation, then a description of how we define and measure alpha will follow. After presenting the experimental results of our studies of attention and alpha, I will review my hypothesis that visual attention and the suppression of occipital alpha are mediated by visual control process, especially efferent processes in cortex associated with the adjustment of the eye. At the end, a criticism of the classical assumptions about the response of the alpha rhythms to visual stimulation is presented and some new kinds of experiments proposed.

A. The Response of the Occipital Alpha Rhythms

The classical concepts of the response of the alpha rhythm emphasized the *singularity* of the response—the single alpha "block" after stimulation, *functional equivalence* of all alpha "blocks," and the *functional identity* of all stages of the single alpha block. In all the studies of "attention" and alpha, these assumptions played their role influencing the methods of stimulus presentation, the collection and analysis of data, and the theoretical treatment of the results. In my view all three assumptions of singularity, functional equivalence and functional identity are either contrary to experimental and clinical evidence or simply unnecessary and superfluous. I shall discuss each of them in the context of our work at Bedford. Before I do, it is necessary to review the kind of definition of alpha that we use.

B. Definition of Alpha

When the EEG is used as an index of behavioral and psychological processes, the requirements of EEG analysis are different from those of an analysis of the EEG as a complex signal per se. In the latter a rapid, finely differentiated description is required such as fast spectral analysis. In the former the degree of differentiation of the index is related to that of the associated behavioral and psychological processes. Features of the EEG must be so described that they match the features of the behavioral process, in the time domain. In the case of fairly slow behavioral changes which are also large-scale a fast, highly differentiated EEG analysis may in fact be an impediment because fast, transitory and finely differentiated changes will occur in the EEG which have no necessary relation to behavior. Here a method for defining and detecting EEG occipital alpha is described which meets the requirements for an index of visual attention.

The occipital EEG is defined as a series of events. An event is either alpha or it is not. This does not mean that the response of the EEG is either/or, only that the EEG meets criteria for our definition or it does not. The series formed by the alternation between alpha and no-alpha events is called the alpha-attenuation series. There is no mechanism implied by the term; it is a name for a familiar phenomenon.

The alpha detection and control system described here is currently in use.[2] Consideration in its design were accuracy, reliability, and convenience. Occipital alpha is easy to detect but because of its low frequency, the minimum detection time is about .1 sec. A band-pass filter with rectification and integration was chosen on the basis of overall performance. Other detection systems offer quicker response times or sharper frequency discrimination but the filter–rectifier–integrator combination has a time constant which best approximates the time constant of the biological system that it is measuring, neither too fast nor too slow. The feedback control system is designed to control visual and auditory displays, to perform routine housekeeping such as controlling clocks, markers, and counters, and to provide maximum flexibility in experiment design.

1. Definition of Alpha for Each Individual

The classical definition of alpha is an 8–12 Hz, nearly sinusoidal signal at a voltage level of between 5 and 150 μV. These are statistical limits and say nothing about an individual's alpha. Individual amplitude and frequency parameters must be determined and used as criteria for setting

[2] The system described here was designed and built by R. Boudrot. Complete description will be published elsewhere.

the alpha detection system. The alpha frequency counted manually over several seconds is used to set the center of a 2-Hz passband. The "static maximum alpha" (eyes closed in the dark after a period of 1 or 2 min) is attenuated or increased at the preamplifier to produce full-scale deflection of the meter in the detection circuit. The threshold amplitude for "dynamic alpha" (alpha under operating conditions) is standardized with the threshold set control. When the filtered signal is equal to or greater than 25% of the static alpha amplitude, response of the relay to an above-threshold alpha in the EEG is between .25–.35 sec.

Raw data is collected in the normal fashion on a Grass Model 7 Polygraph. The amplified but unfiltered raw data appears at a high level output jack (J7) with a potential of 2 V (peak-to-peak) corresponding to a 1-cm pen deflection. This output is processed by a tunable RC-type bandpass filter which has a 24 dB/octave roll off filter function. The output of the filter is bridge rectified then integrated by a critically damped, variable threshold, optical meter relay. The meter is protected from overload with a Zener diode which also serves to limit the "OFF" time delay when an exceptionally high-amplitude alpha period is detected. This easily assembled system offers a settable passband, a settable threshold, repeatability and linearity within 2%, .25-sec response time, ease of calibration and operation, durability, and low cost (see Fig. 4.1).

2. Choice of Parameter Values

Filter. For most subjects, the probability for the occurrence of alpha is higher when the probability for the occurrence of competing brain rhythms is lower. When alpha is present it is usually prominent and dominant. Conversely when the probability of other rhythms is higher, the probability of alpha is lower (Cobb, 1963; Lindsley, 1960). Occipital alpha, which is the most prominent brain rhythm has a frequency stability of ± 1 Hz and is usually an order of magnitude greater than the noise (signal–noise > 10) and 2–10 times the amplitude of other rhythms which are usually 20 μV or less (Cobb, 1963). Our variable passband RC filter has been superseded by newer types with better performance characteristics but it performs adequately in distinguishing the nearly noise-free, nearly coherent alpha signals. With our filter, the shape of the attenuation frequency curve does not change significantly as the passband indicator on the filter is narrowed from 4 Hz down to 1 Hz. There is a large increase in attenuation of the band-pass frequencies with the narrowing of the passband indicator. We have standardized pass indicator settings at 1 Hz above and 1 Hz below the resting alpha frequency.

Threshold. An alpha sensitivity function was obtained using two matched

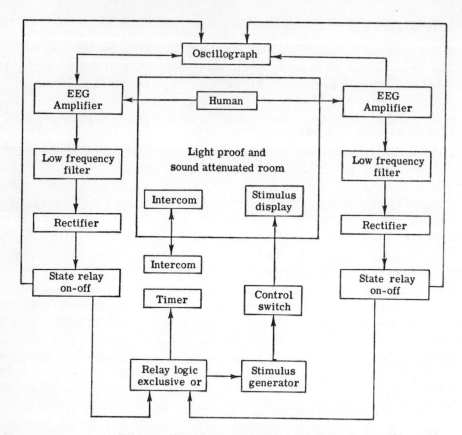

Fig. 4.1. Flow diagram of the apparatus.

recording channels each receiving the same EEG input. One channel was maintained at 25% threshold, the other was varied in successive trials. Data was then collected from a subject and the percentage of time the alpha state relays were ON was computed.

The percentage of alpha on both the constant and variable threshold channel changed over the experiment due to habituation. To correct for this and to express the values relative to the constant threshold, the percentage of alpha with the variable threshold at 25% were averaged with the values on the constant threshold which were the lowest values occurring early in the trial. This number was used to adjust the value obtained with the variable threshold for a particular trial. In this way a correction for habituation was made and the corrected value made relative to the average value at 25%.

The "dynamic alpha" threshold was determined from the inflection in the percentage of alpha-threshold function. The slope between threshold values of 20 and 40% is nearly −1. At threshold which is 25% of the value of the maximum resting value the alpha patterns on the polygraph are sufficiently large and coherent to be recognizable, there is a nearly linear relation between percentage of alpha and detection threshold, and the on and off delays of the detection system are about equal shifting the stimulus in time but maintaining a stimulus duration equal to an alpha duration.

Response time. Since the EEG is used as a *gross* index of relatively *slow* psychological and behavioral processes, we require an EEG index of *large* changes which have a relatively *long* time constant. Note that we are not analyzing the EEG signal per se, but using it as an index of something else. Consequently fast signal detection is not necessary. In fact if the alpha detector has a response time of <.2 sec it may hinder the utility of the alpha feedback method in the study of visual attention, because of the increased rate of detecting transients which are not correlated with behavioral change.

Typical examples of behavioral and psychological times related to attention and orienting are (1) latency (.2 sec) for saccadic eye movements (Stark, Michael, & Zuber, 1969); (2) shifts of attention vary from .1 to 5.0 sec with most shifts greater than .2 sec (Woodworth & Schlossberg, 1954); (3) latency for alpha blocking is .2 sec or greater (Cruickshank, 1937; Cobb, 1963). Most intervals of alpha and alpha blocking are greater than .5 sec (Mulholland, 1972). A response time of .25–.35 sec seems to be a reasonable compromise between matching the system and biological time constants, avoiding noisy response to transients and having the feedback stimulus occur without too much delay. With faster detection, the system is excessively noisy, exhibiting responses which are faster than changes in the behavioral processes we are studying. With longer delays feedback stimulation occurs less often and the variance of alpha intervals increases.

Calibration. The detection system is calibrated by adjusting the gain of the metering circuit to a full-scale deflection corresponding to a 1-cm polygraph pen deflection using a train of simulated alpha waves produced by a variable frequency sine wave oscillator. The frequency of the sine wave (simulated alpha) should be the same as that of the subject's alpha with a passband set at 1 Hz and 1 Hz below the alpha frequency. Normalization between hemispheres or between subjects is accomplished by adjusting the "static alpha" amplitude with the polygraph preamplifier gain control to produce a 1-cm pen deflection. This 1-cm pen deflection at the calibration frequency causes a full-scale deflection in the metering circuit. Normalization reduces the individual or interhemispheric differences in alpha amplitudes. If differences then occur under experimental conditions they are likely to be reliable differences. The time required to calibrate and normalize the two channel detection system is 3–5 min.

3. Feedback Control System

The basic requirement for the feedback control system is to cause a feedback stimulus to occur in response to an alpha–no-alpha event. Additional requirements are event counting, timing, and marking, and flexibility and expandability to encompass a wide range of experiments. In keeping with these basic requirements, the control system allows up to four separate stimuli in any combination of EEG event and stimulus and controlled from either left or right sides. It has a 70-terminal connector panel externalizing key circuit points permitting patching to accomplish experimental goals plus a way of "adding on" functions that are not part of the system. The quantification of alpha–no-alpha events is to the nearest .1 sec. Data acquisition and processing is done by the PDP-12. The various events and data sampling time are marked on the polygraph[3] (see Fig. 4.2).

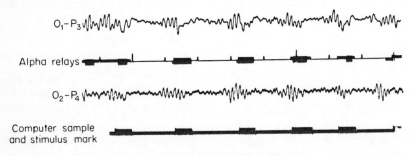

Fig. 4.2. Polygraph record.

C. Experiments on Alpha and Attention

1. Distribution of Alpha and No-Alpha Durations

The event series of alpha and no-alpha events are measured to the nearest .1 sec. The distribution of percentage of cases as a function of duration shows clearly that different conditions involving "visual attention" produce large changes in the alpha-attenuation series.

The following are from a study of 24 children[4] (see Fig. 4.3). Condition

---

[3] Programs for acquisition, measurement, display and analysis of alpha and no-alpha events were developed by Brad Cox and David Goodman. They will be published elsewhere.

[4] This study was in collaboration with Dr. Constance Murray, Lexington, Massachusetts School Department, and Dr. Generoso Gascon, Seizure Unit, Childrens Hospital Medical Center, Boston, Massachusetts.

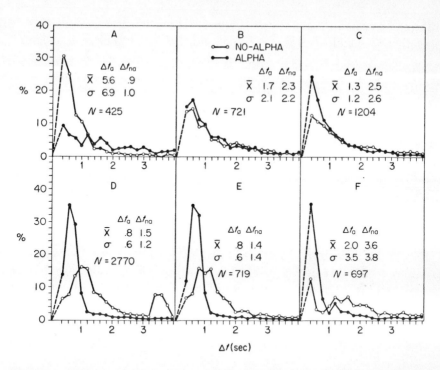

Fig. 4.3. Distributions of Δt_a, Δt_{na} for 24 children. (A) Eyes closed in the dark. (B) Eyes open in the dark. (C) Eyes open, steady light. (D) Eyes open, feedback stimulation (Loop 1). (E) Eyes open, Loop 1 feedback. (F) Eyes open, Loop 2 feedback.

A is eyes closed in the dark. Alpha events range from very brief to 14 sec duration (events greater than 4 sec are not shown). There is no definite central tendency. The intervals of no-alpha are brief with most being less than 1 sec. In condition B, eyes were open in the dark. The change in the distribution functions is clear—alpha durations become briefer, no-alpha longer. Again, most values are 1 sec or less. The distribution functions are quite similar for alpha and no-alpha. In condition C, a steady spot of light was turned on in front of the child. The alpha duration is decreased, no-alpha increased and the distributions are less alike.

In conditions D and E alpha controlled the occurrence of a visual stimulus. When alpha occurred a colored picture was turned on, for no-alpha it was turned off (Loop 1). The distribution functions are changed compared to the steady light condition. Alpha durations are briefer and the central tendency more pronounced. No-alphas are longer still varying over a wider range.

In condition F, alpha feedback was reversed. Alpha caused the picture to be off, no-alpha turned it on (Loop 2). The distribution functions are different from Loop 1 conditions. There are more longer durations (>4 sec) for both alpha and no-alpha (Mulholland, 1968). It is clear that shifts in seeing and looking at visual stimuli produce definite changes in the distribution functions of the durations of alpha and no-alpha events. A feedback path between the alpha and stimulus reduces the variance of alpha and no-alpha intervals (Loop 1).

2. *Time Series of Alpha and No-Alpha Durations*

Alpha and no-alpha durations show a *temporal* variation in relation to the onset of a stimulus, an ocular maneuver or both. The systematic and reproducible variation over time can be estimated by averaging to obtain an average series or by fitting functions to individual series. The values of $\bar{\Delta}t_a$ and $\bar{\Delta}t_{na}$ are functions of the number (N) of events in the series.

Earlier work showed that repeated stimulation was followed by a *disturbance* and a *recovery* of the alpha-attenuation cycle (see Fig. 4.4) (Mulholland & Runnals, 1964b). From the terminology of classical EEG these are average habituation functions. Average durations of no-alpha

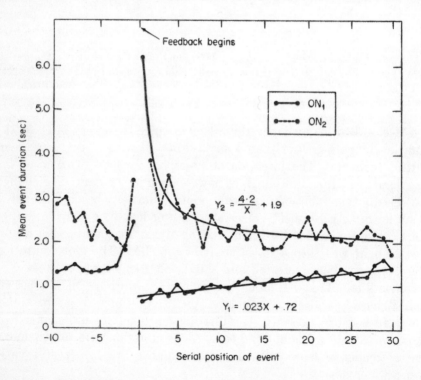

Fig. 4.4. Disturbance and recovery of the alpha-attenuation cycle with feedback stimulation. ON_1 is alpha; ON_2 is no-alpha. [From Mulholland & Runnals, 1964b.]

are initially increased with the onset of stimulation, then decreased; alpha durations are initially decreased then gradually increased.

Similar functions are obtained when eyes are opened in the dark without visual stimuli or when a steady light is turned on or when the subject starts an ocular maneuver such as focusing on a target (Mulholland & Runnals, 1964b; Mulholland, 1968).

Figure 4.5 shows results from the study of children described before. Average alpha and no-alpha series are shown beginning with the onset of various conditions. With eyes closed in the dark alpha durations are generally long and no-alpha brief. When eyes are opened in the dark the typical *disturbance* and *recovery* for the event series are seen. When a steady light is turned on, there is again a disturbance followed by recovery. For the onset of feedback, again a disturbance followed by a recovery.

Similar results from a study of alpha and no-alpha events during various tracking tasks are presented in Fig. 4.6. The subjects were tracking a target $\frac{1}{2}$-in. in diameter about 5 in. in front of them, moving back and forth at regular or irregular motion. They either tracked it accurately with clear focus (focus–track, FT) or blurred tracking with relaxed accommodation (blur–track, BT) or not tracking, simply viewing the target (blur–no-track, BNT). The average alpha and no-alpha series beginning with the onset of the ocular maneuvers are shown in Fig. 4.6. The same kind of disturbance and recovery functions can be seen (Mulholland, 1972).

I hypothesize from these data that a shift of attention from a lower to higher level, induced by stimulation, or by opening the eyes in the dark, or by ocular maneuver is mediated by visual control processes which produce a characteristic disturbance and recovery of the occipital EEG

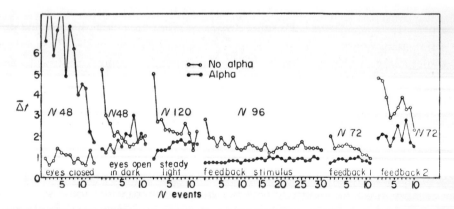

Fig. 4.5. Disturbance and recovery functions of the average alpha-actuation cycle (24 children).

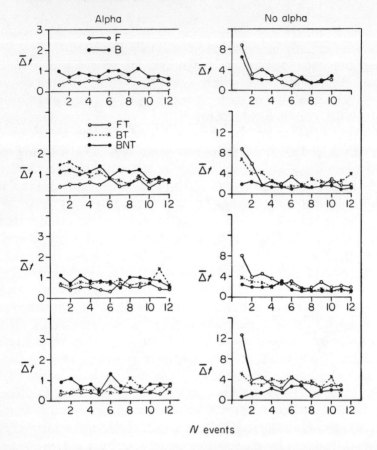

Fig. 4.6. Average disturbance and recovery functions for various ocular maneuvers. The top of the graph is for a stationary target. The lower graphs are for a moving target. See text.

alpha-attenuation cycle. For this process a stimulus is a sufficient but not a necessary condition as evidenced by the disturbance and recovery after the opening of the eyes in the dark. A quantitative approximation to the disturbance and recovery function is

$$\bar{\Delta}t_{\mathrm{a}} = AN + B \tag{1}$$

$$\bar{\Delta}t_{\mathrm{na}} = C/N + D \tag{2}$$

When N is the number (less than 50) of the event starting from the onset of stimulus or ocular maneuver.

In the study of 24 children (see Fig. 4.5), the average hyperbolic and linear functions for the conditions (1) eyes open in the dark, (2) steady light on, and (3) Loop 1 feedback are shown on the right side of Table 4-1.

The individual data were also fitted with these functions and for the majority of 24 subjects the best fit was statistically significant. The individual best fit functions for in single trial are useful for comparing the similarity of the functional response of the EEG from left and right sides. In Fig. 4.7 an example of computer-derived functions is shown for the no-alpha series and the alpha series during visual feedback stimulation. The functions are for a single trial, from a 6-year-old boy. In this case the functions fitted the data well. In other cases the individual functions do not fit the data as well. For this reason, the hyperbolic and linear functions described before apply only to average data, though they are representative of the majority of cases.

Average disturbance–recovery functions for each various experimental conditions were separately estimated by fitting a linear function to the alpha series and a linearized hyperbolic function to the no-alpha series with the method of least squares. Each serial event was associated with a mean and σ based on 24 children. The standard error of the estimate (SE) and the correlation coefficient indicate how well the functions fit the actual data. The functions ± 1 SE include about 68% of the data. For eyes open in the dark and steady light conditions $r = .53$ is significant at the .5 level; $r = .66$ significant at the .01 level. For Loop 1, $r = .35$ is significant at .05 level; .45 at the .01 level. For both alpha and no-alpha the functions of the means, and the standard error of the estimate are least for Loop 1 feedback.

In the feedback conditions, Δt_a includes the average latency: $\bar{\Delta} t_a =$ latency $(\bar{l}) + \bar{L}_2$. Here, $\bar{L}_2$ is the average time between recorded alpha

TABLE 4–1

Estimate of the Statistics of Regression Functions of Δt_a, Δt_{na} on N

$\Delta t_a = AN + B$	Average of regressions			Regression of the average			
	A	B	$r_{y \cdot x}$	A	B	SE	$r_{y \cdot x}$
Eyes open, dark	.07	1.3	$+.44$	.07	1.3	.4	$+.54$
Steady light	.02	1.2	$+.31$	.06	1.1	.2	$+.78$
Loop 1 feedback	.01	.7	$+.44$	.01	.7	.1	$+.76$
$\bar{\Delta} t_{na} = (1/N)C + D$	C	D	$r_{y \cdot f(x)}$	C	D	SE	$r_{y \cdot f(x)}$
Eyes open, dark	3.8	1.2	$+.67$	3.7	1.3	.2	$+.98$
Steady light	3.1	1.6	$+.78$	3.1	1.7	.3	$+.93$
Loop 1 feedback	1.4	1.3	$+.68$	1.4	1.3	.1	$+.87$

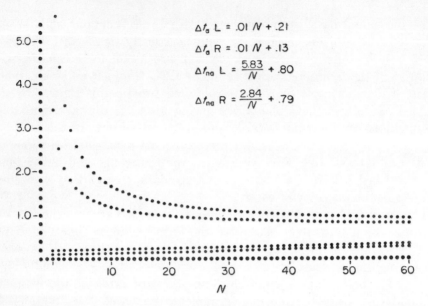

Fig. 4.7. Computer-calculated disturbance and recovery functions for $\Delta t_a \Delta t_{na}$ on right and left sides. Data from a single trial with a 6-year-old child. The best fit correlation coefficients (r) for the four functions are Δt_a, left (.26); Δt_a, right (.24); Δt_{na}, left (.74); Δt_{na}, right (.38).

blocking and state relay off. In this study $\bar{L}_2$ was .3–.4 sec. Systematic changes in the $\bar{\Delta}t_a$ are due to systematic changes in the latency.

For the regression of the average feedback condition (Table 4-1).

$$AN + B = \bar{l} + \bar{L}_2$$

$$.01N + 0.7 - .35 = \bar{l}$$

$$\bar{l} = .01N + .35 \ (\text{sec}).$$

The recorded duration of EEG attenuation after stimulation can be estimated

$$\bar{\Delta}t_{rna} = \bar{\Delta}t_{na} + \bar{L}_2 - \bar{L}_1.$$

$\bar{L}_1$ is the delay between recorded alpha and state relay on (alpha). $\bar{L}_2$ is as before.

$$\bar{\Delta}t_{rna} = (C/N) + D + \bar{L}_2 - \bar{L}_1$$

$$C = 1.40, \qquad D = 1.30, \qquad \bar{L}_1 = 0.25 \text{ sec}$$

$$\bar{\Delta}t_{rna} = (1.4/N) + 1.3 + .1 = 1.4/N + 1.4 \ (\text{sec}).$$

The habituation function is described as a change in the latency and duration of the EEG attenuation after stimulation. In Loop 1 the initial response to the first stimulus had an average latency of .36 sec; average duration of 2.80 sec. After 30 stimulations the average latency was .65 sec; average duration, 1.44 sec. The ratio duration/latency is called the *index of orienting* (IO). After the first Loop 1 stimulus, IO was 7.8, after 30 stimulations it was 2.2. An approximation to IO is the ratio of $\Delta t_{na}/\Delta t_a$ which is sufficient for most experiments.

3. *Instructional Set and Voluntary Attention*

The time series of alpha and no-alpha events can be influenced by voluntary attention and cognitive tasks. The simplest attention task is to have the subject "pay attention" for a series of flashes or to simply view them. With instructions to "pay attention" the subject usually shows longer no-alpha and briefer alpha durations (see Fig. 4.8; Mulholland & Runnals, 1962b). Similar results are obtained when the subject is instructed to be "alert" or to be "relaxed" (see Fig. 4.9; Mulholland, 1968). Counting the stimuli also produce similar changes in the alpha attenuation series (see Fig. 4.10; Mulholland & Runnals, 1962b). There are the expected

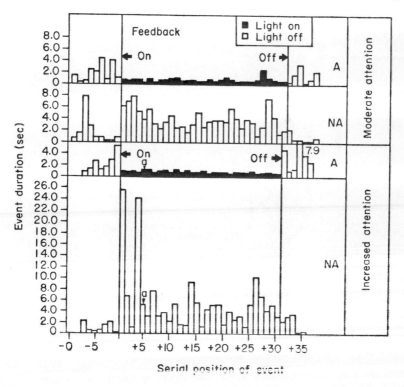

Fig. 4.8. The Δt_a (A) decreases, and Δt_{na} (NA) increases when subject pays attention. [From Mulholland & Runnals, 1962b.]

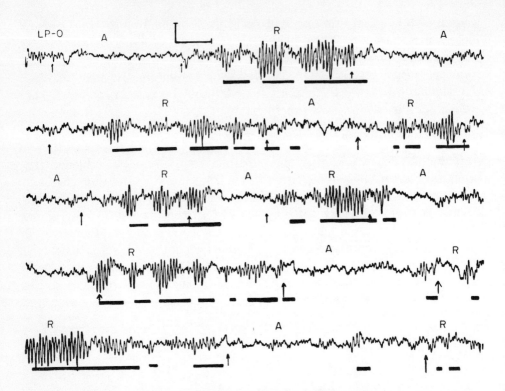

Fig. 4.9. Subject reports he is alert (A) or relaxed (R). The EEG is prominent during the "relax" intervals. [From Mulholland & Evans, 1966.]

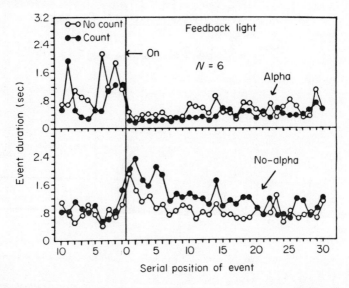

Fig. 4.10. Average Δt_a, Δt_{na} while counting or not counting feedback stimuli. [From Mulholland & Runnals, 1962b.]

individual differences. Some subjects do not show large changes; a few show none at all.

More complex attentional tasks require the subject to "pay attention" or to count the feedback stimuli flashes according to a prearranged schedule, e.g., instructions to "pay particular attention to a particular flash." Using feedback method the series of alpha and no-alpha bursts associated with the "target" stimuli were different from the others compared to control conditions (see Fig. 4.11; Mulholland & Runnals, 1963).

In Fig. 4.12 results for a single subject on a single run are shown. He was instructed to "pay attention" to the 10th, 20th, 30th, and 40th flashes.

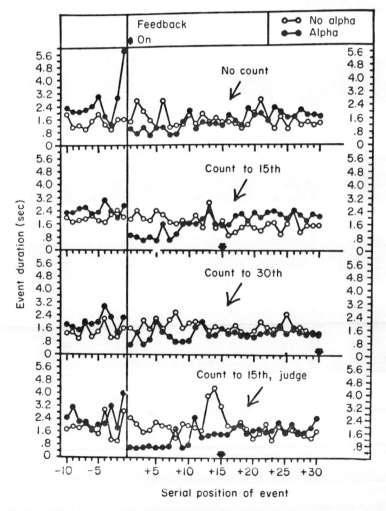

Fig. 4.11. Average Δt_a, Δt_{na} while counting specific feedback stimuli. The bottom graph is for instructions to pay particular attention to the 15th flash and judge its brightness. [From Mulholland & Runnals, 1963.]

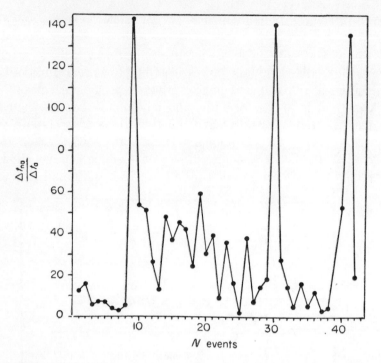

Fig. 4.12. Index of orienting for a single trial with prior instructions to pay attention to the 10th, 20th, 30th, and 40th stimulus (12-year-old boy). [From Mulholland, 1970.]

The number used here was the ratio of $(\Delta t$ no-alpha$)/(\Delta t$ alpha$)$. The response series was changed as scheduled by instructions, with greater orienting at the 10th, 20th, 30th, and 40th response (Mulholland, 1970). In experiments like this we have found that the alpha-attenuation series can be reliably modified by subjects according to a prearranged schedule. There are individual differences. Some show much greater effects than others.

My interpretation of these results is that the subject, using a memory scheme of the instructions, "counts down" using inner speech to the proper stimulus in the series. This is associated with activation and intensification of visual control processes as expectancy increases and the occipital alpha is suppressed for a longer time. The term *internal attention gradient* is used to describe those still-hidden, complicated cognitive and perceptual operations that result in occipital EEG changes on schedule following instructions (Mulholland, 1962).

4. Shifts of Attention and Emotional Stimuli

It is well-known that emotional or evocative stimuli such as pictures of nudes compared to pictures of flowers (Peper, 1970), pictures of sexual activity compared to nonsexual activity (Mander, 1971), emotional words compared to neutral words (Mulholland & Davis, 1966), elicit different degrees of attention and longer durations of alpha blocking. I believe that when they look, people spend a longer time looking at such pictures compared to neutral ones, and the intervals of no-alpha are longer. These changes occur reliably with the feedback method yielding characteristic shifts in disturbance and recovery functions to such stimuli. See Figs. 4.13 and 4.14. The response to the various kind of stimuli can be analyzed in terms of the initial effect, rate of habituation to determine whether the alpha function, no-alpha function, or both are affected.

5. Shifts of Attention from One Stimulus to Another

Ordinarily the disturbance and recovery of the occipital EEG alpha-attenuation cycle is interpreted as a shift in the *level* of attention. In studies where the subject shifts his attention from one stimulus to another, there is no clear evidence in the EEG which permits one to know which

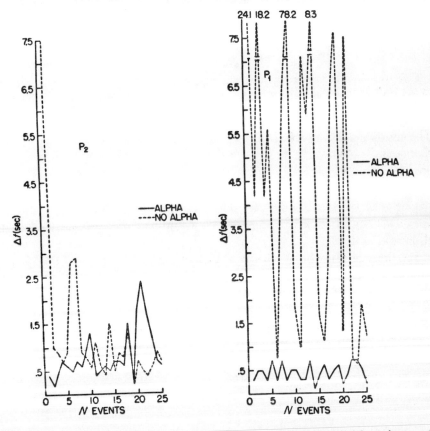

Fig. 4.13. Disturbance and recovery of Δt_a, Δt_{na} for a single trial with a picture of a flower (left) and with a picture of a nude (right). [From Peper, 1970.]

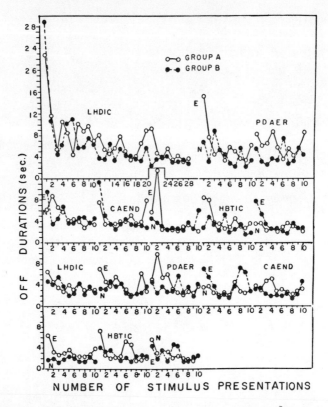

Fig. 4.14. Disturbance and recovery of Δt_{na} with neutral (N), emotional (E), and scrambled words. [From Mulholland, T. & Davis, E. Electroencephalographic activation: Nonspecific habituation by verbal stimuli. *Science*, **152**, 1966, 1104–1106, Fig. 1. Copyright 1966 by the American Association for the Advancement of Science.]

stimulus is being attended to. The next studies demonstrate that feedback EEG can be used to show which stimulus the subject is attending to and looking at.

Previous studies have shown that the length of alpha "bursts" during feedback can be increased by increasing the stimulus delay during feedback (Mulholland, 1968; see Fig. 4.15). The results for the three time delays is clear. The longer the delay the longer the alpha bursts. This effect is a statistical one. As delay increases the number of longer alpha bursts increases. If the delay is too long, the alpha will be episodically and unpredictably attenuated and the stimulus will occur infrequently. Figure 4.16 summarizes the statistical relation between alpha-stimulus delay and alpha durations, latency and the number of alpha events associated with stimulation based on experimental results from five subjects.

This result can be applied to the study of orienting to *one* stimulus when *two* stimuli are linked to alpha. If two stimuli are presented, one with a *brief* time delay, the other with a *longer* time delay, the question is—can

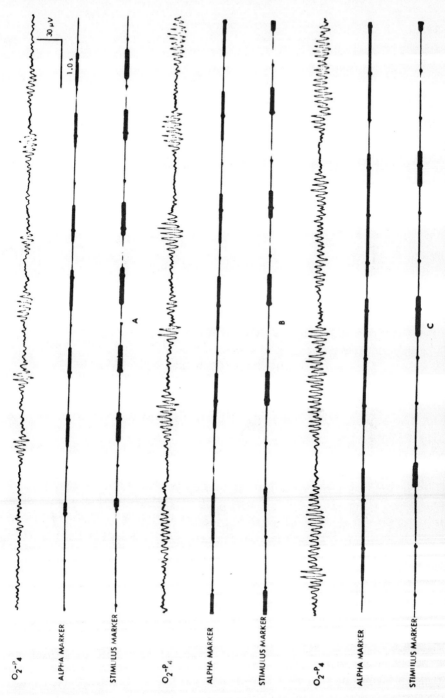

Fig. 4.15. Delayed feedback stimulation is associated with increased Δt_s.

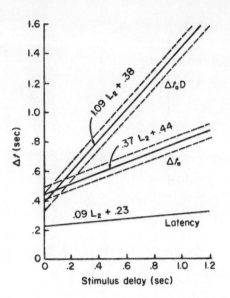

Fig. 4.16. Statistical summary of the relationship between Δt_a and feedback delay. From five normals. At delays $<.25$ sec almost all intervals of alpha are associated with stimulation.

the subject, by selective attention, by selective looking, respond to the feedback stimulus having the long time delay and not to the one having the brief time delay? If he can shift from one stimulus to the other, the EEG should shift from longer to briefer alpha bursts and vice-versa.

Recent results from our laboratory show that some subjects can voluntarily shift from one loop to the other so that the EEG can show which stimulus is "in the loop" and when the shift occurs from one loop to the other. The subject must have well-defined alpha and a definite response to stimulation.

The subject is seated in a simple perimeter. A chin rest is used. On each side, 25° from straightahead are small lights, about 12 in. from the eye. Both lights are controlled by alpha and both are clearly seen by the subject. One light has a long time delay (LTD), the other has a brief time delay (BTD) (.2 sec). In practice sessions the subject is tested with the BTD light, and the LTD light separately. Then the LTD light is connected in the feedback path until about 15–40 alpha-light events have occurred. Then the BTD light is turned on. The result is a change in the EEG from longer to shorter alpha bursts which is often apparent from visual inspection of the record. An abrupt shift of both alpha and no-alpha durations occurs. The computer display of the successive alpha, no-alpha intervals shows the change in the alpha-attenuation series with the presentation of the brief time-delay stimulus though the effects on the alpha durations are most evident (see Figs. 4.17 and 4.18).

In the next conditions both lights are connected in the loop together. The experimenter instructs the subject "I want you to pay attention to the light on the left." Thirty alpha-light events are collected. Then he says "pay attention to the lights on the right." These conditions are practiced until the subject gives predominantly long alpha bursts in association with the light having the long time delay when "paying attention" to it or short alpha bursts when "paying attention" to the light having a brief time delay, taking care that complete habituation to the stimulus does not occur.

In test trials the subject voluntarily shifts attention from one side to the other side while viewing the lights. Subjective attention to the right is indicated by pushing a hand switch which marks the ink record. When paying attention to the left the button is not pushed. The EEG results from three subjects are shown in Figs. 4.19–4.21. One subject who did not exhibit good control stated that she could not ignore the brief time delay light. The results of these preliminary studies were

(1) For most subjects there is a definite change in the EEG alpha bursts in association with the stimulus that the subject reported he was attending to.

(2) For some subjects the EEG changes are not consistent.

(3) Some subjects do not show any effect after a brief training period.

We have also found that if the subject is told to look at the lights he attends to or is not told that he cannot look, the results are like those described above. If the subject is instructed to look straightahead, (both

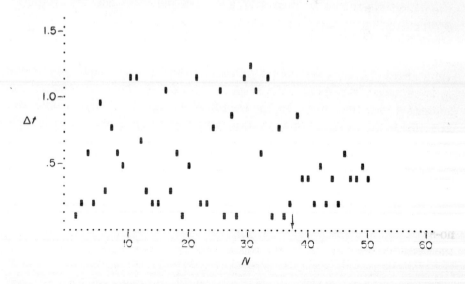

Fig. 4.17. Computer display of Δt_a during feedback stimulation with long time delay and adding a second stimulus with a brief time delay.

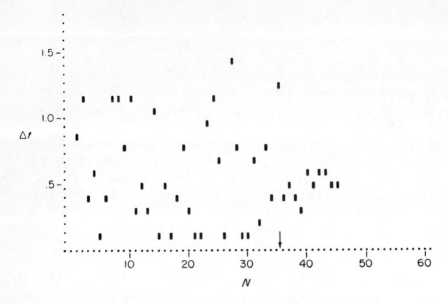

Fig. 4.18. Same as 17. Different subject.

lights can be clearly seen), to shift his attention but *not* his eyes, no differential effect of the attentional variable set has been seen yet. Although much more work is needed, this new method will extend the use of EEG in the study of human orienting, and permit closer correlation of the EEG with changes in looking behavior and subjective reports of attention.

The results shown in Figs. 4.17 and 4.18 indicate that the method of delayed feedback may be employed to study the shift of orienting from a suprathreshold stimulus to another which is just at threshold. First the subject would be habituated to a visual stimulus having a long time delay. Another stimulus connected in the feedback loop would be well below threshold with a short time delay. This stimulus is then increased in graded steps. As the stimulus having a brief time delay enters the threshold range of magnitudes, and the subject reacts to it, there would be a shift from predominantly longer to briefer alpha durations, a decreased variance of alpha durations and increase in durations of no-alpha, i.e., the subject would show EEG changes associated with orienting to a near threshold stimulus. Sokolov has shown that orienting to a threshold stimulus is greater and more prolonged compared to suprathreshold stimuli (Sokolov, 1963). The effect may be transitory as a weak stimulus will rapidly habituate. These methodological suggestions following from preliminary, promising results must be tested further before their usefulness can be fully appreciated.

The remainder of this paper reviews my current hypotheses linking the suppression of alpha to visual control processes. This is followed by a

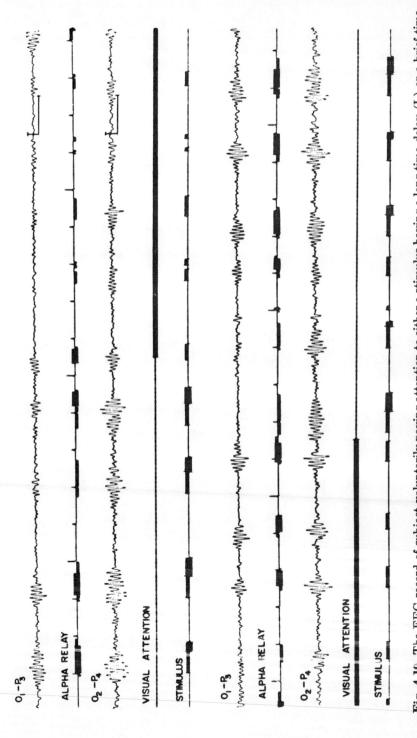

Fig. 4.19. The EEG record of subject voluntarily paying attention to either a stimulus having a long time delay (L) or a brief time delay (R). When paying attention to the stimulus on the right subject pressed a hand switch causing a mark on the polygraph tracing labeled voluntary attention. See text.

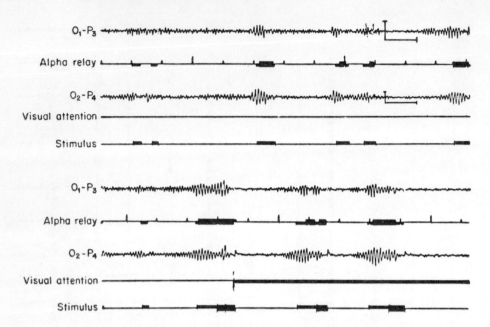

Fig. 4.20. Same as 19. Different subject. BTD on left stimulus.

critical evaluation of three assumptions often made in EEG studies: (1) *singularity* of the responses of the occipital alpha rhythm to visual stimulation; (2) *functional equivalence* of EEG events; (3) *functional identity* during the temporal interval of alpha suppression. Some new kinds of experiments are suggested which may extend the study of visual attention with objective EEG and behavioral methods.

II. NEUROPHYSIOLOGICAL BASIS FOR CHANGES IN THE EEG RELATED TO VISUAL ATTENTION

A. VISUAL CONTROL AND THE OCCIPITAL ALPHA RHYTHMS

Visual control processes refer to the ongoing adjustment of the visual receptor on the basis of information about the target fed back from the retina. It includes processes involved in fixation, lens accommodation, tracking, saccadic and vergence movements, and control of pupillary diameter. A visual stimulus is both *seen* and *looked* at. Visual control does not occur as separate units, e.g., afferent, integrative, and efferent processes. Visual control involves the whole of the visual apparatus and the study of alpha suppression in relation to visual attention requires a consideration of the whole visual processes otherwise a one-sided interpretation will result. This has been the case for the familiar interpretation of

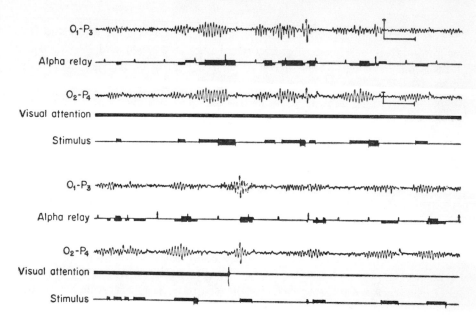

Fig. 4.21. Same as 19. Different subject. BTD on left stimulus.

alpha suppression after visual stimulation, an interpretation which emphasizes the afferent processes, neglecting the receptor adjustment processes.

When Moruzzi and Magoun (1949) introduced the concept of the reticular activating system they laid the groundwork for an interpretation of the desynchronization or "activation" of the electrocorticogram and EEG which has persisted until now. Their discovery that afferent excitation passed along collaterals into the midbrain up to the thalamus and then to extensive regions in the cortex is known to every student of brain research. The emphasis was on *afferent* processes, and the extent and complexity of those processes were shown to be much greater than previously thought. Moreover, they drew an analogy between EEG changes which occur naturally when an animal "alerts to attention" (Magoun, 1954) and the changes after stimulation of the reticular formation. There was no consideration of the possibility that efferent processes occurring in cortex subsequent to the arrival of afferent excitation could also produce cortical activation and EEG desynchronization. This possibility was there even in the anesthetized animal because of the difficulty of suppressing eye movements, i.e., of stopping visual processes. Subsequent research on the oculomotor system with stimulation and lesion techniques, showed that processes involved in eye movement were located in the same zone of the midbrain tegmentum as the reticular activating system (Bender & Shanzer, 1964).

Moreover, visual processes related to pursuit tracking, fixation and lens accommodation are occurring in cortical regions *17*, *18*, and *19* which are the regions from which the parietal–occipital EEG is derived (Robinson, 1968; Wagman, 1964). These visual functions are also involved in the orienting to visual stimuli. Studies of the occipital EEG and accommodative vergence, pursuit tracking and fast eye movements confirm the hypothesis that the occurrence of alpha is linked not to visual attention but to visual control processes (Mulholland & Peper, 1971). A representative experiment from those studies is presented here.

Adult humans with normal corrected vision and who had recordable occipital alpha with eyes open were studied. Recordings were made in a quiet audiometric test room. Three kinds of recordings were obtained: EEG, EOG, and a report of the apparent clearness or subjective clarity (SC) of the target. EEGs were obtained from parietal–occipital electrodes, Pi–O_1, Pi–O_2, or occipital O_1–O_2 in the international nomenclature. The EEG electrodes were attached to the scalp with electrolytic paste and connected to a Grass Model 5 polygraph. An electrode over the mastoid was ground.

The EEG was automatically classified into intervals of alpha and no-alpha (Mulholland, 1968). The definition of alpha was accomplished by means of a band-pass filter, amplifier, and state relay circuit as described before.

The target moved laterally at eye level in the frontal plane through a distance of 5–6 in. Movement of the target was controlled by two variable-speed motors. These were connected by cams to rigid levers which were linked to the target holder. The levers and motors were noisy when the target was moving. By varying the speed of the motors with a manual control, simple and complex movements could be generated. Target motion was recorded from a potentiometer linked to the movement of the target holder. As the target moved, it turned the potentiometer through a small angle. The change of resistance was recorded as a voltage deflection by connecting the potentiometer between the polygraph driver amplifier and ground. The beginning, direction, and end of target motion was recorded, which was sufficient for these studies.

The EOG was recorded with nonpolarizing AgCl (Beckman) electrodes from the inner and outer canthi for each eye. The EOG showed the beginning, direction, and end of eye movements. At the beginning and end of each trial the EOG for extreme left, right, upward, and downward ocular deviation was recorded. A head or jaw support was used for all subjects. When necessary a bite board was used.

Three kinds of eye movements were recorded: a slow accommodative vergence, slow tracking movements, and fast movements. To record accommodative vergence the target was viewed monocularly, one eye being occluded. Then the target was brought near the viewing eye, the occluded eye moved inward (convergence) while the viewing eye moved outward (divergence). For other subjects the target was viewed binocularly and both eyes showed the symmetrical movements of binocular convergence. Change in vergence was usually associated with a change in subjective clearness of the target. The subject was instructed to press a telegraph key whenever the target appeared clear and focused. The key position was marked on the EEG record. Sometimes the report of subjective clarity (SC) lagged behind the recorded change of vergence.

Pursuit tracking movements were distinguished from fast movements by a slower velocity and close correspondence with target motion. They were distinguished from vergence movements by their velocity. Vergence movements were slower and each eye moved in opposite directions.

The EEG, EOG, and subjective clarity (SC) report were recorded while viewing a target moving laterally in a complex, unpredictable trajectory.

Tracking tasks and instructions were focus and track the target (focus–track, FT); relax accommodation until the target is subjectively blurred and continue tracking (blur–track, BT); or relax accommodation and not track (blur–no-track, BNT). The number of experimental trials sometimes varied from subject to subject. For this reason, data for each subject are presented separately. Fourteen subjects were tested. Two subjects showed no alpha under any of the conditions; three did not monitor target clearness reliably. The EEG results for the last three were similar to those obtained by the majority of the remaining nine subjects whose results are presented here.

The quantification of the EEG was based on measures made on the ink tracing:

Alpha index. State relay ON defined alpha; OFF defined no-alpha. From these the series of durations of alpha and no-alpha events were obtained and an estimate of percentage of time alpha.

Maximum alpha amplitude. In each trial the maximum peak-to-peak amplitude of alpha associated with state relay ON was measured in millimeters.

Alpha delay. The delay between the beginning of an experiment trial and the first state relay ON (alpha) was measured.

Total time. The total time (in seconds) for each trial was measured. The beginning of a trial was defined as the ON or OFF interval during which the brief instructions were given over the intercom as prearranged with the subject. These were "focus–track," "blur–track," and "blur–no-track." The total time in each trial was also measured. The mean of total time, percent time "alpha," maximum "alpha" amplitude, and "alpha" delay were analyzed by analysis of variance.

With divergence and a report of a "blurred" target and no pursuit tracking, "alpha" occurs more often, with greater maximum amplitude and sooner (see Table 4-2). For percentage of time alpha the average for FT < BNT for nine subjects; FT < BT < BNT, six subjects. For maximum alpha amplitude FT < BNT, six; FT < BT < BNT, two subjects. For alpha delay FT > BNT, eight subjects; BT > BNT, seven subjects; FT > BT > BNT, four subjects. For total time FT < BNT, four subjects; FT < BT < BNT, no subjects.

Analysis of variance for the differences among conditions FT, BT, and BNT yielded F significant ($p < .05$) for maximum alpha amplitude; F significant ($p < .001$) for percentage of time alpha. The F ratios for total time and alpha delay were not significant. Figure 4.22 illustrates these results. Saccadic eye movements were not reliably associated with a decrease of alpha occurrence.

It is true of control systems using negative feedback that good control

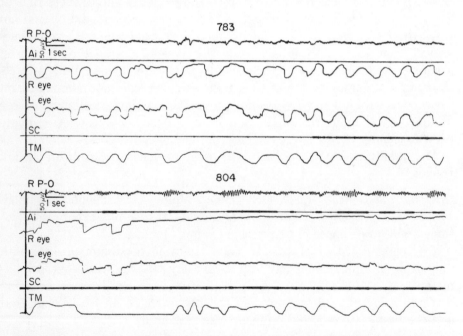

Fig. 4.22. Tracings are: R P-O right parietal-occipital EEG; Ai, alpha index, R eye, L eye, right and left EOG; SC, subjective clarity of target; TM, target motion. The EEG and EOG for a subject tracking with focused vision, defocusing, then not tracking and still defocused. Alpha increases when tracking ceases. [From Mulholland & Peper, 1971.]

TABLE 4-2

Unpredictably Moving Target[a]

Subject	N trials			Total time			$\bar{X}$ percent-time alpha			$\bar{X}$ maximum alpha amplitude (mm)			$\bar{X}$ alpha delay (sec)		
	FT	BT	BNT	FT	BT	BNT	FT	BT	BNT	FT	BT	BNT	FT	BT	BNT
P.W.	3	3	3	117	114	102	23.3	16.2	28.9	10.6	9.0	10.0	1.6	3.3	1.4
W.C.	4	3	3	65	98	80	10.8	17.1	38.8	4.8	4.3	7.0	3.8	2.3	2.0
S.F.	3	3	3	68	64	86	3.8	5.2	34.3	6.3	4.6	10.3	7.7	2.1	1.8
S.L.	3	3	3	112	85	107	1.8	3.4	20.5	4.0	8.0	11.5	9.9	9.2	3.8
R.H.	2	2	2	51	68	41	48.7	80.7	75.4	11.0	8.2	8.0	1.6	.6	.5
R.D.	2	2	2	91	71	79	6.6	9.9	46.3	8.0	7.5	9.5	8.5	1.1	4.4
W.P.	3	3	3	132	171	132	15.1	41.9	44.7	12.0	15.0	16.5	7.6	3.9	1.3
R.G.	3	3	3	180	149	258	9.4	15.1	12.2	10.0	7.5	10.0	3.1	5.2	4.6
A.M.	3	3	3	106	59	70	2.1	13.9	41.1	7.3	11.6	10.6	4.7	6.3	2.6
$\bar{X}$				102.4	97.6	106.1	13.5	22.6	38.2	8.2	8.4	10.4	5.4	3.8	2.5

[a] From Mulholland and Peper (1971).

in terms of frequency response and stability can result even if the components of the system are somewhat noisy, i.e., have an imperfect reliability. The characteristics of a feedback system can be identified even though there is "loose" causal coupling among the component operators. This empirical fact has a methodological counterpart—feedback configurations can be used to detect causal links among variables even though the functional relationship includes noise or unpredictable variation. Thus, if one hypothesizes A causes B or, if A, then B, etc., then connecting B back to A through an external path should produce different effects depending on the sign of feedback from B, i.e., whether feedback is positive or negative. The contrast between these two kinds of feedback effects is an index of the reliability of the link A to B (Mulholland, 1968). For instance, if it were true that a visual stimulus decreased alpha to some minimum and that absence of visual stimulation increased it to a maximum, then connecting the EEG alpha back to the stimulus with negative feedback should produce a stable oscillation between alpha and no-alpha whose frequency would depend on the transfer function of the system. With positive feedback it should go to a limit of maximum or minimum alpha or swing erratically between these limits. Of course, this does not happen because in fact the hypothesis is incorrect—absence of visual stimulus does not increase alpha to a maximum, nor does increasing a visual stimulus decrease it to a minimum. This is already known. There are other variables which must be identified. As these variables are introduced into the feedback system the difference between positive and negative feedback should increase and provide evidence that the variables are, in fact, relevant. In the following experiment, hypothesized variables are connected into the system until the maximum difference between negative and positive delayed feedback was achieved.

The basic feedback connection was between the alpha-attenuation cycle and the visibility of the target which can be stationary or moving. The variables which were introduced were target visibility, target motion, and modes of oculomotor response. The changes of the alpha activation cycle were compared among the various feedback configurations for the time series of duration of alpha events, the duration of no-alpha events and the period (Δt alpha $+$ Δt no-alpha) of the alpha-attenuation cycle. If the experimental variables loaded on the system are causally linked to the EEG response, they should exhibit minimum variation under negative feedback and swing erratically and unpredictably between limits with positive feedback.

In one experiment in my laboratory, E. Peper connected the EEG by an external path to the visibility of the moving target by an external path. Eye-tracking functions were linked to target visibility by instruction to the subject. The experimental set-up was that described previously. When in view the target was always moving in a quasi-sinusoidal path. The subject was instructed to view the target and track it whenever it was visible. Peper found in all cases where alpha was present with eyes open that the EEG showed a very stable alternation between Δt alpha and Δt no-alpha with Loop 1 (alpha → target ON, no-alpha → OFF). With the reverse configuration Loop 2 (alpha → target OFF and no-alpha → target ON), a runaway system with erratic swinging between long periods of alpha and no tracking and no-alpha and tracking was observed. The contrast between negative and positive feedback was clearly greater than what we had observed previously with stationary targets (see Fig. 4.23). It was concluded that the tracking process was linked to the EEG occipital alpha-activation cycle and that Loop 1 was a negative feedback, and Loop 2 a positive feedback configuration.

One can therefore hypothesize quite reasonably that both efferent visual control processes and afferent processes and their integration occurring in cortex are involved in the suppression of alpha after stimulation. Moreover this hypothesis permits an interpretation of transitory suppression of alpha when eyes are opened in the dark or when one "attempts to see" in the dark, without resorting to a demon called "attention." The interpretation of older and recent studies of alpha and attention in terms of visual control processes have been summarized elsewhere (Mulholland, 1968, 1969, 1972; Mulholland & Peper, 1971).

B. A New Experimental Approach to the Classical Theory

The response of the occipital EEG after visual stimulation is not singular, it is a disturbance followed by a recovery of the alpha-attenuation cycle; as shown before. The alternation is not invariant but changes with the availability of visual information. Though looking can be initiated voluntarily it does not continue in the absence of visual stimulation. To start looking again a new command must be given to the visual apparatus. Intervals of alpha and little or no-alpha may reflect in a gross way a "not-look"–"look," a "not-scan"–"scan" system. Such a system would be related to a schedule of the sampling of visual information. When information was high look (no-alpha) samples would be long and no-look (alpha) times briefer. As information became redundant or not relevant, look samples would be briefer and not-look times would be longer. Also, one may see or be aware of stimuli yet not look at them. In this sense, one could be attending to a stimulus, but without *looking* there would be little or no effect on the alpha rhythm.

The habituation of the response to stimulation may be a change in the visual field sampling function in response to an increasingly redundant

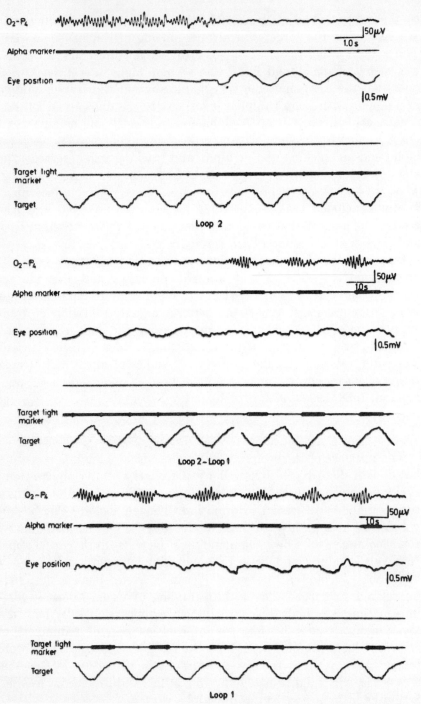

Fig. 4.23. The EEG and EOG record while tracking a moving target whose luminance is controlled by the occurrence of alpha. Transition from Loop 2 feedback to Loop 1. [From Peper, 1970.]

stimulus. This approach lends naturally to a time-series analysis of alpha and no-alpha events during habituation rather than an overemphasis on the singular, no-alpha intervals after successive stimulations.

A second classical assumption was that all alpha events reflect the same level of behavioral or psychological function. For instance all alpha intervals were assumed to indicate a *low* level of visual attention, all no-alpha, low amplitude–fast activity were assumed to indicate a *high* level of visual attention. This assumption of *functional equivalence* is seen in those statistical procedures whereby all alpha events are pooled to get percent-time alpha or where all intervals of no-alpha are lumped together as an index of orienting.

Although direct experimental evidence is lacking, it is worthwhile to consider an alternative hypothesis that all alpha and all no-alpha events are not functionally equivalent. For instance, when habituation to a recurring visual stimulus, as described before, the changes in $\bar{\Delta}t_a$ and $\bar{\Delta}t_{na}$ can be approximated by the function where N is equal to or less than 50.

$$\bar{\Delta}t_a = AN + B$$

$$\bar{\Delta}t_{na} = C/N + D.$$

Behavioral performance, attention, alertness, etc., may not necessarily be functions of alpha versus no-alpha but functions of the habituation functions. It is possible that an interval of alpha occurring just after stimulation is associated with a higher level of visual attention or behavioral alertness than is an interval of little or no-alpha occurring after 30 alpha events. If the stimuli are say, words to be memorized or learned, perhaps learning is complete when habituation reaches an asymptote, etc.

The assumption of functional equivalence is related to the assumption of response singularity because then the initial, singular no-alpha is also at the beginning of the habituation process. The behavioral changes which are observed during that initial, single no-alpha interval may not be true of other intervals of no-alpha, i.e., they may be functions of the habituation function.

A third classical assumption is that all parts of an interval of no-alpha, low amplitude–fast activity, are associated with an identical psychological or behavioral state. For instance, the "blocking" of alpha after visual stimulation is said to reflect a state of arousal, alertness, activation, or increased attention. By means of such concepts the disappearance or suppression of alpha is explained. However, after awhile alpha returns. How is the recurrence of alpha explained? There must be a return to a *lower* level of arousal, alertness, activation, or attention. Obviously the sequence of changes from alpha to no-alpha back to alpha implies a dynamic cycle, another kind of disturbance and recovery *within* the no-alpha interval.

The idea that the EEG activation or desynchronization was composed of different processes was expressed by Sharpless and Jasper (1956). In their terms there are two components to the response of the EEG to stimulation—a *phasic* response and a *tonic* response. Phasic responses have a short latency, brief duration, and do not habituate. Tonic responses have a longer latency, a longer duration, and habituate readily. Sharpless and Jasper showed that different brain processes were involved for phasic compared to tonic responses.

The blocking of alpha to stimulation includes both phasic and tonic components. The latency of an alpha block has to be the phasic latency as it always occurs and is briefer than the tonic latency. The phasic activation may end quickly and, the tonic process, already begun, will continue and alpha will not occur. In this way the processes at the beginning of an alpha block would be phasic while those at the end after the phasic process has subsided would include the tonic process. The longer the duration of desynchronization or alpha suppression the greater the difference between early phasic and late tonic parts of a no-alpha interval. After habituation has occurred, the no-alpha may be due to phasic processes, since Sharpless and Jasper showed that the tonic component became habituated, but not the phasic.

These considerations point to some new kinds of experiments, which test the hypothesis that electrophysiological and behavioral changes may be occurring within the interval of low-amplitude–fast activity. For instance, if a stimulus were systematically delayed so that it was made to occur near the beginning, near the middle, or near the end of an interval of no-alpha would the average evoked response be the same for these three delays? Would the latency of fast eye movement to a new target be the same if the movement occurred just after an interval of no-alpha began compared to a longer delay so that it occurred just before alpha returned? From this paradigm one can imagine studies of stimulus thresholds, pattern recognition using tachistoscopic method, learning and remembering as a function of the amount of delay between the start of the no-alpha interval and the stimulus. By means of such studies, some estimate of the functional changes within the no-alpha interval can be made.

All of these ideas are summarized in the schema of the alpha-attenuation series, presented in Fig. 4.24 (Mulholland, 1969). Some process which is associated with alpha gives way to a suppression of alpha if a critical value is reached. However, after a time the processes reverse moving toward the value favorable for alpha. The series alternates in a complex

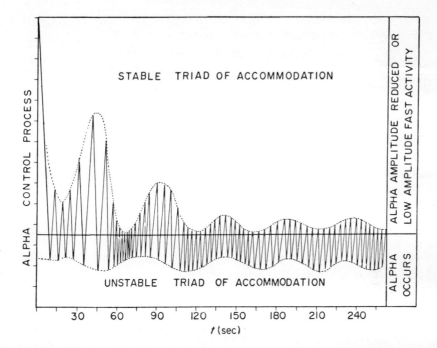

Fig. 4.24. Hypothetical schema of the alpha-attenuation series. [From Mulholland, 1969.]

way. The schema points up the difference between the older and the newer hypotheses. The response is a series, all intervals of all alpha and all intervals of no-alpha may not be functionally equivalent and all parts of a given interval may not be functionally identical. This schema is only a guide to experimentation and may be quite incomplete or incorrect. Nature has an endless capacity to outwit theorists.

The fundamental question of the alpha process is of course still obscure and functional experiments cannot provide an answer. However, when neurophysiology provides the necessary evidence and alpha *is* explained, we shall understand the neurophysiological basis for the observations and the empirical findings already made and verified during the brief history of research on the occipital alpha rhythm in relation to human attention.

1. Practical Applications

In conclusion, I would like to speculate on some applications of feedback EEG in relation to visual control as I see them. Some of these are already close at hand, others require considerable development (Mulholland, 1970). The following groups of applications are intended as an outline.

Alertometers. This would be a system for comparing one visual display with another in terms of the alertness of the viewers. With the aid of a computer, the attentional-looking response of brain rhythms could be averaged and printed out on a graph, an alertograph. Such a system could be mobile, that is, a specially equipped vehicle could be used to sample alertographs in various areas permitting regional and market comparisons. With modern radio telemetry techniques people need not be connected to the brain wave machine by a cable. This would permit study of attentive looking in more natural settings. Such a system would also have application in research on the many variables linked to attentive looking, for instance the ontogenesis or development of attention, and changes due aging.

Attention controllers. In this application a computer is used. It looks at the response of the brain rhythms to the visual stimulus and compares the response against a rule that has been programmed. If the brain response is too little, it changes the visual display according to its program until the proper brain response is achieved. This feature could be incorporated into a teaching machine which would present a warning or alerting signal or change the display to keep the subject paying attention.

A more complex system would require a large variety of visual displays. The rule of the game would be to present visual displays which produced the most brain rhythm reaction. The computer would store the reactions and use this past experience in selecting a visual display. After awhile the computer would make selections which in fact produced the most attentive looking for the longest time. It would be most interesting to find out what this set of "alerting" visual displays was like.

Display controllers. Here the characteristics of a display could be controlled by attentive looking, which is also under voluntary control. For instance, when alpha was suppressed by attentive looking a series of visual displays could be presented at a rapid rate. A much slower rate plus a warning could be given when alpha occurred. In the case where there is a continuing inspection of stimuli required, then the rate of presentation of the various objects would be so regulated by attentive looking that the best inspection would occur. One can imagine a vehicle or machine which is unsafe if the operator is not attentive or alert. Such a machine could be automatically shut down if attentive looking flagged below a critical level.

Attention compensators. This is a special case of display controller. Here the display would magnify or exaggerate the visual display effect of attention to make up for an attention defect. For instance, when a person was not attentively looking at a visual display it would get brighter or clearer or larger, permitting a better reception of it.

Attention trainers. Here the goal would be to use feedback to tell a person when his brain rhythms indicated that he was alert. He would practice until he could voluntarily change the display indicating that attentive looking, or not, was achieved. Such training might help people to improve their attentive-looking behavior. They may learn an improved self-control of attention. Experimental studies show that by feedback training, control of the brain rhythms is improved (Nowlis & Kamiya, 1970; Peper & Mulholland, 1970).

In these applications I have talked about brain wave responses. It would be important also to study eye movement and pupillary changes to make displays controlled by eye behavior. In these ways we may improve the evaluation and automatic control of visual displays in terms of their effect on the orienting response of the viewer.

The Discussion of Dr. Mulholland's Paper

LED BY DR. WILLIAM GRINGS
University of Southern California

Grings: The papers which we have heard thus far have impressed me by the extent to which they give clarity to one of the terms in our program title, namely "psychophysiology." In all cases the presentations have attended to both sides of the definition of that field, that is, to both the psyche and the physiology. Our past discussion questions have been similarly oriented. I expect that the questions for this paper will be divided between the matters of achieving an adequate psychological definition of attention and the deciding among available physiological measures. It takes ingenuity to work on both sides of a concept like attention, and the present paper provides novel integrating material.

The variable of time delay feedback poses a number of questions. One was raised with reference to the auditory detection problem. During the paper there was no mention of work with acoustic stimuli. Have the time delay feedback manipulations been checked out with auditory stimuli in a fashion similar to that used with lights?

Another question concerns the role that specific instructions to the subjects about the time delay variable may have on the variable's efficacy. Such information to the subject will clearly determine his sensorimotor adjustment to the performance task.

For persons interested in conditioning behavior, there is a clear parallel between the operation of the feedback manipulation where two stimuli are involved and other situations involving discrimination among stimuli. The question arises about the resemblance of the feedback manipulation to instances in learning where various forms of differential reinforcement are applied to accomplish discrimination behavior.

Which brings up questions concerning the generality of the gross shift manipulation and the extent to which it can be elaborated or extended. This probably leads to specific procedural matters regarding manipulation of the on–off variable and the extent to which these procedural parameters are critical to the appearance of the phenomena. One question relates to criteria for cut-off and criteria for various kinds of triggering operations.

Open Discussion

Mulholland: With regard to auditory stimulation as feedback, there is a very brief effect. The disturbance of the system does not occur with the same magnitude as with visual stimuli, and it very rapidly habituates. This can be attributed to the role the oculomotor system plays in the orienting of response to any stimulus. In a dark homogenous field, listening to sound stimuli, there will be a brief orienting response, which includes the looking response. This response very rapidly habituates because it is not followed-up by any target feedback. If you use the method for auditory detection, you would have to be observing "on-line," because it would rapidly habituate.

I have to agree that the question of the arbitrary definition of alpha due to the cut-offs and the triggering functions is difficult. We have tried various criteria. We wanted to detect alpha as quickly as we could, but this did not work. Even though we could detect alpha within half a cycle, the system was very noisy, relative to the orienting response. The criterion for the threshold is determined by taking the maximum output, during resting, over a 2–5-min interval. We then examined the probability of making an alpha detection in a series of records with various threshold settings. We got an approximation to a sensitivity function, which was fairly flat when the threshold was high; when the threshold was lowered, the function increased rapidly. The probability of an alpha detection increased very rapidly as threshold went below 20% of the maximum. We set the threshold at the point of inflection of that function where the rate of change of threshold and percent detection attained a slope of -1. If you use that threshold, the stimulus on–off delays tend to be equal. This was a good feature for us, but it is arbitrary. You would get different results if you lowered the threshold.

Dr. Robert Chapman (Eye Research Foundation of Bethesda): You are saying that there are three major things that control alpha: visual input, something about efferent output, and attention? That may be wrong, but I just want to talk about one of them—all your data could be explained by dropping out the efferent aspect of the explanation. In the two-light case, where the subject is supposed to pay attention to one light or the other, he might be shifting his gaze. We know that there is an amplification of the visual input when the visual stimulus falls on the fovea, so we might expect that kind of change; such is a visual input, even though it is brought about by an efferent change that shifted the eyes. The question is whether it is the intent to shift the eye, or whether it is really the change in the afferent (visual) input consequent to that light.

Mulholland: In the two-light experiments there would be all three, input, output, and "attention." I would like to drop attention. Attention, as far as the EEG goes, can be reduced to the input functions and ongoing adjustments of the receptor. That is why I talked about *seeing* and *looking*. When you look at a visible target, you cannot unravel the two, except at the initiation of the process, and if there is a measure of when the efferent process started.

When the subject's eyes are open in the dark, or when the subject intends to look in a certain direction, there may be some kind of relevant attention process. But terms such as "directed attention," "focusing one's attention," are really metaphors for visual control.

Chapman: The specific experiment in which you manipulated the efferent aspect, concerned learning and not learning, that is, tracking and not tracking; this was an instructional procedure. To the extent that the subject defocuses to the point that he blurs, that means the visual input is different. So, again, we have confusion as to what the afferent input is and what the control is; now that can be divorced by a different technique. If you put ancillary lenses in, such that the subject's accommodation cannot overcome it, then you can manipulate what the accommodative response actually is, and separate it from the visual input.

Mulholland: My experiment was not intended to separate input functions from eye movement control functions; it was to test the hypothesis about ongoing monitoring of the target, that is, to determine if the visual attention hypothesis were incorrect. We had the subject monitor the clarity of the target, and then showed, by these complicated ocular exercises, that the alpha shifted as a function of whether or not he was tracking with relaxed accommodation. Monitoring the target has to include what we mean by "visual attention."

The key problem is that when the subject directs his gaze in the dark, you will always confound the attentional, and output variables. My study provides circumstantial evidence in support of the efferent oculomotor hypothesis, and it points to some neurophysiological studies. One might look at the outflow down to the extrinsic ocular muscles and evaluate the EEG desynchronization in terms of what is involved there. I don't think the EEG studies can answer your question. Also looking in the dark blocks the alpha rhythms. This cannot be explained on the basis of change in stimulation.

Chapman: Would you predict that looking in the dark would produce accommodative changes? That would suggest an experiment in which one actually determines what such oculomotor changes are.

Mulholland: If you give a person a task, say "look straightahead in the dark," the eyes will fixate momentarily, then they will drift from that position, since there is no target feedback. If there were not oculomotor changes in the dark, associated with the alpha blocking, then we would have to say that our hypothesis is incorrect. We already know that eyes move when you do this in the dark, but the experiment combining the oculomotor and EEG has not been done. Also, when the subject clenches one fist, then there is a blocking of central alpha in the recording from the opposite hemisphere, followed by blocking on the same side but a little later. If he clenches both fists, alpha blocks on both sides at the same time. If motor responses block the central alpha, then may not oculomotor responses block the posterior alpha?

Dr. Johann Stoyva (University of Colorado): What happens to alpha if the oculomotor system is inactivated, and also if an animal is enucleated?

Mulholland: With regard to a case of binocular enucleation, the alpha was irregular and not well defined; but it did block to auditory stimuli. That really poked a hole in our thinking. Such cases might have muscle remnants that can still receive efferent impulses; there could be cortical processes which would ordinarily eventuate in movement. I asked Dr. Bender, who is an expert on oculomotor systems, if that could happen, but his experience would not permit him to say whether that would be enough to desynchronize the EEG.

There is also a problem with blind subjects. If a person is blind from birth, his alpha is absent; a person who loses his sight later in life may have some alpha. So there seems to be an intimate relationship between the appearance of alpha and the integrity of vision.

All of our work has been concerned with the blocking of alpha, and we can identify conditions that are very likely to block alpha; but we don't have any good explanation for why, when these conditions are not present, the alpha returns. The genesis of the alpha rhythm is still an enigma and constitutes an obstacle for our kind of functional investigation.

Dr. Paul Woods (Hollins College): Your puzzlement regarding the response when the eyes are open in the dark might be answered by considering the past history of the organism. In evolutionary situations, the eyes have been opened *many* times to visual stimuli, perhaps producing conditioning—perhaps a sensory-preparatory hookup allows the brain to respond to the opening of the eyes prior to the onset of the visual input.

Mulholland: Would it be the looking response that we conditioned so that the subject starts to look as soon as he opens his eyes?

Woods: Maybe a conditional central preparatory reaction to the expectation of the stimuli following the output.

Mulholland: Dr. Black comments that "conditioning" of an EEG wave exclusively of something else is increasingly difficult to demonstrate. The suspicion is growing that the conditioning of brain waves involves the conditioning of motor processes. When you open your eyes in the dark, learned responses associated with looking occur, and these could be associated with the transitory blocking of alpha.

REFERENCES

Adrian, E. D. The dominance of vision. *Opthalmological Society, U.K.,* 1943, **63,** 194–207.

Adrain, E. D., & Matthews, B. H. C. The Berger rhythm: Potential changes from the occipital lobes in man. *Brain,* 1934, **57,** 354–385.

Berger, H. On the electroencephalogram of man. In P. Gloor, (Ed.), Hans Berger on the electroencephalogram of man. (Trans.) *Electroencephalography and Clinical Neurophysiology, Suppl.,* 1969, **28,** 75–93. Original published in *Journal fur Psychologie und Neurologie,* 1930, **40,** 160–179.

Bender, M., & Shanzer, S. Oculomotor pathways defined by electric stimulation and lesions in the brainstem of monkey. In M. Bender, (Ed.), *The oculomotor system.* New York: Harper, 1964. Pp. 81–140.

Cobb, W. A. The normal adult EEG. In D. H. Hill, & G. Parr, (Eds.), *Electroencephalography: A symposium on its various aspects.* New York: Macmillan, 1963. Pp. 232–239.

Cruikshank, R. M. Human occipital brain potentials as affected by intensity-duration variables of visual stimulation. *Journal of Experimental Psychology,* 1937, **21,** 625–641.

Evans, C. R., & Mulholland, T. B. *Attention in neurophysiology.* London: Butterworths, 1969.

Lindsley, D. B. Attention, consciousness, sleep and wakefulness. In J. Field, H. W. Magoun, & V. E. Hall, (Eds.), *Handbook of physiology,* Vol. III. Washington, D.C.: American Physiological Society, 1960. Pg. 1553.

Mander, J. Arousal to neutral and sexual stimuli as a function of repressor and intellectualized defense styles and stress. Proposal for Ph.D. thesis, Boston University Graduate School, 1971.

Magoun, H. W. The ascending reticular system and wakefulness. In E. D. Adrian, F. Bremer, & H. H. Jasper, (Eds.), *Brain mechanisms and consciousness.* Oxford: Blackwell, 1954. Pg. 1.

Moruzzi, G., & Magoun, H. W. Brain stem reticular formation and activation of the EEG. *Electroencephalography and Clinical Neurophysiology,* 1949, **1,** 455–473.

Mulholland, T. The electroencephalogram as an experimental tool in the study of internal attention gradients. *Transactions of the New York Academy of Science,* 1962. **24,** No. 6., 664–669.

Mulholland, T. Feedback electroencephalography. *Activitas Nervosa Superior, Prague,* 1968, 10, 410–438.

Mulholland, T. B. The concept of attention and the electroencephalographic alpha rhythm. In C. R. Evans, & T. B. Mulholland, (Eds.), *Attention in neurophysiology.* London, Butterworths: 1969. Pp. 100–127.

Mulholland, T. Automatic control of visual displays by the attention of the human viewer. In C. M. Williams, & J. L. Debes (Eds.), *1st National Conference on Visual, Literacy.* New York: Pitman, 1970. Pp. 70–80.

Mulholland, T. Can you really turn on with alpha? Paper presented to the Masschusetts Psychological Association, Boston College, May 7, 1971.

Mulholland, T. Occipital alpha revisited. *Psychological Bulletin,* 1972, (in press).

Mulholland, T., & Davis, E. Electroencephalographic activation non-specific habituation by verbal stimuli. *Science,* 1966, **152,** 1104–1106.

Mulholland, T., & Evans, C. R. Oculomotor function and the alpha-activation cycle. *Nature,* 1966, **211,** 1278–1279.

Mulholland, T., & Peper, E. Occipital alpha and accommodative vergence, pursuit tracking and fast eye movements. *Psychophysiology,* 1971, **8,** 556–575.

Mulholland, T., & Runnals, S. Evaluation of attention and alertness with a stimulus-brain feedback loop. *Electroencephalography and Clinical Neurophysiology,* 1962, **14,** 847–852. (a)

Mulholland, T., & Runnals, S. A stimulus-brain feedback system for evaluation of alertness. *Journal Psychology,* 1962, **54,** 69–83. (b)

Mulholland, T., & Runnals, S. The effect of voluntarily directed attention on successive cortical activation responses. *Journal Psychology,* 1963, **55,** 427–436.

Mulholland, T., & Runnals, S. Cortical activation during steady and changing stimulation. *Electroencephalography and Clinical Neurophysiology,* 1964, **17,** 371–375. (a)

Mulholland, T., & Runnals, S. Cortical activation by alternate visual and auditory stimuli. *Cortex,* 1964, **1,** 225–232. (b)

Nowlis, D. P., & Kamiya, J. The control of electroencephalographic alpha rhythms through auditory feedback and the associated mental activity. *Psychophysiology,* 1970, **6,** 476–484.

Peper, E. Feedback regulation of the alpha electroencephalogram activity through control of the internal and external parameters. *Kybernetic,* 1970, **7,** 107–112.

Peper, E., & Mulholland, T. Methodological and theoretical problems in the voluntary control of electroencephalographic occipital alpha by the subject. *Kybernetic,* 1970, **7,** 10–13.

Robinson, D. A. Eye movement control in primates. *Science,* 1968, **161,** 1219–1224.

Sharpless, S., & Jasper, H. H. Habituation of the arousal reaction. *Brain,* 1956, **79,** 655–680.

Sokolov, Y. N. *Perception and the conditioned reflex.* Oxford: Pergamon Press, 1963.

Stark, L., Michael, J. A., & Zuber, B. L. Saccadic suppression: A product of the saccadic anticipatory signal. In C. R. Evans, & T. B. Mulholland (Eds.), *Attention in neurophysiology.* London: Butterworths, 1969. Pg. 291.

Wagman, I. H. Eye momvenents induced by electric stimulation of cerebrum in monkeys and their relationship to bodily movements. In M. Bender (Ed.), *The oculomotor system.* New York: Harper, 1964. Pp. 18–39.

Woodworth, R., & Schlossberg, H. *Experimental psychology.* New York: Holt, 1954.

IV

PLACEBO EFFECTS

Contribution to a History of 17
the Placebo Effect

Arthur K. Shapiro

"Those who forget the past are destined always to repeat it."

Santayana

INTRODUCTION

INTEREST in the placebo effect has increased considerably in recent years, more papers on the placebo having appeared in the last four years (35 during 1954–1957) than in all previous years (21 between 1900 and 1954). (See Figure 1.) Indices, journals, texts, and abstract journals are increasingly including the word placebo in their list of references; the word placebo appears more frequently in the title of articles (Table 1); and it is becoming a commonplace in research, as it has been a commonplace in medicine for a much longer period of time. A placebo control is included in double blind studies which also are appearing more frequently in scientific literature.

The sharp increase in "psychiatric"[2] interest in the placebo can be seen illustrated graphically in Figure 1, more articles on this subject having appeared in the last two years (9 during 1956–1957) than in all previous years combined (5 between 1900 and 1956). These last two years have been the only years in which the number of "psychiatric" articles (9) has equaled the

---

[1] This paper was completed at the Massachusetts Mental Health Center, Boston Psychopathic Hospital, and Harvard Medical School.

[2] The term "psychiatric" refers to psychiatric and psychological articles or interest. The term "non-psychiatric" refers to all other medical specialties and workers in areas such as pharmacology, physiology, etc.

---

number of "non-psychiatric" articles (9). Many of these articles comment on the importance of studying the placebo effect. This increased interest is indicative of an important new trend in psychiatry, medicine, and the other sciences.

This paper will be concerned primarily with historical considerations. Special emphasis will be placed on the placebo and placebo effect in this history, and on the history of the use of the placebo and the development of the placebo effect concept. Some of the major contributions to an understanding of this concept will be noted and outlined. Some of the conclusions, implications, and questions stimulated by these historical considerations will be discussed.

The paper will not be concerned primarily with the use and ethics of placebos, with the evidence for the existence of the placebo effect, the magnitude of the placebo effect, or an analysis of the placebo effect. It will not be concerned primarily with the theories that have been advanced to explain the placebo effect, or theories which are suggested by the evidence. This will be reported elsewhere (Shapiro, a, b, c).

MEDICAL (NON-PSYCHIATRIC) HISTORY AND THE PLACEBO EFFECT

Let us begin with the "non-psychiatric" medical history. In the following section the "psychiatric" history will be presented.

Sir William Osler (1905) felt that, "... the desire to take a medicine is one feature which distinguishes man, the animal, from his fellow creatures." It is probable that

Reprinted from *Behavior Science*, Vol. 5, No. 2, April, 1960, 109-135.

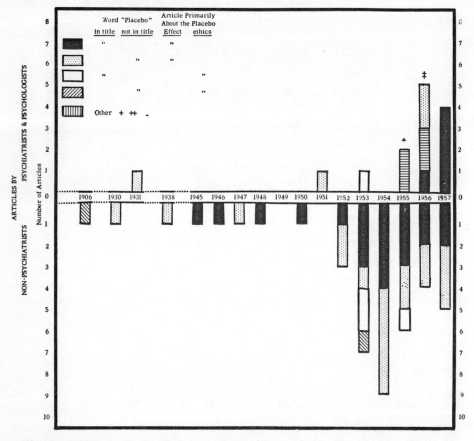

FIG. 1. Papers on the placebo effect and ethics according to year and whether the author was a psychiatrist, psychologist, or non-psychiatrist and whether the word "placebo" appears in the title.*

* Criteria for inclusion of papers in this list and references for the various years will be supplied by the author upon request.

† Both articles with placebo in the title and written by psychiatrists but one appearing in a medical journal (Hofling, 1955) and the other in a psychological journal (Abramson et al., 1955).

†† Both articles with placebo in the title, one written by a psychiatrist and appearing in a medical journal (Fisher & Olin, 1956), the other written by a psychologist as principal author and a psychiatrist as second author and appearing in a psychological journal (Rosenthal & Frank, 1956).

whatever beneficial effects accrued to man's first medication could only have been due to the placebo effect (Modell, 1925; Rivers, 1927). This may be defined at the present time as the psychological, physiological, or psychophysiological effect of any medication or procedure given with therapeutic intent, which is independent of or minimally related to the pharmacological effect of the medication or to the specific effects of the procedure, and which operates through a psychological mechanism. Although the pharmacologic effect of a drug may have been deleterious or of little consequence to the organism, its effect could have been beneficial nevertheless. Indeed, this is the history of medical treatment for the most part until relatively recently, since almost

TABLE I

The Number of Papers Indexed in Various References With the Word "Placebo" in the Title, According to Year and Whether the Author Was a "Non-Psychiatric" M.D. (M.D.) or a "Psychiatric" M.D. or Psychologist (PSY.)*

YEAR	CURRENT LIST OF MEDICAL LITERATURE		QUARTERLY CUMULATIVE INDEX MEDICUS		EXCERPTA MEDICA-NEUROLOGY PSYCHIATRY		DIGEST OF NEUROLOGY AND PSYCHIATRY		PSYCHOLOGICAL ABSTRACTS	
	M. D.	PSY.	M. D.	PSY.	M. D.	PSY.	M. D.	PSY.	M. D.	PSY.
1957	-	-	-	-	-	-	-	1	-	-
1956	3	3	-	-	-	-	-	1	-	-
1955	6	-	-	1	-	-	-	-	-	-
1954	2	-	5	-	-	-	1	-	1	-
1953	4	-	3	-	-	-	-	-	-	-
1952	1	-	-	-	-	-	-	-	-	-
1951	-	-	-	-	-	-	-	-	-	-
1950	3	-	1	-	-	-	1	-	-	-
1949	-	-	-	-	-	-	-	-	-	-
1948	-	-	1	-	-	-	-	-	1	-
1947	1	-	-	-	-	-	-	-	-	-
1946	-	-	1	-	-	-	-	-	-	-
1945	-	-	1	-	-	-	-	-	-	-
1944	-	-	-	-	-	-	-	-	-	-
1943	-	-	-	-	-	-	-	-	-	-
1942	-	-	-	-	-	-	-	-	-	-
1941	-	-	-	-	-	-	-	-	-	-
1940	-	-	-	-	-	-	-	-	-	-
TOTALS	20	3	12	1	0	0	2	2	2	0

*REFERENCES NOT IN EXISTENCE, AVAILABLE OR REVIEWED ARE INDICATED BY A BLANK SPACE. FOREIGN ARTICLES HAVE NOT BEEN INCLUDED.

all medications until recently were placebos (Houston, 1938; Pepper, 1945).

Patients in ancient Egypt, according to the Ebers Papyrus, in 1500 B.C., were often treated with medication such as "lizard's blood, crocodile dung, the teeth of swine, the hoof of an ass, putrid meat and fly specs" (Findley, 1953). No treatments of specific value are found in all the pages of Hippocrates (Houston, 1938). Despite this, and the continued prescription of the "flesh of vipers, the spermatic fluid of frogs, horns of deer, animal excretions, holy oil" (Leslie, 1954) and other bizarre substances, the physician continued to be a useful, respected and a highly honored member of society.

The history of medical treatment concordant with scientific progress in general, is at the same time incredible (Castiglioni, 1946; Garrison, 1921; Haggard, 1929; Haggard, 1933; Haggard, 1934; Goldwyn, 1958; Major, 1954; Major, 1955; Rapport and Wright, 1952; Rivers, 1927; Sigerist, 1958; Zilboorg, 1941). Four of the most famous medications that were used by physicians

up to the 16th and at times during the 18th centuries were: the fabled unicorn's horn to detect and protect against poisons in wines, bezoar stones as antidotes for poisons of all types, theriac as a universal antidote, and powdered Egyptian mummy to heal wounds and as an almost universal remedy. These medications were very expensive and only the wealthy could afford them. Unicorn's horn usually came from the ivory of the narwhal or elephant. Bezoar stones, according to legend, were a crystallized tear from the eye of a deer bitten by a snake. In reality, they were a concretion or gallstone found in the stomachs and intestines of animals such as the goat. Theriac dates back to the experiments of Mithradates and was used up to one hundred years ago. Although the main ingredient was the flesh of vipers, it contained 37 to 63 ingredients, all of which were worthless, and which often required several months to concoct. Several official conferences complained about the adulteration of the powdered mummy from Egypt and the impurity of the unicorn's horns. Powdered mummy presumably came from ground-up mummy in Egypt. Mattioli (an antidote containing 230 ingredients), usnea (the moss scraped from the skull of a hung criminal), crocodile dung, fly specs, eunuch fat were only a few of the more unpalatable drugs. Medical reasoning was primitive: the lungs of the fox were given to consumptives because the fox was a long-winded animal; the fat of a bear, a hirsute animal, was given to those suffering from baldness. Despite the ignorance and superstition, the physician must have benefited his patient because he continued to be held in high esteem.

Consider the treatment that Charles II endured by the physicians of his day: "A pint of blood was extracted from his right arm, and a half-pint from his left shoulder, followed by an emetic, two physics, and an enema comprising fifteen substances; the royal head was then shaved and a blister raised; then a sneezing powder, more emetics, and bleeding, soothing potions, a plaster of pitch and pigeon dung on his feet, potions containing ten different substances, chiefly herbs, finally forty drops of extract of human skull, and the application of bezoar stone; after which his majesty died." (Van Dyke, 1947; for a more complete description, see Haggard, 1929).

Astute observers of their time, such as Montaigne (1946) in the sixteenth century, observed that doctors, in general, were a danger to their patients. Earlier, in the twelfth century, Maimonides (1957), implied this in his statement, "I call him a perfect physician who judges it better to abstain from treatment rather than prescribe one which might perturb the course of the malady." Moliere's satires in the seventeenth century on the medicine of his time are well-known (Garrison, 1921). As late as the seventeenth century, a contemporary of Moliere, Robert Boyle, the father of modern chemistry, after expunging many questionable remedies from the revised pharmacopoeia, included the sole of an old shoe "worn by some man that walked much" which was to be ground into a powder and taken for stomach ache (Haggard, 1929). Oliver Wendell Holmes (1891) said as recently as 1860, that nearly

all the drugs then in use should be thrown "... into the sea where it would be the better for mankind, and all the worse for the fishes." Despite this, sick patients continued to submit to purging, puking, cutting, cupping, blistering, bleeding, freezing, heating, sweating, and shocking.

In 1794, Dr. Ranieri Gerbi, a professor at Pisa, published a manuscript describing a miraculous cure for toothache due to any cause which lasted for a whole year. A worm species, called curculio antiodontaligious, was crushed between the thumb and forefingers of the right hand. The fingers then touched the affected part. An investigatory commission found that 431 of 629 toothaches were stopped immediately. Later, Dr. Carradori, court physician at Weimar, advanced the discovery by substituting a more pleasant ladybird, and an official commission confirmed the immediate relief of toothache in 65–70 per cent of cases. Soon thereafter, an English paper published the following prescription for toothache: "fill your mouth with milk and shake it until it becomes butter, in this way at least three out of four toothaches cease immediately and without fail." (Volgyesi, 1954). This prescription, although pharmacologically ineffective, was more palatable than Pliny's prescription that a mouse be eaten once a month to prevent toothache (Haggard, 1934), or the use of urine as an analgesic mouthwash.

Mistletoe was thought by the ancient druids to have curative virtues against St. Anthony's fire (erysepelas), corns, frostbite, muscular atrophy, apoplexy, infertility, chorea, and bubonic plague (*Spectrum*, 1957, b). It was Galen's drug of choice and thought to be a plant that grows on the oak and hence cannot fall, and naturally should be a specific for the falling sickness (Lennox, 1957). In 1719, however, Colbatch (1719) found it as effective when grown on the lime tree. By the 17th century its powers had spread and it was thought to be effective against edema, impotence, leprosy, syphilis and other diseases. It was thought to be effective against epilepsy from the 17th century and was used by Sir Charles Locock, physician to the queen, who thought epilepsy might be caused by crowded teeth, the practice of onanism, and by a hysterical form connected with the menstrual period (Lennox, 1957)—all of which are completely unrelated to the disease.

A Dr. Raymond at the Salpetriere in Paris found 70 per cent of patients suffering from a variety of diseases, including tabes, were treated successfully by suspending them by their feet, causing the blood to flow into their heads. A collaborator of Bernheim at Nancy, a Dr. Haushalter, reversed the procedure and suspended the patient's head upwards and obtained a similar per cent success in a variety of organic and nervous diseases (Volgyesi, 1954).

One could expand at considerable length on other such examples. Today we know that the effectiveness of these procedures and medications was due to the placebo effect, although little is known about how the placebo effect is effective. Let us continue to explore the historical past in order to learn how not to repeat it.

The placebo effect and the doctor-patient relationship

Although medicine was integrally related to the finest scientific, religious, cultural, and ethical traditions in most periods of history, and despite the ephemeral and/or quite quantitative appearance of drugs or procedures which were truly helpful, one may ask how physicians maintained their position of honor and respect throughout history in the face of thousands of years of prescribing what we now know to be useless and often dangerous medications? Indeed, this would have been a major accomplishment of the physician were it not for the fact that despite the uselessness of the drugs and procedures, nevertheless, the physician truly helped the patient. It was not to the specific medications, however, that the patient responded, but to something inherent in the doctor-patient relationship.[3] Findley

(1953) asks, ". . . if it can fairly be said that scientific medicine began only seven or eight decades ago, what of those who practiced before? Were they ignorant, unscrupulous, fraudulent?" He goes on to say, ". . . that the physician is a vastly more important institution than the drug store," and that even today, "Despite the scientific achievements of this century the physician himself is still the most important therapeutic agent." According to Findley, the effectiveness of this placebo effect lies in the action, ritual, faith and enthusiasm on the part of both the doctor and patient.

Houston (1938), in an early article, discusses the doctor as a therapeutic agent, describing early medicine as a symbol related to the placebo effect. He states that in the early history of medicine the relationship between doctor and patient comprised all that the doctor had to offer the patient. The medicines used were placebos, and, "The great lesson, then, of medical history is that the placebo has always been the norm of medical practice, that it was only occasionally and at great intervals that anything really serviceable, such as the cure of scurvy by fresh fruits, was introduced into medical practice. . . . Their skill was a skill in dealing with the emotions of men. They themselves were the therapeutic agents by which cures were effected. Their therapeutic procedures, whether they were inert or whether they were dangerous, were placebos, symbols by which their patients' faith and their own was sustained." He continues, "The history of medicine is a history of the dynamic power of the relationship between doctor and patient. Through centuries when doctors were doing more harm than good this dynamic force has sustained the medical pro-

---

[3] Another factor contributing to the "success" of these physicians in the past must be considered. Spontaneous recoveries and remissions "can" occur in the course of almost any illness and "may" be unrelated to the administered drugs, doctor-patient relationships and placebo effects. It is very difficult, however, to isolate this factor because of the potential placebo effect in every therapeutic relationship. In addition, the belief of the physician and/or the patient that recovery is a consequence of some activity of the physician would tend to increase the effect of placebos in general. Although this factor must be postulated, it does not negate what is thought to be the more important influence of the doctor-patient relationship in the history of medical treatment.

fession in the esteem of their clientele, it has inspired their fellow citizens with such faith in its values that they were willing to give economic support to the doctor." Houston relates the efficacy of the placebo to the faith of the doctor and patient in the medication, to the faith that the doctor is able to impart to the patient, and to the ameliorative effect of action which the doctor provides in some form.

This view is reiterated by Modell (1955): "It would appear that this placebo action is the one constant in the long history of medical practice. It is the one common denominator, for instance, between the treatment of the Egyptian physician who, in the Papyrus Ebers, prescribed a draught of one-thirty-second part of Tail-of-Mouse with Honey, one third, for cooling the anus, and the treatment of the modern physician who prescribes penicillin for pneumonia. Placebo effect was present in the administrations of the first tribal witch doctor and is equally active today, since it is a component . . . not only of medication, but of every phase and kind of medical treatment."

The frequent reference to the importance of the "art of medicine" implies an understanding of the placebo effect (Bromberg, 1954; Bromberg, 1958; Hailman, 1953; Modell, 1955; Parsons, 1951; Pepper, 1945). Though none of the drugs listed by Hippocrates have proven to be of any usefulness, his observation on the "art of medicine" implies an understanding of the placebo effect and his psychotherapeutic acumen was extremely pertinent (Block, 1957). The famous admonition, loosely paraphrased, "You should treat as many patients as possible with the new drugs while they still have the power to heal," implies a knowledgable appreciation of the placebo effect, a statement which has become so famous that it has been attributed to Trousseau (Findley, 1953; Koteen, 1957; *Spectrum*, 1957, a), Osler (Wayne, 1956), Sydenham (Elkes, 1954) and Nolan D. C. Lewis (Sabshin, 1956). Another historical fact which implies an effect of the placebo has been noted by many authors (Bernheim, 1889; Bromberg, 1954; Grinker, 1958; Horwitt, 1956; Janet, 1925; Sabshin and

Ramet, 1956). Findley (1953) says, "One drug after another has its little day of popularity, then sinks into oblivion. Sheaves of paper by well-intentioned authors testify to their usefulness, but they are quickly replaced by others. This familiar phenomena is perhaps the strongest argument for the validity of placebo therapy, for it means faith endows drugs or treatments with powers which they themselves do not possess." The importance of faith is reflected in the fact that one of the best educated, major religious groups in the United States is able to deny the rational efficacy of any treatment or medicine and to assign all treatment benefits to faith. Houston (1938) remarks on the many reminders of the historical past in the contemporary successful existence of the nostrum vendors, chiropractors and myriads of other varieties of quackery. He also notes that no one considers applying the principles of osteopathy to animals, where it would certainly fail, because the principles are effective only when they involve a human interpersonal relationship, [although it is possible that animals are capable of "placebo-like" reactions also (Gliedman, Gantt, & Teitelbaum, 1957; Wolff, 1946)].

When one considers that the normative history of medical treatment, until relatively recently, has been the history of the placebo effect, one is amazed to find a veritable curtain of silence about it. Houston (1938) likens the pages of medical history to the log of an old-fashioned ocean voyage, in which it was noted that on such a day a whale spouted, or a flying fish was sighted, or a bit of driftwood seen, but in which no mention is made of the huge prevailing fact, that what was constantly seen, almost exclusively, was the unending green waste of water. This circumambient ocean is by analogy the placebo effect.

The Countess of Chinchon is erroneously credited with introducing cinchoma bark, which contains quinine, as a treatment for febrile infections in 1638. Sydenham, by demonstrating that it was specific only for fever of malarial origin, contributed to the end of Galenism and the beginning of scientific medicine (Garrison, 1925; Haggard,

1934; Major, 1954; Major, 1955; Pepper, 1945). It may be considered that this was the first drug that was not a placebo (Findley, 1953; Houston, 1938; Pepper, 1945) because previous to this there was no way to distinguish a placebo from a non-placebo (Pepper, 1945). But even after this period, and even after the beginning of scientific medicine which began seven or eight decades ago, (Findley, 1953; Rivers, 1927; Van Dyke, 1947), one cannot escape noticing the continued resistance to the use of the word "placebo", or the concept underlying the word, in medical parlance, dictionaries, and texts. This is illustrated in the paper by Pepper (1945), which is of interest in that it was the first paper devoted exclusively to the placebo, with the word "placebo" in the title.

History of the word "placebo"

Pepper (1945) eloquently traces the history of the word "placebo" (see also Webster's, 1940, and the Oxford, 1933, Dictionaries). It is the first person singular of the future indicative of the Latin verb "to please"; the word "placebo" itself being equivalent to the phrase "I shall please." The first use of the word dates back to at least the thirteenth century. It appears in the Vespers for the Dead in the Roman Catholic service, the 114th Psalm, in the Vulgate, beginning, "Placebo Domino in regione vivorum. . . ." It was used in the sense of "I will walk before . . . " or "I will please. . . ." It is then found in phrases suggesting sychophancy and servility, and as a noun meaning a flatterer, sychophant or parasite. It was used by Chaucer in both senses, and a character of this type is given Placebo as a proper name. Sir Walter Scott used it in the sense of a soothing sentiment. It is defined as "a commonplace method of medicine" in the 1787 edition of Quincy's *Lexicon* and in the *Philadelphia Medical Dictionary* published in 1808 by John Redman Coxe. Pepper points out that this definition may illustrate the earliest stage of doubt concerning the efficacy of prescriptions of those days, and an approach to the frank admission of a quarter of a century later which appeared in the 1811 edition of

Hooper's *Medical Dictionary* with the definition of the placebo as "an epithet given to any medicine adopted more to please than to benefit the patient."

Thus the placebo appears in medical terminology five hundred years after it was first used in other ways. Let us not be too surprised at this belated appearance, because despite the placebo being freely prescribed during the nineteenth and twentieth centuries, the word placebo did not appear in the index of H. C. Wood's *Therapeutics* whose fourteen editions covered the period from 1875 to 1908, and because, as we shall see later, the resistance to and silence about this important therapeutic agent continues into the more recent history of the placebo.

Placebo effect before 1900

Difficulties are encountered when reviewing the literature prior to 1900. This literature is massive and the indexing is inadequate. The terms placebo and placebo effect were hardly used prior to 1900. This review, therefore, cannot be extensive or exhaustive.

There are, however, many indications that physicians and others of the past (even from earliest times) were cognizant of "placebo-like" phenomena, although this was not referred to as the placebo effect, exhaustively studied or extensively written about. Certainly the full implications of this phenomena were not appreciated.

The observations of Maimonides, Montaigne, Moliere, and Trousseau have been mentioned previously.

Pierre Pomponazzi, an Italian philosopher, uttered these words in the 16th century: "We can easily conceive the marvelous effects which confidence and imagination can produce. . . . The cures attributed to the influence of certain relics, are the effect of this imagination and confidence. Quacks and philosophers know that if the bones of any skeleton were put in place of the saint's bones, the sick would none the less experience beneficial effects if they believed that they were near veritable relics." (Tuke, 1886).

Paracelsus commented in the fifteenth century: "Whether the object of your faith be real or false, you will nevertheless obtain the same effects. Thus, if I believe in St. Peter's statue as I would have believed in St. Peter himself, I will obtain the same effects that I would have obtained from St. Peter;—but that is superstition. Faith, however, produces miracles and whether it be a true or a false faith, it will always produce the same wonders." (Charpingnon, 1864).

It should be noted, however, that these observations are directed not to medical practice, but to religious faith and mysticism as treatment. To Paracelsus' credit belongs his vitriolic opposition to the polypharmacy of his day, the observation that medicine killed and that nature heals. He, however, espoused his own brand of occultism and clung to his own placebo medication, e.g., sympathetic powder, which cured the injuries of a wounded person when applied to the blood-stained garments (Garrison, 1921). Paré was notable for his contributing to the abandonment of many venerable beliefs, e.g., Egyptian mummy, unicorn horn, bezoar stones and boiling oil for cauterization of wounds. He substituted his own placebo for the latter eventually with a concoction consisting of earthworms steeped in turpentine and oil of puppies and lillies (Garrison, 1921).

Oliver Wendell Holmes (1891) first presented his very interesting lecture on *Homeopathy and its Kindred Delusions in 1842*. Although his main concern is with a criticism of homeopathy, he discusses the Royal cure of the King's Evil, the Weapon Ointment, Sympathetic Powder, the Tarwater panacea of Bishop Berkeley and Perkins' Metallic Tractors. He asseverates how patients can benefit "through the influence exerted upon their imaginations," and how they, "all display in superfluous abundance the boundless credulity and excitability of mankind upon subjects connected with medicine." He examines these phenomena in order to illustrate the ease with which numerous *facts* are accumulated to prove the most fanciful and senseless extravagances, and the inefficiency and incompetency of persons without medical knowledge despite wisdom, honesty, and accomplishment. He is cognizant of the role of spontaneous remis-

sion in the natural course of disease, citing a figure of 90 per cent recovery in patients seen in general practice, "provided nothing were done to interfere with the efforts of nature." He is familiar with elemental probability theory and mentions several primitive attempts at controlled studies.

Although Holmes does relegate the majority of drugs then in use to the bottom of the sea, for the most part, he addresses himself to the abuses of the past and those at the periphery of medicine, and not to the mainstream of medical practice of his day. However, there are some implications that he does address himself to the medical practice of his day indirectly and by analogy. This is implied to some extent in the article and especially in the preface to the article.

Although many authors in the past (as today) have given some indication that they were cognizant of "placebo-like" effects (the degree of sensitivity varying considerably), it is striking how this was no guarantee against them becoming subject to a belief in a placebo of their own.

This is dramatically illustrated by the cogent observation of Quimby in 1859, who said, "But through a great many mistakes, and the prescription of a great many useless drugs, I was led to re-examine the question, and came in the end to the position I now hold: the cure does not depend upon any drug, but simply upon the patient's belief in the doctor or the medicine." (Janet, 1925). P. P. Quimby was the immediate predecessor of Mary Baker Eddy and Christian Science.

Paré believed in the puppy ointment and Paracelsus espoused occultism. Trousseau, who was able to say "You should treat as many patients as possible with the new drugs while they have the power to heal," was able to claim diseases (such as neuralgia, nervous dyspnoea, angina pectoris and rheumatism) to be cured, modified and rapidly checked by the use of magnets "which it is impossible to refer to the patient's imagination" (Trousseau, 1833). William Osler was a therapeutic nihilist who battled the irrational polypharmacy of his day. When discussing "Psychical methods of cure, in which faith in something is suggested to the patient," (Osler, 1892), he approvingly quotes Galen as saying, "he cures most in whom most are confident," and Paracelsus encouraging his patients "to have a good faith, a strong imagination, and they shall find the effects." He continues, "Faith in the gods or in the saints cures one, faith in little pills another, hypnotic suggestion a third, faith in a plain common doctor a fourth. . . . Faith in us, faith in our drugs and methods, is the great stock in trade of the profession . . . the touchstone of success in medicine . . . and must be considered in discussing the foundation of therapeutics . . . a most precious commodity, without which we should be very badly off." He points out that doctors do not enjoy a "monopoly in the faith business," and that, "While we doctors often overlook or are ignorant of our own faith-cures, we are just a wee bit too sensitive about those performed outside our ranks." Despite the latter, Osler used cupping, leeching and venesection (and other doubtful medicinal substances) in the treatment of pneumonia, stating, "a timely venesection may save life . . . relieving the pain and dyspnoea, reducing the temperature, and allaying the cerebral symptoms" (Osler, 1892).

It is appropriate to remember the wise words of Janet (1925): "It is only too easy to make fun of stories of miraculous cure. Not merely are sceptics prone to use this weapon of ridicule, but the faithful do the same thing. The devotees of a religion are strongly inclined to attack kindred superstitions. Nothing will persuade the adepts of Lourdes that the miracles worked at the shrine of Aesculapius were genuine. Who could induce the admirers of animal magnetism to take a serious view of such miracles as those of Lourdes: Each one attacks his neighbour, and is quite unaware that his criticisms rebound upon himself."

Placebo effect from 1900 to 1945

Very few articles were written on the placebo between 1900 and 1945. It is difficult to trace such articles because the topic has never been indexed in the Index of the Surgeon General's Library, and not in the Quarterly Cumulative Index Medicus prior to 1945, or in the Current List of Medical Literature prior to 1946. (Table 1) One would have to scour mountains of literature to completely cover the literature during this period. This literature was covered, insofar as it could be, by tracing each reference to its source that came to the author's attention, and by reviewing subjects such as the doctor-patient relationship, therapeutics, faith cures, and suggestibility. Several articles were found which discussed the placebo and placebo effect and which characteristically did not have the word placebo in the title.

Cabot (1906) discusses the ethics of the "Nostrum Evil" referring to the placebo as quackery. In the same year, Fantus (1906), in his text on pharmacy and prescription writing, briefly mentions the positive indications for the use of placebos.

Rivers (1908) studied *The Influence of Alcohol and other drugs on Fatigue* in which he used inert material, not referred to as a placebo, as a control. The latter was designed to taste and appear indistinguishable from the experimental drug. The subjects, or when the experimenter was a subject, had no knowledge of the substances they were receiving. It is one of the earliest anticipations of the double blind procedure. Many methodological variables are considered. It represents a very early understanding of (and greater sophistication than many contemporary investigators about) some of the powerful effects of the placebo in experimentation. It is interesting that no statistical analysis was made of the extensive data, because as recently as 1908 this methodological tool was unavailable. Rivers' (1927) erudition and prescience again appears in his posthumous *Medicine, Magic and Religion*, which was written for the most part prior to 1920. He says, "The action of suggestion can never be excluded in any form of medical treatment, whether it be explicitly designed to act upon the mind or whether ostensibly it is purely physical in character. . . . If we confine our attention to our own culture, it is only within the last fifty or sixty years that there has been any clear recognition of the vast importance of the mental factor in the production and treatment of disease, and even now this knowledge is far from being fully recognized either by the medical profession or the laity. ... Though remedies acting through the mind were probably the earliest to be employed by Man, the knowledge that the remedies act in this way is one of the most recent acquirements of medicine.... Few can now be found who will deny that the success which attended the complex prescriptions, and most of the dietetic remedies of the last generation, was due mainly, if not entirely, to the play of faith and suggestion. The salient feature of the medicine of today is that these psychical factors are no longer allowed to play their part unwittingly, but are themselves becoming the subject of study, so that the present age is seeing the growth of a rational system of psychotherapeutics."

Ayman (1930) discusses the concept of the placebo without mentioning the word in a splendid paper in which he evaluates the therapeutic results in 35 papers on essential hypertension. He found that in every paper complete or partial symptomatic relief was described. Up to 85 per cent reduction in blood pressure was reported. Mistletoe, diathermy, watermelon extract, and Nauheim baths were some of the therapeutic agents listed. Ayman treated forty patients with drops of dilute HCl t.i.d. and 82 per cent showed definite improvement. Many minor and some major side effects were reported. Ayman believed that the common element was the enthusiastic giving or doing of something to the patient.

Much of the material in the very fine article by Houston (1938) has been mentioned previously. In addition, the word "placebo" is used extensively, and some of the factors involved in the placebo effect are discussed. Fantus (1938) expands in greater detail on his previous statement in 1906. He again advises candor and psychotherapy where possible, but briefly discusses the situations in which placebos are indicated— patients with low intelligence and imaginary illnesses. He decries the use of expensive placebos and the widespread use of medication such as vitamins that are prescribed in the spirit of the placebo.

No other articles have come to the author's attention prior to 1945 except for those by psychiatrists which will be discussed later.

As can be seen from Figure 1, prior to 1952, there was less than one article on the placebo effect per year. Despite the demonstration by Ayman as early as 1930 that studies on hypotensive agents were subject to the placebo effect, the vast majority of articles and most research, even up to the present day, is conceived, executed, and reported without adequate controls, indicating a failure to appreciate the powerful effects of the placebo. Some of the variables in research on hypotensive agents have been pointed out in recent articles by Schapiro, Myers, Reiser, and Ferris (1954) and Schapiro (1955). During the last twenty years, not only has the literature on the placebo effect been surprisingly meager, but the principles that follow such understanding have not been absorbed into the mainstream of medical research and practice (Hailman, 1953). The placebo is not indexed or discussed in LaWall's *Four Thousand Years of Pharmacy* (1927) or, as pointed out by Pepper, in modern books on treatment. An issue of the *Memphis Medical Journal* (1941) is devoted to an evaluation of drugs, which included ten articles on the use and abuse of cathartics, vitamins, hormones and other drugs. The word "placebo" is not mentioned though some of the concepts implicit in an understanding of the placebo effect are discussed.

In 1938 one hundred million dollars was spent by the American public for vitamin preparations. The total amount spent on medical care in the same year was approximately one billion dollars (Sanford, 1941). Thus, approximately 10 per cent of the nation's medical expenses was spent for vitamins, which are so often prescribed both knowingly and unknowingly for their placebo effect (*J.A.M.A.*, 1959). Dunlap, Henderson, and Inch (1952) analyzed over 17,000 prescriptions of physicians from representative areas in Great Britain for a one month period. Approximately one third were considered to be in the placebo category. The *British Medical Journal* (1952) editorialized that, "... a bottle of medicine is given as a placebo in about 40 per cent" of the patients seen in general practice, a figure that is close to Cabot's (1906) estimate of 44 per cent of the prescriptions filled by Boston Back Bay drug stores.

Recently the influence of size, color, and taste on the effectiveness of placebos has been discussed, although it should be remembered, that "What constitutes a good placebo cannot be specifically stated, because what may be good for one patient may not be so for another even though he has a similar condition" (*J.A.M.A.*, 1955).

Leslie (1954) discusses the influence of color on the effectiveness of placebos, advising red, yellow, or brown rather than blue or green which are associated with "poisonous or external-use-only liquids." The use of red coloring agents, such as alkaline aromatic solution, has long been standard prescription practice, and officially sanctioned by the United States Pharmacopoeia and the National Formulary. He feels that size is also important, tiny and oversize tablets and capsules being much more impressive than average sized ones, ". . . the tiny ones suggesting great strength and the jumbo ones impressing by its heroic size." The more a tablet resembles aspirin the less effective the psychological effect. It is probable that prescribing nine or eleven drops rather than the usual ten would add to the effectiveness of the placebo effect. Taste has always been important. The aromatic elixir (Wolff, 1946), the compound tincture of gentian (Dubois, 1946; Findley, 1953; Leslie, 1954; Wolff, 1946), and asofetida were standard bitter placebo medications used in the past. A more contemporary bitter solution can be prepared with a 0.1 per cent solution of sodium dehydrocholate. Wolff (1946) finds the ammoniated tincture of valerian to be a very efficacious placebo because of "the riot of tastes and smells in the preparation." It may be pointed out that the simple lactose tablet has fallen into disuse because it can be easily recognized and because it can be tasted and the prescription easily read and interpreted. How much more effective is a strange-tasting drug with a complicated and esoteric appellation?

The gastro-intestinal tract, from one end to the other, has been especially prone to exploitation by the placebo. It would be superfluous at this time to name the hundreds of placebo medications that have been used and continue to be used in the treatment of dyspepsia, gastric distress, irritable bowel, bulemia, constipation, and even for conditions such as peptic ulcer. Purgatives and enemas were known and used prior to Hippocrates. Louis XIII was so enthusiastic about their usefulness that he prescribed them for his hunting dogs. Voltaire advised young men to secure a wife who could give an enema pleasantly and quickly (Seager, 1941). When one considers the limited advantages and probable harmful consequences of emptying the intestinal tract, such as, dehydration, exhaustion, discomfort, loss of nutrition, disturbance of sleep and even possibly death (the mortality from appendectomy being 10 per cent greater if a purgative is taken prior to operation), it is difficult to understand the continued use of these substances (Campbell, 1941). Advertisements for colonic irrigations are seen frequently in most daily newspapers. The expenditure for proprietary drugs of this sort must reach millions of dollars.

The odor of tincture of benzoin makes the inhalation of steam so much more acceptable to patients. The effectiveness of placebos on allergic rhinitis, hay fever, and other nasal conditions is well-known. Headaches respond flagrantly to placebo medication. The effectiveness of Epsom salts used in wet dressings for inflamed areas is not due to the magnesium sulfate which is the active ingredient, because this has no specific cutaneous effect. This is also true of the methyl salicylate used in numerous preparations for sore muscles. Both are effective by virtue of their placebo effect (Leslie, 1954; Hyman, 1946).

The so-called tonics in medicine are notorious placebos. The most active part of the tincture of condurango, a bitter tonic and stomachic, and the fluid extract of cimicifuga nigra, a tonic and antispasmodic, is in their impressive names. Tonics of more recent vintage are the elixir of iron, quinine and strychnine (Findley, 1953; Gold, 1946). Some of the most widely used drugs today are prescribed both knowingly and unknowingly for their tonic or placebo action. Those drugs that are given in inappropriate circumstances or inadequate dosages can be designated as placebo medication. These would include all tonics and most of the vitamin, liver, hormone preparations and a host of proprietary medications, drugs which stimulate and sedate the patient, control and stimulate appetite, the many combinations of drugs with opposing action (the "if-in-doubt" medication) which have recently appeared, and even many potent drugs.

Placebo effect since 1945

The placebo effect is not a phenomenon limited to the past. Dubois (1946) points out that, "You cannot write a prescription without the element of the placebo. A prayer to Jupiter starts the prescription, and it carries the weight of two or three thousand years of medicine" (Findley, 1953; Houston, 1938; Gold, 1946; *Lancet*, 1954; Leslie, 1954; Modell, 1955; Whitehorn, 1958; Wolff, 1946). The prescription is written by the doctor, and although the Latin of the past is disappearing, the polysyllabic names remain. It is then taken to special stores to be filled by specially trained men and is frequently expensive. Any treatment procedure, including all medication, even potent and pharmacologically effective medicines, have potential placebo effects inherent within them (Dubois, 1946; Findley, 1953; Houston, 1938; Gold, 1946; Hyman, 1946; *Lancet*, 1954; Leslie, 1954; Modell, 1955; Pepper, 1945; Rivers, 1927; Whitehorn, 1958; Wolff, 1946).

Let us trace the further development of the word itself.

Dubois (1946) lists three classes of placebo. The first is the pure placebo, such as lactose, which has no possible intrinsic action. The second is the impure or adulterated placebo which contains some active ingredient but which has no effect on the patient's disease. The third is not a placebo itself but is the psychotherapeutic element inseparable from any medication.

Gold (1946, 1954) (who was either responsible for or one of the earliest to use the term "blind-test" for what later became the "double blind procedure," and who has been a major influence in bringing the placebo to the attention of the medical profession) and Clark (1946) view the placebo as a chemical device for psychotherapy.

Gaddum (1954) feels that the placebo is defined as a medicine given more to please than to benefit the patient, and as such, is given to have an effect. He proposed the use of the "dummy tablet" instead, as a form of treatment which is intended to have no effect, which does not aid therapeutic suggestion or work through a psychological mechanism. Beecher (1956 a) differs with Gaddum, feeling that although the word lacks precision it is adequate. Gaddum's idea has not been absorbed into the literature to any extent.

Leslie (1954) widens the definition: "A placebo is a medicine or preparation which has no inherent pertinent pharmacologic activity but which is effective only by virtue of the factor of suggestion attendant upon its administration. The substance may be ingested, injected, inserted, inhaled or applied." Leslie thus adds preparations that are applied to the list of placebos. He also offers a mechanism, suggestion, as part of his definition.

Beecher summarizes the purposes and uses of placebos, ". . . as a psychological instrument in the therapy of certain ailments arising out of mental illness, as a resource of the harassed doctor in dealing with the neurotic patient, to determine the true effect of drugs apart from suggestion in experimental work, as a device for elimination of bias not only on the part of the patient but also, when used as an unknown, of the observer, and finally, as a tool of importance in the study of the mechanism of drug action."

Findley (1953), quoting Houston, divides placebos into three types: 1. The type of drug which the physician knows to be inert, but which the patient believes to be potent. 2. Both the patient and the physician believe the drug to be potent, but which is really inert. 3. The patient and the physician both believe a drug to be helpful but which is actually harmful. Findley's concern is with the failure of some physicians to recognize that they are prescribing placebos, and with the harmful effects which may result.

Despite the aforementioned, the usual definition of the placebo, though with some variation, is similar to that appearing in Dorland's *American Illustrated Dictionary* (1951), where it is defined: "An inactive substance or preparation formerly given to please or gratify a patient, now also used in controlled studies to determine the efficacy of drugs" (Blackeston's, 1956; Oxford, 1933; Shorter Oxford, 1944; Skinner, 1949; Webster's, 1956). This definition is interesting in that it harbors a projective mechanism. Patients are not pleased or gratified by the taking of placebos. It is the doctor who invests the giving of placebos and those patients responding to placebos with a variety of feelings which involve guilt and/or hostility, and which are then projected onto the patient and rationalized as the patient being pleased or gratified. An improved definition of the placebo appears in English and English (1958): "A preparation containing no medicine (or no medicine related to the complaint) and administered to cause the patient to believe he is receiving treatment." However, this definition is inadequate also because it fails to mention that anything offered with therapeutic intent may be a placebo, whether it be given with or without the conscious (or unconscious) knowledge of the doctor or therapist.

Although the placebo is old in history, its use in controlled studies is new and appears frequently in contemporary definitions (*Brit. Med. J.*, 1952; Dorland, 1951; *J.A.M.A.*, 1955; Skinner, 1949).

Beecher, Wolf and Lasagna are of considerable importance to the history of the placebo effect. Beecher (1952; 1955; 1956 a; 1956 b; 1957; Beecher, Keats, Mosteller, & Lasagna, 1953) believes the effectiveness of placebos to be related to the degree of stress or anxiety, the placebo modifying the subjective response to an original sensation or by effecting the reaction component of stress. Wolf's (1950) classic experiments with "Tom" which demonstrated how placebos could reverse the pharmacologic action of drugs and cause end organ changes was an early experimental stimulus to the study of the placebo effect. He showed how placebos could cause extensive "toxic" reactions (Wolf and Pinsky, 1954), and experimentally explored other attributes of placebos (Abbot, Mark, & Wolf, 1952; Hagans, Doering, Ashley, & Wolf, 1957; Wolf, Doering, Clark, & Hagans, 1957). Lasagna has contributed important papers (Beecher et al., 1953; Lasagna, Mosteller, von Felsinger, & Beecher, 1954; von Felsinger, Lasagna, & Beecher, 1955; Lasagna, 1956).

The increased interest in the placebo effect is evident from the data in Figure 1 and Table 1. Articles on the placebo effect have even begun to appear in commercial pharmaceutical journals (*Physician's Bull.*, 1955a, 1955b; *Spectrum*, 1957a). Methodological problems (and the placebo effect indirectly) are explored with increasing frequency in medical journals. Books now contain full chapters on the placebo (Modell, 1955; Hollander, 1958).

The belated interest in the placebo effect

Many authors have commented on the surprising belated interest in the placebo effect. Its potency, widespread use, and therapeutic potentialities have not been acknowledged until recently. Study of its underlying mechanism and dynamics have begun to appear relatively late in the history of medicine.

Houston (1938) wonders how the placebo effect, which is so omnipresent, could have escaped scientific notice for so long a period of time. Pepper (1945) points to the resistance against recognition of the placebo effect that has existed throughout the ages, including the period up to 1945. Dubois (1946) states, ". . . the study of the placebo is the most important step to be taken in scientific therapy." He continues, ". . . although placebos are scarcely mentioned in the literature, they are administered more than any other group of drugs . . . that although few doctors admit that they give placebos, there is a placebo ingredient in practically every prescription . . . that the placebo is a potent agent and its actions can resemble almost any drug." Findley (1953) states that the placebo is the most important therapeutic weapon in the hands of even the modern physician. Leslie (1954) is surprised, ". . . that in the light of their importance and everyday use placebos have until so recently been all but neglected in medical curricula and writings." Lasagna (1956) says, "Considering how profound an effect placebos have . . . it is surprising how little study has been given to identifying the characteristics of placebo reactors." Wayne (1956) comments on the little interest that has been taken on the action of placebos. *Lancet* (1954) editorialized, "Our predecessors paid little attention to such a lowly menial, and published references to it were few. But the spread of scientific methods to the study of materia medica has led to a remarkable improvement in the status of . . . the placebo which until recently . . . has never been regarded as quite respectable."

The situation has changed since 1952 as can be noted from Figure 1. More than seven articles on the placebo have appeared each year since 1953. The word "placebo" itself appears more frequently in articles on the placebo effect specifically, and in titles of articles of all types (Table 1).

Factors responsible for the belated interest in the placebo effect

There are several possible factors for the belated interest in the placebo effect.

The first possibility is that there is a preconscious (or unconscious) perception of the placebo effect which is not verbalized or acknowledged because its revelation would be anxiety provoking or threatening. This is based on the premise that a consideration of the placebo effect has long been obvious and overdue. The energy required for this suppression (or repression) is derived from anxiety related to loss of self esteem and guilt. Placebos are often given to demanding and difficult patients, when the physician is frustrated personally and professionally, when the physician's knowledge, or medical knowledge in general, is inadequate to the presenting problem, when the doctor-patient relationship is deteriorating, when the physician is in a hostile, punitive or disdainful frame of mind, when too busy to do anything else and when there is nothing else to

do because of failure to respond to the usual therapeutic attempts. Physicians often prescribe with the full knowledge, or at least the suspicion, that these substances are placebos, although communicating to the patient, by omission, or commission, that these inert substances are active. The resultant defensiveness and feelings of guilt would add to the difficulty of discussing the placebo with equanimity and carry over to the placebo effect also (Clyne, 1953; Hofling, 1955; Whitehorn, 1958). It may be threatening for some to give up therapeutic methods, abilities or beliefs which required many years to develop and acquire. Others may be threatened by a real or imagined loss of self esteem and prestige among colleagues and in the community and by the threat of uncertainty or loss of magical powers. [Parsons (1951) speaks of the latter in positive terms. He believes that "optimistic biases" are very general and fundamental in human social organization, and are responsible for the pseudo belief in the efficacy of measures, and the magical beliefs and practices that cluster about situations wherein there is an important uncertainty factor and strong emotional interests in the force of action.]

Another factor may be lack of knowledge or rigidity in thinking. If there is no understanding that there is a phenomenon such as the placebo effect, and that all medication has a placebo effect in part, the concept cannot be considered. The consequences are as harmful today as they were in medicine prior to the seventeenth century when it was not known that the effectiveness of almost all medication was due to the placebo effect. A third possibility is an understanding of the placebo effect but a belief that it is unimportant or inadvisable to discuss it. We cannot accept this possibility as plausible, the purpose of this paper being to indicate the converse proposition. The last two factors may be a consequence of the first factor, i.e., the threatening nature of the material making it possible for lack of knowledge, the rigidity in thinking, a belief in the unimportance of and the inadvisability of discussing the placebo.

Factors responsible for the recent interest in the placebo effect

How can we account for the recent increased interest in the placebo effect? Scientific knowledge has continued to increase geometrically. This increase in knowledge includes an understanding of the placebo effect. With the increased number of therapeutically effective drugs there is less of a necessity to rely on drugs with a placebo effect. As a consequence the resistance against acceptance of this phenomenon decreases. Individuals are less threatened and the silence about the placebo effect begins to vanish. Another factor may be the repetitious fanfare heralding the effectiveness of new drugs with which the drug companies are increasingly flooding the market. The vast majority of these preparations are relegated to silent oblivion. Repeated experiences of this nature should influence one's thinking about the placebo effect as a consequence. Public and private financial support of research has increased enormously in recent years. Between 1952 and 1955 alone, there has been a fiscal increase of 77 per cent in government support of life-science research and an increase of 33 per cent in the number of projects (Consolazio and Jeffrey, 1957). Many more individuals are involved in research. The production of scientists, as reflected in the number of doctorates granted each year, has roughly doubled each decade (National Academy of Sciences, 1958). Methodological problems are examined. The placebo effect cannot be ignored.

The influence of psychiatric thinking on the sciences has increased following World War II. Psychologically, psychoanalytically, and socially oriented psychiatrists have entered the medical schools and hospitals in increasing numbers. There is more inter-disciplinary contact and research. It should not be surprising that their concern with psychological factors, symbolism, the doctor-patient relationship, transference and counter-transference should influence scientific thinking in the direction of recognizing the extensiveness of psychological phenomena. Psychiatrists have been active in extending their knowledge to the rest of the

medical profession and especially to the general practitioner. This is reflected in the numerous lectures, conferences, and books, as well as numerous articles which are directed toward the general practitioner or other medical specialist (Balint, 1955; Clyne, 1953; English, 1930; Fisher, 1956; Hofling, 1955; Levine, 1942; Romano, 1952; Salfield, 1953).

Despite this, it is difficult to document because psychiatrists (and psychologists) have published the least number of articles on the placebo effect, and only in recent years have they been concerned with it at all (See Figure 1 and Table 1).

PSYCHIATRY AND THE PLACEBO EFFECT
Placebo effect as a problem in Psychiatry.

Psychiatry is in greater need of the knowledge and of the principles underlying and stemming from the placebo effect than medicine or the other sciences. Psychiatrists manage patients with psychological problems almost exclusively, and are involved in a much more meaningful and closer doctor-patient relationship, a situation which maximizes the placebo potential.

The need for psychiatry to be concerned with the placebo effect is readily apparent from a review of the literature on almost any aspect of psychiatry. Contradictory reports abound in all areas. Although it is not the purpose of this paper to review the literature on therapy and other aspects of psychiatry, some of the highlights should be mentioned. In the treatment of manic depressive psychosis, Bellak (1952) lists fifty odd methods, nearly each one having "... been reported as leading to recoveries and/or improvements." Some of the methods of treatment were: testicular vein blood serum, "own blood" injections, lysate of the hypophysis, epivector serum, refrigeration, aurora-tone films, puppets, and diencephalic radiation. The history of the treatment in schizophrenia is even more impressive in this respect (Bellak, 1948). Horwitt (1956) points out how the papers reporting the pathology of schizophrenia year after year, repeated by each new generation, "... would make the schizophrenic patient a sorry physical specimen indeed: his liver, brain, kidney, and circulatory functions are impaired; he is deficient in practically every vitamin; his hormones are out of balance, and his enzymes are askew." One can find support in the literature for every possible viewpoint about psychiatric treatment. Many papers have appeared which question the efficacy or the possible placebo-like component of psychotherapy (Appel, Lhamon, Myers, & Harvey, 1951; Frank, Gliedman, Imber, Nash, & Stone, 1957; Gliedman, Nash, Imber, Stone, & Frank, 1958; Grinker, 1958; Imber, Frank, Nash, Stone, & Gliedman, 1957; Lewis, 1941; Levitt, 1957; Murphy, 1951; Rosenthal and Frank, 1956; Smith and Wittson, 1957; Whitehorn, 1958), electric convulsive treatment (Brill, Crumpton, Eiduson, Grayson, Hellman, Tichards, Strassman, & Unger, 1957; Bond, & Morris, 1954; Karagulla, 1950; Roth, 1952; Zubin, 1953), insulin coma treatment (Ackner and Harris, 1957; Bourne, 1953; Bourne, 1958; Boardman, Lemas, & Markowe, 1956; Boling, Ryan, & Greenblatt, 1957; Fink, Shaw, Gross, & Coleman, 1958; Leyton, 1953) or the other somatotherapies and psychotherapies in general (Appel et al., 1951; Boardman et al., 1956; Bourne 1957; Clyne, 1953; Diethelm, 1936; Hastings, 1957; Laties & Weiss, 1958; Staudt & Zubin, 1957; Tibbetts and Hawkins, 1956). The papers illustrating the unresolved position of the drugs are too numerous to mention. There are between 20 and 30 tranquilizers on the market, each purporting to be effective in the treatment of psychological illness, not to mention variants of the latter, the numerous combinations of the latter with other drugs and the recent rash of stimulant drugs. The tranquilizers are the fastest growing drugs in history, and it was estimated that in 1957 they would move into second place in sales, reaching about forty million prescriptions totalling 175–200 million dollars in retail sales (Plumb, 1957; Bello, 1957).

Will we appear as wise one hundred years from now as do the compilers of the Paris Pharmacologia of a century ago who said, "What pledge can be afforded that the boasted remedies of the present day will not,

like their predecessors, fall into disrepute, and in their turn serve only as a humiliating memorial of the credulity and infatuation of the physicians who recommended and prescribed them?" (LaWall, 1927). Perhaps recent psychiatric developments in the history of the placebo will gainsay us a place in history as prescient as the Paris compilers of a century ago.

The belated interest of psychiatrists in the placebo effect

Before outlining the contributions of psychiatrists and psychologists, it should be noted that the latter have been the last to become interested in the placebo effect. Without going into the details of Figure 1, there are only 2 papers by Americans which meet the criteria of being written by psychiatrists, with placebo in the title and appearing in American psychiatric journals. A total of 6 indexed papers with placebo in the title by psychiatrists (Table 1) contrasts with the 36 papers by non-psychiatric physicians.

Although one could object that part of the discrepancy can be accounted for by the comparative preponderance of non-psychiatric investigators this cannot account for the greater part of the discrepancy. One would expect the placebo effect to be more the concern of psychiatrists than of other investigators, and reflect itself in articles on the placebo effect and perhaps in articles with the word placebo in the title. By analogy, one does expect and does in fact find more articles on schizophrenia by psychiatric authors than by others.

This situation is again reflected in the most widely known book on the history of psychiatry. Zilboorg (1941) does not mention the placebo or the placebo effect in his *History of Medical Psychology*. There is no discussion of suggestibility which ·at times is equated with the placebo effect. There is only a very brief and inadequate discussion of the doctor-patient relationship from this viewpoint. This is true also of Lewis (1941) *A Short History of Psychiatric Achievement*. Some general histories of medicine do slightly better in this respect although they too are inadequate for the most part. Bromberg

(1954) acknowledges the importance and effectiveness of faith in the magico-religious psychotherapy of the past in his history of psychotherapy, *Man Above Humanity*. He does not discuss, however, faith, suggestibility, or the placebo effect as it applies to medication prescribed in the past or present or to contemporaneous treatment in psychiatry. Parsons (1951) is far more at home with "placebo-like" phenomena in the therapeutic process (although he does not use the term specifically) than the aforementioned authors. He discusses medical practice by way of illustrating a theory of social structure in *The Social System*. Perhaps, because he is a sociologist looking at the therapeutic process from the outside, he can be so much more cognizant of these factors than psychiatrists who are a part of the very process they are observing.

Prior to pursuing this study it was thought that psychologists, by virtue of their careful concern with variables in experimentation, would be cognizant of the placebo effect as an important variable. The converse was found to be true, as indicated by the sparsity of articles published by psychologists (Figure 1) and by the few articles appearing in "Psychological Abstracts" (Table 1). This was further confirmed by the impression that the double blind procedure, which implies an understanding of the placebo effect and which is increasingly being used in clinical studies, is virtually an unknown and unused concept among experimental psychologists who are among the most careful of investigators. Many studies, especially those about which there is some contention, would benefit from a re-evaluation with attention given to this variable.

Psychiatric surprise at the scarcity of articles on the placebo effect

A common feature among psychiatric authors who have written about the placebo effect in recent years is the manifestation of surprise at the scarcity of articles on this subject. It implies that the placebo effect was known but that nobody did anything about it. In another way, it highlights psychiatric belatedness in this area.

Hofling (1955) says, "It is a matter of some curiosity when a group of therapeutic agents in widespread use over a long period of time is largely ignored in medical literature. That this has been the case with placebos is a matter of easy verification. A check of the most widely used textbooks of internal medicine, pharmacology, and therapeutics reveals scarcely any reference to the subject, with nowhere so much as a page devoted to its general discussion."

Fisher (1956) says, although, "Placebo therapy is unique in its timeless potency and popularity . . . it has not achieved full scientific status. . . . Placebo therapy, the most common of all therapies, by paradox has a scanty literature with but few references. . . . The subject receives scant notice in textbooks on treatment, and is often ignored in lectures and courses on therapeutics."

Gliedman et al. (1957) comments, "In recent years, the results achieved by placebo have acquired a limited aura of respectability. The ability of inert compounds . . . to modify a variety of conditions . . . has begun to have a serious impact on medical thinking."

Trouton (1957) says, "Although numerous instances of the surprising efficacy of placebos in a wide variety of conditions have been reported lately, little has yet been done towards providing an explanation of the occurrence of placebo reactions, in terms of psychology." Kurland (1957) comments on the ". . . relatively unexplored areas" of the placebo effect and the paucity of information about this subject. [See also Charcot (1893), Freud (1948, 1950a), Janet (1924, 1925) and Jones (1923a) for similar thoughts on "suggestion."]

Recent interest in the placebo effect appears in psychology. Garner (1958) notes the ". . . seldom reported effects . . ." of the placebo, and says, "Much time and energy would be saved if research workers in this area were familiar with the many points of these papers before they undertook to explain the effect of drugs on patient behavior."

Factors responsible for recent psychiatric interest in the placebo effect

How can this situation be explained? The factors mentioned previously—being threatened, lack of knowledge, rigidity in thinking and disbelief in its importance—can be cited again. In addition, the closer relationship between psychiatrists and patients, with all the implications and consequences of trans-ference and counter - transference phe-nomena, would make it more difficult for the latter to objectively evaluate such phenomena.

It is readily observed that the situation has changed in recent years. (Table 1, Figure 1). In addition to the factors men-tioned previously — increased scientific knowledge, greater numbers of research personnel, concern with methodology, in-creased numbers of psychiatrists in research, etc.—several deserve special emphasis. In the last twenty-five years more therapeutic methods have been introduced into psy-chiatry than ever previously. Many of these methods—psychotherapy, ICT, ECT, re-habilitative (milieu) efforts, lobotomy and drugs—*appear* to be effective in as yet some unelucidated way. This should result in psychiatry being more secure and less threatened, and being able more readily to face scientific problems and criticize ineffec-tive methods more objectively. The evalua-tion of these therapies raises many other problems. The complexity of evaluating contradictory reports, the difficulty of com-paring different investigative methods, and the problem of isolating complex variables, inevitably leads, from many directions, to a consideration of the placebo and the placebo effect. It is perhaps not fortuitous that psy-chiatrists have become interested in the placebo effect following the introduction of the tranquilizing drugs in 1954. (Figure 1).

"Psychiatric" contributions to the study of the placebo effect

Despite psychiatrists' relatively recent concern with the placebo effect, they have contributed perhaps more substantially than all other previous groups of investigators. They have applied their special training and understanding with considerable fruitful-ness.

Discussion of the placebo effect during the nineteenth century revolved around the concept of suggestion. This was stimulated

by the advent of magnetic and hypnotic treatment. This development was not sudden and had historical roots in the past. As pointed out by Janet (1924, 1925), there was a long period of "Miraculous Healing" in which cure was attributed to Gods. A "Meta-physical Stage" followed in which power was invested in a particular person and exemplified by Mesmerism and Christian Science. The "Scientific Stage" (Bernheim, 1889; Janet, 1924, 1925) followed with the advent of hypnotism. These stages stamped their character on discussions of what is now called the placebo effect.

In the latter half of the 19th century many papers appeared on suggestion theory and therapy with particular emphasis on hyp-nosis. Hypnosis was viewed as the scientific attempt to investigate and use the principles of psychotherapy which had acted so blindly in the past (Bernheim, 1889; Janet, 1924, 1925). Suggestion was equated with hyp-nosis and hysteria and most of the papers used these terms as if they were synonymous (Bernheim, 1889; Breuer and Freud, 1957; Charcot, 1925; Ferenczi, 1950; Janet, 1924, 1925; Jones, 1923a, 1923b; Stekel, 1923). Although suggestion and hypnosis are related to the placebo effect and have many common principles, characteristics, and implications for each other, there is evidence (which will not be gone into at the present time) that these phenomena differ from one another in many details (e.g., conversion hysterics are poor placebo reactors, placebo effects can occur without direct, unconscious or conscious suggestions, etc.). For this reason, papers on hypnosis and suggestion per se, unless they have some importance for an understanding of the placebo effect, will not be summarized here (and are readily available elsewhere: Bernheim, 1889; Hull, 1933; Janet, 1925; Schilder, 1956; Weitzen-hoffer, 1953).

Bernheim (1889) demonstrated with many appropriate examples the "suggestive" fac-tors which led to ". . . the possible efficacy of various practices employed for the cure of disease and which have succeeded each other from ancient to modern times." His under-standing of this phenomenon is based on his concept of hypnosis which is thought to be merely an extension or heightening of suggestion operating or present in every individual and involving all of human activity.

Similarly, Janet (1924, 1925), although critical of Bernheim's formulations about suggestibility and hypnosis, is well aware of the "suggestive" factors in the history of medical treatment. Janet criticizes the methodology of those attributing cures to miraculous, magical, religious and other suggestive forms of treatment. He cites the inadequacy of the diagnosis, records and statistical treatment, the poor definition of cure, evidence for cure and verification of the cures, and touches on the failure to formulate specificity, laws and indications for treatment. However, he is well aware that there is enough valid evidence for considering these treatments as truly effective and significant. He discusses the factors in the patient, physician and situation which are thought to underlie these successes: In the patient—enthusiasm, faith, belief, feelings in general, power of the imagination, expectant attention, faith in authority, the importance to the patient of being the object of investigation; in the physician—undoubting enthusiasm, faith, and belief, the unconscious personality of the healer; in the situation—the ritual, mystery and strangeness of the proceedings and the situation, changed environment, repetitive education, and suggestibility factors.

Freud (1950a) is in essential agreement with Janet that the majority of primitive treatments "must be classed under the head of psychotherapy," that this element enters into every therapeutic process, that all physicians use it, that it should be studied rather than used blindly, and that "a condition of expectant faith" was induced to effect cures. Concerning drugs Freud says, "It is not a modern dictum but an old saying of physicians that these diseases (psychoneuroses) are not cured by the drug but by the physician, that is by the personality of the physician, inasmuch as through it he exerts a mental influence." It is of interest that Freud viewed treatment in "hydropathic establishments" as effective, whereas today we would class such a cure as due to the placebo effect. Later, in 1912 and 1913,

Freud (1949; 1950b; 1950c) emphasized the concept of transference, and made it the cornerstone for explaining the success of suggestive cures. Still later Freud (1948) says "Now that I once more approach the riddle of suggestion after having kept away from it for some 30 years, I find there is no change in the situation," and that it is necessary to formulate a concept of suggestion correctly and limit its extended use. He goes on, "But there has been no explanation of the nature of suggestion, that is, the conditions under which influence without logical foundation takes place."

Ferenczi, in 1909 (1950), holds that suggestion, hypnotism and healing of mental conflicts occurs "through repression, displacement and transference of disagreeable complexes," particularly transference of "repressed parental complexes" and of "unconscious libidinal impulses" onto the person of the suggestor, hypnotist, healer and physician.

Jones (1913; 1923a; 1923b) differentiates between two processes in suggestion—verbal and affective suggestion. The latter is more important and the basis for the former. "Affective suggestion" is the basis of therapeutic suggestion, and is "a rapport which depends on the transference of certain positive affective processes in the unconscious . . . " which are ". . . always components or derivatives of the psychosexual group of activities . . . one form of the more general mechanism of displacement, by means of which an affect is transferred from an original, unpleasant and repressed conception to another less acceptable one. . . . It acts by releasing the repressed desires that are finding expression in the form of symptoms, and allowing them to become attached to the idea of the physician, psychologically this means replacement of one symptom by another. . . ."

Hollingsworth (1912), a psychologist, following the lead of Rivers (1908), published a monograph on *The Influence of Caffein on Mental and Motor Efficiency*. Rivers is quoted approvingly and most of the latter's techniques are incorporated into the study.

Glover's (1931) paper on *The Therapeutic Effect of Inexact Interpretation*, although it does not discuss or mention the placebo, is concerned with the factors operating in successful suggestion from a psychoanalytic viewpoint and has many implications for an understanding of the placebo effect. The principle method is thought to be the increased effectiveness of repression, backed by strong transference authority, the specific technique depending on the emphasis placed on various defensive mechanisms.

An excellent (practical and theoretical) discussion of "suggestion therapy" (which includes the placebo as one type of such therapy) appears in Levine's (1942) *Psychiatry and Medical Practice*. He discusses the ethics, indications, contraindications, dangers and theoretical factors from a psychoanalytic view. Diethelm (1936) briefly discusses the ethics of using placebos and comments on the suggestive influence of certain psychiatric treatments. As one of the participants in the 1946 Cornell Conference on Therapy, Diethelm (1946) comments on the little progress in understanding suggestibility (which includes the placebo effect) and stresses the belief on the part of the patient and the physician, and the physician's symbolic value and personality as important factors influencing suggestibility. At this same conference Wolff (1946) relates the placebo effect to his experiments on pain thresholds and to the pill being a potent symbol of the doctor which supports the patient in the former's absence. It symbolizes being cared for and gives emotional support or endorsement. It satisfies needs to feel dependent or may fulfill a need to be punished, and supports the desire to get well.

Appel et al. (1951) tabulate the results of psychotherapy with the neuroses and psychoses. They find it striking ". . . . that individual reports from various sources show little variation from the average improvement rate of 67 per cent in the psychoneuroses and 39 per cent in the schizophrenic illnesses," despite a wide variety of procedures which included reassurance at the one end of a continuum and psychoanalysis at the other end of the continuum. They discuss many of the variables that might have determined these

results, and raise the question about the usefulness of psychotherapy which has not been adequately tested up to the present time. The paper does not mention the placebo effect specifically but considers many of its facets which would be called the placebo effect by other authors.

Hofling (1955), in an insightful article on the placebo effect for general practitioners, widens the concept of the placebo by defining it as, "A therapeutic measure which is administered largely or entirely for a psychologic effect not inherent in its physical or pharmacologic properties." He goes on to discuss the factors influencing the effectiveness, the therapeutic indications and the ethics of placebos. His elucidation of the attitudes and feelings ("counter-transference phenomena") that accompany, result in or result from the prescribing of placebos is of considerable interest and a major contribution to the understanding of the placebo effect. These factors, rarely considered previously, are shown to influence the effectiveness of and the attitudes toward the placebo. This aspect has been the special and unique contribution of psychiatry and has been considered by others in addition (Clyne, 1953; Whitehorn, 1958).

Abramson, Jarvik, Levine, Kaufman, and Hirsch (1955) discuss the placebo effect as related to LSD, enumerate important variables in such studies, list some of the characteristics of placebo reactors, and correlate the placebo effect with responses to the Cornell Medical Index Health Questionnaire, arithmetic test, Rorschach, and the Wechsler-Bellevue Intelligence Scale.

Fisher and Olin (1956) in a clinical study of patients receiving medication with potent autonomic properties (including a placebo in a double blind study), discuss the dynamics of placebo therapy. A broad definition of the placebo is offered, "A placebo may be any object offered with therapeutic intent," and adds that, "The 'placebo reaction' occurs in psychotherapy even without a pill, in the so-called 'transference' cure." Traits of the positive and negative placebo reactor stemming from this study are delineated.

Tibbetts and Hawkins (1956) cite their experiments with physical treatments in psychiatry and relate their findings to the placebo effect. Traits found to characterize the positive placebo reactor are listed. Baker and Thorpe (1957) conducted a clinical study in which a placebo control resulted in significantly greater improvement than a tranquilizer. They list several of the methodological variables of importance in understanding the placebo effect which were felt to be responsible for this astonishing outcome. Trouton (1957) reviews the literature and relates the placebo effect to learning and personality theories. Hoffer (1956) comments on " . . . . the psychologic or placebo factors that no longer can be ignored." He lists three psychological factors that must be considered when drugs are studied, and cites his experiences with LSD in this regard. Psychodynamic and conditional reflex actions of placebos are discussed by Kurland (1957) who offers some tentative conclusions resulting from a study now in progress.

A number of excellent papers on the placebo effect have emanated from a group at the Johns Hopkins Medical School. Psychotherapy and the placebo effect is discussed by Rosenthal and Frank (1956). They review the literature and demonstrate the importance of considering this factor in research and evaluation of psychotherapy. Gliedman et al. (1957) summarize some conditional research studies on dogs and relate placebo reactivity to established learning concepts. Gliedman et al. (1958) elaborate further on the placebo effect in the context of a study comparing short-term psychotherapy with a placebo. Both procedures resulted in similar "symptom reduction" which was not significantly different from one another. They relate the nature of the symptoms relieved to Beecher's concept of the "reaction component of suffering." Although they comment on the limitations of their study, and many others could be raised, it does represent an attempt to study experimentally the effect of the placebo in the very complicated and difficult area of psychotherapy. Whitehorn, in a recent article (1958), defines the placebo

effect as, " . . . . all those psychological and psychophysiological benefits or determinants which quite directly involve the patient's expectations and depend directly upon the diminution or augmentation of the patient's apprehension by the symbolism of medication or the symbolic implications of the physician's behavior and attitudes." This definition adds a dynamic dimension to the usual definition—the expectation and apprehension of the patient. This succinct and insightful article touches on most of the major questions about the placebo effect—theory, psychotherapy, ethics, double blind studies, the doctor-patient relationship, psychodynamics, and the importance of research on this subject. (See also Frank et al., 1957; Imber et al., 1957).

Many of the above articles review the literature on the placebo. Substantial contributions to methodological problems, which involve the use of placebos and indirect concern with the placebo effect, are appearing in increasing numbers by psychiatrists (Feldman, 1956; Horwitt, 1956; Sabshin and Ramot, 1956; Sainz, Biegelow, & Barwise, 1957; Smith & Wittson, 1957; Rashkis & Smarr, 1957a; 1957b).

In 1956 a three day "Conference on the Evaluation of Pharmacotherapy in Mental Illness" was sponsored by the National Academy of Sciences (1956) and should be published in the near future.

DISCUSSION

The placebo effect appears to consist of three factors which are distinct from one another but which are often used interchangeably in the literature.

The first involves methodological errors resulting from variables other than the experimental variable determining results. These errors can arise at any and all stages of an experiment. If the experimental group is not compared with a control group which has been matched, randomized or analyzed for age, sex, acuteness or chronicity of illness, length of hospitalization, diagnosis, prognosis, psychodynamic factors, nutritional and physiological states and a great number of other variables. the experimental results are very likely to be erroneous.

These controls aid in minimizing the omnipresent positive or negative bias of investigators and observors. The effect of spontaneous remission during the course of illness must be considered in the evaluation of therapeutic efficacy. The increasing use of the double blind procedure (Shapiro, Dussik, Tolentino, & Azekoff, 1959) reflects the concern of investigators with these problems.

Studies planned with diligence in every respect, including the use of the double blind procedure, can result in a placebo appearing significantly superior to a tranquilizing drug if the placebo is sweet and the tranquilizer bitter; and if the placebo can be dissolved or easily distinguished from the active drug, the results may reflect, not the effect of medication, but the attitudes of the personnel administering and evaluating the drug (Baker & Thorpe, 1957). The effect of the observer's attitude determining results with tranquilizing drugs has also been demonstrated graphically by Feldman (1956) who found that the reported therapeutic effect of chlorpromazine correlated closely with the physician's attitude to the drug. Many other such examples could be cited.

After examination of the experimental evidence, as well as a consideration of the history of medicine, the literature on the placebo effect, suggestibility, etc., another factor appears which may be a variable but which is different from the usual methodological variables. If all the known and possible variables are controlled or excluded except for this one the results are very likely to be in error. This factor is the placebo effect, the effect of the doctor himself (or some symbolic representative of the doctor) as therapeutic agent (Freud, 1950a; Findley, 1953; Houston, 1938), the most widely used of all agents (Balint, 1955; Cornell Conference, 1946; Fisher & Olin, 1956; Janet, 1924; Jones, 1923a).

This factor assumes special importance because it has dynamic therapeutic effects which are different from simple variables such as age and chronicity of illness. The powerful therapeutic potential of the placebo effect should be further investigated so that its mechanism is understood and its possible uses explored. It may help elucidate some of the problems in psychotherapy and liberate for further inquiry the effects of psychotherapy which appear to be above and beyond the mere result of the placebo effect. The principle(s) underlying the effect of this variable can be extended to non-therapeutic experimental situations which involve an interpersonal relationship with an investigator, or even some symbolic representative of the latter. The effect of the observer or investigator in experimentation requires further exploration.

A third factor is the effect of the placebo when it is an uncontrolled variable in experimental research or therapeutic evaluation which then becomes subject to the methodological errors described previously.

Thus, a clarification of the placebo effect requires that a distinction be made between methodological variables, the placebo effect itself, and the placebo effect as an uncontrolled variable. In addition, as correctly pointed out by Fisher (1956), the placebo should be distinguished from the placebo effect, the placebo being the agent which may or may not result in a placebo effect.

These considerations have important implications for psychiatry. It should stimulate the development of the sensitive methodology required by the complex factors in psychiatry. The perennial misevaluation of new therapies may be avoided or limited. The recent flood of newly introduced therapeutic agents and procedures demands reliable evaluation. It is important to tease out the effects due to specific factors and those due to experimental variables and the placebo effect. It is important to determine whether, to what extent, and why a specific therapy may require a placebo effect to be successful, neither possibly being effective separately but only in combination. As pointed out by Rosenthal and Frank (1956), the effects of psychotherapy may be obscured by under or overevaluation because some patients may respond without therapy, some to any kind, and others only to specific therapy. The effect of the "social milieu" or "psychosocial environment" should be clarified and distinguished from the placebo effect if possible, if it is distinguishable in fact, and not itself a product of the placebo effect (Greenblatt, Levinson, & Shapiro, 1959).

Occasional records of ancient medicine having stumbled upon a useful drug do occur. The inability, however, to scientifically evaluate the specific usefulness of the drug usually resulted in its loss to future generations. The ancient Chinese gave ground-up "dragon bones" to children with convulsions, the calcium being effective for infantile tetany (Haggard, 1933). Burnt sponge, which contains iodine, was used to treat simple goiter (Haggard, 1933). Withering used his digitalis concoction (Fox-glove) for all cases of dropsy, which was regarded as a primary disease (Garrison, 1921; Major, 1955). The recognition that digitalis had a beneficial effect in only certain types of dropsy, that caused by congestive heart failure, and that it was ineffective in renal disease, vitamin deficiency, hypothyroidism, cirrhosis, adrenal malfunction, neoplasm, etc., led to the former's more effective treatment and to advances in the understanding and treatment of the other conditions. Sydenham in the 17th century is credited with a major contribution to the end of "galenicals" in medicine, and the beginnings of scientific medicine, by demonstrating the specificity of cinchoma bark for fever of malarial origin (Garrison, 1921; Haggard, 1929; Haggard, 1934; Major, 1954; Major, 1955; Pepper, 1945).

Although psychiatry is on a much higher level than medicine of that period there are some rough similarities that do not require elaboration.

This paper is not meant to derogate the ingenuity, inventiveness, sensitivity, and value of the individual clinician. The past, present, and future would be bleak indeed if their creative function were superseded by a mechanistic methodology. Scientific methodology rarely if ever creates ideas in itself but is used to test these ideas and concepts. But it is also necessary to recognize the limitations and dangers inherent in the "common sense" method of the clinician. This has been demonstrated clearly in the case of morphine. After all the centuries it has been used, the dosage arrived at in this country is 50 to 100 per cent greater than the one that gives essentially the maximum of pain relief, as determined by careful methodological evaluation. (Beecher, 1952; Denton and Beecher, 1949; Lasagna and Beecher, 1954; Lasagna et al., 1954; Keats, Beecher, & Mosteller, 1950; Lee, 1942). It does not follow, however, that recognition be denied the astute clinician who first used morphine, or those who rediscovered it in other places and at other times, or those who followed reifying its usefulness. Their importance and function is gainsaid. Our concern is with minimizing the errors of the astute clinician and the hyperbole of the less gifted, and with the adding of clarity, objectivity, reliability and sensitivity to the "common sense" and at times the "uncommon sense" of the clinician. This requires concern with methodological problems in general and the placebo effect as a methodological problem in particular. Finally the recognition of the placebo effect, an important variable in methodology, capable of potent and extensive therapeutic effects, requires special attention.

REFERENCES

Abbot, F. K., Mark, M., & Wolf, S. The action of Banthine on the stomach and duodenum of man with observations on the effects of placebos. *Gastroenterology*, 1952, 20, 249.

Abramson, H. A., Jarvik, M. E., Levine, A., Kaufman, M. R., & Hirsch, M. W. Lysergic Acid Diethylamide (LSD-25): XV, The effects produced by substitution of a tap water placebo. *J. of Psych.*, 1955, 40, 367.

Abramowitz, W. The use of placebos in the local therapy of skin diseases. *N. Y. State J. Med.*, 1948, 48: 11, 1927.

Ackner, M. A., & Harris, A. Insulin treatment of schizophrenia. *Lancet*, 1957, I, 607.

Appel, K. E., Lhamon, W. T., Myers, J. M., & Harvey, W. A. Long term psychotherapy. In *Psychiatric treatment. Proc. Ass. Res. Nerv. Mental Dis.*, N.Y., Baltimore: Williams & Wilkins, 1951.

Ayman, D. An evaluation of therapeutic results in essential hypertension. *J.A.M.A.*, 1930, 95, 246.

Baker, A. A., & Thorpe, J. G. Placebo response. *A.M.A. Arch. Neurol. & Psychiat.*, 1957, 78, 57.

Balint, M. The doctor, his patient, and the illness. *Lancet*, 1955, I, 683.

Balint, M. *The doctor, his patient and the illness*. N.Y.: International Universities Press, 1957.

Beecher, H. K. Experimental pharmacology and measurement of the subjective response. *Science*, 1952, 116, 157.

Beecher, H. K. The powerful placebo. *J.A.M.A.*, 1955, 159, 1602.

Beecher, H. K. The subjective response and the reaction to sensation: the reaction phase as site of effective drug action. *Am. J. Med.*, 1956, 20, 107. (a)

Beecher, H. K. Evidence for increased effectiveness of placebos with increased stress. *Am. J. Physiol.*, 1956, 187, 163. (b)

Beecher, H. K. Measurement of pain. *Pharm. Rev.*, 1957, 9, 59.

Beecher, H. K., Keats, A. S., Mosteller, F., & Lasagna, L. The effectiveness of oral analgesics (morphine, codeine, acetylsalicylic acid) and the problem of placebo "reactors" and "non-reactors." *J. Pharmacol. & Exper. Ther.*, 1953, 109, 393.

Bellak, L. *Dementia praecox.* N.Y.: Grune & Stratton, 1948.

Bellak, L. *Manic-depressive psychosis and allied conditions.* N.Y.: Grune & Stratton, 1952.

Bello, F. The tranquilizer question. *Fortune*, May 1957, 162–188.

Bernheim, H. *Suggestive therapeutics.* New York: G. P. Putnam's Sons, 1889.

Block, S. L. Hippocrates on psychotherapy by the general practitioner. *New Eng. J. Med.*, 1957, 256, 559.

Boardman, R. H., Lemas, J., & Markowe, M. Insulin and Chlorpromazine in schizophrenia. *Lancet*, 1956, II, 487.

Boling, L., Ryan, W., & Greenblatt, M. Insulin treatment of psychotic patients. *Am. J. Psychiat.* 1957, 113, 1009.

Bond, E. D. & Morris, Jr., H. H. III: Manic-depressive reactions. *Am. J. Psychiat.*, 1954, 110, 883.

Bourne, H. The insulin myth. *Lancet*, 1953, II, 964.

Bourne, H. Psychotherapy and tranquilizers. *New Zealand Med. J.*, 1957, LVI, 392.

Bourne, H. Insulin coma in decline. *Am. J. Psychiat.*, 1958, 114, 1015.

Breuer, J., & Freud, A. *Studies on hysteria.* New York: Basic Books, 1957.

Brill, N. G., Crumpton, E., Eiduson, S., Grayson, H. M., Hellman, L. I., Tichards, R. A., Strassman, H. D., & Unger, A. A. Investigation of the therapeutic components and various factors associated with improvement with electroconvulsive treatment; A preliminary report. *Am. J. Psychiat.* 1957, 113, 997.

Brit. Med. J. Editorial—The Bottle of Medicine. 1952, I, 149.

Bromberg, W. *Man above humanity—A history of psychotherapy.* Philadelphia: J. B. Lippincott Co., 1954.

Bromberg, W. An analysis of therapeutic artfulness. *Am. J. Psychiat.*, 1958, 114, 719.

Cabot, R. C. The physician's responsibility for the Nostrum Evil. *J.A.M.A.*, 1906, 47, 982.

Campbell, E. G. Use and abuse of cathartics. *Memphis Med. J.*, 1941, XVI, 192.

Carter, A. B. The placebo: Its use and abuse. *Lancet*, 1953, 11, 823.

Castiglioni, A. *Adventures of the mind.* New York: Alfred A. Knopf, 1946.

Cecil, R. A., & Loeb, R. F. *A textbook of medicine.* Philadelphia: W. B. Saunders & Co., 1951.

Charcot, J. M. La foi qui guérit. *Archives de Neurologie*, 1893, 1, 74. Quoted in: Janet, 1924, 1925.

Charpingnon. *Etudes sur la Médecine animque et vitaliste.* Paris: G. Bailliere, 1864. Translated in: Bernheim, 1891.

Clark, Quoted by Dubois, E. F. Cornell Conference on Therapy. *N. Y. State J. Med.*, 1946, 46: 2, 1718.

Clyne, M. B. Letters to the editor—The placebo. *Lancet*, 1953, II, 939.

Colbatch, J. *A dissertation concerning mistletoe: A most wonderful specific remedy for the cure of convulsive distempers.* London: W. Churchill, 1719.

Consolazio, W. V., & Jeffrey, H. L. Federal support of research in the life of science. *Science*, 1957, 126, 154.

Cornell Conference on Therapy. *N.Y. State J. Med.*, 1946, 46: 2, 1718.

DeMaar, E. W. J., & Pelikan, E. W. The use of placebos in therapy and clinical pharmacology. *Mod. Hosp.*, 1955, 84, 108.

Denton, J. E., & Beecher, H. K. New analgesics. *J.A.M.A.*, 1949, 141, 105.

Diethelm, O. *Treatment in psychiatry.* N.Y.: The MacMillan Co., 1936.

Diethelm, O. Cornell Conference on Therapy. *N.Y. State J. Med.*, 1946, 46: 2, 1718.

Dorland, W. A. N. *The American illustrated medical dictionary.* Philadelphia & London: Saunders, 1951.

Dubois, E. F. Cornell Conference on Therapy. *N.Y. State J. Med.*, 1946, 46: 2, 1718.

Dunlap, D. M., Henderson, T. L. & Inch, R. S. A Survey of 17,301 prescriptions on form E 10. *Brit. Med. J.*, 1952, I, 292.

Elkes, J. & Elkes, C. Effect of Chlorpromazine on the behavior of chronically overactive psychotic patients. *Brit Med. J.*, 1954, 11, 560.

English, O. S. On the necessity of applying psychotherapy exclusively. *Med. Rec.*, 1930, 143, 384.

English, H. B., & English, A. C. *A comprehensive dictionary of psychological and psychoanalytic terms.* New York: Longman's Green & Co., 1958.

Fantus, B. *A text book of prescription writing and pharmacy.* Chicago: Chicago Medical Book Co., 1906.

Fantus, B. *General technique of medication.* Am. Medical Association, 1938.

Feldman, P. E. The personal element in psychiatric research. *Am. J. Psychiat.*, 1956, 113, 52.

Ferenczi, S. Introjection and transference. In

Sex in psychoanalysis. New York: Basic Books, 1950.

Findley, T. The placebo and the physician. *Med. Clin. N. Amer.*, 1953, 37, 1821.

Fink, M., Shaw, R., Gross, G. E., & Coleman, F. S. Comparative study of chlorpromazine and insulin coma in therapy of psychosis. *J.A.M.A.*, 1958, 166, 1846.

Fisher, H. K., & Olin, B. M. The dynamics of placebo therapy: A clinical study. *Am. J. Med. Sc.*, 1956, 232, 504.

Frank, J. D., Gliedman, L. H., Imber, S. B., Nash, E. H., & Stone, A. R. Why patients leave psychotherapy. *A.M.A. Arch. Neurol. & Psychiat.*, 1957, 77, 283.

Freud, S. On psychotherapy. *Collected Papers.* Vol. 1, London: Hogarth Press, 1950. (a)

Freud S. The dynamics of the transference. *Collected Papers*, Vol. II, Hogarth Press, 1950. (b)

Freud S. On beginning treatment. Further recommendations in the technique of psychoanalysis. *Collected Papers.* Vol. II, Hogarth Press, 1950. (c)

Freud S. *Group psychotherapy and the analysis of the ego.* London: Hogarth Press, 1948.

Freud S. *An outline of psychoanalysis.* New York: W. W. Norton & Co., 1949.

Gaddum, J. H. Walter Dixon Memorial Lecture: Clinical pharmacology. *Proc. Roy. Soc. Med.*, 1954, 47.

Garner, A. M. *Annual review of psychology.* California: Annual Reviews, Inc., 1958.

Garrison, F. H. *An introduction to the history of medicine.* Phil: W. B. Saunders Co., 1921.

Glaser, E. M., & Whittow, G. C. Experimental errors in clinical trials. *Clin. Sc.*, 1953, 13, 199.

Gliedman, L. H., Gantt, H., & Teitelbaum, H. A. Some implications of conditional reflex studies for placebo research. *Am. J. Psychiat.*, 1957, 113, 1103.

Gliedman, L. H., Nash, Jr., E. H., Imber, S. D., Stone, A. R., & Frank, J. D. Reduction of symptoms by pharmacologically inert substances and by short-term psychotherapy. *A.M.A. Arch. Neurol. & Psychiat.*, 1958, 79, 345.

Glover, E. The therapeutic effect of inexact interpretation: A contribution to the theory suggestion. *Int'l J. Psychoanalysis*, 1931, 12, 397.

Gold, H. Cornell Conference on Therapy, *N.Y. State J. Med.*, 1946, 46: 2, 1718.

Gold, H. In Cornell Conference on Therapy, How to evaluate a new drug. *Am. J. Med.*, 1954, 17, 722.

Goldwyn, R. W. The king's touch for the king's evil. *Harvard Med. Alumni Bull.*, 1958, 32, 18.

Greenblatt, M., Levinson, D. J., & Shapiro, A. K. Placebo effect, social milieu, and the evaluation of psychiatric therapies. *J. Chr. Dis.*, 1959, 9, 327.

Grinker, R. R., Discussion of article by Bromberg, W.: An analysis of therapeutic artfullness. *Am. J. Psychiat.*, 1958, 114, 725.

Hadfield-Jones, R. F. C. A bottle of medicine from the doctor. *Lancet*, 1953, II, 823.

Hagans, J. A., Doering, C. R., Ashley, F. W., & Wolf, S. The therapeutic experiment. *J. Lab. & Clin. Med.*, 1957, 9, 282.

Haggard, H. W. *Devils, drugs and doctors.* New York: Harper & Bros., 1929.

Haggard, H. W. *Mystery, magic and medicine.* New York: Doubleday Doran & Co., Inc., 1933.

Haggard, H. W. *The doctor in history.* New Haven: Yale Univ. Press., 1934.

Hailman, H. F. The blind placebo in the evaluation of drugs. *J.A.M.A.*, 1953, 151, 1430.

Hastings, E. W. Follow-up results in psychiatric illness. *Am. J. Psychiat.*, 1957, 54, 171.

Hoffer, A. Experimental pharmacodynamics and psychobiology. *J. Clin. & Exp. Psychopath.*, 1956, XVII, 376.

Hofling, C. K. The place of placebos in medical practice. *G.P.*, 1955, XI, 103.

Hollander, M. H. *The psychology of medical practice.* Phil.: W. B. Saunders Co., 1958.

Hollingsworth, H. L. The influence of caffein on mental and motor efficiency. *Arch. Psychol.*, 1912, 22, 1–166.

Holmes, O. W. *Medical essays, 1842–1882.* Cambridge, Mass.: The Riverside Press, 1891.

Horwitt, M. K. Fact and artifact in the biology of schizophrenia. *Science*, 1956, 124, 429.

Houston, W. R. Doctor himself as therapeutic agent. *Ann. Int. Med.*, 1938, 11, 1416.

Hull, C. L. *Hypnosis and suggestibility.* New York: Appleton-Century, 1933.

Hyman, H. T. *An integrated practice of medicine.* Philadelphia: W. B. Saunders & Co., 1946.

Imber, S. D., Frank, F. D., Nash, E. H., Stone, A. R., & Gliedman, L. H. Improvement and amount of therapeutic contact; An alternative to the use of no-treatment controls in psychotherapy. *J. Cons. Psychol.*, 1957, 21, 309.

J.A.M.A. The Iatroergic Pill. 1954, 154, 28.

J.A.M.A. Editorial—Placebos. 1955, 159, 780.

J.A.M.A., Council on Food & Nutrition. Vitamin preparations as dietary supplements and as therapeutic agents. 1959, 1, 41.

Janet, P. *Principles of psychotherapy.* New York: The MacMillan Co., 1924.

Janet, P. *Psychological healing. A historical and clinical study.* Vol. 1, London: George Allen & Unwin Ltd., 1925.

Jones, E. The treatment of the neuroses, including the psychoneuroses. In W. A. White and S. Jelliffe, *The modern treatment of neuroses and mental illness.* Philadelphia and New York: Lea and Febiger, 1913.

Jones, E. The action of suggestion in psychotherapy. In *Papers on psychoanalysis*, London: Bailliere, Tindall and Cox, 1923. (a)

Jones, E. The nature of auto-suggestion. In *Papers on psychoanalysis*, London: Bailliere, Tindall and Cox, 1923. (b)

Karagulla, S. Evaluation of electric convulsion therapy as compared with conservative methods of treatment in depressive states. *J. Ment. Sci.*, 1950, 96, 1060.

Keats, A. S., Beecher, H. K., & Mosteller, F. C., Measurement of pathological pain in distinction to experimental pain. *J. Appl. Physiol.*, 1950, 3, 35.

Koteen, H. The use of a "double blind" study investigating the clinical merits of a new tranquilizing agent. *Ann. of Int. Med.*, 1957, 47, 978.

Kraines, S. H. *The therapy of the neuroses and psychoses.* Philadelphia: Lea & Febiger, 1948.

Kurland, A. A. The drug placebo—Its psychodynamic and conditional reflex action. *Behavioral Science*, 1957, 2, 101.

Lancet. Editorial, The humble humbug. 1954, II, 321.

Lasagna, L. Placebos. *Sci. Am.*, 1956, 193, 68.

Lasagna, L., & Beecher, H. K. The optimal dose of morphine. *J.A.M.A.*, 1954, 156, 230.

Lasagna, L., Mosteller, F., von Felsinger, J. M., & Beecher, H. K. A study of the placebo response. *Am. J. Med.*, 1954, 16, 770.

Laties, V. G., & Weiss, B. A critical review of the efficacy of meprobamate in the treatment of anxiety. *J. Chr. Dis.*, 1958, 7, 500.

LaWall, C. H. *Four thousand years of pharmacy.* Philadelphia & London: J. B. Lippincott Co., 1927.

Lee, L. E., Jr., Studies of morphine, codeine and their derivatives; XVI, Clinical studies of morphine, Metopen and Desmorphine. *J. Pharmacol.*, 1942, 75, 161.

Lennox, W. G. The centenary of bromides. *New England J. Med.*, 1957, 259, 887.

Leslie, A. Ethics and practice of placebo therapy. *Am. J. Med.*, 1954, XVI, 854.

Levine, M. *Psychotherapy in medical practice.* New York: MacMillan, 1942.

Levitt, E. E. The results of psychotherapy with children: An evaluation. *J. cons. Psychol.*, 1957, 21, 189.

Lewis, N. D. C. *A short history of psychiatric achievement.* New York: Norton, 1941.

Leyton, S. R. Glucose vs. insulin. *Lancet*, 1953, I, 1253.

Maimonides. Quoted in Baruk, H., *Les therapeutiques psychiatriques.* Paris: Presses Universitaires de France, 1957.

Major, R. H. *A history of medicine.* Vol. I. Springfield, Ill.: C. C Thomas, 1954.

Major, R. H. *Classic descriptions of disease.* Springfield, Ill.: C. C Thomas, 1955.

Masserman, J. H. *The practice of dynamic psychiatry.* Philadelphia: W. B. Saunders, 1955.

Memphis Med. J. Dec. 1941, XVI, 12.

Modell, W. *The relief of symptoms.* Philadelphia: W. B. Saunders, 1955.

Montaigne. *The essays of Montaigne.* New York: Modern Library, 1946.

Murphy, W. F. Problems in evaluating the results of psychotherapy. *A. M. A. Arch. Neurol. & Psychiat.*, 1951, 66, 643.

National Academy of Sciences, National Research Council. Conference on the evaluation of pharmacotherapy in mental illness. Washington, D. C., Sept. 19–22, 1956.

National Academy of Sciences, National Research Council: Production of U. S. scientists. *Science*, 1958, 127, 682.

O'Brien, J. R. Is liver a "tonic"? A short study of injecting placebos. *Brit. Med. J.*, 1954, 11, 136.

Osler, W. *The principles and practice of medicine.* New York: Appleton & Co., 1892.

Osler, W. Medicine in the nineteenth century. In *Aequanimatas.* Philadelphia: P. Blakeston's Son & Co., 1905.

Oxford New English Dictionary. New York & Oxford: Oxford Univ. Press, 1933.

Parsons, T. *The social system.* Glencoe, Ill.: The Free Press, 1951.

Pepper, O. H. A note on the placebo. *Am. J. Pharm.*, 1945, 117, 409.

Physician's Bulletin, The placebo—A neglected agent? Part 1. 1955, XX, 3. (a)

Physician's Bulletin, The placebo—A neglected agent? Part 2. 1955, XX, 48. (b)

Platt, R. Two essays on the practice of medicine. *Lancet*, 1947, II, 305.

Plumb, R. K. Tranquilizer sales, in Science in Review. *N.Y. Times*, Sunday, August 25, 1957, p. E9.

Rapport, S. & Wright, H. *Great adventures in medicine.* New York: Dial Press, 1952.

Rashkis, H. A., & Smarr, E. R. Psychopharmacotherapeutic research. *A.M.A. Arch. Neurol. & Psychiat.*, 1957, 77, 202. (a)

Rashkis, H. A., & Smarr, E. R. Drug and milieu effect with chronic schizophrenics. *A.M.A. Arch. Neurol. & Psychiat.*, 1957, 78, 89. (b)

Rivers, W. H. R. *The influence of alcohol and other drugs on fatigue.* London: Edw. Arnold, 1908.

Rivers, W. H. R., *Medicine, magic and religion.* N.Y.: Harcourt Brace & Co., 1927.

Romano, J., *In teaching psychotherapeutic medicine.* Cambridge: Harvard Univ. Press, 1952.

Rosenthal, D., & Frank, J. D. Psychotherapy and the placebo effect. *Psychol. Bull.*, 1956, 55, 294.

Roth, M. A theory of ECT action and its bearing on the biological significance of epilepsy. *J. Ment. Sc.*, 1952, 98, 44.

Sabshin, M., & Ramet, J. Pharmacotherapeutic evaluation and the psychiatric setting. *A.M.A. Arch. Neurol. & Psychiat.*, 1956, 75, 362.

Sadler, W. S. *Practice of psychiatry.* St. Louis: C. V. Mosby Co., 1953.

Sainz, A., Biegelow, N., & Barwise, C. On a methodology for the clinical evaluation of phenopraxic drugs. *Psychiat. Quarterly*, 1957, 31, 10.

Salfield, D. J. Letters to the Editor—The placebo. *Lancet*, 1953, II, 940.

Sanford, C. H. Exploitation of vitamins. *Memphis Med. J.*, 1941, XVI, 186.

Schapiro, A. F., Psychological factors in evaluation of hypertensive drugs. *Psychosomatic Med.*, 1955, XVII, 291.

Schapiro, A. F., Myers, T., Reiser, M. F., & Ferris, E. B. Blood pressure response to Veratrum and doctor. *Psychosomatic Med.*, 1954, XVI, 478.

Schilder, P. *The nature of hypnosis.* New York: International Universities Press, 1956.

Seager, L. D. Use and abuse of drugs. *Memphis Med. J.*, 1941, XVI, 189.

Shapiro, A. K. The placebo effect in the history of medical treatment (Implications for psychiatry). In Press, *Am. J. Psychiat.* (a)

Shapiro, A. K. Attitudes towards the use of placebos in treatment. Submitted for publication. (b)

Shapiro, A. K. Other papers on the placebo effect in preparation. (c)

Shapiro, A., Dussik, K. T., Tolentino, J. C., & Azekoff, M. The feasibility of "browsing" double-blind studies in large state hospitals, and A "browsing" double-blind study of Iproniazid in geriatric patients; Submitted for publication.

Sigerist, H. E. *The great doctors.* New York: Doubleday & Co., 1958.

Skinner, H. A. *The origin of medical terms.* Baltimore: The William & Wilkins Co., 1949.

Smith, J. A., & Wittson, L. L. Evaluation of treatment procedures in psychiatry. *Dis. Nerv. System*, 1957, XVIII, 1.

Spectrum. The Placebo. 1957, 5, 141. (a)

Spectrum. Mistletoe. 1957, 5, 612. (b)

Staudt, V. M., & Zubin, J., A biometric evaluation of the somatotherapies in schizophrenia. *Psychol. Bull.*, 1957, 54, 171.

Stekel, W. *Psychoanalysis & suggestion therapy.* New York: Moffat Yard & Co., 1923.

Thorner, M. W. *Psychiatry in general practice.* Philadelphia: W. B. Saunders Co., 1949.

Tibbetts, R. W., & Hawkins, J. R. The placebo response. *J. of Ment. Sc.*, 1956, 102, 60.

Trouton, D. S. Placebos and their psychological effects. *J. Ment. Sc.*, 1957, 103, 344.

Trousseau. *Dictionaire de Médicine.* Paris: Libraire de la Faculté de Médecina, 1833. Translated in: Bernheim, 1889.

Tuke, H. *Le Corps et l'esprit. Action du moral et l'imagination sur le physique.* Paris: 1886. Translated in: Bernheim, H., 1889.

Van Dyke, H. B. The weapons of panacea. *Scientific Monthly*, 1947, 64, 322.

Volgyesi, F. A. "School for Patients" hypnosis-therapy and psychoprophylaxis. *Brit. J. Med. Hypnotism*, 1954, 5, 8.

von Felsinger, J. M., Lasagna, L., & Beecher, H. K. Drug-induced mood changes in man. 2. Personality and reactions to drugs. *J.A.M.A.*, 1955, 157, 1113.

Wayne, E. J. "Placebos". *Brit. Med. J.*, 1956, 11, 157.

Webster's New International Dictionary of the English Language. Springfield, Mass.: G. ec. Merriam Co., 1940.

Weiss, E., & English, O. S. *Psychomatic medicine.* Philadelphia: W. B. Saunders Co., 1949.

Weitzenhoffer, A. M. *Hypnotism: An objective study in suggestibility.* New York: Wiley, 1953.

Whitehorn, J. C. Psychiatric implications of the "placebo effect." *Am. J. Psychiat.*, 1958, 114, 662.

Wolf, W. Effects of suggestion and conditioning on the action of chemical agents in human subjects—the pharmacology of placebos. *J. Lab. & Clin. Med.*, 1950, 29, 100.

Wolf, S., Doering, C. R., Clark, M. L., & Hagans, J. A. Chance distribution and the placebo "reactor." *J. Lab. & Clin. Med.*, 1957, 49, 837.

Wolf, S., & Pinsky, R. H. Effects of placebo administration and occurrence of toxic reactions. *J.A.M.A.*, 1954, 155, 339.

Wolff, H. G. Cornell Conference on Therapy. *N.Y. State J. Med.*, 1946, 46: 2, 1718.

Zilboorg, G. *A history of medical psychology.* N.Y.: W. W. Norton & Co., 1941.

Zubin, J. Design for the evaluation of therapy. In *Psychiatric treatment, Proc. Ass. Res. Nerv. Mental Dis.* N.Y.: Williams & Wilkins, 1953.

(Manuscript received April 2, 1959.)

Influences of Suggestion on 18
Airway Reactivity in Asthmatic Subjects

Thomas Luparello, Harold A. Lyons, Eugene R. Bleecker and E. R. McFadden, Jr.

The effect of suggestion on bronchomotor tone was evaluated in a setting in which accurate, rapid, and reproducible measurements of airway resistance (Ra) could be made. Subjects with asthma, emphysema, and restrictive lung disease, as well as normal subjects, were studied. All subjects were led to believe that they were inhaling irritants or allergens which cause bronchoconstriction. The actual substance used in all instances was nebulized physiologic saline solution. Nineteen of 40 asthmatics reacted to the experimental situation with a significant increase in Ra. Twelve of the asthmatic subjects developed full-blown attacks of bronchospasm which was reversed with a saline solution placebo. The 40 control nonasthmatic subjects did not react.

THE INVESTIGATION of bronchial asthma has been concerned with the role of allergic, infectious, psychological, social, endocrinous, and hereditary factors.[1] Up to now, no single causative determinant has been isolated, and it appears that a variety of factors may be involved in the development and continuance of asthma

From the Departments of Psychiatry and Medicine, State University of New York, Downstate Medical Center, Brooklyn, N. Y.

Supported in part by National Institute of Mental Health Research Career Development Award K3MH 15,620 and Grants MH–13439, National Institute of Mental Health, and 5TI–HE 5485, National Heart Institute, U. S. Public Health Service.

Presented in part at the Annual Meeting of the American Psychosomatic Society, Mar. 30, 1968.

The authors wish to thank Mrs. Frances Klugman for her help in the preparation of the manuscript and Miss Eileen Abramoff for her help with the statistics.

Received for publication Apr. 5, 1968.

and in the precipitation of any given acute attack. The effect of psychological stimuli on the precipitation of asthma attacks has been evaluated sporadically over the years. MacKenzie[2] noted bronchospasm in a patient with an "allergy" to roses, when he presented to her an artificial rose. More recently, Dekker and Groen[3] exposed asthmatic subjects to "meaningful emotional stimuli" and were able to measure a decrease in vital capacity in some of the subjects. Each stimulus in that study was specific for a particular subject and represented historical events in the individual's disease process. For example, one subject reported developing asthma attacks at the sight of goldfish in a bowl. When shown an artificial representation of this by the experimenters, the subject developed bronchospasm. Another individual, who had indicted dust as a trigger substance for asthma, reacted with bronchospasm when presented with a sealed glass container filled with dust. Those experiments have demonstrated that certain asthmatics are sensitive to perceptual cues which are capable of affecting bronchomotor tone. However, the heterogeneity of the stimuli employed was such that it was not possible to make meaningful comparisons within the group of subjects. In addition, the respiratory end point chosen was an indirect and relatively insensitive measure of airway obstruction.

The present study was undertaken to overcome these problems and to gain an impression of the prevalence of psychological stimuli as factors in the precipitation of asthma attacks. The independent variable chosen was suggestion, since it could be clearly defined, uniformly applied to all subjects, and easily controlled in a laboratory setting. Changes in airway resistance (Ra) were measured directly by body plethysmography. In addition, it became possible to determine whether the effects of suggestion on bronchomotor tone were unique for asthmatics or were shared by subjects with other lung diseases.

Methods

The data were obtained from 40 asthmatic subjects. The diagnosis of asthma was based on a characteristic history of episodic attacks of reversible bronchospasm associated with a family or personal history or both of allergy, and on an absence of irreversible mechanical defects within the lungs. The subjects were told that they were cooperating in a study related to the control of air pollution and that the experimenters were trying to determine the concentrations at which a variety of substances in the atmosphere would induce attacks of wheezing. It was indicated to each subject that he would be inhaling five different concentrations of an irritant or allergen which the subject had previously indicted as being associated with his asthmatic attacks. The subject was led to believe that he would be exposed to progressively increasing concentrations of this substance, whereas the material actually presented to him, in all instances, was physiologic saline solution. Ra and thoracic gas volume (TGV) were measured in a Collins body plethysmograph, prior to the onset of any test inhalation.[4] Ra and TGV were calculated as the mean of five successive measures of each variable. Resistance was converted to its reciprocal or conductance (Ga) and was expressed as a conductance—thoracic gas volume ratio (Ga/TGV) in order to correct for a variation in lung volume during testing.[5] The normal range for this ratio is 0.13 to 0.35 L.sec./cm. H_2O/L.

After baseline data were obtained, the subjects inhaled over a 30-sec. period ten deep breaths of the suggested "allergen" or "irritant" from a DeVilbiss nebulizer. Following this, Ra and TGV were measured at 1-min. and 4-min. postinhalation intervals, with each measurement representing the mean of 5 determinations at each interval. This procedure was repeated for each new suggested "increased concentration" of the bogus allergen or irritant given to the subject. In the event the subject experienced dyspnea or wheezing, the inhalations were stopped and a placebo in the form of nebulized physiologic saline solution was administered; the subjects were told that they were receiving Isuprel. The Ga/TGV ratios were then determined 3 min. after administering the placebo.

As control subjects, 10 normal individuals, 15 subjects with sarcoid or with tuberculosis (restrictive lung diseases), and 15 individuals with chronic bronchitis were investigated in the same manner, except that they were told the inhalants were 5 different concentrations of industrial air pollutants which cause bronchial irritation and difficulty in breathing.

Results

The data are summarized in Table 1. The mean age of the asthmatic subjects was 25.8 years with a standard deviation (S.D.) of 7.4 years. There were 26 women and 14 men. The mean baseline Ra was 2.22 ± 0.27 cm. H_2O/L./sec. This was associated with a TGV of 2.79 ± 0.49 L. which produced a Ga/TGV ratio of 0.18

TABLE 1. PLETHYSMOGRAPHIC RESPONSES OF TEST SUBJECTS TO THE INHALATION OF SUGGESTED BOGUS ALLERGENS OR IRRITANTS

Subjects	Sex M	Sex F	No.	Age*	Ra*† (cm. H_2O/L./sec.) B‖	Ra*† (cm. H_2O/L./sec.) PI¶	TGV*‡ (L.) B	TGV*‡ (L.) PI	Ga/TGV*§ (L./sec./cm. H_2O/L.) B	Ga/TGV*§ (L./sec./cm. H_2O/L.) PI
Asthmatic	14	26	40	25.8 ± 7.4	2.22 ± 0.27	3.43 ± 1.35	2.79 ± 0.49	3.00 ± 0.74	0.18 ± .05	0.12 ± .05
Normal	4	6	10	23.7 ± 1.8	1.22 ± 0.36	1.39 ± 0.37	2.86 ± 0.41	2.85 ± 0.41	0.32 ± .11	0.28 ± .09
Restrictive	4	11	15	30.0 ± 9.8	2.77 ± 0.82	3.12 ± 0.89	2.12 ± 0.70	2.04 ± 0.64	0.20 ± .07	0.18 ± .05
Bronchitic	10	5	15	51.8 ± 14.8	3.59 ± 1.44	3.95 ± 1.28	3.91 ± 1.02	4.03 ± 1.05	0.09 ± .03	0.08 ± .03

* Values given are the mean and standard deviation.
† Airway resistance.
‡ Thoracic gas volume.
§ Conductance—thoracic gas volume ratio.
‖ Baseline measurements.
¶ Postinhalation measurements.

TABLE 2. EFFECT OF SUGGESTION ON AIRWAY REACTIVITY IN ASTHMATIC SUBJECTS

Asthmatic subjects	No.	Ra (cm. H_2O/L./sec.) B	Ra (cm. H_2O/L./sec.) PI	TGV (L.) B	TGV (L.) PI	Ga/TGV (L./sec./cm. H_2O/L.) B	Ga/TGV (L./sec./cm. H_2O/L.) PI
Clinical asthma attacks	12	2.29 ± 0.60	4.97 ± 0.87	2.71 ± 0.69	3.10 ± 0.85	0.18 ± 0.02	0.07 ± 0.03
Increased Ra with no symptoms	7	2.26 ± 0.35	3.72 ± 0.41	2.57 ± 0.38	2.83 ± 0.67	0.18 ± 0.05	0.10 ± 0.01
No reactions	21	2.16 ± 0.51	2.44 ± 0.49	2.90 ± 0.73	2.99 ± 0.72	0.18 ± 0.05	0.15 ± 0.05

Abbreviations and measurement values are the same as in Table 1.

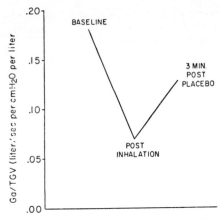

FIG. 1. Mean Ga/TGV ratio values of 12 asthmatic subjects developing clinical signs and symptoms of bronchospasm in response to the inhalation of a supposed allergen or irritant, and the subsequent response following the administering of a placebo.

± 0.05 L./sec./cm. H_2O/L. Following exposure to the suggested allergen or irritant (i.e., saline solution), the Ga/TGV ratios of the entire group fell to an abnormal level (mean Ga/TGV ratio 0.12 ± 0.05; p = 0.001 by t test). This change was effected by an increase in the Ra to 3.43 ± 1.35 cm. H_2O/L./sec., while the TGV only increased to 3.00 ± 0.74 L. This clearly indicated that the Ga/TGV ratios fell because of a disproportionate rise in Ra.

Correlation between baseline values and postinhalation Ga/TGV ratios in the entire group of asthmatics indicated that the changes produced in this ratio were not a function of the initial value (r = 0.05).

Twelve of the 40 subjects developed full-blown clinical attacks of asthma with dyspnea and wheezing. The mean Ga/TGV ratio of these 12 individuals dropped from a baseline ratio of 0.18 ± 0.03 to 0.07 ± 0.03 L./sec./cm. H_2O/L. following inhalation of the supposed noxious substance (Table 2). Following the administration of a placebo, the Ga/TGV ratio rose to 0.13 ± 0.04 L./sec./

cm. H_2O/L. (Fig. 1). An analysis of variance for correlated means reveals significant differences between the baseline values and the lowest Ga/TGV ratios following inhalation of the supposed irritant or allergen, and between this lowest value and that obtained 3 min. following the giving of a placebo. Further analysis by Duncan's New Multiple Range Test showed that there was a significant difference between the baseline levels and the lowest ratio values (p < 0.001) and between the pre- and post placebo administration values (p < 0.001).

Seven of the 40 subjects responded with an increased Ra (Table 2) so that their Ga/TGV ratios fell below accepted normal levels. However, the degree of airway obstruction associated with these changes was not of sufficient magnitude to induce signs and symptoms of acute bronchospasm (Ga/TGV ratio baseline values, 0.18 ± 0.05; Ga/TGV postinhalation values, 0.10 ± 0.01). The remaining 21 asthmatic subjects did not respond to the experimental manipulation (Table 2), and there was minimal change in their Ra (Ga/TGV ratio baseline values, 0.18 ± 0.05; Ga/TGV ratio postinhalation values, 0.15 ± 0.05; p = N.S.). Figure 2 shows the characteristic responses of 2 subjects who reacted to the inhalation of bogus allergens with bronchospasm and the responses of 2 asthmatic subjects who, under similar test conditions, did not react with bronchospasm.

No changes were found in the Ra or Ga/TGV ratios of the normal, restrictive, or bronchitic subjects studied (Table 1). It is of interest to note that the mean baseline Ga/TGV ratio of the bronchitic group was in the abnormal range (Ga/TGV ratio value, 0.09 ± 0.03 L./sec./cm. H_2O/L., and it might be argued that significant changes in the Ra of this population would be missed because of the large baseline TGV. However, several asthmatic subjects were observed who had equivalently abnormal baseline Ga/

TGV ratio values but who still responded to the experimental situation with a marked fall in Ga/TGV ratio values (e.g., a baseline Ga/TGV ratio value of 0.12, followed by a postinhalation Ga/TGV ratio value of 0.04, observed in one subject).

Discussion

The data demonstrate that an appropriately supplied suggestion is capable of influencing the airway caliber of 47.5% of the asthmatic subjects investigated. Bronchoconstriction or dilatation could be accomplished, depending upon the suggestion supplied. This phenomenon was not observed in normal subjects or in subjects with bronchitis or restrictive lung diseases. It cannot be argued that the asthmatics developed their attacks by chance alone under the stresses of the experimental situation, since this would not account for the dramatic re-

versal of the bronchospasm in those subjects who received a placebo under the same test conditions. The following observation illustrates that the response of the subjects was related specifically to the suggestion. One subject, who was given the suggestion that she was inhaling pollen, developed hay fever as well as bronchospasm. As part of another experiment, she was given the suggestion that the inhalant was dust and the subject then had only an asthma attack without hayfever. On a third occasion, following exposure to supposed "pollen," she once more reacted with hayfever as well as asthma.

Although the independent variable in the present study has been referred to as suggestion, it may be that such a designation is an over simplification. It is possible that certain elements of conditioning may also be operating. If an individual has repeatedly associated the

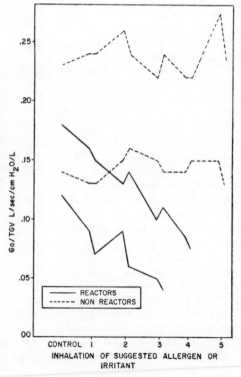

FIG. 2. Solid lines represent the responses of 2 asthmatic subjects who reacted to the inhalation of suggested allergens with bronchospasm (expressed as a fall in the Ga/TGV ratio value). Broken lines represent the responses of 2 asthmatic subjects who did not react to the same test stimulus.

onset of asthma attacks with the presence of a specific agent, it is possible that contiguous stimuli may assume a conditional stimulus value. The present study, however, does not provide sufficient information to permit a distinction to be made about the various types of learning which could be instrumental in bringing about the phenomenon observed in this investigation.

With the demonstration that asthmatics can be divided into two populations—namely, those who react to suggestion with changes in lung mechanics and those who do not, it becomes relevant to inquire about other possible differences between these two populations. For example, are there differences between the two groups in personality, duration of illness, frequency of attacks, or allergic diathesis? These questions cannot be answered on the basis of the available information, and further studies are required before any meaningful comparisons of the two asthmatic populations can be made along these parameters.

The changes in the Ga/TGV ratio observed in the present study occurred primarily because of a fall in airway conductance. The rapidity of both the responses and their reversibility point to a change in smooth-muscle tone as the most likely explanation.[6] In another study, we have demonstrated that atropine is capable of blocking the bronchoconstriction induced by suggestion,[7] indicating that the response of airways to this stimulus is mediated through cholinergic efferent pathways. This hypothesis is in keeping with the observations of Simonsson *et al.*[8] Those authors have shown that stimulation of subepithelial receptors will trigger reflex airway constriction, which is eliminated by atropine blockade of the efferent limb of the reflex arc. The present study indicates that activation of efferent fibers can occur at a central level without direct stimulation of the afferent side. The exact site of stimulation of the efferent fibers and the mechanism by which they are activated is unknown.

Asthma is a complex disease process, the pathogenesis of which remains unknown. In the light of the present findings, a meaningful assessment of the precipitants of asthma and the treatment of any given asthmatic patient must necessarily include an appraisal of the role played by suggestion. If an individual associates a specific agent with the onset of his asthmatic attacks, there is a likelihood that contact with that substance when the asthmatic is aware of it will induce an asthma attack, regardless of whether that agent at that time is physiologically active. Subsequent provocative tests for diagnostic purposes, if done with the subject's knowledge of the test substance, will probably only enhance the asthmogenic potential of that substance. Similarly, the expectations of the patient will have a marked influence on the efficacy of any given therapeutic regimen.

Research related to the psychophysiology of asthma must necessarily institute suitable controls for the influence of suggestion. In such experiments, it often becomes extremely difficult to provide adequate controls for the large number of complex, interacting psychological variables presumed to be operating. In those instances, it is especially important to be sure that the subject is not responding to subtle cues being communicated by the experimenter. Such cues could operate as a suggestion for a particular response, which would then confound rather than clarify the psychophysiology of asthma.

Summary

The effect of suggestion on the pulmonary mechanics of subjects with bronchial asthma, of subjects with restrictive lung diseases, of emphysematous subjects, and of normal individuals was studied by whole-body plethysmography. Following baseline measurements of Ra, each subject was told that he would be inhaling progressively increasing concentrations of an allergen or irritant which would induce bronchospasm. The substance actually given was nebulized physiologic saline solution. After inhalation of the bogus allergen or irritant, the mean Ra of the entire group of asthmatic subjects rose significantly. This was brought about by a marked rise in the Ra of 19 of the 40 asthmatic subjects. Of those 19 asthmatic subjects who reacted, 12 developed full-blown attacks of asthma with wheezing and dyspnea. All asthma attacks were successfully treated with a saline solution placebo, and 3 min. after the inhalation of the placebo, the Ra had returned to baseline levels. The normal subjects and those subjects with restrictive and nonasthmatic, obstructive lung diseases did not react to the inhalation of suggested bogus irritants or allergens with significant changes in Ra.

Downstate Medical Center
450 Clarkson Ave.
Brooklyn, N. Y. 11203

References

1. STEIN, M. "Etiology and mechanisms in the Development of Asthma." In *The First Hahnemann Symposium on Psychosomatic Medicine*. Lea, Philadelphia, 1962, p. 149.

2. MacKENZIE, J. N. The production of "rose asthma" by an artificial rose. *Amer J Med Sci 91:45*, 1886.

3. DEKKER, E., and GROEN, J. Reproducible psychogenic attacks of asthma. *J Psychosom Res 1:58*, 1956.

4. DuBOIS, A. B., BOTELHO, S. Y., and COMROE, J. H., JR. A new method for measuring airway resistance in man using a body plethysmograph: Values in normal subjects and in patients with respiratory disease. *J Clin Invest 35:327*, 1956.

5. BRISCOE, W. A., and DuBOIS, A. B. The relationship between airway resistance, airway conductance and lung volume in subjects of different age and body size. *J Clin Invest 37:1279*, 1958.

6. WIDDICOMBE, J. G. Regulation of tracheobronchial smooth muscle. *Physiol Rev 43:1*, 1963.

7. McFADDEN, E. R. JR., LUPARELLO, T., LYONS, H. A., and BLEECKER, E. R. The mechanisms of action of suggestion in the induction of acute asthma attacks. In preparation.

8. SIMONSSON, B. G., JACOBS, F. M., and NADEL, J. A. Role of autonomic nervous system and the cough reflex in the increased responsiveness of airways in patients with obstructive airway disease. *J Clin Invest 46:1812*, 1967.

V

HEADACHE, MUSCLE TENSION, ANXIETY

EMG Biofeedback and Tension Headache: A Controlled Outcome Study

19

Thomas H. Budznyski, Johann M. Stoyva, Charles S. Adler, and Daniel J. Mullaney

A significant reduction in muscle contraction headache activity was observed in patients trained in the relaxation of the forehead musculature through EMG biofeedback. Training consisted of 16 semiweekly 20 min. EMG feedback sessions augmented by daily home practice. A pseudofeedback control group and a no-treatment control group failed to show significant reductions. A three-month follow-up questionnaire revealed a greatly decreased medication usage in the experimental group.

In the late fifties, two British researchers (1) employed a then unique electromyographic (EMG) integration circuit to show that the resting level of frontalis EMG activity was higher in tension headache patients than normals. Since the immediate cause of pain associated with this common type of headache (more properly called muscle contraction headache) is usually due to a sustained contraction of the scalp and neck muscles (2,3,4), we hypothesized that if patients could be taught to relax these muscles, the pain would be alleviated.

A previous study in our laboratory has indicated that individuals can be trained to lower frontalis tension levels through EMG biofeedback. (5) Subjects in this study reported that there was a generalization of the relaxation to other muscle groups especially in the head and neck area. In view of these observations and the results of the British study, we decided to apply EMG feedback from the frontalis to tension headache.

The results of a pilot study with five patients (6) revealed that the EMG feedback training appeared to be effective in reducing the frequency and severity of tension headaches. However, to rule out the possibility that these results were mainly attributable to either placebo or suggestion effects, we initiated the present study which employed two control groups in addition to the experimental group.

From the University of Colorado Medical Center, Denver, Colorado 80220.

Received for publication October 2, 1972; revision received March 16, 1973.

Address for reprint request: Dr. T.H. Budznyski, University of Colorado Medical Center, 4200 E. 9th Ave. m.s. 2621, Denver, Colorado 80220.

METHOD

Patients

Advertisements placed in a local paper asked for individuals afflicted with frequent tension headaches to participate in a study at the University of Colorado Medical Center. The applicants were offered no pay. A 22-item telephone questionnaire was used to screen out applicants who appeared to have other than muscle contraction headaches. Those who passed the telephone interview next underwent a thorough medical and psychiatric examination in order to rule out the possibility of neurological and other organic disorders and to confirm the diagnosis of tension headache. Typically, this type of headache is characterized by a dull "band-like" pain located bilaterally in the occipital region, although it is often felt in the forehead region as well. It is gradual in onset and may last for hours, weeks, even months.

Following the examination patients were asked to begin daily charting of their headache activity. The purpose of this charting was to provide us with quantitative data on headache levels for the entire course of the study. As shown in Fig. 1 (a hypothetical patient), the charts were 3 by 5 in. cards with the vertical scale representing headache intensity from 0 to 5, with "5" indicating an intense, incapacitating headache. A "4" represented a very severe headache which made concentration difficult, but the patient could perform tasks of an undemanding nature. A "3" headache was painful, but the patient would be able to continue at his job. The "2" level represented a

headache pain level that could be ignored at times. A level "1" headache was a very low level type which entered awareness only at times when attention was devoted to it.

The patient plotted one point for each waking hour, and the headache data were averaged to obtain a weekly score. For example, in Fig. 1, the hourly average for this day would be computed in this fashion:

$$H_D = [(1 \times 3) + (2 \times 4) + (3 \times 3) + (4 \times 4) + (5 \times 2)] \div 24 = 1.92$$

The weekly score would be the simple average of the seven H_D scores for that patient. An average of 1.92 for a week would indicate an extremely high level of headache activity.

In order to establish a baseline level of headache activity, all patients charted headaches for two weeks prior to any training. Data from the pilot study indicated that an average of 0.3 was a moderate level of headache activity. Those patients who scored below this average (approximately 25%) for the two week baseline were not included in the main study but were assigned to a "case study" group. These "case study" patients were not used in the main study, but they were given EMG feedback training. Almost all of these individuals reported a sudden disappearance or decline of headaches soon after their accept-

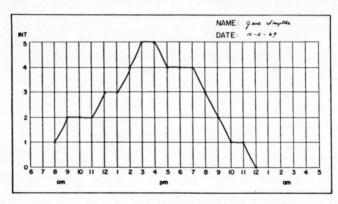

Fig. 1.   Headache rating chart.

ance into the study. However, their headaches usually returned after five to twelve days. This placebo or suggestion response produced genuine wonderment in most of these patients.

All patients who passed the physical and psychiatric interview screen were given the Minnesota Multiphasic Personality Inventory (MMPI). This test was again administered at the end of the training period. Those patients who showed evidence of severe psychological problems as detected by the MMPI were eliminated from the main study although they were allowed to continue training. Dropouts were replaced with patients who answered the second advertisement placed in the paper. Of the 18 patients selected for the study, 2 were male and 16 were female. The mean age was 36 years, with a range of 22–44 years. The mean duration of severe headache activity for groups A, B, and C was 9.6, 6.8, and 6.7 years, respectively. Occupations included secretaries, teachers, housewives, graduate students, nurses, and a writer.

Experimental Design

After the two-week baseline period during which two no-feedback sessions were used to assess pretraining EMG levels, 18 patients were randomly assigned to one of three groups for a total of six in each group. Group A patients received the EMG biofeedback training (the experimental condition). Group B patients also received the "feedback" except that it was tape recorded from Group A (the "pseudofeedback" condition), i.e., the feedback signal produced and heard by the experimental patients was tape recorded and then played back to the Group B patients. Thus, they received noncontingent feedback. Group C received no training but the patients were asked to keep track of their headaches on the daily charts (no-treatment condition).

After the two-week baseline, Groups A and B received 16 sessions of training (ideally, two sessions per week) followed by a three-month follow-up period. Dur-

ing this time the patients charted their daily headache activity. At the end of the three-month follow-up, patients from Groups A and B were brought back for three no-feedback sessions to assess their ability to produce low EMG levels. A questionnaire was also administered to Groups A and B at the end of the three-month follow-up. The questionnaire was particularly designed to assess evidence of symptom substitution and levels of medication usage.

Upon completion of 16 sessions by Groups A and B, Group C patients were allowed to begin feedback training. Similarly, after the three-month follow-up, Group B patients were told that they could, if they so desired, receive additional training of a slightly different sort (real feedback).

Instructions to the Patients

The instructions to Group A patients were as follows:

"Tension headaches are primarily due to sustained contraction or tightness in the muscles of the scalp and neck.

The goal of this study is to learn to relax your muscles so that the tension level never gets too high, and you no longer get headaches. This will involve a great deal of work on your part, both here in the lab, and also at home.

In order to help you learn, we are going to provide you with information as to the level of muscle tension in your forehead region. You will hear a series of clicks in the headphones. The click rate will be proportional to your forehead tension; that is, the higher the tension, the faster the click rate. Your job will be to find out what makes the click rate slow down, because this means lower muscle tension. Try to eliminate those things that make the click rate go faster. Do not try too hard, or this will defeat your goal of deep relaxation. Remember to keep your attention focused on the clicks—do not let your mind wander.

This session will last about 30 minutes.

Remember—do not go to sleep.

Any questions?"

The instructions to Group B patients were as follows:

"Tension headaches are primarily due to sustained contraction or tightness in the muscles of the scalp and neck.

The goal of this study is to learn to relax your muscles so that the tension level never gets too high, and you no longer get headaches. This will involve a great deal of work on your part, both here in the lab, and also at home.

As you relax, it is important to keep out intruding thoughts. The varying click rate you will hear in the headphones will help you to keep out these thoughts. It is very important to keep your attention focused on the varying rate of clicks. Do not let your mind wander.

This session will last about 30 minutes.

Remember—do not go to sleep.

Any questions?"

Patients in this control group were *not* told that the feedback reflected tension levels in their forehead musculature because they could easily have determined that this was not true.

Group C patients were told that they were to chart their headache activity each day and that training would begin after a two-month base-line period. These patients were brought to the laboratory several times during this period for full instrumentation no-feedback sessions in order to encourage them to remain in the study.

Home Practice

Since our pilot study results had indicated the critical importance of daily practice outside the laboratory setting, patients in Groups A and B were told to practice relaxation outside of the laboratory for two 15–20 minute periods every day. No specific relaxation instructions were given for the home practice except that the patients were told to relax in the same way they had in the laboratory—but, of course, without the aid of any instruments.

Instrumentation and Laboratory Procedure

The "BIFS" EMG feedback system (Bio-Feedback Systems, Inc., Boulder, Colorado) was designed to assist individuals in reaching a condition of thorough muscle relaxation by means of information feedback. The unit was able to provide several types of auditory feedback as well as visual feedback. However, for this study, only auditory feedback in the form of a series of click sounds was employed. The frequency of the clicks was proportional to the integrated EMG level. A high EMG level produced a high click rate. As the EMG level declined, the click frequency decreased. The patient, who had EMG electrodes applied to the skin surface over the frontalis muscle, attempted to lower the click rate by progressively relaxing the muscle.

The electrodes (one-half in. diam.; silver, silver-chloride) were placed 1 in. above each eyebrow and spaced 4 in. apart on the patient's forehead. One reference electrode was located in the center of the forehead. Electrode resistances were less than 10,000 ohms. The patient reclined on a couch, in a dimly-lighted, electrically shielded room, and kept the eyes closed.

The EMG feedback unit functions as diagrammed in Fig. 2. An a.c. differential preamplifier with a bandwidth of 120–1000 Hz is used to amplify (gain = 1000) the bioelectric signal generated by the muscle. The amplified EMG signal is then both quantified and converted into a feedback signal by the BIFS. The fluctuating EMG level is changed into a varying click rate. Thus, the patient can "hear" his own muscle activity. The quantification of the EMG is such that a digital readout, available each minute, represents the average level of EMG activity in microvolts (μV) peak-to-peak (p-p) for that minute.

A cassette tape recorder was used to present the feedback clicks, as recorded from experimental patients, to the pseudofeedback control patients.

RESULTS

EMG Levels

In this carefully selected group of

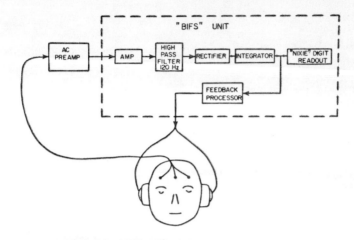

Fig. 2. Functional diagram of the EMG feedback system.

tension headache patients, the level of frontalis EMG during the two baseline weeks averaged slightly over 10 V (p-p) for each group. These values are at least double those shown by young normal subjects in our laboratory. These readings are also a considerable increase over the 6 μV p-p baseline level for the five patients in the pilot study (6) and probably reflect the more stringent selection criteria used in the present study. It is evident from Fig. 3 that the mean EMG level for Group A showed a considerable decrease from the baseline level in the first feedback sessions. The mean EMG level of the Group B patients also dropped somewhat after the baseline sessions; however, the mean value of Group B remained at a higher level than the mean of Group A. The Group B curve also showed a great deal more variation than did that of the feedback group, perhaps not a surprising result since it is characteristic of feedback to decrease the variance of the response.

It was expected that the pseudofeedback Group B patients would show some decrease in EMG level as a result of the focusing of attention on a meaningless and comparatively monotonous stimulus (the "feedback" clicks). Furthermore, the shifting of attention from troublesome, anxiety-evoking thoughts to a relatively neutral stimulus probably also contribut-

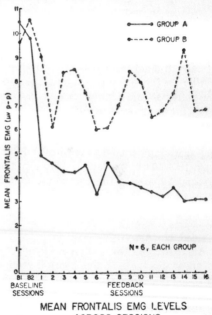

MEAN FRONTALIS EMG LEVELS
ACROSS SESSIONS

Fig. 3. Mean frontalis EMG levels across sessions. Group A—true feedback. Group B—pseudofeedback.

ed to the lowered EMG level. Interestingly, it may be noted that the focusing of attention on a neutral, meaningless thought or word, to the exclusion of other thoughts, is an essential characteristic of many meditative disciplines.

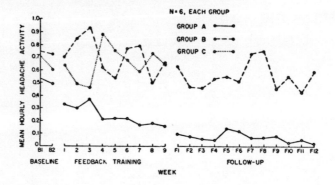

Fig. 4.   Headache activity during feedback training (all 3 groups) and during the three-month follow-up (A and B only). Group A—true feedback. Group B—pseudofeedback. Group C—no treatment.

Although all three groups showed no differences in baseline EMG levels, there was a significant difference ($p < 0.05$ one-tailed) between Groups A and B during the last two weeks of training (Group C did not receive any training).

After the three-month follow-up period, the patients from Groups A and B were tested for three sessions with no feedback. The mean frontalis EMG levels were 3.92 and 8.43 μV p-p for A and B respectively, and again represented a significant difference ($p < 0.01$ one-tailed) between the groups. Apparently the trained group had retained the learning over the three-month period.

Headache Activity

As expected, the averaged headache rating scores for both the A and B groups declined over time (see Fig. 4). However, as Fig. 4 indicates, *baseline* levels of headache activity had been somewhat lower in Group A than in Group B or C. Therefore, a Kruskal-Wallis analysis of variance by ranks was first applied to the baseline headache data. This test showed that the starting levels of the three groups were not significantly different from each other.

Additionally, in order to eliminate the possibility that different baseline levels were contributing to a significant difference between groups, we performed a slope analysis for each group. (7) Only Group A produced a statistically significant decline ($p < 0.001$ when the regression coefficient was tested against the null hypothesis of zero slope).

The headache data for *individual* patients in each group were also analyzed in this fashion. The analysis revealed that four out of six patients in the A group showed significant declines ($p < 0.05$) in headache activity, while in the pseudofeedback control group, only one of six showed a significant decline. None of the C group patients showed a significant decline below baseline levels.

Finally, the Kruskal-Wallis analysis of variance by ranks which had been applied to the baseline headache activity was also used to test differences among the three groups at the end of the training period (weeks eight and nine). At this time there were significant differences in headache activity among the groups ($p < 0.001$).

Correlation Betwen EMG Levels and Headache Activity

When weekly headache activity during the baseline and training weeks was correlated with weekly frontalis EMG levels, the A group data showed a $+0.90$ correlation while the B group showed only -0.05, or essentially no correlation. This result may be due to the fact that the patients receiving the real feedback were

TABLE 1. Number of Patients in Each Group Showing Declines of Ten or More Points on Three MMPI Scales

	Hs	D	Hy
Group A	3	3	4
Group B	2	1	1
Group C	1	1	1

indeed learning to relax in the laboratory and were able to apply this learning outside the laboratory, whereas the pseudofeedback patients generally were unable to do so.

The three-month follow-up data (see Fig. 4) indicated that the B group patients appeared to have stabilized at a mean headache level of about 0.53, whereas the A group was producing very little in the way of headache activity during the last month.

Dropouts

It should be noted that there were four dropouts from the original group B. These were patients who felt that the training was having no effect on their headaches. All of them were experiencing high levels of headache activity when they retired from the study. However, the Group B patients who remained felt that the training was helpful. There were also two dropouts in the C group, but none in the A group. All dropouts were replaced with new patients.

Subjective Reports

While being instrumented prior to the sessions as well as just after the sessions, the patients would often volunteer comments as to their success or lack of it with the training. These comments were later entered into a log book by the technicians. On the basis of these comments, it soon became apparent that in this study, as well as the prior pilot study, the patients passed through several discrete stages in terms of their ability to use a "cultivated" relaxation response to reduce headache activity.

Stage 1. Patient is unable to prevent or abort headaches.

Stage 2. Patient becomes more aware of the tension preceding the headaches and can relax to some degree with a conscious effort. However, he cannot abort headaches.

Stage 3. Patient shows an increasing awareness of the tension, plus he is better able to relax consciously and abort light-to-moderate headaches. The frequency and intensity of headaches is now diminishing.

Stage 4. Patient now seems to relax automatically in the face of stress and does not have to make a conscious effort to do so. The headache activity is now appreciably reduced or even eliminated.

The last stage would seem to indicate that the ability to relax in the face of stress eventually becomes an overlearned habit resulting in a change in life style.

MMPI Results

All the patients were given the Minnesota Multiphasic Personality Inventory (MMPI) before and after the training period. In general, the "before" profile of scores showed that the Hs (hysteria), D (depression), and Hy (hypochondriasis) scales were somewhat elevated (the means for all three groups were in the low 60's). The "after" profiles of all three groups showed reductions in these three scales; however, the only statistically significant mean before-after change occurred in the Hy score of Group A ($p < 0.05$ two-tailed).

Table 1 lists the number of patients in each group who showed declines of 10 points or more on these three scales. The A group produced a total of 10 change-scores equal to or greater than 10 points while Group B showed four, and group C a total of three. A chi-square test performed with the data from this table

TABLE 2.   Drug Usage in Group A (Experimental)

Patient	Before Study	First Half of Training	Second Half of Training	After Training
1	Fiorinal, Valium 3–4 daily	Fiorinal, Valium 3–4 daily	Librium 3–4 daily	Librium 3 per week
2	Darvon, Equagesic (all day)	Darvon, Equagesic (all day)	Darvon, Equagesic seldom	Darvon seldom
3	Valium 4 per day	Valium 1 × day	none	none
4	Anacin—10 per day	Anacin—4 per day	Anacin—2 per week	Anacin—2 per week
5	Darvon—4 per day	Darvon—4 per day	Darvon—2 per day	none
6	none	none	none	none

showed that the three groups were significantly different (p < 0.01) in the number of negative change-scores greater than ten.

The "before" profile showing the elevated triad of hysteria, depression and hypochondriasis is in general agreement with Martin (4) who found the same elevations in a large group of tension headache patients.

Follow-up Data

A four-page post-training questionnaire was used to assess drug usage, evidence of symptom substitution, mood and behavior changes, and interpersonal relationships. All the patients in Groups A and B received this questionnaire after the three-month follow-up period. The patients were asked to rate the severity or frequency of symptoms on a scale of 0 to 3. Ratings were made for four periods: before training, first half of training, second half of training, and after training.

In the A group decreasing severity or frequency was seen in 27 of 28 items. Group B patients rated themselves as decreasing on 23 of 28 items. In both groups the items showing the greatest decreases were depression, tension, anxiety, insomnia, fast heart beat, irritability, persistent thoughts, sexual disinterest, and fear of driving. Lesser decreases in both groups included chest pain, use of alcohol, sweating, and sexual anxieties. The Group A patients in addition registered large decreases in tiredness, apathy, fear of crowds, and compulsive behavior. Patients in both groups saw themselves as improved in relationships with spouses and/or friends.

Although, generally, there was no evidence of symptom substitution, one patient in Group A did report a certain amount of stomach distress as she proceeded through training in deep relaxation. This phenomenon appears to be related to the sudden shift from a predominantly sympathetic autonomic state towards a parasympathetically dominant pattern. This transition does seem to produce an increase in stomach acidity in some individuals. As the patient continues the daily relaxation practice this reaction tends to disappear.

Drug usage decreased dramatically in Group A patients. As seen in Table 2, 4 of 6 went from a rate of 3 to 4 capsules of prescription tranquilizers and pain killers (typically valium, librium, fiorinal, and darvon) per day to only occasional use of the tranquilizer. Another patient in Group A decreased his intake of aspirin from up to 10 per day to 2 per week. The final patient in this group took no medication for his headaches (and did not show a significant decrease in headache activity).

Two of the Group B patients (see Table 3) reported decreases in medication, while three did not change in their usage. One patient switched from a fiorinal-by-day, librium-by-night schedule to librium

TABLE 3. Drug Usage in Group B (Pseudofeedback Control)

Patient	Before Study	First Half of Training	Second Half of Training	After Training
1	Fiorinal—2 per day Librium—2 at night	Fiorinal—2 per day Librium—2 at night	Fiorinal—2 per day Librium—1 at night	Librium—4 day and night
2	Librium—2 per day Aspirin—4–5 day	Librium—1 per day Aspirin—2 per day	Aspirin—1 per day	Aspirin—1 per day
3	Anacin—4–6 per day	same	same	same
4	Meprobamate—3 per day Elavil—2 per day	same	same	same
5	Wigraine Valium	same	same	same
6	Equagesic—3 per day Meprobamate—2 per day	Equagesic—2 per day Meprobamate—1 per day	none	none

day and night. Interestingly, one patient from this group who showed *no* decrease in drug usage had reported a decrease in headache activity.

The questionnaire also required patients to rate their level of headache activity before, during, and after the training. In Group A, five of six rated their headaches as decreasing. One patient indicated no change. Three of the Group B patients rated themselves as decreasing in headache activity, while three others saw no change. One of those who rated her headaches as decreasing did not show a decrease in her daily charting of the headache activity.

Eighteen-month Follow-up. Approximately 1½ years after the completion of feedback training, four of the six Group A patients (two had left Colorado) were contacted. Three of the four previously had shown significant declines in headache activity during training. The three reported that their headaches remained at a very low level (roughly one or two mild headaches a month). Because they now felt more relaxed generally, they no longer engaged in a daily period of deep

relaxation, using this approach only when feeling particularly tense. The fourth patient (who had *not* shown a significant reduction during training) reported that his headaches continued, though at a reduced rate.

"Real" Training for Group B and C Patients. After the three-month follow-up, three patients from the pseudofeedback group (B) decided to try "another type" of training. Two of these people showed significant decreases in their headache scores through the training period. The third individual did not improve significantly.

Five of the Group C patients also received training consisting of 16 sessions of EMG feedback. Their training was initiated after their nine-week "baseline" period was completed. Four of the five showed significant declines in headache activity.

The biofeedback training of the eight former control group patients along with a number of "pilot" headache patients was augmented with cassette tape recordings for home practice. In several instances portable EMG feedback units were used at home as well.

DISCUSSION

The results of an earlier pilot study with five patients (6) had suggested that training in relaxation of the forehead muscles with EMG feedback might be effective in eliminating muscle contraction or tension headaches. That conclusion was further strengthened by the analysis of the data from this second experiment which employed two control groups in addition to the experimental group. It now seems apparent that chronic tension headache patients can learn to decrease their resting forehead EMG levels by 50 to 70% in three to six 20-minute feedback sessions. When they subsequently engage in regular, daily relaxation, the headache activity diminishes considerably. Recently, other laboratories (8,9) have also reported that EMG feedback training is useful in the alleviation of tension headache.

These results are in keeping with a suggestion made independently by Malmo (10) of McGill University Medical School, who has worked extensively with electromyographic recording since the early 1950's. Malmo proposed that systematic muscle relaxation training might well be useful for treating tension headache.

Stages of Progress

As the patients progressed through training, their verbal reports suggested that they first developed a heightened awareness of maladaptive tension levels. This was followed by an increasing ability to remove the tension (and slight-to-moderate headaches) through relaxation. If the patients then applied this new learning to every day stress situations, a change in life style frequently seemed to occur. At this stage, patients typically reported that they no longer overreacted to stress. This "automatic" moderation of arousal level in the face of stress has also been reported by anxiety patients who have received EMG feedback-assisted relaxation training in our laboratory.

Transfer to Real Life

The no-feedback sessions at the end of the three-month follow-up revealed that those patients who had received feedback training still retained the ability to produce low forehead EMG levels. The eighteen-month follow-up interview indicated that most experimental group patients had also managed to keep themselves relatively free of headaches even though they had been chronic headache sufferers for years prior to the training. In this group also, the use of powerful prescription drugs decreased dramatically.

Only one of the pseudofeedback controls produced a significant decline in headache activity over time. This patient was the youngest member of that group. She regularly performed the daily home relaxation practice. Although she was not given specific relaxation instructions, this patient learned to discriminate the internal cues of thorough relaxation such as heaviness and warmth in the arms.

Importance of Daily Practice

This study, as did the pilot study, pointed up the importance of daily home practice. The two experimental group patients who did not show significant declines had found it difficult to carry out the home relaxation assignments. Typically they reported that the hectic state of affairs at home did not permit quiet periods of relaxation. Other patients stated that they would have preferred more explicit relaxation instructions for home use. A few found the daily home practice to be somewhat boring.

Addition to the Basic Technique

In the present study, only a minimal sort of training was employed—EMG feedback from the frontalis muscle. Probably this training could be strengthened considerably. For example, we have recently begun experimenting with two home practice techniques which should add both structure and novelty to the home training. One technique makes use of a 30-minute cassette tape containing relaxation instructions on either side. The other technique utilizes a battery-powered portable EMG feedback unit (Bio-Feedback Systems, Inc.). The tape and portable unit can be employed singly, sequentially, or simultaneously.

Preliminary results indicate that each of these two supplementary methods will be a valuable addition to the minimum procedure used for Groups A, B and C. By now, tapes and portable equipment have been used in the training of some of the approximately 30 tension headache patients (including those from the B and C groups who later received the "real" feedback) who have been trained in muscle relaxation with EMG biofeedback since the completion of this second study. The overall results indicate that roughly 75% showed significant declines in headache activity.

It is possible that some of those who did not show decreases may have been unwilling to give up their headaches. The headaches may have allowed those patients to avoid certain anxiety-arousing situations, or to manipulate others in their family or at work. In these instances, psychotherapy or behavior therapy is required. (11)

Even though EMG feedback training alone is not effective in all cases, the technique would seem to be of considerable value for a substantial proportion of tension headache cases. The training does not involve drugs or other kinds of therapy and can be accomplished with relatively inexpensive portable equipment. Training can be carried out by a technician (or perhaps by the patient himself) under professional supervision. In most instances, beneficial results can be achieved in four to eight weeks. Since many tension headache patients experience pain in the back of the neck and shoulders, it is possible that faster results could be obtained with some of these patients through feedback from these muscle sites. These locations were not used in this study because it is more difficult to obtain precise electrode location here than on the forehead.

A variety of evidence suggests that biofeedback techniques may have applications to stress-related disorders other than tension headache. For example, researchers at the Menninger Foundation (12) have explored the use of skin temperature feedback with migraine patients. In our own laboratory, we have for several years regularly employed EMG feedback techniques in the systematic desensitization of phobias. (13) Insomnia may be another potential application. Drowsiness is a frequent accompaniment of profound muscle relaxation; perhaps EMG (and related) feedback techniques would be useful in some instances of sleep-onset insomnia. Observations in support of such a surmise may be found in Jacobson's writings (14) on progressive relaxation and in the autogenic training literature. (15) It may be noted that both these older approaches systematically train patients in the ability to shift readily into a relaxed, low arousal condition.

This research was supported by the National Institutes of Mental Health, Grant Number MH-15596, and Research Scientist Development Award, Grant Number K01-MH-43361.

We are most grateful to Susan Blom and John Nagel, M.D. for their technical assistance.

REFERENCES

1. Sainsbury P, Gibson JF: Symptoms of anxiety and tension and accompanying physiological changes in the muscular system. J Neurol Neurosurg Psychiat 17:216–224, 1954
2. Ostfeld AM: The common headache syndromes: Biochemistry, pathophysiology, therapy. Springfield, Illinois, Thomas, 1962, p. 19

3. Wolff HG: Headache and other pain. New York, Oxford University Press, 1963, pp. 582–616
4. Martin MJ: Tension headache, a psychiatric study. Headache 6:47–54, 1966
5. Budzynski TH, Stoyva JM: An instrument for producing deep relaxation by means of analog information feedback. J Appl Behav Anal 2:231–237, 1969
6. Budzynski TH, Stoyva JM, Adler CS: Feedback-induced muscle relaxation: Application to tension headache. Behav Ther Exp Psychiat 1:205–211, 1970
7. Snedecor GW, Cochran WG: Statistical methods, 6th ed. Ames, Iowa, Iowa State University Press, 1967, 152–153
8. Wickramasekera I: Electromyographic feedback training and tension headache: Preliminary observations. Amer J Clin Hyp 15:83–85, 1972
9. Raskin M, Johnson G, Rondestvedt JW: Chronic anxiety treated by feedback-induced muscle relaxation. Arch Gen Psychiat 28:263–267, 1973
10. Malmo RB: Emotions and muscle tension: The story of Anne. Psychol Today 3:64, 1970
11. Dengrove E: Behavior therapy of headache. J Amer Soc Psychosom Dent Med 15:41–48, 1968
12. Sargent JD, Green EE, Walters ED: Preliminary report on the use of autogenic feedback techniques in the treatment of migraine and tension headache. Psychosom Med, (in press).
13. Budzynski TH, Stoyva JM: Biofeedback techniques in behavior therapy, in Beitrage der Neuropsychologie zur Angstforschung. Reihe Fortschritte der Klinischen Psychologie, BD 4. Edited by N. Birbaumer, Munchen, Wien, Verlag Urban Schwarzenberg (in press). English version republished in Biofeedback and self-control: 1972. Chicago, Aldine-Atherton (in press) (Edited by D. Shapiro et al.)
14. Jacobson E: Progressive relaxation, 2nd ed. Chicago, University of Chicago Press, 1938, pp. 418–419
15. Schultz JH, Luthe W: Autogenic training: A psychophysiological approach in psychotherapy. New York, Grune & Stratton, 1959

Electromyographic Feedback 20

Training and Tension Headache:
Preliminary Observations

Ian Wickramasekera

Five female Ss diagnosed by neurologists as chronic headache cases and who had failed to respond to a variety of other treatment procedures (*e.g.*, psychotherapy, medication, etc.) were trained to relax their frontalis area with EMG feedback. Ss receiving contingent EMG feedback reduced the frequency and intensity of headache activity but Ss who received non-contingent, but non-frustrative EMG feedback did not reduce headache activity.

Sustained contraction of the scalp and neck muscles appear to be associated with tension headache (Ostfeld, 1962; Wolff, 1963). Electromyographic (EMG) feedback seems useful in the induction of muscular relaxation (Budzynski & Stoyva, 1969, Green, Walters, Green & Murphy, 1969). Budzynski, Stoyva and Adler (1970) described an EMG instrument and feedback training procedure which appeared to reduce both the intensity and frequency of tension headache. Their report was a collection of case studies and lacked several experimental controls. The purpose of the present study was to attempt to replicate their observations with more control, while retaining the merits of the case study method.

METHOD

Instrumentation: EMG Feedback System

The purpose of this instrument is to enable the S to monitor his muscle tension by means of an analog information feedback system. The S hears a tone with a frequency proportional to the EMG activity in the relevant muscle group. The feedback tone tracks the changing EMG level of the muscle. Three surface electrodes are applied either to the forearm extensor one inch below the elbow, or to the frontalis in such a way that the center electrode is centered on the forehead about one inch above the eyebrows. The instrument is constructed so that there is a maximum of 20K unbalanced electrode resistance and a maximum of 30K resistance to ground for each active electrode. The instrument is constructed to eliminate the EKG, EEG and "noise" artifacts.

The S is instructed to keep the tone low by relaxing the relevant muscle group. As the S improves this control, the loop gain of the feedback system is increased, thus requiring him to maintain a lower EMG level in order to hear a low tone. The response of muscle relaxation is shaped by increasing the difficulty of the task in three steps (three sensitivity settings, *i.e.*, low, medium, high). Brief visual feedback was provided only in the first session of training with the

[1] This study was partly supported by a grant from the A.S.C.H. Research Foundation.
[2] Requests for reprints to: 320 East Armstrong Avenue, Peoria, Illinois 61603.

Originally published in *The American Journal of Clinical Hypnosis*, 1972, Vol. 15, 83-85. Copyright, 1972 by the American Society of Clinical Hypnosis.

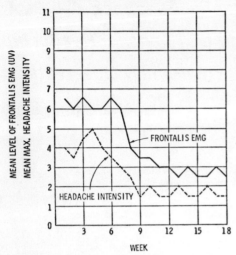

FIG. 1. Headache Intensity and Frontalis EMG Over Time. (0–3 weeks is baseline; 3–6 weeks is non-contingent feedback; 6–18 weeks is contingent feedback)

use of a meter unit calibrated in microamps. The microvolt level, sensitivity setting and meter readout were inter-related. For example, for an S to hold a meter reading of 26 while the sensitivity control is increased from low to medium to high, the S must drop microvolt level from 5.8 to 4.1 to 3.7.

Procedure

Five female Ss diagnosed by neurologists as chronic (6–20 years) tension headache cases, were accepted for the following medical and psychological procedures: (a) Psychological testing (M.M.P.I., SHSS Forms A (pretested prior to EMG feedback training) and B (post-tested after EMG feedback training). (b) Complete physical examination by consulting internist, EEG and examination by consulting neurologist. (c) Next, the patients were given charts on which they were required to keep an accurate record of the intensity and frequency of all headache activity. They were also instructed to cease taking any medication

prescribed for their headaches till the conclusion of the study. (d) There was an initial three week observation period to determine base rates of headache activity. (e) At the end of the three week baseline period, Ss were orientated and instructed (for ten minutes) in the use of the EMG feedback training procedure. The instruction was conducted with "true" or contingent EMG auditory feedback. (f) Next the patients received six sessions of "false" or non-contingent EMG auditory feedback training over a three week period. Each session lasted 30 minutes. Patients did not know they were receiving "false" feedback, hence the study was single blind. The "false" auditory EMG feedback was not randomly generated and hence possibly frustrative in nature. After the orientation period the EMG console was placed on a table behind the Ss chair. The earphones which delivered the auditory feedback were disconnected without the Ss knowledge from the EMG console and connected to a recorder that delivered taped auditory EMG feedback from the actual first six sessions

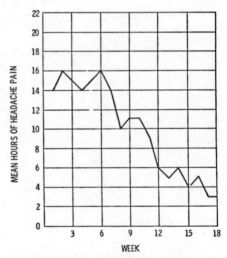

FIG. 2. Headache Activity Over Time. (0–3 weeks is baseline; 3–6 weeks is non-contingent feedback; 6–18 weeks is contingent feedback)

of an *S* successfully trained to relax with "true" or contingent feedback. Hence during the control period *S*s received a pattern of feedback which had the appearance of reality and progress, because the feedback tone declined over time. But the decline was unrelated to anything that the *S* did or did not do during the control period. Informal post-experimental inquiry revealed that the *S*s believed that they were receiving "true" feedback from their own frontalis and that they had improved in their relaxation skills. *S*s continued to keep the record of their headache activity during the "false" feedback period. (g) At the end of the "false" feedback period all patients received six sessions of EMG auditory feedback training with "true" or contingent feedback for another three weeks. Each contingent feedback training session was identical in length (30 minutes) to the previous non-contingent training sessions.

RESULTS

Inspection of the records of all patients appear to indicate no significant difference in the frequency and intensity of headache activity between the baseline period and the non-contingent ("false") EMG feedback period. But there appears to be for all patients significant differences in both intensity and frequency of headache activity between the baseline period and the contingent feedback period. The significant differences in headache activity between the non-contingent and contingent feedback period appears to suggest that the observed differences were probably not a function of placebo efforts (*e.g.*, attention, impressive instrumentation, etc.) These preliminary data seem to suggest that contingent EMG auditory feedback training may be a promising method of reducing the frequency and intensity of tension headache.

REFERENCES

BUDZYNSKI, T. H. & STOYVA, J. M. An instrument for producing deep muscle relaxation by means for analog information feedback. *Journal of Applied Behavior Analysis*, 1969, 2, 231–237.

BUDZYNSKI, T. H.; STOYVA, J. M. & ADLER, C. Feedback induced muscle application to tension headache. *Journal of Behavior Therapy and Experimental Psychiatry*, 1970, 1, 205–211.

GREEN, E. E.; WALTERS, E. D.; GREEN, A. M. & MURPHY, G. Feedback technique for deep relaxation. *Psychophysiology*, 1969, 6, 372–377.

OSTFELD, A. M. *The common headache syndromes biochemistry, pathophysiology, therapy.* Springfield, Illinois: Thomas, 1969.

WOLFF, H. G. *Headache and other pain.* New York: Oxford University Press, 1963.

Joseph D. Sargent, Elmer E. Green,

and E. Dale Walters

A new technique for psychosomatic self-regulation, called autogenic feedback training, was developed by combining biofeedback techniques with autogenic training, a therapeutic method involving simultaneous management of mental and somatic functions. The approach used to control autonomic nervous system functioning was voluntarily increasing blood flow into the hands which is directly related to an increase in hand temperature. By chance, one research subject found that her sudden recovery from a migraine attack coincided with an increase in hand temperature of 10°F in two minutes. This observation culminated in a study of 28 migraine and tension headache sufferers who used hand-warming exercises to regulate their headaches. From this study, regulation of blood flow to the hands seems a useful treatment for migraine attacks. Tension headaches may require a different form of biofeedback training. The encouraging results of this study should provide impetus to other basic research in psychosomatic medicine.

For at least three thousand years, migraine headaches have been a subject of study and discussion. Hippocrates used the expression "hemicrania" and Galen spoke of this entity in his writings. Gradually "hemicrania" evolved into our present word "migraine" (1). The exact cause of migraine is still unknown, although it is clear that symptoms of this type of headache are mediated through the autonomic nervous system.

From 1932 until the time of his death, Wolff probed the pathophysiology of migraine headaches through systematic studies. As a result of his work, it seems likely that there is a "headache stuff" (2) which causes both the edema around blood vessels and the pain which persists long after the prodromal symptoms have subsided. Inability to control the effects of this substance increases the morbidity of migraine attacks.

The migraine syndrome has been defined by many clinicians and investigators. For our purpose the definition as given by Wolff will be used. "The outstanding feature of the migraine syndrome is periodic headache usually unilateral in onset which may become generalized. The headaches are associated with 'irritability' and nausea and often with photophobia, vomiting, constipation, or

From The Menninger Foundation Topeka, Kansas 66601.

The authors wish to thank Nathaniel Uhr, MD and Herbert Spohn, PhD for their helpful editorial comments and Regina Franzen for the assistance in data reduction.

Received for publication December 6, 1971; final revision received April 11, 1972.

Address for reprint requests: Joseph D. Sargent, MD, The Menninger Clinic, Topeka, Kansas, 66601.

diarrhea. Not infrequently the headaches are ushered in by scotomata, hemianopia, unilateral paresthesia, and speech disorders. The pain is commonly limited to the head. Often other members of the patient's family have similar headaches" (3).

In 1953, Wolff, et al, made a study of 119 kindred and found migraine headaches frequently occurring in two to three generations. Three families had evidence of migraine attacks in five generations. The inheritance of this trait is thought to be through a recessive gene with a penetrance of approximately 70 percent (2). This could suggest a common, inherited biochemical defect; however, an environmental factor should also be considered. A personality type characterized as ambitious, perfectionistic, rigid, tense or resentful, yet efficient and poised has been described (4). Emotional crises in these individuals have precipitated migraine attacks.

Tension headaches result from chronic muscle contraction and have a close relationship to emotional conflicts. Onel, et al, have shown that blood flow in the affected muscle is increased (5). Thus, both migraine and tension headaches could possibly be ameliorated by regulation of blood flow via the autonomic nervous system.

Neal Miller in a recent paper has presented research that challenges the concept that "learning" in the autonomic nervous system is a reflection of striate activity. Through animal studies it has been shown that heart rate, gastrointestinal contractions, blood pressure, and the rate of saliva and urine formation, can be directly controlled through "operant conditioning techniques" by way of the autonomic nervous system (6). In humans there is recent scientific evidence for voluntary control of the autonomic nervous system through the training techniques of Yoga (7), biofeedback training (8–11) and the work of Schultz and Luthe on "autogenic training" (12).

Autogenic training, according to Luthe, is a basic therapeutic method of a series of psychophysiologically-oriented approaches which are in contrast to other medical or psychological forms of treatment (12). It involves the simultaneous regulation of mental and somatic functions. The desired somatic responses are brought about by passive concentration upon phrases of preselected words (12). The specific somatic responses in preliminary training brought under voluntary control are heaviness in the limbs, warmth in the extremities, control of heart rate, sense of warmth in the abdomen, and cooling of the forehead.

The usual psychosomatic approach to medicine has emphasized stress as a factor producing dysfunction and pathological change in the patient. Autogenic training evokes changes diametrically opposed to those produced by stress; thus, the autogenic approach has importance for preventive medicine (12).

In treating migraines, Schultz and Luthe reported that the majority of their patients responded with lessened frequency and intensity of headaches with autogenic training exercises. A number of patients reported a cure after several months of practice and learned to interrupt the onset of an attack by starting autogenic exercises as soon as prodromal symptoms appear (12).

Biofeedback training, a recently developed technique, holds promise of accelerating psychosomatic self-regulation. This technique, when combined with autogenic phrases, is called autogenic-feedback training and uses visual and auditory devices to show the subject what is happening to normally unconscious bodily functions as he attempts to influence them by his use of mental, emotional, and somatic visualizations (9). One physiological function experimented with was increasing the hand temperature as an index to the voluntary control of the autonomic nervous system.

The possibility of using autogenic-feedback training for migraine patients was suggested by the experience of a research subject who, during the spontaneous recovery from a migraine attack, demonstrated considerable flushing in her hands with an accompanying 10°F rise in two minutes. Knowledge of this event quickly spread throughout the laboratory and prompted two individuals with migraine to volunteer for training in hand temperature control. One was wholly successful; the other had a partially beneficial result. On the basis of this pre-pilot experience, it seemed useful to conduct further study with a number of headache patients in a clinical setting.

METHODS

Subjects in the pilot study have been either self-referred or referred by physicians in the community. Each patient before participating in the project had a detailed history, complete physical examination, and laboratory tests which included electroencephalogram, skull x-rays, echoencephalogram, chest x-ray, serological test for syphilis, CBC, and urinalysis. Subjects with serious physical and/or psychological disorders were eliminated from the study.

Of 28 subjects there were 22 females and 6 males; all were white. One subject was eliminated from the group because of too brief a period of observation. The age at starting the project ranged from 21 to 63 years. Ten of the subjects with a positive family history of headache had migraine attacks. None of the subjects with tension headaches had a family history of head pain. Twenty subjects fit the definition of migraine headache as defined earlier in the paper by Wolff. Two had questionable migraine attacks. One of the questionable migraine subjects has had continuous right frontotemporal headache for the past three to four years. The other had continuous right mandibular pain for the past several years but also had intermittent right frontotemporal headache. Only the right frontotemporal pain responded to the handwarming exercises. Six subjects had tension headaches.

The patient received instructions in the use of a "temperature trainer" which indicated the differential temperature between the midforehead and the

right index finger. He was also given a typewritten sheet containing autogenic phrases (Table 1). The first group of phrases helped the subject achieve passive concentration and relaxation of the whole body. The second group of phrases focussed on achieving warmth in the hands. After learning the phrases, the participant dispensed with the typewritten sheet and visualized the changes while watching the temperature trainer. A positive response as indicated by the trainer was accomplished by increasing temperature of the hands in comparison with the forehead and helped the subject to learn to observe the changes that occurred in his hands while practicing. Since absolute temperatures were not measured at either site, it is impossible to know whether a positive response indicated an actual increase in hand warmth or a decrease in the forehead temperature. However, it should be noted that a positive response was always associated with a feeling of increased warmth in the hands without any apparent change of feeling in the forehead. Recent unpublished results in our laboratory with experimental subjects indicate that the positive temperature response is almost entirely due to increased hand temperature. The correlation between subjective and objective responses is an important aspect of the training exercises if the subject is to overcome his initial doubt with respect to the control of basic physiological processes. A positive response on the trainer affords the patient confidence in doing his exercises.

Each participant practiced daily with the temperature trainer and kept a record of the practice session on a special data sheet. Pertinent details included the hour of the day, the position (sitting or recumbent), temperature change as shown by the meter and estimation by the patient of his level of concentration, his overall relaxation, and his sense of warmth in the hands. The patient also recorded severity of headache between practice sessions, type of medication, and dosage. Such a record was expected of the participant as long as he remained in the project.

At first the subject was seen on a weekly or biweekly basis until he had a consistent sense of warmth in his hands and positive responses on the temperature trainer. After mastering the handwarming technique he practiced on alternate days without the trainer which later was withdrawn. He was

TABLE 1 Autogenic Phrases

I feel quite quiet . . . I am beginning to feel quite relaxed . . . My feet feel heavy and relaxed . . . My ankles, my knees, and my hips, feel heavy, relaxed, and comfortable . . . My solar plexus, and the whole central portion of my body, feel relaxed and quiet . . . My hands, my arms, and my shoulders feel heavy, relaxed and comfortable. . . . My neck, my jaws, and my forehead feel relaxed . . . They feel comfortable and smooth . . . My whole body feels quiet, heavy, comfortable and relaxed.

I feel quite relaxed . . . My arms and hands are heavy and warm . . . I feel quite quiet . . . My whole body is relaxed and my hands are warm, relaxed and warm . . . My hands are warm . . . Warmth is flowing into my hands, they are warm . . . warm.

---

expected to continue daily practice sessions and was encouraged to use the handwarming to help control tension and headache. In two to four months the frequency of office visits was reduced to once monthly. The expected followup period is two to three years. During his regular office visits pertinent data which may have influenced or precipitated the patient's headaches were recorded.

The clinical investigator's global clinical judgment of each patient's success or failure was compared with the independent assessment by two psychologists of the regression lines of three scales—severity of headache, sum of the potency of the analgesics, and number of analgesics used. The potency scale represented the sum of the strengths of the analgesics used over a 24-hour period. Each analgesic was assigned a number, the extremes of which were aspirin (one) and morphine (seven). The other scale of analgesic usage was the number of different types used in 24 hours. The subjects also rated the severity of the most intense period of headache in each 24-hour period on a five-point scale.

RESULTS

Agreement was reached on 19 subjects and of these 15 had migraine and 4 had tension headaches (Table 2). Of the 15 migraine subjects, 12 were evaluated as improved and 3 as unimproved. Two of the subjects with muscle contraction headaches seemed improved and 2 unimproved.

Of the 8 subjects on whom there was disagreement, 4 had migraine headaches, 2 questionable migraine attacks, and 2 tension-type head pain. The internist judged that improvement occurred in 4 migraine sufferers, 2 with tension headaches, and one of the 2 in the questionable migraine category.

Of the 19 migraine patients 12 (or 63%)

were evaluated as improved by both the internist and two psychologists, while only 2 (or 33%) of the 6 with tension headaches and none of the 2 with questionable migraine attacks were concurred on. No subjects on which there was disagreement were included in the percent improved column. One patient with migraine attacks was not evaluated because of a too brief period of observation.

The exploratory nature of the project and varying lengths of practice with temperature feedback training prohibited any systematic statistical analyses. The period of observation for the evaluated group varied from one month to 22 months, with a mean of 7.7 months.

COMMENTS

Although the agreement between the internist's clinical judgment and the two psychologists' independent assessments was moderately good, the devised scales do not measure all the variables upon which the internist's opinion was based.

For instance, some subjects suffered with more than one type of headache and had not been asked to distinguish between them. Such persons had combinations of migraine, tension, and/or "sinus" headache. A subject could control his migraine headache and still have a record showing little improvement in headache severity if he was troubled with "sinus" headaches as was the case with three participants.

Due to the small number of patients with tension headaches it is not possible

TABLE 2 Classification of Headache Type and Evaluation of Treatment

Type of headache	# of subjects on which there was unanimous agreement		# of subjects on which agreement was not unanimous	Percent improved
	Improved	Unimproved		
Migraine	12	3	4	63
Tension	2	2	2	33
Uncertain	0	0	2	0
Total	14	5	8	

to reach a definite conclusion regarding the effectiveness of handwarming in this entity. However, tension headaches may require a different kind of biofeedback training. The technique developed by Budzynski, Stoyva, and Adler (13) seems promising and in the future we plan to treat patients with such headaches by biofeedback training that produces low electromyographic potentials in the frontalis or trapezius muscles.

At the outset it was hypothesized that decrease in headache severity and type and dose of analgesic used would correspond with clinical judgment of improvement; however, information obtained by the internist during regular interviews did not necessarily correlate with the devised scales. The rapidity and ease with which the patient succeeded in warming the hands contributed greatly in aborting milder headaches. Many patients were improved simply by eliminating such symptoms as nausea or vomiting and others could recognize and handle prodromal somatic manifestations of tension much more easily with the exercises. Both factors contributed to the subjects' sense of improvement. The visits to the emergency room for injections, time spent in the hospital, absenteeism from work, the length of stay at home during an attack, and the altered behavior with family and fellow workers were not directly assessed. All these factors will need future evaluation.

Modifications in the project were made as it progressed. One such change was an individual's recording severity and frequency of headache and medication usage one month prior to training in handwarming so that a baseline for each patient was established.

So far, the majority of patients have had the capacity to produce warmth in their hands within one to eight weeks. A beginner's chief difficulty is the recognition of feeling in the hands associated with rise in skin temperature; to some this may be actual warmth, to others it may be throbbing. Since our experience suggests that most subjects acquire the technique more rapidly than originally thought, the training phase is presently limited to one month. Then the trainer is withdrawn and the subjects are advised to continue daily practice in handwarming. When the participant is able consistently to produce handwarming, he is urged to continue to apply his acquired skill in the prevention and amelioration of the attacks.

The reasons for individual failure varied. One subject lost interest soon after she entered and declared later that she preferred Yoga to handwarming. Two individuals lost interest (they thought the training bordered on mysticism). One individual suffered almost constantly with frontotemporal pain; his exact diagnosis remains unclear. Two faithful participants in the project for one year showed no improvement.

There is need for a more effective treatment modality for tension and migraine headaches. Psychotherapy may be useful for some patients, but it is too often out of reach financially and is an objectionable form of treatment to them. Potent drugs have been developed for management of migraine headaches but often have deleterious side effects. More effective and safer drugs are promised for control of migraine but are still in the experimental phase. Some patients with migraine are not helped by any type of medication. For these, temperature regulation of the hands offers an alternative method of treatment.

The encouraging results of this project should justify not only an expanded evaluation of the effectiveness of temperature training in the control of migraine, but also should provide greater impetus to other basic research in psychosomatic medicine.

SUMMARY

A new technique for psychosomatic self-regulation, called autogenic feedback training, was developed by combining biofeedback techniques with autogenic training, a therapeutic method involving simultaneous management of mental and somatic functions. Autogenic training developed out of the work of Schultz and Luthe and its effects on the body are diametrically opposed to changes elicited by stress.

Research with animals has shown that the autonomic nervous system can be controlled directly by "operant conditioning techniques." Voluntary control of the autonomic nervous system in humans has been demonstrated in Yoga, autogenic training, and biofeedback training.

The symptoms of a migraine attack are mediated through the autonomic nervous system and are often evidenced by increased blood flow in the head. In muscle contraction headaches one group of investigators has demonstrated increased blood flow through the affected muscle. Thus, both migraine and tension headaches might be ameliorated by regulation of blood flow through voluntary control of the autonomic nervous system.

Increased blood flow in the hand is associated with an increase in hand temperature. In this study 28 patients suffering from migraine and from tension headaches used handwarming exercises to ameliorate or abort their headaches. The internist's clinical judgement was compared with the independent assessment of the other two authors' observation of regression lines of three scales—severity of headache, sum of potency of the analgesics used, and the number of pain-relieving medications. The scales consisted of numerical scores obtained from daily records kept by the patient. One patient was eliminated from the group because of too brief a period of observation. Of the remaining 27 participants, agreement was reached on 19. Of these, 15 had migraine and 4 had tension headache. Out of 15 migraine subjects, 12 were improved and 3 unimproved. Twelve migraine sufferers out of a total of 19 (or 63%) were improved.

From this study, temperature regulation of the hands seems a useful adjunct in the treatment of migraine attacks. Tension headaches may require a different type of training. The encouraging results of this study should provide impetus to other basic research in psychosomatic medicine.

REFERENCES

1. Friedman A: The migraine syndrome. Bull NY Acad Med 44:45–62, 1968
2. Goodell H: Thirty years of headache research in the laboratory of the late Dr. Harold G. Wolff. Headache 6:158–171, 1967
3. Wolff H: Headache mechanisms. McGill Med J 15:130–169, 1946
4. Von Storch T: Migraine 1947: A review. Amer Pract 1:631–639, 1947
5. Onel Y, Friedman A, and Grossman J: Muscle blood flow studies in muscle contraction headaches. Neurology 11:935–939, 1961
6. Miller NE: Learning of visceral and glandular responses. Science 163:434–445, 1969
7. Green EE, Ferguson DW, Green AM, and Walters ED: Preliminary Report on the Voluntary Controls Project: Swami Rama. The Menninger Foundation, June, 1970
8. Engel BT and Melmon KL: Operant conditioning of heart rate in patients with cardiac arrhythmias. Cond Reflex 3:130, 1968
9. Green EE, Green AM, and Walters ED: Voluntary control of internal states: psychological and physiological Biofeedback and Self-Control. Edited by T.X. Barber, et al. Chicago, Aldine-Atherton, Inc, 1971
10. Weiss T and Engel BT: Operant conditioning of heart rate in patients with premature ventricular contractions. Psychosom Med 33:301–321, 1971
11. Schwartz GE, Shapiro D, and Tursky B: Learned control of cardiovascular integration in man through operant conditioning. Psychosom Med 33:57–62, 1971
12. Schultz JH and Luthe W: Autogenic Therapy (Vol. I). New York, Grune and Stratton, 1969
13. Budzynski T, Stoyva J and Adler C: Feedback-induced muscle relaxation: Application to tension headache. Biofeedback and Self-Control. Edited by T.X. Barber, et al. Chicago: Aldine-Atherton, Inc, 1971

Chronic Anxiety Treated 22
by Feedback- Induced Muscle Relaxation:
A Pilot Study

Majorie Raskin, George Johnson,
and Joanne W. Rondestvedt

The effects of daily deep muscle relaxation, achieved through electromyographic feedback training, on the symptoms of ten chronically anxious patients were assessed. All ten successfully learned to sustain 25 minutes of profound relaxation of the frontalis muscle with or without feedback. The most striking results occurred when a patient learned to use relaxation techniques at critical times. Three patients learned to use partial relaxation to control previously intolerable situational anxiety and four patients learned to abort tension headaches in the same manner. However, a limited period of relaxation gives insufficient relief from symptoms which endure in time. Only one patient had a marked lessening of his pervasive anxiety and although patients with insomnia learned to put themselves to sleep by relaxing, most experienced frequent awakenings.

An estimated 5% of the United States population is afflicted by chronic anxiety—a persistent or recurrent state of dread or apprehension accompanied by signs of physiological arousal such as palpitations, tremulousness, tachycardia, and dizziness. This painful and disabling state commonly persists for decades.[1] Insight-oriented psychotherapy[2,3] and behavioral therapy[4,5] fail to give satisfactory symptomatic relief in approximately one half the cases. The minor tranquilizers constitute the most

Accepted for publication Nov 16, 1972.
From the Department of Psychiatry, University of California School of Medicine, San Francisco.
Reprint requests to Langley Porter Neuropsychiatric Institute, 401 Parnassus Ave, San Francisco 94122 (Dr. Raskin).

popular treatment of chronic anxiety. The results of studies of the effectiveness of these agents are contradictory and inconclusive.[6-8] Moreover, even our safest and most effective antianxiety agents expose the patient to some risk from unwanted side effects, such as impaired driving proficiency[9,10] and long-term use of these agents for decades may lead to unexpected complications.

In hopes of developing an effective therapeutic regimen we have been exploring the use of feedback-induced muscle relaxation for states of chronic anxiety. Specifically, in this study, we attempted to determine whether the daily practice of deep muscle relaxation would ameliorate symptoms of anxiety in ten chronically anxious patients and alleviate the insomnia and tension headaches which were accompanying disturbances in some of these individuals.

Intervention aimed at teaching relaxation or states of lowered arousal are far from new. In the Eastern practices of yoga and Zen various exercises have been used for thousands of years which allow some individuals to develop remarkable control of the physiological systems that are frequently hyperactive in states of anxiety.[11] More recently, in the past 40 years, two basically physiological approaches to mental and psychosomatic illness have been developed which may also be viewed as attempts to teach volitional control of arousal to patients. These are Jacobson's progressive relaxation[12,13] and Shultz and Luthe's autogenic training.[14,15] The practice of deep muscle relaxation is central to both methods. These two therapies have been credited with considerable success in the treatment of chronic anxiety as well as in the treatment of tension headaches, migraine, asthma, cardiac arrhythmias, and hypertension. We know of no controlled studies to substantiate these results with respect to chronic anxiety.

The current preliminary successes of biofeedback training in the treatment of tension headaches[16] and cardiac arrhythmias,[17] and the suggestion of possible future success in the treatment of migraine[18] and hypertension,[19] have led to renewed interest in the methods and claims of Zen, yoga, progressive relaxation, and autogenic training. In many ways biofeedback techniques represent a modern electronic version of these older approaches. All of these techniques teach the subject to be aware of subtle internal cues and to use these cues to bring about desired psychophysiological states.

The significance of biofeedback training in anxiety has not yet been determined. Budzynski et al[16] used feedback-induced muscle relaxation to successfully treat the tension headaches of five patients. They noted that within eight weeks their patients exhibited "a decreasing tendency to overreact to stress" and postulated that the patients' daily relaxation practice had led to a general lowering of their arousal level. In autogenic training, as well, considerable relief from anxiety is expected within eight weeks of training.[14(p182)] Therefore, we felt that eight weeks of daily relaxation practice in an individual already trained to sustain deep muscle relaxation would be a sufficient period of time to detect some amelioration of anxiety if this technique were to prove successful.

Case Sample

The ten subjects of this study had been troubled by symptoms of anxiety for at least one year before having been admitted to our care for an earlier study and they had remained symptomatic despite two years of treatment with individual psychotherapy and medications. The ten subjects were young adults, with an average age of 27 years, and included six men and four women. All were college graduates and most worked in intellectually demanding positions. All ten patients felt that their symptoms markedly disrupted their lives. These particular ten subjects were chosen for study because of their strong desire for symptomatic relief and because we believed that they would follow a rather exacting treatment regimen.

Each patient had had numerous trials on different medications at varying dosages during the prior two years of treatment. The amount of medication necessary to fully alleviate the symptoms of some of these patients led to an apathy and drowsiness almost as distressing to them as their anxiety. Other patients in this group were disturbed by the idea of relying on drugs indefinitely, particularly when the medications were only partially effective. At the time they entered the study five patients were on moderate doses of chlordiapazide hydrochloride (40 to 80 mg per day) and they remained on the same dosage schedule throughout the study. The other five patients had not used antianxiety agents for some months prior to beginning the study and they remained without antianxiety agents throughout the study.

Method

Relaxation Training and Monitoring.—Patients were taught relaxation in a quiet, somewhat darkened room while reclining on a couch. The muscle feedback instrument and methodology described by Budzynski and Stoyva[20] was used during the study. Surface electrodes were placed on the frontalis muscle. The electromyographic (EMG) activity received from these electrodes controlled the pitch of a tone which was heard through a loudspeaker; the more activity the higher the tone. The patient's instructor, who was seated in the room, faced an instrument panel which displayed a readout of the average level of EMG activity in microvolts for the preceding minute. Each minute was considered a separate trial and the instructor recorded the scores for each trial. Each session lasted for one hour, with training sessions for each patient occurring five times a week.

Instructions to the patient were relatively brief. They were asked to relax with their eyes closed and to purposefully relax specific individual muscle groups. They were then asked to rid their minds of thoughts by concentrating on their breathing or on a pleasant and relaxing image. In all cases we encouraged the patient to experiment, using the tone to tell him what worked best for him in producing deep muscle relaxation.

We considered that the patient was able to maintain deep muscle relaxation when his EMG activity averaged less than $25\mu v$ peak-to-peak per trial for 25 minutes. At this level of relaxation almost no motor unit firing was detectable on an oscilloscope. Once the patient could remain deeply relaxed for 25 minutes training sessions without feedback were interspersed every two to three days. As soon as some progress in relaxing in the laboratory was evident, the patients were instructed to practice relaxation at home.

The eight weeks of daily relaxation practice during which we hoped to see symptomatic relief began when the patient could sustain deep muscle relaxation for 25 minutes with and without feedback. During this time the patients practiced at home for two half-hour sessions daily. They kept charts of the duration and success of their home practice as well as their mood following each home practice session. In addition to home practice each patient was monitored while relaxing in the laboratory at least twice a week. If the patients reported or evidenced any difficulty relaxing, their sessions in the laboratory were made more frequent and feedback was reintroduced.

Assessment of Subjective Relaxation During the Training Sessions.—As part of each session the patient twice rated his subjective feelings of calmness or anxiety on a 10-point scale (0 = profound relaxation and 10 = panic) during two one-minute trials. One rating was made early in the session and one near the end. During the two trials which preceded each self-rating the patient heard no feedback.

Assessment of Symptoms.—For eight weeks prior to the relaxation training, each patient was seen individually, once weekly, by his regular therapist. During this time baselines with regard to anxiety, insomnia, and tension headaches were established. These same ratings were made weekly during the period of feedback training and during the eight weeks of daily relaxation practice.

Anxiety.—Anxiety was assessed using a 65-item mood checklist filled out by the patient. The therapist also rated the patient's anxiety on the basis of his appearance and complaints. The instruments used in this study and their reliability have been described more fully in a prior publication[3] and represent adaptations of established anxiety rating scales.

Sleep Difficulties.—Six patients had insomnia and had taken sedatives nightly for years. They agreed to attempt to try to sleep for one hour without a sedative starting eight weeks before the relaxation training. They kept daily records of how long it took them to get to sleep, whether a sedative was finally used, whether they awakened during the night, and the hour of awakening in the morning.

Headaches.—Four patients were troubled by tension headaches. These were diagnosed by history following the classification of Wolff.[21] They all took pain medications for their headaches and often experienced incomplete relief. They kept daily charts of the frequency, duration, and intensity of their headaches using a quantification technique described by Budzynski et al.[16]

Results

Achievement of Profound Relaxation.—All ten patients reached the criterion point of 2.5μv/min or less averaged over a 25-minute period with and without feedback. The training time varied from two weeks to three months; the average training period was six weeks. Training took longest in patients who responded to their initial brief periods of relaxation with intense anxiety. A mean initial EMG for each individual was calculated by averaging his 15 one-minute trial scores during his first three days of training. The group's mean score was 14.1μv peak-to-peak with a standard deviation of 5.4. During the eight weeks of relaxation practice which followed training the patients maintained EMG levels which ranged from one half to one eighth of their initial values.

During home practice, a major problem for half the patients was that of falling asleep during sessions. The patients experimented with a variety of techniques to prevent sleeping, but most of the patients with this difficulty did not adequately resolve the problem. They frequently had to practice two or three times to obtain one sustained relaxation period. In one case the patient was relaxed in the laboratory on a daily basis in order to obtain relaxation without sleep. Inability to relax because the patient was very nervous was less of a problem. Once the patients had been trained they were generally successful in relaxing at home even when very anxious.

Subjective State During Relaxation Sessions.—On almost all occasions during which the patient sustained 25 minutes of deep muscle relaxation his subjective state at the end of the session was one of tranquility. Rarely, the patients sustained muscular relaxation despite the fact that they were preoccupied with planning or problem solving. Following such sessions the patients stated that their bodies felt relaxed, but that their minds were not. On two occasions we observed dramatic dissociations between muscular tension and anxiety. Both instances involved patients who had learned relaxation rapidly and who prided themselves on their ability to "control the machines," ie, to keep the sound low. These patients experienced profound anxiety, which ultimately disrupted the session, despite the fact that they maintained profound frontalis relaxation.

To more closely explore the relationship between EMG activity and anxiety, we examined each patient's first 15 sessions. Three correlation coefficients were computed for each patient using 15 paired scores: the patient's EMG scores recorded early in each session were correlated with the patient's beginning of the session anxiety scores; the patient's EMG scores recorded late in each session were correlated with the patient's end of the session anxiety scores; and the patient's within session changes in muscle tension were correlated with within session changes in anxiety. These correlations coefficients varied considerably and were not statistically significant. The lowest correlations were found in the patients with lowest initial frontalis activity. There was no relationship between the degree of correlation for each individual and his use or nonuse of medications.

Effects on Symptoms.—Table 1 summarizes the changes in symptom distress which occurred during the eight weeks of practice.

Anxiety.—General symptomic improvement was assessed by comparing the patient's self-rating anxiety scores and the therapist's ratings during the baseline period with the corresponding scores obtained during the period of daily relaxation.

One patient had improved markedly; moving from scores representing consistently high anxiety to scores

Changes in Symptom Intensity				
Symptom		Outcomes		
	No. Patients With Each Symptom	No. Markedly Improved	No. Moderately Improved	No. Unimproved
Anxiety	10	1	3	6
Insomnia	6	1	4	1
Headaches	4	3	1	0

vent expected tension build-ups at a later time they reported no success. Prolonged periods of relaxation following practice generally occurred when conditions were conducive to continued relaxation.

When severe anxiety occurred in social situations all ten patients attempted to use relaxation techniques to control their anxiety. For most patients this was of little value. They found that their ability to relax was limited to a supine eyes-closed posture. However, three patients reported repeated instances of remarkable success in controlling severe situational anxiety using modified relaxation techniques while seated with their eyes open. These were the three patients whose overall scores reflected moderate improvement.

Sleep Difficulties.—The relaxation training had profound effects on the insomnia of five of the six patients with sleep disturbances. These five found that they could put themselves to sleep promptly, almost every night, by relaxing. This had been impossible throughout the eight weeks used for a baseline. Unfortunately, their ability to put themselves to sleep was not accompanied by an equal improvement in other sleep parameters. Without medication, four of the five frequently awakened periodically during the night or at an unusually early morning hour. representing well being or occasionally mild anxiety. Three patients improved moderately in their ratings were consistently lower than before, but still reflected frequent moderate to high anxiety. The other six patients exhibited no change.

During periods of very severe anxiety occurring at home, almost all the patients found that relaxation practice for 30 to 45 minutes would frequently interrupt their episodes of anxiety and leave them feeling much calmer for varying lengths of time (20 minutes to a number of hours). When the patients relaxed early in the day to pre-

The patients could usually relax back to sleep, but they stated that their sleep was not as restful as the sedative-induced sleep they previously experienced. However, their capacity to put themselves to sleep at will markedly decreased their fear of insomnia and they considered their ability to sleep without sedatives to be a major gain.

Headaches.—The four patients with headaches experienced considerable reduction in the frequency and intensity of their headaches. They learned to use relaxation techniques to abort anticipated or beginning headaches and even to diminish the pain of an established headache.

Comment

The primary question this study set out to answer was whether the daily practice of deep muscle relaxation would alleviate the anxiety symptoms of chronically anxious patients. This intervention had beneficial effects on the anxiety of four of ten patients. One patient had a dramatic lessening of all his anxiety symptoms, while the other three learned to use relaxation techniques to decrease previously intolerable situational anxiety. Considering the fact that all of our patients were chronically ill and treatment refractory, these results are promising. The fact that three patients learned to control situational anxiety was particularly encouraging. We are hopeful that more patients can be taught to master their situational anxiety through modifications in our training procedure, for example by using feedback training while the patients are seated with their eyes open. However, daily relaxation per se does not appear to be an effective treatment for the pervasive symptoms associated with chronic anxiety.

The tranquility associated with a limited period of relaxation all too frequently proves transient. In order to achieve satisfactory results in chronic anxiety it appears necessary for the patient to learn to incorporate relaxation into his daily activities. Autogenic training and progressive relaxation are reputedly successful in the treatment of chronic anxiety. It is interesting to speculate that these approaches differed from ours in ways which allowed for greater generalization of the patient's relaxation response to his ongoing life. For example, Shultz and Luthe taught relaxation in a seated posture and placed great emphasis on the patient's ability to relax quickly at will. Jacobson's training was very prolonged, taking months or years, and he attempted to teach his subjects to eliminate unnecessary physical or mental tension whenever it arose. Haugen et al[22] developed a modified version of Jacobson's procedure. Immediately after the patient learned to relax he was instructed to practice relaxation while active, eg, while walking or driving a car. Haugen and associates give an explicit account of how they taught the anxious patient to incorporate relaxation into his every activity. This modified approach was apparently quite successful in the treatment of hundreds of patients suffering from chronic anxiety. Unfortunately, these favorable results are entirely anecdotal.

We were also interested in assessing the effects of daily relaxation on insomnia and tension headaches. These results parallel the effects of relaxation practice on anxiety. In both pervasive anxiety and insomnia the beneficial effects of a finite period of relaxation give insufficient relief. However, the patients who learned to relax themselves to sleep felt that they had made a major gain since they were no longer reliant on the sedatives they had taken for years. In situational anxiety and tension headaches a finite period of relaxation at a critical time can make a major difference to the patient's well being. Our patients' experience with the modification of tension headaches through feedback induced relaxation are entirely in accord with the findings of Budzynski et al.[16]

The fact that a selected group of chronically anxious patients can be taught to achieve a state of lowered arousal consistently without medications is in itself useful, both clinically and experimentally. Our own patients found that relaxation could be used to end prolonged states of intense anxiety. Budzynski and Stoyva[20] have suggested that this state may prove an important adjunct to desensitization, and it may prove useful in other therapies as well.

The ability to study a chronically anxious patient in a nonmedicated, nonanxious state may help clarify certain theoretical issues. For example, Lader and Wing[23] suggest that the anxiety-prone person has an innate deficit in arousal modulation. Considerable evidence does demonstrate that the anxious individual takes longer to decrease his arousal following stimulation than the normal subject.[23(p86)-27] However, the higher the level of ongoing arousal in any individual, the longer it will take him to return to a baseline following stimulation.[23(p141)] Inasmuch as the anxious patient has usually been anxious at the time he was studied, it has never been clear if his homeostatic failure is the cause or result of his anxiety. It will be important to see if anxious patients continue to show slowed adaptation or habituation as compared to normals when both are studied in a state of deep relaxation.

In the present study EMG activity was recorded from the frontalis muscle. This muscle is difficult to relax voluntarily and it frequently remains active, particularly in anxious subjects, despite more general muscular relaxation.[28,29] Therefore, it seems likely that teaching subjects profound relaxation of the frontalis muscle will result in general muscular relaxation. Our own observations, our patients' reports and the observations of others[20] support this assumption. However, the assumption will have to be tested by replicating our studies while simultaneously monitoring several muscles groups.

The low within-subject correlations we found between muscle tension scores and subjective anxiety ratings are in accord with the conclusions of Lader and Mathews.[30] In their recent review they stated that while anxious patients often had higher muscle tension levels than normal individuals, the correlations between EMG scores and anxiety scores were generally low.

Once the patients learned to sustain low frontalis EMG activity for prolonged periods of time they reported that this state was almost always accompanied by subjective tranquility. This stands in marked contrast to the low correlations between subjective anxiety and EMG scores obtained during the training period. There are several possible explanations for these paradoxical results. It may be that sustained profound muscular relaxation is much more potent in lowering central arousal than the sporadic episodes of low muscular activity observed during training. Alternatively, the training procedure may have led the patients to learn cognitive maneuvers which lowered their central arousal and secondarily reduced muscle tension. If this was the case then the analog feedback may have been helpful in allowing patients to select mental states most conducive to lowered central arousal, or it may have been irrelevent in producing subjective relaxation. If the effects of the training procedure were primarily direct central effects then the close association between subjective relaxation and low frontalis EMG levels may have been the result of our simultaneous reinforcement of both subjective relaxation and low frontalis activity. Future studies of relaxation in anxious patients using irrelevant and false feedback as control conditions should help clarify these issues.

These results are encouraging with respect to the use of muscle feedback training in some of the symptoms associated with chronic anxiety. However, the transiency of tranquility associated with a limited period of relaxation suggests that relaxation must be more fully incorporated into the patient's life to produce satisfactory results in decreasing pervasive anxiety. Decades of clinical wisdom concerning the treatment of symptoms of anxiety using psychophysiological approaches are available to us.[12-15,22] Biofeedback technology now makes it possible to teach some of the interventions in a more rapid and efficient manner. Hopefully, continued exploration combining biofeedback training techniques with the older psychophysiological approaches will result in more effective treatment of the chronically anxious patient.

psychophysiological approaches are available to us.[12-15,22] Biofeedback technology now makes it possible to teach some of the interventions in a more rapid and efficient manner. Hopefully, continued exploration combining biofeedback training techniques with the older psychophysiological approaches will result in more effective treatment of the chronically anxious patient.

References

1. Harris A: The prognosis of anxiety states. *Br Med J* 2:649-654, 1938.
2. Miles HHW, Barabee EL, Finesinger JE: Evaluation of psychotherapy with a follow-up of 62 cases of anxiety neurosis. *Psychosom Med* 13:83-105, 1951.
3. Raskin M, Rondestvedt JW, Johnson G: Anxiety in young adults: A prognostic study. *J Nerv Ment Dis* 154:229-237, 1972.
4. Lazarus AA: The results of behavior therapy in 126 cases of severe neurosis. *Behav Res Ther* 1:69-79, 1963.
5. Gelder M: Behavior therapy for anxiety states. *Br Med J* 1:691-694, 1969.
6. Klein DF, Davis JM: *Diagnosis and Drug Treatment of Psychiatric Disorders.* Baltimore, Williams & Wilkins Co, 1969, pp 342-403.
7. Jarvik ME: In Goodman LS, Gilman A (eds): *Drugs Used in the Treatment of Psychiatric Disorders.* London, Macmillan Co, 1970, pp 174-181.
8. Librium and Valium. *The Medical Letter* 11:81-84, 1969.
9. Hollister LE: Complications from psychotherapeutic drugs. *Clin Pharmacol Ther* 5:328, 1964.
10. Drugs and auto accidents. *The Medical Letter* 8:53-54, 1966.
11. Wenger MA, Bagchi BK: Studies of autonomic functions in

practitioners of Yoga in India. *Behav Sci* 6:312-317, 1961.

12. Jacobson E: *Progressive Relaxation.* Chicago, University of Chicago Press, 1938.

13. Jacobson E: *Modern Treatment of Tense Patients.* Springfield, Ill, Charles C Thomas Publisher, 1970.

14. Schultz JH, Luthe W: *Autogenic Training.* New York, Grune & Stratton Inc, 1959.

15. Luthe W: In Barber TX, et al (eds): *Autogenic Training: Method, Research, and Applications in Medicine, Biofeedback and Self-Control.* Chicago, Aldine-Atherton, 1971, pp 633-655.

16. Budzynski T, Stoyva J, Adler C: Feedback-induced muscle relaxation: Application to tension headaches. *J Behav Ther Exp Psychiatry* 1:205-211, 1970.

17. Weiss T, Engel BT: Operant conditioning of heart rate in patients with cardiac arrythmias. *Psychophysiology* 6:636-637, 1970.

18. Sargent JD, Green EE, Walters ED: Preliminary report on the use of autogenic feedback techniques in the treatment of migraine and tension headaches. *Psychosom Med,* to be published.

19. Benson H, et al: Decreased systolic blood pressure through operant conditioning techniques in patients with essential hypertension. *Science* 173:740-741, 1971.

20. Budzynski TH, Stoyva JM: An instrument for producing deep muscle relaxation by means of analog information feedback. *J Appl Behav Anal* 2:231-237, 1969.

21. Wolff H: *Headaches and Other Head Pain,* ed 3. Revised by Dalessio DJ. New York, Oxford University Press, 1972.

22. Haugen GB, Dixon HH, Dickel HA: *A Therapy for Anxiety Tension Reactions.* New York, Macmillan Co, 1958.

23. Lader MH, Wing L: *Physiological Measures, Sedative Drugs, and Morbid Anxiety.* New York, Oxford University Press, 1966.

24. Rubin LS: Autonomic dysfunction as a concomitant of neurotic behavior. *J Nerv Ment Dis* 138:558-575, 1964.

25. Davis JF, Malmo RB, Shagass C: Electromyographic reaction to strong auditory stimuli in psychiatric patients. *Canad J Psychol* 8:177-186, 1954.

26. Clemens TL, Selesnick ST: Psychological method for evaluating medication by repeated exposure to a stress or film. *Dis Nerv Syst* 28:98, 1967.

27. Koepke JE, Pribram KH: Habituation of the vasoconstriction response as a function of stimulus duration and anxiety. *J Comp Physiol Psychol* 64:502-504, 1967.

28. Balshan ID: Muscle tension and personality in women. *Arch Gen Psychiatry* 7:436-448, 1962.

29. Malmo RB, Smith AA: Forehead tension and motor irregularities in psychoneurotic patients under stress. *J Pers* 23:391-406, 1955.

30. Lader MH, Mathews AM: Electromyographic studies of tension. *J Psychosom Res* 15:479-486, 1971.

Behavior Techniques in the 23
Modification of Spasmodic Torticollis

Charles S. Cleeland

Torticollis is a disturbance of the finely tuned movement and postural control of the head and neck, often associated with spasm of the muscles controlling head support and movement. The head is deviated to one side. The etiology of the disorder remains obscure; different investigators have argued that the disorder is either primarily organic[1] or essentially functional[2] in nature. Patients are not often incapacitated by torticollis, although those in vocations requiring close visual monitoring and fine hand-eye coordination may have to find different occupations. In addition, the continual twisting of the neck can cause severe discomfort and is almost universally an embarrassment. Insidious in onset, the twisting of the head in torticollis typically becomes more severe over a period of months, then becomes stable. Spontaneous remissions are rare but have been reported.

Torticollis is relatively refractory to a wide variety of treatments. Those who consider that it is primarily a functional disturbance advocate psychotherapy as the treatment of choice, and successful treatment occasionally has been reported.[3] Those favoring an organic basis for torticollis favor surgical intervention, such as rhizotomy[4] or the placement of stereotaxic lesions in the basal ganglia or thalamic tracts.[5] Studies on the outcome of surgical treatment vary from optimistic to cautionary, and the risk of complications may run high.[6] Many feel that intracranial surgery is unjustified in the disorder, and some reports suggest that various medications may be of considerable benefit to the patient.

The patient's description of torticollis almost always emphasizes the loss of voluntary control; our patients often state that the head "just seems to want to go" in the direction of the torticollis. This description suggested to us the possibility that voluntary control might be relearned, especially if technics were devised to enhance learning effects.

This view had received some support from several different sources. Brierly[8] reported that a simple avoidance-conditioning paradigm was effective in relieving spasm in two patients with torticollis. A relatively mild cutaneous shock was delivered to the arm when a position-sensitive switch worn on the patient's head was activated by head deviation. Studies in normal subjects have shown that the development of a precision in muscle control not normally available can be obtained if the subject has a display of ongoing electromyographic (EMG) activity available to him. Hefferline[9] showed that a single motor unit can be made to increase or decrease its activity when the potential for that unit is amplified and displayed to the subject. Such con-

From the Department of Neurology, University of Wisconsin Center for Health Sciences, Madison 53706.
This study was supported in part by NIH grant 5-POI-NS 03360.
Received for publication May 9, 1973.
Dr. Cleeland's address is Department of Neurology, University Hospitals, University of Wisconsin; 1300 University Avenue, Madison 53706.

trol is possible even when no physical contraction can be reported or observed by the subject. Sasmor,[10] working with Hefferline, reported that motor unit responses could be conditioned in 10 microvolt ranges, and Basmajain[11] showed that subjects can use displays of motor unit activity to produce repeatable complex rhythmic patterns.

These studies suggested that various behavioral technics, more typical of the psychology laboratory than the clinic, might be of some benefit in the modification of torticollis. The following studies were designed to see if patients with torticollis could modify the intensity and frequency of their spasms when the spasm was paired with cutaneous shock, or with an ongoing display of associated EMG activity (feedback), or with a combination of shock and feedback.

Materials and methods

Pilot data indicated that a single pulse shock, when delivered by a position-sense switch, did reduce the frequency of spasmodic activity in four of five torticollis patients studied. The reduction in spasm frequency, however, was only temporary and of little clinical benefit to the patient.[12] The experimental situation therefore was modified in several ways: first, to give the patient continuous "on-line" information about the relative EMG activity in the involved muscles; second, to trigger the cutaneous shock from the initial increase in EMG amplitude (which would deliver shock at the onset of the spasm rather than at its termination, as was true with the position-sense switch); and, third, to deliver shock as long as the spasm was present. All of these modifications were included to achieve optimum speed in spasm reduction and to enhance the possibility of generalization of spasm reduction to situations outside the laboratory.

Surface electrodes were placed near the anterior border and just above the clavicular attachment of both the left and right sternocleidomastoid muscles. Electromyographic activity was recorded, as were the various stimuli (shock and auditory EMG feedback display) that were presented to the subject contingent upon predetermined specified changes in EMG activity. Amplified EMG activity was fed to a voltage-controlled oscillator that,

via an audio amplifier and speaker, presented a tone that varied in pitch proportionate to the EMG activity. Amplified EMG was also fed to an adjustable Schmidt trigger, the output of which could activate a cutaneous shock. Shock was delivered from a stimulator with a step-up isolation transformer that delivered shock to two plate electrodes mounted on the first and second digits. Pulse trains of 10 per second were used, with a pulse duration of 10 msec. The current delivered per pulse ranged from 2 to 4 ma. The shock train was activated as long as the Schmidt trigger threshold voltage was exceeded.

The auditory display heard by the patient was delivered by a speaker in the experimental chamber. The pitch change proportional to the EMG varied through a range of 200 to 1500 Hz. The range was adjusted proportional to the spasm amplitude for each patient. Spasms were recorded on an electric counter activated by the Schmidt trigger. Records of the patient were made both before and after the study either on film or video tape.

Results

Ten patients served as subjects; nine were diagnosed as having spasmodic torticollis and one as having retrocollis (see the table). Patients were classified into three groups according to the degree of response to behavioral treatment: (1) Improvement was considered marked (+ +) if the patient demonstrated no spasmodic activity on follow-up EMG recordings and if the patient reported no spasmodic activity outside the laboratory. (2) A response was considered moderate (+) if the patient displayed reduced spasm frequency on follow-up EMG recordings, was judged by at least two staff neurologists to have significantly reduced head deviation and spasmodic activity, *and* reported consistent reduction of head deviation and spasm outside the laboratory and clinic. (3) Minimal or no improvement (0) was listed if any one of the criteria for moderate (+) could not be met. Patient reporting of improvement alone was not considered objective assessment. Although the two procedures, EMG feedback and shock avoidance training, were applied to all 10 subjects in this group, variations in the treatment technic were dictated by the expression of torticollis in each patient.

DATA FOR NINE PATIENTS WITH TORTICOLLIS AND ONE WITH RETROCOLLIS

	Age	Sex	Symptom duration	Sessions	Initial spasm frequency / 5 minutes	Final spasm frequency / 5 minutes	Shock effect	Initial improvement	Follow-up improvement (duration)
Case 1	15	M	4 months	16	44	3	+	++	++ (18 months)
Case 2	25	F	60 months	6	21	6	+	+	+ (40 months)
Case 3	64	M	36 months	23	188	168	0	0	0 (17 months)
Case 4	50	F	24 months	10	40	1	+	+	+ (18 months)
Case 5	28	M	9 months	8	75	46	+	+	Lost to follow-up
Case 6*	54	F	36 months	8	40	0	+	++	+ (17 months)
Case 7	18	F	2 months	15	11	0	+	++	++ (24 months)
Case 8	54	F	10 months	10	54	11	+	+	0 (20 months)
Case 9	43	F	7 months	8	34	8	0	+	0 (5 months)
Case 10	32	M	6 months	8	28	5	+	++	++ (1 month)

*Retrocollis.

Therefore, a more detailed presentation of the investigation of three patients, one from each outcome classification, will be offered.

Case reports

Case 1. A 15 year old boy had had torticollis to the left for four months. The symptom had become so severe and persistent that he had not attended school for one month. The physical and neurologic examinations were completely within normal limits, with the exception of fixed head position to the left and mild hypertrophy of the patient's right sternocleidomastoid.

Spasm in the right sternocleidomastoid was evident only when the patient made an effort to bring his head to midline. Auditory EMG feedback was made available from surface electrodes attached over the right sternocleidomastoid. The patient was instructed to lower the tone by decreasing right sternocleidomastoid activity, then move his head toward the midline until the tone rose in pitch, then lower the one again. His initial task, then, was to bring his head toward midline in successive steps, with each step contingent on relative relaxation in the right sternocleidomastoid. As with all other patients in this series, sessions consisted of six to eight five minute intervals with a two to three minute intertrial interval. One to two sessions per day were given. With all patients, an attempt was made to "shape" muscle activity by requiring less EMG activity from session to session to activate the feedback display or the shock, or both.

After seven sessions using only the EMG feedback, the patient was able to keep his head in the midline for all trials but with frequent jerky head movements to the left, associated with spasm in the right sternocleidomastoid. At this point, spasm onset was paired with light cutaneous shock (3 ma) to the fingertips, triggered by EMG activity. The shock remained on as long as EMG activity remained above a preset level. Again, "shaping" was used. Shock first was administered only with high amplitude spasm, then with spasms of decreasing amplitude as the sessions progressed. Mean spasm frequency for base-line (no shock) sessions on the

first day of shock administration was 44 for five minutes. Initial and final spasm frequency for each of the first five shock and feedback sessions is presented in figure 1. The spasm frequency was higher than base line during the first session using shock but dropped to below base line by the third session. Shock was paired with spasm for a total of seven sessions. In addition to the gradual spasm reduction from session to session, spasm frequency was reduced from the initial to the final trial during seven of the eight shock sessions. When discharged, the patient was able to hold his head in the midline with essential symmetry of right and left sternocleidomastoid activity. He was able to return to school and resume his usual activities. Some spasm remained, however, and the patient returned weekly for five additional sessions. He has been followed on a bimonthly basis for 30 months, with no evidence of spasm from EMG recording and no resumption of the torticollis. His improvement was classified as marked.

Case 2. A 25 year old woman school teacher had intermittent spasms of the neck and head deviation to the left that had been present for five years before admission. Physical and neurologic examination was described as completely within normal limits with the exception of frequent spasms of the right sternocleidomastoid with head deviation to the left. The patient was unable to position her head in the midline during a spasm.

She was seen for six sessions, receiving both cutaneous shock (3 ma) and tone feedback triggered by spasm. The auditory display was different from that used with other patients in the series in that initial sessions used a pure tone (1000 Hz) auditory display that was present only when a spasm occurred. Although the tone was present for every spasm above the selected amplitude, shock was only intermittently administered, approximately one for every seven spasms. The mean frequency of spasms per five minute trial was initially 20, which was reduced over the six sessions to one to two spasms per trial.

A month after initial shock and feedback sessions, the patient reported continuing im-

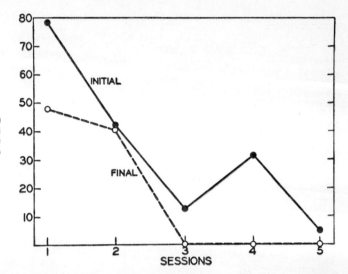

Figure 1. Case 1. Spasm frequency and initial and final five minute base-line trials for the first five sessions using shock and feedback.

provement with an increase in the range of her daily activities. She was followed at bimonthly intervals. At her request, at each interval she received two conditioning sessions, one in the morning and one in the afternoon, to maintain the spasm reduction. Ten months after her initial sessions, the variable-pitch EMG feedback became available and has been used with her since.

Fifteen months after the initial sessions, she reported an increase in the frequency of spasms and was seen for four sessions over a two day period. Spasm again was reduced to the frequency it had been at the end of the initial sessions. She did well for approximately a year until she noticed an increase in the spasm frequency about a month before the birth of her first child. After delivery, the spasm frequency diminished with no intervention, and she has retained the reduced spasm frequency for another year. She has been followed for a total of 40 months. Her improvement was classified as moderate.

Case 3. A 64 year old man had spasmodic torticollis to the right. About two years before admission the patient noticed stiffness of the right side of the neck that slowly developed into a persistent jerking head movement. This movement slowly progressed despite a variety of physical and drug therapies, including trials on amitriptyline hydrochloride, diazepam, and amantadine hydrochloride. Neurologic examination was essentially within normal limits. Marked hypertrophy of the left sternocleidomastoid was noted.

The procedure followed in case 3 was essentially the same as in case 1, except that the initial sessions using EMG feedback only were not necessary because the patient could hold his head in the midline voluntarily. Shock level was 4 ma. Eight sessions were administered while the patient was in the hospital. When he held his head in the midline, a high frequency of spasm activity was noted (as high as one per second on initial base line). Trials represented a combination of shock only, feedback only, and shock and feedback combined. All three methods were associated with substantially lower spasm frequencies during all eight sessions; only one trial of the eight sessions (a total of 40 trials) showed a higher frequency of spasmodic activity than either the initial or final base line for that session. The patient's response is presented in figure 2.

Despite a clinical impression of some reduction in the degree of head deviation and spasmodic activity, session-to-session reduction in spasm frequency was not seen in this patient, other than initial reduction from session one to session two. The contingency trials (shock or feedback or both) continued to suppress the spasm but with little generalization to situations outside the laboratory, and no further reduction was noted in the initial base line for each session. At the patient's request, he was seen on an outpatient basis for an additional 15 sessions. Again, the spasm was suppressed during contingency trials (consistently reduced spasm frequency by one-half to two-thirds). Initial base-line frequency, however, continued to be stable; the patient reported no significant improvement in the spasm generally and the sessions were discontinued.

Other patients studied. Of the other seven patients included in the study (see the table), two were classified as showing marked improvement (total three), two moderate improvement (total three), and two no improvement. One patient was lost to follow-up. This last patient showed improvement in head deviation, as judged by the viewing of presession and postsession video tapes, but the reduction in spasm frequency from initial to

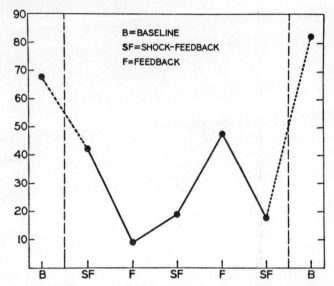

Figure 2. Case 3. Seventh session, illustrating suppression of spasm activity with both shock and shock-feedback (five minute trials).

final base lines was not substantial, and he was placed in the no improvement classification (total unimproved, four). Therefore, 60 percent of the patients were classified as showing moderate or greater improvement.

Two of the three patients showing no improvement on follow-up did show moderate improvement in both spasm frequency and head position immediately after the sessions.

Within one month, however, both had returned to pretreatment base-line levels. Therefore, if improvement were transitory, this was apparent relatively soon after treatment ended.

In all patients, trials with EMG feedback combined with shock were compared with trials in which feedback alone was used. In eight of the 10 patients, shock-plus-feedback trials showed lower spasm frequency than

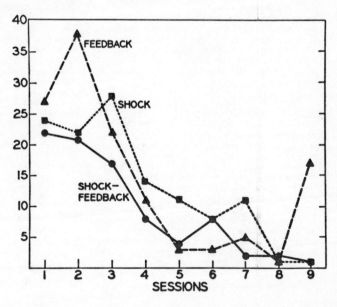

Figure 3. Case 4. Mean trial spasm frequency (five minute trials) for shock, feedback, and shock-feedback conditions for the first nine sessions.

feedback-only trials during more than 50 percent of sessions when shock was administered. These patients were classified as demonstrating a "shock effect" (see the table). Two patients showed little or no further spasm reduction attributable to the addition of shock.

The parameters of shock were different in the pilot study and in the present experiment (single shock delivered by a position switch in contrast with an EMG-triggered shock pulse train that lasted as long as the spasm was present). Therefore, the effect of EMG-triggered shock alone was studied in one patient: Shock trials were presented randomly in all sessions, together with feedback-only trials and feedback-plus-shock trials. For this patient, shock-feedback trials were associated with significantly fewer spasms than shock-only trials ($p < 0.05$) and were associated with fewer spasms than feedback-only trials, although this second comparison was not judged to be statistically significant ($p < 0.10$) (figure 3).

Discussion

Eight of the 10 patients studied showed reduction in the frequency of spasmodic activity of the neck when this activity was paired with cutaneous shock and auditory feedback of myoelectric potentials of the muscles in spasm. The reduction in spasm was rapidly apparent (usually by the second session) and, in seven patients, was progressively reduced from one session to the next. In six of the 10 patients, the sessions had a clear therapeutic benefit that appears to be stable (mean follow-up 19 months). Of the four patients who did not show improvement on follow-up, two showed initial and substantial improvement that persisted outside the laboratory but that was of less than a month's duration. The reasons for this return to base-line spasm frequency in these two patients are unclear.

Contingent cutaneous shock has been used to reduce the frequency of tics in various muscle groups.[13] The use of EMG feedback in reducing muscle tension levels of patients with neck injuries[14] and in reducing tension headaches[15] has been reported. Spasmodic torticollis consists of both spasmodic activity and excessive background EMG activity, usually in one sternocleidomastoid muscle but often spreading to other muscle groups. The com-bination of these two factors may make shock combined with feedback the most effective contingency for reduction of spasm frequency.

The levels of cutaneous shock used in this study were described by the patients as unpleasant but not particularly painful. Yet the shock was associated with decreased spasm frequency in eight of 10 patients. Several patients in the study commented with some surprise that the shock helped them lower spasm frequency even when they were unable to do so unaided. Although it is tempting to ascribe this shock effect to a simple avoidance or escape learning model, the possibility exists that shock may help lower spasm frequency on some imprecisely understood reflex basis. Such a possibility is suggested by Podivinsky,[16] who found that cutaneous tactile stimulation applied to the affected side of the neck tended to block or decrease spasm in torticollis. Whatever the basis of the shock effect, the finding that spasms remained reduced in frequency or were eliminated in six of the 10 patients supports numerous studies that report the difficulty of extinguishing learned behavior produced with shock procedures.[17] It seems logical to assume that, at least in part, slight increases in sternocleidomastoid activity (and change in the feedback signal) became a conditioned or discriminative stimulus for the occurrence of both spasm and shock. Several of the patients commented that the EMG feedback helped them get an "image" of the relative activity of sternocleidomastoid muscles that was not available to them before, and that this heightened proprioception enabled them voluntarily to relax the muscles. EMG feedback alone might be effective as a treatment, although that cannot be determined by the present investigation.

The potential therapeutic benefit of the procedure described is limited by the time demands on both patient and clinician and by the specialized equipment required for the contingencies described, but the procedure may prove of benefit to some patients refractory to other treatment methods. The most significant improvement was shown by patients who were younger and for whom torticollis was a symptom of relatively short duration, although no older patients with torticollis of short duration (less than six months) were included in the study. Some of the patients in this report may well have responded to the more recently reported medical treatments available, although three of the patients were refractory to haloperidol, amantadine hydrochloride, or combinations of these two agents. One of these three patients showed marked improvement with shock-feedback; two were classified as unimproved.

Summary

The effects of EMG feedback and contingent cutaneous shock were studied in 10 patients with involuntary spasmodic activity of the muscles of the neck (nine torticollis, one retrocollis). The combination of shock and feedback was associated with reduced spasm frequency in the laboratory in eight of 10 patients, and sessions using these conditions proved to be of therapeutic benefit in six of the 10 patients studied.

Acknowledgments

The author wishes to thank Dr. Francis M. Forster for suggesting the use of conditioning technics with torticollis, and Ms. Monika Petkus for extensive technical assistance in data collection and data reduction.

REFERENCES

1. Paterson M: Spasmodic torticollis. Lancet 249:556, 1945
2. Fenichel O: The Psychoanalytic Theory of Neuroses. New York, W. W. Norton & Company, Inc., 1945
3. Pattison EM: The patient after psychotherapy. Am J Psychother 25:194, 1970
4. Dandy WE: Operation for treatment of spasmodic torticollis. Arch Surg 20:1021, 1930
5. Cooper IS: Effect of thalamic lesions upon torticollis. N Engl J Med 270:967, 1964
6. Meanes R: Natural history of spasmodic torticollis and effect of surgery. Lancet 2:149, 1971
7. Gilbert GJ: The medical treatment of spasmodic torticollis. Arch Neurol 27:503, 1972
8. Brierly H: The treatment of hysterical spasmodic torticollis by behavior therapy. Behav Res Ther 5:139, 1967
9. Hefferline RF: The role of proprioception in the control of behavior. Trans NY Acad Sci 20:739, 1958
10. Sasmor RM: Operant conditioning of a small-scale muscle response. J Exp Anal Behav 9:69, 1966
11. Basmajain JV: Control and training of individual motor units. Science 141:440, 1963
12. Cleeland CS: Conditioning and the dystonias. Symposium presentation. Canadian Psychological Association. St. John's, Newfoundland, June 1971
13. Yates AJ: The application of learning theory to the treatment of tics. J Abnorm Psychol 56:175, 1958
14. Jacobs A, Felton GS: Visual feedback of myoelectric output to facilitate muscle relaxation in normal persons and patients with neck injuries. Arch Phys Med Rehabil 50:34, 1969
15. Budzynski T, Stoyva J, Adler C: Feedback-induced muscle relaxation: Application to tension headache. J Behav Ther Exp Psychiatry 1:205, 1970
16. Podivinsky F: Role of sensory and emotional inputs in mechanisms underlying involuntary motor activity. Activ Nerv Sup Praha 11:19, 1969
17. Solomon RL, Wynne LC: Traumatic avoidance learning: The principles of anxiety conversion and partial irreversibility. Psychol Rev 61:353, 1954

VI

CARDIOVASCULAR THERAPY

Learned Control of Ventricular 24
Rate in Patients with Atrial Fibrillation

Eugene R. Bleecker and Bernard T. Engel

Six patients with chronic atrial fibrillation (AF) and rheumatic heart disease on stable digitalis regimens were trained to slow and to speed ventricular rate (VR). Two subjects were more consistent in their ability to slow VR; two subjects were more consistent in their ability to speed VR; and the remaining two subjects were able to slow and to speed VR reliably. All subjects were able to control VR differentially during sequential slowing and speeding phases of experimental training sessions. Analyses of R-R interval histograms revealed that all subjects significantly changed the statistical frequency distributions of their R-R intervals. During VR slowing one subject generated a junctional escape rhythm. Another subject produced frequent premature ventricular contractions during speeding of VR under effective B-adrenergic blockade with propranolol. This control of VR in AF is neurally mediated at the level of the atrioventricular node. Studies with autonomic drugs indicate that this central nervous system control of VR in this arrhythmia usually occurs through activation of efferent cholinergic pathways.

Normal men (7–11) and monkeys (12) can be trained to slow, speed, or cyclically slow and speed their heart rates. Normal men can also decrease beat-to-beat heart rate variability (13). Fields (14) demonstrated that rats can be trained to control their P-R intervals.

There is unresolved debate concerning the control of atrioventricular (A-V) transmission and the periodicity and rhythmicity of atrial and ventricular rate

patterns in patients with atrial fibrillation (AF). Bootsma et al. (1) state that ventricular rhythm in AF is random and is not related to alterations in the electrophysiologic properties of the A-V node. These investigators contend that the role of the A-V node is limited to adjusting ventricular rate (VR) by modifying the rate of atrial impulses penetrating the A-V conduction system. Other investigators (2–6) assert that there is demonstrable periodicity and regularity of VR in AF. They further conclude that VR patterns are influenced by the state of A-V nodal tissue, by concealed conduction of atrial beats, and by changes in A-V nodal effective refractory period.

The purposes of the present study are to determine whether patients with chronic AF can be trained to slow and speed VR and to identify some of the autonomic

From the Section of Physiological Psychology, Laboratory of Behavioral Sciences, Gerontology Research Center, National Institute of Child Health and Human Development, Baltimore City Hospitals, Baltimore, Md.

Address for reprint requests: Bernard T. Engel, PhD, Gerontology Research Center, Baltimore City Hospitals, Baltimore, Md. 21224.

Received for publication May 2, 1972; revision received August 7, 1972.

nervous system mechanisms which mediate the voluntary control of VR in AF. The results of this study should help to clarify the intracardiac mechanisms of voluntary cardiac control; and they should resolve some of the questions about the control of VR in patients with AF (18).

METHOD

Six patients with AF were recruited from the Baltimore City Hospitals and Johns Hopkins Hospital cardiac clinics. The only criteria for patient selection were a history of rheumatic valvular heart disease, freedom from serious neurologic disorders, and that each patient was maintained on a stable dosage of a digitalis preparation for at least three months prior to study. Pertinent clinical data for each patient are contained in Table 1. During the three-week period of study each patient was hospitalized on a research ward.

Each patient was trained in the laboratory to speed and to slow his VR. Three first were trained to slow VR while the other three were trained initially to speed VR.

While in the experimental laboratory the subject lay semireclined in a hospital bed in a quiet room. Arrayed in front of the patient was a vertical display of three differently colored lights which provided feedback information about VR. The top light (green) and the bottom light (red) were cue lights which informed the patient about the experimental conditions. The middle light (yellow) was lit whenever the patient produced the correct change in VR, and therefore provided him with beat-to-beat information about his VR.

A typical experimental session began with a 30-min period during which electrocardiographic

TABLE 1. Clinical Data on Patients [a]

Patient	Age	Sex	Diagnosis	Duration CHF	Medications—cardiac (daily dosage)	ECG	Classifi-cation [b]
FP	56	F	RHD MS MI Postoperative mitral commissurotomy History cerebral embolus	2 years	0.25 mg digoxin 5 mg warfarin 25 mg hydrochloro- thiazide KCL	AF VR=60–70 RAD	II B

JB	28	M	RHD
			Aortic and mitral
			  Starr Edwards pro-
			  theses
			History subacute bacterial endocarditis
				3 years	0.25 mg digoxin on even dates
					0.125 mg digoxin on odd dates
					7.5 mg warfarin
						AF
						
						VR=80–90
						
						PVC
						LVH
							II B

WF	62	M	RHD AS AI MI	5 years	0.75 mg digoxin 50 mg hydrochloro- thiazide KCL	AF LVH VR=50–60	III C
EW	31	F	RHD MS MI History duodenal ulcer disease	12 years	0.1 mg digitoxin 100 mg hydrochloro- thiazide	AF VR=70–80 LVH	II B
MW	56	F	RHD MS AI Gout	6 years	0.25 mg digoxin 40 mg furosemide KCL	AF VR=70–80 VPC	II B
WL	57	M	RHD MS MI AI Postoperative mitral commissurotomy (twice)	20 years	0.75 mg digoxin 50 mg hydrochloro- thiazide KCL	AF VR=70–80 LVH	II–III C

[a] Abbreviations: RHD= rheumatic heart disease; AS= aortic stenosis; AI= aortic insufficiency; MI= mitral insufficiency; MS= mitral stenosis; CHF= congestive heart failure; AF= atrial fibrillation; VR= ventricular rate; LVH= left ventricular hypertrophy; RAD= right axis deviation; PVC= premature ventricular contractions; ECG= electrocardiogram.

[b] New York Heart Association Functional and Therapeutic Classifications.

leads were attached, and the patient adapted to the experimental situation and stabilized his VR. During the last 512 sec of this period (the baseline period), automatic data processing equipment monitored and recorded the frequency of the subject's ventricular contractions. The last phase of the experimental sessions was a 1,024-sec training period during which the patient actively tried to control his VR. The specific durations of the baseline period (512 sec) and the training period (1,024 sec) were chosen because the data processing equipment used in these experiments employed a binary counting system to measure time. When the patient was being trained to speed his VR, the green light was lit throughout the entire training period. When the patient speeded his VR above his baseline VR, the yellow light would go on and remain on as long as VR was above baseline VR. As soon as his VR fell below baseline rate, the yellow light would go off. Each subject was instructed to keep the yellow light on as long as possible and he knew that speeding his VR was the correct way to do this. During training to slow VR the procedure was identical to that outlined for speeding except that the red light rather than the green light remained lit, and that relatively slow VR now controlled the yellow light. Of course, no lights were lit during the resting and baseline periods.

After a series of training sessions in slowing VR and a series of training sessions in speeding VR, each patient was tested further under alternating conditions. During the training phase of these sessions the patient was required alternately to speed and slow his VR over four consecutive 256-sec intervals which were signaled by the red and green cue lights. The patient knew that these lights meant he should try to slow and speed VR respectively.

In five patients (WL refused participation) pharmacologic studies were carried out using some or all of the following autonomic drugs—isoproterenol (0.5–2.0 ug/min IV infusion), propranolol (0.075 mg/kg IV in divided 1-mg dosages), atropine (0.05 mg/kg IV in divided 1-mg dosages), and edrophonium (10 mg initially IV followed after 10 min by 1 mg/min IV). The dosage of isoproterenol was adjusted so that resting VR would be increased approximately 25 beats/min. The beta adrenegic blockade achieved with propranolol was sufficient to prevent any change in VR during isoproterenol infusion. The dosage of atropine sulfate used was considered adequate to block transmission of efferent cholinergic pathways but far less than the pharmacologic dosage (0.5 mg/kg) required in animals to prevent the effects of electrical stimulation of the peripheral ends of the cut vagus nerve (15). All drug studies were performed after training in VR control was completed in order to investigate the mechanisms of VR and rhythm changes.

The laboratory apparatus employed in these experiments has been previously described by Weiss and Engel (16).

Data were analyzed statistically in two ways. During the baseline and training periods of each session, electrocardiograms were recorded continuously on an analog tape recorder. These tapes subsequently were played back through a computer which generated R-R interval histograms, both on a visual monitor and on punched paper tape. The R-R interval data were transformed to rates subsequently. Differences between baseline VR and training level VR and between the slow and fast training levels during the alternating sessions were compared by means of T-tests. Rate histograms were generated by standardizing the data within each condition (baseline, slow, fast) and the differences between the distributions of the rate histograms were compared by means of the chi-square statistic. The standardization procedure made the chi-square test independent of differences in central tendency (mean VR) and variability (standard deviation of VR). For the purposes of this analysis eight intervals were generated: $>1.75S + VR$; $1.75S + VR$ to $1.25S + VR$; $1.25S + VR$ to $0.75S + VR$; $0.75S + VR$ to $0.25S + VR$; $0.25S + VR$ to $-0.25S + VR$; $-0.25S + VR$ to $-0.75S + VR$; $-0.75S + VR$ to $-1.25S + VR$; $< -1.25S + VR$, where S is the standard deviation of ventricular rate and the VR is the average ventricular rate for that condition. It should be clear that these tests of distribution are independent of any differences in the mean or standard deviations of VR.

In addition to the statistical procedures described above, individual interval histograms and individual rhythm strips were visually inspected. The frequency of occurrence of premature ventricular contractions was determined by direct count from individual rhythm strips.

RESULTS

Figure 1 graphs mean VR for the entire experimental group during baseline recordings and mean changes in VR during training. Training has been divided into ten trial blocks by averaging temporally related sessions when the number of individual sessions for each phase of training exceeded ten. Mean baseline VR remained relatively stable throughout speeding and slowing sessions but decreased slightly (2.5 beats/min) during differential training. During training to speed VR there is an increase in the magnitude of mean VR changes (-0.5 beats/min to +9.5 beats/min) recorded during successive trial blocks. A similar but less marked trend (-0.8 beats/min to -3.5 beats/min) is noted during VR slowing. In the alternate sessions the performances of the six patients demonstrate consistent differences between the fast

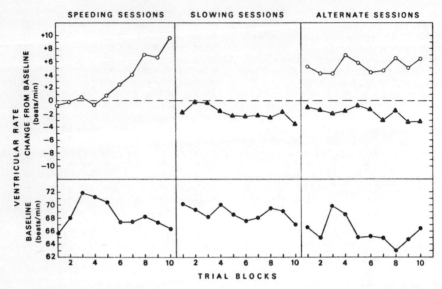

Fig. 1. Mean baseline VRs for all patients during training (bottom graph); mean changes from baseline VR during training (top graph). VR during slowing is represented by ▲ and during speeding by O. Training has been divided into ten trial blocks by averaging temporally related training sessions.

and slow phases of each trial block (average difference in VR is 7.2 beats /min). Table 2 lists the trial-block data for each patient during the differential training sessions.

Table 3 lists the ratio of individual training sessions in which a subject either slowed or speeded VR correctly to the total number of training sessions for that contingency. The results in this table and the trial-block data of Table 2 indicate that FP and JB were more consistent in their ability to slow VR; WF and EW consistently speeded VR; and WL and MW were able to speed and to slow their ventricular rates reliably. Although the initial sessions in VR speeding do not reflect EW's ability to speed VR, once this patient learned this response she performed consistently as illustrated during speeding of VR in alternate sessions. WF and EW were able to speed as much as 30% and 60% respectively above baseline VR during each of several sessions.

The most critical demonstration of a subject's ability to control VR is his ability to speed and slow VR during alternate sessions. All subjects differentiated be-

tween fast and slow cues in this phase of training. Differential control of cardiac rate when comparing the slow and fast phases of each alternate session is statistically significant ($p < 0.05$) in 30% of JB's, 50% of FP's, 70% of MW's, 95% of WF's, and 100% of WL's and EW's alternate sessions.

Figure 2 presents a representative R-R interval histogram for each patient during alternate training sessions. Each histogram is based on all of the ventricular beats which occurred during 512-sec recordings of baseline (middle), speeding (top), and slowing (bottom). These histograms illustrate statistically significant shifts from baseline VR *distribution* achieved by these subjects during voluntary control of VR. Statistically significant shifts in distribution of VR (Table 4) during speeding were noted in WF, JB, and EW; during slowing in FP, MW, JB, EW, and WL. In alternate sessions WF, MW, EW, and WL generated significant differences in distribution of VR between the fast and slow phases of each session. The probabilities in this table were obtained by combining the chi-square val-

TABLE 2. Mean VR (Beats/Min) for Baseline and
Cyclical Fast and Slow Training Trial Blocks [a]

Subject		1	2	3	4	5	6	7	8	9	10	$\bar{x}$
FP	base	51.5	53.0	58.8	51.2	54.0	58.0	53.8	44.5	51.7	55.2	53.2
	fast	48.4	51.1	56.5	49.0	54.5	54.5	54.4	45.6	50.0	59.5	52.4
	slow	46.3	48.7	54.0	46.6	51.0	51.3	50.0	44.5	48.0	55.8	49.6
JB	base	93.5	79.6	88.6	93.4	83.3	79.8	85.8	73.7	79.1	75.6	83.2
	fast	89.7	81.2	84.6	91.1	82.5	80.0	79.0	75.1	76.1	76.3	81.6
	slow	90.0	80.6	84.0	89.6	80.1	78.2	76.8	72.2	72.3	69.6	79.3
WF	base	50.2	52.3	52.8	52.2	55.7	53.3	51.4	52.3	55.6	68.5	54.4
	fast	54.2	56.7	60.3	58.2	61.3	62.0	63.5	65.2	66.8	80.2	62.8
	slow	53.7	52.6	54.2	52.7	57.1	54.6	53.8	56.6	55.3	64.1	55.4
EW	base	75.6	74.5	75.6	71.3	70.5	68.8	73.0	74.2	71.6	68.2	72.3
	fast	106.7	95.6	97.4	94.1	93.8	94.0	90.7	91.5	89.2	86.3	93.9
	slow	82.0	75.4	77.7	73.5	74.0	72.0	73.2	71.9	69.3	68.3	73.7
MW	base	75.0	71.0	85.2	88.1	73.0	72.8	68.6	71.0	72.7	72.0	74.9
	fast	72.0	69.8	88.6	90.8	74.8	75.5	70.8	70.8	73.8	73.5	76.0
	slow	71.0	67.3	85.6	89.5	72.4	72.7	67.7	68.4	69.4	69.1	73.3
WL	base	54.7	59.8	58.2	55.2	54.0	58.4	57.7	62.8	57.7	58.8	57.7
	fast	60.3	62.5	56.0	60.6	58.6	60.3	59.4	69.7	62.1	61.8	61.1
	slow	51.2	55.5	52.0	50.5	52.1	54.5	50.8	56.1	54.6	53.4	53.0

[a] See legend to Fig. 1 for definition of a trial block.

TABLE 3. Ratio of Sessions in Which Each Subject "Correctly" Modified VR to Total Training Sessions for
All Patients

Subject	Slow training sessions	Fast training sessions	Alternate training sessions [a]		
			Alt.	Slow	Fast
FP	17/19	5/17	21/23	19/23	7/23
JB	14/19	10/19	24/31	24/31	9/31
WF	7/17	11/13	20/24	4/24	24/24
EW	7/24	4/10	15/15	3/15	15/15
MW	19/20	11/21	22/25	18/25	17/25
WL	12/12	13/16	12/12	12/12	11/12

[a] Alt. column refers to subject's ability to correctly cyclically control VR during slowing and speeding phases, while the slow and fast columns reflect speeding and slowing of VR with respect to baseline VR.

ues from all of the sessions during each of the conditions. It should be clear that these changes in VR distribution are independent of any changes in the mean or standard deviation of rate.

Studies with autonomic drugs were performed in FP, WF, MW, EW, and JB. Neither isoproterenol, propranalol, nor edrophonium abolished the ability of these subjects to voluntarily modify VR (Figure 3). Atropine abolished differential modification of cardiac rate in FP, WF, MW, and JB (Table 5). However, EW could

still alter VR although less well than previously. EW's performance under autonomic drugs will be presented in detail later. Figure 3 illustrates that similar increases in mean baseline VR were achieved with atropine and isoproterenol infusion, and similar decreases in mean baseline VR were achieved with propranolol and edrophonium infusion.

Patients WF and WL were given extensive training to try to teach them to decrease the variabilities of their ventricular rates. During training to control VR

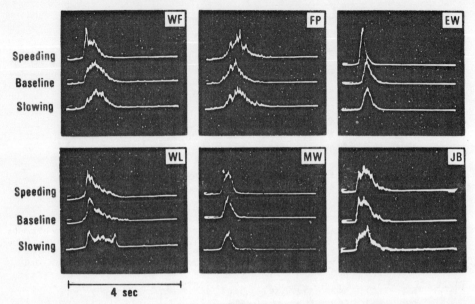

Fig. 2. Representative R-R interval histograms for each patient during alternate training in VR control. Each histogram represents the R-R intervals for all ventricular beats during the 512-sec period of baseline recordings (middle histogram), speeding of VR (top histogram), and slowing of VR (bottom histogram). Time scale for the abscissa of each histogram is 4 sec.

TABLE 4.   Probability Levels of Statistical Differences in VR Distribution During Training [a]

Patient	Slowing B-S	Speeding B-F	Alternate B-S	B-F	F-S
FP	<0.01	NS	<0.05	<0.01	NS
JB	<0.01	<0.01	<0.01	NS	NS
WF	NS	<0.01	<0.05	<0.01	<0.01
EW	<0.01	<0.01	<0.01	<0.01	<0.01
MW	<0.01	*b*	<0.01	<0.01	<0.05
WL	<0.01	NS	<0.01	<0.01	<0.01

[a] Abbreviations: B= baseline; S= slow; F= fast; NS= not significant.
[b] Distribution data were not available.

variability, the yellow light would be on as long as the patient maintained his VR within the predefined limits. As soon as the patient speeded his heart above the upper limit (approximately 7.5 beats above baseline VR), the red light would go on and the yellow light would go off. Similarly, if the patient slowed below the lower limit (approximately 7.5 beats below baseline VR), the yellow light would go off and the green light would go on. WF was able to reduce VR variability from baseline (as measured by the standard deviations of VR) in 14 of 21 sessions, which is statistically significant ($p < 0.05$), and WF reduced VR variability in 24 of 30 sessions, which is statistically significant ($p < 0.05$). However, neither patient showed any evidence of day-to-day reduction in VR variability.

Results in the performance of two subjects require detailed presentation. R-R interval histograms during various stages of slowing and speeding training in

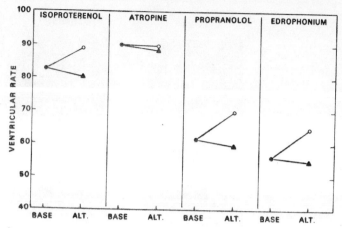

Fig. 3. Effect of autonomic drugs on voluntary control of VR in AF. During alternate training sessions the VRs graphed are mean values for all patients. (O= VR during baseline recordings, O=VR during the speeding phase of the alternate sessions, ▲= VR during the slowing phase of the alternate sessions.)

TABLE 5. Ratio of Sessions in Which Each Subject "Correctly" Modified VR to Total Sessions for Each Drug During Alternate Sessions [a]

Patient	Isoproterenol	Atropine	Propranolol	Edrophonium
FP	3/3	0/2		
JB	2/2	0/2	2/2	1/1
WF		0/2		
EW	2/2	2/2	4/4	1/1
MW	2/2	0/2	2/2	1/1

[a] Correct performance refers to greater than one heartbeat difference during cyclical slowing and speeding of VR.

WL (Figure 4) indicate that during speeding there is a shift in the histograms toward faster VR. During slowing training WL generated an increasing number of slow heartbeats including what appears to be a second mode at the tail of the distribution. This is further illustrated by the histograms from alternate training sessions (Figure 5). During slowing WL generated a bimodal distribution of R-R intervals. One mode occurs at a rate similar to the baseline modal rate while the second peak corresponds to a VR of approximately 40 beats/min. This second grouping of ventricular beats may represent an A-V junctional escape pacemaker which is activated during voluntary VR slowing. Inspection of WL's rhythm strips reveals evidence of numerous fixed R-R intervals of approximately 1.5-sec dura-

tion during voluntary slowing of VR. The QRS complexes are the same configuration and magnitude as WL's usual QRS complex.

Patient EW not only increased VR but also changed cardiac rhythm such that she would have frequent bursts of premature ventricular contractions (PVCs) often in a bigeminal rhythm. EW experienced difficulty slowing VR and during this training she generated runs of PVCs which we reinforced because the yellow light was triggered by the normally directed R wave and a PVC with reversed polarity was perceived by our detection system as a very slow rate (Figure 6). Figure 7 shows two slowing sessions in which EW generated long runs of PVCs that were reinforced as if they represented VR slowing. We then stopped

SPEEDING   SLOWING

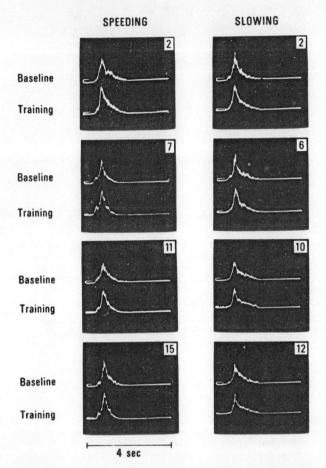

Fig. 4. R-R interval histograms during progressive stages of slowing and speeding training in patient WL. (Number on histogram refers to training session number.)

reinforcement and PVCs only occurred sporadically.

During drug studies EW demonstrated frequent PVCs throughout the period of isoproterenol administration (Figure 8). However, after adequate beta adrenergic blockade with propranolol, EW selectively generated PVCs during VR speeding. This response was so intriguing that two days later the patient was retested with propranolol (sessions 2A and 2B) and again produced PVCs only during periods of speeding of VR (Figure 9). During the two 256-sec speeding phases of propranolol in session 1A, EW emitted 104 and 102 PVCs, respectively; during session 1B she emitted 158 and 175 PVCs;

during session 2A she generated 3 and 22 PVCs; and finally during session 2B she emitted 25 and 69 PVCs, respectively. During the baseline periods and the slowing phases of the alternate sessions there were no PVCs.

DISCUSSION

The results of this study indicate that digitalized patients with AF can be operantly conditioned to modify VR differentially. This control of VR probably is mediated neurally at the level of the A-V node. Studies with autonomic drugs suggest that blockage of efferent cholinergic pathways by the administra-

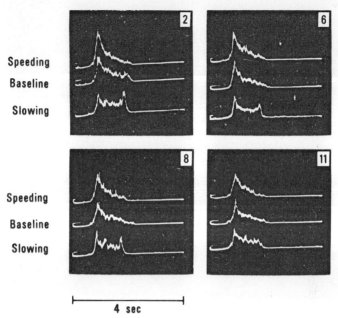

Fig. 5. R-R interval histograms during progressive stages of alternate training sessions in patient WL. The second modal peak during slowing occurs at a VR of approximately 40 beats/min.

tion of atropine sulfate abolishes voluntary control of VR in patients with established AF.

Cyclical control of VR as well as alteration of beat-to-beat VR variability in subjects with normal sinus rhythm would be effected by direct changes in the sino-atrial node pacemaker (17). Unpublished data from this laboratory from patients with third-degree heart block suggest that these patients cannot modify their VR voluntarily. These findings indicate that pacemakers below the A-V node are not under direct central nervous system control, while the present study suggests that voluntary central nervous control of VR can be achieved by direct neural alterations of the A-V node.

During training in control of VR, significant changes in the statistical distribution of VR patterns were noted. Patient WL during slowing of VR generated bimodal distributions of R-R intervals, suggesting that he not only lengthened his R-R intervals, but that he also initiated an A-V junctional escape pacemaker. Analyses of his histograms revealed the second peak to correspond to a VR of about 40 beats/min. Inspection of electrocardiogram rhythm strips revealed R-R intervals of 1.5 sec during training periods of VR slowing. There is evidence that an A-V junctional escape pacemaker in AF is caused by pathologic A-V block which is usually the result of digitalis toxicity (5,19). WL exhibited this escape rhythm during slowing when he may have modified A-V conduction tissue by increasing refractory period and/or increasing conduction time. This patient was chronically maintained on a stable dosage of digoxin. There was no evidence of digitalis toxicity during the immediately preceding baseline recording periods or during temporally contiguous periods of speeding of VR. Increase in vagal tone to the heart by carotid sinus stimulation (20) and by administration of edrophonium chloride (21) have been reported to be useful in the early detection of digitalis excess. One may conclude that this A-V junctional escape rhythm was caused either by direct modification of the A-V node during voluntary VR slowing or that

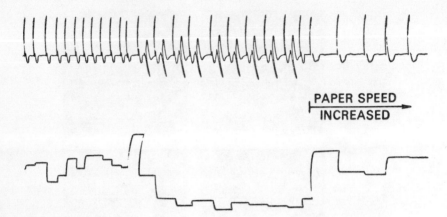

Fig. 6. Cardiotachometer (bottom) and electrocardiographic tracings illustrating the effects of premature ventricular contractions on feedback to patient EW during slow training sessions. The cardiotachometer is triggered by the normally directed R wave. A PVC with reversed electric polarity does not trigger the detection system and is perceived as a slow VR (decrease in magnitude of cardiotachometer tracing).

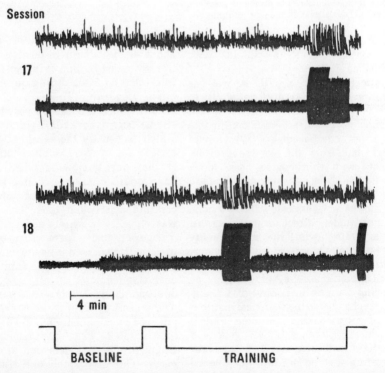

Fig. 7. Cardiotachometer (top) and electrocardiographic (bottom) tracings showing periods of reinforcement of PVCs during slow training sessions 17 and 18 in patient EW. PVCs appear as extra-wide excursions on the electrocardiographic tracings. Note the very slow paper speed.

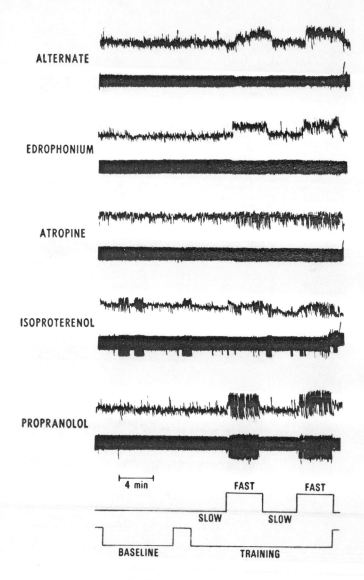

Fig. 8. Effects of autonomic drugs on ventricular rate and rhythm during alternate training sessions in patient EW. PVCs appear as wide excursions on the electrocardiographic tracing (bottom). During isoproterenol administration PVCs occurred throughout the baseline, slow, and fast phases of training. During propranolol administration PVCs are noted only during the speeding phases of the alternate training sessions. Note very slow paper speed. (In the cardiotachometer tracing (upper) higher deflections indicate faster VR while lower deflections indicate slower VR.)

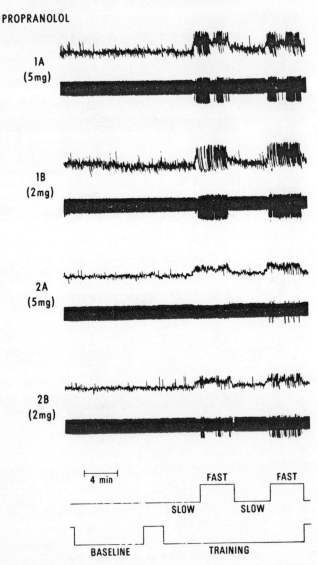

Fig. 9. Electrocardiographic (bottom) and cardiotachometer (top) tracings from the alternate training session in patient EW during which propranolol was administered. These tracings show that PVCs (wide ECG excursions) were generated only during the speeding phases of each alternate training session but none were generated during slow or baseline phases. The intravenous dosage of propranolol is listed under the session number. Propranolol sessions 1A and 1B were run sequentially on one day and propranolol sessions 2A and 2B were run sequentially on a subsequent day.

learned modification of VR was additive to that of digitalis, thereby unmasking latent digitalis toxicity.

An explanation is lacking for patient EW's selective ability to generate PVCs during speeding of VR under the influence of adequate beta adrenergic blockade with propranolol. This subject consistently generated PVCs during each 256-sec speeding interval during the four different alternate sessions performed with propranolol. EW was the only subject who remained able to modify VR and especially perform VR speeding during efferent vagal blockade after a total of 4 mg of intravenously administered atropine. We speculate that this patient was able to speed her VR by way of vagal inhibition (in the presence of propranolol) and by increased sympathetic outflow (in the presence of atropine). We believe this mechanism is atypical since no other patient speeded with efferent vagal blockade with atropine.

Bootsma et al. (1) minimize the function of the A-V node to "scaling of atrial impulses." The present study indicates that the central nervous system, acting on the A-V node, can modify not only VR but can also shift the statistical distribution of ventricular beats. Furthermore, we have noted the generation of an A-V nodal escape rhythm during VR slowing.

Attempts to train two patients to chronically reduce VR variability were unsuccessful. Although changes in vagal tone to the A-V node can modulate VR, these alterations of nervous input to the node apparently are unable to decrease R-R variability sufficiently to produce clinically significant, long-term changes in variability of VR.

It seems worthwhile to investigate further the interaction of training to alter VR in AF with the effects of medications such as digitalis and quinidine. It also seems worthwhile to explore the mechanisms of this technique in relation to electrophysiologic diagnostic procedures such as direct recordings of His bundle electrocardiograms.

We wish to thank Dr. Gustav C. Voigt, chief of the Cardiac Division, Baltimore City Hospitals, for his advice and consultations on the patients. We wish to thank Dr. J. O'Neal Humphries for referring patients WL, EW, and JB from The Johns Hopkins Hospital Cardiac Clinic. We wish to acknowledge our appreciation to Mr. Reginald E. Quilter, who assisted in the development and maintenance of various instruments used in this study, to Miss Diana Dumps for technical assistance in data analysis, and to Mrs. Estelle Carter for secretarial help in the preparation of this manuscript.

REFERENCES

1. Bootsma BK, Hoelen AJ, Strackee J, Meyler FL: Analysis of R-R intervals in patients with atrial fibrillation at rest and during exercise. Circulation 41:783–794, 1970
2. Moe GK, Abildskov JA: Observations on the ventricular dysrhythmia associated with atrial fibrillation in the dog heart. Circ Res 14:447–460, 1964
3. Braunstein JR, Franke EK: Autocorrelation of ventricular response in atrial fibrillation. Circ Res 9:300–304, 1961
4. Horan LG, Kistler JC: Study of ventricular response in atrial fibrillation. Circ Res 9:305–311, 1961
5. Urbach JR, Grauman JJ, Straus SH: Quantitative methods for the recognition of atrioventricular junctional rhythms in atrial fibrillation. Circulation 39:803–817, 1969
6. Battersby EJ: Pacemaker periodicity in atrial fibrillation. Circulation 17:296–302, 1965

7. Shearn DW: Operant conditioning heart rate. Science 137:530–531, 1962

8. Engel BT, Hansen SP: Operant conditioning of heart rate slowing. Psychophysiology 3:176–187, 1966

9. Engel BT, Chism RA: Operant conditioning of heart rate speeding. Psychophysiology 3:418–426, 1967

10. Levine HI, Engel BT, Pearson JA: Differential operant conditioning of heart rate. Psychosom Med 30:837–845, 1968

11. Frazier TW: Avoidance conditioning of heart rate in humans. Psychophysiology 3:188–202, 1966

12. Engel BT, Gottlieb SH: Differential operant conditioning of heart rate in the restrained monkey. J Comp Physiol Psychol 73:217–225, 1970

13. Hnatiow M, Lang PJ: Learned stabilization of cardiac rate. Psychophysiology 1:330–336, 1965

14. Fields C: Instrumental conditioning of the rat cardiac control systems. Proc Natl Acad Sci USA 65:293–299, 1970

15. Goodman LS, Gilman A: The Pharmacologic Basis of Therapeutics, 4th ed. New York, Macmillan, 1970

16. Weiss T, Engel BT: Operant conditioning of heart rate in patients with premature ventricular contractions. Psychosom Med 33:301–321, 1971

17. Miller NE, DiCara L: Instrumental learning of heart rate changes in curarized rats. J Comp Physiol Psychol 63:12–19, 1967

18. Brody DA: Ventricular rate patterns in atrial fibrillation. Circulation 41:733–735, 1970

19. Kastor JA, Yurchak PM: Recognition of digitalis intoxication in the presence of atrial fibrillation. Ann Intern Med 67:1045–1054, 1967

20. Lown B, Levine SA: The carotid sinus: Clinical value of its stimulation. Circulation 33:766–790, 1961

21. Pitt B, Kurland GS: Use of edrophonium chloride (Tensilon) to detect early digitalis toxicity. Amer J Cardiol 18:557–565, 1966

Learned Control of Cardiac Rate 25
and Cardiac Conduction in the Wolff-Parkinson-White Syndrome

Eugene R. Bleecker and Bernard T. Engel

IT has been shown that normal men can be trained to slow, speed and cyclically slow and speed heart rate.[1-4] Patients with premature ventricular contractions can be trained to decrease and to control them.[5] Patients with chronic atrial fibrillation can be trained to change ventricular rate by the modification of vagal tone to the atrioventricular node.[6] Our purpose in this study was to determine whether a patient with intermittent Wolff–Parkinson–White syndrome can learn to control heart rate and also to modify the pathway of cardiac conduction.

CASE REPORT

A 29-year-old woman was admitted to the Gerontology Research Center in 1972. Since the age of 19 she had had episodes of rapid tachycardia associated with dyspnea, syncope and chest pain and treated with combinations of various medications: propranolol, quinidine, procainamide, diphenylhydantoin, digoxin and sedatives. Ten-hour Holter continuous monitoring and exercise treadmill stress tests performed during the last 3 years documented the presence of intermittent conduction typical of the Wolff–Parkinson–White syndrome, sinus tachycardia and supraventricular tachycardias (200 to 240 beats per minute) with a conduction pattern typical of the syndrome. She received only sedatives and analgesics during the month before this study.

From the Section of Physiological Psychology, Laboratory of Behavioral Sciences, Gerontology Research Center, National Institute of Child Health and Human Development, Baltimore City Hospitals, Baltimore, Md. 21224, where reprint requests should be addressed to Dr. Engel.

Reprinted with permission from the *New England Journal of Medicine*, Vol. 288, March 15, 1973, 560-562.

Admission physical examination revealed a normally developed, asthenic woman with a blood pressure of 110/80 and regular pulse rate of 110. An electrocardiogram revealed intermittent Type A conduction typical of the Wolff–Parkinson–White syndrome. The heart was vertical, with a $+70°$ axis. During normal conduction the PR interval was 0.18 second, and the QRS duration 0.07 second. During Wolff–Parkinson–White conduction the PR interval was 0.10 second, and the QRS duration 0.12 second.

METHODS

Training in Heart-Rate Control

The patient was first trained to slow and then to speed and finally sequentially to slow and speed her heart rate. While in the laboratory she lay in a hospital bed. Each session began with a rest period during which electrocardiographic leads were attached, and she stabilized her heart rate. During the last 512 seconds of this base-line period her heart rate was recorded. The last phase of the experimental session was a training period of 1024 seconds when she was trained to control her heart rate. During speeding training, a green light was put on that she could see throughout the entire training period. When the patient speeded her heart rate above the base-line rate, a yellow light went on and remained on as long as the rate was above base line. As soon as the heart rate fell below the base-line rate, the yellow light went off. The patient was instructed to keep the yellow light on, and she knew that speeding her heart rate was the correct way to accomplish this purpose. During slowing training the procedure was identical to that outlined for speeding except that a red light rather than the green light remained on, and that a relatively slow heart rate now controlled the yellow light. After a series of sessions to slow and a series of sessions to speed the rate, she was required alternately to speed and to slow the rate during 4 consecutive 256-second intervals that were signaled by the red and green cue lights. The laboratory apparatus employed has previously been described.[5] Differences between base-line and training heart rates and between the slow and fast training phases were compared by means of t-tests.

Training to Control Cardiac Conduction

After rate training was completed, she was trained to control the prevalence of normal and Wolff–Parkinson–White beats. This control was made possible by selection of a right precordial electrocardiographic lead in which the major QRS deflection of Wolff–Parkinson–White-conducted beats and normally conducted beats were opposite, and then by selectively triggering a clicker from normally conducted QRS complexes only. During training sessions designed to teach her to increase normal conduction she was told to increase the frequency of these sounds. During training to increase Wolff–Parkinson–White conduction she was instructed to decrease the frequency of these sounds. She was then required alternately to increase and decrease the frequency of clicks over consecutive 128-second intervals that were signaled by cue lights. Finally, she was trained to increase normally conducted beats without feedback.

At the conclusion of training, pharmacologic studies were carried out to investigate the mechanisms of rhythm change. The following autonomic drugs were administered: isoproterenol (1.0 to 1.5 μg per minute, intravenous infusion); phenylephrine (0.02 to 0.05 mg per minute intravenously); propranolol (5.0 mg intravenously); and atropine (1.5 mg intravenously). The beta-adrenergic blockade achieved with propranolol was sufficient to prevent any change in heart rate during an isoproterenol infusion. During administration of these drugs the patient tried to increase and decrease normal conduction.

Differences in the frequencies of normally conducted and Wolff–Parkinson–White beats were compared statistically by means of the chi-square test.

RESULTS

Training in Rate Control

The patient decreased her heart rate by an average of 3.4 beats per minute during 26 slowing training sessions: she slowed her rate from base line in 19 of the 26 sessions. She increased it an average of 2.5 beats per minute during 15 speeding training sessions, and she speeded from base line in 11 of the 15 sessions. The most critical demonstration of her ability to control her heart rate occurred during the sequential, alternating phase, when she performed successfully in 20 of 21 sessions, and when the average heart-rate difference between the speeding and slowing segments was 5.5 beats per minute.

Training in Rhythm Control

When she received reinforcement to increase normal conduction, she did so significantly ($p \leq 0.05$) in four of eight training sessions. She also was able to increase Wolff–Parkinson–White conduction significantly in two of three sessions when she was trained to do so.

Her performance during the alternating training sessions was divided into three categories depending on her base-line rhythm. When normal conduction was rare (base-line rhythm less than 10 per cent normal conduction), she was able to increase normal conduction significantly during all five sessions from an average of 1.8 to an average of 18.2 per cent. When normal conduction was moderate (base-line rhythm between 10 and 90 per cent normal conduction) she was able to increase normal conduction significantly in five of seven sessions from an average of 38.1 to an average of 55.9 per cent, and to decrease normal conduction significantly in four of seven sessions to an average of 31.4 per cent. In six of these seven sessions she significantly differentiated between the increase and decrease of normal conduction phases. During sessions when normal conduction was predominant (base-line rhythm greater than 90 per cent), she was able to decrease normal conduction significantly in five of ten sessions, from an average of 99.7 to an average of 90.4 per cent. Figure 1 shows representative electrocardiographic tracings from an alternating session in which she increased and decreased normal conduction.

During the last stage of training the patient was taught to increase normal conduction without feedback. In these training sessions, 128-second periods of feedback were alternated with 128-second periods of no feedback, and she was instructed to increase normal conduction during the entire training session. She increased normal conduction significantly in all eight sessions during both the feedback and the no-feedback phases. The mean proportional increase of normal conduction from base line was 13 per cent during both feedback and no-feedback phases of training.

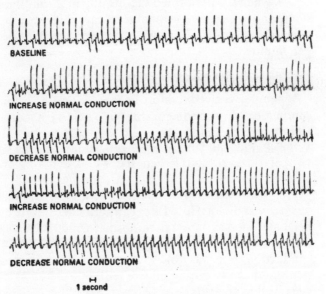

BASELINE

INCREASE NORMAL CONDUCTION

DECREASE NORMAL CONDUCTION

INCREASE NORMAL CONDUCTION

DECREASE NORMAL CONDUCTION

1 second

Figure 1. Representative Rhythm Strips from an Alternate Training Session during Which the Patient was Sequentially Increasing and Decreasing Normal Conduction.

QRS complexes with upright R waves and normal PR intervals were normally conducted.

When heart rate and rhythm were compared, normal conduction tended to be associated with a fast rate although on numerous occasions, the rate was low and she had predominant normal conduction. Drug studies were done to clarify the relation between heart rate and conduction and to identify autonomic mechanisms mediating the patient's performance. Administration of phenylephrine increased Wolff–Parkinson–White conduction and decreased heart rate during the base-line period. During the training session she was able to increase normal conduction from 5 to 12 per cent and also increased heart rate from 82 to 91 beats per minute. During beta-adrenergic blockade with propranolol the heart rate was 81 beats per minute, with 4 per cent normally conducted beats in the base-line period. She was able to increase to 11 per cent normal conduction with an increase in rate of only 2 beats per minute. The administration of atropine, on two different days, resulted in an increase in heart rate and conversion to 100 per cent normal conduction. She was unable to generate Wolff–Parkinson–White conduction during atropine administration. During base line with isoproterenol administration she exhibited 20 per cent normal conduction with a heart rate of 116 beats per minute. She decreased normal conduction to 9 per cent during the "increase" period and decreased normal conduction to 6 per cent during the "decrease" period. Heart rates were 124 and 121 beats per minute respectively.

During follow-up testing 10 weeks after initial training she was able to modify cardiac conduction differentially (Fig. 2).

DISCUSSION

Blockage of vagal tone increased heart rate and produced normal conduction. Vagomimetic effects of phenylephrine increased Wolff–Parkinson–White conduction and decreased heart rate. With faster heart rate during isoproterenol infusion or an exercise treadmill stress test, there was predominant Wolff–Parkinson–White conduction. Since both atropine and either isoproterenol or exercise increase heart rate but have opposite effects on conduction, we conclude that heart rate alone is not the determinant of conduction in this patient. We hypothesize that learned modification of vagal tone to her heart is the mechanism by which she is able to modulate conduction.

A complete discussion of the behavioral mechanisms associated with learned control of cardiac function is beyond the scope of this report; however, we have dis-

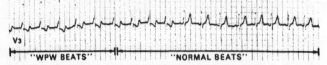

Figure 2. Electrocardiographic Rhythm Strip Taken 10 Weeks after Completion of Training (WPW Denotes Wolff–Parkinson–White).

The patient was able to control differentially her heart rhythm away from the laboratory and without feedback.

cussed some of these factors elsewhere.[7] Other investigators have shown that learned control of cardiac changes is not necessarily mediated by respiratory or skeletal effects.[8] Our observations in this patient suggested that her control was not mediated by modifications of respiration or by modifications in skeletal-muscle activity.

This study integrates technics of behavioral training with the investigation of the physiology of cardiac conduction. Further studies in patients with the Wolff–Parkinson–White Syndrome are indicated to investigate physiologic and clinical applications of similar training. It would be especially worthwhile to carry out these studies in conjunction with pharmacologic agents, His-bundle recordings and epicardial mapping technics.

We are indebted to Dr. Gustav C. Voigt for advice in the care of this patient, and for helpful comments on this manuscript.

REFERENCES

1. Engel BT, Hansen SP: Operant conditioning of heart rate slowing. Psychophysiology 3:176-187, 1966
2. Engel BT, Chism RA: Operant conditioning of heart rate speeding. Psychophysiology 3:418-426, 1967
3. Levene HI, Engel BT, Pearson JA: Differential operant conditioning of heart rate. Psychosom Med 30:837-845, 1968
4. Frazier TW: Avoidance conditioning of heart rate in humans. Psychophysiology 3:188-202, 1966
5. Weiss T, Engel BT: Operant conditioning of heart rate in patients with premature ventricular contractions. Psychosom Med 33:301-321, 1971
6. Bleecker ER, Engel BT: Learned control of ventricular rate in patients with atrial fibrillation. Psychosom Med (in press)
7. Engel BT: Operant conditioning of cardiac function: a status report. Psychophysiology 9:161-177, 1972
8. Miller NE: Learning of visceral and glandular responses. Science 163:434-445, 1969

Instrumental Conditioning 26
of Diastolic Blood Pressure in Essential
Hypertensive Patients

S. Thomas Elder, Z. Rosalbe Ruiz,
Herdis L. Deabler and Robert L. Dillenkoffer

Eighteen male essential hypertensive patients participated in an experiment designed to compare two strategies for controlling high blood pressure. Each strategy was derived from the instrumental learning literature, and the aim was to treat the blood pressure response as an operant and determine the most effective conditioning procedure for manipulating it. The results demonstrate that patients could be conditioned to lower blood pressure by 20% to 30% over a period as brief as four days by providing an external signal and verbal praise contingent upon each reduction in diastolic pressure that met a pre-set criterion.

The modification of glandular and visceral responses through operant conditioning is a recent breakthrough (Miller, 1969; Miller, DiCara, Solomon, Weiss, and Dworkin, 1970) that offers an opportunity for innovation in the treatment and clinical management of psychosomatic disorders. Instrumental control of blood pressure was a natural sequel (Gutman and Benson, 1971), and recent data show that it can be done.

In 1969, Shapiro, Tursky, Gershon, and Stern reported an experiment in which 10 normotensive male subjects received feedback reinforcement for raising their blood pressure, and 10 others were conditioned the same way to lower their blood pressure levels. Reinforcement was made available in the form of an external signal to the subject that he had successfully increased or decreased his systolic pressure, as the case may be. Subsequently, Shapiro, Tursky, and Schwartz (1970) showed that it was possible in a similar manner to train subjects to change their blood pressure up or down independently or concomitantly with increases or decreases in heart rate. Thus, it became apparent that visceral response units could be shaped with a great deal of specificity, as Miller (1969) had asserted earlier, or developed as general response patterns as Shapiro, et al. (1969) demonstrated.

The first report that essential hypertension could be managed by operant conditioning with performance contingent feedback came from Miller's laboratory (Miller, *personal communication*). A female patient learned to lower her blood pressure, and eventually drove it down as much as 30 mm Hg. More recently, Benson,

[1]This study was supported in part with funds made available through the Veterans Administration Hospital, New Orleans, Louisiana, and a preliminary report of the results was presented at the American Psychological Association meetings in Honolulu, 1972. Reprints may be obtained from S. Thomas Elder, Department of Psychology, LSUNO-Lakefront, New Orleans, Louisiana 70122.

Shapiro, Tursky, and Schwartz (1971) successfully conditioned five of seven essential hypertensive patients to lower their systolic pressure as much as 16 to 34 mm Hg.

In view of these intriguing data, the present study sought: (1) to compare two different reinforcement feedback strategies in search of an optimum set of routine clinical operations, and (2) to employ a more stringent test of consequences than Shapiro *et al.* used by examining changes in diastolic as well as systolic pressures.

METHOD

Subjects

Eighteen male patients between 23 and 59 yr of age had all been diagnosed previously as essential hypertensives; their blood pressures at the time of admission to hospital are shown in Table 1. None was receiving medication specifically for their high blood pressure, but many were on central nervous system depressants (*e.g.*, chlordiazepoxide or diazepam), and all had received bed rest and a salt-free diet for at least three days before participating in the study.

Apparatus

The apparatus consisted of a model 1900 London pressureometer, model 1910 alarm module, and model 2400 strip-chart recorder. Except for the addition of a small timing circuit to limit duration of the alarm module signal (red light) to 3 sec, the apparatus was standard and free of modification. With this particular system, it was possible to obtain an indirect measure of systolic and diastolic blood pressure once every 2 min over an extended interval. In addition, this could be done automatically at a distance as great as 25 ft from the subject. Sensitivity was to the nearest 5 mm Hg. As a reliability check, blood pressure was measured on an independent sample of 10 male patients using the London pressureometer and a standard sphygmomanometer. When the two procedures were compared, the systolic pressure scores correlated 0.96 and the diastolic scores correlated 0.84 (p < 0.001 in both instances).

The apparatus was housed in a semi-sound-resistant air-conditioned room. Subjects were observed individually with only one experimenter in attendance.

Table 1

Summary of subjects' raw blood pressures scores (mm Hg) at time of hospitalization, on-set of the experiment, and at follow-up.

	Age	Time of Hospitalization		Basal Pressure (Session 1)		Follow-up (Session 9)	
		Systolic	Diastolic	Systolic	Diastolic	Systolic	Diastolic
Group I (Control)							
1	39	250	115	155	103	144	99
2	45	162	110	169	97	—	—
3	47	200	136	130	87	—	—
4	48	184	120	149	108	—	—
5	52	172	110	150	89	140	88
6	57	170	110	147	85	—	—
Group II (Strategy 1)							
1	28	190	120	155	130	143	94
2	42	170	120	177	116	160	114
3	48	184	120	141	108	—	—
4	49	230	130	148	105	146	108
5	49	200	140	145	95	153	94
6	54	190	102	124	91	—	—
Group III (Strategy 2)							
1	23	170	120	137	101	138	89
2	44	220	126	176	123	123	77
3	47	200	120	151	105	147	102
4	53	170	120	144	88	124	72
5	58	170	95	164	94	121	76
6	59	160	105	150	112	—	—

Procedure

Patients were selected for the study with the assistance of several ward physicians, and assigned to one of three groups in random order. The experimental conditions represented by the three groups were: (I) control (no feedback), (II) strategy 1 in which a signal (3-sec red light) was given to the patient contingent on a reduction in his diastolic pressure, and (III) strategy 2 in which verbal approval was paired with the signal employed in strategy 1.

On the morning of Day 1, each patient arrived at the laboratory on schedule, and was immediately directed to urinate. After that, he was asked to have a seat outside the experimental room, and wait until called. Ten to 20 min later, he was invited into the laboratory and seated in an upholstered straight-back chair facing the signal panel of the apparatus, but away from the pressureometer. Then the cuff was secured to his upper left arm, which rested on the arm of the chair, taking care to position the microphone directly over the brachial artery. Next, his blood pressure was measured automatically every 2 min for a total of 20 successive determinations. No experimental manipulations were made during this session and the mean of these readings was taken as the patient's *basal* systolic and diastolic blood pressures.

That afternoon the subject returned for Session 2, and at that point designated experimental treatments began and were continued at the rate of one training session each morning and afternoon for the next three days. Treatments were discontinued after training session 8, and the patient was not seen again until the follow-up examination (Session 9) one week later.

Positive stimulus feedback such as that employed in strategies 1 and 2 is illustrated in Table 2. On Trial 1 (T1), the subject's basal

diastolic pressure occurred so that no feedback was given. When pressure was found to be 5 mm lower on T3, the feedback signal was presented. The same events occurred on T4 and T5. On T6, the feedback signal was withheld even though the pressure was 105, since the objective was to shape the patient's behavior further. Note that withdrawal of feedback reinforcement on T6 was followed by further reduction in blood pressure which resulted in response-contingent feedback on T7 through T10. On T11, feedback was withheld once more by way of requiring the subject to lower his pressure still more. The utilization of response shaping was considered essential to the success of this experiment. In strategy 2, verbal reinforcement consisted of saying "good" if diastolic pressure was at the criterion, "very good" if it was five units below the criterion, and "wonderful" if blood pressure fell 10 mm Hg below the criterion value.

At no point was the training procedure explained to the patient except to instruct him to lower his blood pressure any way he could. He was advised to hold his gaze on the signal module, and told that whenever the red light appeared it meant that he had succeeded in reducing his pressure by at least a small amount. Patients in the control group were given the same instructions except that no mention was made of the light signal. Then he was told to relax, to avoid thinking about personal problems, and to focus his attention on lowering his blood pressure.

Following Session 8, each patient was asked to return in exactly one week for a follow-up examination. Nine remained in the hospital for more than an additional week and eight appeared voluntarily for follow-up. Nine were discharged before follow-up and three returned

Table 2

Illustration of Training Procedure

T-1	T-2	T-3	T-4
110 (no signal)	110 (no signal)	105 (red light)	105 (red light)
T-5	T-6	T-7	T-8
105 (red light)	105 (no signal)	100 (red light)	95 (red light)
T-9	T-10	T-11	
95 (red light)	95 (red light)	95 (no signal) ...	

for the final session. The Session 9 procedure was identical to that employed in Session 1. The 20 systolic and diastolic scores obtained from each session were averaged and taken as the follow-up score (see Table 1).

RESULTS

To determine whether or not differences in basal blood pressure existed among the three groups before experimental treatments were initiated, systolic and diastolic scores were subjected to one-way analyses of variance. In the former, $F = 0.20$ was obtained, and in the latter $F = 1.71$ was found (with $df = 2/15$, $F = 3.68$ required for significance at the 0.05 level). Then, each patient's raw systolic and diastolic blood pressure scores determined over Sessions 2 to 8 and at follow-up (Session 9) were converted to per cent of basal pressure and subjected to two-way analyses of variance. Raw scores were expressed as per cent of basal pressure in order to bring the distribution characteristics of the data set in line with the assumptions of analysis of variance.

Systolic pressure. The analysis of the data generated over Sessions 2 to 8 failed to yield any significant differences. There was, however, a consistent tendency for the Group III means to decrease over trials, as shown in Figure 1. Similarly, analysis of the follow-up scores failed to yield significant differences, but these, too, have been included in Figure 1 because the apparent decrease developed in Group III over Sessions 2 to 8 tended to persist throughout follow-up.

Diastolic pressure. Analysis of the diastolic data obtained over Sessions 2 to 8 yielded a significant Groups main effect ($F = 3.99$; $df = 2/15$; $p < 0.05$) and a significant Groups X Session interaction ($F = 2.42$; $df = 12/90$; $p < 0.01$). The means contributing to the latter effect have been plotted in Figure 2. Tukey's (a) procedure (Tukey, 1949) was used to evaluate the differences between any set of session means, and this yielded a value of 9.80 at the 0.05 level. Thus, the means of Group III were reliably different from those of Groups I and II over Sessions 3 to 8. In addition, the mean of Group II was different from the Group I mean over

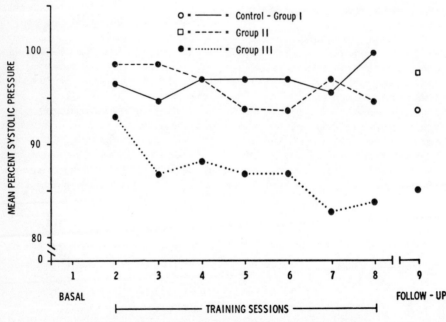

Fig. 1. Mean per cent of basal systolic pressure as a function of sessions.

Sessions 7 to 8. That is to say, strategy 1 began to have a significant decremental effect by Sessions 7 to 8 as compared with strategy 2, which produced a significant and persistent decrement as early as Session 3.

Only 11 of the 18 subjects returned for follow-up examination, rendering analysis of the following-up data difficult. Even so, means of the available data have been included in Figure 2.

DISCUSSION

These data suggest that diastolic pressure is a more suitable dependent variable than systolic blood pressure. Although in essential hypertension both systolic and diastolic pressure are raised, it is a common belief among cardiologists that diastolic pressure is more significant in the development of heart disease. Since systolic and diastolic pressures are not uncorrelated variables, it may be expected that modification of one should be accompanied somewhat by correlated changes in the other, but to what extent instrumental control of one modulates changes in the other must await the collation of additional data.

Another interesting feature of this experiment was the follow-up results. Any routine application of instrumental conditioning to the clinical management of essential hypertension must be predicated on data that demonstrate some persistence of conditioned pressure reduction over time. The data assembled here, coupled with results of an animal experiment by DiCara and Miller (1968), provide a basis for encouragement, but many more data are needed before a firm conclusion regarding clinical use can be drawn.

The present study confirmed the earlier results of Miller (1969) and Shapiro, Tursky, Gershon, and Stern (1969). In addition, it has been shown that diastolic blood pressure can be lowered by as much as 25% over a period of four days, and that this conditioned reduction tends to persist for at least a week after training. Moreover, the most effective strategy for controlling systolic and/or diastolic blood pressure seems to consist of substantial and immediate positive stimulus feedback indicating correct and error

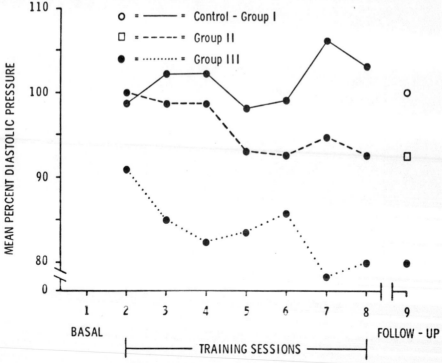

Fig. 2. Mean per cent of basal diastolic pressure as a function of sessions.

responses. Some additional experiments are required to evaluate other strategies, to carry out follow-up evaluations over longer intervals, and to improve the measurement procedures; but the present results bring the management of essential hypertension through operant conditioning one step nearer.

REFERENCES

Benson, H., Shapiro, D., Tursky, B., and Schwartz, G. Decreased systolic blood pressure through operant conditioning techniques in patients with essential hypertension. *Science,* 1971, **173,** 740-742.

DiCara, L. V. and Miller, N. E. Long term retention of instrumentally learned heart-rate changes in curarized rats. *Communication Behavioral Biology,* Part A, 1968, **2,** 19-23.

Gutmann, M. C. and Benson, H. Interaction of environmental factors and systematic arterial blood pressure: a review. *Medicine,* 1971, **50,** 543-553.

Miller, N. E. Learning visceral and glandular responses. *Science,* 1969, **163,** 434-445.

Miller, N. E. Personal communication, 1970.

Miller, N. E., DiCara, L. V., Solomon, H., Weiss, J. M., and Dworkin, B. Learned modifications of autonomic functions: a review and some new data. *Supplement 1 to Circulation Research,* 26 and 27, 1970.

Shapiro, D., Tursky, B., Gershon, E., and Stern, M. Effects of feedback and reinforcement on the control of human systolic blood pressure. *Science,* 1969, **163,** 558-590.

Shapiro, D., Tursky, B., and Schwartz, G. Differentiation of heart rate and systolic blood pressure in man by operant conditioning. *Psychosomatic Medicine,* 1970, **32,** 417-423.

Tukey, J. W. Comparing individual means in the analysis of variance. *Biometrics,* 1949, **4,** 6.

Received 15 May 1972.
(Revision requested 7 August 1972.)
(Revision requested 24 November 1972.)
(Final acceptance 9 April 1973.)

Yoga and Biofeedback 27
in the Management of Hypertension

C. H. Patel

Summary Yogic relaxation and bio-feedback techniques were used in the treatment of 20 patients with hypertension. As a result, anti-hypertensive therapy was stopped altogether in 5 patients and reduced by 33–60% in a further 7 patients. Blood-pressure control was better in 4 other patients, while 4 patients did not respond to therapy. Of these 4 patients, at least 1 had derived indirect benefit by the relief of migraine and depression. The results of this study promise a useful new approach to the treatment of hypertension.

Introduction

MORBIDITY and mortality are directly proportional to increases in blood-pressure.[1] Treatment reduces the complications [2,3] and radically improves the prognosis.[4] The antihypertensive drugs available are not ideal and have many disadvantages.[5] Any new method for reducing blood-pressure is therefore very welcome. Datey et al.[6] demonstrated that yogic exercise (Shavasan), which produces complete mental and physical relaxation, significantly reduces blood-pressure in hypertensive patients. Miller and other workers [7–9] demonstrated that in laboratory animals and man many autonomic functions previously thought to be involuntary can be controlled by operant conditioning.

The "bio-feedback" technique provides continuous visual or auditory displays to show the subject what happens to certain normally involuntary functions of his body as he attempts to influence them by mental, emotional, or somatic means. The correct response is immediately rewarded. This reinforces the subject's efforts to change the physiological variables in the desired directions. This technique has been used with considerable success in laboratory studies of patients with premature ventricular contractions [10] and essential hypertension.[11,12]

I have combined yoga and bio-feedback methods to reduce blood-pressure in a group of hypertensive patients.

Patients

11 women and 9 men were selected from a suburban group general practice (see accompanying table). 16 patients were included in the trial in the order they presented to me for their routine check-ups or for any other medical reason. 4 other patients were selected, to make the group as varied as possible. Each patient (except no. 17) was on antihypertensive therapy.

Patients acted as their own controls. Their past medical records, which went back for from twenty years or more to five years, were examined. Before entering the trial, my own 16 patients were seen by me monthly throughout the period they were known to be hypertensive. Any attempt to reduce their drug dosage increased their blood-pressure. The other 4 patients were seen on three consecutive days to obtain control readings. Their blood-pressures when upright, sitting, and recumbent were recorded on their arrival and again after half an hour's rest. The average of these readings was taken as the pre-trial blood-pressure. 18 patients were White and 2 were Black. Their ages varied from thirty-nine to seventy-eight years (average 57·35 years). When they were first found to be hypertensive their systolic pressure varied from 160 to 230 mm. Hg (average 190) and their diastolic pressure varied from 100 to 150 (average 122 mm. Hg). Their average mean pressure (i.e., diastolic blood-pressure plus one-third of the pulse pressure) was 145 mm. Hg.

When they entered the trial, their systolic pressure varied from 130 to 190 mm. Hg (average 160). Their diastolic pressure varied from 88 to 113 mm. Hg (average 102). The mean blood-pressure at the beginning of the trial was 121. The duration of hypertension varied from one to twenty years (average 6·8 years).

Reprinted by permission from *The Lancet*, November 10, 1973, 1053-1055.

All patients underwent the standard investigations in order to establish the ætiology of hypertension (see table). Symptoms in these patients varied. Tiredness was present in 14, headache in 13, dyspnœa on exertion in 11, dizziness in 9, irritability in 8, chest pain in 6 (angina 2), palpitation in 6, and nervousness and depression in 5. 2 patients had had left ventricular failure over two years before. They had been well controlled on drugs. 2 patients had symptoms of intermittent claudication (1 of these patients has a block in one of the arteries of his right leg). 1 patient had had a cerebrovascular accident about eighteen months before, with only a slight residual weakness at the time of entering the trial. 1 patient had received treatment for myxœdema for more than twenty-five years.

Methods

All patients were seen individually and the technique was explained to them. Patients attended three times a week for half an hour each for three months. Blood-pressure and pulse and respiration-rates were recorded at the beginning and end of each session. Blood-pressure was recorded when standing, sitting, and recumbent. Only blood-pressure when recumbent was recorded in the patients who were either not on any antihypertensive drugs or were being treated by beta blockers. An ordinary clinical sphygmomanometer was used. This was checked frequently against various other sphygmomanometers in the practice. I made most of the recordings, but they were often checked by a nurse or another doctor. All diastolic pressures were recorded in the 5th phase.

Technique

The patient lay on an examination couch with legs slightly apart, arms by the sides, hands supine, and fingers slightly flexed. Eyes were kept closed but falling asleep was avoided. The position of the head was adjusted for comfort. External noise was avoided but no attempts were made to make the room soundproof. During the whole session patients were connected to a relaxometer by two finger electrodes. This machine measures the activity of the sympathetic nervous system indirectly by changes in the skin's electrical resistance. These changes are associated with sweat-gland activity, which can increase without any apparent increase in sweating. The sympathetic activity was turned into an audio signal and the patient tried to reduce the signal or stop it. An increase in pitch of the signal indicated an increase in sympathetic activity, and a decrease indicated relaxation. Strictly speaking, continuous information about blood-pressure should have been fed back to the patient. However, con-

DETAILS OF HYPERTENSIVE PATIENTS

Patient no.	Type	Age	Sex	Duration of hypertension (yr.)	Original B.P. (mean) (mm. Hg)	B.P. on entering trial (mean) (mm. Hg)	B.P. end of trial (mean) (mm. Hg)	Original drugs (mg./day)	Drugs at end of trial (mg./day)	Percentage reduction in drugs
1	T	39	F	20	170/130 (143)	130/100 (110)	120/83 (95)	Reserpine (0·5)	None	100
2	T	43	F	1½	170/120 (133)	143/97 (112)	110/83 (92)	Methyldopa (750)	,,	100
3	T	44	F	14	180/110 (133)	167/100 (122)	130/85 (100)	Rauwolfia (100) Hydroflumethiazide (100)	,,	100
4	E	71	F	9½	220/120 (153)	150/100 (117)	120/80 (93)	Oxprenolol (240)	,,	100
5	E	41	F	1	160/100 (120)	150/100 (117)	110/80 (90)	Oxprenolol (160)	,,	100
6	R	40	M	1+	230/150 (177)	150/113 (125)	120/93 (101)	Methyldopa (1125)	Methyldopa (750)	33
7	I.C.	64	M	9	220/120 (153)	157/97 (117)	140/80 (93)	Guanethidine (60)	Guanethidine (40)	33
8	E	78	F	7	230/130 (163)	190/88 (123)	150/67 (95)	Bethanidine (50) Digoxin and diuretics	Bethanidine (20) Digoxin and diuretics	60
9	E	71	F	1½	220/140 (167)	147/95 (114)	140/85 (103)	Bethanidine (40)	Bethanidine (25)	37·5
10	E	41	M	1½	230/130 (163)	138/100 (113)	103/75 (84)	Clonidine (0·6)	Clonidine (0·4)	33
11	E	75	M	2	220/110 (147)	186/92 (123)	180/77 (109)	Methyldopa (250)	Methyldopa (125)	50
12	E	72	F	3	210/110 (133)	160/100 (120)	140/80 (100)	Oxprenolol (160) Digoxin and diuretics	Oxprenolol (80) Digoxin and diuretics	50
13	E	52	M	5	180/110 (133)	150/103 (119)	113/80 (91)	Rauwolfia (100) Hydroflumethiazide (100)	Unchanged	None
14	E	66	F	2	220/120 (153)	173/92 (119)	123/75 (92)	Rauwolfia (100) Hydroflumethiazide (200)	,,	None
15	R	74	F	8	200/140 (160)	170/110 (130)	130/85 (100)	Oxprenolol (160)	,,	None
16	E	60	M	9	230/130 (163)	180/113 (135)	133/100 (111)	Reserpine (0·75)	,,	None
17	E	60	F	9	200/120 (147)	173/103 (126)	160/105 (123)	Thyroid extract (210) Tranylcypromine (20) Trifluoperazine (2)	Thyroid extract (210) None None	None 100 100
18	E	41	M	3	170/105 (127)	156/102 (120)	147/97 (114)	Rauwolfia (100) Hydroflumethiazide (100)	Unchanged	None
19	E	53	M	3	190/120 (143)	162/97 (118)	160/95 (117)	Guanethidine (25)	Unchanged	None
20	E	62	M	15	180/120 (140)	150/100 (117)	160/110 (127)	Methyldopa (500)	Unchanged (irregularly taken)	None

B.P. = Blood-pressure.
E = Essential hypertension.
R = Renal hypertension.
T = Essential hypertension following pregnancy toxæmia.
I.C. = Intracranial hypertension.

tinuous measurement of blood-pressure requires the introduction of a transducer directly into an artery.

The patient was asked to pay attention to his breathing first. After making sure that it was smooth and regular, he mentally went over the various parts of his body and made them completely limp and relaxed. He made sure that there was no tension left in the muscles of the face, neck, chest, and abdomen. If he wished he could mentally repeat phrases like " my arms are feeling very heavy and relaxed ".[13] Typewritten sheets of instructions and useful phrases were given to each patient so that they could learn and practise relaxation at home. Once they had learnt to relax physically they had to relax mentally. Experience showed that most patients during physical relaxation were able to forget the outside world and often were not aware of their own limbs, but they found it difficult to forget their breathing-movements. They used these as the object for concentration. They concentrated on inspiration and expiration (akin to Dharna in Yoga). They could mentally repeat " Relaxed . . . Relaxed . . ." with every expiration (akin to Yoga Mantra). Patients were free to select their object or idea for concentration. This concentration kept them mentally alert but inwardly aware. At the end of a session each patient was told his blood-pressure levels before and after the session.

The dosage of drugs was adjusted according to the response, and the percentage reduction in dose was calculated.

Results

Subjective improvement was reflected by the favourable comments given voluntarily by some patients during the course of their treatment.

The average mean blood-pressure of 121 mm. Hg at the beginning of the trial was reduced to 101 mm. Hg, despite the 41% fall in the total drug requirement (see table). 5 patients had stopped their antihypertensive drugs altogether. A further 7 patients were able to reduce their drug requirements by 33–60%. There were 4 patients whose drug regimen was unchanged, but their blood-pressure control was better than before the trial began. The remaining 4 patients had not reduced their blood-pressures. 16 patients had derived direct benefit, and, of the 4 patients who did not control their blood-pressure, at least one (no. 17) derived some indirect benefit from the treatment. The frequency and severity of her migraine had been reduced considerably and she was able to stop her antidepressant drug therapy. The 3 patients with hypertension after pregnancy toxæmia did best as a group. 6 men (66%) and 10 women (91%) derived benefit from the present therapy. Both systolic and diastolic blood-pressures were reduced. Their average systolic pressure fell from 160 to 134 mm. Hg and their average diastolic pressure fell from 102 to 86 mm. Hg. There were no significant changes in the pulse-rate, respiration-rate, or body-weight among these patients over the period of therapy.

Discussion

Although many studies have been done to investigate psychological, personality, socio-cultural, and neurohormonal factors,[14-25] the cause of essential hypertension remains unknown. These experiments

and studies, however, suggest that repeated episodes of increased sympathetic discharge with concomitant hormonal release in response to emotional situations in daily life may constitute an intermittently acting trigger factor in the gradual development of chronic hypertension in susceptible individuals. It is postulated that yogic relaxation and meditation reduces the sympathetic discharge[26] in response to the environmental stimuli, making the neurohormonal factors concerned with the production of hypertension ineffective. Mental concentration reduces the external interference, making the subject less aware of the external environment. This increases his perception of his own internal environment. Additionally, helped by bio-feedback, the subject becomes more aware of the smallest changes in the autonomic function (in this case blood-pressure), which allows him to make necessary changes in the control of that function.

I am now studying another series of hypertensive patients, using hypertensive controls matched for age and sex, so that the effect on blood-pressure of repeated blood-pressure measurement and increased medical attention is eliminated.

This study was supported by the research committee of the South-West Metropolitan Regional Hospital Board.

Requests for reprints should be addressed to C. H. P., 11 Upfield, Croydon CR0 5DR, Surrey.

REFERENCES

1. Pickering, G. W. *Am. J. Med.* 1972, **52**, 571.
2. Hamilton, M., Thompson, E. N., Wisniewski, T. K. M. *Lancet,* 1964, i, 235.
3. Veterans Administration Co-operative Study Group on Antihypertensive Agents. *J. Am. med. Ass.* 1970, **213**, 1143.
4. Dollery, C. T., Breckenbridge, A., Parry, E. H. O. *Q. Jl Med.* 1970, **39**, 411.
5. Bulpitt, C. J., Dollery, C. T. *Br. med. J.* 1973, iii, 485.
6. Datey, K. K., Deshmukh, S. M., Dalvi, C. P., Vineker, S. L. *Angiology,* 1969, **20**, 325.
7. Miller, N. E. *Science,* 1969, **163**, 434.
8. Miller, N. E., Dicara, L. V. *in* Bio-feedback and Self Control (edited by J. Kamiya, T. X. Barber, L. V. Dicara, N. E. Miller, D. Shapiro, and J. Stoyva); p. 92. New York, 1971.
9. Shapiro, D., Tursky, B., Gershon, E., Stern, M. *Science,* 1969, **163**, 588.
10. Weiss, T., Engel, B. *Psychosom. Med.* 1971, **33**, 301.
11. Benson, H., Shapiro, D., Tursky, B., Schwartz, G. E. *Science,* 1971, **173**, 740.
12. Shapiro, D., Schwartz, G. E., Tursky, B. *Psychophysiology,* 1972, **9**, 296.
13. Schultz, J. H., Luthe, W. Autogenic Training. New York, 1959.
14. Scotch, N. A., Geiger, J. H. *J. chron. Dis.* 1963, **16**, 1183.
15. Cruz-Coke, R. *Lancet,* 1960, ii, 885.
16. Cruz-Coke, R., Etcheverry, R., Nagel, R. *ibid.* 1964, i, 697.
17. Harris, R. E., Singer, M. T. *in* Hypertension: Neural Control of Arterial Pressure, vol. xvi; p. 104. New York, 1967.
18. Hinkle, L. E., Jr., Wolff, H. G. *in* Explorations in Social Psychiatry (edited by A. H. Leighton); p. 105. New York, 1957.
19. Hinkle, L. E., Jr., Wolff, H. G. *Archs intern. Med.* 1957, **99**, 442.
20. Hinkle, L. E., Jr., Wolff, H. G. *Ann. intern. Med.* 1958, **49**, 1373.
21. Hinkle, L. E., Jr., Wolff, H. G. *in* Proceedings of a Symposium on the Pathogenesis of Essential Hypertension; p. 129. Prague, 1961.
22. Lacey, J. I., Lacey, B. C. *Am. J. Psychol.* 1958, **71**, 50.
23. Lacey, J. I., Lacey, B. *Ann. N.Y. Acad. Sci.* 1962, **98**, 1257.
24. Folkow, B., Rubinstein, E. H. *Acta physiol. scand.* 1968, **68**, 48.
25. Charvat, J., Dell, P., Folkow, B. *Cardiologia,* 1964, **44**, 124.
26. Wallace, R. K., Benson, H. *Scient. Am.* 1972, **226**, 84.

Suppression of Penile 28
Tumescence by Instrumental
Conditioning

Raymond C. Rosen

Penile tumescence was elicited in normal male volunteers by erotic tape-recorded passages. Experimental subjects were provided with immediate contingent feedback [red light] whenever their penile tumescence exceeded a criterion increase. Controls for noncontingent feedback and suppression instructions alone indicate that the instrumental conditioning procedure is particularly effective in modifying this response. Results have implications for etiological formulations and treatment of psychogenic potency disorders.

Penile tumescence in the human male is directly facilitated by parasympathetic vasodilator fibers [nervi erigentes] from the sacral cord (1,2,3). Regardless of the source of stimulation, engorgement of the corpus spongiosum and corpora cavernosa results from this parasympathetically mediated expansion of the arterial lumina. The central role of the autonomic nervous system has led previous researchers to assert that penile tumescence is a totally involuntary response, subject only to reflexive control (4). This conceptualization has greatly influenced etiological accounts as well as treatment approaches to tumescence disorders (5).

Recent research has indicated, however, that some degree of voluntary control of tumescence might be possible (6,7). In

these studies it appeared that instructed subjects were able to voluntarily enhance or suppress tumescence in the presence or absence of visual erotica.

To the extent that tumescence might be subject to voluntary control under certain conditions, it follows that instrumental contingencies could be important in the development and maintenance of the response. Fine differentiation of visceral behavior is possible through instrumental conditioning (8,9), and penile tumescence, being readily detectable, might be particularly susceptible to external contingencies. While changes in heart rate or blood pressure would typically pass unnoticed, penile tumescence in an "inappropriate" social situation could elicit immediate reinforcement, either positive or negative. It is hypothesized, therefore, that such contingencies could play an important role in developing the specificity of control apparent in the normal adult male.

The present study was conducted to ascertain the possible effects of contingent

From the Department of Psychiatry, CMDNJ-Rutgers Medical School, Piscataway, New Jersey 08854.

This research was supported in part by funds from an Office of Education Grant 2-700041 [509].

Received for publication March 16, 1973; revision received May 25, 1973.

feedback on the suppression of elicited tumescence. Specifically, an attempt was made to demonstrate that, under controlled laboratory conditions, an instrumental conditioning procedure could produce substantial suppression of tumescence in normal male volunteers. The effects of such a procedure might have important implications for our understanding of the development of control of tumescence in both normal and disordered males.

METHOD

The laboratory measurement of penile tumescence is readily achieved through the use of a mercury strain-gauge (Parks Electronics) which reflects changes in penile diameter as an approximately linear function of resistance changes in the mercury column within the strain-gauge (10). By defining the criterion of tumescence onset (an increase in penile diameter of approximately 0.5 mm from the flaccid state), it is possible to establish the conditions for the presentation of immediate contingent feedback to the subject. This feedback (a dim red light projected into the darkened experimental chamber) was automatically triggered by a voltage discriminator circuit preset at the criterion strain-gauge level.

The subjects were forty males without any history of sexual dysfunction (undergraduate volunteers who took part in the experiment for academic credit). They were seated in a sound- and temperature-controlled room, where the details of the experiment were explained. Subjects were told that the purpose of the experiment was to determine the effects of erotic stimulation under different conditions. Subjects were encouraged to tell friends that the experiment involved listening to "sexy" tapes, without going into any further details, "so as not to spoil it for them!" As a result, a large source of volunteers was obtained, none of whom appeared to have any preconceptions, other than that they would be sexually aroused by the experiment.

Subjects were instructed to place the strain-gauge around the shaft of the penis, just below the coronal ridge, after the experimenter had left the room. This strain-gauge formed one leg of a Wheatstone bridge circuit (Parks Model 270 Plethysmograph Wheatstone Bridge), which allowed voltage changes to be displayed on a Beckman Type R Dynograph. Figure 1 illustrates the penile volume and finger pulse volume polygraph recordings.

Samples of pulse volume from the finger were obtained from 12 of the subjects. These data were obtained by means of a strain-gauge circuit similar to the penile strain-gauge, but AC coupled to the polygraph. Recording and programming of the experiment were conducted from an adjacent room.

In order to elicit penile tumescence, a series of erotic passages were extracted from popular pornography and tape-recorded in the form of ten minute

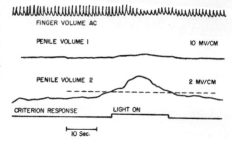

FINGER VOLUME AC

PENILE VOLUME 1   10 MV/CM

PENILE VOLUME 2   2 MV/CM

CRITERION RESPONSE   LIGHT ON

10 Sec.

Fig. 1. Representative portion of the polygraph record from a Contigent Feedback subject. Penile tumescence is displayed on two separate channels (one at a lower gain in order to maintain the full range of the response within the channel). The dashed line across the high gain penile channel indicates the level of the voltage discriminatory switch setting. Whenever penile diameter exceeds this criterion, the marker (lower channel) indicates the duration of the response. Also shown is the finger blood volume record (upper channel) which was recorded from 12 subjects.

segments by a female narrator. The erotic tape-recordings used in the experiment were shown in earlier pilot research to reliably elicit sizeable tumescence in the subject population.

For each of the four experimental sessions, subjects were presented with a different ten-min passage (randomly selected) through Grason Stadler Model TDH earphones. Prior to the onset of the erotic narration, a three-min period of quiet instrumental music was presented, during which time the diameter of the flaccid penis was assessed, and defined as the subject's basal level for that session. Strain-gauge expansion during the subsequent ten min of erotic stimulus presentation was reflected as mm polygraph pen deflection above the resting level. Strain-gauge calibration was checked before experimental sessions by means of a standard aluminum cylinder.

The experiment was divided into two phases: a base-line session and three subsequent treatment sessions. During the base-line (pretreatment) session, all subjects listened to one of the erotic passages while physiological measures were recorded. This session was intended to indicate the tumescence produced prior to treatment.

After this session, subjects were randomly divided into four groups (N=10): (i) *The Contingent Feedback* group was instructed to suppress their erections by turning off a red light which was projected into the experimental room whenever the subject's tumescence exceeded 0.5 mm diameter increase from the basal level. (ii) The *Yoked Feedback* group received similar instructions, but were presented with nonveridical [yoked] feedback. Yoking was achieved through the use of a tape-recording of the feedback record of each of the Contingent Feedback subjects, which was then used to trigger the feedback projection for each of the Yoked Feedback subjects. This meant that the yoked controls received the same order and duration of feedback, but *noncontingently*. The purpose of this Yoked group was to control for the possible intrinsically inhibiting effect of the feedback light irrespective of the contingency. (iii) The *Instructions Only* group were instructed to attempt to suppress tumescence in the presence of the erotic stimulus material. However, they were not provided with any form of prosthetic feedback. In fact, the feedback light was disconnected for this and the following group. (iv) The *No Treatment Control* group received repeated presentations of the erotic material without any inhibition instructions or external feedback. This group was included as a control for possible habituation effects. Subjects in all four groups had available normal tactile feedback from underclothing, skin contact with other body parts, etc.

Subjects in the suppression groups (i, ii, and iii) were all instructed to refrain from any manual suppression of tumescence. Moreover, they were instructed to attend to the tape-recordings as closely as possible as they would subsequently be tested on the content. Random assignment of subjects to experimental groups, and standardization of experimental instructions were used to minimize experimenter bias.

All sessions were spaced approximately one week apart. Postsession questionnaires were administered after the pretreatment, first, and last treatment sessions. These questionnaires were designed to ascertain the subject's awareness of the experimental contingencies, as well as their subjective response to the procedure. Debriefing was conducted after the final [fourth] session.

RESULTS

The most direct measure of the effectiveness of the contingency is the amount of time that the subject's tumescence exceeded the experimental criterion. In order to compare group differences, the mean percentage time above criterion for each group was computed. If a subject's tumescence exceeded the criterion for the entire session, that subject would therefore receive a score of 100% for that session. A subject who had attained complete suppression of tumescence would receive a score of 0% for the session. Figure 2 indicates these time

above criterion data for each of the four experimental sessions (including the initial base-line session).

A one-way analysis of variance on the pretreatment data shows that there were no systematic differences between the groups prior to treatment, i.e., that the groups had in fact been randomly assigned. A two-way analysis of variance (11) of the data from four groups over all four experimental sessions shows that the main effect for groups was significant (p

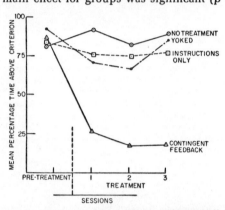

Fig. 2. Average time above criterion (0.5 mm penile diameter increase from flaccid level) of the four groups over the four experimental sessions. Each point on the graph represents the mean time above criterion for ten subjects in one experimental session.

< 0.005), as well as the groups X sessions interaction effect ($p < 0.05$).

A planned comparison of the differences between group means indicates that the Contingent Feedback group was the only group that showed a significant ($p < 0.01$) suppression effect over the three treatment sessions. The No Treatment Control group showed no evidence of an habituation effect. Review of individual records suggested different suppression approaches in the contingent feedback group: (i) After exceeding the criterion a number of times early in the training sessions, some subjects were able to maintain a relatively constant below criterion response for most of the sessions. (ii) Other subjects appeared to use the feedback light to maintain their response at just about criterion level. One subject received as many as 15 feedback presentations in one session.

Finger pulse volume data from twelve of the subjects was analyzed with respect to rate and amplitude. While there was no significant difference between the feedback and no-feedback groups in terms of the overall finger pulse amplitude or rate scores, there appeared to be a suggestive, but not statistically significatnt negative correlation ($r = -0.37$) between penile diameter increase and pulse rate changes: as subjects' penile diameter increased, their pulse rates tended to decrease. However, as the actual pulse rates showed relatively minor changes (2–5 beats/min), and the correlation is rather small, this finding should be cautiously interpreted.

In attempting to assess whether successful suppression of tumescence was associated with decreased attention to the content of the erotic material, the postsession questionnaires were also designed to elicit subjective reactions to the experimental procedure. Subjects were required to answer a number of questions concerning the content of the passages. No significant differences in recall scores emerged. Although subjects in the control conditions tended to rate themselves as having been less successful during the suppression phase, there was no evidence that the yoked subjects doubted the veridicality of the feedback. Moreover, there did not appear to be any systematic pattern of suppression strategies described by subjects (almost half the subjects reported some form of muscular or mental tension, while the remainder attempted to relax in some way).

One final questionnaire finding of note was that subjects appeared to be able to rate reasonably accurately the extent to which they had been successful in inhibiting their tumescence during the session. That is, subjective ratings of suppression correlated significantly ($p > 0.01$) with actual strain-gauge scores.

DISCUSSION

The data from this experiment suggest obtained in this study suggest that penile that if normal male volunteers are provided with precise immediate feedback as soon as their tumescence exceeds a certain criterion, they are able to learn a remarkable degree of control with respect to that criterion. Moreover, results of the control groups suggest that the suppression obtained is not attributable to any of the nonspecific experimental factors. Nor can the results be accounted for solely on the basis of attentional differences between the groups.

It has been demonstrated in animals [12] as well as humans [13] that remarkable specifity of function of the autonomic nervous system can be achieved through instrumental conditioning. The results tumescence, as a parasympathetically mediated response, is particularly susceptible to suppression as a function of external contingencies.

Although this study was conducted on normal subjects in a laboratory situation, tentative clinical inferences can be drawn from the results. Masters and Johnson (5, p. 196) have stated that: "Erections develop just as involuntarily and with just as little effort as breathing." On the other hand, the results of this study suggest that instrumental contingencies could control tumescence in a manner analogous to the control of somatic behavior. This suggests an alternative etiological formulation in certain cases of psychogenic impotence.

It would also appear feasible to extend such instrumental conditioning techniques to the treatment of certain disorders. If, for example, penile tumescence is elicited in the presence of socially unacceptable stimuli [fetishism], a contingent feedback procedure similar to that used in this study might be sufficient to enable the individual to suppress tumescence when necessary. This might prove a more effective, as well as a more humane alternative to current aversion therapy procedures (14, 15).

SUMMARY

Penile tumescence has been widely regarded as an involuntary response, susceptible only to reflexive control. The present study was designed to investigate the possible modification of penile tumescence by instrumental conditioning procedures.

Penile tumescence in this experiment was elicited by erotic tape-recorded passages of approximately 10-min duration. Forty normal male volunteers were randomly divided into four experimental conditions, which included a contingent feedback group, a yoked control, an instructions only, and a no treatment group. All subjects received one pretreatment and three treatment sessions.

Highly significant suppression of tumescence was obtained as a result of the contingent feedback procedure. None of the control groups demonstrated this effect, indicating that the instrumental conditioning procedure is particularly effective in modifying this response.

Postsession questionnaires did not provide any evidence for specific patterns of somatic or cognitive mediation. Finger pulse volume data collected is suggestive of a correlation between tumescence suppression and direct parasympathetic [vagal] control.

These data suggest that instrumental contingencies might play an important role in the development of control of penile tumescence in the human male. This notion could have implications for etiological formulations of certain potency disorders, as well as behavioral therapies for such disorders.

I wish to thank Dr. James Geer, Dr. Gerald Davison, and Dr. John Gagnon for advice and support during the project, and Dr. David Shapiro and Dr. Robert Edelberg for comments on the manuscript.

REFERENCES

1. Learmonth JR: A contribution to the neurophysiology of the urinary bladder. Brain 54:147–176, 1931
2. Weiss HD: The physiology of human penile erection. Ann Intern Med 76:793–799, 1972
3. Katchadourian HA, Lunde DT: Fundamentals of Human Sexuality. New York, Holt, Rinehart and Winston, 1972
4. Masters WH, Johnson VE: Human Sexual Response. Boston, Little Brown, 1966
5. Masters WH, Johnson VE: Human Sexual Inadequacy. Boston, Little Brown, 1970
6. Laws DR, Rubin HB: Instructional control of an auticmic sexual response. Appl Behav Anal 2:93–99, 1969
7. Henson DE, Rubin HB: Voluntary control of eroticism. Appl Behav Anal 4:37–44, 1971
8. Shapiro D, Tursky B, Schwartz GE: Differentiation of heart rate and systolic blood pressure in man by operant conditioning. Psychosom Med 32:417–423, 1970
9. Schwartz GE: Voluntary control of human cardiovascular integration and differentiation through feedback and reward. Science 175:90–93, 1972
10. Zuckerman M: Physiological measures of sexual arousal in the human. Psychol Bull 75:297–329, 1971
11. Winer BJ: Statistical Principles in Experimental Design. New York, McGraw-Hill, 1962
12. Miller NE: Learning of visceral and glandular responses. Science 163:434–445, 1969
13. Katkin ES, Murray EN: Instrumental conditioning of autonomically mediated behavior: Theoretical and methodological issues Psychol Bull 70:52–68, 1968
14. Feldman MP: Aversion therapy for sexual deviations: A critical review Psychol Bull 65:65–79, 1966
15. Rachman S, Teasdale J: Aversion Therapy and Behaviour Disorders: An Analysis. Coral Gables, University of Miami Press, 1969

Biofeedback and Essential 29 Hypertension: Current Findings and Theoretical Concerns

Gary E. Schwartz and David Shapiro

When normotensive and hypertensive subjects are provided with feedback for relative increases or decreases in blood pressure and rewarded for these changes, they can learn to exert some control over their pressure. Biofeedback research on self-regulation of systolic and diastolic pressure, heart rate, and patterns of these functions is reviewed, and a general model of pattern learning is described. Application of these techniques to the control of systolic and diastolic pressure in patients diagnosed with essential hypertension are presented and critically analyzed. Problems of expectancy and motivation, personality and life-style, and biologic constraints are emphasized. It is concluded that biofeedback techniques should be viewed as only one part of a combined behavioral treatment program for hypertensive patients.

E STIMATED TO AFFECT between 15% and 30% of the U.S. population, high blood pressure is a serious medical problem. Concern with hypertension is largely due to its association with increased risk of coronary artery disease and cerebrovascular accidents,[20,21] the major causes of death in the U.S. today.[44] Between 90% and 95% of all cases of hypertension have no known etiology and are labeled "essential." The systematic application of behavioral theory and methods to the study of essential hypertension has occurred relatively recently, even though environmental factors have been long suspected of having an important etiologic role.[15]

Supported by the Milton Fund and the Spencer Fund of Harvard University; the Advanced Research Projects Agency of the Department of Defense and monitored by the Office of Naval Research under Contract N00014-70-C-0350 to the San Diego State University Foundation; NIMH Grant MH-08853; Research Scientist Award MH-20476; Office of Naval Research Contract N00014-67-A-0024; and USPHS Grant 5 R01 HL 14486-02.

Reprint requests should be addressed to Dr. Gary E. Schwartz, Department of Psychology and Social Relations, Harvard University, 1444 William James Hall, Cambridge, Mass. 02138.

© *1973 by Grune & Stratton, Inc.*

For more than 6 yr our laboratories have been concerned with the application of feedback and reward procedures to the self-regulation of blood pressure and other cardiovascular responses in healthy human subjects and patients with essential hypertension. The purpose of this paper is to review and evaluate these data and also to consider current theoretical and practical issues in light of other findings. Included are new data on attempts to train patients with essential hypertension to lower their diastolic pressure using biofeedback techniques.

MEASUREMENT OF BLOOD PRESSURE

In order to provide subjects with feedback for small changes in blood pressure, it is necessary to be able to easily and reliably measure pressure on each beat of the heart. Direct arterial catheterization is not amenable for routine and repetitive laboratory training with human subjects, so alternative monitoring procedures are necessary. After evaluation of various sphygmomanometer techniques, a new system was developed using a constant cuff pressure procedure.[38,43] The reader is referred to Tursky[42] and Benson[3] for recent reviews of blood pressure recording procedures in humans.

Briefly, a blood pressure cuff is wrapped around the upper arm and a microphone is placed at the distal end under the cuff over the brachial artery. If the cuff is inflated to approximately average systolic pressure and held there, whenever systolic pressure rises and exceeds the cuff pressure following a given heart contraction, blood will be forced through the artery under the cuff and a Korotkoff sound will be heard. Conversely, for those heart beats followed by a systolic peak pressure that is less than the occluding pressure of the cuff, blood will not flow through the artery and a Korotkoff sound will not be heard. Using regulated pressure sources and solid state programming equipment, it is possible to establish automatically the cuff pressure at which 50% of the beats are above the pressure in the cuff and 50% are below. This, by definition, is median systolic pressure and corresponds within 2 mm Hg to median pressures obtained using direct arterial catheterization.[43]

Typically, the cuff is inflated for 50 heart beats and then deflated for 30–45 sec to allow blood flow and eliminate discomfort and potential artifacts. The period of inflation consititutes a trial. If the subject raises or lowers his average systolic pressure in a given trial by more than 2 mm Hg, this will correspondingly increase or decrease the percentage of Korotkoff sounds by about 25%. The percentage of Korotkoff sounds in a trial determines how the pressure should be set for the next trial, thus making it possible to track median pressure over trials. Normally the cuff pressure is raised or lowered by 2 mm Hg for ± 25% changes in Korotkoff sounds, and 4 mm Hg for ± 50% changes. The system also provides information on relative changes in pressure on each successive beat of the heart.

In the studies, subjects are provided with binary (yes–no) feedback in the form of lights and tones whenever a coincidence (R spike of EKG plus Korotkoff sound within 300 msec) or anticoincidence (R spike and no Korotkoff sound) occur, depending upon the experimental condition. At median systolic pressure, a coincidence, or presence of Korotkoff sound, indicates a relative increase in pressure; an anticoincidence or absence of Korotkoff sound indicates a relative decrease in pressure. After producing a certain number of such "feedback stimuli," subjects earn a reward in the form of a slide. In normotensive subjects, depending upon the particular experiment, the slides have been landscapes of Boston, pictures from around the world, photos of nude females, and monetary bonuses. In working with hypertensive patients, motivation becomes an important problem, one not easily solved using simple extrinsic rewards.

Before considering the data, it is important to indicate how the concepts of feedback and reward, voluntary control and conditioning are used here, especially in view of previous confusion arising in the literature concerning definition of terms and theoretical interpretations (e.g., Crider et al.[11] and Katkin and Murray[22]). The distinction between feedback and reward is viewed more as a continuum involving the extent of intrinsic incentive value in the stimulus. In the binary feedback–reward procedure described above, the feedback and reward each contain comparable information value about changes in blood pressure. Whether the reward is more "rewarding" than the feedback depends on their relative degree of incentive value for a given subject. One can, however, experimentally separate information components from incentive. For example, in ongoing basic research in our laboratories, subjects receive binary feedback, but the reward is now contingent upon changes in cuff pressure rather than on the number of feedbacks *per se*. Hence the "feedback" reflects phasic (beat by beat) changes while the "reward" is for more tonic changes in pressure.

From a procedural point of view, operant conditioning is simply defined as an experimental technique where the information and incentive value are contained in the same stimulus (the reinforcer). However, to the extent that feedback terminology is more physiologic in nature and more consistent with control theory of biologic machines, it has definite advantages.[9,31]

The distinction between voluntary control and conditioning as *processes* may also be viewed in terms of a continuum, from self-directed to environmentally controlled behavior. From a clinical point of view, the general goal is twofold: to teach patients self-control of their pressure and ultimately have it become habitual and automatic. Therefore, this goal incorporates the common meanings of both voluntary control and conditioning.

SELF-REGULATION OF BLOOD PRESSURE AND HEART RATE: BASIC RESEARCH

Not knowing whether voluntary control of blood pressure was feasible, the initial studies were concerned with whether healthy college students could learn to increase and decrease their systolic blood pressure using the constant cuff pressure system.[38,39] To control for possible complications due to differential instructions and experimenter bias,[29] all subjects were given the same general instructions indicating that their task was to learn how to make the feedback occur as often as possible. They were not told the response was their blood pressure, nor were they told what direction it was to change. The data indicated that (1) subjects could learn to relatively increase or decrease their blood pressure with feedback; (2) systolic pressure changes appeared independent of heart rate, and (3) subjects could not consciously tell which experimental condition they were in, as indicated by interviews and questionnaires—that is, they revealed no consistent cognitive strategies reflecting, for example, a simple "relaxation-tension" dimension.

Although many questions were raised by these first studies, it became clear that the choice of "base-line" values was critical in evaluating relative degree of learned increases and decreases (see also Crider et al.[11]). It has often been assumed that resting values obtained at the beginning of a session will remain constant over the session. In some situations, however, increases will occur due to the arousing nature of the stimuli and the task itself. Or, subjects may habituate to the experimental situation, producing a natural decrease in blood pressure. For example, when a group was included that was given identical stimuli and instructions, but for whom the feedback was in fact randomly related to systolic pressure,[39] the correct feedback for increases or decreases led to *relative* control of blood pressure *vis-à-vis* the declining "base-line" values. While the initial curves had suggested that decreases in pressure were easier to obtain, an opposite conclusion may be drawn when correct base-line estimates are used. The question of appropriate base lines and range of possible values per individual therefore becomes paramount in evaluating clinical effects.[31]

A follow-up study was designed to explore further the dissociation of blood pressure and heart rate and the nature of the subjective experience in self-regulation. Subjects were given the identical binary feedback and reward paradigm, except that feedback and reward was given for increases or decreases in heart rate, while systolic pressure was simultaneously monitored.[40] Under these conditions, subjects learned to increase and decrease their heart rate without differentially affecting their systolic pressure. Again, postexperimental interviews did not reveal any consistent cognitive or somatic processes that distinguished the groups. Subgroup analyses were made of the best learners in both the heart rate control study and in the earlier blood pressure study to further evaluate specificity of learning. Again there was no indication of simultaneous learning in both functions.

Although these data were encouraging from a clinical point of view in suggesting that biofeedback might be used to treat specific symptoms,[36] they did not explain why specificity should occur, nor what the possible constraints might be. A series of studies on the measurement and control of patterns of blood pressure and heart rate were undertaken to provide some answers to these questions.[32-34,37] Schwartz[32] hypothesized that when feedback is given for one response, simultaneous learning of any other response will depend on several factors. One factor is the precise nature of the relation of other responses to the response controlling the feedback (e.g., if two responses were always waxing and waning together, then feedback for one would result in identical feedback for the other as well, and therefore both should show learning and change and in the same direction). The other factor concerns potential biologic constraints that can affect the interrelation of the responses. This analysis suggests that learned specificity will occur to the extent that multi-responses are randomly related over time and that the systems are biologically capable of separating.

A system was developed for tracking both phasic and tonic patterns of blood pressure and heart rate in real time (e.g., isolating $BP^{up} HR^{up}$, $BP^{up} HR_{down}$, $BP_{down} HR^{up}$, $BP_{down} HR_{down}$ responses at each heart beat). To test the hypothesis that pattern learning is possible, subjects were given feedback and reward for each of the four possible patterns. The results showed that subjects readily learned to integrate these responses; in fact, feedback for $BP^{up} HR^{up}$ or $BP_{down} HR_{down}$ led to more rapid learning and produced somewhat larger effects in *both* responses than the earlier feedback for either one alone.[32,33] In addition, subjects were able to voluntarily differentiate these responses, although this proved to be more difficult, especially for the $BP^{up} HR_{down}$ pattern.[32] Analysis of the phasic patterns confirmed that each of the four patterns was equally likely, thus explaining the earlier specificity findings. In addition, by carefully analyzing the natural tonic reactivity in this situation, it was possible to predict the extent and time course of learning for each of the four conditions.

Interestingly, despite the fact that these subjects were relatively uninformed, analysis of the subjective report data showed that subjects became more relaxed as they learned to lower *both* their systolic pressure and heart rate.[32] To the extent that general relaxation is a pattern of decreases in many physiologic systems simultaneously, it is reasonable to assume that decreases in both blood pressure and heart rate will be more associated with subjective relaxation than decreases in either one alone.

In current work on the voluntary control of diastolic pressure, the usefulness of this strategy has been supported. When subjects are given feedback and reward for changes in diastolic pressure, some learning in heart rate also occurs.[37] Analysis of natural phasic integration reveals that these two responses are partially, but not completely integrated. This can explain why heart rate shows some learning, but not as much as is obtained when only heart rate feedback is used. Taking into account base-line constraints and physiologic considerations, it has been possible to predict the degree to which subjects can learn to voluntarily integrate and differentiate their diastolic pressure and heart rate.[34]

Space does not allow a more detailed presentation of the theory and data (see Schwartz[30,31]). However, brief mention of their clinical implications is in order. First is that the simple notion of symptom treatment as employed in behavior therapy may be in error; more careful analysis of patterns reflecting underlying physiologic causes may be needed to utilize feedback more efficiently. For example, in disorders such as angina pectoris, where it is desirable to lower both blood pressure and heart rate,[8] direct feedback for $BP_{down} HR_{down}$ patterns may be in order. Further, since blood pressure reflects the sum total of multi-cardiovascular factors operating at the same time, then exactly which component of the pressure is selected for feedback will influence the degree to which different underlying mechanisms are receiving contingent feedback. Therefore, if it is desirable for certain patients to reduce their peripheral resistance, but feedback is given for small, phasic changes in diastolic pressure, the patient may well be receiving feedback for heart rate-mediated changes, and therefore not learn to control the peripheral factors directly. If the patient becomes "confused" with partially inaccurate feedback, more direct feedback procedures may be required, either singly or in patterns.

On the side of biologic constraints, it is reasonable to assume that to the extent that chronic pathology is present (e.g., in atherosclerosis), self-regulation of neural and hormonal processes may have little effect, at least in the short run. One possible predictor of clinical success with biofeedback may be the extent to which the system is labile and biologically capable of change (e.g., by comparing responses during sleep, exercise, relaxation, and different conditions of environmental stimulation).

CONTROL OF SYSTOLIC PRESSURE IN ESSENTIAL HYPERTENSION

The jump from normotensive college students to hypertensive patients was stimulated in part by operant conditioning experiments with primates. High blood pressure was found to be associated with operant schedules that continuously exerted strong control over the animals' behavior.[16] Chronic high blood pressure was also achieved in other experiments where avoidance of shock was made directly dependent on increased arterial pressures.[4] Further, in these same experiments, blood pressure levels could be reduced to normotensive levels when avoidance of shock was made dependent on decreased pressure. In light of this research in monkeys, the constant cuff pressure feedback technique was applied to patients diagnosed with essential hypertension.[6] Seven patients were studied for five to 16 control sessions during which time stable median systolic pressure was obtained under quiet resting conditions. All patients then received daily feedback sessions for decreasing systolic pressure until no further reductions in blood pressure occured in five consecutive sessions. For the period of the study, all patients were maintained on their prior drug schedule. The results showed that the five patients diagnosed with essential hypertension responded positively to the treatment, showing decreases of 34, 29, 16, 16, and 17 mm Hg with 33, 22, 34, 31, and 12 sessions of training, respectively. Of the other two patients, one did not have elevated systolic pressure and the other had renal artery stenosis with normal renin levels; neither showed significant decreases in pressure.

Although these findings are encouraging, they are only a beginning, and many questions need to be answered before their clinical value can be decided. Despite the fact that extensive control pressures were taken before the feedback sessions, it could be argued that decreases might have also occurred if more resting sessions were used. Furthermore, the novelty of the experimental situation plus expectancy effects may have operated as a "placebo" treatment, and therefore the role of the feedback itself can be questioned. On the other hand, it is hypothesized* that expectancy effects, particularly in behavioral therapies where practice on the part of the patient is necessary for successful outcome, are an essential ingredient for effective therapy.[36] It is conceivable that feedback *plus* suggestion effects can act synergistically, thereby producing larger effects than either alone,[45] although this remains to be demonstrated in a clinical setting.

---

*Editor's note: This need not be merely hypothesized; rather, it has in fact been demonstrated, and even studied quantitatively (see Chapter 3), by Dr. Stroebel on the interaction of effects mediated by suggestion vs. those by autonomic learning.

Other questions that can be raised include: (1) Can patients learn to control their pressure without feedback? Shapiro, Schwartz and Tursky[37] have provided some positive data for this in normal subjects. (2) Will their pressures be lower in the stressful environment outside of the quiet of the laboratory? Pressure taken outside the laboratory in two of the patients studied suggested that this was possible, although the data are not complete enough to draw conclusions at this time. Recently, Sirota, Schwartz, and Shapiro[41] have found that subjects can voluntarily lower their heart rate in anticipation of a stressful stimulus. Furthermore, heart rate slowing through biofeedback and instructions can reduce the perceived noxiousness of the stimulus. Whether hypertensive patients can learn to voluntarily lower their pressure under stressful conditions remains to be demonstrated.

As described by Shapiro and Schwartz,[36] motivation is an important component for success in any form of psychotherapy (both in and out of the therapy situation) and this particularly applies to patients with essential hypertension. Unlike patients who suffer from psychologic problems such as phobia or psychosomatic disorders such as tension headache, patients with essential hypertension typically experience little or no discomfort from their condition. Thus, motivation for change is based on physicians' "threats" that serious problems may arise *in the future* if they do not take care of themselves. Given the difficulty in getting patients to take medication reliably, it would not be surprising if prolonged biofeedback training in and of itself had little long-term clinical value. When the patient with a tension headache reduces his frontalis tension with biofeedback,[10] the reward in terms of relief from pain is relatively immediate and strong; unfortunately, the hypertensive patient experiences little of this.

Further discussion and examples of these and related issues can be found in Schwartz[30,31] and Shapiro.[35]

VOLUNTARY CONTROL OF DIASTOLIC PRESSURE IN ESSENTIAL HYPERTENSION

Based on the findings for systolic blood pressure, in collaboration with H. Benson at the Boston City Hospital, we have recently completed a study using biofeedback for diastolic pressure in seven patients diagnosed with essential hypertension. The basic constant cuff pressure system was employed, although the Korotkoff sound was replaced with cuff oscillations[3] to improve across-session comparisons within subjects. Each patient was studied for either 15 or 20 separate sessions. No instructions or feedback were given during the first five sessions (resting base-line period). During the next five sessions, the patients were asked to "think pleasant thoughts and relax" in order to lower their pressure and they were rewarded for total decrease in pressure at the end of the sessions. Again, no feedback was employed. However, during the next five sessions, information about the level of average blood pressure was fed back to the patients after *each* cuff inflation, and monetary reward was directly related to the decrease in median diastolic pressure. Hence, rather than giving feedback for phasic diastolic changes, tonic changes in level were used instead. In these five sessions, the patients were informed only about decreases in pressure. In the final five sessions, information about increases as well as decreases in tonic diastolic pressure was provided.

The results for these patients proved to be discouraging. Compared to the resting condition average of 102 mm Hg, the remaining three conditions of the experiment yielded average pressures of 104, 102, and 102 mm Hg, respectively. Only one of the patients responded positively, showing a progressive reduction in diastolic blood pressure from 99–85 mm Hg.

Although it is possible to argue that the feedback and reward procedure was not optimal, this is tempered by the fact that *within*-session decreases during the two feedback conditions yielded statistically significant decreases in diastolic pressure of 5 mm Hg. This is comparable to the within-session differences in systolic pressure found in the previous patient group.[6] The latter group showed across-session tonic effects as well. Further, the within-session decreases observed in patients given diastolic-level feedback were twice the magnitude as the within-session decreases observed in normal subjects given diastolic phasic binary feedback.[37] Although other hypotheses can be offered, the one favored at the moment is that in chronic hypertension, diastolic pressure becomes relatively fixed due to chronic changes in the vascular beds leading to increased peripheral resistance. To the extent that systolic pressure is still governed in part by sympathetic nervous system activity resulting in increased cardiac contractility, this neural component may be more readily self-regulated through biofeedback techniques. If substantiated by hemodynamic studies, this would suggest that biofeedback (and other techniques) aimed at lowering sympathetic activity in labile hypertensive patients with increased cardiac output may be the most fruitful direction in which to move.

THE PLACE OF BIOFEEDBACK IN ESSENTIAL HYPERTENSION TREATMENT

If biofeedback is conceptualized as but one possible procedure in therapy, then its potential role can be viewed in perspective. It is now apparent that the procedure is only as "powerful" as the patient allows it to be. Further, to the degree that hypertension is mediated by complex factors including genetics, diet, smoking, behavioral and social stress, plus maladaptive coping mechanisms on the part of the patient, it becomes clear that voluntary control of pressure *per se* will in most cases be limited.

Physiologically, early hypertension is associated with increased cardiac output.[13] From the behavioral side, Gutmann and Benson[15] suggest that the pattern of responses in labile hypertension reflects a repeatedly activated "fight or flight" reaction, related to stressful environmental events that require continuous behavioral adjustment. This preparation for somatic action is not unlike anticipation of active exercise,[27] and not surprisingly it involves increased muscle tension in preparation for aggression or withdrawal. Clinicians have noted that patients with essential hypertension appear as a group to be overly inhibited in expression of anger and anxiety,[1] and these individual differences continue to emerge in current personality research,[28] although writers disagree as to their etiologic significance because of the present lack of prospective studies.[15] Inducing attitudes of constantly being on guard for danger leads to increased pressure (see Graham[14]). Hokanson and colleagues[18] have empirically demonstrated that if normal subjects are angered, their pressure rises and remains high unless they are able to express their aggression. This observation is consistent with cardiovascular research showing that isometric tension leads to sustained elevations in pressure, while isotonic action has less of a pressure-increasing effect, and sometimes may lead to a relative decrease in pressure.[25] Also consistent with this is the common clinical observation that exercise programs (e.g., jogging) sometimes have beneficial effects on high blood pressure, although little systematic research has been performed to date evaluating these claims.

Based on these observations, it would seem fruitful to explore techniques attempting to (1) reduce sympathetic activity in aggressive–anxiety situations by teaching patients to relax somatically; (2) teach patients how to recognize anger–fear situations and express their feelings in a psychologically and physiologically adaptive fashion; and (3) teach patients how to possibly avoid such situations, or change their environment so as to minimize them. Concerning the first factor, techniques include progressive relaxation,[19] autogenic training,[26] certain forms of yoga,[12] and transcendental meditation,[5,7] all of which claim to produce general relaxation that leads to reductions in high blood pressure. In addition, techniques like transcendental meditation claim to reduce anxiety and aggressive tendencies as well, and Schwartz and Goleman have recently found evidence for these changes in the personality of meditators (unpublished data). Of course, direct biofeedback training for muscle relaxation could be very useful in lowering high blood pressure, as recently observed by Mueller and Love (unpublished data).

Concerning the second factor, desensitization procedures and particularly assertive training[46] might be efficiently used to help patients learn how to express their aggressive feelings. Modeling and role-playing situations[2] might also be used to extend this further. To the extent that meditation techniques actually improve one's ability to recognize one's feelings and those of others,[24] these procedures might provide additional benefits. As for the last factor, this requires a change in the patient's motivation and life-style, and various forms of behavioral and verbal psychotherapy might be useful.

Where then does blood pressure biofeedback *per se* come in? This becomes an empirical question. Our hypothesis is that a combined treatment approach (e.g., using both relaxation training *and* direct blood pressure control techniques) may be better than either alone to the extent that the latter directs one's attention to the aberrant system and possibly increases one's awareness and control of it,[9] although it is possible that relaxation alone may be sufficient. Here, the feedback is being used primarily in a "control" sense to help the person develop more direct control over his blood pressure.

On the other hand, biofeedback can also be used as information or as a "monitor," not to be directly controlled but rather as an indicant of success in other spheres. Schwartz[30] has noted that in the same way that a scale helps the obese patient and therapist evaluate success in controlling food intake and/or exercise in order to reduce weight, so can biofeedback be used for pressure changes. By means of the feedback, the patient can learn to recognize what kinds of thoughts, feelings, situations, and actions lead to increased pressure, and how successful he is in changing his life-style and/or environment in order to reduce the pressure. Although it is difficult and expensive to accurately measure pressures in ambulatory patients (e.g., Hinman et al.[17]), less sophisticated procedures might be usefully employed, such as having patients keep track of their pressures throughout the day using a simple self-administered sphygmomanometer procedure. In this way, the patient can learn to utilize any cognitive or somatic "mediator" at his disposal to help him control his pressure.

In his recent textbook, Lachman[23] suggests that some of the major goals of psychotherapy with psychosomatic disorders are as follows:

(1) To help the individual recognize the role of emotion in the development and precipitation of illness generally and of his illness in particular.

(2) To help the individual identify particular—or at least probable—emotion-arousing situations and conflicts that operate for him.

(3) To assist the patient in acquiring control over overt activities associated with emotional arousal. This includes not only training the individual to recognize emotional situations, but also training him to avoid such situations and, if they are encountered, to deal constructively with them. It also includes directing overt behavior toward reducing or dissipating the energy resources and other physiological products generated by emotional reactivity, and directing behavior toward constructive activities and away from destructive responses.

(4) To achieve modification in amplitude, duration, and frequency of deviations of autonomic reactions from pathogenic values to normal or optimal levels.

(5) To help the individual to acquire, insofar as possible, direct control of his own autonomic reactions. (pp. 177–178)

Traditionally, biofeedback has been seen as primarily affecting the fifth goal. It is suggested that feedback can be used in the other four goals as well. However, it would appear that for psychosomatic problems—especially for disorders such as hypertension—combined procedures attacking the problem at many levels will be necessary to produce meaningful and long-lasting clinical effects.

ACKNOWLEDGMENT

We thank H. Benson for his helpful comments and S. Cronan for typing the manuscript.

REFERENCES

1. Alexander F: Psychosomatic Medicine: Its Principles and Applications. New York, Norton, 1950

2. Bandura A: Principles of Behavior Modification. New York, Holt, Rinehart & Winston, 1969

3. Benson H: Methods of blood pressure recording: 1733 to 1971, in Onesti G, Kim KE, Moyer JH (eds): Hypertension: Mechanisms and Management. New York, Grune & Stratton, (in press)

4. Benson H, Herd JA, Morse WH, et al: Behavioral induction of arterial hypertension and its reversal. Am J Physiol 217:30, 1969

5. Benson H, Rosner BA, Marzetta BR: Decreased systolic blood pressure in hyper-

tensive subjects who practiced meditation (abstract). J Clin Invest (in press)

6. Benson H, Shapiro D, Tursky B, et al: Decreased systolic blood pressure through operant conditioning techniques in patients with essential hypertension. Science 173:740, 1971

7. Benson H, Wallace K: Decreased blood pressure in hypertensive patients who practiced meditation (abstract). Circulation 46:II-130, 1972

8. Braunwald E, Epstein SE, Glick G, et al: Relief of angina pectoris by electrical stimulation of the carotid-sinus nerves. N Engl J Med 227:1278, 1967

9. Brener J: A general model of voluntary control applied to the phenomena of learned cardiovascular change, in Obrist PA, Black AH, Brener J, et al (eds): Cardiovascular Psychophysiology. Chicago, Aldine (in press)

10. Budzynski T, Stoyva J, Adler C: Feedback-induced muscle relaxation: Application to tension headache. J Behav Ther Exp Psychiatry 1:205, 1970

11. Crider A, Schwartz GE, Shnidman SR: On the criteria for instrumental autonomic conditioning: A reply to Katkin and Murray. Psychol Bull 71:455, 1969

12. Datey KK, Deshmuk SN, Dalvi CP, et al: "Shavasan": A Yogic exercise in the management of hypertension. Angiology 20:325, 1969

13. Eich RH, Cuddy RP, Smulyan H, et al: Hemodynamics in labile hypertension. Circulation 34:299, 1966

14. Graham DT: Psychosomatic medicine, in Greenfield HS, Sternbach RA (eds): Handbook of Psychophysiology. New York, Holt, Rinehart & Winston, 1972

15. Gutmann MC, Benson H: Interaction of environmental factors and systemic arterial blood pressure: A review. Medicine 50:543, 1971

16. Herd JA, Morse WH, Kelleher RT, et al: Arterial hypertension in the squirrel monkey during behavioral experiments. Am J Physiol 217:24, 1969

17. Hinman AT, Engel BT, Bickford AF: Portable blood pressure recorder: Accuracy and preliminary use in evaluating intradaily variations in pressure. Am Heart J 63:663, 1962

18. Hokanson JE, Burgess M, Cohen MF: Effects of displaced aggression on systolic blood pressure. J Abnorm Soc Psychol 67:214, 1963

19. Jacobson E: Progressive Relaxation. Chicago, Univ of Chicago Pr, 1938

20. Kannel WB, Dawber TR, Kagan A, et al: Factors of risk in the development of coronary heart disease. Ann Intern Med 55:33, 1961

21. Kannel WB, Schwartz MJ, McNamara PM: Blood pressure risk of coronary heart disease: The Framingham study. Dis Chest 56:43, 1969

22. Katkin ES, Murray EN: Instrumental conditioning of autonomically mediated behavior: Theoretical and methodological issues. Psychol Bull 70:52, 1968

23. Lachman SJ: Psychosomatic Disorders: A Behavioristic Interpretation. New York, Wiley, 1972

24. Lesh TV: Zen meditation and the development of empathy in counselors. J Hum Psychol 10:39, 1970

25. Lind AR, Taylor SH, Humphreys PW, et al: The circulatory effects of sustained voluntary muscle contraction. Clin Sci 27:229, 1964

26. Luthe W: Autogenic training: Method, research and application in medicine. Am J Psychother 17:174, 1963

27. Obrist PA, Webb RA, Sutterer JR, et al: The cardiac–somatic relationship: Some reformulations. Psychophysiology 6:569, 1970

28. Pilowsky I, Spalding D, Shaw J, et al: Hypertension and personality. Psychosom Med 35:50, 1973

29. Rosenthal R: Experimenter Effects in Behavioral Research. New York, Appleton-Century-Crofts, 1966

30. Schwartz GE: Biofeedback as therapy: Some theoretical and practical issues. Am Psychol 28:666, 1973

31. Schwartz GE: Toward a theory of voluntary control of response patterns in the cardiovascular system, in Obrist PA, Black AH, Brener J, et al (eds): Cardiovascular Psychophysiology. Chicago, Aldine (in press)

32. Schwartz GE: Voluntary control of human cardiovascular integration and differentiation through feedback and reward. Science 175:90, 1972

33. Schwartz GE, Shapiro D, Tursky B: Learned control of cardiovascular integration in man through operant conditioning. Psychosom Med 33:57, 1971

34. Schwartz GE, Shapiro D, Tursky B: Self-control of patterns of human diastolic blood pressure and heart rate through feedback and reward (abstract). Psychophysiology 9:270, 1972

35. Shapiro D: Operant-feedback control of human blood pressure: Some clinical issues, in Obrist PA, Black AH, Brener J, et al (eds): Cardiovascular Psychophysiology. Chicago, Aldine (in press)

36. Shapiro D, Schwartz GE: Biofeedback and visceral learning: Clinical applications. Semin Psychiatry 4:171, 1972

37. Shapiro D, Schwartz GE, Tursky B: Control of diastolic blood pressure in man by feedback and reinforcement. Psychophysiology 9:296, 1972

38. Shapiro D, Tursky B, Gershon E, et al: Effects of feedback and reinforcement on the control of human systolic blood pressure. Science 163:588, 1969

39. Shapiro D, Tursky B, Schwartz GE: Control of blood pressure in man by operant conditioning. Circ Res 26, 27:27 (Suppl 1), 1970

40. Shapiro D, Tursky B, Schwartz GE: Differentiation of heart rate and blood pressure in man by operant conditioning. Psychosom Med 32:417, 1970

41. Sirota A, Schwartz GE, Shapiro D: Effects of feedback control of heart rate on judgments of electric shock intensity (abstract), in Shapiro D, Barber TX, DiCara LV, et al (eds): Biofeedback and Self Control 1972: An Aldine Annual on the Self Regulation of Physiological Processes and Consciousness. Chicago, Aldine, 1973

42. Tursky B: The indirect recording of human blood pressure, in Obrist PA, Black AH, Brener J, et al (eds): Contemporary Trends in Cardiovascular Psychophysiology. Chicago, Aldine (in press)

43. Tursky B, Shapiro D, Schwartz GE: Automated constant cuff-pressure system for measuring average systolic and diastolic blood pressure in man. IEEE Trans Biomed Eng 19: 271, 1972

44. United States Department of Health, Education and Welfare, Vital Statistics, vol 2, part A. Washington, DC, Government Printing Office, 1967, p 1

45. Walsh DH: Effects of instructional set, reinforcement and individual differences in EEG alpha feedback training (abstract), in Shapiro D, Barber TX, DiCara LV, et al (eds): Biofeedback and Self Control 1972: An Aldine Annual on the Self Regulation of Physiological Processes and Consciousness. Chicago, Aldine, 1973

46. Wolpe J: Psychotherapy by Reciprocal Inhibition. Stanford, Conn, Stanford Univ Pr, 1958

Self-Control of Cardiac 30
Functioning: A Promise as Yet Unfulfilled

Edward B. Blanchard and Larry D. Young

The research in the operant conditioning or self-control of four cardiac functions, heart rate level, heart rate variability, blood pressure, and cardiac arrhythmias, is reviewed. Although the fact of the self-control of these functions seems well established, with few exceptions the magnitude of change is statistically significant rather than clinically significant. A few studies, all involving numerous training sessions, have reported large magnitude changes. Several methodological issues are raised and discussed. Finally, alternative modes of achieving self-control of cardiac function, such as progressive relaxation and Yoga exercises are discussed.

Since the mid-1960s an increasing number of articles on the topic of the operant conditioning and/or establishment of self-control of cardiovascular processes in humans have appeared in the literature. These articles hold out the promise, either implicitly or explicitly, of being able to treat cardiovascular disorders by psychological, rather than pharmacological, means. However, a critical examination of this literature, which is the principal purpose of the present article, reveals that, for the most part, this promise is, as yet, unfulfilled. With rare exception, the results are reported for changes in cardiovascular functioning of normal subjects instead of patients and the magnitude of change reported has been of a *statistically* significant, rather than *clinically* significant, magnitude.

The research is summarized in terms of the four cardiovascular responses studied, with particular emphasis on the magnitude of change obtained. From this summarization, several methodological issues become apparent and are subsequently discussed.

HEART RATE

In Table 1 are summarized the studies involving change in heart rate as the dependent variable. Omitted from this table, and from intensive consideration by this review, are studies by Shearn (1962), Frazier (1966), and Brener (1966), all of which used a shock avoidance procedure. Basically these studies allowed the subject to avoid mild but painful electrical shocks by emitting a heart rate of the appropriate magnitude. These studies, which did show that subjects could learn some degree of heart rate control, are omitted because such a paradigm was not thought to be relevant for clinical practice.

Inspection of Table 1 reveals that each experimenter has tended to use his own individual method of determining if subjects can change their heart rate. Although, with three exceptions, the magnitude of the change in heart rate achieved is quite small, ranging 1–7 beats per minute, nevertheless, it seems fairly well established that small, but statistically significant, changes in heart rate can

[1] Preparation of this manuscript was supported in part by Grant 1R01HL14906-01 from the National Heart and Lung Institute, Robert W. Scott, principal investigator. The authors wish to thank W. Stewart Agras and Mischel Hersen for their critical comments on earlier versions of this manuscript.

[2] Requests for reprints should be sent to Edward B. Blanchard, Psychiatry Department, University of Mississippi Medical Center, Jackson, Mississippi 39216.

TABLE 1

SUMMARY OF SELF-CONTROL OF HEART RATE

Authors	Desired response	Independent variables						Controls	Results
		Reinforcement	Feedback type	Subjects informed of response	Trial length	Trials per session	Number of sessions		Magnitude of heart rate change
Engel & Hansen, 1966	Decrease HR	3¢ per second of correct response	Binary visual	No	25 minutes	1	6	Yoked	E: −.5 BPM (range: 2.6 to −2.6 BPM) C: 5.6 BPM
Engel & Chism, 1967	Increase HR	3¢ per second of correct response	Binary visual	No	25 minutes	1	6	Yoked	E: 5.9 BPM (range: 4.2 to 9.8 BPM) C: 3.0 BPM
Levene, Engel, & Pearson, 1968	Alternately increase and decrease HR	None	Binary visual	No	1 minute	25	Varied from 2–4 (until response was learned)	None	E: 4.8 BPM on increase trials (2 of 5 subjects showed consistent alternation) −2.5 BPM on decrease trials
Brener & Hothersall, 1966	Alternately increase and decrease HR	None	Binary auditory	No	50 IBIs (50 seconds)	8	1	None	E: HR > base line on 85% of beats on increase trials. HR < base line on 55% of beats on decrease trials (HR < base line on 80% of beats n post decrease trial)

Note. Abbreviations: E = experimental, C = control, BPM = beats per minute, HR = heart rate, IBI = interbeat interval.

Table 1—(*Continued*)

Authors	Desired response	Independent variables			Trial length	Trials per session	Number of sessions	Controls	Results
		Reinforcement	Feedback type'	Subjects informed of response					
Brener & Hothersall, 1967	Alternately increase and decrease HR	None	Binary auditory	No	50 IBIs (50 seconds)	22	2	None	E: 8–10 BPM difference between increase and decrease trials
Brener, Kleinman & Goesling, 1969	Alternately increase and decrease HR	None	None	Yes	50 IBIs (50 seconds)	29	1	None	E: 1–3 BPM difference between increase and decrease trials
	Alternately increase and decrease HR without feedback	None	Binary auditory for 100%, 50%, and 0% of trials	Yes	50 IBIs (50 seconds)	18	2	None	100% feedback significantly better (by 2–3 BPM difference between increase and decrease trials) than 0% feedback; 100% feedback showed 10 BPM difference at second trial; second session performance significantly better than first session
Johns, 1970	Increase and decrease HR	None	Binary auditory	E: Yes	70 seconds	19	1		E: raise: 4.6 BPM; lower: no change

Table 1—(*Continued*)

Authors	Independent variables							Controls	Results
	Desired response	Reinforcement	Feedback type	Subjects informed of response	Trial length	Trials per session	Number of sessions		Magnitude of heart rate change
				C1: Yes C2: No C3: No				C1: Information no feedback. C2: No information-feedback. C3: No information-no feedback	C1: raise: no change; lower: −2.3 BPM C2: no change C3: no change
Finley, 1971	Decrease HR	None	Proportional visual	No	5 minutes	11	1	Inaccurate feedback	E: −1.7 BPM feedback versus no feedback E versus C: −1.5 BPM
Sroufe, 1971	Increase HR	None	Proportional visual	Yes	5 minutes	3	1	None	E: 10 BPM for shallow versus deep respiratory volume
Peters, Scott, & Gillespie, 1971	Increase HR Decrease HR	Contingent commercial television	None	No	20 minutes	1	13 10	Single subje Single subject	19 BPM −19 BPM
Headrick, Feather, & Wells, 1971	Alternately increase and decrease HR	None	Proportional auditory	No	1 minute	10	1	None	E: raise: 3.3 BPM; lower: no change
	Increase and decrease HR	None	Proportional visual	Yes	1 minute	1	12	Single subject	E: raise: 30 BPM; lower: −5 BPM
Bergman & Johnson, 1971	Increase and decrease HR	None	None	Only experimental subjects	6 IBIs (5 seconds)	30	1	Uninformed subjects	raise: E>C, +1.5 BPM lower: no difference E versus C

Table 1—(*Continued*)

Authors	Independent variables								Results
	Desired response	Reinforcement	Feedback type	Subjects informed of response	Trial length	Trials per session	Number of sessions	Controls	Magnitude of heart rate change
Blanchard, Young & McLeod, 1972	Increase and decrease HR	None	Proportional visual	Yes	1 minute	10	1	None	Low aware subjects could raise (2.9 BPM) and lower (−2.8 BPM) HR from own base line
Blanchard & Young 1972	Increase and decrease HR	None	Proportional visual and proportional auditory	Yes	1 minute	8	2	No feedback	E combined: raise: +4.2 BPM; C.3 BPM; lower: −3.3 BPM C −2.2 BPM
Scott, Blanchard, Edmunson, & Young, 1972	Increase HR	Contingent commercial television or 1¢/10 second correct response	Binary visual	No, then yes	20 minutes	1	34	Single subject	16 BPM with contingent money
	Decrease HR			Yes			52		−16 BPM, decided clinical improvement 30 BPM
	Increase HR			No			18		
Stephens, Harris, & Brady, 1972	Increase and decrease HR	1¢/second of correct response	Proportional visual and proportional auditory	Yes	5 or 30 minutes	8 or 1	17	Single subject	Increase=23 BPM decrease=5 BPM
					5 or 60 minutes	4 or 1	18		Increase=24 BPM
					5 minutes	8	10		Increase=15 BPM decrease=6 BPM
					5 or 60 minutes	8 or 1	12		Increase=29 BPM

Table 1—*(Continued)*

Authors	Desired response	Reinforcement	Feedback type	Independent variables Subjects informed of response	Trial length	Trials per session	Number of sessions	Controls	Results Magnitude of heart rate change
Bergman & Johnson, 1972	Increase HR	None	Binary visual for half of subjects in all groups E_1 = none E_2 = heart sounds	E_1 and E_2 = yes C = no	20 seconds	30	1	Uninformed, no feedback	Binary visual feedback ineffective as reinforcer; informed, instructed subjects E_1 & E_2 > C: 1.8 BPM E_1 = E_2

be obtained through giving subjects feedback or reinforcement. However, these changes, though of sufficient magnitude to be statistically significant, are not clinically significant. For the purposes of this review, a change in response is considered to be clinically significant if it is equal to either 20% of the base rate or, in the case of an abnormally high response, the change is such as to return the response to the normal range.

The three studies which have demonstrated large magnitude changes in heart rate include a single subject whom Headrick, Feather, and Wells (1971) ran for 14 sessions and who demonstrated within-trial increases in heart rate of 30 beats per minute for the short 1-minute trial. Recently Stephens, Harris, and Brady (1972) have reported on four normal subjects who were run under a complex combination of feedback and reinforcement conditions for 10–18 sessions of trials varying 5–60 minutes. In all four subjects clinically significant within-trial increases in heart rate were obtained, ranging 15–29 beats per minute; moreover, two of the subjects were able to decrease their heart rate 5–8 beats per minute from base line. A final study by Scott et al. (1972)[3] reported clinically significant increases in heart rate of 16 and 25 beats per minute in two normal subjects which were maintained over three consecutive daily sessions. More importantly, a stable (over daily sessions) 16 beats per minute decrease in heart rate was obtained in a patient suffering from tachycardia. Coincident with the decrease in heart rate (in the latter subject) were several clinical improvements including obtaining gainful employment. This last case is the only reported direct clinical application of the studies of heart rate conditioning to date.

The methodological issues and conflicts which have arisen in this area are presented next.

Operant Conditioning versus Self-Control

The first issue is one of terminology, yet it extends beyond mere semantics. Engel and

[3] R. W. Scott, E. B. Blanchard, E. Edmundson, & L. D. Young. An improved shaping procedure for clinical cardiac control. Paper presented at Southeastern Psychological Association meeting, Atlanta, 1972.

his associates refer to their operations as operant conditioning. In addition to visual feedback, their subjects were given small sums of money for accumulated experimental time during which their heart rate was in the appropriate direction relative to a criterion heart rate. Stephens et al. (1972) followed a similar procedure.

Most of the other studies of heart rate change are described in terms of self-control established through external sensory feedback. It is possible, of course, to construe all of these studies as examples of operant conditioning in which the reinforcement is knowledge of having successfully emitted the correct response. On the other hand, it is equally possible to construe the reinforcement, especially that used by Bergman and Johnson (1972), in informational terms as binary feedback, since subjects receive reinforcement if they are correct and do not receive it if they are not making the correct response.

If one considers knowledge of results to be a reinforcer, feedback and reinforcement are inextricably confounded in the feedback studies. Therefore, it is not possible to settle the question by merely giving one group of subjects feedback and a second group reinforcement, and then comparing their performance. However, it would be possible to determine if the reinforcement used by Engel has an effect above that achieved by feedback by comparing the performance of groups of subjects run in Engel's paradigm with and without monetary reinforcement.

Type of Feedback

There are two dimensions in the classification of types of feedback used. The first is sensory modality. Feedback has been given to subjects by either auditory or visual means, or by both, with no apparent rationale given for preferring one mode to the other. Blanchard and Young (1972), in their study of the relative efficacy of these two modes, made both within- and between-subject comparisons, and found no statistical advantage for one sensory modality over the other. Thus it would seem that the decision as to which sensory modality one should use, particularly in a clinical procedure, must rest on factors other than efficacy.

In describing the second classification dimension, we have introduced some new terminology which may require explanation. By *binary* feedback we refer to a situation such as that in studies by Engel and his associates and by Brener and his associates wherein the subject's heart rate in terms of interbeat intervals, the reciprocal of heart rate, is compared to some criterion on a beat-by-beat basis. After each comparison, the subject is automatically informed as to whether or not he has met or exceeded the criterion by the presence or absence of the feedback signal, respectively. This class of feedback has been delivered in either the auditory mode (Brener, Kleinman, & Goesling, 1969) or the visual mode (Engel & Chism, 1967b; Engel & Hansen, 1966).

By *proportional* feedback, we refer to a situation such as that in studies by Finley (1971), Sroufe (1971), Blanchard et al. (1972) in which the subject is provided with direct knowledge of heart rate on a beat-by-beat basis. With this kind of feedback, the subject is told not only if he is right or wrong as in binary feedback, but also by how much. At the time of this review no one has compared binary and proportional feedback with regard to relative efficacy.

Knowledge of Response by the Subject

Whether or not the subjects should be informed of the particular response which they are to change is an issue in the field of heart rate control which provokes almost as much mixed opinion as the particular feedback arrangement to use. From Table 1 one can see that researchers are fairly well divided as to whether or not to inform the subjects of the nature of the response. For example, Brener changed his policy on informing the subjects: in his first two studies (Brener & Hothersall, 1966, 1967) the subjects were not informed; in his later study (Brener et al., 1969) they were informed.

This difference of opinion seems to date back to the early work of Engel and his associates. For reasons which are unclear in their reports, they elected not to inform subjects what response was related to the feedback and reinforcement. Engel and Hansen (1966) found, post hoc, that subjects who did not correctly infer the response that was related to the feedback and reinforcement contingency showed evidence of learning the heart-rate-slowing response whereas four of their five "nonlearners" correctly guessed that heart rate was the response. In a second study (Engel & Chism, 1967b) although all five subjects showed evidence of heart rate speeding, four of the five subjects did not know the nature of the response.

Bergman and Johnson (1972) have taken a step toward resolving this issue by treating awareness of the response as an independent variable. Of two groups of subjects receiving no feedback of heart rate, those informed of the response raised it significantly higher ($\Delta \bar{X} = 1.8$ beats per minute) than uninformed subjects trying to control an unspecified response. Interestingly, a third group of subjects who were both informed and given feedback in the form of heart sounds did no better than the informed, no-feedback subjects.

One would hope that further research in this area will show that knowledge of the response being changed, at the very least, has no detrimental effect since in a clinical application of these procedures one would prefer to be able to inform patients fully about the procedure.

Types of Control Groups

Several different policies on control groups have been followed in these studies. One policy has been to use no formal control group, but instead to use subjects as their own controls by comparing heart rate during experimental trials to that recorded during some other period. This within-subject control policy was followed by Blanchard, Young, and McLeod, 1972; Brener and Hothersall, 1966, 1967; Brener et al., 1969; Headrick et al., 1971; Levene, Engel, and Pearson, 1968; and Stephens et al., 1972.

A second policy on control groups, which has been followed by Engel and Hansen (1966) and Engel and Chism (1967b), is the use of yoked controls. In this procedure the control subject receives the same feedback signal as the experimental subject to whom he is yoked. A similar form of false feedback has been used by Finley (1971).

Church (1964) has pointed out the statistical and methodological fallacies inherent in the use of yoked controls. Examination of the results for subjects given some form of false feedback reveals that the performance of these yoked control subjects tends to deteriorate, that is, their responses are in the wrong direction. For example, in the study of heart-rate-slowing by Engel and Hansen (1966) the control subjects achieved a mean increase in heart rate of 5.6 beats per minute. Furthermore, Finley's (1971) control subjects showed an increased heart rate ($\Delta \bar{X} = .8$ beats per minute) when they received false feedback as contrasted to times when they received no feedback. Comparisons of changes in heart rate for experimental and control subjects thus yield spuriously large effects because of capitalizing on differences which include the deterioration of the controls.

The appropriate control condition would be one in which subjects receive the same instructions as the experimental subjects but no feedback. The inclusion of an instructed, no-feedback control has been followed by Blanchard and Young (1972), Bergman and Johnson (1972), Brener et al. (1969), Johns (1970), and Sroufe (1971).

Changes in Heart Rate in the Absence of Feedback or Reinforcement

The use of a no-feedback condition enables one to detect if subjects can significantly change their heart rate in the absence of external feedback or reinforcement. The results on this point are mixed. Bergman and Johnson (1971) found both significant increases and decreases for very brief (4–6 seconds) trials in the absence of any feedback. In a later study, described above, Bergman and Johnson (1972) found that subjects instructed to increase heart rate but given no feedback did as well as similarly instructed subjects who received a form of auditory feedback.

Although the subjects of Brener et al. (1969) who received feedback on 100% of the trials showed significantly greater heart rate control than those subjects who received no feedback, the latter group did show a small ($\Delta \bar{X} = 2.4$ beats per minute) but significant difference between raise and lower trials. However, since the results were reported as differences, no directional statement can be made from their data. Both Johns (1970) and Blanchard and Young (1972) found that their no-feedback control subjects could lower heart rate but could not raise it ($\bar{X} = -2.3$ beats per minute, $\bar{X} = -2.2$ beats per minute, respectively). At this point one cannot conclude definitely that feedback enables subjects to change heart rate in either direction more than subjects who are similarly instructed but receive no feedback.

Another way of viewing this question is to examine how well subjects who have been trained to control heart rate with feedback can control their heart rate in the absence of feedback. This is a point of considerable clinical significance since transfer of the self-control that patients learn in an experimental setting to their natural environment is essential. Brener et al. (1969) found significantly greater generalized self-control for subjects given feedback on 100% of trials than to subjects given no feedback.

Sroufe (1971), working primarily with heart rate variability (to be discussed later), has achieved similar results. His subjects, who were taught to control heart rate variability through paced respiration and who were given proportional visual feedback, showed significant transfer of self-control to a no-feedback state after only a brief (5-minute) training period.

Respiratory Effects

An issue in the field of self-control of cardiac function surrounded by much controversy is the relative importance of mediational variables. Although mediation by means of cognitive or unspecified skeletal muscular mechanisms has been suggested, the primary focus of the mediation controversy has been on the effects of respiratory variables. Experimental procedures designed to answer whether or not the obtained heart rate change resulted from respiratory changes fall into four general categories. Although no investigator failed to monitor respiration, some did little else. Brener and Hothersall (1966) and Brener et al. (1969) report monitoring respiration but do not mention any instructions concerning breathing nor do they report any analyses of the observed differences.

Blanchard and his associates (Blanchard et al., 1972; Blanchard & Young, 1972) and Engel and his associates (Engel & Chism, 1967b; Engel & Hansen, 1966; Levene et al., 1968) gave all subjects in their investigations the explicit instructions not to change their breathing pattern from normal. Again, however, only monitoring and visual inspection of the data were used to reach the conclusions that respiration did not change significantly and that the observed heart rate differences did not result from respiratory changes. Levene et al. (1968) did carry the investigation a step further, however, by teaching two subjects whose respiration rates were variable to duplicate their earlier respiration rate through a pacing technique. This resulted in changes in heart rate variability but not in overall heart rate.

The third approach to the problem, namely, manipulation of respiration rate to insure its constancy during heart rate conditioning sessions, was employed by Brener and Hothersall (1967), Johns (1970), and Sroufe (1969) and basically consists of having subjects pace their respiration to a metronome or rhythmic puff of air set at their adaptation respiration rate. Even with respiration rate held constant experimentally, subjects were still able to alter their heart rate significantly in the appropriate direction. However, as Sroufe pointed out, ability to control heart rate appears to deteriorate with any session when the subject is attempting to control two systems simultaneously.

The final method used (Finley, 1971; Headrick et al., 1971; Hnatiow & Lang, 1965; Lang, Sroufe, & Hastings, 1967) to insure that changes in heart rate were not the result of respiratory differences is to monitor, analyze, and control statistically through covariance analyses any systematic variations in respiration that are found. There have been no significant relationships between heart rate change and respiratory changes with two minor exceptions: Headrick et al. (1971) found a significant correlation between breathing amplitude and heart rate for only one subject; and Hnatiow and Lang's (1965) single significant correlation was between average heart rate deviation during the final no-feedback period and the average inspiration to total cycle ratio for the final feedback period.

A summary of cardiorespiratory relations is not complete without the inclusion of two studies which focus specifically on them. In the earlier investigation (Engel & Chism, 1967a) 20% changes in respiration rate sustained for a 10-minute period did not cause changes in average heart rate. However, an inverse relation was noted between respiration rate and heart rate variability. Sroufe's (1971) series of three experiments was broader in scope since he manipulated respiratory volume in addition to respiration rate. His results confirmed the earlier finding of Engel and Chism (1967a) that changes in respiration rate affect only heart rate variability with increases in respiration rate producing a more stable heart rate. However, changes in respiratory volume affected both the level and variability of heart rate with deeper breathing producing a higher but more variable heart rate.

In light of the evidence, monitoring of respiratory variables seems mandatory for those investigations attempting to show heart rate control. However, monitoring alone is not sufficient; the effects of respiratory changes must be controlled either experimentally or statistically to eliminate this possible source of confounding. As Sroufe (1971) has so aptly observed, "The fact that cardiac control is possible with respiration experimentally controlled merely suggests that subjects *can* control rate independent of respiration, not that respiration is of minor importance [p. 654]."

Sroufe's (1971) research carries several implications and suggestions for subsequent research in the area of heart rate self-control, particularly clinical studies: Since respiration and skeletal muscle activity are more discriminable than cardiac activity, they might profitably be used early in training and gradually faded as the desired response is acquired. As Sroufe (1971) showed, utilization of these or similar techniques improved the transfer of the learned cardiac control from periods where feedback is present to periods where it is absent; ultimately, utilization improved the first step in establishing generalization from the experimental chamber to the natural environment.

HEART RATE VARIABILITY

Lang and his associates have been the principal researchers investigating the self-control of heart rate variability. All of their studies have used the same basic experimental procedure: The experimental subjects are given proportional visual feedback of their heart rate and asked to keep it within ±3 beats per minute of a set point (their mean preexperimental heart rate). Dependent measures are the standard deviation of the distribution of interbeat intervals and time on target (within the ± beats per minute range).

In the first study (Hnatiow & Lang, 1965) experimental subjects performed significantly better than yoked controls who received false feedback and who were told only to track the visual display, with no mention of controlling it.

The second study (Lang, Sroufe, & Hastings, 1967) was a refinement of the first to include additional controls. Subjects in the experimental group again received proportional visual feedback of heart rate, were told what the feedback display represented, and were instructed to try to keep their heart rate within a 6 beat per minute range. Those in one control group received the same instructions but the feedback display of their yoked experimental partner. The other two control groups were not informed concerning what the visual display represented, and were told only to track the visual display.

The experimental group was significantly better at reducing heart rate variability than any of the controls. Of special note are the within-subject analyses which showed that the experimental subjects improved significantly from no-feedback to feedback-available conditions. The control subjects yoked to the experimental subjects, who were also supposed to control heart rate, did poorest, supporting our previous criticism of this control procedure.

In the third study of this series (Sroufe, 1969), subjects again were given either true or false proportional visual feedback of heart rate and told to keep it within a specified range. The purpose of the study was to control for respiration effects and the possibility that subjects were reducing heart rate variability through respiratory means. Thus three groups were taught, over several sessions, to breathe at a fixed rate, while a fourth group had no restrictions placed on their breathing. All subjects received two training sessions before data were collected in a third session of 1-minute trials. Again, subjects given true feedback showed significant reductions in heart rate variability during times it was available compared both to no-feedback periods and to subjects receiving false feedback. For subjects breathing at fixed rates, performance tended to deteriorate over time while no such deterioration was found for subjects not under respiratory restriction.

Interestingly, a final study in this series (Hnatiow, 1971) failed to replicate the early findings of better control by subjects receiving feedback than the yoked controls in spite of using identical equipment and procedures.

To date, Lang and his associates have reported no clinical application of their procedure. In fact, all of their work has been with normal college students.

Blood Pressure

In Table 2 are summarized the studies involving change in blood pressure as the dependent variable.

In all of their blood pressure control studies, Shapiro and his colleagues at Harvard have used the same basic experimental procedure: A subject receives binary feedback, both visual and auditory, as to whether his blood pressure is at or in the appropriate direction away from a criterion blood pressure value on each heart beat; in addition to this sensory feedback, the subject receives a reinforcement of a brief presentation of a slide of either a nude, a landscape, or an indication of small financial reward on some fixed-ratio schedule for a blood pressure response in the appropriate direction.

The method of delivering this feedback involves inflating an arm cuff to a pressure very close to either systolic or diastolic blood pressure, depending on which is of interest, then varying the pressure in small increments and noting the presence or disappearance of Korotkoff sounds within a specified time interval after each heart beat. Feedback delivery is dependent upon the appropriate response. For example, in trying to shape a decrease in systolic blood pressure, feedback would be given the subject if no Korotkoff sound was detected following the R wave of the electrocardiogram. Had a sound been detected, indicating that the systolic pressure was above the cuff pressure, no feedback would be given. Typically subjects are given 25 trials per session with a trial being 50 interbeat intervals long.

As can be seen in Table 2, with the exception of their recently completed clinical trial (Benson, Shapiro, Tursky, & Schwartz, 1971), the magnitude of change in blood pressure has been rather small, averaging less than 1 millimeter of mercrury per trial for subjects who were increasing blood pressure and about 2–3 millimeters of mercury per trial for subjects lowering their blood pressure. Using as an index of the efficacy of their procedure the average blood pressure on the final block of five trials, the average amount of increase in blood pressure has been 1–2 millimeters of mercury while the average decrease in subjects lowering blood pressure has been 4–6 millimeters of mercury.

Despite their impressive series of studies, many of the criticisms previously leveled at the research on self-control of heart rate can be supplied to the blood pressure self-control studies. First and foremost, it is not possible to tell what are the active ingredients in the Shapiro procedure since subjects receive both binary auditory and visual feedback as well as reinforcement on some fixed ratio schedule. Whether reinforcement contributes to the efficacy of the procedure is not known, nor are the relative efficacies of the types of feedback.

A second problem with these studies has been the failure to include a no-feedback control in order to evaluate the efficacy of their combination of procedures over merely instructing subjects to lower their blood pressure. In one study (Shapiro et al., 1970a) a group reinforced on a random basis was included. Results showed that groups reinforced for raising or lowering blood pressures, while different from each other, did not differ from this group which was reinforced randomly.

TABLE 2

SUMMARY OF SELF-CONTROL OF BLOOD PRESSURE

| Authors | Desired response | Reinforcement | Independent variables | | | | | | Controls | Results |
			Feedback	Subjects informed of response	Trial length	Trials per session	Number of sessions		Results: magnitude of blood pressure change
Shapiro, Tursky, Gershon, & Stern, 1969	E_1 = Increase systolic BP E_2 = Decrease systolic BP	Slides of nudes FR 20	Binary auditory & visual	No	65 seconds	25	1	None	E_1: −.8 millimeters Hg $E_1 > E_2$ E_2: −4.8 millimeters Hg
Shapiro, Tursky, & Schwartz, 1970a	E_1 = Increase systolic BP E_2 = Decrease systolic BP	Slides (1/3 nudes, 1/3 landscapes, 1/3 money . . . 10–25¢) FR 20	Binary auditory & visual	No	50 IBI	25	2	Random reinforcement (50% probability for each IBI)	1. E_1: 2.3 millimeters Hg; C: 0 millimeters Hg $E_1 > C = E_2$
	E_1, C, E_2 = Decrease systolic BP								2. E_1: −2.0 millimeters Hg; C: −2.0 millimeters Hg; E_2: −4.5 millimeters Hg. $E_1 = C > E_2$
Shapiro, Tursky, & Schwartz, 1970b	E_1 = Increase HR E_2 = Decrease HR	Slides of nudes FR 20	Binary visual for all subjects plus half received binary auditory & other half proportional auditory	Yes	50 IBI	25	1	None	E_1: HR = .8 BPM; BP = .5 millimeter Hg E_2: HR = 5.0 BPM; BP = −.5 millimeter Hg For BP $E_1 = E_2$
Schwartz, 1972	HR-BP Integration & differentiation	Slides (landscapes, nudes, money) FR 12	Binary auditory & visual	No	50 IBI	25	1	None	HR = BP Integration easier to achieve than HR = BP differentiation

Note. Abbreviations: E = experimental, Hg = mercury, IBI = interbeat interval, HR = heart rate, BP = blood pressure, FR = fixed ratio.

Table 2—(*Continued*)

Authors	Desired response	Reinforcement	Feedback	Subjects informed of response	Trial length	Trials per session	Number of sessions	Controls	Results; magnitude of blood pressure change
Shapiro, Schwartz, & Tursky, 1972	E_1 = Increase diastolic BP; E_2 = Decrease diastolic BP	Slides (landscapes, nudes, money) FR 20	Binary auditory & visual	No	50 IBI	35	1	None	E_1: 7/10 increased BP, $\bar{x}$=4.0 mm. voluntary control maintained in extinction; E_2: 8/10 decreased BP $\bar{x}$= −2.0 mm.
Schwartz, Shapiro, & Tursky, 1971	E_1=Increase HR & Systolic BP; E_2 = Decrease HR & Systolic BP	Slides (landscapes, nudes, money) 5¢/slide FR 12	Binary auditory & visual	No	50 IBI	40	1	None	E_1: HR =1.2 BPM; BP=2.2 millimeters Hg; E_2: HR= −6.0 BPM; BP= −4.8 millimeters Hg; $E_1 > E_2$
Benson, Shapiro, Tursky, & Schwartz, 1971	Decrease systolic BP	Slides (landscapes, nudes, money) 5¢/slide FR 20	Binary auditory & visual	Yes	50 IBI	30	8-34 conditioning sessions $\bar{x}$=21.7	None	$\bar{x}$= −16.5 millimeters Hg (Range: =.9 to −33.8 millimeters Hg)
Brener & Kleinman, 1970	Decrease systolic BP	None	Proportional visual	Yes	50 seconds	20	2	To pay attention to feedback display	E (Session 1): −16 millimeter Hg; (Session 2): −10 millimeter Hg. C (Session 1): No change; (Session 2): No change
Hnatiow, 1971	Decrease systolic BP variability	None	Proportional visual	E Yes C No	5 minutes	3	1	Track display of yoked partner	E=C on blood pressure variability reduction E reduced blood pressure more than C (but this was not the task)

Thus to date, this group of investigators has shown primarily that subjects reinforced for raising blood pressure are different from subjects reinforced for lowering blood pressure.

Despite the methodological problems with these studies, the Shapiro group certainly deserves praise for their pioneering work in this area. Recently they have focused on self-control of diastolic blood pressure (Shapiro et al., 1972) and the degree of integration and differentiation of the cardiovascular system (Schwartz, 1972; Schwartz, Shapiro, & Tursky, 1971). The former line of research, using the same basic experimental paradigm, has shown that diastolic blood pressure can be altered significantly by this procedure and, of much interest from a clinical point of view, that the changes show some degree of stability after the feedback and reinforcement are no longer available. In the latter research area, a fair degree of independence of heart rate and blood pressure have been shown.

The study by Benson et al. (1971) answers one of our major criticisms leveled at the blood pressure self-control research, namely, the exclusive reliance on normal subjects. Benson applied Shapiro's basic blood pressure control procedure to a group of seven hypertensive patients. Their average systolic blood pressure during the final base-line periods was 165 millimeters of mercury. Clinically significant decreases in blood pressure were obtained in five of the seven patients ($\bar{X} = 22.6$ millimeters of mercury).

As with the heart rate studies which showed large scale changes in that response, numerous trials were necessary to obtain this magnitude of change ($\bar{X} = 21.7$ conditioning sessions of 25 trials each). While no data are available on the stability of the change when the feedback was no longer available, or on the degree of transfer of the decreased blood pressure outside of the laboratory, these results are provocative enough to warrant following up and certainly to increase the clinical promise held out by this research.

As can be seen in Table 2 there has been only one important study of blood pressure self-control conducted by an investigator outside of the Shapiro group at Harvard, and that is by Brener and Kleinman (1970). This study, which utilized a form of proportional visual feedback, has several commendable features: The size of the change in blood pressure, approximately 15 millimeters of mercury in the first session and approximately 12 millimeters of mercury in the second, is considerably larger than that reported by Shapiro and his colleagues with normal subjects, and is of a magnitude which could be clinically significant. Second, control subjects who received the same type of feedback of their own blood pressure but were not instructed to change their blood pressure were used and showed no overall change in blood pressure. A further control group is needed, however, in which subjects, who are instructed to try to lower blood pressure, receive no feedback.

The form of feedback used within the classification system presented previously is closest to proportional visual feedback. Subjects were able to view a manometer which continuously displayed pressure in the occluding staff. The cuff pressure, and hence the feedback received by subjects, oscillated about the individual subject's systolic blood pressure. An interesting aspect of this procedure was the taking of blood pressure on the left index finger rather than upper arm. Such a procedure minimizes the problem ischaemia.

The size changes in blood pressure obtained by Brener and Kleinman's procedure are much larger than those obtained by Shapiro and his colleagues in a similar length of time on a similar population of normotensive college-age males. One could speculate that the major reason for this difference is that Brener and Kleinman's subjects received a form of proportional feedback whereas Shapiro's subjects received binary feedback delivered both ·visually and aurally.

CARDIAC ARRHYTHMIAS

Although there have been several brief reports (Engel & Melmon, 1968; Weiss & Engel, 1970) on the operant conditioning of cardiac arrhythmias, most of the data seem to be summarized in one article (Weiss & Engel, 1971). The latter study contains detailed reports on eight patients suffering from premature ventricular contractions who were all treated in approximately the same experimental paradigm.

The paradigm was, for the most part, a replication of the procedures used in Engel's three previous studies. Patients were given binary visual feedback as to whether their heart rate was at or beyond the desired heart rate in the appropriate direction. In this study, contrary to the previous work with normals, patients were fully informed of all the details of the experiment, especially the response being monitored and also were not given monetary rewards for time accumulated in the correct direction. Despite the omission of this tangible reinforcer, the authors still describe their study in terms of "operant conditioning" rather than self-control through feedback.

Most patients were run under four conditions and some under a fifth. These were, in the usual order, heart rate speeding, heart rate slowing, alternately speeding and slowing heart rate for 1–4 minute trials, and then control of heart rate variability. In this final condition, subjects received binary feedback (light onset) when their heart rate stayed within a 10-beat range. The nature of this feedback arrangement also provided subjects with feedback of the occurrence of each premature ventricular contraction. The fifth condition, in which four of the patients were run, consisted of a gradual removal of feedback. Feedback was alternately presented and removed; the initial ratio of 1 minute of feedback to 1 minute without was extended to 1 minute on and 7 minutes off. Interestingly, in this final phase subjects did as well without feedback as with it, indicating that true self-control had been learned.

Four of the eight patients had a significantly reduced frequency of premature ventricular contractions after the training procedure as measured in the ward and at a follow-up 3–21 months afterward. A fifth patient did not have a significant reduction in premature ventricular contractions rate but did learn to recognize their occurrence and was able to control them at home through resting. The other three patients showed no evidence of learning to control premature ventricular contractions.

Total number of training sessions ranged 22–77 with a mean of 57.5. The five cases which can be considered successes all had 47 or more training sessions. Our reanalysis of these results show that improvement is significantly (by $p = .05$, Fisher's exact probability test) related to receiving 47 or more training sessions.

Weiss and Engel deserve commendation for the following two related techiques for extending their procedures into the area of clinical application: first, eliminating the necessity for external feedback to control the cardiac dysfunction, and more importantly, monitoring premature ventricular contraction rate outside the experimental chamber. The degree of generalization observed in this latter procedure is especially encouraging. Generalization of learned control of cardiac functioning to the natural environment, true self-control, is the desired clinical terminal behavior.

There are two obvious criticisms which can be leveled at this otherwise excellent clinical study. The first is the lack of a controlled group of patients who were either untreated or given some equally time-consuming and involving placebo task. This criticism is obviated to some degree because of the prolonged base-line period prior to the experimental phase during which premature ventricular contractions were noted. The documented history of premature ventricular contractions ranged 3 months–8 years with a mean of 3.0 years. Despite this, one would hope that a next step would be a controlled outcome study of the procedure.

The second criticism is the obvious confounding of several aspects of the training procedure. One does not know whether the entire sequence of training procedures is necessary or only part of it. Thus a next step would be to isolate which parts of the training procedure are necessary, facilitative, or superfluous, in order to improve efficiency.

ALTERNATIVE METHODS OF CARDIAC CONTROL

There are at least two additional lines of research which are related to the area of self-control of cardiac function: (*a*) the use of progressive relaxation as developed by Jacobson (1938) and (*b*) the use of various Yogic exercises and related forms of mediation. In both of these a significant degree of change in various cardiac functions has been produced.

Progressive Relaxation

Jacobson (1939) reported on the effects on blood pressure of training in and subsequent use of his system of muscle relaxation. His conclusions, which tended to be more qualitative than quantitative, were that there is a general relation between decreases in blood pressure and decreases in muscle activity as shown by the electromyogram and that training in "progressive relaxation" results in greater decreases in electromyogram activity than self-induced relaxation without training. He presented blood pressure data on 14 normotensive subjects, 9 of whom had been trained in progressive relaxation. These data, both systolic and diastolic blood pressure, were collected after a 15-minute adaptation period during which the subjects rested in a supine position and again after 45 minutes of self-induced relaxation. Analyses of these data by the present authors revealed significant decreases in both systolic blood pressure ($\Delta \bar{X} = 8.0$ millimeters of mercury; $F = 19.9$, $df = 1/12$, $p < .01$) and diastolic blood pressure ($\Delta \bar{X} = 7.8$ millimeters of mercury; $F = 11.5$, $df = 1/12$, $p < .01$), but no differences between the trained and untrained subjects in degree of reduction achieved. It should be noted that the magnitude of change in blood pressure in this study exceeds that reported by Shapiro and his colleagues in any of their studies of normotensive subjects (see Table 2) and compares favorably with the results reported by Brener and Kleinman (1970).

In a second study, Jacobson (1940) reported decreases in heart rate associated with relaxation training. Heart rate was measured initially after a 15-minute adaptation period during which the subjects rested in a supine position and later after 45 minutes of progressive relaxation. The average decrease in heart rate was 6.5 beats per minute. Analysis of this data *by the present authors* shows this change to be highly significant ($t = 5.59$, $p < .001$).

In a more recent study, Paul (1969) reported on physiological changes in college-age females who were treated for 30 minutes by either (a) a brief form of progressive relaxation training, (b) hypnosis induction and suggestions of relaxation, or (c) self-instructed

relaxation. Heart rate data were collected during a 10-minute adaptation period and at the end of training. The progressive relaxation training group showed significantly greater changes in heart rate than the other two groups with reductions of approximately 8 beats per minute occurring in both sessions. It seems possible that Paul's subjects were not completely adapted when the initial heart rate recording was made which could account for part of the magnitude of change.

In a later report Paul and Trimble (1970) compared subjects given training in brief progressive relaxation either by tape recording or by a therapist present in the room. The latter condition led to significantly greater decreases in heart rate; however, the tape-recorded relaxation treatment did result in a group mean decrease in heart rate of approximately 4 beats per minute which is comparable to the results reported by most other investigators.

It thus seems that training in deep muscle relaxation, even of an abbreviated form, can lead to decreases in heart rate comparable to those achieved by most of the studies in the biofeedback area. This finding leads us to speculate that the operant conditioning or self-control procedures are possibly only inefficient methods of teaching subjects to relax.

Yoga

Although many claims of phenomenal degrees of self-control among Yogis had been made, few scientific data were collected on this subject until the 1950s when Wenger and his associates (Wenger & Bagchi, 1961; Wenger, Bagchi, & Anand, 1961) made systematic autonomic recordings from over 50 Yogis in India. In one study of three Yogis who claimed to be able to stop their heart, Wenger et al. (1961) found (a) absence of radial pulse, (b) absence of most heart sounds, (c) blood pressure radically increased, but (d) no stoppage of the heart and, in fact, (e) very little slowing in heart rate. They concluded that these subjects were utilizing thoracic muscle interference with venous return which led to a radical decrease in blood flow.

A fourth Yogi claimed only to be able to slow his heart rate and did so, demonstrating increases in interbeat intervals from a base line of approximately 1.0 second to slightly over 2 seconds for several beats (equivalent to changes in heart rate from 60 beats per minute to 30 beats per minute. The authors concluded that no muscle interference was apparently used; rather, the alterations seemed to be due to vagal innervation.

A similar example of voluntary cardiac arrest was reported by McClure (1959) in the case of a 44-year-old Caucasian male. This patient, who showed no cardiac irregularities, could voluntarily go into cardiac arrest for periods of approximately 5 seconds, increasing the interbeat interval of his heart rate from normally 1.0 second to over 5 seconds. Although the patient did not know the mechanism involved, McClure concluded that it was due to vagal innervation and was entirely unrelated to respiration rate.

Three systematic studies of the effects of Yoga exercises and meditation on cardiac function have recently been reported. Datey, Deshmukh, Dalvi, and Vinekar (1969) studied the effects of training in the Yogic exercise called "Shavasan" on 47 hypertensive patients. The patients, whose original blood pressures were in the range 160–270/90–145, all received training in Shavasan for unspecified lengths of time. The typical training course was described as requiring 3 weeks of daily 30-minute sessions. Results were reported for three groups of patients: (*a*) 10 not on medication; (*b*) 22 whose hypertension was controlled by drugs; and (*c*) 15 whose hypertension was not adequately controlled by drugs. In all cases blood pressure was reported as the diastolic pressure plus one-third of the pulse pressure. For those not on medication blood pressure was reduced in 9 out of 10 cases with the average reduction being 27 millimeters of mercury ($p < .05$). In the second group the effects of training in Shavasan were evaluated in terms of the reduction in patients' drug dosage necessary to keep their blood pressure under control. In 13 of 22 patients, the drug dosage was decreased by 33% or more, with an average reduction for those 13 patients of 68%. In the third group the effects were evaluated in the same fashion and drug dosage was reduced by at least 33% in 6 of 15 patients. This study seems to show that a chronic course of train-

ing in yogic exercise had a clinically significant effect on a majority of the hypertensive patients studied, and would warrant investigation in a controlled-outcome study.

In the first of two studies of similar design Wallace (1970) studied the physiological effects of "transcendental meditation," as taught by the Maharishi Mahesh Yogi. Physiological responses of 15 "normal" college students, who had been practicing "transcendental meditation" for from 6 months to 3 years, were monitored both for 30 minutes prior to a 20–30 minute meditation period and during the latter period. In the five subjects for whom heart rate was measured, an average decrease of 5 beats per minute was observed. It was not stated, however, whether or not the magnitude of change was statistically significant.

In a more elaborate study of similar design, Wallace, Benson, and Wilson (1971) monitored physiological responses of 36 subjects who had been practicing "transcendental meditation" for an average of 29 months. The principal results of comparisons between the meditation period and the 30 minutes immediately preceding, during which subjects were resting comfortably, were significant changes in electroencephalogram and oxygen consumption. There was also a small but significant ($p < .05$) decrease in heart rate ($\Delta \bar{X} = -.3$ beats per minute), but no change in blood pressure.

These studies, though not of the controlled-outcome format in which a "no-treatment" or "attention-placebo" group is monitored, are highly suggestive that Yoga and other Eastern forms of exercise-meditation training can have important clinical application in the field of cardiac self-control. Certainly the changes achieved are of sufficient magnitude to warrant exploring this line of research as well as the ones discussed previously.

CONCLUSIONS

The self-control of several cardiac functions, acceleration, deceleration, and variability of heart rate and increases and decreases in blood pressure, has been amply demonstrated in normal subjects. However, with few notable exceptions the magnitude of change obtained has been small, the duration for which control was manifested has been brief, and the generalization of the changes obtained in the experimental chamber rarely demonstrated. Future research in this area must follow two directions if the promise it holds out is to be fulfilled: (*a*) there is now a need for chronic studies involving many trials to obtain large-scale changes; (*b*) there is also a need for more direct application of this work to clinical populations. Finally, as was pointed out in the final section of this paper, alternative modes of obtaining changes in cardiac functioning such as training in progressive relaxation, transcendental meditation, or various Yoga exercises, may prove to be more fruitful approaches to obtaining clinically significant changes than the operant-conditioning–feedback techniques reviewed in the main body of this paper. Only comparative outcome studies, conducted on a chronic basis, can answer this question, but certainly it is deserving of an answer.

REFERENCES

BENSON, H., SHAPIRO, D., TURSKY, B., & SCHWARTZ, G. E. Decreased systolic blood pressure through operant conditioning techniques in patients with essential hypertension. *Science*, 1971, 173, 740–742.

BERGMAN, J. S., & JOHNSON, H. J. The effects of instructional set and autonomic perception on cardiac control. *Psychophysiology*, 1971, 8, 180–190.

BERGMAN, J. S., & JOHNSON, H. J. Sources of information which affect training and raising of heart rate. *Psychophysiology*, 1972, 9, 30–39.

BLANCHARD, E. B., & YOUNG, L. D. Relative efficacy of visual and auditory feedback for self-control of heart rate. *Journal of General Psychology*, 1972, 87, 195–202.

BLANCHARD, E. B., YOUNG, L. D., & McLEOD, P. G. Awareness of heart activity and self-control of heart rate. *Psychophysiology*, 1972, 9, 63–68.

BRENER, J. Heart rate as an avoidance response. *Psychological Record*, 1966, 16, 329–336.

BRENER, J., & HOTHERSALL, D. Heart rate control under conditions of augmented sensory feedback. *Psychophysiology*, 1966, 3, 23–28.

BRENER, J., & HOTHERSALL, D. Paced respiration and heart rate control. *Psychophysiology*, 1967, 4, 1–6.

BRENER, J., & KLEINMAN, R. A. Learned control of decreases in systolic blood pressure. *Nature*, 1970, 226, 1063–1064.

BRENER, J., KLEINMAN, R. A., & GOESLING, W. J. The effects of different exposures to augmented sensory feedback on the control of heart rate. *Psychophysiology*, 1969, 5, 510–516.

CHURCH, R. M. Systematic effect of random error in the yoked control design. *Psychological Bulletin*, 1964, 62, 122–131.

DATEY, K. K., DESHMUKH, S. N., DALVI, C. P., & VINEKAR, S. L. "Shavasan": A yogic exercise in the management of hypertension. *Angiology*, 1969, 20, 325–333.

ENGEL, B. T., & CHISM, R. A. Effect of increases and decreases in breathing rate on heart rate and finger pulse volume. *Psychophysiology*, 1967, 4, 83–89. (a)

ENGEL, B. T., & CHISM, R. A. Operant conditioning of heart rate speeding. *Psychophysiology*, 1967, 3, 418–426. (b)

ENGEL, B. T., & HANSEN, S. P. Operant conditioning of heart rate slowing. *Psychophysiology*, 1966, 3, 176–187.

ENGEL, B. T., & MELMON, L. Operant conditioning of heart rate in patients with cardiac arrhythmias. *Conditional Reflex*, 1968, 3, 130.

FINLEY, W. W. The effect of feedback on the control of cardiac rate. *Journal of Psychology*, 1971, 77, 43–54.

FRAZIER, T. W. Avoidance conditioning of heart rate in humans. *Psychophysiology*, 1966, 3, 188–197.

HEADRICK, M. W., FEATHER, B. W., & WELLS, D. T. Unidirectional and large magnitude heart rate changes with augmented sensory feedback. *Psychophysiology*, 1971, 8, 132–142.

HNATIOW, M. Learned control of heart rate and blood pressure. *Perceptual and Motor Skills*, 1971, 33, 219–226.

HNATIOW, M., & LANG, P. J. Learned stabilization of cardiac rate. *Psychophysiology*, 1965, 1, 330–336.

JACOBSON, E. *Progressive relaxation*, Chicago: University of Chicago Press, 1938.

JACOBSON, E. Variation of blood pressure with skeletal muscle tension and relaxation. *Annals of Internal Medicine*, 1939, 12, 1194–1212.

JACOBSON, E. Variation of blood pressure with skeletal muscle tension and relaxation. II. The heart beat. *Annals of Internal Medicine*, 1940, 13, 1619–1625.

JOHNS, T. R. Heart rate control in humans under paced respiration and restricted movement: The effect of instructions and exteroceptive feedback. *Dissertation Abstracts International*, 1970, 30, 5712–5713.

LANG, P. J., SROUFE, L. A., & HASTINGS, J. E. Effects of feedback and instructional set on the control of cardiac rate variability. *Journal of Experimental Psychology*, 1967, 75, 425–431.

LEVENE, H. I., ENGEL, B. T., & PEARSON, J. A. Differential operant conditioning of heart rate. *Psychosomatic Medicine*, 1968, 30, 837–845.

McCLURE, C. M. Cardiac arrest through volition. *California Medicine*, 1959, 90, 440.

PAUL, G. L. Physiological effects of relaxation training and hypnotic suggestion. *Journal of Abnormal Psychology*, 1969, 74, 425–437.

PAUL, G. L., & TRIMBLE, R. W. Recorded vs. "live" relaxation training and hypnotic suggestion: Comparative effectiveness for reducing physiological arousal and inhibiting stress response. *Behavior Therapy,* 1970, **1,** 285–302.

SCHWARTZ, G. E. Voluntary control of human cardiovascular integration and differentiation through feedback and reward. *Science,* 1972, **175,** 90–93.

SCHWARTZ, G. E., SHAPIRO, D., & TURSKY, B. Learned control of cardiovascular integration in man through operant conditioning. *Psychosomatic Medicine,* 1971, **33,** 57–62.

SHAPIRO, D., SCHWARTZ, G. E., & TURSKY, B. Control of diastolic blood pressure in man by feedback and reinforcement. *Psychophysiology,* 1972, **9,** 296–304.

SHAPIRO, D., TURSKY, B., GERSHON, E., & STERN, M. Effects of feedback and reinforcement on the control of human systolic blood pressure. *Science,* 1969, **163,** 588–590.

SHAPIRO, D., TURSKY, B., & SCHWARTZ, G. E. Control of blood pressure in man by operant conditioning. *Circulation Research,* 1970, **26** (Suppl. 1:27–32.) (a)

SHAPIRO, D., TURSKY, B., & SCHWARTZ, G. E. Differentiation of heart rate and systolic blood pressure in man by operant conditioning. *Psychosomatic Medicine,* 1970, **32,** 417–423. (b)

SHEARN, D. W. Operant conditioning of heart rate. *Science,* 1962, **137,** 530–531.

SROUFE, L. A. Learned stabilization of cardiac rate with respiration experimentally controlled. *Journal of Experimental Psychology,* 1969, **81,** 391–393.

SROUFE, L. A. Effects of depth and rate of breathing on heart rate and heart rate variability. *Psychophysiology,* 1971, **8,** 648–655.

STEPHENS, J. H., HARRIS, A. H., & BRADY, J. V. Large magnitude heart rate changes in subjects instructed to change their heart rates and given exteroceptive feedback. *Psychophysiology,* 1972, **9,** 283–285.

WALLACE, R. K. Physiological effects of transcendental meditation. *Science,* 1970, **167,** 1751–1754.

WALLACE, R. K., BENSON, H., & WILSON, A. F. A wakeful hypometabolic physiologic state. *American Journal of Physiology,* 1971, **221,** 795–799.

WEISS, T., & ENGEL, B. T. Operant conditioning of heart rate in patients with premature ventricular contractions. *Psychosomatic Medicine,* 1971, **33,** 301–321.

WENGER, M. A., & BAGCHI, B. K. Studies of autonomic functions in practitioners of Yoga in India. *Behavioral Science,* 1961, **6,** 312–323.

WENGER, M. A., BAGCHI, B. K., & ANAND, B. K. Experiments in India on "voluntary" control of the heart and pulse. *Circulation,* 1961, **24,** 1319–1325.

(Received April 10, 1972)

Comment on Self-Control 31
of Cardiac Functioning: A Promise
as yet Unfulfilled

Bernard T. Engel

Criticizes Blanchard and Young's definition of a clinically significant heart rate change, indicating that only one tachyarrhythmia—sinus tachycardia—is exclusively a heart rate problem. Based on more current data, it is suggested that the original review should have been subtitled, "A promise met, but whose limits are not yet known."

In their generally scholarly and comprehensive review of studies of cardiac self-control in man, Blanchard and Young (1973) introduced a definition of a clinically significant change of heart rate.[1] They called clinically significant any change in rate which was "equal to either 20% of the base rate or, in the case of an abnormally high response . . . [a] change . . . such as to return the response to the normal range [p. 150]." I hope that these criteria are not adopted in the psychophysiological literature.

The cardiological criteria for tachyarrhythmias are quite precise (Hurst & Logue, 1970)—since Blanchard and Young considered only tachycardia, I will limit my discussion to these arrhythmias. Among all of the tachyarrhythmias only one—sinus tachycardia—can be said to be exclusively a problem of heart rate. All of the other tachyarrhythmias are associated with abnormal sites of origin of impulse formation in the heart. Usually, if the site of impulse formation is corrected to the normal, sinus nodal pacemaker, the heart rate returns to normal *within a single beat*. Only in the case of sinus tachycardia can one even consider a clinically significant effect ex-clusively in terms of heart rate, and in this arrhythmia the clinically significant effect is to reduce heart rate below 100 beats per minute. Incidentally sinus tachycardia, when it occurs without relation to organic heart disease, is a benign arrhythmia which is often normal as in the case of exercise.

It is meaningless to talk of a clinically significant effect in a person who has not been diagnosed as medically ill. Therefore, almost none of the laboratory work on learned control of heart rate in normals can be interpreted as having any clinical significance. The medical importance of this work lies in the fact that it suggested that appropriate clinical studies should be done. In this regard it is unfortunate that the publication lag of the article by Blanchard and Young has been so great. Based upon what I know of the evidence today, a more appropriate subtitle for their review would have been: A promise met, but whose limits are not yet known.

REFERENCES

BLANCHARD, E. B., & YOUNG, L. D. Self-control of cardiac functioning: A promise as yet unfulfilled. *Psychological Bulletin*, 1973, 79, 145–163.

HURST, J. W., & LOGUE, R. B. *The heart.* (2nd ed.) New York: McGraw-Hill, 1970.

(Received April 6, 1973)

[1] Requests for reprints should be sent to Bernard T. Engel, Gerontology Research Center, National Institute of Child Health and Human Development, Baltimore City Hospitals, Baltimore, Maryland 21224.

VII

EEG APPLIED TO EPILEPSY AND SLEEP

Neurophysiologic and Clinical Studies of Sensorimotor EEG Biofeedback Training: Some Effects on Epilepsy

32

M. B. Sterman

THE ALPHA RHYTHM, once hailed as "the wave of the future," has proved somewhat disappointing as a bioelectric phenomenon in operant conditioning experiments. The so-called "alpha state," which was initially advertised as a unique and pleasant mind trip, has not been unequivocally endorsed, and at least some subjects have found it to be clearly undesirable.[2,24] Questions have been raised also in relation to the degree of learning achieved in biofeedback studies of the alpha rhythm. While evidence indicates that subjects can learn to increase or decrease the amount of alpha activity with feedback,[15,19] it has proved impossible, thus far, to produce levels exceeding those that occur spontaneously during intervening rest periods (Lynch and Paskewitz[18]). Additionally, it has been suggested that other physiological responses mediate the EEG changes observed, and that instructional set is just as effective as biofeedback in altering alpha production.[3,18] Moreover, it is clear today that there are at least three semi-independent foci of alpha rhythm activity on the human cerebrum that could each be related to a different brain process.[16] Some of the more subtle conceptual and technical problems in this area have been discussed in depth recently by Black.[4]

These problems need not dampen our enthusiasm about the eventual utility of EEG biofeedback training. In fact, it is possible to identify neuroelectric patterns that can be associated directly with specific neural processes. Furthermore, the use of biofeedback techniques can significantly increase the occurrence of these patterns, thereby modifying the behavioral functions they mediate. Our laboratory has been involved in studies of this nature for the past 6 yr. I will attempt to review some of our more salient findings in this regard, and to show how our basic animal research studies have led to a new approach in the treatment of epilepsy.

In the past, we had utilized electrophysiologic recording and stimulation techniques in the cat for the study of brain mechanisms related to sleep. In one particular investigation, pairs of small electrodes had been placed on the dura over several functionally defined cortical regions. Among these was the sensorimotor area, consisting of the region adjacent to the cruciate (central) sulcus in the cat. Recordings from these localized electrodes in the behaving animal disclosed several different rhythmic EEG patterns specific to a given cortical area, and associated uniformly with certain classes of behavior.[20] Of particular interest in this regard was a 12–14-cps rhythm appearing over sensorimotor cortex during the voluntary suppression of movement.[26,27,28] We felt that this rhythm

Reprinted by permission of Grune & Stratton, Inc. and the author from *Seminars in Psychiatry*, Vol. 5, No. 4, 1973, 507-524.

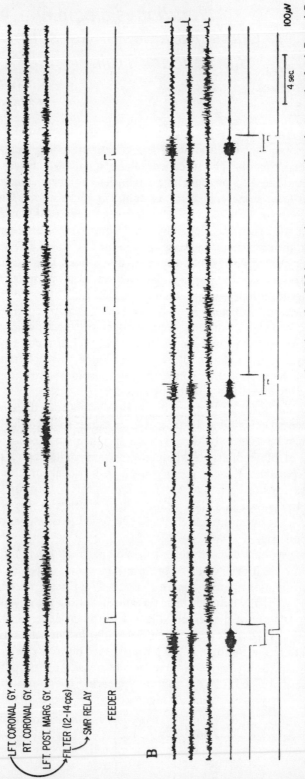

Fig. 1. Typical EEG samples from two groups of cats trained oppositely with regard to operant sensorimotor responses. Record *A* (conditioned LVE EEG response) are data from an animal trained to suppress the SMR, and maintain a low voltage, fast EEG in sensorimotor cortex, in order to receive food. Record *B* (conditioned SMR EEG response) is from a cat trained to produce the SMR for food.

might provide a bioelectric label for the neural process of motor inhibition and proceeded to examine the phenomenon in greater detail. Due to its origin, we had termed this activity the "sensorimotor rhythm" or SMR. The discrete nature of the SMR made it an excellent candidate for operant EEG conditioning. By providing food or positive brain stimulation as a reward for the production of SMR activity, we were able to train cats to control the rhythm with even greater ease than comparable conditioning of motor responses (Fig. 1).

The SMR-trained cats assumed stereotyped, motionless postures in order to produce the rhythm. It was clear from this study that the absence of movement was necessary but not sufficient for the production of the SMR. The essential motionlessness, however, provided an excellent opportunity for the study of other aspects of physiology. In trained animals, the SMR response was accompanied by a sustained decrease in tonic motor discharge and in cardiac rate (Fig. 2), while respiration became exceedingly regular.[6] We were interested also in the physiologic basis of this rhythm and carried out a series of studies to determine its origin.[12,13] The simultaneous recording of electrical activity in subcortical structures together with the cortical SMR quickly focused our attention on the ventrobasal area of the thalamus. Here, and particularly in the nucleus ventralis posterolateralis, we observed high voltage, 12–14-cps activity, which closely paralleled cortical SMR activity. Single unit recordings from cells in this nuclear group disclosed two fundamentally different patterns of discharge dur-

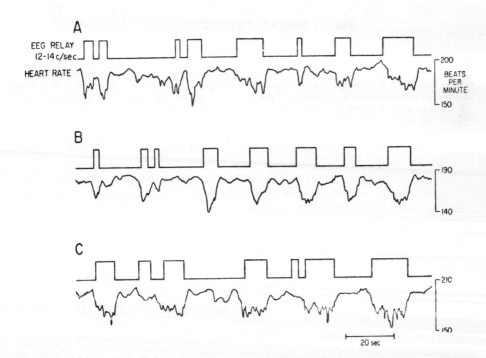

Fig. 2. Heart rate associated with sequential 12–14-cps EEG activity. Traces *A, B,* and *C* were obtained from different animals. Brief as well as long episodes of conditioned EEG activity were associated with a decrease in heart rate. The depression in heart rate was approximately the same during consecutive episodes of the conditioned EEG rhythm. (From Chase and Harper.[6])

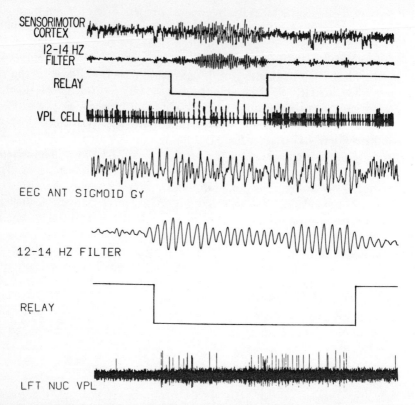

Fig. 3. Extracellular single-unit discharge patterns characterizing the two basic response types recorded from cells in the nucleus ventralis posterolateralis of the cat during trained SMR production. The record in the upper trace exemplifies the pattern change noted in approximately 80% of the units recorded and shows a shift from irregular high frequency discharge to a burst and silence configuration during SMR activity. The lower record, recorded at a slightly faster sweep speed, shows the response obtained in the remaining units studied, which was a shift from low base-line rates to a specific rapid discharge associated with the SMR. It is likely that the burst-silence pattern was characteristic of the larger transmission elements of VPL.

ing the SMR (Fig. 3). The most frequently observed change in relation to the occurrence of a conditioned SMR response was to a pattern of alternating bursting and silence. A smaller number of cells displayed a specific increase in discharge rate during the SMR. These and other observations were consistent with the well-documented electrophysiology of sensorimotor cortex and indicated that the SMR resulted from some form of gating or oscillation in thalamo–cortical–thalamic pathways, as suggested by the model of Andersen and Andersson.[1] The neural organization responsible for the rhythm represented a specific state of the central nervous system that followed the onset of motor quiescence but that was independent of that onset and of resulting motor postures. Other studies have shown that neuronal activity in a number of brain structures concerned with motor control is significantly dampened in relation to the occurrence of the SMR.

In addition to neurophysiologic studies we examined the *behavioral* consequences of SMR biofeedback training in cats. Utilizing untrained and oppositely trained control groups (Fig. 1), we established that sleep was significantly modified by SMR training. Sleep EEG spindles were enhanced and the number of motor disturbances (characteristic postural adjustments, etc.) during sleep diminished in the SMR-trained groups.[26] Moreover, the overall amount of time spent in sleep was reduced, due to a significant shortening of the recurrent sleep epochs in this polycyclic sleeper.[17] Perhaps the most dramatic observation of change related to SMR training was a surprising resistance to drug-induced seizures.[27] The convulsant studied was monomethylhydrazine, for which normative dose–response functions had been derived previously. This compound is highly toxic, producing convulsions in the cat at a dose of 7 mg/kg. It is thought to elicit generalized seizures by disrupting the metabolism of cerebral inhibitory interneurons, in much the same manner as strychnine.[7,11] Animals overtrained with SMR biofeedback showed a significantly prolonged latency to seizure at a dose of 9 mg/kg, and two of the tested animals failed to convulse at all, while clearly manifesting all other symptoms of toxicity related to this drug.

These observations led us to view EEG biofeedback from a somewhat different position than the rest of the field. The question of learning was not at issue and somatic mediation had been ruled out. What then could account for the apparent increase in seizure threshold observed in our trained animals? Could it be that this unusual opportunity for activation of motor inhibitory pathways had in some way altered the connectivity of these pathways? It is well known that denervation or disuse of neural components leads to profound changes in synaptic morphology and biochemistry.[8,22] These changes appear to be directed toward an increase in excitability at the expense of signal resolution. We hypothesized that *overuse* might produce opposite changes in synaptic organization leading to decreased excitability and greater signal specificity. Bliss et al.[5] were surprised and, in fact, disappointed to find that repeated stimulation of a central neural pathway led to a decrease in the probability of transmission, which was opposite to their expectations. But, indeed, this is precisely what one might anticipate if overuse produced cellular changes opposite to disuse, as suggested above. The implications of such a model were remarkable. Could EEG biofeedback provide a means of selectively overstimulating discrete neural networks and thereby decrease excitability in the mechanisms that they subserved? While continuing to seek neurophysiologic support for this concept, we were encouraged also to pursue similar biofeedback studies in man and to examine their utility in relation to epilepsy.

It should be noted that the human EEG is a good deal more complex than that of the cat. A number of classification systems have been evolved for the description of its component frequencies and rhythms, the most familiar of which are the waking alpha, beta, and theta rhythms and the slow wave (delta) and spindle (sigma) configurations of sleep. The human EEG is a sea of low voltage electrical activity in a constant state of flux. Our experience has indicated that functional pattern changes can occur not only in relation to the states of consciousness but, within a given state, in relation to a myriad of variables, such as time of day, time of month (in females particularly) and even events of the previous day or hour! Also, in man it is difficult to evaluate the nonspecific influence of cognitive variables and the specific influences of drugs, such as caffeine and nicotine, not to mention the plethora of patent medicines that one can encounter. Moreover, few studies have obtained substantial EEG samples over extended periods of time, so little can be said about the overall nature of individual variability in such important parameters as frequency, topography, and symmetry. Finally, what is seen is to a large extent determined by the equipment and analytic procedures utilized and the conventions of recording dictated by the history of electroencephalography. We have learned to appreciate these problems through our own experiences, and from them have developed a sense of caution in evaluating studies that appear to overlook these realities.

The techniques utilized originally in these studies were similar in principle to those used in our animal work. The equipment developed to detect SMR activity in cats consisted of a Neuro Feedback Instruments frequency analysis channel, made up of a calibrated precision attenuator and active frequency filter with a relay output. The relay output from the frequency analysis channel was directed to a feedback-logic channel. The unit was sharply tuned to respond to 12–14 cps activity (Fig. 4), and could be adjusted in its sensitivity-duration characteristics to provide for shaping of the desired EEG response.

Electrode placements and application techniques have evolved during the course of these studies. In our earlier work, a bipolar pair of cup electrodes was situated across the estimated central sulcus at sites approximately 1 cm anterior and posterior to C3, according to the international 10–20 system.[25] Currently, we are shifting placements to the medial–lateral plane, with one lead off vertex approximately 10% of the interaural distance and the other just lateral to C3 (see, for example, Fig. 9). Both needle and cup electrodes are used, depending on the patient, and bilateral recordings are uniformly obtained.

The basic EEG feedback unit consisted of a console containing two rows of ten small lamps. The logic channel activated an electronic counter that operated this unit. Each criterion response advanced illumination of the top row of lamps, which was accompanied in each instance by the sounding of a single chime. Each ten criterion responses (which illuminated the entire top row) activated, successively, the lamps in the bottom row, accompanied by a double chime. During the course of these studies, several new feedback modes were added to this system. One consisted of a single large lamp display above the basic console that glowed in intensity as a direct function of the amount of appropriate EEG signal generated. The discrete output of the basic unit was used, also, to operate a slide projector that presented pictures on a screen in front of the patient. These pictures consisted of sequences depicting nature scenes or providing for the completion of a picture puzzle. Different patients have preferred one or the other of these reward modes or a combination of several. This variable was manipulated so as to achieve optimal training from each patient.

We had chosen to study a small but select group of subjects. This strategy was dictated primarily by our model but was also consistent with our resources. Since we proposed that EEG biofeedback might alter neural organization through directed "exercise" of specific functional pathways, it was reasonable to assume that such an objective would require prolonged training. This approach could be compared more favorably with an attempt to create, through

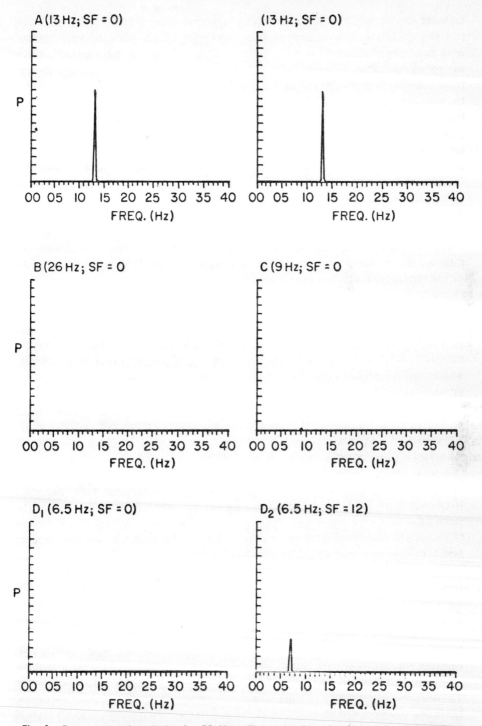

Fig. 4. Power spectral analysis of a 50 μV oscillator signal at the frequencies indicated as recorded through our SMR feedback system. Note the specific response to the 13-Hz signal and the lack of response to harmonics of this frequency or to other frequencies.

training, a concert pianist or to retrain a disabled limb rather than with the objectives of most biofeedback studies. Accordingly, six patients were studied over periods ranging at this point from 6–20 mo. Four of these patients were epileptics and two suffered from spinal cord lesions. Four control subjects have been studied also, but these received less systematic attention. The epileptic patients selected in this initial study suffered from a variety of seizure disorders as indicated in Table 1. This situation was desirable, since it was possible that SMR biofeedback might prove more effective with some patterns than with others.

Each patient was familiarized with the apparatus and procedure in our biofeedback laboratory. They were then seated in front of the feedback unit and electrodes placed over appropriate cortical areas. EEG data were recorded on a ten-channel Grass Model 6 polygraph. The polygraphic display also included filter relay and reward outputs from the neuro-analyzer (see, for example, Fig. 7). A digital counting display provided the operator with a continuous update of the patient's progress. Extensive base-line EEG recordings were obtained where possible, but in all cases at least 3–5 min of data were gathered. At the end of the base-line recording period, the subject was instructed to relax and think positive thoughts in order to find the mental state that would produce activation of the feedback apparatus. This suggestion was based on previous experience with SMR feedback training.[24] Feedback was provided for a period of 20–40 min, depending on the state of the patient, and followed by a 3–5 min post-training baseline recording. Such training sessions were repeated a minimum of three times a week.

After 10 mo of training, one patient was provided with a portable home feedback unit and, thereafter, was recorded only several times per month in the laboratory. This unit contained an EEG preamplifier, a 60 Hz notch filter, a voltage amplifier, a frequency analysis channel and a single lamp display whose intensity directly reflected the occurrence of 13-cps activity. With the use of this unit the patient was able to obtain daily feedback training. Amplitude and frequency settings were calibrated during the intermittent laboratory training sessions.

The detailed description of our methods provided above was deemed important for those who wish to understand our approach. The results of our studies, however, will merely be reviewed here, since a comprehensive exposition of these new data is being prepared currently for the more appropriate context of a scientific journal. I wish also to acknowledge the collaboration of my associates, L. Macdonald and R. Stone, in this effort.

Data from four normal controls, two quadriparetics and four epileptics indicate that 12–14-cps activity can, indeed, be recorded over the rholandic or central cortical region in man. The amount, or operant level, of this activity prior to biofeedback training is low, with bursts occurring at widely spaced intervals. These bursts can usually be obtained only with the detection system set to respond to very low amplitude signals (3–6 μV) in this frequency band. When comparable recordings from other brain regions were passed through the detection system at the identical setting, little if any 12–14-cps activity was observed (Fig. 5). After at least 2 wk of training, the number and duration of these bursts

Table 1. Summary of Human SMR Studies*

Subject	Age	Pathology	Date Started Training	Post-Training Observations EEG	Clinical
K.H.	7	Mixed seizure disorder (major motor and PMV)	1/3/72	Significant decrease in polyspike and slow wave patterns; normalization	Significant reduction of major motor seizures, petit mal, and absence attacks (seizure-free for several periods of 2–4 mo)
M.F.	23	Major motor disorder (focal)	8/24/71	Significant decrease in focal spike discharge; normalization	Significant reduction in grand mal seizures from pretraining rate of 2/mo of 0.5/mo (seizure-free for several periods of 2–5 mos)
S.H.	18	Mixed seizure disorder (petit mal variant)	7/31/72	Significant decrease in polyspike and spike-wave discharge; normalization	Reduction of major motor seizures; decreased PMV manifestations.
D.K.	46	Adult petit mal	8/2/72	Unilateral suppression of 3/sec; spike-wave pattern	Frequent break-up clinical seizures; longest seizure-free periods in history of disorder
N.Y.	36	Quadriparetic (spinal cord compression)	3/29/72	Development of 6–8 Hz slow wave over central region (same true of all above patients)	
J.B.	24	Quadriparetic (spinal cord compression)	11/15/72	Development of profound 12–14 Hz; SMR pattern over central region	

*As of June 1, 1973.

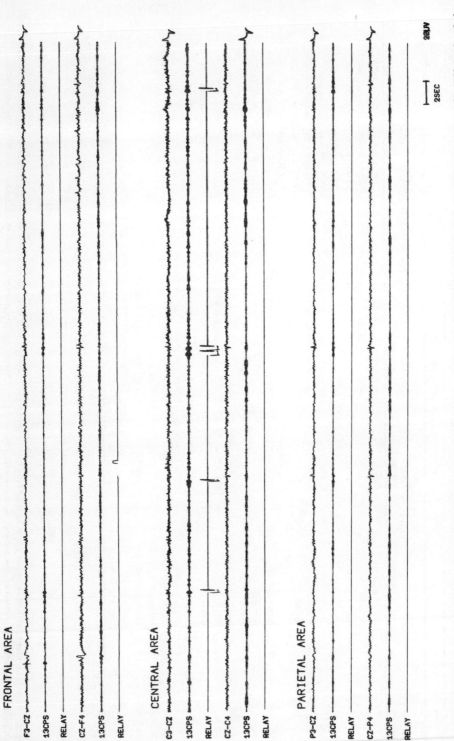

Fig. 5.   One approach to localization and quantification of the human SMR involved the use of our feedback unit as a 12-14-cps detection system. Shown here are simultaneously recorded bipolar EEG tracings, equated for voltage and fed through the unit with all settings kept constant. These recordings were taken from frontal (Fz-F3), central (Cz-C3), and parietal (Pz-P3) leads of the left and right hemispheres in a naïve subject during the initial SMR training session.

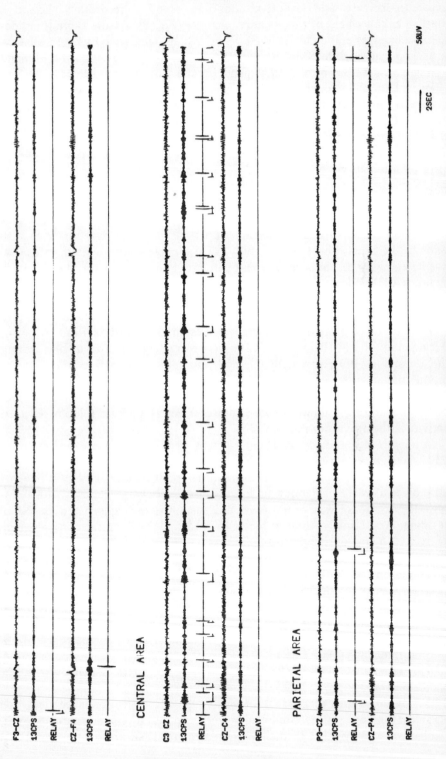

Fig. 6. This is an identical evaluation of SMR localization and quantity as operant performance. Note the specificity of 12–14-cps activity from rholandic cortex and the marked increase in production resulting from training. In this case, however, the subject was well trained in SMR shown in Fig. 5.

began to increase, and several months later identical recordings showed a marked enhancement of this localized activity (Fig. 6). At the same time, detectable changes gradually emerged in the visually analyzed EEG. In all subjects, some increase in SMR amplitude was observed. However, the ultimate voltages achieved appeared to depend on the category of subject involved (Fig. 7). Our epileptics showed the smallest increase in amplitude (the bulk of rewarded bursts still occurring with low voltages which, to our surprise, appeared often to reflect an activation of the EEG); one of the quadriparetic patients showed the greatest increase ($>20 \mu v$), and normals were intermediate. These differences will be discussed below.

In addition to visual analysis of EEG patterns during training, these data were recorded on magnetic tape once per week and subjected to computer evaluation. Sequential 17-sec epochs of sensorimotor cortex EEG activity were subjected to Fast Fourier transform and plotted isometrically, so as to provide a continuous analysis of spectral density for periods ranging in duration from 3–10 min. In the initial phase of the study, such analyses were limited to central cortical activity on the side of the brain providing signals for the feedback device. Occipital leads were also recorded at this time. During the summer of 1972, this procedure was modified to provide for bilateral central cortical monitoring, and thereby a longitudinal analysis of EEG symmetry. These techniques allowed us to determine extant periodicities in the patient's EEG prior to, during, and after SMR training. They were extremely useful in demonstrating the abnormal EEG patterns of our epileptic patients as well as the ongoing modulation of such well-known EEG patterns as the alpha and theta rhythms. Because of the low voltages characteristic of the SMR and its intermittent occurrence during training sessions, power spectral analyses seldom reflected activity in this frequency range.

In all subjects studied significant changes were seen in the distribution of EEG frequencies during training. Normal subjects showed a reduction in occipital and central alpha activity during SMR performance. Epileptic patients all showed a decrease in abnormal low frequency discharge patterns with training. This decrease was progressive and sustained throughout the period of training. Additionally, these subjects showed a slowed central cortical alpha pattern (6–8 cps) during performance. With continued training, this theta activity was also diminished. In some patients, these changes were clearly more profound on the side of the brain where EEG patterns were being reinforced (Fig. 8). A 9-wk discontinuation of training was initiated in three patients at the end of 1972. Seizure manifestations in these patients were clearly exacerbated during this period, after a delay of 4–6 wk. This change in clinical condition was profoundly reflected in the power spectral analysis by a recurrence of abnormal frequencies and a decay of previously developed higher frequency activity (Fig. 9). EEG pattern characteristics in quadriparetic patients will not be elaborated here.

During the course of operant conditioning, our epileptic subjects showed significant changes, also, in clinical seizure manifestations. All patients experienced an improvement in their particular clinical patterns. Both grand mal

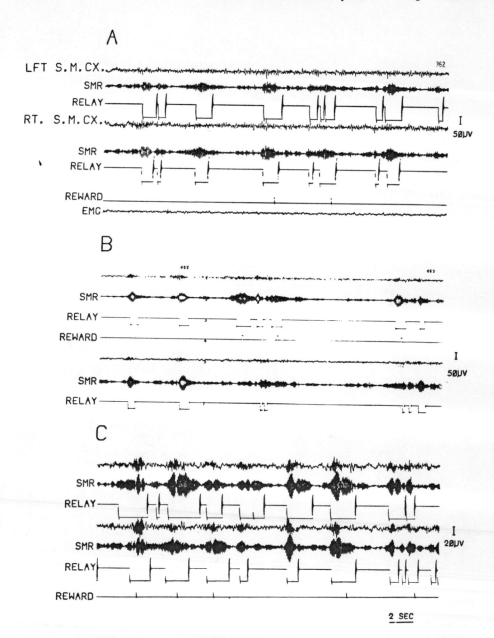

Fig. 7. Typical EEG recordings during SMR performance in three trained subjects. In each case, left and right sensorimotor cortex EEG tracings are shown together with associated 12-14-Hz filter activity, depicting the presence of this frequency independently of its amplitude, and relay activation when feedback criteria are achieved. Feedback is indicated by the reward maker. In *A*, the record was obtained from a patient with focal grand mal epilepsy, in *B*, from a normal control subject, and in *C*, from a quadriparetic patient. Note the relationship between SMR amplitude in the EEG tracings and the dimension of phasic motor excitability, extending from abnormal sensitivity in the epileptic to pathologic depression in the quadriparetic.

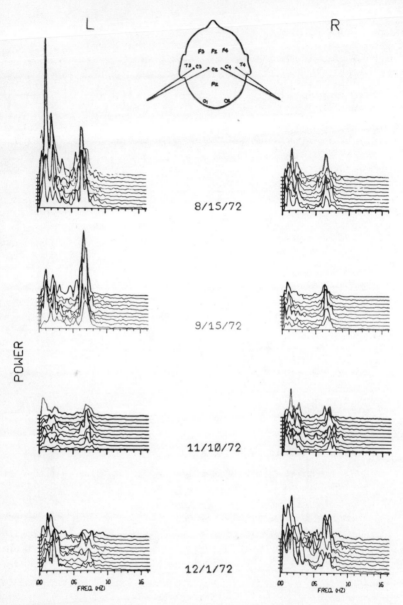

Fig. 8. Power spectral analyses of EEG data from left and right sensorimotor cortex are shown here as obtained over a 5-mo period of training in an epileptic patient. Each graph consists of sequential 17-sec epochs plotted isometrically, providing data from a continuous 3-min period of record. Note that this subject showed abnormally slow frequencies bilaterally that were most marked from the left sensorimotor cortex. In addition, a peak at 7 Hz, characteristic of epileptics, is seen. During the course of training, there were significant decreases in these abnormal frequencies on the left hemisphere, from which EEG signals were operantly reinforced, while frequency patterns from the right hemisphere did not change significantly during this same period. The records evaluated here were obtained during regular biofeedback training sessions and were not disrupted by any sustained seizure discharge. After several months of training, this patient would occasionally show unilateral subclinical seizures limited to the right hemisphere and not accompanied by a loss of consciousness. The occurrence of these seizures was consistent with the EEG asymmetry that had developed.

Fig. 9. The power spectral analyses shown here are similar to those presented in Fig. 8, but are compressed so as to present frequency analysis from continuous 10-min epochs of EEG recordings. In each instance, the records analyzed represent the first 10 min of training in a particular session. This subject had begun training in January 1972; however, bilateral recordings were initiated for the first time in August. The data presented here show the progression of change in component frequencies during the subsequent 4-mo period. They indicate relatively normal EEG frequencies, contrasting sharply with the grossly disordered patterns characteristic of this patient prior to training. The high density peak at 6-8 cps was characteristic of our epileptic subjects. Note the absence of any alpha manifestation and the gradual decrement of central 6-8 cps activity with continued training. There was an indication, also, of more marked change in the reinforced left hemisphere. Two months after the experimental termination of training, this subject showed exacerbated epileptic symptoms. His altered condition was clearly reflected in the power spectral analysis obtained on return to the laboratory.

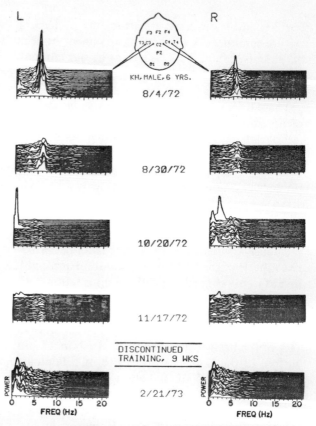

and petit mal manifestations were reduced. The lowest rates of clinical seizure activity in the history of their respective disorders were uniformly achieved within several months of the initiation of training. The best results were obtained in this regard from a 23-yr-old female patient suffering from focal grand mal epilepsy, and a 7-yr-old male patient with serious brain damage resulting in generalized and mixed seizure patterns (Table 1). Less remarkable changes were observed in patients with absence and petit mal variant disorders. All three of the subjects whose training was discontinued in December of 1972 experienced a return to pretraining levels of seizure activity within 6 wk. Upon the reinitiation of biofeedback training these subjects returned rapidly to the previous condition of improved control.

We have less systematic data on the behavioral effects of SMR biofeedback training. Subjects have consistently reported increased general awareness and an improved ability to sustain attention, in accordance with the typical reports of a relaxed, but alert and focused state of mind during successful performance. All subjects found the SMR training experience to be pleasant in nature. Two of the epileptic patients, whose clinical condition made education difficult if not impossible, demonstrated a marked improvement in school performance. In our 7-yr-old subject, severe problems of hyperactivity had compounded his seizure condition. A marked improvement in behavior control was reported by his parents and teachers, as well as by our laboratory staff, after several months of training. Finally, subjective reports during the course of training also suggested that the quality of sleep was improved during this period.

These briefly described observations indicate that 12–14-cps activity can be recorded over the central cortical region in man during wakefulness, that biofeedback techniques can successfully facilitate the occurrence of this activity, and that epileptics can benefit from extensive training in its production. While these statements are clearly substantiated by our findings, there are still many primary questions which must be dealt with. Why is the SMR difficult to observe in some subjects, and why is it manifest at such low voltages in man compared to the cat? Is the SMR indeed a separate EEG entity, or is the 12–14-cps designation inappropriate, the rhythm being of broader range and relating to previously described motor cortex EEG patterns? To what extent might alternative aspects of the biofeedback situation account for the observed improvement in EEG and clinical epileptic manifestations? Finally, why did our epileptic patients demonstrate a return to their previous clinical conditions following discontinuation of training?

Recordings in our animal preparations were obtained directly from the surface of the brain, while those in our human subjects were obtained from the surface of the skull. The presence of a laminated, bony calvarium results in higher resistance and, therefore, lower voltage recordings from humans. We have some reasons to believe that the SMR is obscured under these circumstances, and overshadowed by the relatively high voltage alpha and theta frequencies characteristic of man. However, in some patients, waking 12–14-cps activity may occur at relatively high voltages. We observed this in one man who suffered from a spinal cord compression leading to quadriparesis. After several training sessions this subject showed prominent bilateral SMR bursts over central and frontal cortical areas. In sleep recordings obtained from this patient, it was noted that spindle burst activity, associated with sleep EEG patterns, was also markedly enhanced. It is interesting to note that a similar enhancement of spindle activity has been reported from a teenage girl who had been isolated and restrained during development.[23] Moreover, this child demonstrated high-voltage SMR bursts in the waking state, according to the authors. The significance of these observations may be revealed if we consider certain other facts. In the few normal subjects we have trained, a clear 12–14-cps EEG pattern became apparent after several weeks of performance. While lower in voltage than in the quadriparetic patient, SMR activity in these subjects was nevertheless clearly observed. Also, with extensive training many of our epileptic subjects have shown repeated clear-cut bursts of rhythmic 12–14-cps activity. If one considers the behavior of these various subject groups in relation to corresponding EEG patterns, it is possible to hypothesize a relationship between general level of motor activity and the occurrence of the SMR. Individuals in whom motor behavior was curtailed, either actively or passively, showed high voltage SMR discharge. Conversely, subjects characterized by decreased thresholds for motor discharge (for example, epileptic and hyperkinetic patients) showed a minimal expression of SMR activity in the EEG. Normal subjects appeared to be intermediate between these extremes in terms of SMR manifestations. The motor mechanisms that underlie the appearance in the EEG of the SMR may be facilitated by inactivity and suppressed by somatic hyperactivity. It is interesting to note in this regard that the cats utilized in our experiments are normally maintained in standard laboratory cages, which, by their nature, substantially limit motor behavior. The profound SMR recorded in the cat may result, in part, from the restricted life space of this animal and his consequent inactivity.

These facts suggest that the SMR may indeed be a specific and functionally meaningful EEG phenomenon related to brain mechanisms that mediate motor suppression. However, it is also possible that such mechanisms are less specific than we suppose and are reflected by rhythmic activity of a broader frequency range. Thus, the so-called "en arceau" or "wicket rhythm,"[9] a somewhat slower rhythm that is blocked by movement in man, may likewise reflect the activity of this same motor suppression process, as we have suggested previously.[13] If so, training of this frequency from sensorimotor cortex may produce effects similar to those reported here. This is an empirical problem that can be resolved with further investigation.

It is a well-known fact that certain epileptics show clinical improvement associated merely with admission to a hospital. Extensive attention and concern, as well as the unique characteristics of a research laboratory, could produce similar "secondary gain" effects. The epileptics who have come to our program are seeking desperately to find a solution to their substantial medical problem. In at least one instance, an attempt to retain such a patient in our study for control procedures was not successful; the lack of positive results after several months led to his withdrawal from the program. Efforts to explain the need for control data did not impress this individual. For this reason, and due to limited resources in our laboratory, we have not established a control training group of epileptics. Ultimately, such an addition will be essential. However, there are some reasons to believe that such controls would be useful only from a technical point of view. Most of our epileptic patients have shown progressive clinical improvement, even after periods of training in excess of 1 yr. One might expect that secondary gain related to attention and novelty would be dissipated after so long a period of involvement. This progressive improvement has been apparent, also, in the objective EEG records obtained from these patients. As mentioned before, in several patients there is evidence of a unilateral EEG change in the hemisphere from which EEG signals were led to our feedback unit. Since both sides of the brain have experienced all other variables, one can conclude that the significant variable here was the biofeedback training. Additionally, one patient has been working at home with a portable unit for approximately 1 yr. This subject has demonstrated an even greater improvement in her clinical condition during this period of training out of the laboratory.

Conceivably, any situation that provided for sustained periods of relaxation and the focusing of attention on cerebral activities could produce effects similar to those noted here. We have found, however, that other EEG rhythms are diminished in the course of SMR biofeedback training. Thus, the alpha rhythm is clearly suppressed during SMR performance in a well-trained subject. The final answer to this question awaits studies in which other EEG and behavior phenomena are reinforced and the influence upon epileptic manifestations determined. From the data available we are encouraged to believe that the SMR effects are specific.

Finally, the model that we used to think about our biofeedback efforts rests upon the assumption that such changes would occur due to neuronal reorganization and that they might be long-lasting in nature. However, we have found that discontinuation of training after 6 mo in three patients resulted in a reversal of benefits previously achieved. It was difficult to determine the precise time course leading to exacerbation of symptoms. The three patients notified our laboratory of their worsened condition almost simultaneously, within a period 4–6 wk after training had been discontinued. This "withdrawal" effect came as a surprise to us. In accordance with our model, we could attribute this change to a kind of neuronal supersensitivity following upon a period of reduced activation of the SMR-related motor circuits. The time course of events associated with development of disuse supersensitivity in isolated cerebral cortex has been estimated at 2–4 wk.[21,22]

Our findings with SMR biofeedback in epileptics have been very encouraging thus far. We are cognizant of the fact that many interpretations of these results are possible, and that the mechanism of neural reorganization that we propose will be difficult to establish. Nevertheless, results have indicated a change in the epileptic process in all patients. Our future objectives in these studies will be to carry out some of the controls mentioned above, to evaluate the suggested relationship between EEG and behavior restriction, and to seek better and more efficient methods to accomplish SMR biofeedback training. While this approach may never provide a "cure" for epilepsy or other disease states of neural origin, it does suggest a desirable alternative to current chemical therapies.

REFERENCES

1. Andersen P, Andersson SA: Physiological Basis of the Alpha Rhythm. New York, Appleton-Century-Crofts, 1968, pp 1–235

2. Beatty J: Operant conditioning of the alpha rhythm. Presented at Learned Control of Physiological Functions (workshop) Winter Conference on Brain Research, Vail, Colo, 1972

3. Beatty J: Similar effects of feedback signals and instructional information on EEG activity. Physiol Behav 9:151–154, 1972

4. Black AH: The operant conditioning of central nervous system electrical activity, in Bower GH (ed): The Psychology of Learning and Motivations, vol 6., New York, Academic Press, 1972

5. Bliss TVP, Burns BD, Uttley AM: Factors affecting the conductivity of pathways in the cerebral cortex. J Physiol 195:339–367, 1968

6. Chase MH, Harper RM: Somatomotor and visceromotor correlates of operantly conditioned 12–14 c/sec sensorimotor cortical activity. Electroenceph Clin Neurophysiol 31:85–92, 1971

7. Clark DA, Bairrington JD, Bitter HL, et al: Pharmacology and toxicology of propellant hydrazines. Review 11–68, USAF School of Aerospace Medicine, Brooks A.F.B., Texas, 1968

8. Colonnier M: Experimental degeneration in the cerebral cortex. J Anat 98:47–53, 1964

9. Gastaut H, Terzian H, Gastaut Y: Etude électro-corticographique de la reáctivité des rythmes rolandiques. Rev Neurol 87:176–182, 1952

10. Globus A: Neuronal ontogeny: Its use in tracing connectivity, in Sterman MB, McGinty DJ, Adinolfi AM (eds): Brain Devel-

opment and Behavior, vol. 13. New York, Academic Press, 1971, pp 253–263

11. Goff WR, Allison T, Matsumia W, et al: Effects of 1, 1-dimethylhydrazine (UDMH) on evoked cerebral neuroelectric responses. AMRL-TR-67-67, Aerospace Medical Research Laboratories, Wright-Patterson Air Force Base, Ohio, September, 1967

12. Harper RM, Sterman MB: Subcortical unit activity during a conditioned 12–14 Hz sensorimotor EEG rhythm in the cat. Fed Proc 31:404, 1972

13. Howe RC, Sterman MB: Cortical-subcortical EEG correlates of suppressed motor behavior during sleep and waking in the cat. Electroenceph Clin. Neurophysiol 32:681–695, 1972

14. Howe RC, Sterman MB: Somatosensory system evoked potentials during waking behavior and sleep in the cat. Electroenceph Clin Neurophysiol 34:605–618, 1973

15. Kamiya J: Operant control of the EEG alpha rhythm and some of its reported effects on consciousness, in Tart C (ed): Altered States of Consciousness: A Book of Readings. New York, Wiley, 1969

16. Lehmann D: Multichannel topography of human alpha EEG fields. Electroenceph Clin Neurophysiol 31:439–449, 1971

17. Lucas EA, Sterman MB: A polycyclic sleep–wake cycle in the cat: Effects produced by sensorimotor rhythm conditioning. Exp Neurol (in press)

18. Lynch JJ, Paskewitz DA: On the mechanisms of the feedback control of human brain wave activity. J Nerv Ment Dis 153(3):205–217, 1971

19. Nowlis DP, Kamiya J: The control of electroencephalographic alpha rhythms through auditory feedback and the associated mental activity. Psychophysiology 6:476–484, 1970

20. Roth SR, Sterman MB, Clemente CD: Comparison of EEG correlates of rein-forcement, internal inhibition and sleep. Electroenceph Clin Neurophysiol 23:509–520, 1967

21. Rutledge LT, Ranck JB Jr, Duncan JA: Prevention of supersensitivity in partially isolated cerebral cortex. Electroenceph Clin Neurophysiol 23:256–262, 1967

22. Sharpless SK: Isolated and deafferented neurons: Disuse supersensitivity, in Jasper H, Ward AA, Pope A (eds): Basic Mechanisms of the Epilepsies. Boston, Little, Brown, 1969, pp 329–348

23. Shurley JT, Natani K: Sleep EEG patterns in a fourteen-year-old girl with severe developmental retardation. Presented at the 80th Annual American Psychological Association Convention, Honolulu, 1972

24. Sterman MB: Studies of EEG biofeedback training in man and cats. Highlights of 17th Annual Conference: VA Cooperative Studies in Mental Health and Behavioral Sciences, St. Louis, 50–60, 1972

25. Sterman MB, Friar L: Suppression of seizures in an epileptic following EEG feedback training. Electroenceph Clin Neurophysiol 33:89–95, 1972

26. Sterman MB, Howe RC, Macdonald LR: Facilitation of spindle-burst sleep by conditioning of electroencephalographic activity while awake. Science 167:1146–1148, 1970

27. Sterman MB, LoPresti RW, Fairchild MD: Electroencephalographic and behavioral studies of monomethyl hydrazine toxicity in the cat. Technical Report AMRL-TR-69-3, Air Systems Command, Wright–Patterson Air Force Base, Ohio, 1969

28. Sterman MB, Wyrwicka W, Roth SR: Electrophysiological correlates and neural substrates of alimentary behavior in the cat, in Morgane JP, Wayner M (eds): Neural Regulation of Food and Water Intake. Ann NY Acad Sci 157:723–739, 1969

EEG Biofeedback and Epilepsy 33

Bonnie J. Kaplan

It has been reported that biofeedback training of a 12-14 Hz rhythm recorded from rolandic cortex has significantly reduced the seizure incidence in four human epileptics (Sterman & Friar, 1972; Sterman, 1973). In cats this rhythm, labeled the sensorimotor rhythm (SMR), is correlated with the suppression of movement. Previously, the only rhythm described in humans as a neural correlate of behavioral inhibition was the central mu rhythm, also called the wicket rhythm or rhythme en arceau (Chatrian, Petersen & Lazarte, 1958; Gastaut & Bert, 1954). Cental mu is synchronous activity of 9 ± 2 Hz, recorded from central cortex; it blocks to contra-lateral limb movement.

The present research tested biofeedback training in human epileptics of two types of scalp-recorded EEG activity: 12-14 Hz activity and low frequency synchrony. Two epileptics (JS and SM) received 12-14 Hz biofeedback and reinforcement for three months, in an attempt to replicate Sterman and Friar's results. When no effect was seen, SM and two new patients (AS and MD) were given biofeedback training of low frequency synchronous activity, believed to be a mixture of central mu and alpha. The major difference between this technique and that of Sterman's was the filtering system. In addition to prefiltering with an analog filter, the EEG was also passed through a PDP-12 programmed to function as a digital filter.

Three dependent variables were used: evaluations of clinical EEG's, seizure incidence, and changes in power spectra (fast Fourier transforms of EEG epochs). Following 12-14 Hz training for JS and SM, none of the three variables had changed. Following reinforcement of lower frequency synchrony, the following changes occurred: for SM, there were two medication changes which were clearly responsible for her reduced seizures and change in power spectra. For AS, seizure incidence decreased. For MD, seizure incidence decreased, plus there was a change in her clinical EEG. Neither AS nor MD had any medication changes.

The results are not interpreted as being causally related to the biofeedback training of the patients' EEG synchrony, because there was no change in that rhythm apparent in the power spectra. Since both AS and MD experience more seizures during stress, the results are interpreted conservatively as demonstrating the effect on seizure incidence of learning to function at a lower level of arousal.

Reprinted from *Proceedings of the Biofeedback Research Society,* 1974, 16.

Reduction of Seizures and 34

Normalization of the EEG Following

Sensorimotor Biofeedback Training

William W. Finley

Sensorimotor rhythm (SMR) biofeedback training was attempted in a
13 year old male with frequent atonic seizures. Prior to SMR training
the S was averaging almost eight clinical seizures an hour. The SMR
filter was set at 12 ± 1 H_z with unusually steep slopes ranging from 75
to 188 db per octave. The input of the filter was "buffered" by high
voltage "clippers". Feedback was presented to the S as a blue light accompanied by a tone which occurred whenever the S produced 3 to 4 wave
forms of 12 H_z activity equal to or exceeding 18 uV. Feedback to the S
was automatically interrupted whenever epileptiform activity was detected
by means of a 5.5 H_z filter with skirts rolling off at 20 db per octave.
These special precautions assured that the S would be reinforced only for
the production of 12 ± 1 H_z activity. Feedback training was conducted
over a period of approximately three months. In that time the S's percentage of SMR increased from about 10%, prior to training, to 65% by the
34th training session. Correspondingly, his rate of clinical seizures
decreased by a factor of about 10. Moreover, the duration of his clinical
attacks decreased with training and he showed a significant reduction in
percentage of epileptiform discharges. For a period of one week, beginning
on training trial 29, noncontingent feedback was introduced in place of
contingent or correct feedback. Within one day the S's rate of seizures
increased five-fold. The SMR decreased from about 45% to 30%. All of
the results summarized above were interpreted as being consistent with
the hypothesis that the SMR is related to processes involved in the inhibition of epileptogenic activity.

Reprinted from *Proceedings of the Biofeedback Research Society*, 1974, 17.

Effect of Daytime Alpha Rhythm 35
Maintenance on Subsequent Sleep

Q. R. Regestein, G. H. Buckland, and G. V. Pegram

The sleep of five subjects was studied electroencephalographically to investigate whether the prolonged daytime maintenance of EEG alpha rhythm under feedback conditions affects sleep on the following night. Each of the subjects slept in the laboratory during two separate five-night periods, Monday through Friday, at least a week apart. During Thursday of each study, the subject spent twelve hours producing money-reinforced alpha or nonalpha depending on the experimental paradigm. Mean percentages of the various sleep stages and total sleep times were compared between postfeedback nights and control nights. The sleep stages did not appear to be differentially affected, but a significant decrement of total sleep time was noted between the post-alpha-conditioning night and the controls. Thus, production of high amounts of alpha rhythm during the day may be associated with a slightly decreased sleep need.

Introduction

Daytime experiences change nocturnal sleep patterns. Stoyva et al. report that extreme distortion of visual field by means of spectacles during the day increases the amount of REM sleep at night (1) although there is disagreement on this finding (2). Daytime exercise is said to increase the percentage of stage IV

Q. R. Regestein, MD, is from the Peter Bent Brigham Hospital, Boston, Massachussetts; G. H. Buckland, MS, is with NASA, Ames Research Laboratory, Moffett Field, California; G. V. Pegram, PhD, is with the Neurosciences Program at the University of Alabama, Birmingham, Alabama.

This work was done at the Aeromedical Research Laboratory, Holloman Air Force Base, New Mexico.

Received for publication December 21, 1972.

Address for reprint requests: Q. R. Regestein, MD, Peter Bent Brigham Hospital, 721 Huntington Avenue, Boston, Massachussetts 02115.

sleep on the night following it (3), and traumatic or otherwise intense experience is associated with a much shortened latency of REM sleep (4). Prolonged isolation and monotony associated with several months' residence at the South Pole entail diminished stage IV and stage REM sleep (5). All of these daytime experiences may impose unusual conditions of arousal upon the individual, and we wished to test whether or not artificially manipulating daytime arousal patterns would affect the subsequent nocturnal sleep patterns. In addition, we wished to appraise whether or not prolonged maintenance of alpha rhythm had any recuperative effect such that changes in the amount of alpha produced by a subject during the day might alter his nocturnal patterns. Scott (6) reports that social isolation, exercise, and no talking, all increase subsequent REM time slightly. Amongst rats, those exposed to an enriched environment have significantly more slow-wave sleep, compared with those kept in isolation (7), although five hours of restraint or raising animals with relative activity restriction made no difference to subsequent sleep stage (8,9).

Methods

Subjects

Five subjects were picked from a population of 23 individuals screened for the capacity to produce a high percentage of alpha rhythm under EEG feedback conditions. Details are given elsewhere (10). Briefly, twenty-three advertising respondents were tested over a half-hour baseline, a half-hour practice period, and a four-hour performance period in the production of alpha rhythm for a monetary reward. Five of these subjects who produced the highest percentage of alpha (an average alpha percentage of 70% for four hours) were asked to participate in the EEG conditioning and sleep study to be reported here.

Routine and Equipment

Each of the subjects slept in the laboratory during two separate five-night periods, Monday through Friday, at least a week apart. They arrived shortly before their usual bedtime, were affixed to a standard electroencephalogram (EEG) lead (C₃- or C₄-mastoid), submental electromyogram (EMG), 2 electroocular (EOG) electrodes between the outer canthus of each eye and a ground electrode in the middle of the forehead. Beckman bipotential microelectrodes were used with NASA thin electrode jelly pressured onto the pelletized surface. The horny, insulating layer of the skin was scratched off beneath each electrode site, the area scrubbed with acetone, and the electrode firmly affixed by means of an electrode collar. Adhesive strips were wound around the head circumference and across the vertex in a manner that prevented the electrodes from being pulled loose. A test

of this placement revealed that the resistance rose from about 1000 ohms to about 5000 ohms over twenty-four hours, and that the subject habituated to this treatment. The electrode leads were connected to a small Signatron telemetry unit whose frequency response somewhat attenuated 1 Hz activity. The video transmission was picked up by an antenna in the electrically screened room, and relayed to subcarrier discriminators, which decomposed the video into EEG, EOG and EMG. This information was recorded on a Grass model 6 EEG machine, and read according to standard sleep criteria (11).

The subject slept on a standard hospital-type bed, in a ventilated dark room, ten feet by six feet in area, and was monitored from approximately 11:00 P.M. until the time he spontaneously emerged in the morning.

On the fourth day of the five-day study (each Thursday) the subjects came to the laboratory to produce as much alpha rhythm as possible during a twelve-hour period. At another time, but under exactly the same conditions, the subjects were required to produce a nonalpha rhythm for reinforcement. All participants were paid contingent upon the amount of alpha or nonalpha they produced. Immediately after the twelve-hour biofeedback experiment, meals were provided in the experimental room. The electrode montage was then changed from parietal-occipital for maximal alpha recording to standard sleep leads for the night recording.

Percentages of the standard sleep stages and the total sleep times for nights following alpha production, nights following nonalpha production, first nights (Mondays), and control nights (Tuesdays, Wednesdays and Fridays) were averaged separately.

Results and Discussion

The means for the sleep stages and the total amount of sleep for each experimental condition are presented in Table 1. The mean percentage of each sleep stage and the total sleep time across subjects were compared by means of t-tests. There was

TABLE 1. Sleep Percentages of Total Recording time for Experimental, First Night, and Control Nights

	N	A	I	II	III	IV	REM	Total
After alpha day	5	6.9	5.4	55.6	11.8	1.1	19.1	380.8
(SD)		(2.9)	(1.2)	(10.9)	(12.7)	(1.8)	(4.0)	(57.1)
After nonalpha day	5	8.6	6.1	54.3	9.4	1.1	20.4	417.5
(SD)	(4.1)	(1.3)	(2.8)	(3.7)	(.74)	(5.6)	(69.3)	
First nights	5	7.2	6.2	60.6	10.4	2.5	13.0	434.9
(SD)		(6.0)	(4.2)	(12.3)	(7.6)	(3.5)	(3.6)	(23.2)
Control nights	29	7.0	6.3	58.7	9.2	1.6	17.1	433.2
(SD)		(3.7)	(3.5)	(8.0)	(7.7)	(2.2)	(5.0)	(45.4)

no significant difference between the percentages of sleep stages 1, 2, 3, 4, or REM for either experimental condition when compared to the control nights. However, the decrement of total sleep time for the night following alpha production compared with the control nights proved statistically significant ($p < 0.028$). Latencies to onset of slow wave sleep yielded no significant differences. The quantity of Stage 4 was probably reduced due to the attenuation of 1 Hz activity by the telemetry unit. While this is not desirable, it is very doubtful that this artifact would have any bearing on this experiment since all conditions, experiment and control, had the same frequency limitation. It is also important to remember that the percentages presented in Table 1 represent total recording time, which would naturally show more awake and less Stage 4 than the percentages of sleep time alone.

The amount of the alpha percentage produced per subject during the twelve-hour experimental period within a single condition, alpha or nonalpha production, did not correlate with the total sleep time. It was also observed that performance on the alpha production task was uncorrelated with performance on the nonalpha production task (10). There was a tendency toward a decrease in the amount of REM sleep of the first nights versus the control nights ($p < 0.09$) partially confirming one feature of the "first-night effect" (12).

The data indicated that twelve hours of producing relatively high amounts of EEG alpha rhythm are associated with a decrement of total sleep time. This effect emerges at higher confidence levels than the first-night effect in the small population tested. The effects of physical and social isolation cannot account for the sleep time decrement, since the nonalpha condition entailed similar isolation. To our knowledge, innate constitutional differences, certain stimulating drugs, and affective disorders constitute the principal classes of factors lowering total sleep time. Given the novelty of specific brain wave production as a consciously-controlled, noninvasive technique of possibly decreasing subsequent sleep need, further study would seem warranted.

Summary

The sleep of five individuals was studied electroencephalographically after prolonged daytime maintenance of EEG alpha rhythm to note whether alpha production changed the following night's sleep. The five subjects had shown the highest capacity to produce abundant alpha rhythm during another study which utilized twenty-three subjects on a five-hour alpha-feedback paradigm. Each of the subjects slept in the laboratory during two separate five-night periods, Monday through Friday, at least a week apart. On one Thursday the subject spent twelve hours in the laboratory attempting to produce maximal amounts of alpha via feedback techniques, and on another Thursday, twelve hours of maximal nonalpha was produced. For the sleep data, Tuesday, Wednesday, and Friday nights were used as controls across subjects, with Monday nights used for habituation and Thursday nights the experimental night. Mean percentages of the various sleep stages and total sleep times were compared beween the alpha and the nonalpha nights and control nights. No differences amongst the standard sleep stages between postalpha or postnonalpha nights were observed, but a decrement of sleep time was noted between the control nights and the postalpha nights. Thus, production of high amounts of alpha rhythm does not appear to affect the discrete stages of sleep but may be associated with a slightly decreased sleep need.

REFERENCES

1. Stoyva J, Zimmerman J, Metcalf D: Distorted visual feedback and augmented REM sleep. Presented to the Association for the Physiological Study of Sleep, Santa Fe, March 1970
2. Allen SR, Oswald I, Tagney J: The effects of distorted visual input on sleep. Presented to the Association for the Physiological Study of Sleep, Bruges, June 1971
3. Baekeland F: Laboratory studies of effects of presleep events on sleep and dreams. Int Psychiat Clin 7:49–58, 1970
4. Greenberg R, Pearlman CH, Gampel D: War neuroses and the adaptive function of sleep. Brit J Med Psychol 45:27–33, 1972
5. Natami K, Shurley JT, Pierce CM: Fluctuations in sleep stage patterns as a generalized response to environmental stimulation. Presented to the Association for the Physiological Study of Sleep, Bruges, June 1971
6. Scott J: Some environmental conditions affecting REM time. Presented to the Association for the Physiological Study of Sleep, Bruges, June 1971
7. Tagney J: Rearing in an enriched or isolated environment: Sleep patterns in the rat. Presented to the Association for the Physiological Study of Sleep, New York, May 1972
8. Altman JL, Whitehead WE, Rechtschaffen A: Effects of five hours restraint stress on subsequent sleep in the rat. Presented to the Association for the Physiological Study of Sleep, Bruges, June 1971
9. Webb WG, Friedman J: Attempts to modify the sleep patterns in the rat. Physiol and Behav 6:459–460, 1971
10. Regestein QR, Pegram GV, Cooke B, Bradley D: Alpha rhythm percentage maintained during four and twelve hour feedback periods. Psychosom Med 35:215–222, 1973
11. Rechtschaffen A, Kales A: A manual of standardized terminology, techniques and scoring system for sleep stages of human subjects. Public Health Service, US Government Printing Office, Washington DC, 1968
12. Agnew HW, Webb WB, Williams HL: The first night effect: An EEG study of sleep. Psychophysiology 2:363–366, 1966

VIII

OBESITY AND SELF-CONTROL

New Therapies for the **36**
Eating Disorders

Albert Stunkard

New approaches to psychotherapy, which appear more effective than traditional ones in modifying several kinds of disturbed behavior, have recently been applied to the eating disorders. Patients with both anorexia nervosa and obesity have responded to behavior modification, and experience with obesity has already been sufficient to permit the development and description of relatively specific behavioral programs. These programs have been used to compare behavior modification in a systematic manner with a variety of alternate treatment methods. Every one of eight such studies has reported results favoring behavior modification, an unusual example of unanimity in this heterogeneous and complex disorder. Furthermore, some new experimental designs developed in these studies are making a significant contribution to the study of psychotherapy and the elucidation of its effective components.

I N RECENT years new and distinctive forms of psychotherapy have commanded increasing attention as evidence mounts that they are more effective than traditional techniques in a variety of disorders. These new treatments, known as behavior modification, behavior therapy, and experimental analysis of behavior, comprise a heterogenous series of techniques, bound together by

Accepted for publication Aug 19, 1971.
From the Department of Psychiatry, University of Pennsylvania, and the Philadelphia General Hospital, Philadelphia, and the Center for Advanced Study in the Behavioral Sciences, Stanford, Calif.
Reprint requests to Department of Psychiatry, University of Pennsylvania, Philadelphia 19104 (Dr. Stunkard).

the efforts of their proponents to apply the findings and methods of experimental psychology to disorders of human behavior. The most consistent evidence of their effectiveness comes from the treatment of obesity where their superiority over other methods has been demonstrated in nine different studies. This essay reviews these studies, describes the application of behavior modification techniques to obesity, and outlines some of the increasingly sophisticated experimental designs which are elucidating the effective elements of psychotherapy. It seems particularly important that psychiatrists know of these developments, for behavior modification has grown up largely outside their purview and, at times, in the face of their opposition. The extent of the leadership exercised by psychologists and social workers is nowhere better illustrated than in the "medical" problem of obesity: physicians participated in only one of nine studies described here.

The distinctive characteristic of the various methods of behavior modification is the belief that behavior disorders of the most divergent types are learned responses and that modern theories of learning have much to teach us regarding both the acquisition and extinction of these responses.[1] Furthermore, proponents of behavior modification have been distinguished by their explicit statements of methods and goals, and their willingness to put their results on the line for comparison with other forms of treatment. Illustrative of these methodological concerns, behavior therapists have been among the first to recognize the power, as a dependent variable in psychotherapy research, of weight change in pounds, and they have turned to the treatment of obesity in order to utilize this measure. It is ironic that psychiatry, so sorely in need of measures to evaluate therapeutic success and failure, has taken so long to recognize the sensivity, reliability, and validity of weight change as such a measure.

Anorexia Nervosa

The characteristics and potential of behavior modification can perhaps best be introduced, as they were to me, by the description of a behavioral approach to anorexia nervosa. Three case reports had suggested that behavioral techniques could modify the under-eating of anorexic patients and produce weight gain.[2-4] Not until behavioral analysis, however, revealed an unexpectedly prominent feature of the disorder was it possible to apply an effective behavioral technology to a series of patients.[5,6] This feature was hyperactivity, and its use in therapy illustrates the simplicity and power of behavior modification in this chronic, often intractable, disorder.

Pedometer measurements of patients hospitalized for treatment of anorexia nervosa revealed that they walked an average of 6.8 miles per day, as compared with a mean daily value of 4.9 miles for women of normal weight living at home. This observation suggested that opportunity for physical activity might serve as a reinforcement for increased food intake or, as the program came to specify, weight gain. Accordingly, the patient's access to physical activity was made contingent upon weight gain. Specifically, she was permitted a six-hour unrestricted period outside the hospital on any day that her morning weight was at least 0.5 lb above her previous morning's weight. No comment was made concerning the level of activity or food consumption, thus avoiding direct confrontation over eating.

Less than one week after this regimen was instituted, the first three patients responded with a rapid and consistent increase in body weight. They averaged gains of 4 lb per week during six weeks of hospitalization. These results rank with the best reported in the medical literature, including series of patients treated with far more aggressive measures (bed rest, tube feeding, very large doses of chlorpromazine and insulin).[7-14]

The effectiveness of this approach led us to apply it, with modification, in three additional patients, all of whom responded with similarly gratifying weight gains. An instructive example was a 17-year-old girl admitted in a state of profound inanition and weighing 22.7 kg (50 lb) (height, 149.9 cm [4 ft 11 in]). The patient's behavioral repertoire was so limited that a search for a potential reinforcer was at first unsuccessful. Soon after chlorpromazine treatment was begun, however, the patient began to complain of its sedative effects. Her complaints suggested a new reinforcement contingency.

We prescribed decreases in chlorpromazine dosage proportional to the amount of weight gained on the previous day: on any day that followed a loss or no change in weight, the patient received 400 mg; a 0.25-lb gain resulted in a decrease to 300 mg; a 0.5-lb gain resulted in a decrease to 200 mg; a 0.75-lb gain resulted in a decrease to 100 mg; and a 1-lb gain resulted in a decrease to no drug. This patient averaged a gain of 6 lb per week, despite the consequent radical decrease in chlorpromazine dosage! Moreover, the results made it clear that the therapeutic efficacy of the behavioral approach did not depend upon hyperactivity or any other specific symptom. Rather, any suitable contingency may serve as the reinforcer in behavioral therapy. This finding was particularly indicative to me of the effectiveness of this form of treatment.

Obesity—First Applications

Spurred by the surprising success of a simple behavioral technique in the treatment of a condition as stubborn as anorexia nervosa and by encouraging case reports of the effectiveness of behavioral modification in obesity,[15-20] I attempted to apply its principles to the treatment of two obese persons. Taking the anorexia nervosa paradigm as my model, I decided to make a small number of reinforcements contingent upon weight changes measured at first once and later as often as four times a day. In the case of one patient, a cooperative roommate offered to take over such unpleasant chores as doing dishes or taking out the garbage on the day following one during which the patient lost weight. The second patient's wife, herself a psychologist, agreed to make sexual intercourse contingent upon her husband having lost weight that day.

After an initial loss of 20 lb, the weights of both patients stabilized and they eventually stopped treatment. Paradoxically, it appeared that obesity posed a greater challenge to behavior modification than did the more stubborn anorexia nervosa. Other attempts to apply behavioral therapy to obesity also suggest that the task is more complicated than experience with anorexia nervosa had indicated. Most of these attempts were based on a 1962 paper by Ferster et al[21] who presented a detailed behavioral analysis of eating and means of control.

The Behavioral Program

Perhaps it would be well, at this point, to describe a typical behavioral program for the treatment of obesity. Since our program[22] is derived, as were most others, from Ferster et al,[21] and is similar to the other programs, I will describe it in some detail. Four principles are involved.

Description of the Behavior To Be Controlled.—The patients were asked to keep daily records of the amount, time, and circumstances of their eating. The immediate results of this time-consuming and inconvenient procedure were grumbling and complaints. But eventually each patient reluctantly acknowledged that keeping these records had proved very helpful, particularly in increasing his awareness of how much he ate, the speed with which he ate, and the large variety of environmental and psychological situations associated with eating. For example, after two weeks of record-keeping a 30-year-old housewife reported that, for the first time in her life, she recognized that anger stimulated her eating. Accordingly, whenever she began to get angry, she left the kitchen and wrote down how she felt, thereby decreasing her anger and aborting her eating.

Modification and Control of the Discriminatory Stimuli Governing Eating.—Most of the patients reported that their eating took place in a wide variety of places and at many different times during the day. It was postulated that these times and places had become so-called discriminatory stimuli signaling eating. The concept of a discriminatory stimulus derives from the animal laboratory, where such stimuli as the flashing of a light or sounding of a tone may signal to an animal that pressing a lever will produce food pellets or other reward. Since the reinforcer never occurs without the discriminatory stimulus, in the language of learning theory, the stimuli come to "control" various forms of behavior. In an effort to decrease the potency of the discriminatory stimuli that controlled their eating, patients were encouraged to confine eating, including snacking, to one place. In order not to disrupt domestic routines, this place was usually the kitchen. Further efforts to control discriminatory stimuli included using distinctive table settings, perhaps an unusually colored place mat and napkin. In addition, patients were encouraged to make eating a pure experience, unaccompanied by other activity such as reading, watching television, or arguing with their families.

Development of Techniques To Control the Act of Eating.—Specific techniques were utilized to help patients decrease their speed of eating, to become aware of all the components of the eating process, and to gain control over these components. Exercises included counting each mouthful of food eaten during a meal, placing utensils on the plate after every third mouthful until that mouthful was chewed and swallowed, and introducing a two-minute interruption of the meal.

Prompt Reinforcement of Behaviors That Delay or Control Eating.—A reinforcement schedule, using a point system, was devised for control of eating behavior. Exercise of the suggested control procedures during a meal earned a certain number of points. These points were converted into money, which was brought to the next meeting and donated to the group. At the beginning of the program, the groups decided how the money should be used and they chose highly altruistic uses. Each week one group donated its savings to the Salvation Army and another to a needy friend of one of the members, a widow with 14 children.

It has, in the past, been fairly easy to assess any outpatient treatment for obesity because the results have been so uniformly poor and the treatments themselves so obviously inadequate. (Inpatient treatment, with its potential for greater control of the patient has of course been more successful in weight reduction. Its usefulness has been limited, however, by the almost invariable regaining of weight after discharge.[23,24]) I have summarized my own and my colleagues' results with outpatient treatment quite simply: "Most obese persons will not stay in treatment for obesity. Of those who stay in treatment, most will not lose weight, and of those who do lose weight most will regain it."[25] Attrition rates vary between 20% and 80%. Only 25% of those who enter treatment lose as much as 20 lb; only 5% as much as 40 lb.[26] Against this background, the results obtained by Ferster et al, whose subjects averaged weight losses of only 10 lb, must be considered poor. Against this same background, moreover, the significance of a report on "Behavioral Control of Overeating"[27] is at once apparent. For in this report, Stuart, using a treatment program based on Ferster et al's, described the best results yet obtained in the outpatient treatment of obesity.

A Landmark in the Treatment of Obesity

Stuart's results are summarized in Fig 1 and show the weight losses, over a one-year period, of eight patients who remained in treatment (the initial study group had included ten patients). Three, or 30% of the original sample, lost more than 40 lb and six lost more than 30 lb. These results are the best ever reported for outpatient treatment of obesity, and they constitute a landmark in our understanding of this disorder. Even the absence of a control group does not vitiate the significance of the study.

Certain features of the report deserve attention: First, the expenditure of time was not exorbitant. In fact, the study took no longer than a number of others which achieved far poorer results. At the beginning of the treatment program, patients were seen in 30-minute sessions held three times each week for a total of 12 to 15 sessions. Thereafter, treatment sessions were scheduled as needed, usually at two-week intervals, for the next three months. Subsequently, there were monthly sessions and finally "maintenance" sessions were provided as needed. The total number of sessions during the year varied from 16 to 41.

The specific behavioral techniques applied by Stuart are similar to those used in other studies and described previously. One important feature of this study was that the regimen specified a rigid set of "how to do it" instructions for each of the first 12 in-

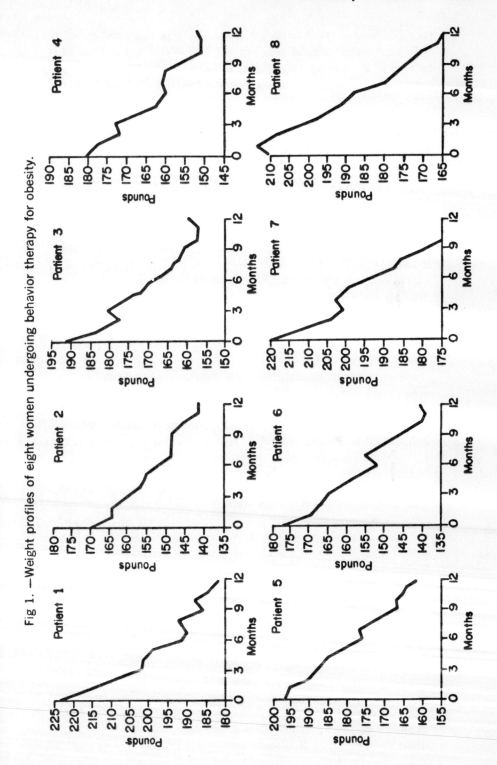

Fig 1. —Weight profiles of eight women undergoing behavior therapy for obesity.

terviews. Within this framework, however, there was great opportunity for the exercise of creativity by both the therapist and the patient. For example, Stuart noted that for patients suffering from a "behavioral depression," eating may be the only readily available reward or reinforcement. For these individuals, the therapist must cultivate a reservoir of positively reinforcing responses. Two patients in the series were helped to develop such responses—an interest in caged birds and in growing African violets respectively. In contrast to the other studies described here, all of which used group therapy, Stuart treated his patients individually.

Use of No-Treatment Controls

In 1969, Harris reported a well-controlled study which utilized behavioral techniques to control eating in mildly overweight college students.[28] Two treatment groups, of three male and five female students each, were compared with a control group of eight students. In order not to discourage them, and thereby bias the results, the controls were told that they could not enter treatment at once because of a conflict in schedules, but that they would receive treatment later. Treatment sessions were held twice weekly for the first two months and then on a more irregular basis for the second two months.

The results are illustrated in Fig 2. The mean weight loss for the experimental group was 10.5 lb as compared with a weight gain of 3.6 lb for the control group, a difference that was very highly significant ($P < .001$).

Although the results in the treatment group are clearly far superior to those in the no-treatment control group, they are not as good as others reported in the literature, when judged by the criteria I have mentioned: only 21% of Harris' subjects lost 20 lb and none lost as much as 40 lb. A major reason for these results was that her subjects were less obese than those studied by other investigators.

An interesting and perhaps significant aspect of the study is the note that E (the experimenter) lost 27 lb. As Harris continues in the quaint language of the psychological literature, "the modeling effect of E, who went from fat to moderate with the pretest Ss and from moderate to thin with the Ss in the final study, was commented upon by many of the subjects." Harris noted that several variables may have contributed to the outcome besides the planned experimental procedures. She suggests that "a much more controlled study, in which various techniques and combinations of procedures are isolated, would be necessary to discover their differential effects."[28]

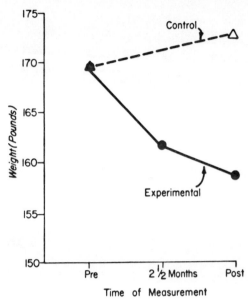

Fig 2.—Mean weights for experimental and control subjects.

Precisely such an investigation was carried out by Wollersheim.[29] Her work is representative of a small but extremely valuable group of studies that are elucidating the effective components of psychotherapy.

Introduction of Alternate-Treatment Controls

Wollersheim's elegant study attempted to disentangle the contributions of various techniques by establishing four experimental conditions: (1) "focal" (behavioral) treatment, 20 patients; (2) nonspecific therapy, 20 patients; (3) social pressure, 20 patients; and (4) control groups of persons promised treatment but not yet receiving it, 19 patients.

The study thus contained three treatment groups (1, 2, and 3) and three control groups (2, 3, and 4) for the behavior modification group. Subjects were, again, mildly (10%) overweight female college students. Four therapists treated groups of five subjects under each of the three treatment conditions. A course of treatment consisted of ten sessions extending over a three-month period.

Wollersheim's findings are illustrated in Fig 3. They showed that at the end of treatment and at eight weeks follow-up, the focal group's results were superior not only to the no-treatment control's, but also to those of the other two treatment groups. The "social pressure" group had participated in 20-minute sessions

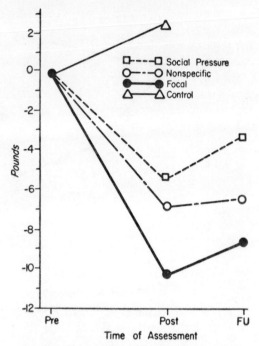

Fig 3.—Mean weight loss of the focal (be-havioral) treatment group, the two alterna-tive treatment control groups, and the no-treatment control group. Treatment lasted three months and follow-up (*FU*) occurred eight weeks later.

based upon those of TOPS (Take Off Pounds Sensibly).[30] The ses-sions included a weigh-in, verbal praise for weight loss, encour-agement for failure to lose weight, and the wearing of such TOPS artifacts as a star for weight loss, a sign in the form of a pig for weight gain, and a sign reading "Turtle" for no change in weight. The purpose of this technique is to foster a high positive ex-pectation for losing weight and to develop and use special pres-sure to help subjects reduce.

The purpose of a "nonspecific therapy" group was to control for the effects of group treatment that resulted from such nonspecific factors as increased attention, "faith," expectation of relief, and presentation of a treatment rationale and meaningful "ritual." The rationale presented to the subjects in this group was that they needed to develop insight into the "real and not readily recogniz-able underlying reasons" for their behavior and to discover the "unconscious motives" underlying their "personality make-up." Each subject was told that as she obtained insight and better un-derstanding of the "real motives and forces" operating within her personality, she would find it easier to accomplish her goals and lose weight.

In each group, not only weight loss but also responses to an eating-patterns questionnaire were used as dependent variables. Here, too, the focal therapy group changed more than the other three, reaching statistically significant results on three of six factors: "emotional and uncontrolled overeating," "eating in isolation," and "between meal eating."

More Alternate-Treatment Controls: Therapy Without a Therapist

Hagen, following up the work of Wollersheim, accepted her finding that behavior modification was the most effective method for the treatment of obesity.[31] He turned his attention to a further refinement—determining whether the results obtained were due only to the specific behavioral techniques used or were dependent also upon the interpersonal influence of the therapist. Hagen constructed an experimental design similar to Wollersheim's. The various treatment groups were compared with each other and with a control group promised treatment but not yet receiving it: (1) group (behavioral) therapy, 18 subjects; (2) bibliotherapy (use of a written manual), 18 subjects; (3) group and bibliotherapy combined, 18 subjects; and (4) the group promised treatment but not yet receiving it, 35 subjects.

The 90 subjects in his study were also mildly (10%) overweight female college students. They were randomly assigned to one of four experimental groups in such a way that the groups were comparable in relation to the obesity of their members. Three therapists treated six subjects each in the group therapy and combined therapy conditions. Ten treatment sessions were held over a three-month period.

The results of treatment are shown in Fig 4. The greatest weight loss occurred in the group and bibliotherapy combined group, which lost an average of 15 lb during treatment and regained 2 lb during the four-week follow-up period. The difference in weight loss between this group and the other two treatment groups was, however, not statistically significant. There was a significant difference ($P < .01$) between its results and those of the no-treatment group. Wollersheim's eating-patterns questionnaire also elicited results from all three treatment groups that were similar to those from her "focal" group, but demonstrated no change in the control group.

Hagen's work showed that it is possible to treat obesity effectively by using a written manual that embodies behavioral ther-

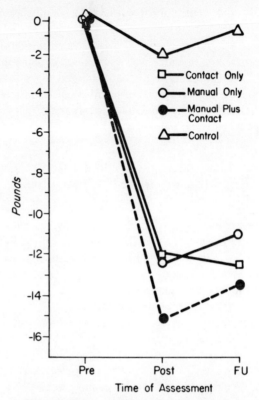

Fig 4.—Mean weight loss of the three treatment groups and of the no-treatment control group. The former lost significantly more weight than the latter, but there was no significant difference in weight loss between the three treatment groups. Treatment lasted three months and follow-up occurred one month later.

apy principles. Moreover, this treatment is apparently as effective as one that utilizes therapists. These results further confirm the effectiveness of behavioral principles in the treatment of obesity.

A Study With a Crossover Design

Stuart has recently completed a study that used the patient as his own control in what is known as a crossover design.[32] The results are summarized in Fig 5. The subjects were divided into two cohorts which contained three moderately obese women each. During a preliminary five-week period they kept careful records of their weight and food intake. Group 1 then received twice weekly treatment sessions of about 40 minutes, for 15 weeks. Meanwhile,

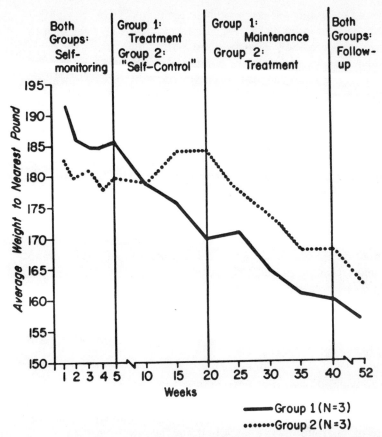

Fig 5.—Weight changes in two groups of women undergoing behavior therapy for overeating.

group 2 was given diet-planning materials and an exercise program (both of which were also offered to group 1). Group 1 lost an average of 15 lb while the control group *gained* an average of 4 lb. At the end of the 15 weeks, group 1 continued with the program on its own, while group 2 received 15 weeks of the same treatment group 1 had received (group therapy plus diet planning and exercise). Under these circumstances, group 1 lost an additional 9 lb, but at a slightly lower rate than when it was under active treatment. Group 2, on the other hand, which had gained weight during the preceding 15 weeks, lost 15 lb. Both groups continued to lose in the subsequent 12 weeks without further treatment.

Treatment of Severe Obesity

Another dimension of the behavioral approach to obesity was

provided by a study of severely obese patients (78% overweight).[22] Two cohorts of eight and seven patients respectively were seen in weekly group therapy sessions lasting about two hours, for three months. The therapists were a male experimental psychologist with a strong background in learning theory but little clinical experience, and a female research technician with no previous experience in therapy. Two control groups received supportive psychotherapy, instruction about dieting and nutrition, and, upon demand, appetite suppressants. Their male and female therapy team consisted of an internist just completing a psychiatric residency, who had had extensive experience in the treatment of obesity, and a research nurse.

The results of treatment of the two cohorts are summarized in the Table. The control group's losses are comparable to those to be found in the medical literature—none lost 40 lb and 24% lost more than 20 lb. By contrast, 13% of the behavior modification group lost more than 40 lb and 53% lost more than 20 lb. Although the differences between the behavior modification and control groups for weight losses over 20 and 40 lb are not statistically significant, the difference for weight losses over 30 lb is ($P = .015$ by Fisher exact probability test). Furthermore, those who had lost weight during treatment continued to lose weight during the following year.

The weight losses for each subject are plotted in Fig 6. Two findings should be noted: First, in each cohort the median weight loss for the behavior modification group was greater than that for the control group—24 lb versus 18 lb for the first cohort; 13 versus 11 for the second. Second, there is far greater variability of results in the behavior modification groups ($F = 4.38, P < .005$). Because of this variability the difference in weight loss between the behavior modification and control groups did not reach statistical significance.

Testing the Limits of the Behavioral Approach

Recently three further studies, on strikingly dissimilar populations, have demonstrated the remarkably wide range of circumstances in which behavior modification may be effective in the treatment of obesity. The first population consisted of long-term schizophrenic patients in a Veterans Administration Hospital,[33] the second of a heterogeneous group of Dutch men and women,[34] and the third of obese women in a general hospital.[35] As in three of the foregoing studies, follow-up data on the first two of these showed significantly greater weight loss among behavior modification subjects than among those who received other forms of treatment.

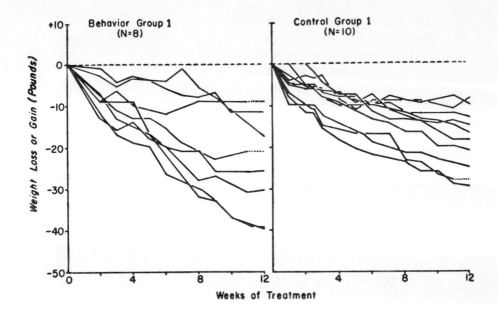

Fig 6, *Above and below.*—Weight changes of patients in the two cohorts. Dotted lines represented interpolated data based upon weights obtained during follow-up. Note greater weight loss of behavior modification groups and greater variability of this weight loss as compared with that of the control group.

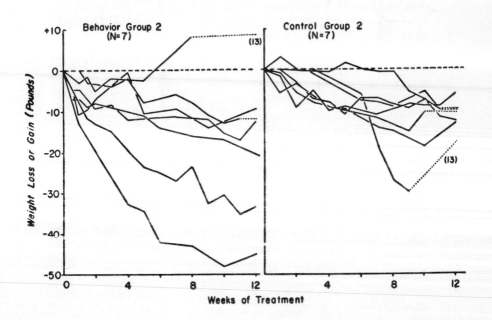

The first of these studies was carried out to explore the management of the obesity which so frequently develops among schizophrenic patients during prolonged hospitalization.[33] Seven men, matched for degree of overweight, were assigned to each of three groups—behavior modification, group therapy, and diet only. Treatment was carried out over a six-week period with a four-week followup. Behavior modification consisted of a penalty schedule involving forfeiture of part of $5 weekly allowance for failure to lose weight during the previous week. Weight loss carried no reward other than assuring the patient of his regular allotment. Group therapy sessions were held once each week for one hour, and consisted of weighings with encouraging comments for weight losses and discussion of reasons for gains and losses. Both treatment groups lost significantly more weight than the diet only group during the six-week treatment period. But the behavior modification subjects lost significantly more weight during the four-week follow-up than did the group therapy subjects.

In the second study the Dutch investigators chose as their subjects university students and others recruited by a variety of means, including advertisements in women's

Results of Treatment: % of Groups Losing Specified Amounts of Weight

Weight Loss	Behavior Modification Groups (No. = 15)		Control Therapy Groups (No. = 17)		Average Medical Literature End of Treatment
	After Treatment	One-Year Follow-up	After Treatment	One-Year Follow-up	
More than 40 lb	13%	33%	0%	12%	5%
More than 30 lb	33%	40%	0%	29%	···
More than 20 lb	53%	53%	24%	47%	25%

magazines.[34] Two behavior modification groups of 15 subjects each were compared with 15 subjects in a traditional diet-therapy group and 15 no-treatment controls. The program consisted of a four-week treatment period with follow-ups at six weeks and five months. At the end of four weeks, all three treatment groups had lost more weight than those who had received no treatment, and one of the behavior modification groups had lost more than the other two treatment groups. At the five-month follow-up, both behavior modification groups, one of which had continued to lose weight and the other of which had maintained its weight loss, had performed significantly more effectively than the diet therapy group, which had regained most of the weight it had lost.

The results of the third study, reported only briefly, again favored behavior modification.[35] Eleven obese women treated with this modality lost more weight than did nine obese women treated by conventional group psychotherapy (15 vs 6.6 lb). Furthermore, in an interesting parallel to the results reported by Penick et al, this 8.4-lb difference in weight loss was not statistically significant, largely because of the very great variability in the behavior modification group (W. Shipman, written communication, May 15, 1971).

Comments and Conclusions

The studies we have reviewed are an impressive example of the kind of contribution which behavior therapists are making to the scientific study of psychotherapy. These workers have introduced experimental designs of a sophistication and power unprecedented in psychotherapy research: they may well be laying the foundations of a truly cumulative science of psychotherapy.

Two further aspects of behavior modification may be less well appreciated by psychiatrists: the possibility of exercising great creativity on the part of both patient and therapist and the encouragement of patients to assume an unusually high degree of responsibility for their own treatment.

Creativity in Behavior Modification.—An unflattering view of behavior modification sees in it mechanistic manipulations to produce trivial changes in overt behavior at the expense of the patient's inner freedom and uniquely human qualities. Such polemics may cite the examples of systematic desensitization of phobias or the conditioned aversion therapy of alcoholism, treatments based upon respondent (pavlovian) conditioning. Whatever the merit of the criticism of these treatments, it is hardly relevant to behavioral measures, such as those reviewed here, which utilize primarily operant (skinnerian) conditioning. A closer look at these measures may help to clarify this point.

A behavioral analysis begins with a careful study of the environmental variables that control the patient's symptomatic behavior. These variables may be divided for convenience into antecedent events, which may precipitate the behavior, and consequent events, which may help to reward and maintain it. For example, understanding a particular episode of binge-eating requires precise information about what was happening to the patient just before the breakdown in eating control occurred. Similarly, it is important to ascertain the immediate effects upon the patient's feelings, on her husband's behavior, and, in fact, upon any significant aspect in her life. Stuart[36] has recently outlined a useful schema for a behavioral analysis and we have described earlier the kind of therapeutic program which can be constructed out of these analyses of specific behaviors.

I was persuaded of the value of such a method of proceeding as I considered the degree to which it specified techniques for the treatment of obesity which I had evolved empirically over nearly 20 years of treatment of obese persons. It contrasted sharply with the recommendations for treatment derived from psychodynamic theories. Such theories, for example, cautioned against considering with the patient his specific acts of overeating and consequent weight gains. For they saw in these acts merely symptoms of an underlying conflict. Any small benefits which might accrue from concern with these symptoms, it was taught, were likely to be far outweighed by distraction of patient and therapist from their primary task of resolution of the pathogenic conflicts. Such resolution, and only such resolution, could lead to a lasting cure.

Quite early, experiences with patients convinced me that such a course was countertherapeutic, and I began to discuss their eating behavior with my patients, focusing in ever greater detail upon specific acts of overeating. I had been content to explain these departures from accepted teaching as necessary adaptations to the special circumstances of the eating disorders. So, when I encountered an approach which prescribed what I was already doing, its appeal was immediate. This approach, moreover, went further to suggest potent new measures of great creativity. What is the source of this creativity?

Central to a behavioral analysis is the search by patient and therapist for solutions to problems which are at the same time both relatively modest and potentially soluble. By limiting therapeutic concern to discrete, clearly specified behaviors, this approach reduces the potentially limitless field of therapeutic encounter and permits patient and therapist to concentrate their efforts on a more limited number of variables than is possible with traditional therapies. By focusing a great deal of attention upon relatively small problems the probability of solving them is greatly increased. And, the experience of success, even in small matters, encourages the patient to continue the process of defining manageable problems and seeking solutions to them. It is hard to do justice to the remarkable creativity evoked in the course of this endeavor. The few examples described in this review can only suggest the kind of innovative measures which, in remarkable scope and diversity, have been applied to the treatment of obesity.

Responsibility in Behavior Modification.—The particular relevance of focusing upon environmental variables in the treatment of obesity is emphasized by Schachter's recent demonstration of the extent to which the eating behavior of many obese persons is under environmental control.[37] He found, for example, that obese persons were far more influenced than non-obese persons by such "external" factors as palatability, time of day, and availability of food, and far less influenced by such "internal" factors as hunger, measured by self-report, and by length of time after eating.

The high degree of environmental control of the food intake of obese persons may help to explain the failures of both routine medical management and of traditional insight therapy. Obese persons often adapt easily to general medicine's authoritarian-physician-dependent-patient relationship and lose some weight to please the doctor. Failure to deal with the environmental variables which play such an important part in the patient's eating, however, leaves him vulnerable to their influence, and sooner or later he breaks his diet. This transgression strikes at the special qualities of this kind of doctor-patient relationship, which then begins to lose its potency. Overeating recurs and a vicious cycle ensues.

The obese person who enters psychiatric treatment frequently fares little better. Insight therapy, with its focus on inner drives, motives, and conflicts, all too often ignores environmental factors in the control of food intake as thoroughly as does general medical treatment. Further, by holding out hope for an eventual solution to obesity through the resolution of conflict, it can foster magical expectations which distract the patient from more mundane concerns of greater therapeutic potential.

In contrast to this neglect by traditional therapies of the environmental influences to which the obese person seems so vulnerable, behavior modification helps him to focus his attention upon them. Not only is he encouraged to observe and make a detailed record of these influences on his eating behavior, but he is also shown how to use this information to plan and carry out tasks to help him gain control over this behavior. The difference between behavior modification and more traditional therapies is particularly notable in the extent of the demands each makes upon the obese patient in the interval between visits to the therapist. In contrast to the limited demands of traditional therapies, behavior modification makes it possible for the patient to invest a great deal of hard work in his treatment. The apparent dependency of successful outcome upon the amount of work invested encourages patients to assume an unusually high degree of responsibility for their own treatment. This increase in the opportunity for the exercise of personal responsibility may prove to be one of behavior modification's major contributions to treatment in psychiatry.

In conclusion, both greater weight loss during treatment and superior maintenance of weight loss after treatment indicate that behavior modification is more effective than previous methods of treatment for obesity. Further, the experimental designs developed to assess these treatments constitute a significant advance in the study of psychotherapy. (Since submission of this review, a comprehensive description of a behavioral approach to obesity has been published by Stuart and Davis.[38])

This study was supported in part by grant MH-15383 from the National Institute of Mental Health.

References

1. Eysenck HJ: Editorial. *Behav Res Ther* 1:1-2, 1963.
2. Bachrach AJ, Erwin W, Mohr JP: The control of eating behavior in an anorexic by operant conditioning techniques, in Ullmann LP, Krasner L (eds): *Case Studies in Behavior Modification*. New York, Holt Rinehart & Winston, 1965, pp 153-163.
3. Hallsten EA Jr: Adolescent anorexia nervosa treated by desensitization. *Behav Res Ther* 3:87-91, 1965.
4. Leitenberg H, Agras WS, Thomson LE: A sequential analysis of the effect of selective positive reinforcement in modifying anorexia nervosa. *Behav Res Ther* 6:211-218, 1968.
5. Blinder BJ, Freeman DMA, Ringold A, et al: Rapid weight restoration in anorexia nervosa. *Clin Res* 15:473, 1967.
6. Blinder BJ, Freeman DMA, Stunkard AJ: Behavior therapy of anorexia nervosa: Effectiveness of activity as a reinforcer of weight gain. *Amer J Psychiat* 126:1093-1098, 1970.
7. Williams E: Anorexia nervosa, a somatic disorder. *Brit Med J* 2:190-195, 1958.
8. Dally P, Sargant W: A new treatment of anorexia. *Brit Med J* 1:1770-1773, 1960.
9. Russell GH, Mezey AG: An analysis of weight gain in patients with anorexia nervosa treated with high calorie diets. *Clin Sci* 23:449-461, 1962.
10. Crisp AH: Clinical and therapeutic aspects of anorexia. *J Psychosom Res* 9:67-78, 1965.
11. Crisp AH: A treatment regime for anorexia nervosa. *Brit J Psychiat* 112:505-512, 1966.
12. Dally P, Sargant W: Treatment and outcome of anorexia. *Brit Med J* 2:293-295, 1966.
13. Groen JJ, Feldman-Toledano Z: Educative treatment of patients and parents in anorexia nervosa. *Brit J Psychiat* 112:671-678, 1966.
14. Browning CH, Miller SI: Anorexia nervosa: A study in prognosis and management. *Amer J Psychiat* 124:1128-1132, 1968.
15. Erickson MA: The utilization of patient behavior in the hypnotherapy of obesity. *Amer J Clin Hypn* 3:112-116, 1960.
16. Thorpe JG, Schmidt E, Brown PT, et al: Aversion relief therapy: A new method for general application. *Behav Res Ther* 2:71-82, 1964.

17. Meyer V, Crisp AH: Aversion therapy in two cases of obesity. *Behav Res Ther* **2**:143-147, 1964.

18. Cautela J: Covert sensitization. *Psychol Rep* **20**:459-468, 1967.

19. Kennedy WA, Foreyt J: Control of eating behavior in an obese patient by avoidance conditioning. *Psychol Rep* **22**:571-576, 1968.

20. Wolpe J: *The Practise of Behavior Therapy.* Oxford, England, Pergamon Press, 1969, pp 204, 205, 216, and 217.

21. Ferster CB, Nurnberger JI, Levitt EB: The control of eating. *J Mathetics* **1**:87-109, 1962.

22. Penick SB, Filion R, Fox S, et al: Behavior modification in the treatment of obesity. *Psychosom Med* **33**:49-55, 1971.

23. Maccuish AC, Munro JF, Duncun LJP: Follow-up study of refractory obesity treated by fasting. *Brit Med J* **1**:91-200, 1968.

24. Swanson DW, Dinello FA: Follow-up of patients starved for obesity. *Psychosom Med* **32**:209-214, 1970.

25. Stunkard AJ: The management of obesity. *New York J Med* **58**:79-87, 1958.

26. Stunkard AJ, McLaren-Hume M: The results of treatment for obesity. *Arch Intern Med* **103**:79-85, 1959.

27. Stuart RB: Behavioral control of overeating. *Behav Res Ther* **5**:357-365, 1967.

28. Harris MB: Self-directed program for weight control: A pilot study. *J Abnorm Psychol* **74**:263-270, 1969.

29. Wollersheim JP: The effectiveness of group therapy based upon learning principles in the treatment of overweight women. *J Abnorm Psychol* **76**:462-474, 1970.

30. Stunkard AJ, Fox S, Levine H: The management of obesity: Patient self-help and medical treatment. *Arch Intern Med* **125**:1067-1072, 1970.'

31. Hagen RL: *Group Therapy Versus Bibliotherapy in Weight Reduction,* thesis. University of Illinois, Champaign, 1969.

32. Stuart RB: A three-dimensional program for the treatment of obesity. *Behav Res Ther* **9**:177-186, 1971.

33. Harmatz MG, Lapuc P: Behavior modification of overeating in a psychiatric population. *J Consult Clin Psychol* **32**:583-587, 1968.

34. Jongman JG: *Vermagerings-Therapieen,* thesis. Psychologisch Laboratorium van de Universiteit van Amsterdam, Amsterdam, 1969.

35. Shipman W: *Behavior Therapy With Obese Dieters,* annual report of the Institute for Psychosomatic and Psychiatric Research and Training. Chicago, Michael Reese Hospital and Medical Center, 1970, pp 70-71.

36. Stuart RB: *Trick or Treatment: How and When Psychotherapy Fails.* Champaign, Ill, Research Press, 1971, pp 183-194.

37. Schachter S: Obesity and eating. *Science* **161**:751-756, 1968.

38. Stuart RB, Davis B: *Slim Chance in a Fat World: Behavioral Control of Obesity.* Champaign, Ill, Research Press, 1971.

Self-Regulation and its Clinical Application: Some Additional Conceptualizations

Frederick H. Kanfer and Paul Karoly

Behavior modification in the early seventies appears to be moving away from peripheralistic, "open-loop" conceptions of human behavior. Theorists and investigators are increasingly turning their attention to the variance contributed by man's unique response capabilities, typically summarized under the labels of *language, cognition,* or *self-processes* (see, for example, Bandura, 1969; Cautela, 1970; Kanfer, 1970, 1971; Kanfer & Phillips, 1970; Lazarus, 1971; Marston & Feldman, 1970; Murray & Jacobson, 1970). In psychotherapy there is a growing search for techniques by which the individual can assume major responsibility for effecting response changes, for only if the patient himself can master the control over his own behavior and over his environment can we expect therapy to have enduring effects and to prepare him for initiating preventive or therapeutic actions under new and unforeseen circumstances. If we can identify

This paper, prepared especially for the present volume, was supported, in part, by Research Grant MH 17902–02 from the National Institute of Mental Health, U.S. Public Health Service, to Frederick H. Kanfer.

Zeitgeist while in its midst, we might point out that the changes within behavioral psychology are but a reflection of a general relaxation of social and institutional pressures for conformity or standardization of conduct, and the emergence of a "Do your own thing" ethic that runs counter to formal (and informal) normative control over individual action. Thus, we are faced with the paradox that, while we may accept the controlling influence of the social environment over behavior (which strict behaviorists would have us do), the breakdown of external governance and its structural permanence requires greater continuity and responsibility on the part of the individual.

The present paper is an attempt to outline a developing theoretical view of the process by which people effect changes in established (habitual) patterns of behavior. Several techniques of *instigation* therapy have been proposed that attempt to integrate external (therapist) control with the patient's private or covert response capabilities (Kanfer & Phillips, 1970), and these continue to receive clinical support and conceptual attention (see, for example, Mahoney, 1970; McFall, 1970). However, a systematic overview of the pivotal behavioral process in this treatment approach, the *self-control sequence*, has not yet been offered by behavior therapists. We plan, therefore, to propose some ideas that would lay the groundwork for a functional analysis of the social setting in human affairs within which self-control and related processes are usually embedded. To date, this area has been examined primarily from a philosophical and moral point of view. The psychiatric orientation has generally been purely descriptive or intrapsychic, with self-control equated with ego strength, superego development, and similar nonempirical, unitary-trait conceptions (Klausner, 1965; Mischel, 1971). In contrast, the model presented here has been formulated to permit tests of its utility via experimentation. The reader will discern the elements and underlying rationale for the present position in the preceding review by Kanfer and Phillips (pp. 417–427 of this volume).

Self-Control and Self-Regulation

We begin with the assertion that self-control *as a process* (superordinate to the various mechanisms of which it is comprised) can best be viewed as a special case of self-regulation. As Kanfer has stated:

> While self-regulatory behaviors generally result in some modification of one's own behavior or of the environmental setting, self-control is characterized as a special case in which there is some underlying motive for *nonexecution* of a response sequence which, under other circumstances, would be predicted to have a high probability of occurrence. Self-control always involves a situation in which there is potentiality of execution of highly

probable behaviors, but instead a response of lower probability occurs. The interest is in the variables which effect the reduction of the occurrence of the probabilities of such behaviors (1970, pp. 214–215).

Recently, a more specific componential analysis of the regulatory process has been offered (Kanfer, 1971). A brief look at this model will aid the present explication.

When conditions are such that behavior chains are not run off smoothly, for example, when a choice point is reached, when an external event interrupts and refocuses one's attention, when one's activation level changes or when the expected consequences of behavior are not forthcoming, then a process of *self-monitoring* is hypothesized to go into effect. Utilizing the input from the external environment and from response-reduced cues (both modified by the individual's social learning history), the person is in a position to *self-evaluate*, that is, to make a discrimination or judgment by comparing the data from the various input sources with a subjectively held *performance standard* (criterion). If the outcome of the comparison is favorable (that is, if the individual judges that he has exceeded the standard level), a positive *self-reinforcement* (SR+) is the result. If the outcome is unfavorable, negative consequences (self-presented aversive stimulation, SR−) ensue. The sequence may, thus, be illustrated:

$$\text{self-monitoring} \longrightarrow$$
$$\text{self-evaluation} \longrightarrow$$
$$\text{self-reinforcement}$$

An S-R analysis of self-regulation focuses on the maintenance of behavior chains in the absence of external support, emphasizing the key role of self-reactions.[1] The goal of self-control, on the other hand, is a change in the probability of executing a final response in a chain. It involves the introduction, by the individual, of techniques designed to insure the nonoccurrence of the terminal link [or the occurrence of a response with initially low probability]. That which unites self-control and the process of self-regulation is the identity of the component mechanisms, with the exception of the performance standard. In self-control situations, the standard (usually based on norms or past experiences) is provided by a kind of *performance promise* or *contract* made by the example, "No more than five cigarettes a day, so help me!"), or in interaction with another person (such as a parent, spouse, or therapist). The antecedents of self-control lie in the discrepancy between self-observation and the performance promise, followed by potential self-reinforcement operations aimed at reducing this discrepancy. Verbal or motoric, the self-reinforcing event is always self-initiated and made contingent upon a self-prescribed (or therapist-prescribed) contract for behavior change.

It has been suggested that the standard (contract or promise) in therapy has utility in directing the change process. We will examine next the factors associated with the directive function of contracts over the execution of desired behaviors.

Social Contracts and Negotiations

The view that man behaves in accordance with written and unwritten social rules is not new. However, the study of cultural and situational parameters that

[1] Research in each of these areas has been accumulating at a rapid pace; thus the review by Kanfer and Phillips (pp. 417–427 of this volume) is only partially up-to-date.

influence the form and direction of individual behavior has been pursued more rigorously by sociologists and social psychologists than by personality theorists. Working from a developmental perspective, investigators in the area of socialization have defined the shift of control from socializing agents to individuals (internalization of rules, moral development) as the most important social learning event of childhood. Sociologists have viewed the social contract as the sine qua non of organized society. And, on a different level, economists depict the process of exchange of goods and services as resting on a foundation of contractual order and rational bargaining. Philosophers have expended much energy in the analysis of man's "nature" as a rule-forming, rule-following, and rule-breaking creature, while adding some rule of their own about man's proper rational and logical behavior. And, finally, we might note that the interpretation and enforcement of legal contracts and agreements (including the aversive consequences for failure to fulfill them) constitute a large share of the practice of law and penology.

Approaching self-control as a process that includes contract negotiation (with oneself or others), the behavioral psychologist must turn his attention, first, to defining the terms ("What is a contract, promise, or statement of intention?"), performing a functional analysis ("Under what conditions are intentions stated, and what maintains them?"), and relating his concepts to the larger theoretical network ("How and when do intentions or promises or so-called therapeutic contracts lead to the actual execution of self-controlling behavior?").

The Contract

Basically, a contract is an agreement that describes particular behaviors that must be engaged in by the contractors, under specific conditions. Typically, some mode of enforcement is provided. Nonfulfillment of the terms of the contract is clearly identifiable and the imposition of sanctions (consequences) is agreed upon in advance. A contract provides one means of social monitoring that clearly incorporates the elements of discriminative and contingency control. Our lives are fraught with situations of a contractual nature, varying in specificity and controlling power for enforcement (for example, employer-employee, buyer-seller, teacher-pupil, parent-child, and, most relevant for the current argument, therapist-client).

The concept of a therapeutic contract is basic to analytic thinking (Freud, 1913; Menninger, 1958). It has also been proposed by theorists of a behavioral persuasion (see, for example, Pratt & Tooley, 1964; Sulzer, 1962). A distinguishing feature of the behavior therapy contract is its specificity, including the specification of controlling devices, in contrast to the vague, almost mystic nature of the psychoanalytic contract. Regardless of the therapist's theoretical orientation or the symptomatic behavior under consideration, a working arrangement between the therapist and client as regards the nature, place, manner, frequency, timing, and range of intervention steps to be taken by both parties generally facilitates achievement of treatment goals. However, in the light of the present theoretical framework, the contract takes on a different and unique coloration. The intention statement or performance promise (used here synonymously), as a variant of the performance standard, is a central construct in the system of propositions applied to the understanding of self-control in humans. When brought into the therapy room, the intention (now developing into a "contract") is no less a basic ingredient

in an SR analysis of behavior change, although it is now enmeshed in a highly complex social setting. Remaining within our model, then, we ask, "What are the relevant antecedents of intention statements?", "Under what conditions are they made and maintained?", and, following Kanfer and Saslow (1965), "Can the patient match his behavior to his intentions?" The remainder of this paper will be devoted to suggesting some tentative answers to these questions.

Intention Statements as Verbal Operants

Intention statements may be looked upon as a class of verbal operants which specify behavioral outcomes. When applied by an individual to himself, these verbal behaviors are often termed *intentions, plans, predictions, promises,* or *resolutions*." They parallel the class of responses called *contracts* and *agreements* when they are made in the presence of other people. These operants serve a specific role in the verbal community, approximating what Skinner (1957) calls *autoclitics*. That is, they are descriptive of the speaker, indicating something of his condition, a property of his behavior, or the circumstances responsible for that property ("qualifying" autoclitics). In extended interactions, autoclitics are useful to the listener and to the speaker (as a listener) in improving behavior predictions. Intention statements, related to self-control situations, are made because they permit the individual to "edit" or monitor his behavior more effectively in the context of new information about himself, and allow him to decide what action, if any, need be taken. "I am going to give up tobacco!" is a declaration of intent that follows from the informational input. "People younger than I are dying from lung cancer every day. And cigarettes cause lung cancer." Casting the same process in somewhat moralistic terms, Premack (1970) has described the cigarette smoker as ready to quit when he discovers his membership in "an ethically repugnant class," such as weak-willed, setting a bad example, or the like. At this point the smoker decides to exert self-control. Thus, Premack regards the main antecedents of self-control as the presentation of information about oneself that is strongly discrepant with the person's avowed self-image. In our view, the class of antecedents are much more varied and can include external as well as self-generated prescriptions for achieving a desired end-state.

It is important to keep in mind that, regardless of the conceptualization about the determinants of the stated intent, the statement is itself a behavior that can be the terminal link of the chain leading to a declaration. Or, it may be an instructional cue for execution of the intent. Thus, these verbal operants do not always constitute components of a self-control sequence. Even if they are originally a part of the behavior chain leading to execution, they may not continue to function as such. Therefore, let us examine more closely the variables that affect the making of an intention statement. The first group will cover factors that serve to increase the probability of the occurrence of verbal intention statements. A second set of variables will be discussed that can effect decreases in the frequency of emission of these behaviors. It is clear that in any situation combinations of these influences will determine the net effect.

What Promotes Intention Statements?

The probability of emitting a verbal operant of the intention or contract class is presumed to be high under the following conditions:

1. When the individual responds to cues in his environment (external or internal) that signal the conflictual nature of his current behavior pattern. According to our model, this behavior is an invariant early component of the self-control sequence. A person may reach for a cigarette and be interrupted by a television commercial of the American Cancer Society; or a heavy drinker may be reminded, en route to his favorite tavern, of a friend who has recently died of an ailment aggravated by alcohol consumption.

2. When the person is suffering from the aversive effects of the behavior to be controlled. Examples are the smoker during a coughing fit and the drinker in the throes of a hangover.

3. When the person is either satiated with respect to the undesirable behavior or when, for other reasons, the probability of making that response is low. Examples might be the obese person immediately after eating, a homosexual after several exhausting encounters, or a lover who has been jilted by his sweetheart.

4. When the probability of social approval for making intention statements is high. This might be the case when others are talking about their good intentions or when the verbal operant is also an S^D for reinforcement from another person (a hidden *mand*), like the promise of a lover, during lovemaking, to quit carousing or the promise of a child, just prior to getting his dessert, not to hit his little sister.

5. When the intention statement is made to a person who is unlikely or unable to monitor (verify) the final execution of the controlling behavior. An example would be a promise about behavior that is to take place

in another location or about behavior that is not normally accessible (public). A vow made in church to put an end to "evil" thoughts represents such an instance.

6. When the behavior to be controlled is infrequent or if execution is intended in the distant future. "I swear I'll never get drunk at another Christmas party at the office!" is an oft-heard example of this condition.

7. When the intention statement produces negative reinforcement or the contingent removal of some aversive stimulus. Examples would be the morning newspaper reader who promises to pay more attention to his wife in order to put an end to her nagging or the sibling in a headlock vowing not to "borrow" his brother's toys.

8. When the person's reinforcement history for intention statements has generally been positive and has been accompanied by the desired short-term outcome. The parent who forgives and forgets when his child vows never again to invite friends to their home without permission or when the child promises to study harder illustrates the way in which histories for "empty promises" are built up by reinforcement—often in the form of escape from aversive consequences.

An individual's history also interacts with any of the above conditions to influence the probability of verbal intention operants. And, even in the absence of any of the above setting characteristics, a person with a positive history of emitting intention statements would tend to show a relatively high probability of employing them.

At the same time, our analysis suggests several conditions that would lower the probability of verbal intention oper-

ants. These factors are of interest for an understanding of the conditions that reduce the requirement for a self-control sequence, since failure to make the initial intention statement obviates the progression of the response chain leading to controlling behavior. For example, the smoker or drinker who has *never* stated (to himself or others) the intention to quit, although behaving in ways that are topographically similar to the conflictual behavior of many smokers and drinkers, cannot be said to display a lack or failure of self-control. His behavior is simply not in the domain of responses that we have defined as self-control. Let us now look at those situations that produce decrements in the probability of emission of intention operants. These include settings in which:

1. The probability of social disapproval for intention statements of a specific sort is high. This is the case when significant others disagree with the proposed goals. Parents may disagree with their daughter's plan to go on a crash diet, for example, or parents may punish any declaration of independence, autonomy, or self-reliance made by their child.

2. The probability of execution of the controlling response is generally *known* to be low. A common example is the decreasing frequency with which growing children make intention statements concerning physical feats that border on the impossible. However, when one moves into a new environment, in which knowledge about the feasibility of a particular behavior is different, then the probability of making the intention statement again varies.

3. The general expectancy for ultimate reinforcement for executing the controlling response is low. If one were going to be in the company of total

strangers or uninterested individuals for a long while, then exerting control over a chronically conflictual behavior (drinking, smoking, eating, gambling, and so on) would not elicit the hoped for social support and approval.

4. The person has a history of prior unsuccessful executions and has experienced aversive consequences during his attempts at change. Examples might be a smoker who, during withdrawal from cigarettes, becomes irritable and jeopardizes his job or long-standing friendships or a patient who has been unsuccessful in changing after several therapy experiences.

5. A considerable social punishment is attached to the eventual nonfulfillment (nonexecution) of the intent. An example would be the signing of a formal contract to buy a home (in this case cash deposits are used to further deter the likelihood of nonexecution). Engagement and marriage are the result of intention statements with well-known (fabled?) aversive consequences associated with the failure to "love, honor, and obey."

Verbal intention operants can be separated into two broad types. They can be either *overt*, made in the presence of an audience (and thus subject to social reinforcement and public monitoring), or *covert*, emitted to oneself (vocally or subvocally). The latter type would be expected to be subject to the same discrimination process (self-evaluation) and the same contingencies of reward and punishment. However, intention statements made privately should generally be less reliable, since no *social* consequences for nonfulfillment need be feared. Public commitment is, therefore, a highly desirable step (as is evidenced

by the apparent success of groups like "Weight Watchers" and "Alcoholics Anonymous").

Executing Contract-Fulfilling Behaviors

If we view the *intention-execution* sequence along a time line (from T_0, the initial making of the intention operant, T_{N-x}, the first execution of the controlling response, to T_N, the final period when the controlling response is no longer required to produce the desired end-state), it becomes clear that some immediate consequences (payoff) of intention statements or of first attempts at execution can serve to undermine the progress of the entire sequence. Getting the person to "stick to the bargain" is a crucial problem in self-control technology, and one that has scarcely been touched (Mahoney, 1970). Our own experience and reports from other clinicians attest to the ubiquity of the self-defeating (and client-defeating) tendency of people to provide social rewards for statements of intentions to change. The probability of an individual reaching T_N is, partly, a function of the clinician's or the listener's ability to refrain from "locking" him in at T_0 with undeserved approval for what is, at that stage, merely a verbal response. Like any behavior that is immediately rewarded, intention operants will be maintained by the "audience" effect. But they will have little value in cueing later responses in a sequence which, after all, is directed toward controlling target behavior already under strong positive reinforcement. A similar fate can be expected when a person who has been rewarded for promises not followed by execution now rewards himself for the mere intention. Given the common social practice of rewarding plans or promises per se and an individual's history of partial reinforcement for such behaviors, the making of intention statements represents a class of operants that should be highly resistant to extinction. Ideally, then, intention operants made early in the change program might best be followed by mild aversive stimuli, with positive reinforcement reserved for sustained execution of self-control.

The probability of initiating behavior that leads to fulfillment of the contract, or the exercise of self-control, can be viewed as a function of the following additional variables:

1. The explicitness or clarity of the contract. A contract with high execution potential is one that specifies the desired outcome in detail, provides the individual with performance standings against which to judge progress, sets time limits for achieving T_{N-x} and then T_x in the not too distant future, clearly delineates the consequences (especially the ultimate positive outcome of self-control), and outlines the steps and methods for the achievement of the desired goal.

2. The "mutuality" of control in the therapy or helping relationship. When working in the area of self-control there is, perhaps, a tendency to underplay the importance of external (social) control. It is frequently necessary for the therapist to exert control initially in order to insure that his client achieves the goal of self-mediated behavior change. It is especially important that the therapist be able to uphold his "end" of the contract.

3. The individual's skill and experience in engaging in the instrumental responses necessary for execution. When therapy includes training in specific techniques of self-control, the nature of training, the effectiveness of the mechanisms employed, and partial success in initial attempts will influence the chances of successful self-control. As the person's behavior changes, the environment must "cooperate" to the extent that stimulus conditions and potential reinforcement contingent upon execution of the undesirable behaviors are altered.

4. The continuous use of self-monitoring that relates execution behavior to the changes in the undesirable behavior. Obviously, inadequate feedback at this stage can undermine programmatic efforts directed at behavioral change.

5. The persistence of the aversive consequences of the undesirable behavior beyond the time at which the intention statement is made. If the intention statement alone alleviates aversive consequences, the behavior no longer has conflictful outcomes and self-control is not needed. The common assertion that a person is trying and promises to try even harder often achieves this reduction of aversive social consequences.

6. Past experience as a basis for the expectation of success or failure of a self-control program. For example, undertaking a successful reducing program often leads people to take steps toward instigating changes in other areas of behavior.

7. The consequences of the comparison by the individual with his desired behavioral goal still differs from feedback from his current behavior. Clearly the discrepancy should have an aversive effect, if the program of self-control is to continue to the point of ultimate elimination of the undesirable response. In this regard, Premack (1970) has argued that an emotional component accompanies

any decision to change. If, over time, the emotion is reduced, the probability of final execution is diminished. In clinical settings, unlike experiments, goals cannot be viewed as absolute or constant, but must be continually reevaluated in the light of the changing organism.

Summary

The preceding section attempts an analysis of the factors contributing toward the making of an intention statement (contract), and the relationship of this response class to the execution of the behaviors specified in the intention. It is proposed that a *social contract model* has heuristic value for the conceptualization and analysis of the determinants of self-directed behaviors, both in therapy and in the fulfillment of self-initiated behavioral change. A special case, related to self-control, is one in which the contract is not negotiated between two persons, but by one person in interaction with himself. This situation reflects the self-generation of standards for behavior, upon which reinforcement is contingent.

The importance of timing and the nature of reinforcement during the sequence of behaviors from commitment to execution was also discussed. Implications are noted for maximizing the probability of execution of a stated response by appropriate clinical techniques. The analysis has led to outlining a series of factors whose influence on self-control is plausible but needs to be verified by experimentation. The central feature of this is an attempt to clarify further the process of self-control by examining the role of intentions as necessary precursors of initiation of self-control.

References

BANDURA, A. *Principles of behavior modification*. New York: Holt, Rinehart and Winston, 1969.

CAUTELA, J. R. Covert reinforcement. *Behavior Therapy*, 1970, 1, 33–50.

FREUD, S. Further recommendations in the technique of analysis (1913). Reprinted in P. Rieff (Ed.), *Freud: Theory and technique*. New York: Collier Books, 1963.

KANFER, F. H. Self-regulation: Research, issues, and speculations. In C. Neuringer & J. L. Michael (Eds.), *Behavior modification and clinical psychology*. New York: Appleton-Century-Crofts, 1970.

KANFER, F. H. The maintenance of behavior by self-generated stimuli and reinforcement. In A. Jacobs & L. Sachs (Eds.), *The psychology of private events*. New York: Academic Press, 1971.

KANFER, F. H., & PHILLIPS, J. S. *Learning foundations of behavior therapy*. New York: Wiley, 1970.

KANFER, F. H., & SASLOW, G. Behavioral analysis: An alternative to diagnostic classification. *Archives of General Psychiatry*, 1965, 12, 529–538.

KLAUSNER, S. Z. (Ed.) *The quest for self-control*. New York: Free Press, 1965.

LAZARUS, A. *Behavior therapy and beyond*. New York: McGraw-Hill, 1971.

MAHONEY, J. J. Toward an experimental analysis of coverant control. *Behavior Therapy*, 1970, 1, 510–521.

MARSTON, A. R., & FELDMAN, S. Toward the use of self-control in behavior modification. Paper presented at the convention of the American Psychological Association, Miami Beach, 1970.

McFALL, R. M. Effect of self-monitoring on normal smoking behavior. *Journal of the Counseling and Clinical Psychologist*, 1970, 35, 135–142.

MENNINGER, K. *Theory of psychoanalytic technique*. New York: Harper, 1958.

MISCHEL, W. *Introduction to personality*. New York: Holt, Rinehart and Winston, 1971.

MURRAY, E. J., & JACOBSON, L. I. The nature of learning in traditional and behavioral psychotherapy. In A. E. Bergin & S. L. Garfield (Eds.), *Handbook of psychotherapy and behavior change*. New York: Wiley, 1970.

PRATT, S., & TOOLEY, J. Contract psychology

and the actualizing transactional-field. *International Journal of Social Psychiatry*, 1964, Congress issue, 51–69.

PREMACK, D. Mechanisms of self-control. In W. Hunt (Ed.), *Learning mechanisms of control in smoking*. Chicago: Aldine, 1970.

SKINNER, B. F. *Verbal behavior*. New York: Appleton-Century-Crofts, 1957.

SULZER, E. S. Reinforcement and therapeutic contract. *Journal of the Consulting and Clinical Psychologist*, 1962, **9**, 271–276.

On the Possibilities of 38
Self-Control in Man and Animals

David Premack and Brian Anglin

Most basic motivational processes are two-organism processes. This is true of both reward and punishment and equally true of the aversive procedures escape and avoidance. The reinforcer or punisher is vested in one organism; the criterial performance which is to be punished or rewarded is vested in a second organism. (The first organism may substitute for itself a machine that will duplicate its judgment and operate upon the second organism appropriately. But whether the first device is an organism or a machine substituting for an organism, the classic motivational procedure is a two-device action.) The infant certainly and even the child are sufficiently monitored by second organisms to assure the necessary contact upon which classic two-organism procedures depend. Similarly, for institutionalized populations—inmates of prisons, hospitals, and schools, the classic procedure should be feasible. But are they applicable to society? Is the noninstitutionalized adult adequately supervised to be effectively controlled by classic motivational procedures? Many social scientists think not. John Whiting (1959), for example, summed up the difficulties for classic procedures with such phrases as "One cannot put a policeman in every livingroom" and suggested that the basic control in society comes from mechanisms other than that of the external contingency. In one of three alternative mechanisms which Whiting claims to find in society, the individual believes in ghosts. We may see the subject as being alone, out of reach of any supervisorial second organism, but he does not see himself as alone. In his own mind he is never alone. Watched over continually by ghosts or spirits, he measures his behavior against the criterion of these agents no less than against that of a supervisorial agent which we would agree was there. Whiting offered some hypotheses about the child rearing which produces this solution and the general character of the society in which this is found, but they need not concern us here.

In the second system, the person believes in an omniscient God. This differs from the first system, principally in that God is not solely vengeful like the ghosts but is also merciful. Thus He not only punishes bad behavior but also rewards good behavior.

The third system, dominant in Western culture, puts the supervisorial organism into the recipient organism—if not the organism, then the values of the supervisorial organism. The effect is to vest both roles of the motivational procedure in one organism. How this is done, if indeed it is done at all, has not been adequately clarified. Called internalization or socialization, there are several theories, but

[1] The article was supported in part by Grant MH-15616 from the National Institute of Health. The authors are indebted to G. Culbertson and E. Lovejoy for many helpful discussions.

[2] Requests for reprints should be sent to David Premack, Department of Psychology, University of California, Santa Barbara, California 93106.

the process itself has not been stated with as much straightforwardness as one would want for so apparently important a process. On the basis of what evidence do we infer socialization, and what are the necessary and sufficient conditions for bringing about that evidence? If the process exists, it should be possible to describe it with enough clarity so that it could be developed in an animal, or if the animal is incapable of the process, then it should be possible to show why this is so. That is mainly what we are considering, though it will be necessary to pause along the way and consider some related topics.

SOCIOLOGY OF REWARD

Consider first that critics of the external contingency may - dismiss it too hastily. In noting the difficulty of lodging police under every bed, the critic may misunderstand the social structure of reward and punishment. Is it only the police who punish and the mother who rewards? It seems more accurate to consider that the prototypic external contingency, contained in the mother–child relation, is not abrogated when the child leaves home. Instead it is supplanted by other relations. The child exchanges judgment by the mother for judgment by peers and other agencies; at the same time he himself becomes a judge of others. No individual comes out from under the external contingency simply by leaving home. Nevertheless, these are merely plausible arguments against rejecting the external contingency as a feasible instrument for the control of a noninstitutionalized population. The argument is not worked out in detail, and grave difficulties arise when we attempt to support the argument with data.

For example, how many rewards or punishments do you receive a day, how many do you give in the same period, and what are the major determinants of each process? The amusement or perplexity that these questions may occasion only underscores our inability to answer them. Who rewards whom in an open society? Does A reward B who rewards A in return, or does B reward C who then rewards D, etc.? What is the social structure of reward? It seems somewhat suspicious that no one appears to have the slightest idea of how many times he is rewarded or rewards someone else in a day. Partly this may be so because as each person looks back on his day he is not sure what is to be counted as a

reward, either from the point of view of a recipient or donor. For instance, should he count his lunch as a reward, and if he does, what responses should he consider it to have reinforced? There is no book that could rightly be called the "Sociology of Reward," nor would it be an easy matter to write such a book.

The difficulty of writing such a work does not become clear until one tries to collect the kind of data that such a book would require. By the 1960s it had become quite popular to attribute so-called mental illness to abnormal reinforcement histories; appropriate behaviors had not been adequately shaped by proper amounts, kinds, or schedules of reward; punishment too had been used inappropriately. But what constitutes a proper or normal reward history? If an inappropriate reinforcement history could be compared with an appropriate one, then perhaps we could say what deviations man can tolerate; or how deviations combine with certain predispositions to produce aberration. But the learning explanation without appropriate base data is just another promissory note in the long history of debits that has been the fate of mental health programs.

To get some idea of what the external contingency looks like outside of the Skinner box, we obtained permission to observe people in their homes. We planned to start in a simple way by counting the occasions on which people reward one another. But since one can not tell a reward by its appearance, the first problem was to decide what to count. The people we observed were mothers and children at lunch time. Only the child ate, the mother either skipped lunch or ate at another time, and the behavior before us was primarily verbal, the mother and child conversing. What constitutes a response in the case of verbal behavior and how do you classify it? We divided both the mother's and child's speech into semantic categories on the basis of such topics as sports, school, self, etc. Treating the child as recipient and the mother as donor, we kept a record of the kind of response the mother made following each response by the child. A matrix with mother's response classes on the vertical and child's on the horizontal showed that frequency was concentrated along the diagonal, which meant that mothers typically preserved the semantic topic of the child. If the child talked about sports, she responded in kind, occasionally changing the subject (more so, probably, than would occur in a conversation between equals).

Were there any rewards in these lunch scenes, and if there were, what was the behavior being rewarded? We treated the mother's verbal responses to the child as possible rewards and undertook to test their actual effect by observing what happened to the child's speech upon the removal and subsequent restoration of the mother's speech. If the mother's response to the child rewarded his utterance, eliminating the mother's response should reduce the frequency of the child's speech; the subsequent restoration of the mother's reply should restore the child's speech to its former level.

After obtaining stable base lines, which took several months, we obtained the mother's cooperation for the next step of the experiment. Mothers agreed that when the child spoke either about himself or about sports—child categories with relatively high and stable base lines—they would either not reply at all or would reply in one of the other semantic categories. For instance, when the child talked about sports, the mother was to change the topic (or not reply at all), and when the child spoke about himself the mother was not to reply at all (or to change the topic).

A check of the mother's ability to code the child's speech showed that they had little difficulty with that task. The first suggestion of any difficulty did not come until later: several mothers reported spending a restless night, rehearsing their plan either not to reply or to reply in a topic different from the one in which the child spoke. And indeed, despite their good intentions and nighttime rehearsals, in the morning the mothers were quite unable to carry out their plan. Two separate experiments involving several months of base data went down the drain for that simple reason. Thus the main thing we learned so far is that the mother must be trained beforehand. Not replying or consistently changing the topic apparently so conflicts with normal speech that without special training the average speaker cannot do it.

The plan had been to compare the frequency of the child's speech in the preselected categories under base-line and experimental conditions. Clearly, however, a change in frequency of the predicted kind would not automatically qualify the mother's behavior as a reward. Her effect upon the child's behavior could equally well be that of a stimulus. This difficulty is not restricted to the present example but would apply to other interactions between mother and child, which in principle would seem to be the major source of reward for the child.

Consider another source of difficulty in the attempt to do ecological studies on reward. What unit of the child's behavior should be treated as the locus of reward? We circumvent this problem in the lab by interpolating an arbitrary event at a preselected site in the sequence. But we cannot interpolate arbitrary events in the ecological study. The point there is to assess the frequency and consequence of reward that may already be present. The question is not, Can you reward behavior in everyday life but rather, Is it rewarded? And if so how? And to what degree? Without going into detail, we would suggest that if the mother is rewarding the child, it is probably not in her individual topic-duplicating comments. More likely, the mother's comments help to keep the child on a semantic track, enabling him to work his way through to some dimly envisaged conclusion. This suggests that the rewarded unit of the child's behavior may be more comparable to the paragraph than the sentence. It also suggests that the same comment by the mother may have profoundly different reward values depending on when in the child's progress the mother makes the comment. Notice that this view does not solve any methodological problems. In brief, we can speculate freely about the role of the external contingency in everyday life; but obtaining actual data on the ecological role of reward is another matter.

ONE-ORGANISM VERSIONS OF THE TWO-ORGANISM PROCEDURES

In principle, the uncertainties that arise in applying the external contingency outside the laboratory could be overcome if motivational processes that typically involve two organisms could be carried out with one organism. We have already encountered one version of this proposal in the conscience or the superego. By merit of internalized values, one organism is said to check or restrain itself in a way that duplicates the restraint that would ordinarily come from a second organism. But the superego or conscience is a limited version of a more general proposal. In the general proposal every operation that goes on at the level of two devices can also be arranged with one device.

We end up not only with self-reward but also with self-punishment, self-extinction, etc. Skinner (1953) was among the first perhaps to advocate this view, though without offering any data. More recently, Kanfer and Marston (1963), Bandura (e.g., 1971), Homme (1965), and others have attempted to test and extend the formulation.

That all classic two-organism processes can be duplicated on a one-organism basis is a powerful claim and would have far-reaching implications if true. In its scope the claim is reminiscent of one by Bandura, according to whom all effects that can be produced by direct experience can also be produced indirectly, merely by observing an appropriate model undergo the direct experience. On this view a subject could eliminate an undesirable response by observing the (repeated) extinction of the response in a model. But if the present claim is correct, the second organism could be dispensed with altogether. The subject should be able to extinguish his own responses. If he can increase the frequency of his responses by rewarding them, he should be able subsequently to extinguish them by withholding reward. When we consider vicarious motivation and self-motivation together, in the first of which the subject need only observe a second organism and in the second of which he can dispense with the second organism altogether, we may see the external contingency vanish into insignificance. The emphasis given this procedure in the laboratory may come from its susceptability to experimental attack. For that reason it may have been an appropriate if not a necessary starting point. But in conjecturing about the ecology we may be misled by the laboratory popularity of the external contingency. Along with vicarious and self-motivational processes, the external contingency may be but one of three ways in which behavior is modulated, and for adult members of society perhaps the least important of the three. These are only possibilities, of course; the data available on this subject are too tenuous to allow any conclusions.

SELF-REWARD

The discussion in the rest of the paper is restricted to only one of the possible forms of self-motivation, namely, self-reward. Presumably it is representative of self-motivational processes generally, so that whatever we find out about it can be applied to the other forms.

Self-Praise as Self-Reward

Bandura (1971) and his associates attempted to combine vicarious processes with self-reward. The basic paradigm involved two groups of children, each of which observed a model play a game. In one case the model was strict with himself and praised his performance sparingly; In the other case he was lenient and praised his performance freely. When the children were subsequently given an opportunity to play the same game, there was a correspondence between the amount of praise the children observed the model give himself and the amount they gave themselves. Children in both groups played the game about equally well; but those who had watched the lienient model praised themselves significantly more often then those who had watched the strict model.

The weakness of these studies is that they equated self-praise with self-reward. We can tell an instance of self-praise merely by looking at the behavior of the child. But we cannot identify an instance of self-reward in the same way. In order to be considered a reward, self-praise must increase the frequency of the response class that it follows. Unfortuntately, that point was not tested. Moreover, the incidental evidence that these studies provide indicates that self-praise could not be equated with self-reward. Although the two groups differed significantly in the frequency of self-praise, they did not differ in the amount they played the game. Barring a ceiling effect, this would disqualify the self-praise as a reward.

The would-be self-reward in these studies included not only congratulating oneself verbally but also giving oneself a piece of candy. Several years earlier we had found that with most middle-class children the opportunity to eat candy would not reward playing a game; on the contrary, playing the game would reward eating the candy (Premack, 1959). Of course, it is not difficult to find differences between the two studies. But the fact of the rewardability of eating by playing combined with the failure of self-praise (and candy eating) to increase the frequency of the referent response suggests that though modeling worked and self-praise definitely took place in the Bandura studies, the self-praise was nonetheless not a reward.

We have since completed other studies that lead to the same conclusion. Briefly, they suggest that frequency of praise is a characteristic of the model's behavior no different from that of any other, such as the height to which he raises his arm in play or the frequency with which he plays, and that the child models the one characteristic as he does the other. But the self-praise is no more a reward of the response class that it follows than are the other modeled behaviors a reward of the response class they follow. The most persuasive demonstration of this point would be to show that the child is capable of modeling such combinations as high self-praise and low frequency of play and low self-praise and high frequency of play. We are testing that now.

Although these studies suggest that praising one's self—or doing so on the basis of a model—may not be rewarding, they do not of course disprove the possibility of self-reward. On the positive side, they suggest a methodological rule that one follow in attempting to study self-reward. Do not ask whether or not an event is self-rewarding until it is first shown that the event is a reward when applied in the classical manner. We see no reason to believe that events which are not rewards when applied in a classical way by a second party should become rewards when an individual applies them to itself. It would be foolish to claim categorically that there are no such cases, but they would not seem to be the most favorable starting point. On the other side of the coin, perhaps there are some events that lose effectiveness when passed from the hands of the second party to those of the first party, but we would think them to be few, few enough so that the least risky research strategem is to start out with events that are clearly rewarding when applied by a second party.

Self-praise is anomalous with respect to this requirement—as is shown by this example. In the course of bowling with his daughter, a father occasionally remarks of his daughter's performance, "That's a good shot." Occasionally he says the same of himself when he makes a good shot. Now the daughter copies the father and sometimes says of her own performance, "That's a good shot." We have "that's a shot" said of the daughter on two occasions, once by the father and once by the daughter when she copies her father and praises herself.

What is the reward value of self-praise relative to that of direct praise? If the father's praise had no reward value, how much value could the daughter's copy of the father's praise have? One plausible assumption is that reward value of self-praise is proportional to

that of direct praise. But the two may be independent; what varies with direct praise may not be reward value of self-praise but simply the probability that the child will engage in self-praise. We know that a child is more likely to copy the praise of a model whom it likes; still, on those occasions when it does copy a relatively disliked model, what is the reward value of the self-praise? Unfortunately, the Bandura studies did not establish that if the model praised the child for playing the game, this would itself serve as a reward. Thus, for all we know, the apparent failure of self-praise to serve as a reward came from the simple fact that praise by the model would not have been a reward. This is not at all implausible in view of the referent response. Playing games is a highly probable response in children, so high that praise may have little effect on it.

We can sidestep these interesting but presently unanswerable questions by using a more static event as a reward, one that tends to remain the same both when it is dispensed by the other one and by the self. Consider two studies that meet these conditions in at least some degree. Kanfer and Marston (1963) attempted a literal test of Skinner's formulation, according to which self-reward occurs when the reward is both applied and received by the same organism. After giving college sophomores incomplete training on paired-associate learning, they divided the subjects into three groups and gave all groups further training on the paired-associate task. The groups were differentiated in terms of the feedback they received for correct responses. One control group received standard feedback, another one no feedback, while members of the experimental group were instructed to say "correct" whenever they thought the response they had made was correct. The performance of the group given standard feedback improved; that of the group given no feedback deteriorated; that of the experimental group remained unchanged. Kanfe and Marston concluded that "correct" was a reward since when said on would-be correct occasions it prevented deterioration.

But the effect may just as well be attributed to memory. "Correct" seems better viewed as information that tells the subject which responses he is to repeat on subsequent occasions (e.g., Dulaney, 1962; Estes, 1969). Which interpretation one favors will depend on how one interprets paired-associate learning in the first place. But it may not be necessary to settle this issue in order to agree that if the efficacy of self-reward is accurately reflected by the slight effect shown in this experiment, then the process is of no practical concern, whatever its theoretical status. Reward is notable in part because of the sheer magnitude of its effect. Perhaps self-reward was weak in this study because classical reward was also weak. Unfortunately the magnitude of the two effects cannot be compared; one group was "rewarded" for correct responses alone, whereas the other group "rewarded" itself for at least some responses which though guessed to be correct were actually incorrect. The desired comparison can be found in a study by Bandura and Perloff (1967); also the contingent event used in that study was more clearly a reward.

Bandura and Perloff: A Paradigmatic Study

In the Bandura and Perloff (1967) study, several groups of children were shown a device and told that by operating it they could obtain tickets which could be exchanged for toys. The device consisted of a crank connected to a column of lights; 5 turns of the crank turned on the bottommost light and 20 the topmost light. After being given a brief opportunity to try out the device, the children were asked to indicate which light they would require of themselves before giving themselves a ticket. The main control group consisted of subjects each of whom was·yoked to a subject in the experimental group; the control subject was given the ticket whenever he met the same criterion his counterpart imposed upon himself. Other control groups were used to establish the base line for responding when no ticket was given, when no tickets were given but the subject was asked beforehand to set a criterion, etc.

Both the experimental group and the yoked control turned the crank reliably more than the appropriate control groups. Boys showed a greater increase with reward than with self-reward, but girls showed as much increase when they gave themselves tickets for a self-selected criterion as they did when someone else gave them a ticket for a criterion someone else had chosen. In both cases the magnitude of the effect was of the order we typically associated with reward.

These results would seem to fulfill the criteria for self-reward. First, in keeping with the methodological rule suggested earlier, the event tested as a self-reward was shown to serve as a reward when applied in the classical manner. Second, the subject gave the reward to himself. Indeed, not only did the subject give himself the item but he did so only when he met a standard and one that he selected himself.

Denial as a Precondition for Reward

The two basic operations in reward are the delivery of the reward and the imposition of a response requirement upon which delivery of the reward is contingent. Thus to engage in self-reward, an individual must not merely give himself the reward but impose upon himself a criterion which he must meet before giving himself the reward. It is not at all difficult for one organism to impose a criterion upon a second organism; that can be done as easily as delivering the reward. But there is a great asymmetry in the difficulty of the two operations when they are carried out by a single organism. Giving oneself a desired item is easy; denying it to oneself until one has met a standard is a different matter.

Self-denial is a precondition for self-reward; how this basic precondition is realized is what we will attempt to describe in a moment. But do not suppose that self-reward in being dependent upon denial is in any way different from classical reward. Although this fact is concealed by inadequacies in the traditional account of reinforcement, classical two-organism reward is as much dependent upon denial as self-reward is upon self-denial. Indeed, there is a sense in which all reward begins with denial.

Suppose the subject is a thirsty rat, the would-be reward is water, and the criterion is running in a wheel. According to the customary account of reward, there should be no difficulty in using water to reinforce running in a thirsty rat. Water is a reward for a thirsty rat, it would be said, and making it contingent upon running should reward running. However, unless the contingency imposes a condition of denial upon the rat, water will not reward running.

Suppose the base level of running and drinking are 20 and 100 seconds, respectively, per 10-minute session. Thus on the average the rat is five times as likely to drink as it is to run. We arrange a contingency in which each time the rat runs for one second it receives an opportunity to drink for 5 seconds. What will be the consequence of this contingency? Nothing—the rat will not run more than its base level. Contingencies that permit the animal to drink base level without running more than base level do not entail denial and do not produce reinforcement. The failure is further shown in would-be extinction sessions. If the contingency is disrupted, and running no longer produces water, the rat still does not exceed its base level of running (Premack, 1965).

The failure is predictable from the assumption that a probability differential is a necessary condition for reinforcement. Suppose the rat were given not a contingency between run and drink but a series of 1-second opportunities to run and a series of 5-second opportunities to drink. In view of the base ratio of run to drink (1:5), the probability that the rat will utilize the 1-second run opportunities and the 5-second drink opportunities should be approximately equal. But reinforcement requires that one response be more probable than the other. A contingency in which the two responses are equally probable should not and does not produce reinforcement.

Standards: The Restraining Force

The basic problem in self-reward is self-denial. The subject must withhold from himself a preferred event until he meets a criterion on a nonpreferred event. The individual must therefore be equipped with a restraining force that will enable him to withhold the preferred event from himself. Thus, the aspect of the child's performance that most needs explanation is the fact that the child did not simply take the ticket without turning the crank at all or turning it more than base level. Interesting, too, is the fact that the child apparently had no difficulty indicating the amount of crank turning that it considered appropriate. Presumably, most of the children had never operated a comparable device, yet on the basis of a very small sample they reached a decision as to what to require of themselves. This aspect of the child's behavior also needs to be explained.

The restraining force can be produced in more than one way, though some ways will be better than others. Perhaps the most direct attack on this problem could be made simply by punishing the subject whenever it attempted to respond to the preferred event without first meeting the criterion. Mahoney and Bandura (in press) have provided an instructive animal example of this case. Pigeons were first taught to peck a key for food, after which the magazine was made available to the bird *before* it pecked the key. As the duration of the magazine presentation was increased, even the well-trained pigeon began to eat before pecking on the key. The bird was then punished for doing so by having the magazine abruptly withdrawn. Only a few trials of this kind were necessary to suppress the undesired response and to teach the bird to peck before eating. The bird imposed the criterion on itself—pecking before eating—because it was punished when it did not.

To what extent does this simple case do justice to what we assume to be involved in socialization? It is open to criticism on at least two basic grounds.

First, the effect of punishment, like that of reward, is temporary. We can predict, therefore, that when the punishment is terminated, the preferred response will not remain suppressed and the subject will go back to eating without pecking. Indeed, when a failure to peck before eating was not punished, this was the outcome; the birds ceased to peck altogether and simply ate from the open magazine. Restraint based on punishment is too subject to extinction. Notice how this breakdown underscores the problem pointed out by critics of the external contingency. Once the child leaves home and is no longer subject to punishment, control will collapse, quite as it did in the above experiment when punishment was withdrawn from the pigeons.

An already mentioned approach to the ecological version of this problem is to transfer the mother's role to new supervisorial agents. Agents whose contact hours with the subject were sufficient to subserve the needs of the external contingency could then mete out the punishment. Perhaps with an appropriate intermittent schedule the contact hours required would not be incompatible with the other needs of the system. (The wife could punish the husband's transgressions and still have time to cook supper and look after the children.) Lacking ecological data on the external contingency, we cannot exclude this alternative, however implausible it may seem. Indeed, a behavior engineer (in the employ of a totalitarian state) might solve the problem easily. Rather than make one supervisorial agent responsible for all the punishment, he would distribute the responsibility over all the agents whom the subject was likely to contact in a day. If not only the wife but also the boss, union chief, butcher, etc., reprimanded the subject on timely occasions, the integrated effect might keep the subject in line indefinitely.

But notice the senselessness of self-reward in such a situation. If agents are needed to make self-reward possible, to maintain the subject's restraint through punishing him, why not drop the self-reward and simply have the same agent reward the subject? The point of self-reward is to eliminate the need for a second agent. But if the restraining force, upon which self-reward depends, cannot be maintained without second agents, then what is the point of self-reward? Is punishment more effective than reward? Would it require fewer man hours than two-organism reward? Or is an image of self-control preserved by having the subject hand himself reward? These seem dubious gains.

Consider also that agents who were capable of imposing punishment would have no problem handling reward. An agent who was in a position to punish a subject would also be in a position to reward him. But the opposite is equally true. The first step in rewarding an organism is to confiscate the reward, that is, to gain control over those stimuli for which the species is most likely to respond and to maximize the probability of responding by deprivation procedures. Any agent that can do that to an organism can certainly punish it also. In summary, for self-reward to make sense, we need a restraining mechanism that does not itself depend indefinitely upon a second organism.

Restraint Built on Avoidance

Punishment is not the only way to build a restraining force, nor is it a particularly good way. Avoidance, if it has no other liabilities, would overcome the main drawback of punishment; it is known to produce exceptional resistance to extinction. As has often been pointed out, in avoidance, as long as the subject responds it cannot discover that the contingency was discontinued, whereas in both punishment and reinforcement it is exactly by responding that it can discover such changes. Avoidance, moreover, would not seem to

introduce any new problem, as would be the case, however, if we tried to improve upon punishment by, for example, increasing the severity of the punisher. Although intense shock produces greater resistance to extinction, it does so by greater suppression in the first place, in the extreme case by reducing the referent response to zero. This would be an unacceptable approach if some form of the suppressed response were necessary for the survival of the subject or the species. For instance, if Mahoney and Bandura tried to use severe punishment to retard extinction, they would run the risk of birds that not only would not eat before pecking but would not eat at all. In general, it would seem dangerous to attempt to restrain either eating or copulation by severe punishment.[3]

Attachment and Withdrawal of the Mother

Avoidance may solve the extinction problem, but we can draw still closer to the human paradigm by eliminating electric shock as the contingent event while retaining the avoidance paradigm. Shock would not seem to be an accurate parallel of the major contingent event in the human case. Probably the basic contingent event in human socialization is simply withdrawal of the mother. Her potency as a contingent event is made possible by the infant's attachment to her. The basis of the attachment is suggested in the work of Harlow (1958), Sackett (1970), Mason (1970), and others. The infant is apparently subject to periods of both hypostimulation and hyperstimulation about which it can do little but which the mother can relieve with species-

---

[3] The possible advantage of basing self-restraint on avoidance could be tested for in the Mahoney-Bandura situation. If the bird were first taught to peck to avoid shock (substitute another response for the key peck which is known to be inappropriate for pigeon avoidance) and was then also taught to peck for food, it might be peculiarly slow in discovering discontinuations in the shock. The tendency to peck should be strong, based both on avoidance and reward, perhaps with appropriate avoidance parameters stronger than the tendency to eat from the open magazine. With support from reward, few if any additional shocks might be needed to sustain keypecking. Unfortunately, we were unsuccessful in finding any cases in the literature in which responding was initiated with avoidance and the avoidance response then transferred to positive reward, either with or without unsignaled termination of the shock.

specific responses (Kessen & Mandler, 1961), for example, by playing with the infant in the first case and by holding and stroking it in the other. We have watched a quiescent infant, simply upon being exposed to a bedstead with painted figures, burst into smile, gurgle, and arch its back in order to direct its gaze at the figures. Conversely, who has not seen screaming infants subside with relief upon being held and stroked?

Although typical laboratory avoidance is based upon the removal of a noxious event, avoidance could also be based upon preventing the removal of a positive event. An avoidance response is effective when it reduces the frequency of electric shock (Herrnstein & Hineline, 1966). But if the contingent event were the withdrawal of food, for example, an avoidance response would be effective if it reduced the frequency with which food was withdrawn.

In order for avoidance to be based upon reducing the frequency with which a positive event is withdrawn, there must be a base frequency with which the event is withdrawn independent of the subject's behavior; even as in the typical case, there is a base frequency with which electric shock is presented independent of the rat's behavior. Avoidance responding has a simple precondition: the world inflicts untoward events upon its inhabitants at some base frequency independent of the inhabitant's behavior. The subject can avoid or at least reduce the frequency of the untoward event by responding in a prescribed fashion. Thus we can incorporate the withdrawal of the mother into this scheme by assuming there to be a base frequency at which the mother withdraws herself independent of the child's behavior.

The infant is given unconditional access to the mother; as the prime source of both relief and excitement, she becomes a potent stimulus. As the infant turns into the child, his access to the mother is no longer unconditional. Once exempted from judgment, he comes increasingly under judgment in proportion to his increasing self-sufficiency. He must behave in prescribed ways to insure continued contact with the mother. That is, an increasing proportion of his behavior comes to be judged "good" or "bad," and the consequence of the judgment is felt in the rate in which the mother withdraws herself. "Good" behavior produces a rate of withdrawal less than that of the base rate; "bad" behavior a

rate of withdrawal greater than that of the base rate. In brief, there is a base rate at which the mother absents herself irrespective of the child's behavior. But the child can operate upon that rate, either increasing or reducing it by behaving in a "good" way or a "bad" way.

A part of the mother's effectiveness comes from the high probability that the dependent organism will seek out and respond to the caretaker organism. Evidence of this is occasionally seen strikingly in young chimpanzees. When a young chimp is rebuked with special severity for some infraction, it may leap upon its trainer, not to attack him as the shaken trainer fears but rather to cling to him and seek assurance. Interestingly, if the value the infant assigned to the caretaker is proportional to the relief that the caretaker brings, exceptionally high values should be assigned by infants who suffer neglect or inconsistent care, provided they are cared for at all. The events underlying human socialization appear to be neatly interlocked. The mother's species-specific responses, issued without condition, assuage and delight the infant—leading him to form an attachment, making him vulnerable to her loss, so that as a child he learns to perform in preselected ways in order to reduce the frequency which she leaves.

Will similar considerations explain the apparent role of toilet training in Western socialization? First, since socialization works through judgment on behavior, it should work best through behavior that is inescapable, that occurs often, and that can be readily detected (without continual scrutiny) through its products. With some behaviors the child could avoid judgment simply by avoiding the behaviors, or by performing them covertly, but not so with elimination. Secondary gains may come from the fact that bowel and bladder control teach the child an anticipatory cognizance of its own body, to sense internal stimulation, a skill that can be applied more broadly later on. Toilet training also involves a feature basic to all human evaluation: some acts are neither good nor bad but are good conditional upon place and manner of performance, a precursor of style. Nonetheless, according to this analysis, socialization need not fasten on toilet training. Elimination could be replaced by any other behavior that was equally inescapable, detectible, and frequent.

Rule Induction and Generalized Self-Judgment

The use of avoidance and of basing the contingency upon withdrawal of the caretaker are features of the training program. They lead to a restraining force of a particular kind, one with qualities different from those that would be formed by different training programs. Yet, certain basic qualities of the restraining force cannot come from the training program but must come from the organism. In particular, the subject must be capable of processing the inputs provided by the training in such a way as to form a generalized restraining force, one that can be applied in situations other than those used in the training. If the subject does not show transfer, there is little if anything that can presently be done at the level of the training program to foster transfer.

No child in the Bandura-Perloff study is reported to have had difficulty defining an acceptable level of performance for himself. Although the apparatus was unlikely to have been quite like any the child had previously experienced, after only a brief sample, each child stated what he thought to be an acceptable performance level for himself. Doubtless the uniqueness of the apparatus could have been greatly increased without troubling the child. The child's ability to make such judgments can be understood by assuming that he has abstracted from previous experience what amounts to a general rule stating how hard he must try in order to perform acceptably. "Hard" could be defined on a number of grounds—the discomfort he is to bear or an image of his own performance compared to an ideal performance, for example. Although, unfortunately, we cannot specify the parameters of the child's rule, it seems reasonable to assume that he can identify what constitutes "trying hard" in almost any situation. Indeed, the child can probably also distinguish situations that are and are not relevant to him, thus situations where he can perform without being subject to judgment.

Socialization

An explication is solid when we can show either how to produce a desired outcome in an animal or when we can state why the animal is incapable of the outcome. In the case of language, for example, we attempted to state first principal exemplars and then for each exemplar a training program that would instill it (Premack, 1971). This is the evidential or "proof-of-the-pudding" part of the explication. But the explication is sadly incomplete until it becomes possible to state the cognitive mechanisms that are a precondition for the performances. We anticipate an inventory of cognitive mechanisms—used in classification of stimuli, storage and retrieval, and problem solving generally—and then an assessment of species in terms of the inventory. At that point, it should be possible to predict whether or not a species can acquire a language, whether or not it can be socialized, and so on.

A child is socialized when its behavior conforms to certain rules, not only in the training situation but in the world at large. The substantive content of the rule is not critical and presumably will vary from culture to culture, even from one sector of society to another. Despite differences in content, all rules will take the same logical form, conditional or biconditional. Some examples from our society are: "You may keep something you have found provided you first have made an effort to find the owner." "To fail without trying is despicable, but if you tried and then failed that is forgivable." The problem is to train the animal so that it will show generalized conformity to conditional or biconditional rules.

Training Program

The training program described here is based on rats since the present facilities do not permit using more appropriate species. Additional compromises have been made with regard to the attachment process, makeup of the contingent event, and even perhaps the dependent variables. The justification for describing the program is that, hopefully, socialization will be made clearer by describing a poor program rather than none at all.

The rat is housed in an apparatus that makes possible automatic sensing of nine of its behaviors, specifically: eating Food A or B, drinking Liquid C or D, grooming, sniffing at Point X, chewing Object Y, occupying a perch, standing up in Area L. Base data are collected giving the distributions of the burst durations for each of these classes. We then arbitrarily impose the following classification: a burst that exceeds K seconds is good: bursts less than G seconds are bad (K and G defined for the individual rat from its base data). Instances of good behavior are followed by a distinctive stimulus (tantamount to "good") and a consequence designed to increase frequency. Instances of bad behavior are followed by a different stimulus ("bad") and a consequence that is designed to decrease the frequency. Although there is apparently considerable latitude in which behaviors can be designated good and bad, the judgment cannot be entirely arbitrary for the outcome must be compatible with the survival of the species.

The consequence assigned to the two classes is manipulated by three tapes, each of which programs a certain frequency of electric shock (we were not able to manage withdrawal of the caretaker organism with the rat). The middle or base tape delivers two shocks per minute independent of the rats behavior. Thus, the rats ambience is not untroubled; there is instead a certain level of metaphysical grit in its world and it is delivered by the middle tape.

The rat can escape the middle tape either by good or bad behavior. Each instance of good behavior switches control to the low-frequency tape, delivering only .5 shocks per minute, for 3 minutes, after which control returns automatically to the middle tape. An instance of bad behavior has essentially the opposite effect: the high-frequency tape, delivering four shocks per minute, takes over for 3 minutes. Grooming in one rat and urinating in a nondesignated quadrant of the cage in another are treated differently. There is no good form of these behaviors. Instead all grooming and all urinating in the contraindicated location are judged bad, even as nondefensive aggression and premarital copulation are (or once were) tabooed in our society. We have the impression that the nobly aspiring or self-sacrificing type of character may be honed through abstinence or the total denial of strong behavior; grooming is of this sort in the rat, and by absolutely denying it to the rat we may open its way to glory. A more complicated program, better simulating the human case, would take into consideration transients in the rat's behavior. The contingency would not be a fixed .5 or four shocks per minute but rather would be sensitive to the sequential character of the subject's behavior. A run of "good" behavior would soften the blow given the next instance of a "bad" behavior, even as a run of "bad" behavior might harden the blow. A more serious question concerns the volume of the subject's behavior that needs to be subjected to judgment. We have the impression that in some households the volume may be small, whereas in others very little of the child's behavior escapes scrutiny. Is there an optimal volume?

The program above describes the second of two phases into which we divided socialization, the judgmental phase, in which contingencies are applied increasingly to the behavior of the ambulatory child. The first phase, in contrast, concerns the helpless infant; rather than being submitted to judgment, he is nurtured by the mother, which paves the way for subsequently using her withdrawal as the main contingent event. Phase 1 may have an added affect; because of the child's attachment to the mother, punishment meted out by her may be especially effective, though perhaps only because it contains the added threat of her withdrawal. Unfortunately, simulating maternal behavior in the rat is more difficult than in species for which the trainer has only to substitute his own behavior for that of the mother. We are trying only a limited simulation of Phase 2. With some rats, the nine commodities—food, water, etc.—sensed at Phase 2 are not available continuously but are presented discontinuously, their delivery always preceded by what we call the mother stimulus. These rats will later be moved into the child–mother phase and be submitted to judgment like the first rats which skipped the infant–mother phase.

The short-range objective of the training is to increase the frequency of the good behavior and decrease that of the bad behavior. But that outcome, which should be an immediate effect of the contingencies, is an almost accidental feature of the long-term objective of socialization. If the socialization program achieves no more than these changes in frequency, then it will have failed. The overriding objective of socialization is to provide an inductive basis for the formation of rules of conduct. In the rat we tested for this outcome by examining the behaviors that were *not* encompassed by the contingencies. Of the nine behaviors sensed, we have set four aside for this purpose. Two tests of transfer are possible. First, transfer can be shown by an appropriate change in the burst distribution of the four classes that were *not linked* to the contingencies. We could say of such an outcome that a rule which the subject induced on the basis of the five classes that were linked to the contingencies was applied to response classes that were not so linked. If the subject were a child we would describe the outcome along these lines: The child has been taught to "try hard" in the case of a certain set of behaviors and now tries hard in the case of all behavior. A second and less interesting kind of transfer would consist of showing that despite a new stimulus situation the five behaviors linked to the contingency would continue to show the appropriate changes.

The rat could fail to show transfer for any of several reasons. It might fail because (*a*) there is no such thing as socialization; or (*b*) there is such a process but we have not succeeded in extracting the critical operations; or (*c*) the operations are appropriate but the procedure must begin when the rat is an infant; or (*d*) the rat need not be an infant but the mother stimulus is not an effective simulation; the punishment is forceful only when the subject links the punishment causally to an agent, and though the rat is capable of inferring causality and assuming agency it will not assume agency for the present mother stimulus; or (*e*) the mother stimulus is an adequate simulation but the rat is cognitively incapable of inducing rules. Of this set we discuss the last alternative.

There is massive indirect and some direct evidence that man copes with exemplars by inducing the rules that can be used to generate them. The indirect evidence comes from language. The ability both to speak and receive productively and to produce and comprehend sentences not previously experienced can be understood only by assuming a set of rules capable of generating the sentences.

But the evidence in the case of language is almost too massive to be persuasive. As experimentalists we prefer smaller more bounded cases in which it may be possible to get a closer look at what is going on. Consider some of the work on miniature languages, introduced by Esper (1925) in the 1920s, taken up again in the 1950s by the reemergence of psycholin-behavior might harden the blow. A more serious question concerns the volume of the subject's behavior that needs to be subjected to judgment. We have the impression that in some households the volume may be small, whereas in others very little of the child's behavior escapes scrutiny. Is there an optimal volume?

The program above describes the second of two phases into which we divided socialization, the judgmental phase, in which contingencies are applied increasingly to the behavior of the ambulatory child. The first phase, in contrast, concerns the helpless infant; rather than being submitted to judgment, he is nurtured by the mother, which paves the way for subsequently using her withdrawal as the main contingent event. Phase 1 may have an added affect; because of the child's attachment to the mother, punishment meted out by her may be especially effective, though perhaps only because it contains the added threat of her withdrawal. Unfortunately, simulating maternal behavior in the rat is more difficult than in species for which the trainer has only to substitute his own behavior for that of the mother. We are trying only a limited simulation of Phase 2. With some rats, the nine commodities—food, water, etc.—sensed at Phase 2 are not available continuously but are presented discontinuously, their delivery always preceded by what we call the mother stimulus. These rats will later be moved into the child–mother phase and be submitted to judgment like the first rats which skipped the infant–mother phase.

The short-range objective of the training is to increase the frequency of the good behavior and decrease that of the bad behavior. But that outcome, which should be an immediate effect of the contingencies, is an almost accidental feature of the long-term objective of socialization. If the socialization program achieves no more than these changes in frequency, then it will have failed. The overriding objective of socialization is to provide an inductive basis for the formation of rules of conduct. In the rat we tested for this outcome by examining the behaviors that were *not* encompassed by the contingencies. Of the nine behaviors sensed, we have set four aside for this purpose. Two tests of transfer are possible. First, transfer can be shown by an appropriate change in the burst distribution of the four classes that were *not linked* to the contingencies. We could say of such an outcome that a rule which the subject induced on the basis of the five classes that were linked to the contingencies was applied to response classes that were not so linked. If the subject were a child we would describe the outcome along these lines: The child has been taught to "try hard" in the case of a certain set of behaviors and now tries hard in the case of all behavior. A second and less interesting kind of transfer would consist of showing that despite a new stimulus situation the five behaviors linked to the contingency would continue to show the appropriate changes.

The rat could fail to show transfer for any of several reasons. It might fail because (*a*) there is no such thing as socialization; or (*b*) there is such a process but we have not succeeded in extracting the critical operations; or (*c*) the operations are appropriate but the procedure must begin when the rat is an infant; or (*d*) the rat need not be an infant but the mother stimulus is not an effective simulation; the punishment is forceful only when the subject links the punishment causally to an agent, and though the rat is capable of inferring causality and assuming agency it will not assume agency for the present mother stimulus; or (*e*) the mother stimulus is an adequate simulation but the rat is cognitively incapable of inducing rules. Of this set we discuss the last alternative.

There is massive indirect and some direct evidence that man copes with exemplars by inducing the rules that can be used to generate them. The indirect evidence comes from language. The ability both to speak and receive productively and to produce and comprehend sentences not previously experienced can be understood only by assuming a set of rules capable of generating the sentences.

But the evidence in the case of language is almost too massive to be persuasive. As experimentalists we prefer smaller more bounded cases in which it may be possible to get a closer look at what is going on. Consider some of the work on miniature languages, introduced by Esper (1925) in the 1920s, taken up again in the 1950s by the reemergence of psycholinguistics, and given some nice twists recently by Smith (1966) and his associates.

In Smith's work the subject is read a list of items, for example, pairs of letters PL, QS, RT, etc., constituting part of a matrix formed by placing one list of letters on the horizontal array and another on the vertical. Each cell of the matrix then consists of a letter–letter pair. The experimenter eliminates the pairs lying on the diagonal, takes the remaining pairs, scrambles them, and reads them to college sophomores. Subsequently the subjects are asked to recall what they were read. The most interesting errors in this task are not those of intrusion like letters not included in the original list but grammatical errors like recall of the letter pairs that lie along the diagonal, which the subject was not given but which are compatible with the matrix and which are recalled significantly more often than any other kind of error.

Although the data are scanty, we have similar evidence from chimpanzees. We have given them lists of nonverbal material generated by matrices, in which, for example, the vertical consisted of three bottles, the horizontal three trinkets, and each cell of a trinket in a bottle. We eliminated the content of the diagonal, gave them the remaining 6 objects, and in what amounts to a delayed match to sample, required them to select from a set of 18 or more objects the 6 they were shown. The 2½- to 3½-year-old chimps have great difficulty with this problem; but Sarah who is about 10 years old gives results that are comparable to those of 4- to 6-year-old children. Both the ape and the children tend to select the grammatical intrusion, items that belong to the matrix but are not actually shown to them.

Standards, conscience, superego, call it what you like, can also be seen as rules induced on a structure, one generated by the mother's sense of what is proper and improper. Now, however, the exemplars are not letter pairs or trinkets in bottles but the behaviors for which the child receives different outcomes: reward and punishment, punishment and avoidance, some combination of motivational procedures that increase and reduce frequency.

No more than the college sophomore absorbs nonsense syllables without organizing them in some fashion does the child passively absorb frowns and kisses. Why was he punished for this and admired for that? The mother, tirelessly generating from a system instilled in her as a child, attempts to justify, with explanations that are often neither consistent nor elegant. Nevertheless, most of us find a way of systemitizing the contingencies for better or worse. We end up summarizing the exemplars with such phrases as "try hard," "put your shoulder to the wheel," "always give your best," and the like.

The disposition to induce rules is apparently not confined to man. Cognitive dispositions long reversed for man seem to be more primitive than we have supposed. Symbolization, for example, the use of one item to represent another item, can be found in the ape (Premack, 1971). Nevertheless, we are doubtful that the rat will induce rules on the basis of the training we are giving it, and we would be more confident if the subjects were apes. Yet in working with rats there is always this compensation. If the process can be found with a rat, then it must be real.

SUMMARY

● Basic motivational procedures are two-organism procedures. The behavior of a first organism is observed and judged by a second organism; if and only if it meets certain criteria does the second organism operate upon the first one.

● Anthropologists and other students of society argue that the kind of contact between individuals required by classic motivational procedures is unlikely to be realized in open society. It will work in children and in institutionalized populations generally. But is the noninstitutionalized adult subject to adequate supervision for the external contingency to work? Those who answer no have devised alternatives—belief in ghosts, God, and also the conscience of internalization of parental values.

● But this judgment may be hasty: the individual does not escape supervisory agencies merely by leaving home. The role once played by the mother is transferred to peers, spouse, employers, etc.

● This argument is plausible and probably correct. But a host of problems confronts the attempt to obtain data on the functioning of the external contingencies in the ecology. How many rewards or punishments do you get and give per day? What is the social structure of reward? These questions, basic to the supposed operation of the external contingency in society, are so far unanswered. Our attempt to answer some of them, even in a modest and preliminary way, encountered severe difficulties. What is the unit of behavior that is undergoing reward or punishment? We answer this in the laboratory by brute force, by interpolating arbitrary events, either on artificially constructed response sequences (e.g., bar press) or on natural ongoing behavior (e.g., heartbeat), and then compare the behavior before and after the interpolation. But in the ecology we cannot finesse the question of units in this way. There we are interested in the effect of events that are already present, not in those we interpolate. The role of the external contingency in non-institutionalized adults, indeed of all classic motivational procedures, is thus even today largely a matter of conjecture.

● The most interesting alternative to two-organism forms of control is one-organism control or self-control. This has been defined, for example, as the case in which the reward is both given and received by the same organism. This is an unfortunate formulation, however, for it calls attention to a superficial aspect of self-reward while concealing the basic aspect. The significant aspect of self-reward is not that the organism hands himself the reward but rather that he requires a criterion performance on his part before giving himself the reward. Self-denial is a prerequisite for self-reward in exactly the same way that denial is a prerequisite for classic reward. In both cases the organism must be denied access to the would-be reward, must be required to meet a criterion before being given access to the reward, and even then allowed as much of the reward as it would take normally, only if it responded more than it would usually on the base response.

● Since what we call a reward is merely a response (or stimulus associated with the response) that is more probable than another response, to postulate self-reward is to require that the organism not allow itself to make its most probable response. Self-reward is reasonable therefore only if we can devise a suitable restraining force, a means by which the organism can prevent itself from behaving in a preferred way.

● We described a two-stage procedure by which an organism might be equipped with a mechanism of self-denial which would serve to make self-reward possible. In the first and nonjudgmental phase, the infant develops an attachment to the mother, based perhaps on species-specific responses that modulate the infant's arousal level. But rather than face the complex task of simulating rat maternal behavior, we treat this phase merely by presenting basic stimuli discontinuously, always preceded by the mother stimulus.

● In the second phase, simulating the mother-child relation, judgments are made on the subject's responses, some called good and others bad. The two response categories are subjected to different outcomes, avoidance subjected to different outcomes, avoidance and punishment in the present experiment, designed to increase and reduce their frequencies, respectively.

● Electric shock is used as the contingent event in the present experiment, but only as a reluctant compromise for it seems likely that the main contingent event in human socialization is withdrawal of the mother.

● Partly for comic relief but also for other reasons, we divested toilet training of its more colorful connotations and justified its role in

Western socialization in engineering terms. Elimination is inescapable, relatively frequent, and highly detectable; other behaviors with like properties might be substituted without loss.

● Resistance to extinction may possibly be maximized by an avoidance schedule in which "good" responses reduce the frequency with which the mother widthdraws herself from the child. Such a schedule presupposes a base frequency with which the mother withdraws herself independent of the child's behavior and was simulated by introducing a base frequency of electric shock independent of the rat's behavior.

● Although the immediate effect of the contingencies is to change response frequencies, the long-term evidence of their effect lies in the facts of transfer. Response classes not bound to the contingencies should show the same kind of changes as those that are bound. In the case of a child trained with such a program, we could say "he was taught to try hard in the case of not hitting his younger brother, keeping his room neat, not talking back to the teacher; but now he tries hard in everything —in going to Sunday school, getting good grades, etc." Socialization leaves the child with a generalized sense of "trying hard," so that he needs only a small sample of a new situation in order to decide what constitutes "trying hard."

● "Trying hard" is the generalized name of all "good" responses, that is, of avoidance responses that reduce the frequency with which the mother withdraws herself.

● Transfer of this kind is most readily explained by rules, by the induction of a system capable of generating or giving back the exemplars one has experienced. Although we typically think of rule induction in problem solving and cognition, there is no reason to exclude it from motivation. Moral systems would seem to be a prime example of rule induction in the motivational domain.

● The gravest weakness of the present experiment is the species. Rats may be only weakly rule inducing, if at all, and it will be desirable to redo the work with primates. Yet if the lowly rat can be socialized, who could doubt the reality of the process?

REFERENCES

ARONFREED, J. *Conduct and conscience.* New York: Academic Press, 1968.

BANDURA, A. Vicarious-and-self-reinforcement processes. In R. Glaser (Ed.), *The nature of reinforcement.* New York: Academic Press, 1971.

BANDURA, A., & PERLOFF, B. Relative efficacy of self-monitored and externally imposed reinforcement and systems. *Journal of Personal and Social Psychology,* 1967, **7,** 111–116.

DULANY, D. E., JR. The place of hypotheses and intentions: An analysis of verbal control in verbal conditioning. In C. W. Eriksen (Ed.), *Behavior and awareness.* Durham, N. C.: Duke University Press, 1962.

ESPER, E. A. A technique for the experimental investigation of associated interference in artificial linguistic material. *Language Monographs,* 1925, **1,** 5–46.

ESTES, W. K. Reinforcement in human learning. In J. T. Tapp (Ed.), *Reinforcement and behavior.* New York: Academic Press, 1969.

HARLOW, H. F. The nature of love. *American Psychologist,* 1958, **13,** 673–685.

HERRNSTEIN, R. J., & HINELINE, R. N. Negative reinforcement as shock frequency reduction. *Journal of the Experimental Analysis of Behavior,* 1966, **9,** 421–430.

HOMME, L. E. Perspectives in psychology: XXIV. Control of coverants, the operants of the mind. *Psychological Record,* 1965, **15,** 501–511.

KANFER, F. H., & MARSTON, A. R. Human reinforcement: Vicarious and direct. *Journal of Experimental Psychology,* 1963, **65,** 292–296.

KESSEN, W., & MANDLER, G. Anxiety, pain and inhibition of distress. *Psychological Review,* 1961, **68,** 293–404.

MAHONEY, M. J., & BANDURA, A. Self-reinforcement in the pigeon. *Learning and Motivation,* in press.

MASON, W. A. Motivational factors in psychosocial development. *Nebraska Symposium on Motivation,* 1970, **18,** 37–61.

PREMACK, D. Toward empirical behavior laws: I. Positive reinforcement. *Psychological Review,* 1959, **66,** 219–233.

PREMACK, D. Reinforcement theory. *Nebraska Symposium on Motivation,* 1965, **14,** 123–180.

PREMACK, D. Language in chimpanzee? *Science,* 1971, **172,** 808–822.

SACKETT, G. P. Unlearned responses, differential rearing experiences, and the development of social attachments by Rhesus monkeys. In, *Primate behavior: Developments in field and laboratory research.* Vol. 1. New York: Academic Press, 1970.

SEARS, R. R. Identification as a form of behavioral development. In D. B. Harris (Ed.), *The concept of development.* Minneapolis: University of Minnesota Press, 1957.

SKINNER, B. F. *Science and human behavior.* New York: MacMillan, 1953.

SMITH, K. H. Grammatical instructions in the recall of structured letter pairs: Mediated transfer or position learning? *Journal of Experimental Psychology,* 1966, **72,** 580–588.

WHITING, J. W. M. Sorcery, sin and the superego: A cross-cultural study of some mechanisms of social control. *Nebraska Symposium on Motivation,* 1959, **7,** 174–195.

(Received August 28, 1972)

IX

GENERAL ARTICLES AND REVIEWS

Biofeedback Procedures 39
in the Clinic

Thomas H. Budzynski

A host of researchers and clinicians are exploring the clinical possibilities of biofeedback techniques. However, unwarranted claims and expectations, as well as strong placebo effects, render a proper evaluation of these procedures somewhat difficult. Nevertheless, certain approaches would appear to be quite effective. Applications to tension and migraine headache, anxiety, and insomnia can now be described. There is a suggestion that biofeedback training may be helpful as a preventive program with regard to stress-related disorders.

THE CLINICAL APPLICATION of biofeedback is such a rapidly evolving field that the techniques described in this paper may well be revised beyond recognition before another 12 mo have passed. However, if this flurry of activity could be "frozen" at this time, one would no doubt find a continuum of emphasis on biofeedback in clinical settings that ranged from heavy to none at all. The fact that biofeedback in general has captured the imagination of both the layman and the professional has made a determination of its efficacy quite difficult. Preliminary research results, often amplified in significance by the popular press, become "fact" before being tested in the crucible of professional criticism. Poorly designed biofeedback equipment and quality units misused by inexperienced but eager clinicians have contributed to the confusion regarding the effectiveness of these procedures. And, finally, it is getting more difficult to find naïve subjects who do not bring a host of expectations to each biofeedback study, thus contributing to strong placebo effects.

Even though unrealistic expectations and inadequate or misused equipment continue to cloud the picture somewhat, it is possible nevertheless to point

---

Reprint requests should be addressed to Dr. Thomas H. Budzynski, University of Colorado Medical Center, 4200 E. Ninth Avenue, Box 2621, Denver, Colo. 80220.

© 1973 by Grune & Stratton, Inc.

out several bright spots in the application of biofeedback to clinical disorders. For example, normative data slowly are becoming more available as system parameters are standardized. Certain types of biofeedback appear to be more useful than others. Clinicians are discovering how to use biofeedback in the context of existing therapies. Reliable equipment manufacturers are responding to the needs of both researcher and clinician in providing systems that vary in complexity, yet give accurate quantified results as well as precise information feedback. In addition, it is a fact that biofeedback procedures are being explored in a variety of clinical settings including medical centers, hospitals, mental health clinics, behavior therapy clinics, private practice, and a few professionally staffed clinics specializing in biofeedback therapy.

WHAT CAN BIOFEEDBACK PROVIDE IN A CLINICAL SETTING?

Biofeedback training essentially has three main goals: (1) the development of increased awareness of the relevant internal physiologic functions or events; (2) the establishment of control over those functions; and (3) the transfer or generalization of that control from the training site to other areas of one's life.

Awareness of the Event

Before voluntary control can be established over some aspect of one's physiology that ordinarily functions below the level of awareness, relevant knowledge of the event must be made known to the subject. Relevant knowledge may include the presence or absence of the event, as is the case with some EEG feedback systems, or an indication of the level of the event, as is the case with EMG; or both, as provided by certain sophisticated EEG feedback systems. Thus, the tracking system should be sensitive, accurate, artifact-free, and it must provide meaningful information feedback.

Voluntary Control Over the Function

Gradually, through a process of trial and error and hypothesis testing, the patient evolves strategies for controlling the feedback and thus the response. As he becomes more successful he learns to associate certain thoughts, as well as proprioceptive and interoceptive sensations, however subtle, with changes in the feedback. It is an interesting fact nevertheless, that a patient may develop some degree of control even before he is able to verbalize what it is that he is, or is not, doing. With continued training he is able to express what he is *not* doing, and finally, what he *is* doing, e.g., producing sensations of floating, or heaviness, or warmth in his limbs, and excluding certain thoughts.

Transfer of Control

The ability to verbalize control strategies enhances transfer from the clinic or laboratory to "real life." Therefore, the patient should be encouraged during the training phase to describe his sensations, as well as his successful and unsuccessful strategies. Often the patient will use a phrase or series of phrases that will become conditioned to the desired physiologic pattern. The autogenic training formulae of Schultz and Luthe[17] are very useful for this purpose. In fact, Green et al.[8] were the first experimenters to combine autogenic training phraseology and biofeedback. Other researchers who have employed autogenic-type phrases to enhance biofeedback learning and transfer are Budzynski and Stoyva[2] and Love.[13]

Jacobson's progressive relaxation exercises[10] are also helpful in the initial stages of biofeedback training. These exercises, along with certain of the autogenic formulae, and other specialized instructions, can be placed on cassette tapes for use in the clinical setting, as well as for home practice. For the past 8 mo we have used clinic and home practice cassette tapes at the Applied Biofeedback Institute. They are now an integral part of the therapy programs. It appears that a patient is more inclined to do the home practicing if he can listen to a tape recording. The patient's progress from one tape to another is based on his ability to demonstrate a certain level of control over a particular function. Home practice cassettes also ease the transition of the patient away from the biofeedback equipment. Of course, the transfer is never completed until the patient can successfully demonstrate his newly developed ability under real-life aversive conditions.

Self-perceived Progress

If the successful pursuance of the three goals can be implemented, then biofeedback training can be of great value in clinical settings. For example, the use of feedback equipment with adequate quantification capability allows the therapist to specify target behaviors in terms of desired physiologic parameters at each stage of training. Thus, the patient perceives that he is progressing as he meets each criterion in turn.

Moment-to-moment knowledge of results provided by the feedback, as well as charts and graphs illustrating longer-term changes, provide objective evidence of progress. The confidence gained from this illustration of increasing control seems to generalize to other areas of the patient's life. Leitenberg,[12] for example, have shown that providing a subject with information about his performance has therapeutic effects.

WHAT BIOFEEDBACK CANNOT PROVIDE IN A CLINICAL SETTING

Although biofeedback training alone can result in positive change, it may be made more effective when used in conjunction with other therapy procedures. This is especially true if factors in the patient's environment appear to be contributing to his problem. These trouble areas of the patient's day-to-day existence may never be brought to light if he interacts only with a biofeedback machine. It is true that biofeedback training alone may help him to cope with these difficulties, however, the problems themselves can act to prevent progress with the training. The patient may find himself dwelling on problem-related thoughts during the training sessions, or he may find it difficult to practice at home.

A more troublesome situation for the therapist occurs when the patient is getting positively reinforced for maintaining his maladaptive behavior, or when he uses his symptoms to avoid certain feared situations. This may also manifest itself as an inability to progress in training and/or a reluctance to practice at home. A good relationship between therapist and patient can reduce, or at least help uncover, some of these motivational problems.

In short, biofeedback is simply a mirror reflecting some aspect of physiology. The patient really must want to learn to use the mirror in developing control over this response. An important part of the therapist's task is to maintain this motivation.

SPECIFIC BIOFEEDBACK THERAPY PROCEDURES

Since biofeedback is useful for altering and bringing under control physiologic responses, this training would seem to be particularly suited to disorders characterized by maladaptive physiologic patterns such as are evident in cases of tension and migraine headaches, essential hypertension, certain types of epilepsy, Raynaud's disease and cardiac arrhythmias. However, only a few of the possible clinical applications have been adequately researched. Requirements such as lengthy base lines, proper control conditions to guard against habituation and placebo effects, control of medication, and meaningful evaluation procedures, render such research with humans a gruelling and time-consuming task.

With equipment design and training procedures evolving at a rapid rate, it is often difficult for the researcher to "freeze" design and training for the length of time it takes to complete an adequate experiment. For example, the tension headache studies carried out at the University of Colorado Medical Center[4,5] involved a "bare bones" procedure. Patients in the second of these two studies were given only EMG (electromyographic) feedback from the forehead musculature for 16 sessions of 20 min each. They were asked to practice relaxing twice a day at home but were told only to do what they had learned in the training sessions. In spite of this simplified procedure approximately 70% of the patients showed significant reductions in headache activity.

Following the completion of the study, the control group patients were offered the real training. In this instance the "bare bones" procedure was augmented by cassette tape relaxation instructions, as well as portable EMG feedback units for home use. These additional measures seem to provide a greater incentive for practicing outside the laboratory.

The transfer of control to real life is enhanced not only by the daily home practice periods but also by reminding the patient to make frequent checks of his general tension level during the day. If he found himself tense, he was to attempt to relax for a short period (30 sec to 3 min). This practice can be implemented by placing a small sliver of brightly colored tape on the wrist watch dial. Thus, each time the patient looks at his watch the tape reminds him to scan around for tension spots. Incidentally, we have found that the color and shape of the tape reminder should be changed at least once a week; otherwise, people tend to habituate and subsequently ignore it. Since we ask our tension headache patients to chart headache intensity every hour, the wrist watch tape serves also as a reminder to complete this task.

Clinical Procedures for Headache Conditions

One of the more interesting conclusions arising from the work with tension headache at the University of Colorado Medical Center and the study of migraine headache at the Menninger Clinic[16] is that EMG feedback alone is quite effective for tension headache but not for migraine, whereas peripheral temperature feedback is effective for migraine but not for tension headache. Consequently, a careful differential diagnosis should be made prior to biofeedback training. Following this, an attempt should be made to determine the circumstances associated with the onset of the headaches as well as the present environmental contingencies that may be maintaining the headaches. The patient is told that he will have to maintain an hourly (if he has tension headaches) or daily (if he has migraine headaches) record of the headache intensity. He is also told that he must practice relaxing at home or at work twice daily, and that the degree of relaxation for each of these sessions must be charted. The patient is taught also to record the type and amount of medication on the headache intensity chart.

It is very important to ascertain from the patient when during the day he feels he can take time to relax. Although most patients will have agreed to follow all the instructions to this point, some patients balk when asked to be specific about home practice times. The therapist may have to review with the patient each day's activities, hour by hour, in order to find appropriate times for the relaxation practice. The patient is also instructed to inform his immediate family of the necessity for privacy and quiet during the home practice periods. If he has a private office at work he is told to have his secretary hold all calls and visitors during the 20-min practice periods.

In most instances a 2-wk base line of charting headaches and medication is taken before training is begun. Following the base-line period, training is initiated with twice-a-week sessions. An abbreviated form of Jacobson's tense-relax procedure is used during the first two or three sessions in order to provide the patient with at least a gross awareness of differing levels of tension in his muscles. A measure of arm and frontalis EMG levels is taken before and after each session. The patient is given a cassette tape with tense-relax instructions for home use. He is told to practice twice a day and to rate the degree of relaxation achieved on a scale of 0 to 5.

The next phase of training involves EMG biofeedback from the forearm extensor. Autogenic-type phrases are coupled with the physiologic changes resulting from the feedback training. These auto-suggestive phrases also help to bring about the desired changes signalled by feelings of heaviness and warmth in the limbs. A cassette tape with the autogenic formulae allows the patient to practice at producing the changes outside the clinic.

When the patient can maintain his forearm tension below a certain level $(3\mu V)$, and when he can feel the heaviness and warmth sensations in his limbs, the feedback can be transferred to the forehead. Surface bioelectric activity in the forehead area is reflective of not only frontalis tension but jaw (masseter and temporalis) muscle tension, eye movements, and eye muscle tension. The diminution of all these signals contributes to a general decrease in arousal level.[7,9] A third cassette tape, building on the prior learning, is used for home practice during the forehead-training phase.

Eventually, the patient learns to reduce forehead bioelectric activity below 3μV while sustaining the warmth and heaviness sensations in his limbs. The patient then practices at keeping the forehead EMG low with his eyes open in an upright sitting posture. The feedback can be withdrawn gradually at this point to check the patient's ability to maintain relaxation in the absence of feedback.

A final phase of the biofeedback training for tension headache involves a "stress management" procedure. While receiving forehead EMG feedback, the patient visualizes, as vividly as possible, a variety of stressful situations. While doing so, he attempts to maintain relaxation, or, at least to recover quickly if aroused momentarily. As in the prior phase of training the feedback is gradually removed as the patient learns to sustain a relaxed physiology in the presence of stressful thoughts. At this point, the patient is encouraged to attempt to maintain an *optimal* arousal level in the face of real life stressors, and to try relaxing *after* the stressful situation is over (see Stoyva and Budzynski[19]). Typically, the duration of training to this point is approximately 15 1-hr sessions or 8 wk.

Migraine patients receive training similar to those with tension headaches except that peripheral temperature feedback is introduced after the EMG feedback training. It has been our experience at the clinic that migraine patients quite often have cold hands (70°–80°F). They also tend to have somewhat lower forehead EMG levels than tension headache patients. Consequently, a shorter EMG training period is required before temperature feedback is initiated. The rationale for the EMG training with migraine cases is that the response of painfully dilated blood vessels in the head represents a rebound phenomenon occurring as a result of an initial over-reaction to stress. If this initial response to the stressor can be modified through relaxation training, then perhaps the rebound response will be weaker. Feedback of temperature information from the hand, a technique pioneered by Sargent et al.[18] appears to be effective in the postponement, alleviation, or prevention of migraine headaches.

For this phase of training, the patient hears an auditory analog of the skin temperature of the hand. When he can maintain regularly a temperature greater than 90°F, the patient is asked to do this with visual feedback only. He will next attempt to do so without feedback. A final phase of training for migraine patients involves the same stress management procedure as employed with the tension headache patients, except that finger temperature is used as the feedback information source.

BIOFEEDBACK USED TO FACILITATE BEHAVIOR THERAPY (SYSTEMATIC DESENSITIZATION)
Drug Dependency Problems (With Migraine Patients)

Even after they have learned to control their muscle tension and temperature responses, some migraine patients find it all but impossible to give up or even decrease their daily drug intake. These are patients who tend to have particularly severe headaches if they fail to take rather large amounts of drugs, such as three to four cafergot suppositories, some valium, and a number of aspirin each day. Rather than risk getting an extremely painful headache, these patients begin taking their medication at the first sign of such an event. Some patients maintain a daily prophylactic dosage and then augment this with additional amounts as a headache seems imminent. Unfortunately, through the years many events become conditioned to the headache pain. Thus, a heightened irritability, a slight feeling of depression, a tense neck musculature, a weather change, an argument with a friend or relative, or a party can signal the onslaught. The response of taking large amounts of medication at this point avoids the headache pain and thus strengthens the response. When asked to give up their medication (even a little at a time), and substitute their newly developed ability to control peripheral warmth, these patients may become very anxious, and therefore, more disposed to headaches.

Consequently, a period of systematic desensitization is required to reduce this anxiety before the medication reduction can begin. The desensitization hierarchy includes scenes in which the patient visualizes himself giving up a progressively greater amount of medication. Upon completion of the hierarchy, the patient is encouraged to begin a very gradual withdrawal from his medication.

Eventually, migraine patients find they can exist without medication except in extreme circumstances or in cases of menstrual cycle headaches that occur once or twice each cycle. Typically, the patients find that they can accomplish the hand-warming in the face of headache onset cues. However, if they are unable to accomplish this warming in 15 min, it is an indication that the headache onset has progressed too far and they will need some medication. This procedure gives the patient a chance to try altering his physiology before giving in to medication. In three cases of menstrual cycle migraine headaches, the hand-warming was difficult to accomplish and the patients usually resorted to medication at these times.

Treatment-refractory Anxiety

Although the research and clinical results with headache conditions appear somewhat compelling, such is not quite the case with biofeedback applied to anxiety problems. A recent study by Raskin et al.[15] indicated that three of ten chronically anxious patients improved moderately, and one showed marked improvement as a result of frontalis EMG feedback training.

Treatment-refractory Insomnia

In this same group of patients,* greater changes were seen in insomnia: of a total of six, four moderately improved and one markedly improved. Since all

---

*Of these ten patients, four also had headache symptoms. Here the results were much better: three improved markedly and one moderately.

ten of these patients were considered to be treatment refractory (they had remained symptomatic despite 2 yr of treatment with individual psychotherapy and medication), and considering the fact that the biofeedback training was not augmented by other relaxation training, the results are indeed promising.

Circumscribed Phobias

After some 5 yr of experimentation at the University of Colorado Medical Center with a variety of biofeedback procedures for anxiety, we have evolved certain programs based on the type of anxiety response shown by the patient. As a general rule, the more specific the anxiety stimulus, the shorter the relaxation training and desensitization time required,[2,3] Experience with some 60 patients has led us to the conclusion that relaxation training may not be required for patients with very circumscribed phobias. Typically, the desensitization can be completed before the patient faces an in vivo phobic stimulus. In most instances he can confront it at a time of his own choosing.

Social Phobias

However, anxiety disorders in which the precipitating stimuli are more common in the environment, such as with social phobias, appear to be characterized by higher arousal levels, and require a thorough period of relaxation training and desensitization.

Generalized Phobias

Lader and Mathews[10] have explored the relationship between the diffuseness of the anxiety and arousal level. Using spontaneous fluctuations of the galvanic skin response (GSR) as a measurement of arousal, they discovered that patients with more generalized phobias exhibited a significantly greater number of fluctuations than did normals or specific phobia patients. These researchers also discovered that those patients with generalized anxiety took much longer to habituate to an auditory stimulus than did normals or the specific phobia group. These conclusions are particularly interesting if the behavior therapy procedure known as systematic desensitization is considered to be an habituation phenomenon.

Thus, Lader and Mathews would view a patient with diffuse anxiety as manifesting a high level of arousal that may be maintained by a wide variety of stimuli, or by stimuli that are prevalent in the patient's environment. Lader and Mathews also predict that any improvement following desensitization would be short-lived in the absence of a *relatively permanent* decrease in arousal.

Agoraphobia

Lader and Wing[11] made the observation that agoraphobic patients have much anxiety even under resting conditions. They suggested that this condition may trigger episodes of positive feedback that are seen clinically as panic attacks. Furthermore, Marks[14] noticed that agoraphobic patients who had recently overcome their fears through systematic desensitization could experience a panic attack that would undo the effects of weeks of treatment. Raskin et al.

stated that, "In order to achieve satisfactory results with chronic anxiety it appears necessary for the patient to incorporate relaxation into his daily activities."[15]

From the above observations, it has become apparent that patients with chronic generalized anxiety should be given thorough training in the achievement of low arousal states, and, furthermore, that they should be taught to maintain a normal arousal level in the face of everyday stress. If these goals are not achieved, the diffuse anxiety patient may become resensitized after completing systematic desensitization.

Achievement of Low Arousal

The concept of altering one's physiology in order to decrease the experience of anxiety has physiologic concomitants, however difficult they may be to measure. It is generally agreed that these physiologic correlates of anxiety are in the direction of heightened arousal. However, the arousal pattern, or profile of responses, for one individual may differ from that of another. Thus, the profile for one patient may be characterized by a large increase in frontalis EMG, and in another patient by a decrease in hand temperature. A third may show a suppression of the alpha EEG brain wave rhythm. Individuals tend to maintain their profiles across different stress conditions—a tendency labelled response sterotype or response specificity.[6] It simply means that a given individual, on different occasions, probably will show the greatest response to stress or anxiety in one particular system.

Perhaps the most efficient approach to biofeedback training for anxiety would involve the monitoring of several physiologic systems while the patient is made to feel slightly anxious or under stress. In this situation, that system (cortical, autonomic, or skeletal muscle) found to be most reactive would be the best prospect for the application of biofeedback. For example, if the patient is asked to think about an anxiety-arousing situation, or is asked to do mental arithmetic, his physiologic responses will change in the direction of increased arousal. This arousal pattern will reveal which response is most reactive.

At the Applied Biofeedback Institute, we have found it useful to use EMG as the initial feedback type. Training with EMG proceeds until the patient can maintain EMG levels below $3\mu V$ over the frontalis and the forearm extensor. When the patient has learned to meet these criteria, feedback of another type is employed if necessary. Criteria for these other responses are evolving as well; for example, we also train patients to develop and maintain skin temperatures of 90° F or more on the hands. In view of the observation of Lader and Mathews[10] that a relaxed individual will exhibit from one to three spontaneous GSR responses per minute, perhaps a maximum of two per minute could be used as a GSR criterion. Cool, damp hands are a common condition in chronically anxious individuals. A high rate of spontaneous GSR activity and decreased hand temperature are reflective of sympathetic arousal. The biofeedback training for individuals with chronic anxiety is thus designed to decrease general arousal, thereby promoting an autonomic, cortical, and skeletal motor profile characteristic of relaxed, and therefore, unanxious patients.

At this stage of training the patient is encouraged to try out his newly developed skills in real-life situations. The confidence to do this can be strengthened by means of several procedures. Systematic desensitization of relevant anxiety hierarchies (see Budzynski and Stoyva[2,3] and Wickramasekera[20]), role rehearsal, and assertive training are some of the behavior therapy approaches that can be employed. One procedure that appears to be of value involves the visualization of anxiety-arousing situations until the anxiety is definitely felt. With well-trained patients, the visualized anxiety situations must be grossly exaggerated in order to produce feelings of anxiety. The patient is receiving feedback of EMG, GSR, or temperature at this time, and is thus aware of the physiologic effects of the anxiety. He then attempts to recover from the heightened arousal by lowering the feedback indicators. We have found that a patient learns to do this in the space of one or two training sessions. Convinced that he can recover successfully with feedback, the patient then practices without feedback. "Recovery training" of this sort provides the patient with the confidence that even if he should begin to experience anxiety outside the clinic, he can bring himself under control. Armed with this knowledge, the patient is less likely to avoid situations that were formerly anxiety-provoking in nature. Hence, he has a greater probability of undergoing in vivo desensitization on his own.

The process of falling asleep involves a lowering of arousal that is indicated by decreasing muscle tonus and heart rate, as well as a decrease in brain wave frequencies. Typically, the relaxed, eyes-closed alpha rhythm begins to slow and diminish in amplitude as theta (4–7 Hz) begins to increase. We felt, therefore, that a useful program for sleep-onset problems would involve muscle relaxation followed by the shaping of drowsy brain wave rhythms.

Thus far, we have trained 11 sleep-onset insomnia (SOI) patients with EMG feedback and theta EEG feedback. Six of the 11 have improved, three dramatically. Five showed no improvement for a variety of reasons.

In general, we have found that individuals with SOI show high EMG levels and an activated EEG. However, several patients could produce very low EMG levels as a result of prior training with various relaxation techniques. These individuals, however, did *not* show evidence of drowsy brain rhythms (theta EEG). Two were able to acquire control over theta by means of theta feedback, and their sleep subsequently improved. The other low EMG patient could not increase theta and did not improve.

The assumption that patients with high levels of muscle tension have difficulty producing theta rhythms was tested in an experiment by Sittenfeld et al.[18] The study compared the ability of normal subjects with high and low muscle tension to produce an increase in theta activity through biofeedback. The results clearly showed that high EMG subjects required prior EMG feedback before theta EEG training was effective. Low EMG subjects, on the other hand, were able to increase their theta activity through theta feedback without the prior EMG training.

Procedures to increase the base operant of theta other than by lowering EMG are being explored at the present time.[1]

Additional support for the application of EMG biofeedback to insomnia comes from the study by Raskin et al.[15] Five of six patients with sleep disturbances learned to put themselves to sleep without medication. This was reported to have markedly decreased their fears of insomnia, even though the patients also stated that their sleep was not as restful as the sedative-induced sleep previously experienced. It is very possible that the medication problem (withdrawal fears and physiologic reactions) with insomnia patients is similar in kind to that encountered in migraine cases. Thus, insomnia patients who regularly take medication before bedtime may benefit from a medication-withdrawal systematic desensitization prior to the actual in vivo gradual withdrawal from medication.

CONCLUDING REMARKS

An accumulating body of clinical and research evidence suggests that biofeedback represents a relatively effective technique for the shaping of self-control over certain physiologic events. These events are usually autonomous in that they tend to occur automatically and below the level of awareness. When these internal events fall outside the normal range of functioning, they constitute maladaptive behaviors that can lead to feelings of anxiety, or the appearance of such stress-related disorders as migraine and tension headaches, certain cardiovascular problems, and sleep-onset insomnia, to name a few. Through biofeedback training, patients learn to maintain their physiology within a normal range of functioning.

In addition to the alleviation or elimination of the symptoms of stress-related disorders, biofeedback training could constitute a preventive technique to enable individuals to better cope with the stress of a "future shock" environment. Furthermore, the development of self-control of internal functions at an early age might represent one of the most effective programs for the prevention of those disorders that produce the highest incidences of morbidity and mortality in our industrialized, fast-paced culture.

REFERENCES

1. Budzynski T: Some applications of biofeedback-produced twilight states. Fields Within Fields ... Within Fields 5:105, 1972. Republished in Shapiro D, et al (eds): Biofeedback and Self-Control: 1972. Chicago, Aldine-Atherton, in press

2. Budzynski T, Stoyva J: Biofeedback techniques in behavior therapy, in Birbaumer N (ed): The Mastery of Anxiety. Contribution of Neuropsychology to Anxiety Research. Reihe Fortschritte der Klinischen Psychologie, Bd. 4, München, Wien: Verlag, Urban & Schwarzenberg, 1973, in press. English version republished in Shapiro D, et al (eds): Biofeedback and Self-Control: 1972. Chicago, Aldine-Atherton, in press

3. Budzynski T, Stoyva J: EMG biofeedback and behavior therapy, in Jurjevich R (ed): Direct Psychotherapy, vol 3: International Developments. Coral Gables, Fla, University of Miami Press, in press

4. Budzynski T, Stoyva J, Adler C: Feedback-induced relaxation: Application to tension headache. J Behav Ther Exp Psychiatry 1:205, 1970

5. Budzynski T, Stoyva J, Adler C, et al: EMG biofeedback and tension headache: A controlled outcome study. Psychosom Med (in press)

6. Engel BT: Response specificity, in Greenfield N, Sternbach R (eds). Handbook of Psychophysiology. New York, Holt, Rinehart & Winston, 1972, p 571

7. Gellhorn E: Motion and emotion. Psychol Rev 71:457, 1964

8. Green E, Green A, Walters E: Voluntary control of internal states: Psychological and physiological. J Transpersonal Psychol 2:1, 1970

9. Jacobson E: Progressive Relaxation (ed 2). Chicago, Univ of Chicago Pr, 1938

10. Lader MH, Mathews AM: A physiological model of phobic anxiety and desensitization. Behav Res Ther 6:411, 1968

11. Lader MH, Wing L: Physiological Measures, Sedative Drugs, and Morbid Anxiety. London, Univ of Oxford Pr, 1966

12. Leitenberg H, Agras W, Thompson L, et al: Feedback in behavior modification: An experimental analysis in two phobic cases. J Appl Behav Anal 1:131, 1968

13. Love WA: Problems in therapeutic application of EMG feedback. Presented at the Annual Meeting of the Biofeedback Research Society, Boston, 1972, unpublished

14. Marks IM: Fears and Phobias. New York, Academic Press, 1969, p 207

15. Raskin M, Johnson G, Rondestvedt T: Chronic anxiety treated by feedback-induced muscle relaxation. Arch Gen Psychiatry 28:263, 1973

16. Sargent J, Green E, Walters E: Preliminary report on the use of autogenic feedback techniques in the treatment of migraine and tension headaches. Psychosom Med 35: 129–135, 1973

17. Schultz J, Luthe W: Autogenic Training. New York, Grune & Stratton, 1959

18. Sittenfeld P, Budzynski T, Stoyva J: Feedback control of the EEG theta rhythm. Presented at the American Psychological Association Meeting, Honolulu, 1972

19. Stoyva J, Budzynski T: Cultivated low arousal—An anti-stress response?, in DiCara LV (ed): Recent Advances in Limbic and Autonomic Nervous System Research. New York, Plenum, in press

20. Wickramasekera I: Instructions and EMG feedback in systematic desensitization: A case report. Behav Ther 3:460, 1972

The Role of Expectancy and 40
Physiological Feedback in Fear Research:
A Review with Special Reference to
Subject Characteristics

Thomas D. Borkovec

Review of the expectancy literature in fear research indicates that a subject characteristic of intensity of fear is related to whether demand characteristic effects confound treatment effects. Review of physiological feedback studies suggests the potentially important role of physiological cues in maintaining and/or modifying fear behavior. Together, the two areas indicate that more research effort should be devoted to (a) the interaction of motoric, verbal, and physiological components of fear and (b) the role of individual differences, particularly at the physiological level, in those components and their modification.

Increased attention has been recently devoted to the effects of expectancy and physiological feedback in analogue fear studies. Expectancy manipulations operationally involve administration of therapy procedures with vs without therapeutic instructions. Physiological feedback studies focus on the effects of amplified physiological signals (real or false) or the effects of actual manipulation of general arousal on fear behavior. Both of these research approaches will be viewed here as involving the manipulation of discriminative stimuli in the fearful subject's experimental environment which set the occasion for certain subsequent verbal and motoric behavior in that environment. The purpose of the present paper is to review and relate the relevant studies in these seemingly separate areas and to draw implications for outcome research with special reference to subject characteristic factors.

EXPECTANCY

Wilkins (in press) has correctly cautioned researchers to avoid the circularity involved in positing an internal "expectancy" construct as an explanation of behavior or behavioral change. This problem can be over-

[1] Based in part on a paper presented at the Purdue Psychotherapy Symposium, April 13, 1972.

[2] Requests for reprints should be sent to Thomas D. Borkovec, Department of Psychology, University of Iowa, Iowa City, Iowa 52240.

come by viewing expectancy manipulations (presence or absence of therapeutic instructions) as discriminative stimuli or demand characteristics (Orne, 1959; Bernstein, in press) influencing posttest fear behavior. That is, implicit or explicit communication is made to the subjects in the therapeutic instruction conditions that the posttest is an assessment of the successfulness of the therapy sessions in *changing* their fear behavior (high demand for improved overt behavior), while subjects in the non-therapeutic condition are given no suggestions that they are to display posttest behavior different from their pretest behavior (low demand for improved behavior).

The traditional control for such nonspecific therapy factors has been the use of placebo conditions. The complimentary nature of the crossed expectancy design to the placebo control is seen in Table 1. The usual comparison has been between the treatment and placebo conditions, both of which are presented as effective therapeutic procedures (e.g., Paul, 1966). Both conditions are assumed to equate expectancy (an assumption that has been recently questioned by Baker and Kahn (1972) and Borkovec and Nau (in press) and the critical difference is presumably the treatment component alone. If treatment is found to be superior to placebo on outcome measures, the conclusion is usually drawn that something "active" in the treatment itself was the cause of the improvement. A crossed expectancy factor, on the other hand, allows *identical* matching of treatment conditions on the active treatment procedure and attempts to vary only the subject's "expectancy" about the effect the procedure is presumed to have on his subsequent behavior. The choice of either design is, of course, a matter of the aim of the investigation: efficacy of a treatment procedure vs the contribution of therapeutic suggestion to a treatment procedure. But two additional implications may

TABLE 1
Placebo and Crossed Expectancy Designs

	High demand for improved behavior	"Active" treatment effects	Low demand for improved behavior
(1) Treatment with non-therapeutic instructions		X	X
(2) Treatment with therapeutic instructions	X	X	
(3) Placebo with therapeutic instructions	X		
(4) Placebo with non-therapeutic instructions			X

follow from the crossed expectancy design: (a) A treatment procedure which produces improvement greater than a placebo condition, regardless of expectancy instructions, is indeed a powerful modification technique and includes some active ingredient separate from demand effects. (b) A treatment procedure which produces improvement greater than a placebo condition only under therapeutic instructions may be a powerful technique, but its effectiveness resides either in the power of its face validity to the subject or in the interaction of its face validity and its active ingredients. That active ingredients can interact with expectancy conditions has been demonstrated even in drug research (e.g., Dinnerstein and Halm, 1970).

While the above discussion indicates the potentially important role that the crossed expectancy factor can play in coming to conclusions about the active ingredients of treatment procedures, the data thus far collected employing this design have been equivocal. Ten of these studies (McGlynn, Mealiea, & Nawas, 1969; McGlynn & Mapp, 1970; McGlynn & Williams, 1970; Lomont & Brock, 1971; McGlynn, 1971; McGlynn, Reynolds, & Linder, 1971a; McGlynn, Reynolds, & Linder, 1971b; Howlett & Nawas, 1972; McGlynn, 1972; McGlynn, Gaynor, & Phur, 1972) have demonstrated that systematic desensitization is equally effective with or without therapeutic instructions, while nine others (Efran & Marcia, 1967; Leitenberg, Agras, Barlow, & Oliveau, 1969; Marcia, Rubin, & Efran, 1969; Oliveau, Agras, Leitenberg, Moore, & Wright, 1969; Parrino, 1971; Borkovec, 1972; Miller, 1972; Persely & Leventhal, 1972; Rappaport, 1972) found therapeutic expectancy superior to nontherapeutic expectancy within therapy conditions (including desensitization, implosion, and operant shaping).

In one attempt to eliminate the confusion, McGlynn, Reynolds, and Linder (1971b) tested the hypothesis that the timing of the therapeutic instructions (pre-treatment instructions alone vs pre- plus intra-treatment instructions) was the major determinant in demonstrating the expectancy effect. They found no difference between these two therapeutic desensitization conditions and neither differed from a non-therapeutic desensitization group, while all three conditions showed greater improvement than pseudo-desensitization and no-treatment groups. The discrepant data remained unexplained.

While other procedural variations may have contributed to the contradictory results in the expectancy literature (Davison & Wilson 1973; Wilkins, in press), it is proposed that the subject characteristic differences may also play an important role. Bernstein (in press) has argued that the influence of demand characteristics can be reduced if investigators are careful to select truly phobic subjects for their research. This

TABLE 2
Crossed Expectancy Factor Studies Demonstrating and Failing to Demonstrate
Expectancy Effects and Their Self-Report and Behavioral
Subject Selection Criteria

Studies demonstrating an expectancy effect	Subject selection criteria	
	Self-report[a]	Behavioral approach[b]
Efran & Marcia, 1967	"very much afraid or terror" (6 or 7 on a 7-pt. scale)	bare hand
Leitenberg *et al.*, 1969	"definitely tense, extremely tense, or terror" (3, 4, or 5 on a 5-pt. scale)	bare hand
Marcia *et al.*, 1969	"very much afraid or terror" (6 or 7 on a 7-pt. scale)	bare hand
Oliveau *et al.*, 1969	"definitely tense, extremely tense, or terror" (3, 4, or 5 on a 5-pt. scale)	bare hand
Parrino, 1971	"much fear, very much fear, or terror" (5, 6, or 7 on a 7-pt. scale)	bare hand
Borkovec, 1972	"much fear, very much fear, or terror" (5, 6, or 7 on a 7-pt. scale)	bare hand
Miller, 1972	"fearful"	lift object briefly
Persely & Leventhal, 1972	"very much afraid or terror" (6 or 7 on a 7-pt. scale)	bare hand
Rappaport, 1972	"much fear, very much fear, or terror" (5, 6, or 7 on a 7-pt. scale)	no pretest
Studies demonstrating no expectancy effect		
McGlynn *et al.*, 1969	"intense fear"[c]	gloved hand
McGlynn & Mapp, 1970	"intense fear"[c]	gloved hand
McGlynn & Williams, 1970	"intense fear"[c]	10-in. wooden pointer
Howlett & Nawas, 1972	reported inability to touch object with gloved hand	12-in. wooden pointer
Lomont & Brock, 1971	"terror" (7 on a 7-pt. scale)	approach no closer than 3 ft
McGlynn, 1971	"intense fear"[c]	gloved hand
McGlynn *et al.*, 1971a	"intense fear"[c]	gloved hand
McGlynn *et al.*, 1971b	"intense fear"[c]	gloved hand
McGlynn, 1972	"intense fear"[c]	gloved hand
McGlynn *et al.*, 1972	"intense fear"[c]	gloved hand

[a] *S* was excluded from participation if he reported less fear than indicated.
[b] *S* was excluded from participation if he touched object as indicated.
[c] 7 on a 7-pt. scale.

would suggest that perhaps the contradictory results among the expectancy studies reflect a greater proportion of more fearful subjects in studies failing to demonstrate the expectancy effect. As seen in Table 2, a review of the selection criteria employed in the expectancy studies supports this notion. Studies failing to find an expectancy effect employed only those subjects who reported the highest level of fear on their respective self-report scales; studies demonstrating expectancy effects allowed a range of fear report within their scales. Secondly, with one exception (Miller, 1972), the latter studies employed a less stringent behavioral selection criterion. Finally, in three of the studies using less stringent selection criteria and favoring the expectancy effect (Leitenberg *et al.*, 1969; Oliveau *et al.*, 1969; Parrino, 1971), subjects had several exposures to the actual feared object during the course of treatment. As Lomont and Brock (1971) have suggested, the demand for showing improvement during these exposures was clearly greater for subjects in the therapeutic condition ("these exposures are to assess your progress") than for those in non-therapeutic condition ("these exposures are to refresh your memory"). It is known from other research that mere repeated exposure results in increased improvement (Rachman, 1966; Borkovec & Craighead, 1971) and that therapeutic suggestions of improvement produce significantly greater approach change than simple repeated exposure (Borkovec, 1973).

The above review of expectancy studies suggests the following hypothesis: External demand characteristics for improved overt behavior in outcome studies have a greater effect on low, fearful subjects than on high, fearful subjects *within* the analogue phobic population. This hypothesis implies that many analogue outcome studies (those using some or all low, phobic subjects) may primarily reflect a demand effect (in agreement with Bernstein & Paul, 1971) or a demand by subject characteristic interaction effect. How the investigator defines intensity of fear, then, becomes an extremely important decision which may influence the extent and direction of the effects which his treatment and extra-treatment variables will have on outcome.

PHYSIOLOGICAL FEEDBACK

While verbal, overt behavioral, and cognitive aspects are often included in behavioral definitions of anxiety, the physiological component has long held an important position (e.g., Wolpe, 1958; Speilberger, 1966; Paul, 1969; Mathews, 1971). The role of physiological responses to be stressed here is somewhat similar, functionally, to the role of expectancy manipulations presented above. As a response-produced stimulus, physiological reactions may serve as discriminative cues for subsequent verbal, behavioral, and cognitive responses. Stampfl and Levis (1969) have indicated the importance of including interoceptive stimuli as part of the CS complex in the implosive treatment of anxiety, while recent case studies (Everaerd, 1970; Furst & Cooper, 1970) suggest that such cues may be the crucial component in the maintenance, and the efficient elimination, of some types of neurotic disturbances. Most of the experimental evidence for the importance of internal cuing and its influence on emotional behavior come from studies presenting physiological feedback (false or real) during treatment or test conditions, or from studies directly manipulating arousal level prior to testing. The use of real autonomic feedback has been reported effective in modifying autonomic functioning in experimental subjects (Brener & Hothersall, 1966; Lang, Stroufe, & Hastings, 1967; Budzynski & Stoyva, 1969; Green, Walters, Green, & Murphy, 1969; Grim, 1971) and clinical patients (Jacobs & Felton, 1969; Budzynski, Stoyva, & Adler, 1970). Such studies are suggestive of the potential effect that a subject's internal responding may have on subsequent behavior, if the subject is made aware of such feedback through amplified signals. Much of the remaining research has stemmed from the work of Schachter and his co-workers (Schachter & Singer, 1962; Schachter & Wheeler, 1962; Schachter, 1964; Nisbett & Schachter, 1966). The theory of emotion based on their research suggests that nonspecific arousal interacts with environmental cues in determining overt emotional behavior. Thus, a subject will label a feeling state as a particular emotion depending on the environmental cues available to him when he cannot identify the source of the arousal.

False Feedback Manipulations

Koenig and Del Castillo (1969) demonstrated the potentially important role of physiological cues in maintaining fear responses. Awareness of the onset of extinction trials in an aversive conditioning paradigm was shown to facilitate extinction of conditioned GSR, while false feedback indicating continued emotional responsivity to the CS retarded GSR extinction in both aware and non-aware conditions. Similarly, Wilkins (1971a) found that false feedback can influence the emotionality of a subject's interpretation of environmental stimuli. Presented with ambiguous auditory messages, subjects receiving high arousal feedback reported more emotional interpretations of the messages than subjects receiving low arousal feedback.

In the area of fear reduction, Valins and Ray (1967) produced approach improvements in snake phobics by manipulating heart rate feedback during slide presentation of feared stimuli. Both Sushinsky and Bootzin (1970) and Gaupp, Stern, and Galbraith (1972) failed to replicated this effect, but both studies in an appropriate effort of control, included a problematical behavioral pretest. First, this may have guaranteed more fearful subjects who, given the expectancy literature discussed above, are less susceptible to demand effects. Secondly, during a pretest snake exposure, subjects will experience fear (physiological cues, avoidance, etc.) prior to the weaker exposure (slides of snakes). Despite the use of the treatment task and false feedback to demonstrate to the subject that she is not fearful, a subject may respond more in accord with her own past experience with the *in vivo* situation than with an experimenter's feedback devices and tasks (Bandura, 1969; Davison & Wilson, in press), if there is no reason for the subject to believe that her pretest reaction is likely to change as a consequence of the experimental task. This was indeed the case, since in both studies subjects were run under non-therapeutic (low demand) instructions. Within-group analysis in the Gaupp *et al.* (1972) study demonstrated, incidentally, the possible importance of actual feedback: subjects showing EKG decreases over slide presentations displayed greater posttest approach than subjects showing no change or increases in EKG. A third attempted replication of the Valins and Ray (1967) experiment was also unsuccessful. Kent, Wilson, and Nelson (1972), pointing to the use of money incentives for increased approach in the Valins and Ray study, used a "conventional" approach posttest and failed to find significant differences between experimental and control groups (although the differences were apparently in the Valins and Ray direction). The discrepancy appears to be between the use of high (money) vs low demand posttests.

Taken together, the above studies suggest that false feedback may modify fear behavior in low fearful subjects if pretest experience does not mitigate the effects of the feedback stimulus and if posttesting is done under conditions high in demand for improved overt behavior. Borkovec and Glasgow (in press) recently obtained data partially supporting this hypothesis. Fearful subjects were randomly assigned to a Solomon four-groups design (pretest vs no-pretest and heart-rate feedback vs non-feedback during snake-slide presentation). Posttesting was performed under high demand instructions. As predicted, non-pretested subjects receiving heart-rate feedback displayed greater posttest approach than non-pretested subjects receiving the same signals described as electronic noise. No differences were found between feedback and non-feedback groups who had been exposed to a pretest. Additionally, actual heart-rate during slide presentation was greater in the pretested groups than the non-pretested groups across feedback conditions, suggesting a mitigating influence of actual feedback on false feedback effects.

Finally, in a snake-fear study assessing the interaction of demand characteristics (suggested improvement vs no suggested improvement instructions) and false feedback (heart rate increasing vs decreasing during posttest), Borkovec (in press) found pulse rate reductions over testings only under the condition of strong demand and increasing feedback. Approach behavior was complexly determined by an interaction of feedback and subject characteristics, and is discussed later.

Arousal Manipulations

Aside from the correlational evidence in Gaupp *et al.* (1972) and Borkovec and Glasgow (in press) only three experimental studies have assessed the influence of what might be considered direct manipulation of real feedback on subsequent phobic behavior. In the first, Anthony and Duerfeldt (1970) presented half of their subjects with training task exposures to the feared stimulus involving minimal tension. Subjects in this condition were asked to repeatedly move the feared object to "their point of slightest tension." The other half of the subjects were asked to move the object to "their point of maximum tension, all the tension you can stand." The latter group showed significantly less approach improvement than the former on the posttest. In the second study (Rimm, Kennedy, Miller, & Tchida, 1971), subjects underwent drive-induction (threat of snake exposure, threat of shock, or frustration), drive-reduction (relaxation or music), or no-task control conditions. The relaxation group displayed significantly greater approach than the three drive-induction groups and greater approach than the music group, while the control condition was significantly different from snake threat and frustration conditions. Given that posttesting was performed under low demand conditions (no implications that drive tasks were expected to influence approach), the main difference among the groups was the presence or absence of physiological arousal cues during the immediately following posttest exposure. Low arousal subjects displayed the greatest approach, despite the fact that all but one of the arousal manipulations occurred under a context irrelevant to the phobic stimulus. Finally, Borkovec (1972) demonstrated that both systematic desensitization and implosive therapy successfully reduced physiological arousal responses to phobic stimulus exposure, but only those subjects receiving therapeutic instructions within those therapy groups displayed increased approach. Hypothetically, modified internal cues were thus discriminative of increased approach only when instructional sets resulted in labelling internal cue change as indicative of improvement.

Earlier, it was concluded that external demand for improved overt behavior has a greater affect on low, fearful subjects than on high, fearful subjects. Given the physiological feedback research, two corollary hypotheses can be offered: (a) External demand cue manipulation will affect fear behavior to the extent that actual, internal physiological cues are absent. Subjects for whom the physiological component is very strong will be little affected by demand cues suggesting improvement; physiological cues will maintain fear behavior until such cues and/or their functional relationships with subsequent behaviors are changed. (b) Actual physiological cue manipulation will reduce (or maintain) fear behavior in the presence of external demand cues discriminative of nonfear (or fear) behavior.

IMPLICATIONS

Two common sense and related implications follow from these hypotheses, yet little research effort has been addressed to them. The first implication is that human behavior involves a complex set of somewhat separate, but certainly interacting, response systems. The separateness of verbal, motoric and physiological indices of fear is seen in the typically low intercorrelations (Lang, 1968), and the evidence that solely changing verbal behavior (Hart, 1966; Suinn, Jorgensen, Stewart, & McGuirk, 1971), verbal associations (Hekmat & Vanian, 1971), or motor behavior (Leitenberg *et al.*, 1971) can produce fear reduction. Of greater importance and veridicality to human behavior, however, is the potential interaction of the three response systems. Intercorrelation may be low due to different lag time of change in the different systems (Mathews, 1971). And the fact that desirable change can occur from treatment of any isolated system suggests only that therapy packages should be developed which systematically modify every response system involved, in the most efficient and efficacious way (Lang, 1968). Unfortunately, little research has been directly aimed at untangling the interacting effects of the three response systems on each other, although the evidence of their potential interaction is clear (Wilkins, 1971b).

The second implication involves the importance of individual differences in fear behavior and its maintaining conditions. Given the various response systems (verbal, cognitive, motoric, and physiological) and their interrelationships, it can be reasonably suggested that individuals differ in terms of which response system or systems play the primary, functional role in the fear response and/or how those systems interrelate. The remainder of this discussion will be devoted to individual differences at the physiological level.

Bernstein and Paul (1971) strongly state that "it is incumbent upon *E* to employ as Ss only persons who can be shown to display significant and therefore clinically relevant increases in physiological arousal and cognitive distress (i.e., anxiety) as a result of the presence of the presumed eliciting stimulus object." Yet subjects in most analogue studies are matched on behavioral avoidance and equated on self report indices of fear. This leaves physiological reactivity, rarely assessed or controlled. Almost all analogue studies, then, employ phobic selection criteria which in no way directly tap a response system considered of major importance in the definition of anxiety. Oddly enough in many studies, physiological measurement is absent even from posttest improvement induces, even though the treatment techniques often asssesed (e.g., systematic desensitization, implosive therapy) depend to some extent on classical autonomic conditioning paradigms for their theoretical underpinnings. Thus, despite elaborate matching and random assignment procedures, it is quite likely that some studies incorporate few subjects for whom physiological reactivity and internal cues are functionally important in their fear behavior. Even with an equal sampling of high and low reactivity subjects, there is little guarantee that random assignment (with usually small n) equates treatment groups within a study on this potentially important variable.

If the physiological component of fear behavior is important and if selection criteria of many studies ignore this factor, resulting inevitably in either poor representation of such responses or lack of information about its representation, then what is to be said about the results of such studies? What type of underlying extinction or counterconditioning principle can be tested if a treatment technique primarily designed to modify a particular response system is applied to subjects for whom that response system is functionally irrelevant? It is not surprising that manipulations such as reinforcement, modeling, demand characteristics, placebo, repeated testing, etc., produce significant changes in approach behavior. Such effects can be expected if one assumes that avoidance behavior and reports of fear can be established and/or maintained by reinforcement, modeling, demand characteristics, suggestion, and lack of opportunity to behave toward the "feared" object. To reiterate the two hypotheses, in the absence of strong physiological cues, other response systems are more easily modified via external stimuli; in the presence of strong physiological cues, such cues need to be modified before other external manipulations can efficiently influence other response systems.

One study (Borkovec, in press) directly addressed the issue of individual differences in physiological reactivity and their influence on changes in approach behavior. Analogue snake-phobic subjects strong vs weak in actual reactivity and strong vs weak in self-reported autonomic activity were exposed to repeated testing under various suggestion and physiological feedback conditions. The absence of strong internal cues, as defined by actual reactivity, was found to be related to approach change in two separate studies. Two of eight groups in the second study showed discrepant results, one due to high pretest performance. The second group, however, involving subjects strong in both perceived and actual reactivity prior to posttest displayed surprisingly superior posttest approach. Correlated with its approach improvement was this group's substantial pulse rate reduction at posttest. While no cause-and-effect conclusion can be drawn, this result does similarly lead to the hypothesis that in the presence of strong internal cues (subjects strong in both perceived and actual reactivity), such cues need to be modified before other cues (e.g., suggested improvement) can affect approach behavior.

Three other recent studies lend further support to the importance of individual differences in physiological reactivity and their relation to outcome in analogue research. Lang, Melamed, and Hart (1970) report a finding which strongly suggests that subjects for whom the physiological component of the fear response appears important respond best under desensitization therapy. Specifically, greater outcome improvement was found among subjects displaying high heart rates during reportedly fearful scenes and greater heart rate decrease over repeated presentations of scenes. Subjects not as autonomically responsive and not reporting fear correlated with responsivity showed less fear reduction at posttest.

Grim (1971) found that muscle tension increased state anxiety among subjects initially low in self-reported anxiety but decreased anxiety among initially high anxiety subjects. Further, real physiological (respiration) feedback facilitated decreases in anxiety among all relaxing subjects except those with initial, low anxiety scores.

Finally, Farmer and Wright (1971) tested the anxiety-inhibiting effects of muscle relaxation as a function of individual differences in muscle tension as measured by Fisher and Cleveland's (1958) body image Barrier scores. In a typical analogue snake-phobia study, high and low Barrier subjects received desensitization-with-relaxation, desensitization-with-muscle-tension, or no treatment. Relaxation was found to successfully reduce fear in both subject groups, but to a greater extent among high Barrier subjects, while only low Barrier subjects showed improvement under muscle-tension conditions. The authors suggest that the most efficient elimination of conditioned anxiety would be achieved by inhibiting a subject's maximum physiological response system.

The present paper, of course, would propose that the most efficient elimination of fear behavior would be achieved by modifying that response system or systems most functionally involved in the behavior, be it physiological or otherwise. The effectiveness of desensitization and implosive therapy techniques may in part be due to the extinction of conditioned autonomic responses. That active ingredient will be important to the extent that that response system is functionally important to the subject's fear behavior, i.e., with high physiological reaction (high phobic) subjects. But, considering fear behavior as involving a set of interacting response systems, such changes are, necessarily, only part of the explanation. Elimination of physiological cues, however, formerly maintaining the fear behavior and mitigating the effects of external stimuli, allows the opportunity for the other response systems to be influenced by therapeutic context or other external demand characteristics. Thus, all the variables listed by Wilkins (1971b) as contributing to desensitization effectiveness (i.e., expectancy, therapist reinforcement, information feedback, controlled attention shifts, and exposure to contingencies of non-avoidant behavior) are indeed important to the extent that they modify cognitive, self-report, and overt behavioral response systems. These variables may account for most of the changes in studies employing typical analogue phobic subjects. In studies of intensely fearful subjects, on the other hand, modification of internal cues may often be necessary before manipulation of other variables will influence remaining response systems.

REFERENCES

ANTHONY, R. M., & DUERFELDT, P. H. The effect of tension level and contingent reinforcement on fear reduction. *Behavior Therapy*, 1970, **1**, 445–464.

BAKER, B. L., & KAHN, M. A reply to "Critique of 'Treatment of insomnia by relaxation training': Relaxation Training, Rogerian Therapy, or demand characteristics." *Journal of Abnormal Psychology*, 1972, **79**, 94–96.

BANDURA, A. Principles of behavior modification. New York: Holt, Rinehart and Winston, 1969.

BERNSTEIN, D. A. Behavioral fear assessment: anxiety or artifact? In H. Adams & P. Unikel (Eds.), *Issues and trends in behavior therapy*. Springfield: Charles C Thomas, in press.

BERNSTEIN, D. A., & PAUL, G. L. Some comments on therapy analogue research with small animal "phobias." *Journal of Behavior Therapy and Experimental Psychiatry*, 1971, **2**, 225–237.

BORKOVEC, T. D. Effects of expectancy on the outcome of systematic desensitization and implosive treatments for analogue fear. *Behavior Therapy*, 1972, **3**, 29–40.

BORKOVEC, T. D. The effects of instructional suggestion and physiological cues on analogue fear. *Behavior Therapy*, 1973, **4**, 185–192.

BORKOVEC, T. D., & CRAIGHEAD, W. E. The comparison of two methods of assessing fear and avoidance behavior. *Behaviour Research and Therapy*, 1971, **9**, 285–291.

BORKOVEC, T. D., & GLASGOW, R. E. Boundary conditions of false heart-rate feedback effects on avoidance behavior: a resolution of discrepant results. *Behaviour Research and Therapy*, in press.

BORKOVEC, T. D., & NAU, S. D. Credibility of analogue therapy rationales. *Journal of Behavior Therapy and Experimental Psychiatry*, in press.

BRENER, J., & HOTHERSALL, D. Heart rate control under conditions of augmented sensory feedback. *Psychophysiology*, 1966, **3**, 23–28.

BUDZYNSKI, T. H., & STOYVA, J. M. An instrument for producing deep muscle relaxation by means of analogue information feedback. *Journal of Applied Behavior Analysis*, 1969, **2**, 231–237.

BUDZYNSKI, T., STOYVA, J., & ADLER, C. Feedback-induced muscle relaxation: application to tension headache. *Journal of Behavior Therapy and Experimental Psychiatry,* 1970, **1,** 205–211.

DAVISON, G. C., & WILSON, G. T. Processes of fear-reduction in systematic desensitization: cognitive and social reinforcement factors in humans. *Behavior Therapy,* 1973, **4,** 1–21.

DINNERSTEIN, A. J., & HALM, J. Modification of placebo effects by means of drugs: effects of aspirin and placebos on self-rated moods. *Journal of Abnormal Psychology,* 1970, **75,** 308–314.

EFRAN, J. S., & MARCIA, J. E. Treatment of fears by expectancy manipulation: An exploratory investigation. *Proceedings of the 75th Annual Convention of the American Psychological Association,* 1967, **2,** 239–240.

EVERAERD, W. T. Reading as the counterconditioning agent in a cardiac neurosis. *Journal of Behavior Therapy and Experimental Psychiatry,* 1970, **1,** 165–167.

FARMER, R. G., & WRIGHT, J. M. Muscular reactivity and systematic desensitization, *Behavior Therapy,* 1972, **2,** 1–10.

FISHER, S., & CLEVELAND, S. E. Body image and personality. Princeton: Van Nostrand, 1958.

FURST, J. B., & COOPER, A. Combined use of imaginal and interoceptive stimuli in desensitizing fear of heart attacks. *Journal of Behavior Therapy and Experimental Psychiatry,* 1970, **1,** 87–89.

GAUPP, L. A., STERN, R. M., & GALBRAITH, G. G. False heart-rate feedback and reciprocal inhibition by aversive relief in the treatment of snake avoidance behavior. *Behavior Therapy,* 1972, **3,** 7–20.

GREEN, E. E., WALTERS, E. D., GREEN, A. M., & MURPHY, G. Feedback technique for deep relaxation. *Psychophysiology,* 1969, **6,** 271–277.

GRIM, P. F. Anxiety change produced by self-induced muscle tension and by relaxation with respiration feedback. *Behavior Therapy,* 1971, **2,** 11–17.

HART, J. D. Fear reduction as a function of the assumption and success of a therapeutic role. Unpublished master's thesis, University of Wisconsin, 1966.

HEKMAT, H., & VANIAN, D. Behavior modification through covert sematic desensitization. *Journal of Consulting and Clinical Psychology,* 1971, **36,** 248–251.

HOWLETT, S. C., & NAWAS, M. M. Exposure to aversive imagery and suggestion in systematic desensitization. In Rubin, R. D., Fensterheim, H., Lazarus, A. A., & Franks, C. M. (Eds.), *Advances in behavior therapy.* New York: Academic Press, 1971. Pp. 123–135.

JACOBS, A., & FELTON, G. S. Visual feedback of myoelectric output to facilitate muscle relaxation in normal persons and patients with neck injuries. *Archives of Physical and Medical Rehabilitation,* 1969, **50,** 34–39.

KENT, R. N., WILSON, G. T., & NELSON, R. Effects of false heart-rate feedback on avoidance behavior: an investigation of "cognitive desensitization." *Behavior Therapy,* 1972, **3,** 1–6.

KOENIG, K. P., & DEL CASTILLO, D. False feedback and longevity of the conditioned GSR during extinction: some implications for aversion therapy. *Journal of Abnormal Psychology,* 1969, **74,** 505–510.

LANG, P. J. Fear reduction and fear behavior: problems in treating a construct. In J. M. Shlien (Ed.), *Research in psychotherapy,* American Psychological Association, Washington, D. C., 1968. Pp. 90–102.

LANG, P. J., MELAMED, B. G., & HART, J. A psychophysiological analysis of fear modification using an automated desensitization procedure. *Journal of Abnormal Psychology,* 1970, **76,** 220–234.

LANG, P. J., STROUFE, L. A., & HASTINGS, J. E. Effects of feedback and instructional set on the control of cardiac-rate variability. *Journal of Experimental Psychology,* 1967, **75,** 425–430.

LEITENBERG, H., AGRAS, W. S., BARLOW, D. H., & OLIVEAU, D. C. Contribution of selective positive reinforcement and therapeutic instructions to systematic desensitization. *Journal of Abnormal Psychology,* 1969, **74,** 113–118.

LEITENBERG, H., AGRAS, S., BUTZ, R., & WINCZE, J. Relationship between heart rate and behavioral change during the treatment of phobias. *Journal of Abnormal Psychology,* 1971, **78,** 59–68.

LOMONT, J. F., & BROCK, L. Cognitive factors in systematic desensitization. *Behaviour Research and Therapy,* 1971, **9,** 187–195.

MARCIA, J. E., RUBIN, B. M., & EFRAN, J. S. Systematic desensitization: Expectancy change or counterconditioning. *Journal of Abnormal Psychology,* 1969, **74,** 382–387.

MATHEWS, A. M. Psychophysiological approaches to the investigation of desensitization and related procedures. *Psychological Bulletin,* 1971, **76,** 73–91.

McGLYNN, F. D. Experimental desensitization following three types of instructions. *Behaviour Research and Therapy,* 1971, **9,** 367–369.

McGLYNN, F. D., MEALIEA, W. L., & NAWAS, M. M. Systematic desensitization of snake-avoidance under two conditions of suggestion. *Psychological Reports,* 1969, **25,** 220–222.

McGLYNN, F. D., & MAPP, R. H. Systematic desensitization of snake-avoidance following three types of suggestion. *Behaviour Research and Therapy,* 1970, **8,** 197–201.

McGLYNN, F. D., & WILLIAMS, C. W. Systematic desensitization of snake-avoidance under three conditions of suggestion. *Journal of Behavior Therapy and Experimental Psychiatry,* 1970, **1,** 97–101.

McGLYNN, F. D., REYNOLDS, E. J., & LINDER, L. H. Experimental desensitization following therapeutically oriented and physiologically oriented instructions. *Journal of Behavior Therapy and Experimental Psychiatry,* 1971a, **2,** 13–18.

McGLYNN, F. D., REYNOLDS, E. J., & LINDER, L. H. Systematic desensitization with pre-treatment and intra-treatment therapeutic instructions. *Behaviour Research and Therapy,* 1971b, **9,** 57–64.

McGLYNN, F. D. Systematic desensitization under two conditions of induced expectancy. *Behaviour Research and Therapy,* 1972, **10,** 229–234.

McGLYNN, F. D., GAYNOR, R., & PHUR, J. Experimental desensitization of snake-avoidance after an instructional manipulation. *Journal of Clinical Psychology,* 1972, **28,** 224–227.

MILLER, S. B. The contribution of therapeutic instructions to systematic desensitization. *Behaviour Research and Therapy,* 1972, **10,** 159–170.

NISBETT, R. E., & SCHACHTER, S. Cognitive manipulation of pain. *Journal of Experimental Social Psychology,* 1966, **2,** 227–236.

OLIVEAU, D. C., AGRAS, W. S., LEITENBERG, H., MOORE, R. C., & WRIGHT, E. D. Systematic desensitization, therapeutically oriented instructions and selective positive reinforcement. *Behaviour Research and Therapy,* 1969, **7,** 27–34.

ORNE, M. T. On the social psychology of the psychological experiment: with particular reference to demand characteristics and their implications. Symposium paper presented at American Psychological Association Convention, New York, 1961.

PARRINO, J. J. Effect of pretherapy information on learning in psychotherapy. *Journal of Abnormal Psychology,* 1971, **77,** 17–24.

PAUL, G. L. *Insight vs desensitization in psychotherapy.* Stanford: Stanford University Press, 1966.

PAUL, G. L. Physiological effects of relaxation training and hypno.ic suggestion. *Journal of Abnormal Psychology,* 1969, 74, 425–437.

PERSELY, G., & LEVENTHAL, D. B. The effects of therapeutically oriented instructions and of the pairing of anxiety imagery and relaxation in systematic desensitization. *Behavior Therapy,* 1972, 3, 417–424.

RACHMAN, S. Studies in desensitization. III. speed of generalization. *Behaviour Research and Therapy,* 1966, 4, 7–15.

RAPPAPORT, H. The modification of avoidance behavior: Expectancy, autonomic reactivity, and verbal report. *Journal of Consulting and Clinical Psychology,* 1972, 39, 404–414.

RIMM, D. C., KENNEDY, T. D., MILLER, H. L., & TCHIDA, G. R. Experimentally manipulated drive level and avoidance behavior. *Journal of Abnormal Psychology,* 1971, **78,** 43–48.

SCHACHTER, S. The interaction of cognitive and physiological determinants of emotional state. In L. Berkowitz (Ed.), *Advances in experimental social psychology,* Vol. 1, New York: Academic Press, 1964. Pp. 49–80.

SCHACHTER, S., & SINGER, J. E. Cognitive, social, and physiological determinants of emotional state. *Psychological Review,* 1962, 69, 379–399.

SCHACHTER, S., & WHEELER, L. Epinephrine, chlorpromazine and amusement. *Journal of Abnormal and Social Psychology,* 1962, **65,** 121–128.

SPIELBERGER, C. D. Theory and research on anxiety. In C. D. Spielberger (Ed.), *Anxiety and behavior.* New York: Academic Press, 1966. Pp. 3–20.

STAMPFL, T. G., & LEVIS, D. J. Learning theory: an aid to dynamic therapeutic practice. In L. D. Eron and R. Callahan (Eds.), *Relationship of theory to practice in psychotherapy.* Chicago: Aldine, 1969. Pp. 85–114.

SUINN, R. M., JORGENSEN, G. T., STEWART, S. T., & McGUIRK, F. D. Fears as attitudes: experimental reduction of fear through reinforcement. *Journal of Abnormal Psychology,* 1971, **78,** 272–279.

SUSHINSKY, L. W., & BOOTZIN, R. R. Cognitive desensitization as a model of systematic desensitization. *Behaviour Research and Therapy,* 1970, 8, 29–34.

VALINS, S., & RAY, A. A. Effects of cognitive desensitization on avoidance behavior. *Journal of Personality and Social Psychology,* 1967, 4, 400–408.

WILKINS, W. Perceptual distortion to account for arousal. *Journal of Abnormal Psychology,* 1971a, **78,** 252–265.

WILKINS, W. Desensitization: social and cognitive factors underlying the effectiveness of Wolpe's procedure. *Psychological Bulletin,* 1971b, **76,** 311–317.

WILKINS, W. Expectancy of therapeutic gain: an empirical and conceptual critique. *Journal of Consulting and Clinical Psychology,* in press.

WOLPE, J. *Psychotherapy by reciprocal inhibition.* Stanford: Stanford University Press, 1958.

Biofeedback as Therapy:
Some Theoretical and Practical Issues

Gary E. Schwartz

A central component in psychotherapy is the use of corrective feedback. This has been especially evident during the past 15 years with the emergence of many new approaches to treatment, including behavior therapy, sensitivity and encounter groups, and what have sometimes been called "video" therapies. In all of these approaches, the patient receives some form of augmented feedback about his own behavior, be it gradual shaping using contingent reinforcement, the reaction of other people in a group setting to the patient's feelings and actions, or the images and sounds of the patient–therapist interaction using videotape replays. Under the right conditions, with suitable motivation or incentives, the patient may develop awareness or "insight" into his own behavior and may learn new ways of experiencing and dealing with his environment.

In a similar vein, the growth of biofeedback can be seen as the development of new, more refined techniques for providing an individual with feedback for specific physiological processes and, with appropriate incentives, these procedures enable him to modify and control what were once considered "involuntary" and "automatic" functions such as heart rate, blood pressure, and brain waves. Actually, the growth of biofeedback simultaneously came out of two somewhat different traditions. One was operant conditioning, where early researchers (in the 1960s) such as Shapiro, Kimmel, Miller, and DiCara viewed the goal of research as demonstrating that operant control of visceral and glandular processes could be obtained in humans using contingent reinforcers such as money, and in animals with reinforcers such as electrical stimulation of reward centers in the brain. At about the same time, Kamiya, Brown, and others became interested in seeing whether human subjects could learn to discriminate higher nervous system activity and

associated subjective states by providing them with external feedback such as brief lights or tones for specific electroencephalogram changes. It was reasoned that through the feedback and resulting discrimination, subjects would be able to develop voluntary control over these functions.

It is important to consider the history and scope of the issues raised by this research in order to more fully appreciate its implications and applications to clinical treatment. In particular, biofeedback has stimulated renewed interest in concepts such as voluntary control and consciousness and in the central question of the degree to which man can modify and control his behavior in the face of opposing forces in the environment. Consequently, the role of the individual patient in taking responsibility for the maintenance and control of his own health becomes of paramount importance. Although biofeedback is a form of behavior therapy, this does not alter the basic issues involved, especially since questions of self-control and cognition are becoming central issues in current behavioral approaches to treatment.

Over 250 papers have been published on the use of operant-feedback techniques in the control of physiological processes, and four volumes reprinting much of this work are now available (Barber et al., 1971; Kamiya et al., 1971; Stoyva et al., 1972; Shapiro et al., 1973). My wish is not to review this work, nor to cover all the potential clinical applications to date, since this material has been recently reviewed elsewhere (Shapiro & Schwartz, 1972).[2] Rather, this article considers some of the important issues or problems involved in clinically applying biofeedback techniques to the individual patient. Toward this end, I will discuss some of our basic and clinical research on the voluntary

---

[1] This article is based on an invited address presented at the Third Annual Brockton Symposium on Behavior Therapy, April 1972. Requests for reprints should be sent to Gary E. Schwartz, Department of Psychology and Social Relations, Harvard University, 1444 William James Hall, Cambridge, Massachusetts 02138.

[2] Potential applications discussed in this article include essential hypertension, cardiac arrhythmias, tension and migraine headaches, rumination, Raynaud's disease, anxiety and fear reduction through relaxation and systematic desensitization, pain reduction through alpha training, meditation and yoga, attention and learning, and sexual behavior.

control of human cardiovascular responses, for it illustrates many of the problems involved.

Basic Research

The possible application of biofeedback to the control of essential hypertension (high blood pressure of unknown etiology) first requires the development of a suitable blood pressure measurement and feedback system. A prerequisite for any biofeedback application is the accurate sensing and processing of physiological activity, and, not surprisingly, one of the reasons why the field took so long in developing was that readily available biomedical technology, including accurate programming equipment, has only appeared in the past 15 years.

Actually, the technology for sensing and recording human blood pressure on a continuous basis was already available, but it was not practical for routine laboratory work since it required surgical insertion of a pressure-transducing tube into an artery. On the other hand, while the traditional stethoscope and blood pressure cuff procedure used by the physician was neither aversive nor dangerous, it was too intermittent (one could only obtain about two readings per minute) and too inaccurate to make it satisfactory ás a feedback device. However, using new pressure-regulating devices and solid-state circuitry (coupled with an extension of blood pressure measurement theory), it was possible to modify and automate a constant cuff pressure system to accurately measure median blood pressure (± 2 millimeters of mercury) and at the same time provide the subject with binary (yes–no) feedback at each heart beat for increases or decreases in blood pressure (Tursky, Shapiro, & Schwartz, 1972). The details of this system need not concern us here—the point is to highlight the general problem of being able to detect and measure the function in question so that it can be easily and practically used by the patient.

In our basic research (as well as clinical) studies to date, we have typically used the procedure of giving the subject binary feedback for small, desired changes in blood pressure (or heart rate) at each beat of the heart and, after producing a certain number of correct responses, of giving the subject a reward or incentive in the form of a slide.[8] The

slides might be landscapes of Boston, pictures from around the world, photos of nude women, or numbers reflecting monetary bonuses. As will be seen, in multisession work involving patients, maintaining interest and motivation can become an important problem, one not easily solved by using simple extrinsic rewards.

In the first two studies (Shapiro, Tursky, Gershon, & Stern, 1969; Shapiro, Tursky, & Schwartz, 1970a), the basic question was whether healthy college students could learn to raise or lower their systolic blood pressure in a single session. All subjects received the same general instructions, and only the contingency of the feedback and reward was varied between groups. To control for possible instructional effects, subjects were not told what the bodily function was, nor were they told in what direction the function was to change. The results indicated that subjects reinforced for increases in blood pressure were able to raise or maintain their pressure, while subjects reinforced for decreases in systolic pressure were able to lower their pressure over the session. Another group given random reinforcement showed that its average pressure fell about midway between the increase and decrease groups, suggesting that the two contingent groups controlled their pressure above and beyond the nonspecific effects of the instructions, the stimulation afforded by the feedback and reward, and quiet sitting in a lounge chair for 40 minutes (Crider, Schwartz, & Shnidman, 1969). Interestingly, postexperimental questionnaires revealed that subjects were not aware they had actually controlled their blood pressure, nor did they realize the direction their pressure had changed.

Some questions consistently raised by this research were, What were the subjects doing or thinking to control their blood pressures? Were they getting excited or relaxed? Were they thinking specific thoughts, or possibly tensing their muscles in some way? Hence, questions of cognitive or somatic mediation were considered to be important, especially by those researchers interested in the theoretical question of whether operant conditioning of autonomic activity per se had in fact taken place (Katkin & Murray, 1968). As it turned out, the blood pressure data proved to be convincing in this regard, because when heart rate (a related cardiovascular function) was analyzed, no differences were found between groups. In other words, the subjects had not learned simply to raise or lower overall autonomic arousal, even within the

---

[8] An analysis of contingent reinforcement as a stimulus containing both information (feedback) and incentive (reward) value is discussed in Schwartz (in press) and Schwartz and Shapiro (in press), the latter completed just prior to publication.

cardiovascular system. In a later study (Shapiro, Tursky, & Schwartz, 1970b), when subjects were trained to raise and lower their heart rate using a similar binary feedback and reward technique, the subjects now learned to control their heart rate, without similarly affecting their systolic blood pressure. Altogether, findings of specificity of learning such as these were seen as important prerequisites for the application of biofeedback training to clinical problems (Shapiro & Schwartz, 1972), since alleviation of the "symptom" was desired without corresponding "side effects" such as those sometimes produced by drugs.

However, questions of mediation and specificity are more complex than originally envisioned (Schwartz, 1972) and have important implications for therapy (Schwartz, in press). On the one hand, the therapist is not usually concerned with obtaining a "pure" effect from a scientific point of view, but wants any combination of factors that will produce large, long-lasting, generalizable, and safe effects. Thus, if for a given hypertensive patient it was found that training in general muscle relaxation alone produced the most rapid and massive decreases in pressure, this would be clinically valuable. Cognitive and somatic mediation, if useful, is of significance to the therapist.

On the other hand, the therapist may be concerned with what else is changing when a person is given biofeedback for a particular function. In fact, there are instances where the therapist may be interested in *patterns* of responses. For example, the desired goal for those hypertensive patients having normal heart rates may be to lower stroke volume and/or peripheral resistance rather than to change heart rate per se. However, in reducing pain in patients suffering from angina pectoris, the desired goal may not be to lower just blood pressure, or heart rate, but rather to lower both functions simultaneously, since by decreasing rate and pressure, the heart requires less oxygen, which in turn leads to reduced pain (Braunwald et al., 1967). In other words, it becomes important not only to be able to predict under what conditions side effects may occur, but also how one might produce them in specific cases.

One approach to this problem is to analyze carefully what else is simultaneously being "reinforced" when feedback and reward are given (Schwartz, 1972, in press). Returning to the blood pressure–heart rate example, if systolic blood pressure and heart rate were so related over time that increases

in one of them were always associated with increases in the other, and vice versa, then when an experimenter chose to give feedback and reward for one, he would unwittingly provide the identical contingency for the other as well. Therefore, from learning (or feedback) theory we would expect that both functions should in fact be learned simultaneously and in the same direction. If these two functions were so related that whenever one increased the other simultaneously decreased, and vice versa, then if feedback and reward were given for one, the other would simultaneously receive the opposite contingency. Both functions should also be learned, only now in opposite directions. However, since neither of these results was empirically obtained, it would follow that systolic blood pressure and heart rate are unrelated in such a way that binary feedback for one results in some form of simultaneous random reinforcement of the other.

Assuming for the moment that this conclusion is true, the next question that arises is, How could a person be taught to control both of them? One approach that follows from the above analysis is to give the feedback and reward only when the desired pattern of responses occurs. In theory, it should be possible to teach a person to voluntarily integrate his systolic blood pressure and heart rate (make both functions increase or decrease together), or to differentiate them (make them go in opposite directions) by providing feedback and reward for the desired pattern. In subsequent studies, it has been verified that systolic blood pressure and heart rate are only integrated 50% under resting conditions (they spontaneously change from beat to beat in the same direction only half of the time) and that subjects can learn voluntarily to make them go together (Schwartz, 1972; Schwartz, Shapiro, & Tursky, 1971) or apart (Schwartz, 1972) when given feedback for the appropriate pattern.

Thus, the interrelationships among bodily functions over time, as well as the exact nature of the contingency (feedback) involved, control the degree to which learned specificity or patterning occurs. Although this type of formulation may provide a useful first step in the prediction and control of multifunctions using biofeedback, it must be incomplete, for it treats physiology as if it operated in a vacuum, without constraints. However, physiological (and associated cognitive) constraints do exist and must be taken into account (Schwartz, 1972). The extent to which simple predictions from learning or feedback theory fail can reveal the exact nature of the constraints involved.

For example, it is easier for subjects to learn to make their systolic blood pressure and heart rate go together than to make them go apart (Schwartz, 1972). Furthermore, feedback for integrating these functions produces somewhat larger effects and more rapid learning than feedback for either single function alone. In addition, when subjects are taught to lower both functions simultaneously, they now begin to report feelings of relaxation and calmness, states one would expect to be associated with more general autonomic relaxation. Altogether, it would seem that in the process of trying to understand and extend biofeedback techniques to patterns of responses, the research uncovers more about the nature of the physiological systems themselves and their relation to cognition.[4]

The combined behavioral–biological approach to biofeedback outlined here has a number of implications for treatment. One is that the clinician should carefully evaluate exactly how he administers feedback to an individual patient, so that he is better able to precisely determine and control what the patient will and will not learn. Understandably, this applies not only to simple discrete-digital feedback, but to more complex forms of continuous-analog feedback as well. For example, if a patient is receiving analog feedback for beat by beat changes in heart rate, and he has sinus arrhythmia (heart rate rising and falling with each breath), the subject will be simultaneously receiving feedback for respiration, and he may modify it accordingly. The clinician should be aware of this possibility and should make a rational decision as to whether or not such learning is desirable.

For applications involving the self-control of more complex states like anxiety or fear, it becomes important to determine what function, or pattern of functions, occurs in these states for the individual patient. It is well known that individuals differ in their autonomic specificity and that situations may evoke different patterns (Lacey, 1967); thus, it makes good sense that the feedback be

selected so as to optimize its integration (correlation) with the problem in question.

As for the question of constraints, it follows that if it is possible to clinically evaluate the flexibility or variability of the function(s) in question, it may be possible to assess whether biofeedback will ultimately work for a given patient. For example, if a patient wtih fixed hypertension (possibly due to excessive hardening of the arteries) has blood pressure levels constantly elevated above normal, it seems unlikely that biofeedback will have any significant effect on purely physiological grounds. Evaluating the potential for organ change (e.g., by taking sleep measurements) may be a useful screening technique. It follows that early diagnosis of the individual for preventive feedback training before the organ system is seriously damaged may be the most meaningful application to psychosomatic medicine.

Before considering further issues raised by clinical work, it may be useful to show how this model applies to animal biofeedback research, where curare is used to paralyze the muscles. Miller (1969) and DiCara (1970) have argued that by paralyzing the muscles with curare, the question of somatic mediation is eliminated. However, all the curare procedure (using moderate doses) does is eliminate potential feedback from actual muscle contraction; it does not stop the rat from struggling and tensing his muscles "in his head." According to the model, to the extent that heart rate and muscle activity are naturally integrated at the level of the brain, reinforcement for the former will result in consistent reinforcement of the latter as well, regardless of the actual state of the muscles.[5] A. H. Black (personal communication, 1971) has found that when he teaches a curarized dog to "move in his head," that is, to produce or inhibit theta waves from the hippocampus (in a nonparalyzed dog, theta occurs when the dog makes voluntary movements), heart rate simultaneously increases or decreases as well. Recently, Goesling and Brener (1972) have found that teaching a rat to tense or relax prior to curare greatly influences his later ability to raise or lower his heart rate while under curare. Hence, the question of mediation is complex, especially at the level of the brain, and one

---

[4] These findings have been extended, and predictions of the model replicated, in current research on the voluntary control of diastolic blood pressure and heart rate (Schwartz, Shapiro, & Tursky, 1972; Shapiro, Schwartz, & Tursky, 1972). The approach also has been applied to the voluntary control of EEG alpha and heart rate (Schwartz, Shaw, & Shapiro, 1972), but this material will not be reviewed here.

[5] Although there is good psychophysiological evidence for believing that heart rate and somatic activity are centrally integrated (Obrist, Webb, Sutterer, & Howard, 1970), this does not imply that other autonomic responses are also so integrated.

must evaluate (*a*) relations between responses, (*b*) the nature of the reinforcement contingency, and (*c*) natural biological, environmental, and "state" constraints in order to understand and predict exactly what is being learned (Schwartz, in press).

Preliminary Clinical Applications to Essential Hypertension and Raynaud's Disease

We have attempted to apply the general procedures developed in the basic research to patients diagnosed with essential hypertension (Benson, Shapiro, Tursky, & Schwartz, 1971). First, the seven patients participated in from 5 to 16 control sessions, during which blood pressures were taken under resting conditions. Then systolic blood pressure feedback and reward sessions were initiated and continued until no further reductions in blood pressure occurred for 5 consecutive sessions. The number of conditioning sessions varied from 8 to 34, with a mean of about 22 sessions. The results showed that six of the seven patients decreased their pressure by as little as 3.5 millimeters of mercury and by as much as 33.8 millimeters of mercury (mean decrease for all patients was 16.5 millimeters of mercury). Interestingly, the one patient who failed to show any decrease in blood pressure was later diagnosed to have renal artery stenosis, which relates back to the question of biological constraints.

Although these findings are encouraging, they are a long way from demonstrating that biofeedback can be a clinical treatment for hypertension. First, it is not known whether patients can control their pressure without the feedback, or even if the feedback was the significant factor in the research. Placebo variables may have been operating and can only be evaluated by the use of the appropriate control groups (Shapiro & Schwartz, 1972). On the other hand, as in all forms of therapy, positive expectations on the part of the patient may well be a prerequisite for positive gains, especially in behavioral therapies where patient cooperation and practice are necessary for change.

Related is the general question of patient motivation. As described in the review of the clinical research (Shapiro & Schwartz, 1972):

Central to all forms of psychotherapy is patient motivation and involvement. The question, at the simplest level, is how to motivate patients to spend the necessary time practicing the desired behavior. With severely retarded and/or emotionally disturbed children, reinforcers such as food, candy, or other desired objects (e.g., watching a fan spin) are often necessary for modifying the behavior. However, with less severe problems, therapist praise, praise from significant others in the patient's environment, or self-reinforcement (a sense of competence) may be more than sufficient. One predictor of success in psychotherapy is the extent to which the patient's problems are causing him pain or suffering. With regard to biofeedback, Miller has suggested that feedback for controlling the function in and of itself may be all that is necessary. However, as progress is made, and the novelty of the situation wears off, what will keep the patient working at the task? In our experience with patients suffering from essential hypertension, a potpourri of rewards was successful, including money for participating and for succeeding (most of these patients were on welfare and thus the money they earned was quite significant), slides of scenes around the world, and general, non-specific praise from the physician and research assistant running the sessions. However, this was an experiment, and the patients were receiving a sizeable monetary reward. One wonders whether they would have spent the same number of hours trying to control their blood pressure in the absence of such incentives, which are impractical on a large-scale basis. In this respect, learning to control physiologic processes is like any other self-control procedure (e.g., dieting) since sacrifice on the patient's part may be necessary for the sake of health [p. 180].

Actually, the hypertensive patient may be a special case, more similar to the average cigarette smoker than to the headache patient. Although the pain caused by tension or migraine headaches is relatively immediate, as is its relief, it may be years before the potential harm from high blood pressure or smoking is experienced directly by the patient. Hence, it is understandable why headache patients are willing to pay for experimental biofeedback treatment (T. Budzynski, personal communication, 1971), while we must pay our research hypertensive patients to potentially help themselves.

The question of motivation leads to another important problem: namely, whether the patient is able, or willing, to control his bodily functions in the hectic, rapidly changing environment outside of the laboratory. It is well known that environmental stressors can augment, or even cause, psychosomatic disorders, and it should not be surprising if many patients desire biofeedback for their blood pressure, just as they take medicine for their stress-related stomachaches. Simply put, the typical patient would rather change his body than change his lifestyle or his environment, the two factors which together augment or cause the bodily dysfunctions in the first place. In this context, it would seem reasonable that biofeedback should be viewed as but one approach to the treatment of the "total person," realizing that to "cure" a problem such as hypertension will require more than just the patient consciously attempting to lower his pressure. Similar views concerning behavioral therapies in general have been stressed by Lazarus (1971).

A good example of this point comes from one of our hypertension patients who, during the feedback sessions, was successful in lowering his pressure. Over the five daily sessions of a typical week, he might lower his pressure by 20 millimeters of mercury and thus earn a total of over $35. However, we consistently noticed that after the weekend, he would enter the laboratory on Monday with elevated pressures again. In interviews with the patient, the problem became clear. After earning a sizable amount of money, the patient would go to the race track on the weekend, gamble, and invariably lose. The likelihood of teaching this patient to "relax" while at the race track through simple laboratory blood pressure feedback would seem slim, indicating that there is a need to work on other aspects of the patient's behavior (e.g., by changing the contingencies of reward) and personality which are related to the high pressure.

Depending on the particular function, dysfunction, and patient involved, biofeedback training may take many sessions. Getting the patient committed to spending this amount of time is difficult enough; getting him to travel to the laboratory for each session often becomes a formidable problem. For this reason, the development of home feedback devices, coupled with weekly consultation with the physician and/or therapist, appears to be a fruitful direction in which to move. In addition, the use of portable feedback devices makes it possible for the patient to evaluate his progress under different environmental conditions outside of the laboratory, and this may significantly enhance the potential for generalization.

Whether or not the patient can learn to control these processes without feedback is still an open and important question. Procedures for "weaning" the patient from the feedback need to be worked out (Weiss & Engel, 1971). However, patients may be able to learn certain cognitive or somatic strategies which they then can use without feedback. One example of this comes from a patient we were experimentally treating for Raynaud's disease, a problem of peripheral constriction and reduced blood flow that under extreme conditions can lead to gangrene in the hands and feet. Symptoms of Raynaud's disease include a feeling of "cold" in the afflicted area that can be quite painful. The patient was a man in his early sixties with very cold feet; this patient was somewhat unusual in that he was a practicing psychoanalyst who came for behavioral treatment of his problem. Briefly, blood volume was recorded simultaneously from the big toes of each foot, and the patient was given binary feedback for each heart beat that was followed by a small increase in blood volume. The feedback and reward procedure was modeled after the blood pressure work, and similar slides were used. Although placebo and expectancy effects cannot be discounted (and were probably operating), over 10 sessions he began to show large increases in blood volume, particularly in the left foot, the foot initially selected for feedback and reward. In the middle of a later session, we then switched to providing feedback and reward for the right foot, which subsequently reached similar increases in overall blood volume. This finding of relative specificity was not surprising, because it was observed on the polygraph that spontaneous dilations and constrictions frequently occurred in one foot and not the other, and therefore the feedback was really contingent to the particular foot controlling the programming equipment, while the other simultaneously received a form of random reinforcement.

This particular patient was unusually inclined toward "free association" and interpreted the purpose of the slides as diverse material for him to covertly free associate to. In one of the later sessions, the slide projector accidentally jammed and, rather than showing a slide, flashed just a white, bright light on the screen. This proved to be a fortunate accident, for the patient began free associating to the sun, warmth, beaches, and so forth, and he reported that these thoughts were particularly helpful in warming his feet. Furthermore, these "hot thoughts," as the patient described them, were the images he used to control his feet outside of the laboratory. Interestingly, this procedure proved to be highly adaptive for him since if his feet got cold, even while he was doing therapy with patients, he reported that all he had to do was "turn on his hot thoughts" for a few moments and he felt relief. Whether or not he actually was able to control his feet out of the laboratory is not known, nor it is known if these images were really the significant mechanisms by which he controlled his blood volume. Nonetheless, the case illustrates the potential use of cognitive mediation in the development of self-control of bodily processes.[6] While this patient remained symptom free for about a year and a half, he later contacted us indicating that his symptoms had returned and that he desired further training.

This patient was highly educated (and high up on the socioeconomic ladder), experienced and comfortable in laboratory situations, and greatly desirous and expectant of success. The other Raynaud's patient we have tried to work with so far was from a lower-middle-class background, inexperienced and wary of the laboratory setting, and of questionable motivation and expectancy concerning exactly what the feedback really was and what it was supposed to help her to do. This woman was seen for fewer than 10 sessions, and there was little indication of clinically meaningful (as opposed to statistical) increases in blood volume in her hands. Although it is not known if further training would have yielded large enough changes to constitute therapeutic success, this seems unlikely since she appeared to have a severe case of the disease (she was being considered for a sympathectomy); and on top of this, we had little success in improving her attitude and reactions toward the whole situation. Her experience illustrates how personality and individual differences make it impossible to provide a simple "cookbook" approach to questions such as "What should I tell the patient?" or "What kinds of incentives should I provide?" On the other hand, to the extent that specific instructions direct a patient's attention to certain aspects of his behavior or lead him to utilize certain strategies in learning control, it can be speculated that what the patient is told, and what he is asked to do, may depend on both the specific nature of

the desired function(s) to be changed and the personality of the patient.[7]

Summary and Conclusions

Biofeedback is clearly an important discovery, one that may prove to have some value in medical and psychological treatment. However, there are many problems that need to be solved, particularly when applied to the individual patient. Biofeedback, if used in conjunction with other medical and psychological techniques, may be useful with certain patients. However, in the face of specific biological and environmental constraints, I am somewhat pessimistic about its application to chronic physical disease, particularly in the absence of other therapeutic procedures.[8] Emphasizing the problems involved is not meant to discourage experimental attempts at clinical application. Although a combined behavioral–biological approach that emphasizes (*a*) the natural relations between responses, (*b*) the exact manner that the feedback and reward is given, and (*c*) biological, cognitive, and environmental constraints is indicated, it is not implied that all of these factors need to be taken into account before using biofeedback in a specific case. Rather, the purpose of the article is to illustrate potential areas of inquiry and evaluation that may be clinically useful.

Even if "direct" voluntary control of certain bodily functions or patterns of functions proves to have little therapeutic value, biofeedback per se can still serve an important function—to signal both the therapist and the patient that the patient is currently thinking, feeling, or doing specific things that are detrimental to his physical or emotional health. In the same way that a scale helps direct the therapist and his obese patient in learning how to reduce food consumption and/or increase exercise in order to control weight,

---

[6] Specific cognitive control of skin temperature (relative dilation in one hand and constriction in the other through hypnosis and imagery of warmth and cold) has recently been reported by Maslach, Marshall, and Zimbardo (1972). Further evidence for cognitive control of cardiovascular activity due to specific thought processes can be found in Schwartz (1971) and Schwartz and Higgins (1971).

[7] For example, if a subject is instructed to close his eyes and to think a neutral word over and over in a relaxed fashion, a reduction in a number of psychophysiological responses (a pattern) may occur, such as those seen in certain forms of meditation (Wallace, 1970).

[8] Learning to relax a chronically tense (but otherwise healthy) muscle with biofeedback, for example, would seem to be a more likely candidate for success. Also, in this case the response in question is likely to be already under some voluntary control since it is part of the motor system. This point would similarly apply to learning to control certain electroencephalographic rhythms, to the extent that they involve self-regulatory sensorimotor processes.

biofeedback for visceral and neural disorders may be so employed as well. By means of immediate, augmented feedback (with its associated increased bodily awareness), the patient may be able to learn new ways of coping *behaviorally* with his environment, or he may be able to alter his *life-style* in such a way as to keep his physiological processes within safer limits. In this respect, biofeedback is really similar to current psychotherapies, for they all provide corrective feedback.[9]

[9] It might be noted that this approach to the use of biofeedback removes the negative clinical implications suggested by recent difficulties in replicating large magnitude effects in the curarized rat (N. E. Miller & L. V. DiCara, personal communication, 1972). Rather than trying to eliminate those overt somatic "mediators" capable of producing large autonomic changes, the goal here is to deliberately use them to produce more physiologically adaptive reactions (e.g., through breathing exercises or other yoga procedures).

REFERENCES

BARBER, T. X., DiCARA, L. V., KAMIYA, J., MILLER, N. E., SHAPIRO, D., & STOYVA, J. (Eds.) *Biofeedback and self-control, 1970: An Aldine annual on the regulation of bodily processes and consciousness.* Chicago: Aldine-Atherton, 1971.

BENSON, H., SHAPIRO, D., TURSKY, B., & SCHWARTZ, G. E. Decreased systolic blood pressure through operant conditioning techniques in patients with essential hypertension. *Science,* 1971, **173,** 740–742.

BRAUNWALD, E., EPSTEIN, S. E., GLICK, G., WECHSLER, A. S., & BRAUNWALD, N. S. Relief of angina pectoris by electrical stimulation of the carotid-sinus nerves. *New England Journal of Medicine,* 1967, **227,** 1278–1283.

CRIDER, A., SCHWARTZ, G. E., & SHNIDMAN, S. R. On the criteria for instrumental autonomic conditioning: A reply to Katkin and Murray. *Psychological Bulletin,* 1969, **71,** 455–461.

DiCARA, L. V. Learning in the autonomic nervous system. *Scientific American,* 1970, **222,** 30–39.

GOESLING, W. J., & BRENER, J. Effect of activity and immobility conditioning upon subsequent heart rate conditioning in curarized rats. *Journal of Comparative and Physiological Psychology,* 1972, **81,** 311–317.

KAMIYA, J., DiCARA, L. V., BARBER, T. X., MILLER, N. E., SHAPIRO, D., & STOYVA, J. (Eds.) *Biofeedback and self-control: An Aldine reader on the regulation of bodily processes and consciousness.* Chicago: Aldine-Atherton, 1971.

KATKIN, E. S., & MURRAY, E. N. Instrumental conditioning of automatically mediated behavior: Theoretical and methodological issues. *Psychological Bulletin,* 1968, **70,** 52–68.

LACEY, J. Somatic response patterning and stress: Some revisions of activation theory. In M. H. Appley & R. Trumbull (Eds.), *Psychological stress.* New York: Appleton-Century-Crofts, 1967.

LAZARUS, A. A. *Behavior therapy and beyond.* New York: McGraw-Hill, 1971.

MASLACH, C., MARSHALL, G., & ZIMBARDO, P. G. Hypnotic control of peripheral skin temperature: A case report. *Psychophysiology,* 1972, 9, 600–605.

MILLER, N. E. Learning of visceral and glandular responses. *Science,* 1969, **163,** 434–445.

OBRIST, P. A., WEBB, R. A., SUTTERER, J. R., & HOWARD, J. L. The cardiac-somatic relationship: Some reformulations. *Psychophysiology,* 1970, **6,** 569–587.

SCHWARTZ, G. E. Cardiac responses to self-induced thoughts. *Psychophysiology,* 1971, **8,** 462–467.

SCHWARTZ, G. E. Voluntary control of human cardiovascular integration and differentiation through feedback and reward. *Science,* 1972, **175,** 90–93.

SCHWARTZ, G. E. Toward a theory of voluntary control of response patterns in the cardiovascular system. In P. A. Obrist, A. H. Black, J. Brener, & L. V. DiCara (Eds.), *Cardiovascular psychophysiology.* Chicago: Aldine, in press.

SCHWARTZ, G. E., & HIGGINS, J. D. Cardiac activity preparatory to overt and covert behavior. *Science,* 1971, **173,** 1144–1146.

SCHWARTZ, G. E., & SHAPIRO, D. Biofeedback in essential hypertension: Current findings and theoretical concerns. *Seminars in Psychiatry,* in press.

SCHWARTZ, G. E., SHAPIRO, D., & TURSKY, B. Learned control of cardiovascular integration in man through operant conditioning. *Psychosomatic Medicine,* 1971, **33,** 57–62.

SCHWARTZ, G. E., SHAPIRO, D., & TURSKY, B. Self control of patterns of human diastolic blood pressure and heart rate through feedback and reward. *Psychophysiology,* 1972, 9, 270. (Abstract)

SCHWARTZ, G. E., SHAW, G., & SHAPIRO, D. Specificity of alpha and heart rate control through feedback. *Psychophysiology,* 1972, 9, 269. (Abstract)

SHAPIRO, D., BARBER, T. X., DiCARA, L. V., KAMIYA, J., MILLER, N. E., & STOYVA, J. (Eds.) *Biofeedback and self-control, 1972: An Aldine annual on the regulation of bodily processes and consciousness.* Chicago: Aldine, 1973.

SHAPIRO, D., & SCHWARTZ, G. E. Biofeedback and visceral learning: Clinical applications. *Seminars in Psychiatry,* 1972, **4,** 171–184.

SHAPIRO, D., SCHWARTZ, G. E., & TURSKY, B. Control of diastolic blood pressure in man by feedback and reinforcement. *Psychophysiology,* 1972, 9, 296–304.

SHAPIRO, D., TURSKY, B., GERSHON, E., & STERN, M. Effects of feedback and reinforcement on the control of human systolic blood pressure. *Science,* 1969, **163,** 588–589.

SHAPIRO, D., TURSKY, B., & SCHWARTZ, G. E. Control of blood pressure in man by operant conditioning. *Circulation Research,* 1970, 26(Suppl. 1), 27, I-27 to I-32. (a)

SHAPIRO, D., TURSKY, B., & SCHWARTZ, G. E. Differentiation of heart rate and blood pressure in man by operant conditioning. *Psychosomatic Medicine,* 1970, **32,** 417–423. (b)

STOYVA, J., BARBER, T. X., DiCARA, L. V., KAMIYA, J., MILLER, N. E., & SHAPIRO, D. (Eds.) *Biofeedback and self-control, 1971: An Aldine annual on the regulation of bodily processes and consciousness.* Chicago: Aldine-Atherton, 1972.

TURSKY, B., SHAPIRO, D., & SCHWARTZ, G. E. Automated constant cuff pressure system to measure average systolic and diastolic blood pressure in man. *IEEE Transactions on Biomedical Engineering,* 1972, **19,** 271–275.

WALLACE, R. K. Physiological effects of transcendental meditation. *Science,* 1970, **167,** 1751–1754.

WEISS, T., & ENGEL, B. T. Operant conditioning of heart rate in patients with premature ventricular contractions. *Psychosomatic Medicine,* 1971, **33,** 301–321.

Autonomic Stability and 42
Transcendental Meditation

David W. Orme-Johnson

Physiological indices of stress were found to be lower in people who regularly practiced Transcendental Meditation ($N=14$) than in nonmeditating control subjects ($N=16$). During normal waking (eyes open) a noxious loud tone (100 db, 0.5 sec, 3000 Hz) was presented to subjects a mean of once every 53 sec at irregular intervals. The stress reaction to each tone, as indicated by the galvanic skin response (GSR), was compared for the two groups. Habituation of the GSR to tones was faster for meditators than for controls, and meditators made fewer multiple responses during habituation, indicating greater stability in response to stress. In two other experiments, meditators were found to make fewer spontaneous GSR's than control subjects, both during meditation, as compared with rest (eyes closed), and while out of meditation with eyes open. Thus meditators were found to be more stable than controls on three autonomic indices: rate of GSR habituation, multiple responses, and spontaneous GSR.

Transcendental Meditation (TM) is a mental technique of deep relaxation which was adapted for Westerners from the Vedic tradition of India by Maharishi Mahesh Yogi. TM has been shown to produce a physiologic state of restful alertness which is different from sleep, dreaming, hypnosis, or waking [1, 2, 3, 4]. The regular experience of this state is reported to alleviate drug abuse [5, 6, 7, 8]

From the Department of Psychology, The University of Texas at El Paso, El Paso, Texas

A modified version of this paper was presented at the Stanford Research Institute, Menlo Park, California, August 5, 1971, and at the Second International Symposium of the Science of Creative Intelligence, Humboldt State College, Arcata, California, August 22, 1971.

Received for publication December 16, 1971; final revision received December 20, 1972.

Address for reprint requests: David Orme-Johnson, Ph.D., Maharishi International University, 1015 Gayley Avenue, Los Angeles, California 90024.

and a variety of psychosomatic disorders [1]. Meditators typically report that they progressively acquire more emotional stability and less susceptibility to the debilitating effects of stress as a benefit of meditating [9, 10, 11, 12, 13]. The present study is an initial investigation of the effects of TM on two indices of stress, spontaneous fluctuations in skin resistance (GSR or galvanic skin response) and GSR habituation.

Spontaneous GSR is defined as fluctuations in skin resistance which occur independently of ambient noise or movements by the subject. The frequency of spontaneous GSR is one way of defining the lability or stress level of an individual [14, 15, 16]. When a person is angry or fearful the frequency rises [17], as it does when adrenaline and nonadrenaline levels increase [18]. Stimulants [19] and environmental stresses of various kinds also elevate the frequency of spontaneous GSR (18, 20, 21, 22, 23). Within a given situation, some individuals (stabiles) consistently show lower frequencies of spontaneous GSR than other individuals (labiles). Stabiles exhibit more effective behavior than labiles in a number of situations. For example, they are better able to withstand stresses (18, 23, 24) and they score higher on Barron's Ego Strength scale which measures general ability to cope with environmental pressures (25). Stabiles are less impulsive on motor tasks (26) and have quicker perceptions (Embedded Figures Test) (27). They also are less conditionable to aversive stimuli than labiles (16, 28, 29, 30). Thus, for stabiles, present behavior is less likely to be restricted by past conditioning.

The frequency of spontaneous GSR is also correlated with the rate of GSR habituation. When tones are repeatedly presented to subjects, stabiles habituate faster on the GSR than labiles (14, 15, 31, 32, 33). Rapid habituators tend to be more extroverted than introverted (34) and psychologically normal persons habituate more rapidly than schizophrenics (35). When schizophrenics were measured and then retested in five weeks, those who habituated faster on the second testing had better hospital discharge records than the slow habituators (36). This research indicates a correlation of rapid habituation with improved mental health. Furthermore, rapid habituation is characteristic of species higher on the philogenetic scale, and it may be considered as a more highly evolved form of adaptation than slow habituation (37). The present investigation compared the rate of GSR habituation between meditator and nonmeditator groups. Three weeks later, these two groups were compared on spontaneous GSR. The investigation of spontaneous GSR was then replicated using new groups of subjects.

METHOD

Subjects

The initial study of GSR habituation and spon-taneous GSR (EXP I) was with eight subjects of college background in the meditator and nonmeditator groups. Both groups consisted of three females and five males and the mean age of the meditators was 24 years (range 19–33 years) and the mean age of nonmeditators was 28 years (range 19–40 years). The meditators were obtained through the University of Texas at El Paso Center of the Students International Meditation Society, and each had been instructed in meditation by a teacher qualified by Maharishi to teach Transcendental Meditation. All meditators regularly practiced TM (twice a day for 15–20 minutes each time), and they had been meditating from two to 36 months, with a mean of 15 months.

The second study (EXP II) of spontaneous GSR was of a different group of eight meditators (three females and five males) and eight nonmeditators (two females and six males) who planned to start the practice of TM in two weeks. Two of the meditators were not included in the final data analysis, one because he began meditation during a rest control period, and the other because she had a history of unwarned shocks in a psychological laboratory. This left six meditators, two females and four males, whose ages ranged 19–40, with a mean age of 24 years. The ages of nonmeditators in the second study ranged 13–40 years with a mean age of 23 years. The six meditators in the second experiment had been meditating regularly for a mean of 24 months (range 2–54 months). Of the 14 meditators, four had been in the experimental room before. Of the 16 nonmeditators, five had been in the experimental room before. The experimenter personally knew nine of the meditators before the experiment and seven of the nonmeditators.

Apparatus

The tone used in the habituation study was generated by a Maico Audiometer and delivered through earphones monaurally. The GSR was recorded on a Lafayette Polygraph which used the exosomatic (Féré) method of applied current. Silver-plated contoured electrodes, 4 x 6 cm on the palm and 1.5 x 2 cm on the middle finger, were used with Hewlett Packard Electrolyte Redux creme electrode paste. The experiment was conducted in a quiet room with a temperature thermostatically controlled at 72°F. Subjects were seated in a comfortable chair placed in front of and facing away from the table containing the audiometer and polygraph, so that subjects could not see the apparatus, but the experimenter, seated quietly at the table, could observe any movements made by the subject.

Procedure

Subjects were invited into the experimental room and asked to sit in the chair. The electrodes were attached and subjects were instructed, "I am going to measure your response to some loud tones played through these earphones. Please just sit comfortably until I indicate that we are finished." The earphones were then put on the subject and the experiment began.

The tone was 100 decibels SPL, 3000 Hz, 0.5 sec, and was presented an average of once every 53 sec, with a range 10–190 sec between stimulus presentations. The GSR was allowed to recover and/or stabilize before the next tone was presented. Tones were presented until three consecutive responses of an amplitude of less than 0.35 K ohms occurred, and this was the criterion for habituation. Response measures used were latency, or the time from the onset of the tone until the onset of the response, half-life, which is the time taken to recover half of the maximum deflection of the response, and amplitude or the maximum deflection of the responses. Half-life was determined by means of a transparent overlay described by Edelberg (38).

Spontaneous GSR, which has been shown to be relatively stabile over time (33), was measured three weeks later for the subjects from the habituation experiment. Seven subjects from each group were able to come back for this measure. Spontaneous GSR was measured during three periods, 10 min of rest, eyes open (all subjects); 10 min of rest, eyes closed (nonmeditators), or 10 min meditation; and 10 minutes of rest, eyes open (all subjects). Subjects were invited in and instructed, "I am going to take some physiological measures, GSR, while you are resting. Sit down; make yourself comfortable. All you have to do is rest for 30 minutes, then we will be finished. (Electrodes were attached.) I would like for you to rest with your eyes open for 10 minutes, then I will signal you to close your eyes for 10 minutes of rest (or meditation), then I will signal you again to open your eyes for 10 minutes. Sit comfortably. It's important not to move your hand, so make yourself comfortable. If you have to scratch or something, that's okay, go ahead and scratch. I'm going to start now, so just sit comfortably for 10 minutes with your eyes open." Basal resistance was measured before and after each 10 min period, and spontaneous GSR

was measured during each period. A spontaneous response was defined as a sudden decrease in resistance of 100 ohms or more followed by a recovery of resistance, and only responses which occurred independently of noise or movement were scored as "spontaneous." In the second spontaneous GSR study, the same procedure and instructions were used as in the above study.

RESULTS AND DISCUSSION

Habituation

For the first 11 trials, habituation was similar for meditators and nonmeditators. During this period the latency and recovery time of responses (half-life) did not differ significantly between the two groups. (See Table 1.) Neither did response amplitude for the first 11 trials; a chi square for goodness of fit between the mean amplitude curves for meditators and controls over the first 11 trials was not significant ($x^2 = 12.5$, $df = 10$, $0.3 > P > 0.2$). However, although habituation was initially similar for the two groups, meditators habituated in significantly fewer trials than nonmeditators.

These results are consistent with the findings of others that response amplitude is initially similar for fast and slow habituators (14). (See Table 1 and Figure 1.) The mean number of trials to criterion was 11.0 for meditators and 26.1 for nonmeditators. In addition, three of the nonmeditators never met criterion before

TABLE 1   Results of Habituation Study Latency and Half-Life for the First 11 Trials

	Latency (sec)		Half-Life (sec)		Trials to Criterion		Multiple Responses to First Tone	
	M	S	M	S	M	S	M	S
Meditators	2.26	0.31	11.9	10.22	11.0	4.81	1	0.92
Nonmeditators	2.70	0.68	17.5	9.74	26.1	12.8	2.25	1.28
t tests df = 14	t = 1.6, NS		t = 1.12, NS		t = 3.13, P < 0.01		t = 2.23 P < 0.05	
Randomization test a					P < 0.01			

aSiegel S: Nonparametric Statistics for the Behavioral Sciences. New York, McGraw-Hill, 1956, pp. 152–156 the session had to be terminated, whereas all meditators reached criterion.

Insert A in Figure 1 shows that meditators also made fewer multiple responses than controls. The difference between the two groups on the mean number of multiple reponses to the first tone was statistically significant (see Table 1), but the curves do not significantly differ otherwise. For both groups, the number of multiple responses decreased during habituation, indicating that the wave form of the GSR tends to stabilize as habituation progresses.

To summarize, when noxious tones were presented to the two groups, the GSR was initially more stable and habituated faster for meditators than for controls.

Spontaneous GSR Exp I, Subjects from the Habituation Study

with 18.25 per 10 minutes for controls during rest, eyes closed (see Figure 2 and Table 2). During the two periods of rest, eyes open, meditators made a mean of 8.71 responses per 10 minutes, compared with 21.0 per 10 minutes for control subjects. Thus, meditators were more stabile than control subjects out of meditation as well as during meditation.

The frequency of spontaneous GSR was significantly correlated with trials to criterion during habituation ($r=0.73$) for the combined data of the two groups. This result is consistent with several studies in the literature showing that stable subjects habituate faster than labile subjects (14, 15, 31, 32, 33). The correlation between the frequency of spontaneous GSR measured in this experiment and number of

The mean basal resistance during rest, eyes open, did not differ significantly between the two groups in either EXP I or

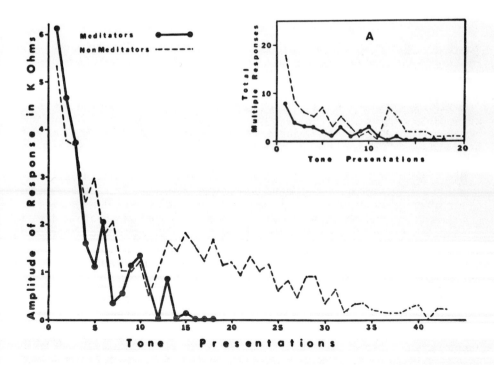

Fig. 1. This figure shows the mean response amplitude as a function of serial tone presentations for the meditator and nonmeditator groups. Insert A shows the total number of multiple responses for each group over tone presentations.

TABLE 2   100 ohm or Greater Spontaneous GSR/10 min

Exp. I	Meditation or Rest, Eyes Closed		Rest, Eyes Open		Basal Resistance (in K ohms)	
	M	S	M	S	M	S
Meditators	6.14	6.90	8.71	4.57	45.3	9.7
Nonmeditators	18.25	10.56	21.0	11.77	44.2	7.6
t test $df = 12$	$t = 2.56$, $P < 0.05$		$t = 2.57$ $P < 0.05$		NS	
Randomization test[a]	$P < 0.05$		$P < 0.05$			
Exp. II	M	S	M	S	M	S
Meditators	2.66	2.34	9.75	3.43	41.0	11.8
Nonmeditators	29.13	20.86	34.25	20.14	38.8	14.3
t test $df = 12$	$t = 3.55$, $P < 0.01$		$t = 3.37$, $P < 0.01$		NS	
Randomization test[a]	$P < 0.01$		$P < 0.01$			

[a]Siegel S: Nonparametric Statistics for the Behavioral Sciences. New York, McGraw-Hill, 1956, pp. 152–156

EXP II. (See Table 2.) Because basal resistances were equivalent for the two groups, the more convenient resistance measures were used to measure spontaneous GSR rather than conductance units.

Meditators were found to be more stabile as measured by a low frequency of spontaneous GSR than controls. During meditation, the mean rate of spontaneous GSR's was 6.14 per 10 min, compared multiple responses during habituation was also significant ($r = 0.75$). Thus, a more stable individual, as measured by spontaneous GSR, is also more stable during habituation.

Spontaneous GSR, Exp II, Nonmeditators Who Planned to Start TM

The results of this experiment showed that subjects planning to start meditation made more spontaneous GSR than subjects already meditating. (See Figure 2 and Table 2.) Nonmeditators made a mean of 34.25 responses per 10 min during the two rest, eyes open periods, compared with 9.75 responses per 10 min for meditators.

There was a small but fairly consistent decrease in spontaneous GSR going from rest, eyes open, to meditation. Out of 13 measurements in the two experiments, spontaneous GSR decreased 10 times, increased twice, and stayed the same once during meditation ($p = 0.038$, Sign test). For controls, closing the eyes didn't have any consistent effect on spontaneous GSR. It decreased six times out of 15.

Approximately 20% of the responses made in the two experiments were correlated with movement by the subject and were not included in the above data analysis. A rationale could be made that they should be included in the analysis because spontaneous GSR and movement-correlated GSR may have a common source. For example, an anxiety provoking thought may produce both spontaneous GSR and a shifting of posture. Therefore, an analysis was made of the total GSR fluctuations over 100 ohms; total GSR = spontaneous GSR + movement-correlated GSR. This inclusion of movement-correlated GSR in the analysis

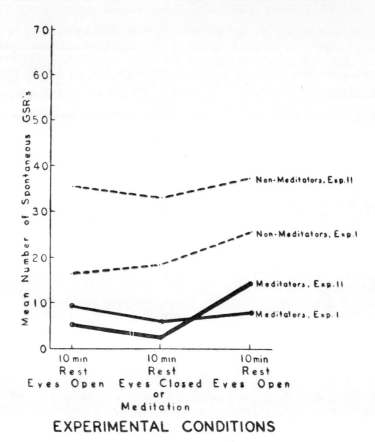

Fig. 2. The mean number of spontaneous GSRs for the various experimental conditions for the indicated groups is shown. "Exp. 1" refers to subjects from the habituation study, and "Exp. II" refers to the experiment in which the control group was composed of nonmeditators who planned to start TM.

modified the interpretation of the results of EXP I, but does not change the interpretation of EXP II or the interpretation of combined results of the two experiments. Meditators and nonmeditators did not differ significantly on the mean number of movement-correlated responses in EXP I, and total GSR (15/10 min for meditators, 25/10 min for non-meditators) did not show a significant difference. However, the interpretation of EXP II was essentially unchanged by including movement produced GSR in the analysis, and the combined data on total GSR for the two experiments was statistically different for the two groups (mean meditator = 14.17/10 min, mean

nonmeditator = 29.11/10 min: $t=3.03$, $df=26$, $p < 0.01$).

During meditation, basal resistance increased for 12 out of 13 individuals ($p=0.004$, Sign test) consistent with Wallace's (2) finding that basal resistance increases during meditation. During rest, eyes closed, for control subjects, basal resistance increased 7 out of 15 times, a nonsignificant change.

Familiarity with the experimental conditions (laboratory and experimenter) is an important determinant of autonomic arousal (39). In the present experiment, subjects from the two groups had a similar amount of prior exposure to the laboratory and acquaintance with the experimenter, with a slight advantage for meditators (see section on subjects). However, additional data on eight meditators attending a teacher training course at Humboldt State College supports the conclusion that the low resting levels of sympathetic activity by meditators seen in the present experiment is not just due to laboratory familiarity. Of the eight college age subjects at Humboldt, only one subject previously knew the experimenter or had been in the experimental room before. The resting levels of spontaneous GSR for this group were $M=7.15/10$ min, $S=5.9$, quite low when compared with the present control subject data. These results support the conclusion that the practice of Transcendental Meditation itself is responsible for the autonomic stability observed in meditators.

SUMMARY

Rapid GSR habituation and low levels of spontaneous GSR are reported in the literature to be correlated with physiological and behavioral characteristics associated with good mental health, e.g. behavioral and autonomic stability, less motor impulsivity, stronger ego, outgoingness, field independence, less susceptibility to a variety of stresses, and less susceptibility to acquiring conditioned stresses. In the present study rapid GSR habituation and low levels of spontaneous GSR were observed in practitioners of Transcendental Meditation. Eight meditators and eight nonmeditators were presented with 100 db, 0.5 sec, 3000 Hz tones at irregular intervals at a mean of once every 53 sec. Meditators habituated in a mean of 11 trials and nonmeditators in 26.1 trials, a statistically significant difference. In addition, meditators made fewer multiple responses in the recovery limb of the GSR to the first tone. In a second experiment three weeks later, meditators made fewer spontaneous GSR fluctuations (100 ohm or greater) than nonmeditators.

A third study showed that nonmeditators planning to begin TM made higher resting levels of spontaneous GSR than meditators. By three criteriá of autonomic stability: rate of habituation, number of multiple responses, and spontaneous GSR, meditators were more stabile than control subjects.

The author wishes to thank Richard Moore, Tom Rosell, and David Beaver for their assistance in the data analysis, Dr. John Bristol for his interest and support of the project, George Kavanagh for doing the photographic work, Mrs. Dorothy Alderman and Mrs. Carolyn Skriiko for typing the manuscript, and the Human Resources Research Organization, Division No. 5 for the use of their computer and photographic facilities.

REFERENCES

1. Wallace RK: The Physiological Effects of Transcendental Meditation: A Proposed Fourth Major State of Consciousness. Los Angeles, Herbert Herz Co., 1970

2. Wallace RK: Physiological Effects of Transcendental Meditation. Science 167:1751–1754, 1970

3. Wallace RK, Benson H, Wilson AF: A wakeful hypometabolic physiologic state. A J Physiol 221:795–799, 1971

4. Wallace RK, Benson H: The physiology of meditation. Sci Amer 226: 84–90, 1972

5. Benson H; Yoga for drug abuse. N Eng J Med, 281:20, 1969

6. Benson H, Wallace RK: Decreased drug abuse with Transcendental Meditation—a study of 1,862 subjects, in Drug Abuse, Proceedings of the International Conference. Philadelphia, Lea & Febiger, 1972 (edited by CJD Aarafonetis), pp. 369–376.

7. Otis L: Survey results presented in plates 15, 16, in Scientific Research on Transcendental Meditation. Los Angeles, MIU Press, 1972

8. Brautigam E: The effect of Transcendental Meditation on drug abuses. Unpublished research report, Dec 1971. (Copies may be obtained from SIMS, 2202 Pico, Santa Monica, Cal.)

9. Schultz T: What science is discovering about the potential benefits of Meditation. Today's Health 50 No. 4: April, 1972

10. Towards pinning down meditation. Hospital Times, May 1, 1970

11. Keil P: Pillar to post. California Business, January 4, 1971

12. Kanellakos DP: Voluntary Improvement of Individual Performance: Literature Survey. Menlo Park, Cal. Stanford Research Institute Report 24–29, 1970

13. Robbins J, Fisher D: Tranquility Without Pills, All About Transcendental Meditation. New York, Peter H. Wyden, 1972

14. Katkin ES, McCubbin RJ: Habituation of the orienting response as a function of individual differences in anxiety and autonomic lability. J. Abnorm Psychol 74:54–60, 1969

15. Mundy-Castle AC, McKiever BL: The psychophysiological significance of the galvanic skin response. J Exp psychol 46:15–24, 1953

16. Stern JA: Stability-lability of physiological response systems. Ann NY Acad Sci 134:1018–1027, 1966

17. Ax Af: The physiological differentiation between fear and anger in humans. Psychosom Med 15:433–442, 1953

18. Silverman AJ, Cohen SI, Shmavonian BM: Investigation of psychophysiologic relationships with skin resistance measures. J Psychosom Res 4:65–87, 1959

19. Greiner TH, Burch NR; Response of human GSR to drugs that influence the reticular formation of brain stem. Fed Proc 14: 346, 1955

20. Katkin ES: Relationship between manifest anxiety and two indices of autonomic response to stress. J Pers Soc Psychol 2: 324–333, 1965

21. Katkin ES: The relationship between a measure of transitory anxiety and spontaneous autonomic activity. J Abnorm Psychol 71:142–146, 1966

22. Rappaport H, Katkin ES: Relationship among manifest anxiety, response to stress and the perception of autonomic activity. Unpublished manuscript, State University of New York at Buffalo, Department of Psychology, 1967

23. Zuckerman M: Perceptual isolation as a stress situation. Arch Gen Psychiat 11:255–276, 1964

24. Burch GE, Cohn AE, Neuman C: A study by quantitative methods of spontaneous variations in volume of the fingertip, toe tip and posterio-superior portion of the pinna of resting, normal, white adults. Amer J Physiol 136:433–447, 1942

25. Alexander AA, Roessler R, Greenfield N: Ego strength and physiological responsivity. Arch Gen Psychiatry 9:142–145, 1963

26. Lacey JI, Lacey BC: The relationship of resting autonomic cyclic activity to motor impulsivity, in The Brain and Human Behavior. HC Solomon, Baltimore, Williams and Wilkins, 1958 (Edited by S Cobb and W Pennfield)

27. Hustmyer FE Jr., Karnes, E: Background autonomic activity and "analytic perception." J Abnorm and Soc Psychol 68:467–468, 1964

28. Stern JA, Stewart MA, Winokur G: An investigation of some relationships between various measures of galvanic skin response. J Psychosom Res 5:215–223, 1961

29. Martin J: Variations in skin resistance and their relationship to GSR conditioning. J. Ment Sci 106:281, 1960

30. Spence KW: A theory of emotionally based drive (D) and its relation to performance in simple learning situations. The Am Psychol 13:131–141, 1958

31. Geer JH: Effect of interstimulus intervals and rest-period length upon habituation of the orienting response. J Exp Psychol 72:617–619, 1966

32. Koepke JE, Pribram KH: Habituation of GSR as a function of stimulus duration and spontaneous activity. J Comp Physiol Psychol 61:442–448, 1966

33. Johnson LC: Some attributes of spontaneous autonomic activity. J Comp Physiol Psychol 56:415–422, 1963

34. Scott ED, Wilkinson D: Adaptation as related to the introversion-extroversion dimension. U. S. Public Health Service, National Institute of Mental Health Report, Grant M1106956-01, 1962

35. Israel NR: Individual differences in GSR orienting response and cognitive control. J Exp Res Person 1:244–248, 1966

36. Stern JA, Surphlis W, Koff E: Electrodermal responsiveness as related to psychiatric diagnosis and prognosis. Psychophysiology 2:51–61, 1965

37. Vedyayev FP, Karmanova IG: On the comparative physiology of the orienting reflex, in Orienting Reflex and Exploratory Behavior. Washington, D. C., American Institute of Biological Sciences, (Edited by LG Vororin, AN Leontiev, AR Luria, EN Sokolov, OS Vinogradova), 1965 pp. 261–265

38. Edelberg R: The information content of the recovery limb of the electrodermal response. Psychophysiology 6:527–539, 1970

39. Sternback RA: Principles of Psychophysiology. New York and London, Academic Press, 1966, pp. 111–138

Mystical States of 43
Consciousness: Neurophysiological and Clinical Aspects

Ernst Gellhorn and William F. Kiely

The relationship of the trophotropic and ergotropic systems of auto-nomic-somatic integration and their relevance to a variety of emotional states and levels of consciousness is reviewed. The importance of proprioceptive afferent feedback to the reticular formation and hypothalamus for the maintenance of ergotropic responsivity is indicated together with the beneficial clinical effects of certain behavior therapies which employ skeletal muscular relaxation as a technique for modifying central nervous system arousal. The neurophysiological basis of Asian and Oriental meditation exercises is reviewed as well as the basis of Yoga ecstasy. EEG patterns in states of meditation indicate that conditions reflective of trophotropic dominance are compatible with full awareness. The failure of habituation of alpha-blocking by sensory input would appear to indicate that some ergotropic influence continues to be exerted upon the cerebral cortex in the meditation state and seems in some way to be a correlate of the heightened perceptual sensitivity reported by such subjects. Clinical observations suggest that certain formerly drug-dependent adolescents and young adults have achieved psychological benefit from systematic practice of meditation. Its potential for therapeutic benefit in certain states of anxiety, phobia, and psychosomatic disorder is suggested.

The burgeoning of interest in altered states of consciousness prevalent among ad-

[1] Professor Emeritus of Neurophysiology, University of Minnesota Medical School. Mailing address: 15 Wendover Drive, Charlottesville, Virginia 22901.

[2] Associate Professor of Psychiatry and Medicine, University of Southern California School of Medicine, 1200 North State Street, Los Angeles, California 90033. This work was supported by Grant MH-06552-07, National Institutes of Health, Bethesda, Maryland.

olescents and young adults in North America and Western Europe in recent years was initially focused around the use of psychedelic and mood-altering drugs. More recently, many of the same young people have taken up Oriental and Asian consciousness-altering exercises in an effort to discover or to achieve psychological peace, a sense of integrity and harmony. Because of the widening interest in mystical states among mental health professionals, a

TABLE 1

The Effects of Stimulation of the Ergotropic and Trophotropic Systems

Autonomic Effects	Somatic Effects	Behavioral Effects
A. Stimulation of the Ergotropic System		
Augmented sympathetic discharges: 1. Increased cardiac rate, blood pressure, sweat section 2. Pupillary dilation and contraction of nictitating membrane 3. Inhibition of G.I. motor and secretory function	Desynchrony of EEG, increased skeletal muscle tone, elevation of certain hormones: adrenaline, noradrenaline, adrenocortical steroids, thyroxin	Arousal, heightened activity and emotional responsiveness
B. Stimulation of the Trophotropic System		
Augmented parasympathetic discharges: 1. Reduction in cardiac rate, blood pressure, sweat secretion 2. Pupillary constriction and relaxation of nictitating membrane 3. Increased G.I. motor and secretory function	Synchrony of EEG, loss of skeletal muscle tone, blocking of shivering response, increased secretion of insulin	Inactivity, drowsiness, and sleep

theory to explain the underlying neurophysiological basis of such altered states of consciousness is offered herein together with some observations regarding possible clinical implications of the theory.

In a series of reviews (8–12) one of us has discussed the relation of the trophotropic and ergotropic systems to various emotional and cognitive states. As first pointed out by Hess (14) the influence of the parasympathetic and sympathetic branches of the autonomic nervous system is not confined to visceral targets but alters somatic functions as well including the skeletal muscles and the cerebral cortex. Dependent on the site and parameters, stimulation of the hypothalamus and the brain stem leads either to the ergotropic or trophotropic syndrome. The ergotropic syndrome consists of an increase in sympathetic discharges and in skeletal muscle tone and also of a diffuse cortical excitation (desynchronization of EEG potentials as in awakening). The trophotropic syndrome is associated with increased parasympathetic discharges, relaxation of skeletal muscles and lessened cortical excitation (increased synchrony as in sleep). It has been recognized in the unanesthetized animal that steady increase in the ergotropic-trophotropic ratio brings about behavior changes from deep sleep to wakefulness and finally to emotional excitement.

Such effects may be produced in two fundamentally different ways: 1) by directly stimulating the "centers" of the ergotropic or trophotropic systems in the hypothalamus or other cerebral areas; and 2) by indirectly altering the activity of the ergotropic and trophotropic systems. This may be accomplished through the cerebral cortex or by changing the degree of afferent discharges impinging on the hypothalamus and reticular formation. It has been shown in particular that propioceptive impulses are very effective in this respect. Reduction of proprioception through curare-like drugs greatly reduces the ergotropic responsiveness of the hypothalamus and diminishes hypothalamic-cortical discharges (7). Moreover, the loss of muscle tone through the effects of these drugs produces behavioral sleep (15). The beneficial effect of muscular relaxation upon states of heightened ergotropic responsivity as in neurosis (16, 17, 22, 29) is thought to be due to this mechanism (see Tables 1 and 2).

THE PHYSIOLOGICAL BASIS OF MEDITATION
AND ECSTASY

The striking production of altered states of consciousness (meditation and ecstasy) by Yoga and Zen monks—and, more recently, among American students of so-called transcendental meditation (26)—has furnished additional examples of the rela-

TABLE 2
Reciprocity between Ergotropic and Trophotropic Systems

1. Shift in Ergotropic-Trophotropic Balance through Trophotropic Stimulation

Excitation of Trophotropic System	Effects on Ergotropic System
a) Reflexly through baroreceptors by raising sino-aortic pressure b) Directly through low frequency stimulation of medulla oblongata, supraoptic area, caudate nucleus, or basal forebrain area	a) Autonomic: inhibition of sympathetic discharges to pupil, nictitating membrane, heart, sweat glands b) Somatic: synchrony in EEG, lessened skeletal muscle tone c) Behavioral: inhibition of sham rage

2. Shift in Ergotropic-Trophotropic Balance through Ergotropic Stimulation

Excitation of Ergotropic System	Effects on Trophotropic System
a) Reflexly through baroreceptors by lowering sino-aortic pressure b) Directly by stimulation of posterior hypothalamus or mesencephalic reticular formation	a) Autonomic: reduction in tonic state of oculomotor (3rd) nerve; diminution in parasympathetic responsivity b) Somatic: lessening of recruitment responses in EEG

3. Shift in Ergotropic-Trophotropic Balance through CNS lesions

Reduction in Ergotropic Tone by Lesions Placed in:	Effects on Trophotropic System
a) Posterior hypothalamus b) Mesencephalic reticular formation c) Transecting brainstem at intracollicular level	increase in parasympathetic reactions: reduction in blood pressure, cardiac rate, and skeletal muscle tone cortical synchrony in EEG somnolence
Reduction of Trophotropic tone by lesions in: a) Septal and anterior hypothalamic areas b) Medial thalamic nuclei c) By midpontine transection	Effect on Ergotropic System increased blood pressure and cardiac rate heightened arousal and activity desynchrony in cortical EEG

tionship of body relaxation to emotional and cognitive states and suggests possible therapeutic value in the learning of such techniques of altering consciousness.

The physiological change which accompanies the mental state of meditation is a shift in the trophotropic-ergotropic balance to the trophotropic side. The EEG shows four stages as the subject develops proficiency in meditation as judged by the Zen master. The presence of alpha potentials, regardless of whether the eyes are open or closed, characterizes stage I. These potentials increase in amplitude in stage II and decline in frequency in stage III, whereas in stage IV theta potentials appear (18). The decrease in heart and respiratory rate (1) and in oxygen consumption—the latter due to the relaxation of skeletal muscles—confirms the interpretation that a shift in the trophotropic-ergotropic balance, with dominance of the trophotropic system, is involved (26, 27). Since this state is associated with reciprocal changes in the tonicity of the ergotropic system—referred to as trophotropic tuning (7, 10, 11)—one would expect that the meditation state would ex-

hibit a diminution in ergotropic tone. The increase in skin resistance noted during meditation (26, 27) shows that in fact the ergotropic tone is lessened: the sympathetic discharges to the sweat glands are diminished.

The marked increase in trophotropic discharges during the meditation state does not lead to sleep, suggesting that some degree of ergotropic excitation exists and counteracts the increased trophotropic discharges. Study of the arousal reaction (blocking of alpha potentials through an acoustic stimulus) discloses that this response quickly disappears on repetition under control conditions, whereas such habituation is absent during the meditation state. The arousal reaction is part of the orienting reflex (19, 24, 25) which involves diffuse activation of the ergotropic system. Numerous investigations have shown that, when the ergotropic system is excited, habituation of the orienting reflex is delayed or abolished, whereas excitation of the trophotropic system tends to accelerate habituation. Thus, section of the brain stem in the mid-pontine region, which intensifies diffuse cortical desynchronization, greatly delays habituation (21), and similar effects are produced by excitatory drugs such as LSD. It is of considerable interest that the subjective experience of some practitioners of Zen or Yoga meditation matches in many respects the heightened sensory awareness and the sense of uniqueness in perceptual experience of many LSD users during the "transcendental" state described by some experienced users of this drug. It is suggested that in some way the lack of habituation of alpha blocking by sensory input is a correlate of this heightened perceptual sensitivity.

On the contrary, the opposite effect is exerted by depressant drugs, such as chlorpromazine, and procedures which induce states of dominance of the trophotropic system, such as stimulation of the septal area (6), or sectioning of the brain stem at the intracollicular level (21). Under these conditions the EEG shows delta potentials (as in sleep) and an acceleration of the habituation of the arousal reaction. In the light of these experiments it is suggested that during meditation there are not only increased trophotropic discharges, leading to an increase in the amplitude and decline in frequency of the alpha potentials, but also concomitant ergotropic discharges which prevent the alpha dominance from passing into the state of sleep.[3] Relatively weak excitation has been shown to induce only partial activation of the ergotropic system (10) and is, therefore, compatible with a trophotropic influence upon the alpha potentials in the EEG and, concomitantly, with an absence of habituation of the ergotropic arousal reaction during the meditation state.[4]

[3] The presence of trophotropic combined with ergotropic discharges in meditation is not based on excessive ergotropic discharge, with overflow into the trophotropic system, as suggested by Gellhorn (8, Chapter IV; and 10) to be the basis of pathological phenomena such as hallucinations, delirium etc. The ergotropic discharges in meditation are rather weak, since they do not block the alpha potentials.

[4] The recent work of DiCara *et al.* (5) and Shapiro *et al.* (23) has furnished further evidence for the occurrence of partial ergotropic reactions in operant conditioning (See Gellhorn, 9, for the literature).

The meditation state is not the only variety of altered consciousness which may be achieved during Yoga trance. Among Indians who have practiced Yoga for years, states of more profound alteration are attained which are designated as ecstasy. Psychophysiological study of Yogis during ecstasy experience reveals that although the EMG records showed no increase in tonic activity over several hours during the progress toward and concomitant with the ecstatic state, there was an acceleration of the heart rate during the ecstasy experience, and following the trance, cardiac slowing (rebound) below the control level took place before the pre-experimental state was reached. The EEG changes were startling. The alpha frequency increased by one to three per second and decreased in amplitude while faster potentials (15–30/sec) appeared. In the ecstatic phase peak values of 40 to 45 per second with an amplitude of 30 to 50 μv were recorded. The return to the norm was preceded, as in the cardiac rate, by a rebound during which the alpha frequency slowed to seven per second. Clearly, in trained subjects unusual degrees of mental concentration and corresponding levels of cortical excitation may be attained during complete muscular relaxation (4). It is quite clear that in meditation a state of trophotropic dominance, and in Yoga ecstasy a state of ergotropic dominance, prevails in the cerebral cortex as indicated by characteristic changes in the EEG. Habituation experiments have apparently not been performed in states of ecstasy, but it seems certain that in this state of ergotropic dominance habituation is even more suppressed than during meditation (28).

CLINICAL IMPLICATIONS

Physiologically and psychologically, the states of consciousness produced by the Zen and transcendental techniques of meditation seem distinct from common states such as wakefulness or sleep, and distinguishable as well from the spectrum of states elicitable through hypnosis. There would, in fact, appear to be nothing physiologically distinctive of the hypnotic state, but rather that a range of affective and behavioral patterns may be hypnotically induced whose physiological correlates are indistinguishable from those characteristic of the waking state. The principal psychological distinction from the normal would appear to be the suspension of autonomous will or intentionality. In the latter respect, there would appear to be some degree of overlap between hypnosis and the states of consciousness associated with meditation and ecstasy.

There is, however, a remarkable parallelism between the state of Yoga ecstasy and that of REM sleep and dreaming. A state of cortical and visceral arousal is common to both as is the associated inhibition of skeletal muscle tone in trunk and limbs. A loss of distinctiveness in the sense of time and space, and vivid perceptual imagery with condensation of imagined persons and events are psychological correlates of both dreams and the state of ecstasy. Further study of the correspondences of these states of altered consciousness is in order as is their relationship to certain psychotic states.

The recently burgeoning adolescent and young adult "counter-culture," with its associated exploration of altered states of consciousness elicitable by psychedelic, stimulant, and sedative drugs and its more recent growth of interest in Asian and Oriental philosophy, has provided one of us (WFK) with clinical experience suggestive that certain beneficial effects are achievable through meditation techniques. A group of anxiously depressed, impulsive-driven adolescents and young adults, formerly dependent upon psychedelic or other dangerous drugs, have been observed to have eliminated drug use and to have substituted daily practice of Zen or of transcendental meditation as the central or guiding focus of their lives. Although no detailed physiological or objective psychological studies are available from these young patients to support the fact of changes in their central nervous system balance, there is clinical evidence of significant emotional and behavioral change. Such individuals report a heightened sense of *inner-directed self-con-*

trol as a result of their meditation practices in contrast to the anxiety-provoking *loss-of-control* experienced under the influence of psychedelic and other drugs. There is evidence, as well, of much improved clarity in cognitive function and in emotional-behavioral integration. A much larger group of similar drug-abusing youngsters treated by more conventional psychiatric methods, including psychoactive drugs, has failed to demonstrate much clinical benefit.

The EEG changes and relaxation of skeletal muscle induced by meditation indicate that this state is accompanied by a shift in T-E balance to the trophotropic side. Similar changes in autonomic-somatic function may be effected by related techniques such as are involved in autogenic training (22), progressive relaxation (17), and systematic densensitization (29). In none of these techniques, however, has there been reported physiological evidence of such remarkable subcortical-cortical patterning of electrical activity as is the case in the meditation and yoga exercises. Wolpe's (29) technique would, in fact, appear to depend, in part at least, on gradual habituation to an anxiety-producing and, therefore, ergotropically acting stimulus. In contrast, as has been indicated, the state of meditation is accompanied by the absence of habituation to the alpha-blocking response to ergotropic stimuli such as an acoustic tone or light flash.[5]

There is reason to believe that transcendental meditation, an easily learned technique (20) in contrast to the rigorous training involved in Zen and Yoga exercises, may be useful clinically in the treatment of psychosomatic tension states, anxiety, and phobic reactions. Its application in the therapy of disorders such as essential hypertension, bronchial asthma, "brittle" juvenile diabetes mellitus, and a number of other psychosomatic disorders would likewise suggest itself. The basic disturbance of trophotropic-ergotropic balance in such disorders has been discussed at length elsewhere (13). Psychopharmacologic agents restoring

[5] The physiological distinction between adaptation to anxiety-producing stimuli in the case of Wolpe's technique and habituation to the cortical arousal reaction may require further analysis (19).

T-E reciprocity at the subcortical level have been of fundamental importance in the therapy of such psychosomatic diseases but have often been less than satisfactory in effecting long term benefit. If the highly successful replacement of emotional turmoil by relative calm, accomplished by certain of the former drug-abusing young people referred to, is replicable by victims of the psychosomatic problems mentioned, a worthwhile addition to overall therapy will have been achieved. Preliminary work (2) is suggestive that this may be the case.

GENERAL SUMMARY

1) The patterns in the EEG in states of meditation and ecstasy show that states of trophotropic, as well as of ergotropic, dominance are compatible with full awareness.

2) The reduction of skeletal muscle tone in Jacobson's, Schultz', and Wolpe's relaxation therapy leads to a loss in ergotropic tone of the hypothalamus (7), a diminution of hypothalamic-cortical discharges, and, consequently, to a dominance of the trophotrophic system through reciprocal innervation. In the unanesthetized animal, cortical synchrony and a sleep-like state may be maintained for hours by elimination of proprioceptive impulses through neuromuscular block by curare and related drugs. Persons engaged in the meditation process assume the Zen-sitting, or lotus position, which is compatible with complete muscular relaxation, while the attention rids itself of mental imagery, ideas, or specific sensory awareness. This results in a state of *emptiness* of consciousness (3) without *loss* of consciousness. The emptiness of consciousness is the psychological concomitant of the shift in the ergotropic-trophotropic balance to the trophotropic side. To maintain this state requires a conscious *effort*, which may be reflected in a mild stimulation of the ergotropic system indicated by the loss of habituation of the arousal reaction. Intensification of this effort, and, thereby, an increase in excitation of the ergotropic system, without increase in muscle tone, is achieved by the trained Yogi and results in the experience of ecstasy.

3) Under conditions of strong afferent (nociceptive or proprioceptive) stimulation, the ergotropic system (including its sympathetic components) tends to discharge as a whole. Partial discharges of the ergotropic and trophotropic systems, including their autonomic components, occur on the other hand when less intensive stimulation or conditions of lesser excitability are employed. Purposeful relaxation of the skeletal muscles is accompanied by reduction in ergotropic system excitation, yet allowing for relatively strong ergotropic cortical effects in ecstasy without increasing skeletal muscle tone. Still milder degrees of ergotropic activity, noted in the meditation state by the failure of habituation of the arousal reaction, are compatible with trophotropic dominance in the EEG but not with behavioral sleep.

4) The data show that proprioceptive impulses are not necessary for the production and maintenance of trophotropic and ergotropic cognitive and emotional states but they play an important role in facilitating and modifying these states as the comparison between ecstasy and rage on the one hand, and meditation and sleep on the other, indicates.

5) Clinical observations suggest that meditation (26), progressive relaxation (17), autogenic training (22), and systematic desensitization (29) induce a shift in the T-E balance to the T side and, thereby, tend to be of therapeutic value in states of E-dominance (E-tuning). The possible advantage of meditation as a mode of therapy in certain forms of neurosis and psychosomatic disorder is suggested.

REFERENCES

1. Allison, J. Respiration changes during transcendental meditation. Lancet, *1*: 833–834, 1970.
2. Benson, H. Letter to editor. N. Engl. J. Med., *281*: 1133, 1969.
3. Buytendijk, F. J. Über den Schmerz. Psyche (Stuttgart), *9*: 436–452, 1956.
4. Das, N. N. and Gastaut, H.: Variations de l'activite electrique du cerveau, du coeur et des muscles squelettiques au cours de la meditation et de l'extase yogique. Electroenceph. Clin. Neurophysiol. [Suppl.], *6*: 211–219, 1957.

5. DiCara, L. V. and Miller, N. E.: Instrumental learning of systolic blood pressure responses by curarized rats: dissociation of cardiac and vascular changes. Psychosom. Med., *30:* 489–496, 1968.

6. Endroczi, E., Doranyi, J., Lissak, K., and Hartman, G.: The role of the mesodiencephalic activating system in the EEG arousal reaction and conditioned reflex activity. Acta Physiol. Pol., *24:* 447–464, 1964.

7. Gellhorn, E.: The influence of curare on hypothalamic excitability and the electroencephalogram. Electroenceph. Clin. Neurophysiol., *10:* 697–703, 1958.

8. Gellhorn, E. *Principles of Autonomic-Somatic Integrations: Physiological Basis and Psychological and Clinical Implications.* Univ. of Minn. Press, Minneapolis, 1967.

9. Gellhorn, E. Neurophysiologic basis of homeostasis. Confin. Neurol., *30:* 217–238, 1968.

10. Gellhorn, E. Central nervous system tuning and its implications for neuropsychiatry. J. Nerv. & Ment. Dis., *147:* 148–162, 1968.

11. Gellhorn, E. Further studies on the physiology and pathophysiology of the tuning of the central nervous system. Psychosom., *10:* 94–104, 1969.

12. Gellhorn, E. Emotions and the ergotropic-trophotropic systems. Psychol. Forsch., *34:* 48–94, 1970.

13. Gellhorn, E. and Kiely, W. F. Autonomic Nervous System in Psychiatric Disorder. In: J. Mendels, ed. *Textbook of Biological Psychiatry.* Wiley-Interscience, New York. In press.

14. Hess, W. R. *On the Relations between Psychic and Vegetative Functions.* Schwabe, Zurich, 1925.

15. Hodes, R. Electrocortical synchronization resulting from reduced proprioceptive drive caused by neuromuscular blocking agents. Electroenceph. Clin. Neurophysiol., *14:* 220–232, 1962.

16. Jacobson, E. *Progressive Relaxation.* U. of Chicago Press, Chicago, 1938.

17. Jacobson, E. *Biology of Emotions.* Thomas, Springfield, 1967.

18. Kasamatsu, A. and Hirai, T. An electroencephalographic study on the Zen meditation (Zazen). Folia Psychiat. Neurol. Jap., *20:* 316–336, 1966.

19. Lynn, R. *Attention, Arousal, and the Orientation Reaction.* Pergamon, Oxford, 1966.

20. M. Mahesh Yogi *The Science of Being and Art of Living.* International SRM, London, 1967.

21. Meulders, M. *Etude Comparative de la Physiologie des Voies Sensorielles Primaires et des Voies Associatives.* Editions Arscia S. A., Brussels, 1962.

22. Schultz, J. W. and Luth, W. *Autogenic Training.* Grune and Stratton, New York, 1959.

23. Shapiro, D., Tursky, B., and Schwartz, G. E. Differentiation of heart rate and systolic pressure. Psychosom. Med., *32:* 417–423, 1970.

24. Sharpless, S. and Jasper, H. Habituation of the arousal reaction. Brain, *79:* 655–680, 1956.

25. Sokolov, Y. N. *Perception and the Conditioned Reflex.* MacMillan, New York, 1963.

26. Wallace, R. K. Physiological effects of transcental meditation. Science, *167:* 1751–54, 1970.

27. Wallace, R. K., Benson, H., and Wilson, A. F. A wakeful hypometabolic physiologic state. Amer. J. Physiol., *221:* 795–799, 1971.

28. Wenger, M. A. and Bagchi, B. K. Studies of autonomic functions in practitioners of Yoga in India. Behav. Sci., *6:* 312–323, 1961.

29. Wolpe, J. *Psychotherapy by Reciprocal Inhibition.* Stanford U. Press, Stanford, 1958.

Sleep-Onset Imagery: 44
A Model for Naturally-Occurring
Hallucinatory Experiences?

Johann Stoyva

Psychophysiology, as the name implies, involves both physiological and psychological observations. If we grant that psychology can be divided into a behavioral component and an experiential one, then, psychophysiology may be thought to embrace three levels of observation—the physiological, the behavioral, and the experiential—the latter indexed by verbal report.

One's first reaction might be to view such an approach as a strategy designed to produce a maximum of confusion. But we think this is not the case—or at least not necessarily! The thesis advanced here is that the combined use of physiological and psychological data can be a fruitful method of experimental inquiry—useful both as a means of gathering evidence about psychological phenomena, and as a method for discovering new relationships. Further, with the addition of the information feedback principle, a new dimension is grafted to psychophysiological methodology. The emerging technique of feedback psychophysiology can, we believe, be valuable not only in exploring a variety of mental processes, but also in teaching individuals to produce certain psychological states at will.

Biofeedback Training and Alterations in Thought Processes

Practically since their inception, there has been speculation that biofeedback techniques could be useful in altering thought processes. This

[1] Supported by Grant Number MH-15596, National Institute of Mental Health; Research Scientist Development Award No. K01-MH-43361-01, National Institute of Mental Health; and Bioengineering Neurosciences Grant NS-08511, National Institute of Health (for development work by the University of Colorado Medical Center Bioengineering Department on the instrumentation system described in this paper).

seems often to be the case, although a great deal remains to be learned.

Feedback training in alpha and in muscle relaxation generally result in a shift away from the thinking of ordinary wakefulness—the subject is more immersed in his internal world, feels relaxed, is in a nonstriving, letting go mode. During muscle relaxation, a number of bodily sensations may be experienced—heaviness, warmth, drowsiness, hovering. When profound relaxation occurs, thought processes shift from action and decision-oriented thinking to a fleeting, visual imagery over which the individual has diminishing voluntary control as he drifts off to sleep.

Also occurring under low arousal conditions is the 4–7 Hz theta rhythm. This rhythm occurs just prior to the onset of Stage 2 spindling sleep, and is associated with drowsiness and, we believe, with muscle relaxation. It is also associated with imagery, mostly visual in nature. The imagery is of an involuntary, emergent type—if the subject tries to produce it, he fails; rather, he must let it happen.

Foulkes (1966) has likened hypnagogic or sleep-onset imagery to a series of disconnected photographic "stills," which is also an apt description for much of theta imagery. Frequently, though, theta images are vivid enough to acquire an hallucinatory intensity, i.e., they seem real. In these instances, the imagery can be better likened to a succession of unrelated film clips, each clip focused on a single scene. Some examples: A handful of old coins sliding off a green velvet cloth; a garden implement; a ship being launched; a stooped figure in a dark overcoat hurrying down a country road; a forest meadow with a freshly dug grave in the middle of it—overhead, a V-formation of geese flying south; someone jumping over a little freshet of water caused by the sudden melting of snow.

The group which has worked most extensively with theta feedback has been Green, Green, and Walters (1970) at the Menninger Foundation. They, too, find that theta is associated with vivid imagery. A major interest of this group is to explore the role of hypnagogic reverie in creativity.

Some Biofeedback Experiments

An attractive feature of theta training is that, at least for many individuals, it offers a means of putting the subject into a condition in which he will experience imagery of hallucinatory intensity. There is a major practical problem, however. When a subject is in theta he seems dissociated from his surroundings, and we are still uncertain whether a subject in this condition will continue to pay any attention to the feedback signal—although this may be a skill which improves with practice.

A matter of first importance is how best to teach subjects to produce theta. One approach is to begin immediately with theta feedback. However, it may be better to conduct the training in two phases—an initial phase of muscle relaxation training, followed by a second phase in which training is shifted to direct feedback of theta. The aim of this second approach is to break the training into two easier-to-master stages. Learning to produce theta is a subtle task; and the base operant level of the rhythm is generally low—often too low to generate a usable feedback signal. But a condition of muscle relaxation is associated with an increase in theta EEG frequencies. Thus, if the subject first attains a deeply relaxed condition as a prelude to theta training, he will have something to work with when he later begins the task of acquiring feedback control of theta. Experiments to test this two-step training are currently being conducted in our laboratory as part of the doctoral dissertation by Miss Pola Sittenfeld.

The foregoing two-phase technique could be considered part of a more general approach aimed at the shaping of low arousal conditions (suggested by Dr. Budzynski). Thus, beginning his training from a point of alert wakefulness, the subject would be gradually led in the direction of sleep. Over several sessions, he would first train in the production of alpha, next in producing mixed alpha and theta frequencies, then in the production of theta frequencies. Later in his training the subject would attempt to produce a particular low arousal condition in the absence of any feedback. An objective criterion for his ability to attain a given low arousal condition could be assessed electroencephalographically, e.g., how readily is he able to produce theta, and how does his performance compare with that of untrained subjects?

Another facet of the research would involve sampling the mental activity associated with alpha, with mixed alpha and theta rhythms, and with theta frequencies. The data would be examined for regularities across subjects. Within-subject regularities would also be investigated since Foulkes (1966) has stated that individual differences are a prominent feature of sleep-onset imagery.

It seems likely that feedback techniques could be profitably employed to increase imagery retrieval from twilight states. Ordinarily, when a subject is roused from a sleep-onset condition and asked to report his thoughts, he frequently finds it difficult to return to a drowsy state. Feedback training, especially in muscle relaxation and in producing theta, can assist the subject in knowing what he must do to return to the drowsy condition in which imagery is likely to occur.

Subjects can also be allowed to signal when they are experiencing imagery, for example, by using a finger switch. By this means, we have found that subjects will press the "imagery switch" 8–12 times in the course of a 20-min session of theta training (although these subjects were not asked to report any details until after the end of the session).

A useful technique for increasing hypnagogic recall has been described by Tart (1969). The subject lies on his back, but keeps one arm in a vertical position, balanced on the elbow. As the subject drifts into sleep, muscle tonus drops, and his arm falls. This awakens him, thereby allowing him to take note of whatever imagery or thinking was in progress. A refinement of this technique has been developed by Green *et al.* (1970) who use a tilt detector consisting of a mercury switch finger ring. Whenever a subjects' hand deviates from the vertical, the mercury switch circuit closes and a chime is sounded.

With theta training it seems likely that we could produce some different-from-normal conditions. For example, we could explore the experiential consequences of hovering for extended periods in the theta zone. Under everyday circumstances, such as falling asleep, we drop through our sleep-onset phase in a matter of seconds or a few minutes. What if subjects were kept in theta for a long period of time, for example, 30–50 min? Perhaps the imagery would reveal new properties, for example, become more intense or more dreamlike. A possible means of keeping someone in theta for extended periods would be to provide him with a feedback signal whenever he began drifting out of the theta band. Give him a high-pitched tone if he slipped in the direction of sleep, a low-pitched tone if he moved toward normal wakefulness.

BETWEEN SLEEP AND WAKEFULNESS

Biofeedback training in alpha control and particularly in muscle relaxation have a quieting effect on the individual; they lower his arousal level and nudge him into a condition close to sleep. This borderland between wakefulness and sleep seems to be especially propitious for evoking alterations in consciousness—an observation which deserves more attention than has so far been bestowed on it in the Anglo-American literature. For example, in hypnotic induction there is much emphasis on relaxation, on quieting oneself, on listening only to the hypnotist's voice. And, as Gill and Brenman (1961, pp. 57–58) have emphasized:

 . . . we see a significant departure from normal, *waking* modes of thought: instead of relatively stable, logical kind of thought—which for the most part employs words as its material—we see the emergence of fluid, archaic forms which often employ visual images and symbols as material, forms which do not follow the ordinary rules of logic, and which moreover are not bound to realistic limitations of time and space.

In autogenic training, a technique which has been extensively used in treating stress-related disorders, emphasis is placed on attaining the "autogenic shift" or *Umschaltung*—a condition for which passive concentration is held to be absolutely essential. In its physiological aspects, this condition involves a shift to parasympathetic predominance in the autonomic nervous system—as evidenced by muscle relaxation, slowed heart rate and respiration, increased skin temperature. Experientially, sensations of flowing warmth are often reported, as is a light quality in the visual field (eyes are closed). Luthe (1965) and others, however, point out that the autogenic shift is not characterized by drowsiness.

Koestler (1964), in his stimulating book, emphasizes that reverie states (which probably occur in the border zone between waking and sleep) figure prominently in literature about creative thinking. For example, Kekulé's conception of the benzene ring originated in a drowsy, reverie state—it was a warm summer's evening, and the famous chemist dozed as his omnibus made its way through the streets of London. The German psychiatrist, Kretschmer (quoted in Koestler, 1964, p. 325), has emphasized that:

> . . . creative products of the artistic imagination tend to emerge from a psychic twilight, a state of lessened consciousness and diminished attentivity to external stimuli. Further, the condition is one of "absent-mindedness" with hypnoidal over-concentration on a single focus, providing an entirely passive experience, frequently of a visual character, divorced from the categories of space and time, and reason and will.

A. HYPNAGOGIC IMAGERY

A valuable contribution of recent sleep research has been the finding that hypnagogic or sleep-onset experiences are surprisingly common. In fact, they are an everyday occurrence. Generally, though, we fail to notice them, or forget them.

Some of the earliest research on hypnagogic imagery was conducted by Silberer (1951) shortly after the turn of the century. He described his approach as a "Method of evoking and observing certain symbolic hallucinatory phenomena." Silberer, a German philosopher, could not have been lacking in old-fashioned will-power, for he would force himself to try to solve problems while in a drowsy condition. Then he would rouse himself and note the images which had slipped into consciousness. Silberer maintained that in this drowsy condition there is a transformation in the thought process—from mental activity of an intellectual character to thinking of a visual, symbolic type. Drawing from his self-observations, Silberer (1951, p. 202–204) provided many instances of this transformation.

Example 1. My thought is: I am to improve a halting passage in an essay.
Symbol: I see myself planing a piece of wood.
Example 7. In opposition to the Kantian view, I am attempting to conceive of time as a "concept."
Symbol: I am pressing a Jack-in-the-Box into the box. But every time I take my hand away it bounces out gaily on its spiral spring.[5]

Contemporary electrophysiological studies of sleep-onset by Foulkes, Rechtschaffen, and their associates have established that sleep-onset imagery, like dreaming, is an everyday occurrence. Thus, Foulkes and Vogel (1965) found that when their subjects were "awakened" close to sleep-onset they recalled some specific mental experience over 90% of the time.

Pilot research by these investigators had suggested that there was an orderly sequence of different types of mental activity with progressive stages of sleep-onset—fragmentary visual material passed into more extended and self-involved "dreamlets" as the EEG shifted from alpha rhythm to spindling sleep. This hint was confirmed in a detailed study of hypnagogic imagery (Foulkes & Vogel, 1965) in which subjects were awakened from each of four sleep-onset EEG patterns: (1) Alpha EEG with rapid eye movements (REMs), (2) alpha rhythm with slow rolling eye movements (SEMs), (3) descending stage 1 sleep (predominance of theta rhythms), and (4) descending Stage 2 sleep (13–16 Hz spindle bursts prominent). As a group, the subjects showed a clear progression toward increasingly hallucinatory material as they drifted toward sleep. Distribution of hallucinatory dreamlike experiences was as follows:

Alpha REM reports	29%
Alpha SEM reports	47%
Descending Stage 1 reports	74%
Descending Stage 2 reports	80%

Recent research suggests that this sleep-onset zone may provide clues as to the necessary conditions for dreaming. A vexatious observation in sleep research has been the finding that dreams are not confined to REM sleep, but are sometimes reported from non-REM sleep as well (see Foulkes, 1966). Why? An experiment by Zimmerman (1970) may help provide an answer. In this study there were two extreme groups—a *light sleeper group*, subjects easily awakened by an auditory signal; and a *deep sleeper*

---

[5] Later investigators have generally failed to find such a continuity between problem-oriented thinking and the hypnagogic imagery immediately succeeding it. This continuity may have resulted from the unusual nature of Silberer's approach, in which he forced himself to solve problems while in a drowsy condition rather than permitting himself a free flow of imagery.

group, subjects who needed much more intense auditory stimulation to wake up. When awakened from non-REM sleep, the light sleeper group showed a far higher incidence of dreamlike recall than did their opposite numbers (71% compared to 21%). Subjects in the light sleeper group were also more aroused physiologically as measured by heart rate, respiration, body temperature levels, spontaneous awakenings, and gross body movements while asleep (Zimmerman, 1967).

Zimmerman's conclusion was that a moderate level of physiological arousal may be necessary in order for dreaming to occur. Consequently, dreamlike experiences could be expected to occur both at sleep-onset and during those epochs of non-REM sleep in which a moderate level of physiological arousal is present. Support for this position comes from an intriguing study by Hersch *et al.* (1970) in which arousal level during non-REM sleep was deliberately increased by chemical means. Catheterized subjects, serving as their own controls, were given intravenous norepinephrine injections during non-REM sleep. An equal number of saline control injections were made, also during non-REM sleep. Awakenings after the norepinephrine injections yielded a significantly greater proportion of dreamlike reports—as assessed by degree of emotionality, type of imagery, etc.

ON THE CONDITIONS FOR HALLUCINATORY ACTIVITY

West's theory. Why should imagery and hallucinations blossom so readily in this twilight terrain between waking and sleep? A theory addressed to this question has been advanced by West (1962). He begins with the observation that in a variety of altered states of consciousness—hypnosis, hypnagogic imagery, dreaming, Zen and Yoga meditation, sensory isolation experiences—certain common conditions are present. West postulates that a major predisposing condition for hallucinatory activity is a reduction in the level or variety of external sensory input to the brain. As the sensory isolation literature in particular has emphasized (Bexton, Heron,& Scott, 1954), ordinary levels of sensory input exercise an organizing and inhibiting effect on consciousness. When sensory input is substantially reduced or made extremely monotonous, it loses its customary organizing effect on the processes of consciousness.

A second requirement for the evocation of hallucinatory activity is the maintenance of an arousal level sufficient to permit awareness. West characterizes this condition as one of "residual awareness." Self-awareness is still present; there is some appreciation of one's own thoughts, feelings, and sensations, but there is a disengagement from one's surroundings— the reality moorings have been severed. Though hard to define operationally, residual awareness is associated with the conditions pertaining to sleep onset, rather than with the comparatively high arousal of active wakefulness or with the low arousal and minimal mental activity of Stage 3 and Stage 4 sleep.

The basic tenet of the theory is that a reduction or impairment of sensory input together with an arousal level sufficient to permit residual awareness is a condition likely to produce hallucinatory experiences. According to West (1968, p. 268) ". . . when the usual information input level no longer suffices completely to inhibit their emergence, the perceptual traces may be 'released' and reexperienced in familiar or new combinations." [6]

Similar conclusions were reached by Zimmerman (1970) with respect to when the experience of dreaming is likely to occur. As already mentioned, Zimmerman maintains that what is essential for the experience we call dreaming is not the presence of REM sleep, but a given (moderate) level of arousal in the absence of reality contact. Thus, dreaming could be expected to occur in non-REM sleep if arousal level were sufficiently high—a hypothesis confirmed by the abovementioned experiment of Hersch *et al.* (1970).

Some additions to West's theory. We believe that West's theory underscores some major determinants of naturally occurring hallucinatory experiences, i.e., those hallucinations which can be made to occur without drugs or surgical intervention. We also believe that on the basis of recent work, particularly in the biofeedback area, the theory can be made more specific and given greater explanatory power in terms of generating testable propositions. In our opinion, the following additional postulates serve to define further those proposed by West:

1. In the production of hallucinatory experiences it is important to reduce not only external sensory input but to reduce internal or proprioceptive input as well. As mentioned earlier, we have found muscular relaxation, with its accompanying reduction of CNS input (see Gellhorn, 1964), conducive to the evocation of hypnagogic material.

It will be remembered that relaxation of the musculature also plays an important role in autogenic training, and in the induction of hypnosis. Conversely, tensing up the musculature acts to eliminate a low arousal condition and the associated alterations in consciousness. For example, a person may tense his muscles to keep from dozing off in a lecture.

2. A second additional postulate is that the ability to shift to a condition of "passive volition" is critical for the attainment of those twilight states

[6] Whether the basic mechanism is an active release process as West maintains, or simply a passive slowing down, is difficult to test at this point. So the question will be left open.

in which imagery and hallucinatory activity are likely to occur. This passive volition characteristic, as Green *et al.* (1970) have termed it, has been noted in several types of biofeedback training, e.g., in work with alpha, theta, and EMG activity. In autogenic training it has been termed passive concentration. As Deikman (1971) has recently emphasized, this ability is required for what he terms the "receptive mode of consciousness"—a mode he regards as essential to the attainment of contemplative states.[7]

3. Also important in the induction of twilight states is a change in autonomic function, a shift from sympathetic predominance to one of parasympathetic predominance. Gellhorn (1964) maintains that the mechanism of this shift is a resetting of hypothalamic balance. A reduction in proprioceptive input, as produced by muscular relaxation, causes hypothalamic balance to change to a parasympathetic pattern.

As the subject moves from alert wakefulness toward sleep, respiration and heart rate decline, skin temperature increases, muscle tension diminishes, and EEG patterns display a change toward slower frequencies. This physiological shift seems to be intimately linked with the altered quality of thinking which occurs in the twilight or sleep-onset state, a point emphasized in the autogenic training literature (Schultz & Luthe, 1959; Stokvis & Wiesenhütter, 1961).

A related point is that the magnitude of the physiological shift seems important. That is to say, the changes in consciousness are greater if a subject goes from high arousal to low arousal than if he merely goes from a moderate level of arousal to a low arousal condition. Why this should be, we are uncertain. Perhaps it is a contrast effect; or possibly there is a greater build-up of some active inhibitory or disinhibitory neural process if the change in arousal level is great; perhaps a large shift generates more internal stimuli. Lest too much stress be put on this observation, its preliminary nature should be emphasized—however, it should be readily open to empirical test.

---

[7] Deikman conceives of two fundamental ways in which waking consciousness operates, (a) an "active" mode—the striving, adaptive, goal-oriented, consciousness of everyday life, and (b) a "receptive" mode, characterized by a lack of striving, a "letting go," calmness, and a quiet receptiveness. This receptive mode has been little emphasized in Western cultures, and most people seem only vaguely aware of it. But writings of the Eastern mystical disciplines suggest that the receptive mode of consciousness could be cultivated and made voluntarily accessible to those willing to do the training. Whether the condition of passive volition is required for *all* biofeedback learning, or only for acquiring feedback control over those responses characteristic of low arousal (e.g., alpha, theta, muscle relaxation), is not yet known.

Also worth noting is that the shift to parasympathetic predominance seems also to be associated with both a change in affect, and a broadening of the range of consciousness. As Koestler (1964) has perceptively remarked, sympathetic predominance is linked to emotions in which the range of awareness is restricted—anger and fear, for example. Parasympathetic functioning he states is associated with subtler emotions—wonder, religious and esthetic experiences, contemplation—emotions characterized by a broader range of awareness.

SUMMARY OF ARGUMENT

The events of consciousness can be scientifically studied to the extent that we are able to make testable inferences about them. One area which has made use of testable inferences about consciousness is contemporary dream research. The basic approach has involved the *combined* use of physiological measures and verbal report—as, for example, in the research which has explored mental activity during the various phases of sleep.

It is argued here that the combined use of verbal report and physiological measures can be profitably extended to the study of certain waking mental activity as well—particularly with the addition of the information feedback principle, which adds a new dimension to the basic methodology. The emerging technique of feedback psychophysiology can be valuable both in exploring mental activity and in teaching individuals to produce some psychological states at will.

Biofeedback techniques have been useful in producing the low arousal state bordering on sleep. In this low arousal state there are characteristic changes in the nature of the thought process—reality-oriented thinking is supplanted by imagery, often of an hallucinatory intensity.

It is argued that the conditions conducive to such low arousal, sleep-onset experiences have broader implications in helping to specify the circumstances under which naturally occurring hallucinatory experiences are likely to arise (phenomena such as dreams, hypnagogic imagery, the hallucinations of hypnosis, and sensory isolation). The major predisposing conditions are (1) a reduction in sensory input, to the brain—both external and internal (proprioceptive) input are important, (2) a shift to a non-striving, passive volitional mode of consciousness, (3) a shift to a low arousal condition characterized by a predominately parasympathetic response pattern in the autonomic nervous system.

REFERENCES

Aserinsky, E., & Kleitman, N. Regularly occurring periods of eye motility and concomitant phenomena during sleep. *Science*, 1953, **118**, 274–284.

Bexton, W. H., Heron, W., & Scott, T. H. Effects of decreased variation in sensory environment. *Canadian Journal of Psychology*, 1954, **8**, 70–76.

Berger, R. J., & Moskowitz, E. Failure to confirm a directional relationship between rapid eye movement and dream imagery. *Psychophysiology*, 1970, **6**, 640–641. (Abstract)

Berger, R. J., & Oswald, I. Eye movements during active and passive dreams. *Science*, 1962, **137**, 601.

Black, A. H. The direct control of neural processes by reward and punishment. *American Scientist*, 1971, **59**, 236–245.

Budzynski, T. H., & Stoyva, J. M. An instrument for producing deep muscle relaxation by means of analog information feedback. *Journal of Applied Behavior Analysis*, 1969, **2**, 231–237.

Budzynski, T. H., Stoyva, J. M., & Adler, C. S. Feedback-induced muscle relaxation: Application to tension headache. *Behavior Theory and Experimental Psychiatry*, 1970, **1**, 205–211.

Deikman, A. J. Bimodal consciousness. *Archives of General Psychiatry*, 1971, **25**, 481–489.

Dement, W., & Kleitman, N. The relation of eye movements during sleep to dream activity: An objective method for the study of dreaming. *Journal of Experimental Psychology*, 1957, **53**, 339–346.

Ferster, C. B. Essentials of a science of behavior. In J. T. Nurnburger, C. B. Ferster, & J. P. Brady (Eds.), *An introduction to the science of human behavior*. New York: Appleton, 1963, Pp. 197–345.

Foulkes, D. *The psychology of sleep*. New York: Scribner, 1966.

Foulkes, D., & Vogel, G. Mental activity at sleep onset. *Journal of Abnormal Psychology*, 1965, **70**, 231–243.

Gellhorn, E. Motion and emotion: The role of proprioception in the physiology and pathology of the emotions. *Psychological Review*, 1964, **71**, 457–472.

Gill, M. M., & Brenman, M. *Hypnosis and related states*. New York: International Universities Press, 1961.

Green, E., Green, A., & Walters, D. Voluntary control of internal states: Psychological and physiological. *Journal of Transpersonal Psychology*, 1970, **1**, 1–26.

Hersch, R. G., Antrobus, J. S., Arkin, A. M., & Singer, J. L. Dreaming as a function of sympathetic arousal. *Psychophysiology*, 1970, **7**, 329–330. (Abstract)

Jacobson, E. *Progressive relaxation*. (2nd ed.) Chicago: Univ. of Chicago Press, 1938.

Jacobson, E. *Modern treatment of tense patients*. Springfield, Illinois: Thomas, 1970.

Kamiya, J. Operant control of the EEG alpha rhythm and some of its reported effects on consciousness. In C. T. Tart (Ed.), *Altered state of consciousness*. New York: Wiley, 1969. Pp. 507–517.

Kennedy, J. L. A possible artifact in electroencephalography. *Psychological Review*, 1959, **66**, 347–352.

Koestler, A. *The act of creation*. New York: Macmillan, 1964.

Lewis, H. B., Goodenough, D. R., Shapiro, A., & Sleser, I. Individual differences in dream recall. *Journal of Abnormal Psychology*, 1966, **71**, 52.

Lippold, O. Origin of the alpha rhythm. *Nature*, 1970, **226**, 616–618.

Luthe, W. (Ed.) *Autogenic training: Correlationes psychosomaticae.* New York: Grune & Stratton, 1965.

Mulholland, T. Feedback electroencephalography. *Activitas Nervosa Superior (Praha),* 1968, **10,** 410–438.

Platt, J. R. Strong inference. *Science,* 1964, **146,** 347–353.

Roffwarg, H. P., Dement, W. C., Muzio, J. N., & Fisher, C. Dream imagery: Relationship to rapid eye movements of sleep. *Archives of General Psychiatry,* 1962, **7,** 235–258.

Schultz, J. H., & Luthe, W. *Autogenic training: A psychophysiological approach in psychotherapy.* New York: Grune & Stratton, 1959.

Silberer, H. Report on a method of eliciting and observing certain symbolic hallucination-phenomena. In D. Rapaport (Ed.), *Organization and pathology of thought.* New York: Columbia Univ. Press, 1951. Pp. 195–207.

Stokvis, E., & Wiesenhütter, E. *Der Mensche in der Entspannung,* (2 Auflage). Stuttgart: Hippokrates Verlag, 1961.

Stoyva, J. M. The public (scientific) study of private events. In E. Hartmann (Ed.), *Sleep and dreaming.* Boston: Little, Brown, 1970. Pp. 353–368. (Republished in T. X. Barber, L. V. DiCara, J. Kamiya, N. E. Miller, D. Shapiro, J. Stoyva (Eds.), *Biofeedback and self-control,* 1970; *An Aldine annual on the regulation of bodily processes and consciousness.* Chicago: Aldine Publishing Co., 1971.)

Stoyva, J. M., & Kamiya, J. Electrophysiological studies of dreaming as the prototype of a new strategy in the study of consciousness. *Psychological Review,* 1968, **75,** 192–205.

Tart, C. T. (Ed.) *Altered states of consciousness.* New York: Wiley, 1969.

West, L. J. A general theory of hallucinations and dreams. In L. J. West (Ed.), *Hallucinations.* New York: Grune & Stratton, 1962. Pp. 275–291.

West, L. J. Hallucinations. In J. G. Howells (Ed.), *Modern perspectives in world psychiatry.* Edinburgh: Oliver & Boyd, 1968. Pp. 265–287.

Zimmerman, W. .B. Psychological and physiological differences between "light" and "deep" sleepers. Unpublished doctoral dissertation, University of Chicago, 1967.

Zimmerman, W. B. Sleep mentation and auditory awakening thresholds. *Psychophysiology,* 1970, 1970, **6,** 540–549.

45

Yoga, Hypnosis, and Self-Control of Cardiovascular Functions

Ambellur N. D. Frederick and Theodore X. Barber

During the past century reports have been filtering
back from India concerning yogis who can exercise voluntary control over autonomic functions. Among the more
dramatic of these reports are those claiming that yogis
can stop the heart and can markedly vary the temperature
of the skin.

Some Ss under "hypnotic trance" have also been said
to show an increased heart rate following direct suggestions
that the heart is beating faster and a decreased heart
rate when given suggestions to slow the heart. It has also
been claimed that "hypnotized" Ss show changes in skin
temperature when they are given the suggestion to think of
cold or warmth(Barber, 1970).

The purpose of this study is to evaluate cardiac and
vasomotor phenomena observed in studies with yogis and
to compare these phenomena with those observed in experimental hypnosis.

CARDIAC FUNCTIONS

Five studies have been conducted that bear directly
on the claim that yogis can stop the heart(Anand & Chhina,
1961; Green, Ferguson, Green, & Walters, 1971; Hoening,
1968; Satyanarayanamurthi & Sastry, 1958; Wenger, Bagchi,
& Anand, 1961). A critical evaluation of these studies
leads to the following conclusions:
    1. There is no evidence that yogis can stop the
heart. Sensitive measures, such as the electrocardiogram

and finger plethysmograph, consistently showed that there was heart activity during the yogis' attempts at heart stopping. However, as will be seen below, some yogis were able to attenuate heart sounds and the radial pulse.

2.   The ability to attenuate the heart sounds(without stopping the heart) was achieved by use of the Valsalva maneuver. During this maneuver the inhaled breath is held with the glottis closed, and the muscles of the thorax and abdomen are stongly contracted. The consequent increase in intrathoracic pressure obstructs the thin-walled veins in the thorax and interferes with the venous return to the heart. Since heart sounds are produced by the heart's contracture over the contained blood and the closure of the valves, and since there is little blood returning to the heart, the heart sounds become attenuated or inaudible. Also, the strong contractions of the thoracic muscles produce a murmur that helps to obscure the heart sounds.

3.   The ability to attenuate the radial pulse is due to contractions of the pectoralis, latissimus dorsi, and other muscles of the arm, chest, and back. These contractions, together with the pressure of the arm against the side, lead to mechanical compression of the brachial artery and an attenuation of the pulse.

4.   Since early workers did not use sensitive instruments, such as the electrocardiogram, they falsely concluded that yogis could stop the heart voluntarily. This invalid conclusion was derived from (a) the ability of some yogis to attenuate heart sounds when tested by auscultation with a stethoscope and (b) the ability to attenuate the radial pulse when tested by palpation. Both of these indices can be absent without a stoppage of the heart.

Although yogis do not stop the heart, some yogis have shown changes in heart rhythm that have not yet been fully explained. Wenger et al.(1961) studied a 37-yr. old male who had about 5 yr. of yogic training. He was able to slow his heart markedly from 63 to 25 beats per min. An increase in the P-R interval and a marked decrease or disappearance of the P wave was noted for periods up to 3 sec.

Rao, Krishnaswamy, Narasimhaiya, Hoenig, and Govindaswamy(1958) and Hoenig(1968) have both discussed another instance of a yogi who showed unusual cardiac manifestations. While buried in a pit, this yogi's heart rate varied from 100 to 40 bpm. in a cyclical manner every 25 min. This cyclical variation in heart rate was not correlated with other observations such as EEG or respiratory rate. Also, this yogi showed no other cardiac abnormality.

More recently, Green et al.(1970) noted that a trained yogi produced about 17 sec. of atrial flutter when he attempted to stop the heart. The yogi stated that he produced the cardiac manifestation by a "solar plexus lock" which may have been his term for the Valsalva maneuver. Green, et al. also reported that the polygraph briefly recorded a heart rate of 300 bpm. during the experiment. It is not clear whether this was a polygraph artifact or a genuine phenomenon.

The ability of some yogis to accelerate and decelerate the heart has also been noted in some hypnotic Ss who have been given the suggestion that the heart is beating faster or slower(Barber, 1970). These changes in heart rate appear to be correlated with changes in levels of arousal or activation. Barber(1970) has summarized the studies in this area by noting that "Cardiac acceleration or deceleration can be produced in some subjects by various types of suggestions or instructions given under either hypnotic or waking conditions [p. 159]." There is also evidence indicating that voluntary control of the heart rate is more common than has at times been supposed and is not discontinuous from other known psychophysiological phenomena(Barber, 1970).

VASOMOTOR FUNCTIONS

Wenger and Bagchi(1961) report the case of a yogi who was able to perspire at will on his forhead between 1½ and 10 min. after he started concentrating on warmth. This man lived in Himalayan caves during part of two winters. The intense cold disturbed his meditation and he was advised by his guru to concentrate on warmth. He was also asked to visualize himself in hot places. After 6 mo. of practice, he was able, when thinking about warmth, to produce a feeling of warmth and perspiration from the forehead. Along similar lines, Green et al.(1970) found that a trained yogi could produce a temperature difference of $2° - 7°F.$ on the same hand between the hypothenar and thenar eminences. The yogi did not specify how he carried out this feat but the principles involved may be similar to those following.

Localized vasoconstriction and vasodilation(and a concomitant localized skin temperature alteration) can be induced by various types of suggestions or instructions given to Ss who have not received yogic training. Menzies

(1941) demonstrated that some normal individuals show vasodilation and vasoconstriction in a limb when instructed to
recall previous experiences involving warmth or cold to the
limb respectively. McDowell(1959) found that a good hypnotic
S showed erythema with vasodilation and increase in skin
temperature of a leg following suggestions that the leg was
immersed in warm water. Hadfield(1920)noted that localized
changes in skin temperature could be induced by suggestions
given to a person in the waking state. In this case, S had
exercised vigorously before the experiment and the temperature
of both hands had reached 95°F. When it was suggested that
his right hand was becoming cold, the temperature of his right
palm fell to 68°F. while the temperature of the left palm
stayed at 94°F. Next, when it was suggested that his right
hand was becoming warm, the temperature of his hand rose to
94°F. in 20 min.

More recently, Zimbardo, Maslach, and Marshall(1970)
presented experimental data showing that some individuals
can exercise cognitive control over skin temperature.
Three trained hypnotic Ss were first asked to relax deeply
and then to make one hand hot and the other cold. The E
suggested several images and encouraged Ss to generate
their own imagery which might be helpful in increasing or
decreasing hand temperature. All three Ss were able to
lower the temperature of one hand by about 2° to 7°. Two
of the three Ss were able to raise the temperature of the
other hand by about 2°C.

The above data suggest that a substantial proportion
of normal individuals might be able to produce localized
changes in skin temperature. Apparently, the process of
vividly imagining cold gives rise to vasoconstriction and
the process of vividly imagining warmth gives rise to
vasodilation. Of course, vasoconstriction in turn produces a drop in skin temperature and vasodilation produces
a rise in skin temperature. We venture to predict that
intensive research will be conducted in the near future
to develop methods for teaching individuals to manifest
this type of control over skin temperature.

REFERENCES

Anand, B.K., & Chhina, G.S. Investigations of Yogis
    claiming to stop their heart beats. Indian Journal
    of Medical Research. 1961, 49, 90-94.

Barber, T.X. LSD, Marihuana, Yoga, and Hypnosis. Chicago: Aldine, 1970.

Green, E.E., Ferguson, D.W., Green, A.M., & Walters, E.D. Voluntary Control Project: Swami Rama. Topeka: Menninger Foundation, 1970.

Hadfield, J.A. The Influence of Suggestions on Body Temperature. Lancet, 1920, 2, 68–69.

Hoenig, J. Medical Research on Yoga. Confinia Psychiatrica, 1968, 11, 68–89.

McDowell, H. Hypnosis in Dermatology. In J.M. Schneck (Ed.), Hypnosis in Modern Medicine. (2nd ed.) Springfield, Ill: Charles C Thomas, 1959.

Menzies, R. Further Studies of Conditioned Vasomotor Responses in Human Subjects. Journal of Experimental Psychology, 1941, 29, 457–482.

Rao, H.V.G., Krishnaswamy, N., Narasimhaiya, R.L., Hoenig, J., & Govindaswamy, M.V. Some experiments on a "yogi" in Controlled States. Journal of the All-India Institute of Mental Health, 1958, 1, 99–106.

Satyanaryanamurthi, G.V., & Sastry, P.B. A Preliminary Scientific investigation into some of the unusual Physiological Manifestations Acquired as a Result of Yogic Practices in India. Wiener Zeitschrift fuer Nervenheilkunde, 1958, 15, 239–249.

Wenger, M.A., & Bagchi, B.K. Studies of Autonomic Functions in Practitioners of Yoga in India. Behavioral Science, 1961, 6, 312–323.

Wenger, M., Bagchi, B.K., & Anand, B.K. Experiments in India on "voluntary" control of the heart and pulse. Circulation, 1961, 24, 1, 313–1, 325.

Zimbardo, P., Maslach, C., & Marshall, G. Hypnosis and the Psychology of Cognitive and Behavioral Control. Stanford, Calif.: Stanford University, 1970.

Needles and Knives: Behind the 46 Mystery of Acupuncture and Chinese Meridians

John F. Chaves and Theodore X. Barber

Of all the things that have come down to us from the ancient Chinese cultures, acupuncture is surely one of the most puzzling. Why does a needle in the skin during surgery make things hurt less rather than more? So far Western science has been at a loss for good answers. Now two pain researchers have come up with six factors which may help to explain just how it works.

John F. Chaves, Ph.D., is a Senior Research Psychologist at the Medfield Foundation, Medfield, Massachusetts. His primary research interest has been in pain, audition and other sensory processes.

Theodore X. Barber, Ph.D., has been Director of Psychological Research at the Medfield Foundation and Medfield State Hospital since 1959. He is president-elect of the Massachusetts Psychological Association. Barber is author of *Hypnosis: A Scientific Approach* and *LSD, Marihuana, Yoga and Hypnosis*, and co-editor of the annuals on *Biofeedback and Self-Control*.

During recent years, physicians from the United States, Canada and England have flocked to China in unprecedented numbers, and one of the wonders they have observed there first-hand is the successful use of acupuncture to relieve surgical pain. Their eyewitness accounts of this phenomenon have set off intense and widespread discussion in articles in the popular press as well as in a series of papers in medical journals.

At least part of the interest in the subject seems to be due to the aura of mystery surrounding it. Acupuncture is billed as an ancient, and therefore inscrutable, Chinese medical art, and it seems to be generally assumed thus far that it defies any rational explanation in Western scientific terms. More than that, the dramatic successes claimed for acupuncture seem to imply that Western science has been somewhat delinquent in failing to delineate certain important factors pertaining to the nature of pain and its control.

Reprinted with permission from *Human Behavior*, September 1973, 19-24.

We do not accept these implications. On the contrary, we believe that there are factors already known but usually overlooked by Western medicine that can help to explain the success of acupuncture in attenuating pain in surgery.

It's true that acupuncture is very old. The treatment of specific illnesses such as arthritic disorders and gastrointestinal diseases goes back at least 5,000 years. However, it wasn't until 1959 that the Chinese started using acupuncture to produce analgesia in surgery and its use has accelerated since 1968.

During the 14 years that acupuncture has been employed in surgery, the thin needles have been typically inserted at points remote from the location where analgesia is desired. For instance, when a gastrectomy is performed, four acupuncture needles are placed in the pinna or lobe of each ear. Moreover, they are commonly placed in innocuous locations such as in the limbs or the pinnae, remote from major organs, blood vessels or nerve trunks. The needles usually penetrate only a few millimeters, and rarely more than two centimeters, beneath the epidermis. When acupuncture is used for surgery, the needles are not simply inserted; instead, they are either twirled and vibrated by the acupuncturist or electricity is applied to them. In a typical procedure, continuous electrical stimulation is applied to the acupuncture needles from a six- or nine-volt battery at a frequency of 120 to 300 cycles/minute, beginning about half an hour before and continuing throughout the operation. However, it is important to note that *electrical* stimulation does not appear to be essential to the success of acupuncture analgesia. In fact, many times surgery is performed using only manual stimulation of the needles.

The traditional Chinese theory of why this works is beguiling and per-haps adds to the confusing mystery of acupuncture. This theory assumes that there are 12 meridians or channels, called Ching lo, running vertically down the body. These meridians are thought to carry a life energy (Qi or Ch'i). The flow of this energy is believed to maintain a balance between two forces, the Yin and the Yang. Yin is viewed as the weak, female, negative force while Yang is the strong, male, positive force. Yin meridians are associated with such organs as the liver, kidneys and spleen, while Yang meridians are associated with such organs as the stomach, gall bladder and intestines

Disease, the Chinese think, is a reflection of the imbalance of Yin and Yang forces. Thus, disease is cured by inserting acupuncture needles in appropriate locations to correct the imbalance. Consequently, to produce analgesia for surgery, it is necessary to insert acupuncture needles into meridians that control the appropriate organs. And since the meridians are thought to run through the whole body, the points of insertion may be quite remote from the points where analgesia is desired.

Although this ancient theory of acupuncture still appears to have many advocates in China, it certainly is acceptable to few if any Western-trained scientists. It isn't even accepted by all Chinese surgeons. Drs. Pang L. Man and Calvin H. Chen of Northville State Hospital in Michigan, noted that some Chinese surgeons "totally disregarded the recognized spots on the meridians" and used almost any spot to produce surgical analgesia, making it appear that the traditional theory of acupuncture points may be misleading.

Dr. Felix Mann, an English physician who has written several books about acupuncture and who, at one time, accepted the traditional theory, now argues, "... I don't believe meridians exist. A lot of acupuncture is based on meridians, and you will see from my theory, I think the meridians of acupuncture are not very much more real than the meridians of geography. And likewise with the acupuncture points." He goes on to note, "The Chinese have so many interconnections in their acupuncture theory that one can explain everything just as politicians do." Patrick Wall, an English physiologist at University College in London, is more succinct in his opinion of meridians, stating, "There is not one scrap of anatomical or physiological evidence for the existence of such a system."

There is at least one Western scientific explanation of how acupuncture works. This is Ronald Melzack's and Patrick Wall's gate control theory of pain. It has been perhaps the first attempt to apply a theory of pain that has any degree of acceptance among Western scientists.

We will examine this theory in more detail later, but briefly stated it asserts that pain depends, in part, on the relative amounts of activity in large A-beta fibers, activated by nonpainful stimuli, and small c-fibers, activated by pain-producing stimuli. Increasing the activity of the A-beta fibers is thought to close a spinal "gate" in the substantia gelatinosa, a section of the spinal cord, preventing the further transmission of information from the c-fibers. As applied to acupuncture, it is assumed that acupuncture needles selectively stimulate the A-beta fibers and that the high level of activity in the A-beta fibers closes the "gate" and thus inhibits pain.

Whichever theory one accepts, the Chinese or the Western gate theory, it is generally assumed that if the acupuncture needles are inserted in the appropriate locations and are either twirled manually or electricity is applied to them, sufficient reduction in pain is produced so that the patient can tolerate major surgical procedures. But the notion that the reduction in pain is due to the effects of the needles has diverted attention from other possible explanations. We believe there are six such factors that may offer a more realistic explanation of why acupuncture seems to work.

1. Beliefs and Lack of Anxiety

The widespread assumption that acupuncture is routinely employed with surgical patients in China is false. The chief delegate of a group of Chinese physicians who visited the United States in the fall of 1972 expressed concern "lest the Americans misunderstand (acupuncture analgesia) as an established, standard technique in China." Dr. E. Grey Dimond, of the University of Missouri Medical School at Kansas City, who visited China, writes, "The decision to use acupuncture anesthesia depended on the full enthusiasm and acceptance by the patient." Patients who are anxious, tense or frightened are given general anesthesia. As Dr. F. Z. Warren observed, Chinese surgeons typically select patients for acupuncture according to the following criteria: "They decide whether the type of operation would be suitable, whether the patient would be too hysterical, whether the patient believes firmly in Mao's teaching, or would Mao's teaching carry him through." Since general anesthesia is available for surgery in China, the motivation to forego general anesthesia and to undergo surgery with acupuncture is probably due, according to Dr. Dimond, to the "...immense pressure to comply and participate in the current Mao Thought Program which is a fundamental requirement for life in China." Before surgery with acupuncture is commenced, the patient and the attending physicians recite quotations from Chairman Mao's book and Mao's picture faces the patients in every operating room. At the end of the operation, the patients thank Chairman Mao for the surgery.

Other cultural factors intensify the Chinese people's acceptance of acupuncture. In some localities in China, the insertion of acupuncture needles is practiced by laymen about as casually as individuals in Western countries take aspirin tablets. In some parts of China, Dr. Ian Capperauld, a visiting surgeon from Edinburgh, saw that "young children practice inserting needles into one another's arms, legs and face to become proficient both as user and as a recipient."

It should be emphasized also that the Chinese learn early in life to expect little or no discomfort during surgery, even when the surgery is performed without drugs and without acupuncture. One eyewitness, British physician P. E. Brown, recalls:

While visiting a children's hospital we saw a queue of smiling 5-year-olds standing outside a room where tonsillectomies were being carried out in rapid succession. The leading child was given a quick anaesthetic spray of the throat by a nurse, a few minutes before walking into the theatre unaccompanied. Each youngster in turn climbed on the table, lay back smiling at the surgeon. opened his mouth wide, and had his tonsils dissected out in the extraordinary time of less than a minute. The only instruments used were dissecting scissors and forceps. The child left the table and walked into the recovery room. spitting blood into a gauze swab. A bucket of water at the surgeon's feet containing thirty-four tonsils of all sizes was proof of the morning's work. This tonsillectomy technique is significant inasmuch as it indicates that, without recourse to acupuncture, the Chinese

patient is conditioned from early childhood to accept surgical interference with his body with the full knowledge that it is going to be successful and he will experience little or no discomfort.

2. Special Preparation and Indoctrination Prior to Surgery

Patients who are selected for surgery with acupuncture receive rather special treatment preoperatively. Usually, the patient comes to the hospital two days before the operation and the surgeons explain to him exactly what they are going to do, show him just how they will operate, and describe what the acupuncturist will do and what effects the needles will have. The patient is asked to talk to other patients who have had the same kind of surgery and he is also given a set of acupuncture needles so that he can try them on himself.

Dr. Capperauld observed, "Acupuncture anesthesia tended to work better in nonemergency situations in which the patients had a few days indoctrination prior to operation. Emergency operations were done usually under conventional spinal techniques."

Although this kind of special preoperative preparation and indoctrination for surgery is not employed in the United States, there is evidence to indicate that "preoperative education," even if very limited, can have a beneficial effect on surgical patients. For instance, Dr. Lawrence D. Egbert of Harvard found that a five- or 10-minute preoperative visit by an anesthesiologist had a greater calming effect on surgical patients than two mg./kg. of pentobarbital sodium. Moreover, patients who were informed about the kind of postsurgical pain they might experience required smaller doses of narcotics for postsurgical pain than uninformed controls. An unexpected bonus was that the informed patients were discharged from the hospital sooner than the controls.

Thus, it appears that the preoperative period for special preparation and indoctrination for acupuncture works to ease the patient's anxiety, to strengthen his "belief and trust in acupuncture," as Patrick Wall says, and to lessen his need for large doses of pain-relieving drugs.

Dr. Felix Mann has recently provided further support for the notion that the patient's belief in the effectiveness of acupuncture is crucial to its success. Working in England with 100 volunteer subjects, he attempted to use acupuncture to produce analgesia to pinpricks that were severe enough to draw blood. He failed to get satisfactory results in at least 90 percent of the subjects, a tremendous contrast to the success rate reported in China. Mann omitted just one vital step that Chinese physicians include: the effort to convince subjects ahead of time that acupuncture would be highly effective.

3. Suggestions for Pain Relief

In addition to the preoperative indoctrination, the patient's belief that acupuncture will mitigate pain is continually bolstered by direct and indirect suggestions even during the operation itself. Even when acupuncture is used to treat specific diseases, Dr. James L. Rhee, an anesthesiologist from the University of California Medical Center noted, "... the acupuncturists whom I have watched work, load their therapy with suggestions."

The effectiveness of indirect suggestion has been evident for years in Western medicine. As far back as 1889, Dr. C. Lloyd Tuckey wrote:

There are few cases of this kind more remarkable than one related by Mr. Woodhouse Braine, the well-known chloroformist. Having to administer ether to an hysterical girl who was about to be operated on for the removal of two sebaceous tumors from the scalp he found that the ether bottle was empty, and that the inhaling bag was free from even the odor of any anesthetic. While a fresh supply was being obtained, he thought to familiarize the patient with the process by putting the inhaling bag over her mouth and nose, and telling her to breath quietly and deeply. After a few inspirations she cried, "Oh, I feel it; I am going off," and a moment after, her eyes turned up, and she became unconscious. As she was found to be perfectly insensible, and the ether had not yet come, Mr. Braine proposed that the surgeon should proceed with the operation. One tumor was removed without in the least disturbing her, and then, in order to test her condition, a bystander said that she was coming to. Upon this she began to show signs of waking, so the bag was once more applied, with the remark, "She'll soon be off again," when she immediately lost sensation and the operation was successfully and painlessly completed.

Working under primitive conditions in a prisoner of war hospital near Singapore during World War II, Australian surgeons found to their surprise that "the mere suggestion of anesthesia" was sufficient to perform minor surgery on the soldiers without apparent pain. More recent experiences in Bulgaria show that suggestions of anesthesia are at times enough to carry out major surgery with little pain.

Placebos are also a way of implanting mental suggestion. Dr. J. D. Hardy et al, in *Pain Sensations and Reactions,* published in 1952, reported that pain thresholds could be elevated 90 percent over control levels when an inactive drug was administered with the suggestion that it was a strong analgesic. Moreover, placebos have been found to be effective in alleviating postsurgical pain as well as chronic pain in many patients.

A series of studies conducted in our laboratory showed that suggestions of anesthesia are also effective in attenuating experimentally induced pain. In one study, suggestions of insensitivity attenuated cold-pressor pain and in another study suggestions of anesthesia reduced the pain produced by a heavy weight applied to a finger. Using the same pain stimulus on the finger, we found that the mere expectation of pain attenuation led to a reduction in pain, although larger reductions were obtained when subjects were asked to vividly imagine pleasant experiences.

4. Distraction Produced by Acupuncture Needles

The insertion and subsequent stimulation of the acupuncture needles is accompanied by various sensations. At times, the electric current that is applied to the needles is strong enough to produce rather strong muscular contraction. Also, the needles are manipulated by hand or stimulated electrically for 20 to 30 minutes prior to surgery and the patient often feels "sore" at the needle sites. Sometimes a slight aching sensation has been reported when the needle has been properly placed, and some patients say the acupuncture needles produce severe pain. Dr. Mann found with his brave pinprick subjects that in order to reduce the pain of pinpricks it was necessary, in most cases, to increase the pain produced by the acupuncture needles "... to more or less torture levels." In describing his own sensations while undergoing acupuncture for the relief of postsurgical abdominal pain, James Reston noted that the needles "... sent ripples of pain racing through my limbs and, at least, had the effect of diverting my attention from the distress in my stomach."

Thus it appears that the various sensations produced by the needles can serve as distractions. Present evidence indicates that distraction is an effective way of lessening pain. One study by S. L. H. Notermans found substantial increases of 40 to 50 percent in the pain threshold when subjects were distracted by performing an irrelevant task, in this case inflating a manometer cuff.

Psychologists F. H. Kanfer and D. A. Goldfoot showed that pain could be reduced by three types of distracters: observing interesting slides, self-pacing with a clock and verbalizing the sensations aloud. Similarly, Barber et al demonstrated that experimentally induced pain could be reduced by various kinds of distractions such as listening to an interesting tape-recorded story, adding numbers aloud and purposively thinking of pleasant events.

Counterirritation can also be an effective distraction. Studies conducted more than 30 years ago showed that experimentally induced pain could be lessened by several kinds of counterirritations including heat, cold, vibration, electric stimulation and static electricity. The same researchers, G. D. Gammon and I. Starr, also found that counterirritation worked in alleviating clinical pain. In one group of 60 clinical patients, 90 percent enjoyed at least some degree of relief, although the most effective type of counterirritation varied from patient to patient.

If such a wide variety of distractions can work to attenuate pain, clearly the acupuncture needles themselves can serve as effective distracters. But even in addition to the needles, some acupuncture patients receive special deep breathing exercises which they later are requested to carry out during the operation itself. By focusing their attention on their breathing, the patients may be provided with an additional useful distraction.

5. Use of Narcotic Analgesics, Local Anesthetics and Sedatives

Popular accounts often neglect to state that narcotic analgesics, local anesthetics and sedatives are often used when patients undergo surgery with acupuncture. Drs. Man and Chen state that the Chinese routinely administer 50 to 60 mg. of meperidine hydrochloride (Demerol) in an intravenous drip during an operation with acupuncture.

Of the six cases described by Dr. Dimond, five received a pain-relieving drug. One patient was given phenobarbital sodium the night before surgery for the removal of a brain tumor, but she did not receive any pain-relieving drugs during the actual surgery. Although she was described as "conscious, but very weak," she tolerated the operation without signs of pain. This was indeed a remarkable case, but it should be noted that brain tissue is generally insensitive to the surgeon's scalpel. Moreover, in other eyewitness reports of operations for cerebral tumor carried out with acupuncture, it is emphasized that the surgeons infiltrated the scalp with 50 milliliters of 0.125 percent procaine before the incision was made.

Dr. Capperauld also learned that sedatives, analgesics and local anesthetics were typically administered, which led him to ask, "The real question to be answered, therefore, is which therapy, the acupuncture needle or the concomitant Western medication, is the adjunct?" In some cases, the drugs that are given during acupuncture fail to control pain; that is, the patient complains of intolerable pain and general anesthe-

sia is administered. Dimond estimated that this kind of failure occurred in China in at least 10 percent of the selected patients. During a recent three-week visit to China, Dr. Marcel Gemperle failed to find a single case where acupuncture produced complete insensitivity and, in one case, the patient screamed and moved about on the operating table during surgery.

6. Overestimation of Surgical Pain

In Western medicine, anesthetic or analgesic agents are almost always used during major surgery. Therefore, there is little scientific information about base-line levels of pain experienced by surgical patients who have not been anesthetized. However, even during the preanesthetic era (prior to the 1840s) some patients undergoing major surgery without drugs, according to contemporary accounts, "bravely made no signs of suffering at all." In one such operation carried out in the early 1800s, a woman who underwent a mastectomy tolerated the surgery ".... without a word, and after being bandaged up, got up, made a curtsy, thanked the surgeon and walked out of the room."

Patients of this type probably represented only a small minority, but they illustrate the major importance of determining base levels of pain when evaluating procedures such as acupuncture.

The available knowledge indicates that surgical procedures produce anxiety and fear, but they usually give rise to less pain than is commonly believed. In summarizing the relevant evidence, Sir Thomas Lewis, an English physician, emphasized that, although the skin is very sensitive, the muscles, bone and most of the internal organs are relatively insensitive. More precisely, the skin is sensitive to a knife cut, but the underlying tissues and internal organs are generally insensitive *to incision*, although they are generally sensitive to other forms of stimulation such as traction or distention. For example, Dr. Lewis noted that the subcutaneous tissue gives rise to little pain when it is cut and slight pain is elicited when muscles are incised. Most of the internal organs also produce little or no pain when they are cut; these include the liver, spleen, kidneys, stomach, jejunum, ileum, colon, lungs, surface of the heart, esophageal wall and uterus. Traction upon the hollow viscera, however, is painful. Also, the surgeon's incision produces pain when it cuts the skin and other external tissues, such as the conjunctiva, the mucous membranes of the mouth and nasopharynx, the upper surface of the larynx and the stratified mucous membranes of the genitalia and also when it cuts a small number of deeper tissues, such as the deep fascia, the periosteum, the tendons and the rectum.

In the early 1900s, a German surgeon, Dr. K. G. Lennander, published a series of case reports showing that major abdominal operations can be accomplished painlessly using only local anesthetics, such as cocaine, to dull the pain of the initial incision through the skin. Dr. J. F. Mitchell also reported an extensive series of major operations performed with local anesthetics used to produce insensitivity of the skin. These included: limb amputations, thyroidectomies, mastectomies, suprapubic cystostomies, laparotomies, excision of glands in the neck and groin, herniorrhaphies, cholecystostomies and appendectomies.

Dr. Mitchell confirmed Lennander's observation regarding the surprising insensitivity of internal organs. For example, he described the following:

The skin being thoroughly anesthetized and the incision made, there is little sensation in the subcutaneous tissue and muscles as long as blood vessels, large nerve trunks and connective tissue bundles are avoided....

The same insensibility to pain in bone has been noted in several cases of amputation, in removal of osteophytes and wiring of fractures. In every instance after thorough cocainization of the periosteum, the actual manipulations of the bone itself have been unaccompanied by pain. The patients have stated that they feel and hear the sawing, but it was as if a board were being sawn while resting upon some part of the body.

The data presented by Lewis, Lennander and Mitchell suggest that the pain associated with major surgical procedures may not always be as great as is usually supposed. It is certainly clear that the amount of pain is not related in any simple way to the extent of surgical intervention. If a patient is relaxed and not anxious and if he can tolerate the initial incision through the skin, it appears that many major surgical procedures can be accomplished without much additional pain. The administration of small or moderate doses of narcotic analgesics and sedatives, as is usually done with acupuncture, makes the patient's task that much easier.

Chinese surgeons who use acupuncture conduct their operations very slowly and carefully. Rib-spreaders employed during thoracotomies are opened slowly. Also, surgeons avoid putting traction on such tissues as the pleura and peritoneum, which are known to be sensitive to this kind of stress. When these tissues are stretched, acupuncture patients grimace, sweat and show other signs of experiencing extreme pain just as would be expected on the basis of the data summarized by Lewis. Acupuncture is difficult to use in abdominal surgery because it is hard to avoid putting traction on these tissues and because acupuncture does not produce adequate relaxation of the abdominal muscles.

All of these factors point to some

major difficulties in using the gate control theory to account for acupuncture analgesia. The gate theory, it will be remembered, holds that the stimulation of certain nerve fibers closes a gate in the spinal cord and blocks off the sensation of pain. First of all, the "gate" is a hypothetical entity that has not been established anatomically. Even if the "gate" were shown to exist, the gate control theory, as originally formulated, could only account for analgesia in the vicinity of the nerves stimulated by the acupuncture needles. However, as we noted earlier, acupuncture needles are inserted at points far removed from the area where relief is desired. A related difficulty is that many of the locations commonly employed in acupuncture, such as the head or ear lobes, would be ineffective in closing the spinal "gate." Thus, it becomes necessary to postulate the existence of a second "gate," presumably located at some higher level of the nervous system, in order to account for the efficacy of needles inserted at these locations. While it is not easy to rule out this possibility entirely, neither is it satisfactory simply to make up new "gates" on an *ad hoc* basis to account for anomalous findings.

Wall, who is one of the original coauthors of the gate control theory, has admitted, "My present guess is that ... it will emerge that acupuncture does not generate the specifically pain-inhibiting barrages for which I was looking." However, Melzack, the other coauthor of the theory, has recently argued that the theory is relevant to acupuncture. Nevertheless, while the gate control theory may appear to be useful in explaining the successes of acupuncture, it is very difficult to see how this theory can explain its failures. Why is it necessary for acupuncture patients to believe in its effectiveness? If acupuncture needles can close the "gate," why is it necessary to administer narcotic analgesics, sedatives and local anesthetics to acupuncture patients? Why is the

"gate" capable of reducing the pain of surgery in China but incapable of reducing the pain of pinpricks in England? Unfortunately, the gate control theory fails to provide answers to these important questions. It appears to us that speculations about the physiological basis for acupuncture may be premature.

It has sometimes been suggested that a physiological theory of acupuncture is needed to explain anecdotal reports in the popular press, which suggest that acupuncture may be useful in performing surgery with rabbits, horses and other mammals. Of course, these statements in newspapers and magazines cannot be evaluated until such time as non-anecdotal studies are presented which, at least, utilize minimal controls. Since there is much evidence demonstrating that many mammals, including rabbits and horses, can tolerate extremely painful stimuli when they are appropriately restrained, controlled studies may find that acupuncture is not especially helpful in operating on mammals.

As more data become available, we will be able to identify additional factors to help explain this phenomenon. It remains to be demonstrated, however, that acupuncture needles exert any specific analgesic effects beyond the six factors we have discussed in this article. Certainly, future attempts to explain the success of acupuncture in easing surgical pain should take these factors into serious consideration.

We would argue that the success of acupuncture analgesia underscores the importance of psychological factors in the control of pain. Obviously, more research is needed to determine the relative importance of the six factors outlined here and to identify additional factors that could help to explain the phenomenon. Providing the basis for a more comprehensive explanation of why acupuncture works will be an exciting area for future research.

SELECTED ABSTRACTS

10. Silverman, S. Z., & Campos, J. J. (University of Denver) **Operant HR conditioning in the infant and young child.** This study tested whether groups of infants and toddlers could learn operant control of HR. Others had previously shown that infants can readily be skeletally conditioned with conjugate reinforcement. This technique, whereby the intensity of a sensory reinforcer is proportional, or inversely proportional, to the rate of an operant response, seemed ideally suited for reinforcing children's HR changes. The first step in the research involved testing adult Ss to determine whether HR could come under operant control by means of this conjugate reinforcement method. We found that Ss clearly and significantly changed HR in the reinforced direction. The second step was to test children, 10 in each of three age groups: 1, 2, and 3 years old. As with adults, reinforcement consisted of one of two cartoon films, which varied in brightness proportionally (or inversely proportionally, according to condition), with HR. Half the Ss in each age group were reinforced for HR increases, half for HR decreases. Each group was given 6 4-min training sessions, preceded by 1.5 min baselines. There also was 1 extinction session. Results showed no evidence of operant HR control in the 1 and 2 year olds. However, the 3 year olds showed divergent HR curves as a function of training condition in both acquisition and extinction phases of the study, suggesting that HR operant control may be possible at least as early as 3 years of age.

11. Shucard, D. W. (National Jewish Hospital and Research Center) **Effects of instructional set on visual evoked potentials.** Visual evoked potentials (EPs) were recorded under two conditions of instructional set (suggestion) and two conditions of flash intensity using a sequence of three stimuli for each condition. The relative influence of these variables and subject suggestibility on EPs recorded from scalp vertex leads was investigated. The results indicated that (1) instructional set influenced both amplitude and latency of EP peaks. There was a general sharpening and decrease in the latency of EP components as a function of set. Although the direction of amplitude change appeared to be generally independent of the direction of change suggested by the experimenter, both the strategy and suggestibility of S appeared to influence EP amplitude. In general suggestion produced an increase in EP peak amplitude for the appropriate stimulus whether S was instructed that the stimulus would be brighter or dimmer than the others in the sequence. (2) Set combined with stimulus intensity change produced the highest EP peak amplitude scores. (3) No systematic EP amplitude decrease occurred to the sequence of three stimuli. Amplitude decrease across a series of stimuli has been frequently reported and referred to as fatigue or EP habituation. The lack of a systematic decrease in amplitude in this study suggests the importance of subject set in experiments utilizing average evoked potentials.

14. Sandler, L. S. (University of Manitoba), **& Schwartz, M.** (University of Cincinnati) **Differential effects of selective attention and stimulus probability upon the evoked potential and the contingent negative vari-**

ation. The question of the relationship between the P300 component of the Evoked Potential (EP) and the Contingent Negative Variation (CNV) is much in debate at present. The purpose of this study was to help in the clarification of this issue by manipulating factors that can be expected, from the literature, to have either similar or opposite effects on these two electrical responses. The effects of both selective attention and stimulus probability on the CNV and the P300 component of the EP were examined. Previous findings would suggest that making a stimulus relevant should enhance both the CNV and P300, while decreasing its probability should enhance P300 while attenuating the CNV. To the extent that opposite effects are possible, the responses can be interpreted as stemming from different mechanisms. The basic experimental paradigm in all conditions was for a warning click (S_a) to be followed 1000 msec later by either S_{b1} (high tone) or S_{b2} (low tone). Before each condition, S was told which tone was relevant, i.e., required a response, and the probability of its occurrence (100%, 80%, 50%, 20%). Each S participated in all conditions. CNV and P300 measures were obtained to both stimuli in all conditions. Repeated measures analyses of variance of the CNV and P300 data demonstrated that both experimental manipulations had significant effects upon the amplitude of P300, whereas no such effects were found for the CNV. Thus, the position that P300 amplitude changes are not related to changes in selective attention, but to a nonspecific arousal function, is disputed. Additionally, the notion that the CNV and the P300 effects represent the same process was questioned, and alternate explanations explored.

21. Kahn, S D., Swint, E. B., & Bowne, G. W. (Georgia Mental Health Institute & Emory University School of Medicine) **A film demonstration of biofeedback technology in which covert operants control the visual environment.** This film illustrates a basic methodology for linking covert operants to the perceptual field, while quantifying the relevant data by computer. The system is illustrated by showing a closed-loop biofeedback system in which single motor units are allowed to control a figure-ground projector system, with the option of giving the S auditory feedback as well. The use of a small dedicated real-time computer (PDP-12A) to analyze the physiological data on-line is also shown. The experimental paradigm selected to illustrate the system demonstrates the acquisition of voluntary control over the discharge of a single motor unit, and the simultaneous suppression of surrounding motor units. The S achieves this task utilizing the information obtained by visual and auditory feedback. Since the discharge of a single motor unit cannot ordinarily be discriminated by interoceptive feedback, this paradigm may also be used to study certain unconscious cognitive processes. For example, when the S is unaware that he is determining the figure-ground relationships of his perceptual field, his motor unit "behavior" may reveal stimulus preferences that are uncontaminated by those social factors and demand characteristics of the experiment which would ordinarily affect conscious choice.

29. Lynch, J. J., Mills, M. E., Thomas, S. A., & Malinow, K. (University of Maryland Medical School) **The effects of pulse-taking on the cardiac functioning of patients in a coronary care unit.** During the past few years a series of studies have noted that social interactions often have marked, and at times, profound effects on cardiovascular functioning. In light of these reports, studies were initiated to explore the cardiac reactions of patients in a Coronary Care Unit to analogous social stimuli. This report will focus on one such "social interaction"—cardiac reactions of patients in a Coronary Care Unit (CCU) to a nurse taking the patient's pulse. The patients were chosen at random after having been admitted to the CCU a minimum of 12 hrs prior to our observations. Each patient's EKG was continuously recorded for a 5 to 10 hr period. Every major event and social interactions that occurred in the CCU during this period were noted. Both the patient and most of the individuals who normally interacted with the patient were unaware of our observations and recordings. Observations on 2 patients in the CCU have revealed that major changes in cardiac rate and rhythm often occur while a nurse is taking the pulse and may begin on the very first heart beat after the nurse touches the patient's arm. In addition to major rate changes, we have observed frequent increases in premature ventricular contractions, changes in atrial blocking ratios, and various other ectopic cardiac reactions to pulse taking. Coupled with our observations of the cardiac reactions elicited in these patients during other social interactions, these data suggest that careful attention must be paid to the entire social milieu of Coronary Care Units.

31. Levenson, R. W., & Strupp, H. H. (Vanderbilt University) **Simultaneous feedback and control of heart rate and respiration rate.** Thirty Ss were asked to either increase or decrease their heart rate (HR), relative to a pre-trial baseline period, while keeping their respiration rate (RR) at its baseline level. Ss were provided with external feedback of their HR and RR independently, via a digital display device which presented numerical representations of their current HR and RR relative to baseline rates. The amount of feedback was varied on different trials to consist of either no feedback, HR feedback, or HR and RR feedback. HR and RR data were quantified on-line by a digital computer and were analyzed in terms of (1) HR inter-beat-interval (IBI) changes; (2) RR inter-cycle-interval (ICI) changes, (3) the number of heart beat intervals which were in the instructed (i.e., increase or decrease) direction; and (4) the number of heart beat intervals in the instructed direction *and* accompanied by respiration intervals at the baseline rate. Data analysis revealed that Ss were reliably able to produce HR changes regardless of the amount of feedback available, but that parallel changes in RR accompanied these HR changes. These RR changes occurred in spite of specific instructions not to use breathing changes to effect HR change and regardless of whether feedback of RR was available. On the basis of the combined measure of HR and RR intervals which met the instructed criteria, it was concluded that Ss were unable to produce HR change without accompanying RR changes. Implications of this finding for the general question of mediation in autonomic control research and for future studies using human Ss were discussed.

32. Perez-Cruet, J. (Johns Hopkins University School of Medicine) **Operant conditioning of Wenckebach periods in the rhesus monkey.** Previously it has been shown that disorders of conduction in the heart can be conditioned using Pavlovian techniques. The present study was designed to study whether it is also possible to condition EKG changes operantly. A total of 22 rhesus monkeys were studied at different periods for 6 yrs (1961–1967). Operant performance was programmed under a contingent reinforcement schedule (CRF) based on reinforcements of occasional Wenckebach periods spontaneously occurring in these monkeys. Later the CRF schedule was changed to a fixed ratio schedule (FR) where the Wenckebach periods

were also used as a contingent variable. FR 2 and FR 3 were attempted. Reinforcement consisted of an artificial orange juice (Tang) dissolved in a 1:3 solution and delivered automatically by EKG monitoring equipment immediately after the appearance of a Wenckebach period. Six rhesus monkeys showed operant conditioning of Wenckebach periods by the third day of training. Operant heart rate conditioning in the form of a mild bradycardia was also observed as reported previously. This study shows that disorders of conduction in the heart can be conditioned either operantly or by Pavlovian methods. These findings suggest that the underlying physiological and neurotransmitter mechanisms of these two types of cardiac conditioning may be similar.

38. Paskewitz, D. A., & Orne, M. T. (Institute of the Pennsylvania Hospital and University of Pennsylvania) **On the reliability of baseline EEG alpha activity.** Considerable consistency is known to exist between alpha densities for a given S obtained in standard situations on different occasions. The stability of alpha density over several sessions is further augmented in a feedback situation. Though Ss' absolute alpha density is greatly affected by different feedback conditions, a S's initial baseline level is the single most important predictor of his response to feedback—underlining the need for establishing methods to evaluate the reliability of a S's baseline. A study was carried out to clarify the nature of variations observed in alpha baseline levels over several days. Analysis indicated that most discrepancies from the S's modal alpha were in the direction of decreased alpha density, and were associated with independent evidence of drowsiness. Electrooocular records, obtained simultaneously, were scored blind; the slow rolling eye movements typically associated with early sleep onset served to clearly separate the periods of diminished alpha density from those which corresponded to the individual's modal level. It was also possible, utilizing the EEG alone, to show that the relative variation in 15-sec period density scores during the baseline period is highly correlated with the presence of slow eye movements. Different methods for correcting alpha density baseline scores for drowsy periods were assessed. The implications of these findings for studies using alpha density as a criterion measure are discussed. (Supported in part by the Advanced Research Projects Agency of the Department of Defense and was monitored by the Office of

Naval Research under Contract N0014-70-C-0350 to the San Diego State College Foundation)

39. Kaszniak, A. W. (University of Illinois at Chicago Circle) **Dichotic auditory vigilance during feedback-enhanced EEG alpha.** Several investigators have suggested that relatively high concentrations of alpha activity are associated with a narrowing of perceptual awareness, and that increases in alpha, produced by feedback training, may reflect an increasing ability to ignore distracting stimuli. The hypothesis was tested that alpha enhancement, following feedback training, would be concomitant with decreased task peripheral accuracy, as well as increased task central accuracy. A dichotic auditory vigilance task tested this in 17 Ss previously trained to enhance and inhibit alpha. The vigilance task consisted of the presentation of two differing series of nonsense syllables occurring simultaneously in the right and left ears, with a target syllable being specified. Target syllables occurring in the right ear were made task central by instructing Ss to pay particular attention to this ear. Each S completed the vigilance task once while trying to enhance alpha (alpha "on"), and once while trying to suppress alpha (alpha "off"). A significant difference in amount of alpha activity, between alpha "on" and alpha "off" conditions, demonstrated effectiveness of the feedback training. Analysis of vigilance task performance revealed decreased accuracy for target syllable detection in the left ear during alpha "on," while right ear accuracy remained the same between conditions. This supports the hypothesis of decreased task peripheral accuracy during alpha enhancement, but not that of increased task central accuracy. Results are discussed in relation to both conditioned and spontaneously occurring alpha activity.

45. Christie, D. J., & Kotses, H. (Ohio University, Athens, Ohio) **Bidirectional operant conditioning of the cephalic vasomotor response in humans.** The objective of the current research was to determine the possibility of operantly conditioning the human cephalic vasomotor response. An attempt was made to condition this response over an extended period of training in 8 volunteer male Ss, 4 of which were conditioned to constrict while the remaining 4 were conditioned to dilate. All Ss underwent 6 30-min training sessions on 6 consecutive days. The first 3 consisted of a 5 min rest period followed by a 25 min conditioning period. The rein-

forcement procedure during the conditioning period involved avoidance of a white noise (85 dB) stimulus which was presented automatically. The duration of the noise was adjusted every 30 sec so that each S received approximately 5 sec of white noise for each 30 sec period throughout the conditioning phase. During the last 3 sessions, a 5 min rest period was followed by a 25 min conditioning period during which dependent measures were recorded. For purposes of analysis, this phase was broken-up into 25 1-min segments each consisting of a 30 sec conditioning interval (S_d) and a 30 sec control interval (S_Δ). The positional level of the last beat that occurred in each S_Δ interval served as the criterion for white noise presentation in the succeeding S_d interval. An analysis of variance on the sixth session revealed that Ss exhibited vasodilation and vasoconstriction relative to their control periods ($p <$ .05). From these results it was concluded that the human cephalic vasomotor response was amenable to operant conditioning techniques.

50. Frese, F. J., & Kotses, H. (Ohio University, Athens, Ohio) **Effects of massed and distributed practice on operant deceleration of heart rate.** This study was designed to test the effects of massed versus distributed practice in operant deceleration of human HR. Fifteen male undergraduates were assigned to one of three groups consisting of a Massed group and two Distributed Practice groups. Practice sessions were separated by 2.5 hrs and 24 hrs in the latter two groups. HR was recorded for all S for a 60 min period of conditioning following a 20 min baseline period. The Massed group completed this procedure in 1 80-min session while the Distributed Practice groups were required to participate in 4 20-min sessions. In the Distributed Practice groups a 3 min baseline period preceded each of the last 3 sessions. During conditioning a 50 dB continuous white noise was automatically presented on a beat-to-beat basis whenever Ss' HR dropped below a pre-established criterion level. A shaping procedure was employed such that criterion levels were adjusted by 2 bpm whenever the S attained the criterion level for a 2 min period. Comparisons were made between baseline measures and measures taken during training in each of the three groups. For the Massed group, training effects were referred to the initial 20 min baseline period, while the pre-session baseline served as the reference point in the Distributed Practice groups. Statistical tests revealed that the conditioning technique employed was capable of producing significant HR decelerations. These were detected primarily in the Distributed Practice groups with the 24 hr group showing the greatest amount of decrease.

54. Harrison, R. S., & Raskin, D. C. (University of Utah) **Learned control of HR variability during feedback and no-feedback conditions.** Previous studies have demonstrated that feedback techniques can be used to train Ss to control HR variability, but the ability of Ss to transfer that control to a no-feedback situation has not been confirmed. Twenty pairs of Ss were given true HR feedback (TF) or false feedback (FF) in a yoked-control design. All Ss were instructed to try to control HR variability while HR feedback was continuously displayed on a meter and to try to continue to control their HR variability when the HR feedback meter was turned off. During feedback display periods, Ss that received true HR feedback showed reliably better control of HR variability than their yoked controls. When the meter was turned off, Ss in the TF group were able to keep their HR within the specified zone for longer periods of time than the FF Ss. However, TF Ss had also achieved lower mean HRs at the end of the display periods. Therefore, the apparent ability of TF Ss to control HR variability during the no-feedback period may have resulted from their lower mean HR prior to the no-feedback periods and was not necessarily a result of the control learned during feedback display periods. Analysis of respiration and skin resistance indicated no evidence of a relationship between HR responses and changes in respiration and skin resistance.

58. Hirschman, R. (Kent State University) **Effects of anticipatory bogus heart rate feedback in a negative emotional context.** Previous research has demonstrated that bogus heart rate feedback can affect judgments of positive emotional stimuli. The present investigation examined the effects of anticipatory bogus heart rate feedback on verbal as well as electrodermal responses to negative emotional stimuli. Forty-eight female Ss were exposed to heart increase, heart no change, noise increase, or noise no change feedback, while observing 10 autopsy slides. Ss in the heart-increase and noise-increase conditions heard a continuous pulse rate vary between 66 and 72 bpm every 5 sec. Twenty sec preceding slide onset the rate increased in 5 sec segments from 72 to 100 bpm. Ss in heart-no-change and noise-no-change groups heard only a continuous pulse rate vary between 66 and 72 bpm every 5 sec. As expected the heart conditions resulted in significantly greater electrodermal activity, both preceding and in response to the slides, as well as significantly greater self reports of discomfort and slide unpleasantness as compared to the noise conditions. The most pronounced responses were associated with the heart-increase condition. Since no differences in electrodermal activity were found among groups prior to the experimental manipulation, the physiological effects were attributed to the differences in the perceived arousal conditions which were experimentally introduced. These results suggest that a cyclic cognitive-visceral link may occur in anticipation of an emotionally arousing stimulus.

59. Kinsman, R. A., O'Banion, K., & Robinson, S. (National Jewish Hospital and Research Center, Denver) **Continuous information feedback and discrete post-trial informative feedback during muscle relaxation training.** Training to relax the frontalis muscle using continuous information feedback (CIF) was compared to discrete post-trial informative feedback (DIF) in this study. CIF was a stream of clicks, the rate of which continuously tracked changes in frontalis muscle action potential. DIF was verbal feedback, delivered immediately after each trial, indicating that the average muscle action potential either increased or decreased with respect to the previous trial. A total of 64 Ss were assigned randomly to four conditions of a factorial design determined by the presentation or nonpresentation of CIF and DIF during training. All Ss received 3 baseline (no feedback) trials followed by 10 128-sec training trials on 3 successive days. Average muscle action potential in mv measured peak-to-peak was obtained on each trial for all Ss. Before delivery of any post-trial feedback, one-half of the Ss in each condition guessed whether they relaxed more or less than on the preceding trial. The results indicated that for overall training the CIF condition produced a significant decrease in muscle action potential from Day 1 baseline (33%), most of which occurred on the first day (28%). This decrease was maintained during the nonfeedback baseline trials preceding the training trials on the second and third training days. DIF resulted in a lesser, nonsignificant decrease (11%), but produced consistent improvement across the training days. Ss in the condition receiving neither CIF nor DIF showed no change (0%)

from baseline levels. Examination of post-trial guesses showed that Ss receiving CIF guessed correctly about their performance more often than Ss in the other conditions. These results indicate the superiority of CIF over an alternative feedback modality, DIF, and suggest that awareness of performance is related to the efficacy of continuous feedback modalities in training of instrumental control of muscle relaxation.

71. Sirota, A. D. (Pennsylvania State University), **Schwartz, G. E., & Shapiro, D.** (Harvard Medical School) **Effects of feedback control of heart rate on judgments of electric shock intensity.** Twenty female Ss (aged 21–27) were instructed either to increase (N = 10) or to decrease (N = 10) their heart rate while anticipating electric shock. They were also provided with visual and auditory feedback and monetary incentives for the appropriate heart rate changes. The experiment consisted of 72 trials of 15-sec duration each, half followed by electric shock delivered to the left forearm on a random schedule. By the end of conditioning, heart rate in the Increase group was significantly greater by 13 bpm than in the Decrease group during the anticipatory periods. Phasic heart rate changes showed similar differences, with shock trials producing elevations in heart rate over no-shock trials for the Increase but not for the Decrease group. Shock ratings were significantly higher for Increase Ss, but this difference appeared on the earliest trials. However, when Ss in each group were subdivided into Cardiac-Reactors and Non-cardiac-Reactors on the basis of a post-experimental questionnaire designed to measure awareness of physiological states during fear or anxiety, a highly significant subgroup by trial interaction evolved. Increase Cardiac-Reactors rated the shocks as increasing in intensity over the trials whereas Decrease Cardiac-Reactors showed decreases in their ratings. Non-cardiac-Reactors showed no such differentiation. These data suggest that a conditioned and instructionally mediated change in an autonomic response can affect subjective reaction to painful stimuli, particularly in Ss for whom such a change is relevant in terms of their normal awareness of autonomic functioning in fearful situations.

New Therapeutic Modality 48
for Treatment of Spasmodic Torticollis

J. Brudny, B. B. Grynbaum, and J. Korein

Nine patients with spasmodic torticollis, of varying degrees of severity and duration, were included in a larger ongoing study of E.M.G. feedback in learning control of abnormal motor activity. Clinical observations led to the belief that augmenting priprioceptive feedback from affected muscles will contribute to improvement of dyskinesa seen in spasmodic torticollis. Auditory and visual displays of integrated myoelectric potentials, monitored from affected muscles, were used in this study. The instantaneous presentation of changing levels of visual and auditory displays reflected closely the functional state of the involved muscles (tension and/or relaxation). Learning the volitional change of levels of the E.M.G. feedback displays resulted in learning volitional control of muscle activity. When such learned control seemed to be adequate, the E.M.G. feedback was withdrawn and patients were followed periodically for reexamination and reinforcement of volitional control of muscle activity, when needed. All nine patients showed considerable improvement and retained the newly learned control of neck muscles activity for significant periods of time. External sensory information, reflecting closely the functional state of affected muscles, could apparently augment or substitute for a defect in the servo-mechanism of patterned volitional movements and aid in reestablishing the integrity of sensory motor interaction. The study implies that teaching voluntary control of muscle activity in spasmodic torticollis with aid of additional external sensory information is possible. Such technique may represent a significant advance in treatment of spasmodic torticollis.

Reprinted from the *Archives of Physical Medicine and Rehabilitation*, 1973, Vol. 54, 575.

NAME INDEX

Hofer, M. A., 25
Hoffer, A., 237
Hofling, C. K., 218n, 230, 231, 233, 236
Hokanson, J. E., 337
Holland, J. G., 61
Hollander, M. H., 229
Hollingsworth, H. L., 235
Homme, L. E., 426
Hooper, 223
Horwitt, M. K., 222, 231, 237
Hothersall, D., 46, 49, 50, 56, 57, 66, 347,
    348, 349, 458
Houston, W. R., 219, 221, 222, 223, 226, 228,
    229, 238
Howard, J. L., 471n
Howlett, S. C., 455, 456
Hull, C. L., 234
Humphrey, D. R., 96, 116
Humphreys, P. W., 55
Humphries, J. O'Neal, 307
Hurst, J. W., 360
Hyman, H. T., 227, 228

Imber, S. B., 232, 237
Inch, R. S., 226

Jacobs, A., 458
Jacobson, E., 281, 355, 356, 443, 489
Jacobson, L. I., 413
Janet, P., 222, 224, 225, 233, 234, 235, 238
Jarvik, M. E., 236
Jasper, H. H., 206
Jeffrey, H. L., 231
Johns, T. R., 348, 349
Johnson, H. J., 347, 348
Jones, E., 233, 234, 235, 238
Jorgensen, G. T., 461

Kahn, M., 454
Kamiya, J., 149, 152, 153, 155, 159, 161,
    209, 468
Kanfer, Frederick H., 413n, 413, 414, 415n,
    416, 426, 427, 513
Karagulla, S., 232
Katkin, E. S., 15, 331, 469
Katz, R. A., 61
Kaufman, M. R., 236
Keats, A. S., 229, 239
Keenan, B., 127
Kekulé, 495
Kennedy, T. D., 460
Kennelly, B. M., 55
Kent, R. N., 459
Kessen, W., 431
Kimmel, 468
Klausner, S. Z., 414
Kleinman, R. A., 20, 60, 347, 354, 356

Klompus, Barbara, 120
Klugman, Frances, 244n
Koelle, G. B., 33
Koenig, K. P., 458
Koester, A., 495, 500
Koteen, H., 222
Kretschmer, 495
Krishaswamy, N., 504
Kurland, A. A., 233, 237

Lacey, J., 471
Lachman, S. J., 338
Ladar, M. H., 282, 283, 448, 449
Lang, P. J., 349, 350, 351, 458, 461, 463
Lasagna, L., 229, 230, 239
Laties, V. G., 232
LaWall, C. H., 226, 232
Lazarte, 382
Lazarus, A. A., 413, 473
Leao, A. A. P., 36
Lee, L. E., Jr., 239
Leibrecht, Bruce C., 122n, 122, 123, 124,
    127, 128
Leitenberg, H., 443, 455, 456, 457, 461
Lemas, J., 232
Lennander, K. G., 515
Lennox, W. G., 220, 221
Leslie, A., 219, 227, 228, 230
Levene, H. I., 56, 57, 60, 66, 67, 348, 349
Leventhal, D. B., 455, 456
Levi-Montalcini, R., 25
Levine, A., 236
Levine, M., 231, 236
Levinson, D. J., 239
Levis, D. J., 458
Levitt, E. E., 232
Lewis, Nolan D. C., 222, 232
Lewis, Thomas, 514, 515
Leyton, S. R., 232
Lhamon, W. T., 232
Lind, A. R., 55
Linder, L. H., 455
Lindsley, D. B., 175
Lloyd, A. J., 122, 123, 124, 127, 128
Locock, Sir Charles, 220
Logue, R. B., 360
Lomont, J. F., 455, 456, 457
Love, 337
Love, W. A., 443
Lovejoy, E., 423n
Luria, A. R., 3
Luschei, Erich S., 96, 120
Luthe, W., 269, 273, 281, 443, 495, 499
Lynch, J. J., 363

Macdonald, L. R., 370
MacKenzie, J. N., 244

SUBJECT INDEX

R-R interval, 295-306
and Wolff-Parkinson-White syndrome,
310-12
Electrocorticogram, 197
Electroencephalography (EEG)
alteration of, 150-54, 164, 177-82, 186,
189-99, 202-4, 385, 485, 522
environmental variables and, 154, 367
phasic and tonic responses, 206
"sensorimotor rhythm," 365, 383
similarity to evoked potentials, 71
sleep spindles (sigma), 367, 493, 496
use as biofeedback tool, 149, 174, 190,
207-9, 363, 382, 450, 493, 521
see also, Alpha rhythm; Non-alpha rhythm
Electromyography (EMG)
ecstasy state of Yoga, 487
use as biofeedback tool, 142-44, 253-63,
265-67, 274, 277, 287-92, 444, 447,
450
change in, 49, 50, 53, 54, 385
correlation with operant bursts,112-14,
116-17, 119
single motor unit (SMU) control,
122-28
suppression of, 25
Electrooculography (EOG), 198-200, 204,
385
Electrophysiology, 78
see also, Electroencephalography;
Neuronal activity
EMG. *See* Electromyography
Emphysema, 244, 250
EOG, 198-200, 204, 385
Epilepsy, 267-80, 382, 383
Ergotropic system, 484-89
ESB, 131-32

Fear. *See* Anxiety
Feedback. *See* Biofeedback

Geisser-Greenhouse test, 168
Grand mal. *See* Epilepsy

Hallucinations, 6, 497-500
Headache
migraine, 445-47
autogenic feedback training, 268-73
drug dependency, 446-47
tension (muscle contraction)
EMG biofeedback training, 253-63,
265-67, 274, 277, 278, 281, 444, 445
Heart rate. *See* Physiological alterations
Homeopathy, 224
Home training practice, 443, 444-46
Hypertension, 315-20, 321-23, 329-38, 357,
469-73

Hypnagogic imagery, 495-97
Hypnosis, 3, 234-36, 488, 494
and heart rate control, 503, 505
and vasomotor control, 503, 506
Hypothalamus. *See* Diencephalon

Immunosympathectomy, 25
Insomnia, 278, 280-81, 447-48, 450-51

Mao Thought Program, 510
Medical history, 219-34
Medicine
as art, 222
history of, 219-34
see also, Physician; Placebo
Meditation. *See* Transcendental Meditation;
Yoga; Zen
Medulla. *See* Brain stem
Mental illness. *See* Psychosis
Meridians (Ching lo), 509
Mesencephalon, midbrain, 197
Midbrain, 197
Minnesota Multiphasic Personality Inventory
(MMPI), 255, 259, 266
Motor activity
associated with operant bursts, 116
without kinesthetic feedback, 130-44
single motor unit (SMU) control, 122-28
Motor neuron. *See* Neuron, motoneuron
Muscles
associated with operant bursts, 116-19
depolarization, 118
retrocollis, 287, 288, 291-92
tension, 49, 53-58, 523
torticollis, 286-92
see also, Headache, tension

Nerve
peroneal, 132, 133, 135, 141
sciatic, 131, 132
tibial, 132, 133
Neuron
motoneuron, 118
alpha, 131, 144
gamma, 131
see also, Neuronal activity
Neuronal activity
afferent, 197, 203, 211, 484, 489
destruction of, 130-44
conditioning by adjacent neurons, 107-12
control of, 127-28
efferent, 173, 197, 203, 211, 295-97
and evoked potentials, 71-76, 78-85,
100-105
overuse, 367
and voluntary movement, 96
see also, Electroencephalography; Neuron